Time Out

London Guide

Penguin Books

PENGUIN BOOKS

Published by the Penguin Group
Penguin Books Ltd, 27 Wright's Lane, London W8 5TZ, England
Penguin Books USA Inc., 375 Hudson Street, New York, New York 10014, USA
Penguin Books Australia Ltd, Ringwood, Victoria, Australia
Penguin Books Canada Ltd, 10 Alcorn Avenue, Toronto, Ontario, Canada M4V 3B2
Penguin Books (NZ) Ltd, 182-190 Wairau Road, Auckland 10, New Zealand

Penguin Books Ltd, Registered Offices: Harmondsworth, Middlesex, England

First published 1989
Second edition 1990
Third edition 1992
Fourth Edition 1994
10 9 8 7 6 5 4 3 2 1

Printed by William Clowes Ltd, Beccles, Suffolk NR34 9QE

Edited and designed by
Time Out Magazine Limited,
Universal House,
251 Tottenham Court Road,
London W1A 1BZ
Tel: 071 813 3000
Fax: 071 813 6001

Editorial
Managing Editor
Peter Fiennes
Editor
Philip Harriss
Writer/researchers
Charlie Godfrey-Faussett, David Hutcheon

Design
Art Director
Warren Beeby
Designers
Iain Murray, John Oakey
Ad Make-up
Martin Harrison

Advertising
Group Advertisement Director
Lesley Gill
Sales Director/Sponsorship
Mark Phillips
Advertisement Sales
Christopher Seth, Steve Barker
Display Production Manager
Sally Webb
Advertising Assistant
Philippa Bowes

Administration
Publisher
Tony Elliott
Managing Director
Mike Hardwick
Financial Director
Kevin Ellis
Marketing Director
Gillian Auld
Production Manager
Mark Lamond

Reprographics by Rapida
136 Tooley Street
London SE1

Contents

About the Guide

The fourth edition of the *Time Out London Guide* has been comprehensively revised and updated. Once again, it covers the whole of London, not just the major tourist traps. Of course, we have visited and critically reviewed the major attractions, but we also take you to the sights, streets, shops, venues and restaurants that other guide books rarely reach.

Time Out magazine has been covering the capital's arts and entertainment for over 25 years. Its critics and reviewers cover all aspects of London life: film, theatre, comedy, art, music, dance, sport, eating out and much more. If you want to know what's going on in London, consult *Time Out*.

All the information was checked and correct at time of going to press, but owners and managers can change their arrangements at any time. It's always best to phone before you set out to check opening times, the dates of exhibitions, admission fees and other important details. In particular, we have tried to include information on access for the disabled, but once again, it's wise to phone first to check your needs can be met.

PRICES

The prices listed throughout the guide should be used as guidelines. Fluctuating exchange rates and inflation can cause prices, in shops and restaurants especially, to change rapidly. If prices or services somewhere vary greatly from those we have quoted, ask whether there's a good reason. If not, go elsewhere. Then, please let us know. We try to give the best and most up-to-date advice, so we always want to hear if you've been overcharged or badly treated.

TELEPHONES

All seven-digit London numbers are prefixed by either 071 or 081: 071 for central London and 081 for the rest of Greater London. If you're in an 071 area, you'll have to dial 081 and then the phone number to reach someone in the suburbs; in an 081 area dial 071 for central London. If you're phoning to someone in the same band, no prefix is needed.

CREDIT CARDS

Throughout the guide, the following abbreviations have been used for credit cards: **A/c** Account customers; **AmEx** American Express; **DC** Diners' Club; **EC** Eurocheque card; **JCB** Japanese credit card; **LV** Luncheon vouchers; **MC** Mastercard/Access; **SC** store's own card; **TC** travellers' cheques in any currency; **$TC**, **£TC**, **FTC**, and so on: travellers' cheques in US dollars, sterling, French francs, or other specified currencies; **V** Visa/Barclaycard.

LET US KNOW

It should be stressed that the information we give is impartial. No organisation or enterprise has been included in this guide because its owner or manager has advertised in our publications. We hope you enjoy the *Time Out London Guide*, but if you disagree with any of our reviews, let us know. Your comments on places you have visited are always welcome and will be taken into account when compiling future editions of the guide. There's a reader's reply card at the back of the book.

Introduction

I confess. I'm an addict. And if you don't want to get addicted too, you should use this book with extreme caution.

It started while I was at school. One of my teachers tried to entice a group of children up to London to see some Shakespeare – Jonathan Pryce in *Hamlet*. I didn't really want to try it, but my friends pushed me into it. Besides, I thought, where was the harm? I could take it or leave it, I thought. I was wrong.

Soon, I was coming up not just for day trips, but for weekends. Pogoing to punk bands at the Hope & Anchor. Sitting through Bergman movies at the National Film Theatre. Strolling down the King's Road and trying to make a cup of coffee last the whole afternoon. Oh, I fought against it. Sometimes I'd manage weeks – months – of abstinence. Then I'd convince myself I'd finally conquered my guilty cravings, so it couldn't hurt if I tried just one last time... And that would be it. Hooked again.

In the end, I gave myself up to it. I rented a flat in north London, hardly caring that all my relations knew, and really let myself go.

I started fairly light at first: blockbuster films in Leicester Square, West End musicals, heck-ling at Speaker's Corner, late Saturday nights clubbing it, burgers in American-style diners. But soon that wasn't enough, and I sought out the hard stuff: poetry readings in politically correct bookshops; Kav Kavanagh's rock 'n' roll jiving lessons; experimental theatre in small sweaty rooms above pubs; even the odd hit of modern dance.

It was never enough. The more of London I tried, the more I wanted. You could even, with the right contacts, or a guide book like this one, indulge all day and all night.

Finally, my habit got so bad I couldn't afford to keep up with the payments. So, like others before me, I turned to dealing: working on, and eventually editing, *Time Out*, London's best-selling listings magazine. We serve up over 70 galleries and museums, 170 films, 120 plays and 750 gigs a week. More than enough to get any-one addicted to London.

So take a tip from someone who's been there. If you want to experience the best that London has to offer, you've come to the right place. Just don't say you weren't warned. It might start to become a habit.

Dominic Wells, Editor, *Time Out* magazine

JAWS
OPEN

10 A.M.

LONDON ZOO
CONSERVATION IN ACTION

For more information ring the **ZOOLINE** *on* **0891 505 767.**
T.I.S. plc, EC1A 9DL. Calls cost 36p per minute cheap rate and 48p per minute at all other times.

Essential Information

Facts that give you the low-down on London. Read this before you set foot on the streets.

London calling: old, red telephone boxes.

There are some things you need to know right at the start of your visit to London. Most are listed here, but we've given the complex transport system a section to itself; *see chapter* **Getting Around: Arriving in London**. For more detailed information which you may need once ensconced in the city, *see chapter* **Survival**.

Visas

A valid passport is all that is required for a stay of up to three months in the UK if you are an EC national, or if you live in a Commonwealth country (unless you come from Nigeria, Ghana, India, Bangladesh, Sri Lanka or Pakistan).

If you're a resident of certain non-Commonwealth countries, including USA, Japan, Austria, Finland, Iceland, Mexico, Sweden and Switzerland, you'll be allowed to visit Britain without a visa. If you do need a visa, apply to the British Embassy, High Commission or Consulate in your own country before leaving. The visa allows you to stay for a maximum of six months. If you want a work permit, *see chapter* **Survival: Working in London**. The work permit should be arranged before you enter the UK.

To procure visas to other countries, you'll need to contact the embassies concerned (*see chapter* **Survival: Embassies**). But, for a fee, **Rapid Visa** or **Worldwide Visas** will handle all the paperwork

for you. However, certain countries, including Italy, Canada, Guyana and Japan, require personal applications.

Home Office

Immigration and Nationality Department, Lunar House, Wellesley Road, Croydon CR9 2BY (081 686 0688). East Croydon BR. **Open** 8.30am-4pm Mon-Fri.
The immigration department of the Home Office deals with queries about immigration matters, visas and work permits for citizens from Commonwealth and a few other countries.

Rapid Visa

Top Deck House, 131-135 Earl's Court Road, SW5 (071 373 3026). Earl's Court underground. **Open** 9am-6pm Mon-Fri; 9.30am-1pm. **Credit** £TC.
Avoid the aggro of sorting out visas and let RV take the strain. You needn't be British to use the service and it costs £11.

Worldwide Visas

9 Adelaide Street, WC2 (071 379 0376). Charing Cross underground. **Open** 9.30am-6.30pm Mon-Fri; 10am-2pm Sat.
If you want an extension to your UK Visa for up to six months, Worldwide should be able to sort out all the red-tape, though it will cost about £150. The company can also arrange visas to other parts of the world.

Customs

For citizens of non-EC countries and for anyone buying duty-free goods, the following import limits apply, when entering the UK:
• 200 cigarettes **or** 50 cigars **or** 250 grams (8.82 ounces) of tobacco.
• 1 litre of spirits (over 22 per cent alcohol), **or** 2 litres of fortified wine (under 22 per cent alcohol), **or** 2 litres of sparkling and non-sparkling wine.
• 50 grams (1.76 ounces) of perfume.
• 500 grams (1.1lb) coffee.
• 100 grams (3.52 ounces) tea.
• Other goods to the value of £36 for non-commercial use.
• The import of meat, meat products, fruit, plants, flowers and protected animals is restricted or forbidden.
• There are no restrictions on the import and export of currency.

Historic Maritime Greenwich

The Place Where Time Begins

Set your watch by Greenwich Mean Time, visit the clipper ship Cutty Sark, the Queen's House and the world first Fan Museum. Shop at the arts, crafts and antiques markets. Enjoy good food from a selection of excellent restaurants and entertainment at a wide variety of venues.

Greenwich - for a great time, anytime

For further information & FREE Guide Book:
Greenwich Tourist Information Centre,
46 Greenwich Church St, London SE10 9BL.
Telephone: 081-858 6376.

Since the Single European Market agreement came into force at the beginning of 1993, EC nationals over the age of 17 have been able to import limitless goods for their personal use, if bought tax paid (ie not duty-free). But Customs officials may need convincing that you do not intend to sell any of the goods.

Insurance

It's advisable to take out insurance for your personal belongings. Medical insurance is often included in travel insurance packages, and it's important to have it unless your country has a reciprocal medical treatment arrangement with Britain (*see chapter* **Survival: Health**). All EC citizens will need to produce one of forms E110, E111, or E112.

Make sure you're insured before you leave home, since it's almost impossible to arrange once you've arrived in London.

Money

The currency in Britain is **pounds sterling** (£). One pound equals 100 pence (p). 1p and 2p coins are copper; 5p, 10p, 20p and 50p coins are silver; and £1 is a yellow coin. Thereafter, money becomes paper notes: the blue £5 note, the orange £10 note, the purple £20 and the green £50 note.

You can exchange foreign currency at either banks or bureaux de change. But if you're here for a long stay, you may need to open a bank or building society account. To do this, you'll probably need to present a reference from your bank back home, and certainly a passport as identification. **Barclays Bank**,

155 Brompton Road, SW5 (071 581 4000), deals exclusively with non-residents.

Banks

Bank opening hours can vary considerably. Minimum hours are 9.30am-3.30pm Mon-Fri, but some branches are open until 5pm. Nat West branches open until 5.30pm include 94 Kensington High Street, South Kensington Station, Regent Street, and the Strand. Cashpoint machines are outside most branches; they're usually open 24 hours daily.

Banks generally offer the best exchange rates. Commission is sometimes charged for cashing travellers' cheques in foreign currencies, but not for sterling travellers' cheques, provided you cash the cheques at a bank affiliated to the issuing bank (obtain a list when you buy the travellers' cheques). Commission is charged if you change cash into another currency. You always need identification, such as a passport, when exchanging money.

Bureaux de Change

If you cash travellers' cheques or buy and sell foreign currency at bureaux de change, you'll be charged for it. No consumer organisation controls the practices of the bureaux so commission rates – which should be clearly displayed – vary. **Chequepoint** (25 London branches) and **Lenlyn** (20 London branches) are reputable bureaux.

The major rail and underground stations in central London have bureaux de change, and there are many in tourist areas. Most are open 8am-9pm, but those listed below are open 24 hours daily.

Starting off

On the first day of your visit to London, there are three essential purchases to make, to help you explore this glorious city without wasting cash or time.

• **A Travelcard**. This ticket enables you to travel within certain zones in London on any train on the underground system, all London Regional Transport (LRT) buses (the red ones) and most British Rail trains operating within London. It can be used after 9.30am Monday to Friday, and all day Saturday and Sunday. *See chapter* **Getting Around: Public Transport** for more details of tickets.

• **A street atlas**. Buy either the *A-Z Atlas of London* or the *Nicholson London Streetfinder*. Both have a street index, and cost about £3.50 (from most newsagents and bookshops). Use the atlas in conjunction with this Guide.

• *Time Out* **magazine**. Find out what's cooking in the capital by buying a copy of London's weekly listings mag (price £1.50 from most newsagents). As well as telling you which films, plays, bands, orchestras and art exhibitions are in town, *Time Out* also gives details (in the 'Around Town' section) of all the festivals, shows, guided walks and events taking place each week.

Chequepoint
548 Oxford Street, W1 (071 723 2646). Marble Arch underground.

Chequepoint
222 Earl's Court Road, SW5 (071 370 3238). Earl's Court underground.

Chequepoint
58 Queensway, W2 (071 229 4268). Bayswater or Queensway underground.

Opening Times

For all our listings in this guide we give full opening times, but in general, shops open 9am-6pm Monday to Saturday. Several stores stay open later; we've listed a selection in *chapter* **Early Hours**. Arcane, ridiculous laws govern Sunday trading (it's illegal to sell tinned sweetcorn, but legal to sell frozen sweetcorn, for instance); many corner shops in the suburbs open on Sunday to sell food, but most specialist shops and larger stores remain closed. Things are in a mess, and some supermarkets openly flout the law. Torn between its doctrinaire commitment to free trade, and its pandering to the religious lobby, the Tory Government is dithering over whether to change the legislation.

Pub licensing laws make Britain a laughing stock. A few years ago they were eased, but a special licence is still needed for a pub to serve alcohol after 11pm. The majority of West End pubs are open 11am-11pm Monday to Saturday; noon-3pm and 7-10.30pm Sunday.

Poste Restante

If you intend to travel around Britain, you can ask friends from home to write to you care of a post office for up to one month. Your name and **Poste Restante, London** must be clearly marked on the letter: they are sent to the London Chief Post Office, King Edward Street, EC1. Bring your passport or ID card to collect your mail. For post office services within London, *see chapter* **Survival: Post Offices**.

Public Holidays

On public holidays (known as **Bank Holidays**) many shops remain open, but the public transport service is less frequent. The exception is Christmas Day: apart from a few restaurants (booked-up weeks in advance), and shops run by non-Christians, almost everything closes down as the English lock themselves in, eat and watch telly.
Good Friday Friday 1 April 1994; Friday 14 April 1995.
Easter Monday Monday 4 April 1994; Monday 17 April 1995.

May Day Holiday Monday 2 May 1994; Monday 1 May 1995.
Spring Bank Holiday Monday 30 May 1994; Monday 29 May 1995.
Summer Bank Holiday Monday 29 August 1994; Monday 28 August 1995.
Christmas Day Sunday 25 December 1994. Monday 25 December 1995.
Boxing Day Monday 26 December 1994 (Tuesday 27 December also taken as holiday); Tuesday 26 December 1995.
New Year's Day Sunday 1 January 1995 (Monday 2 January taken as holiday); Monday 1 January 1996.

Telephone

To phone London from outside the UK, you must first dial the international code (it varies from country to country), followed by 44 (the code for Britain), then the nine-digit number starting with 71 or 81 (ie omitting the first 0). For phone calls made from London *see chapter* **Survival: Telephones**.

Time

Every year (on 27 March 1994, 26 March 1995) we put our clocks forward by one hour to give British Summer Time (BST). In autumn (22 October 1994, 29 October 1995) the clocks go back by one hour to Greenwich Mean Time (GMT).

Tipping

In Britain it's accepted that you tip in taxis, minicabs, restaurants, hairdressers, hotels and some bars (not in pubs). The amount can be anything up to 15 per cent.

Tourist Information

The **London Tourist Board** runs the information centres listed below; the information centres will also supply a free map of central London. You can also ring Visitorcall on 0839 123456 which is a recorded information service with different lines providing information on places to visit, entertainment and events. Phone 071 971 0026 for a card listing the services.

Heathrow Terminals 1, 2, 3
Underground Station Concourse, Heathrow Airport. **Open** 8.30am-6pm daily.

Liverpool Street
Underground Station, EC2. **Open** 8.15am-6pm Mon-Sat; 8.30am-4.40pm Sun.

Selfridges
Basement Services Arcade, Selfridges, Oxford Street, W1. Bond Street underground. **Open** (shop hours) 9.30am-7pm Mon-Wed; 9.30am-8pm Thur, Fri; 9.30am-6.30pm Sat.

Victoria Station Forecourt
Victoria Station, SW1. **Open** 8am-7pm daily.

Getting Around

Few Londoners manage to move smoothly around this massive metropolis, but following these tips should help.

London's transport system is the busiest in western Europe: you'll be vying with millions of commuters and Londoners for that elusive seat on the underground. Yet compared to other European capitals, the level of subsidies for public transport is very low. But take time to get to know the system, work out your route carefully, and travelling on public transport can be an excellent insight into London life.

Arriving in London

To & From the Airports

Heathrow
Underground: *Piccadilly Line* **Times** *from Heathrow* 5.08am-11.33pm Mon-Sat; 6.40am-10.57pm Sun. *From Piccadilly Circus to Heathrow* 5.46am-12.21pm Mon-Sat; 7.04am-11.25pm Sun. **Tickets** *from central London* £2.80; £1.20 under-16s.
Airbus A1 from Grosvenor Gardens, SW1 *(Victoria underground/BR);* A2 from Woburn Place, WC1 *(Tottenham Court Road underground);* Euston Bus Station, Marylebone Road, NW1 *(Baker Street underground)* or Oxford Street, W1 *(Marble Arch underground).* **Times** 6.40am-8pm daily, every 20 mins until 3pm, then every 30mins. **Tickets** £5 single, £8 return; £3 single, £5 return under-16s.
The Piccadilly Line underground (dark blue on the underground map, *see* **Maps of London**) is the fastest and cheapest way of travelling between Heathrow and central London (50-60 minutes from Piccadilly Circus). The Airbuses A1 and A2 are also recommended: the journey takes 60 to 80 minutes (information 071 222 1234).
Taxi fares are high (£20 or more). Heathrow is just off the M4 motorway, about 15 miles (25km) west of central London. The journey from central London can take less than an hour, except during the rush hour, when travel is to be avoided if possible.

Gatwick
Gatwick Express train *(071 928 2113/5100). Victoria underground/BR.* **Times** *from Victoria railway station* 5.30am-8pm (every 15 mins), 4.30-5.30am, 8pm-1am (every half hour), 1-4am (every hour on the hour), daily. **Tickets** £8.50 adults; £4.25 under-15s.
Flightline 777 bus *(081 668 7261). Victoria underground/BR.* **Times** *from Victoria Bus Station* (approx once an hour) 6.35am-11.25pm daily. **Tickets** £7.50 single, £8.50 return, £11 period return; half-price under-15s; free under-5s.
Driving to or from Gatwick (about 30 miles/50km south of central London) is usually a nightmare as the route takes you through narrow, congested, south London roads. The Gatwick Express train is much the fastest service, taking approximately 30 minutes; trains run through the night. The regular Flightline 777 bus is cheaper but takes an average of 75 minutes. Both train and bus will take you to **Victoria Station** *(see below)*.

London City Airport
King George V Dock, Silvertown, E16 (071 474 5555).
It takes a journey of about 45 minutes by taxi between this new East London airport and the West End (cost: about £11; distance: about 10 miles/16km). The cheapest way to go is by rail; the BR station at Silvertown is five minutes' walk from the airport entrance. Trains run from 6.15am until 11.57pm. To get to the West End, change at Stratford onto the Central Line (red on the underground map, *see* **Maps of London**). The journey takes about 45 minutes and costs about £4. The fastest and by far the most pleasant way to get to or from the airport is to catch a riverbus boat *(see below* **Water Transport: Commuter Services**). A (free) bus runs between Canary Wharf pier and the airport. The bus journey takes about 15 minutes (longer in the rush hour). The riverbus travels between Canary Wharf and Charing Cross in the West End, taking about half an hour.

Stansted Airport
Stansted, Essex (0279 680500).
Stansted Express train *(071 928 5100). Liverpool Street underground/BR.* **Times** *from Liverpool Street railway station* (every half hour) 5.30am-11pm Mon-Fri; 6.30am-11pm Sat; 7am-11pm Sun. **Tickets** £9.80 adults; £4.90 under-15s.
London's newest airport lies about 35 miles (60km) north-east of central London. It has its own motorway exit, junction 8, on the M11; the journey to London takes about one hour. The Stansted Express train takes 40 minutes, and runs between the airport and **Liverpool Street** station *(see below)*. Expect to pay around £35 for a taxi to London, more after midnight.

To & From the Coach Station
Victoria Coach Station
164 Buckingham Palace Road, SW1 (071 730 0202).
If you arrive in London by scheduled coach, chances are you'll end your journey here. The National Express coach company runs services all over the British Isles, including Ireland, Scotland and Wales, from Victoria. Many other coach companies also operate from this terminus. The Coach Station is situated about 2 miles (3km) south-west of the West End. To reach Victoria underground and railway station from here will take a good ten minutes' walk (north, up Buckingham Palace Road). From Victoria underground station you can take the Victoria (light blue), District (green), or Circle (yellow) underground lines, or one of a myriad red buses.

To & From the Railway Stations
All London's major rail stations have their own underground station, within easy walking distance of the over-ground platforms. Below, we've listed which underground lines serve each station, giving the line's colour on the underground map *(see* **Maps of London**). All these termini are in Zone 1 *(see below* **Public Transport: Fares**) of the underground system.

Charing Cross *Strand, WC2 (071 928 5100).*
Suburban trains from the South East terminate here.
The station is just to the south of the West End.
Charing Cross is on the Bakerloo (brown), Jubilee
(silver), and Northern (black) underground lines.
Euston *Euston Road, NW1 (071 387 7070).* Inter-City
trains from the North and North West and a suburban
line from Watford terminate at Euston. The station lies
about 1½ miles (3km) north of the West End, and
about half a mile (1km) south-west of King's Cross
Station. Euston is on the Northern (black), and
Victoria (light blue) underground lines.
King's Cross *Euston Road, N1 (071 278 2477).* Inter-City
trains from the North and North East terminate
here. The station is about 2 miles (3km) north-east of
the West End. King's Cross is on the Circle (yellow),
Hammersmith & City (pink), Metropolitan (purple),
Northern (black), Piccadilly (dark blue) and Victoria
(light blue) underground lines.
Liverpool Street *Liverpool Street, EC2 (071 928
5100).* Fast trains from East Anglia, Stansted Airport,
and suburban services from east and north-east
London terminate here. The station is to the east of the
City, about 3 miles (5km) east of the West End.
Liverpool Street is on the Central (red), Circle
(yellow), Hammersmith & City (pink), and
Metropolitan (purple) underground lines.
Paddington *Praed Street, W2 (071 262 6767).* Fast
trains from the South West, West and North West
terminate at Paddington. The station is about 1½ miles
(2½km) north-west of the West End. Paddington is on
the Bakerloo (brown), Circle (yellow), District
(green), and Hammersmith & City (pink)
underground lines.
Victoria *Terminus Place, SW1 (071 928 5100).* The
fast trains from the Channel Ports terminate here, as
do trains from Brighton and Gatwick. The station is on
the Victoria (light blue), District (green) and Circle
(yellow) underground lines, about 2 miles (3km)
south-west of the West End.
Waterloo *York Road, SE1 (071 928 5100).* Fast trains
from Portsmouth, Southampton and Dorset, together
with suburban services from south-west London
terminate at Waterloo. The station is near the South
Bank, about half a mile (1km) south of the West End.
Waterloo is on the Bakerloo (brown) and Northern
(black) underground lines.

Public Transport

The underground system, commonly referred
to as the tube, is generally faster than buses,
although it's not recommended during the rush
hour (7-10am, 5-7pm, Monday to Friday) if you
don't like crowds, heat and standing up. If you
have the time, travelling by bus is less crowded and stressful and gives you a better under-
standing of the layout of the city.

The underground system and buses within
the London area are both run by **London
Regional Transport (LRT)**, which has a 24-
hour, seven-day enquiry telephone service on
071 222 1234. This provides information about
routes, fares and times for buses, the underground and the London lines operated by
British Rail (BR). In addition, there is a constantly up-dated 24-hour recorded information
service on 071 222 1200.

LRT Travel Information Centres

These Centres provide free maps and Night-
bus timetables. They also give information
about the underground, the Docklands Light
Railway and the day-time buses, plus some
details on British Rail's London routes. You can
find them in the following stations:
Euston (open 7.15am-6pm Mon-Sat; 8.30am-4.50pm Sun).
Heathrow station terminals 1, 2, 3 (open 7.15am-6pm
Mon-Sat; 8.15am-6pm Sun).
King's Cross (open 8.15am-6pm Mon-Sat; 8.30am-
5pm Sun).
Oxford Circus (open 9am-6pm Mon-Sat).
Piccadilly Circus (open 9am-6pm daily).
Victoria (open 8.15am-7.30pm Mon-Sat; 8.45am-
7.30pm Sun).

Travellers With Disabilities

For disabled people, LRT publishes a booklet
called *Access to the Underground*, which gives
information on lifts and ramps at individual
underground stations. It costs 70p and is available from London Regional Transport, Unit for
Disabled Passengers, 55 Broadway, SW1H
0BD (071 918 3312) and at **Travel Information
Centres** *(see above)*. The unit also provides
details on buses for the disabled and Braille
maps for the visually impaired. The Docklands
Light Railway has wheelchair access at all its
stations. More information can be found in
chapter **Survival: Visitors With Disabilities**.

Fares

LRT bus and underground fares are based on
a zone system. There are five zones which
stretch 12 miles (20km) out from the centre of
London *(see* **Maps of London***)*. It's advisable
to get the correct ticket; in a draconian campaign to prosecute fare evaders, LRT threatens
with relish to give you a criminal record as well
as a hefty fine.

Travelcards
The most economical way to get about is to buy a
Travelcard, usable on the underground, buses (but not
Night buses), British Rail's Network SouthEast,
Docklands Light Railway, and some Green Line services.
It is sold at all underground stations. From January 1994,
the one-day Travelcard costs £3.50 for all zones and can
be used from 9.30am weekdays; all day Saturdays,
Sundays and public holidays.

Passes
Passes are available in different combinations of zones
(central only, one zone, two zones, and so on); and for
various periods of time – the weekly costs £27.20 for all
zones, the monthly costs £104.40 all zones. Passes are
valid at any time of day and can be purchased from various newsagents, underground stations, and Network
SouthEast stations within the zones. You'll need a passport-sized photograph.

Child's Fare
On all London buses, tubes and British Rail's Network
SouthEast trains, children are classified as under 16

years of age. Under-fives travel free. Under-16s pay a child's fare until 10pm, but 14- and 15-year-olds must carry Child Rate Photocards (these are free and available from underground stations and post offices in the London area). The child's one-day travelcard costs £1.30 and covers all zones. The weekly card costs £7.95 and the monthly is £30.60 for all five zones.

The Underground

London has the world's biggest underground train system, yet the service to some residential districts is often shambolic. The government is reluctant to subsidise public transport, so travel is more expensive in London than in Europe.

Smoking is illegal anywhere on the underground.

Crime on London's underground system is nowhere near as bad as on New York's subway. Minor harassment (mostly begging) goes on, however, and women are more frequently approached. Be careful about getting into an empty tube carriage on your own and beware of pickpockets.

Using the System
If you haven't a **Travelcard** (*see above*), tickets can be bought from a station ticket office or from the self-service machines, now in most stations. Put your ticket through the new automatic checking gates, or show it as you pass through the barriers. You must hold on to your ticket until you have passed the barriers at your destination.

Underground Timetable
Tube trains run daily, except for Christmas Day, starting at around 5.30am Monday to Saturday, 7am Sunday. You won't usually have to wait more than ten minutes for a train; during peak times the service should run every couple of minutes. Last underground times vary according to lines and journeys: they're usually between 11.30pm and 1am on week nights, and 11.30pm on Sundays (but you can catch some trains after midnight).

The Docklands Light Railway (DLR)
(Travel enquiries 071 222 1234).
The DLR is administered as part of the underground system. It's a hi-tech service that runs on a raised track from Tower Gateway (a short walk from Tower Hill underground) to the tip of the Isle of Dogs. Unfortunately, the service has been plagued by mechanical and computer failures. Major engineering work means that the service can be limited in the evenings or at weekends, but from Mondays to Fridays it runs from 5.40am to 9.30pm and by March 1994 it should be running at weekends too.

Buses

Buses are the best way to see London, but they are subject to endless delays in the rush hour. The famous open-backed, red double deckers were designed to fit London's roads and many still work after 30 years. The new buses, bigger and more ungainly, are actually slower and block traffic.

Travelling At Night

Night buses run through central London from about 11pm to 6am, about once an hour on most

routes. Virtually all pass through **Trafalgar Square**, which is the best place to head for if you're unsure which bus to get. Night buses have the letter 'N' before the number.

Green Line Buses

Green Line buses serve the suburbs and towns within a 40-mile (64-kilometre) radius of London. The main departure point is Eccleston Bridge, SW1. For information on schedules and fares telephone 081 668 7261.

British Rail

Network SouthEast is run by British Rail and criss-crosses London and the suburbs. Most routes interchange with at least one main underground line and you don't have to buy a separate ticket if you have an LRT Travelcard.

British Rail Travel Enquiries
(24-hour information 071 928 5100).

Taxis

The traditional London taxis are called black cabs even though they can now be red, blue, green or even white. All licensed black cabs should have a 'For Hire' sign and a white plate on the back of the vehicle stating it is permitted to carry four or five people (depending on the model).

To get a licence, drivers of black cabs must pass a rigorous test (called 'The Knowledge') to prove they know where every street is and the shortest route to it. If you have any complaints, take a note of the cabbie's number (which s/he should wear on the left lapel) and the number of the cab (which should be displayed below the Fare Table inside the cab, and on the back plate). Complaints should be made to the **Public Carriage Office** (071 230 1631; enquiries on 071 230 1632; open 9am-4pm Monday-Friday).

Minicabs

Over long distances, minicabs are usually cheaper than black cabs, especially at night and weekends. Always ask the price when you book and confirm it with the driver.

Minicabs can't be hailed in the street; you should avoid drivers touting for business (common at night) as it's illegal, and they're probably not insured. Below we have listed some reputable services.
Atlas Cars *(071 602 1234).*
Embassy Cars *(081 560 5346).*
Greater London Hire *(081 340 2450).*
Lady Cabs *156 Essex Road, N1 (071 272 1992).* One of several branches of a north-London-based taxi service run by women, solely for women.

They're the wrong side of 30, but we love 'em: London's Big Red Buses.

Transport Hire

Car Hire

To hire a car you must have at least one year's driving experience with a full current driving licence. If you are an overseas visitor your current driving licence is valid in Britain for a year. If you live in the European Community (EC), Australia or New Zealand, and want to drive for longer than one year, you must exchange your licence for a British one; it costs about £15, and the appropriate form is available at any post office. Otherwise, you must re-take a driving test.
Avis *(Central reservations 081 848 8733)*. **Open** 8.30am-6pm Mon-Fri; 9.30am-4pm Sat. **Credit** A, AmEx, DC, £TC, V. You must be over 23 to hire a car. Chauffeur-driven cars are available – luxury models include Porsches and Rolls-Royces. Check the phone directory for the nearest Avis branch. Cheapest rental is £41.50 per day, inclusive, and there's a seasonal summer rate of £169.50 inclusive for 7-day hire.
Practical Used Car Rental *111 Bartholomew Road, NW5 (071 284 0199). Kentish Town underground/BR.* **Open** 8.30am-5.30pm Mon-Fri; 8.30am-noon Sat. Credit A, V. This franchise is the cheapest car hire in the country. The age limit is 22 with credit card ID, otherwise it's 25 years old. All cars have full AA cover and are, really, as good as new. The cheapest rental, of a four door Fiat Uno, costs only £26.12 per day, inclusive.

Cycle Hire

Cycling is an excellent way of getting around town. It's faster than going by car (motor traffic moves at 11 miles/17.7 kilometres an hour, if you're very lucky) and you don't have to rely on public transport. But there are drawbacks. Apart from inhaling car fumes, you're risking life and limb. Assertive riding is an important safety measure as are reflective armbands.
On Your Bike *52-54 Tooley Street, SE1 (071 378*

6669) London Bridge underground/BR. **Open** 9am-6pm Mon-Fri; 9.30am-5.30pm Sat. **Hire** from £6 per day; from £15 per weekend; from £25 per week. **Deposit** £50-£200. **Credit** A, V. Three- to ten-speed bikes, mountain bikes and tandems are available for hire.
Yellow Jersey Cycles *44 Chalk Farm Road, NW1 (071 485 8090). Camden Town or Chalk Farm underground/ Primrose Hill BR.* **Open** 9am-6pm Mon-Sat; 11am-5pm Sun. **Hire** mountain bikes from £15 per day, £60 per week. Only a spanner's throw from Camden Market. Most of the staff are friendly and know what they're talking about. There's a limited hire service.

Motorbike Hire

Scootabout *59 Albert Embankment, SE1 (071 582 0055). Vauxhall underground/BR.* **Open** 9am-6pm Mon-Fri; 9am-1pm Sat. **Credit** A, AmEx, DC, £TC, V. Any driver's licence, British or foreign, qualifies you to drive a 50cc moped. The hire charge for a Honda 100 goes from £30.40 per day including unlimited mileage and helmet, and from £117 per week. A Honda CBR 1000 can be hired for £70.50 per day, or £305 per week. No deposit is needed for credit card users, but if you pay by cheque or cash, you will have to pay between £100 and £350 deposit. All prices include helmet, mileage, AA membership and insurance.

Water Transport

Up until mid-August, 1993 you could sail on stylish catamarans up and down the Thames between Greenwich, Charing Cross and Chelsea Harbour. Sadly, however, the Riverbus Partnership, which had been struggling to keep its head above water for some time, finally went under. On the last riverbus to sail from Charing Cross Pier on Friday 20 August there was one passenger, not enough to keep the company afloat. As we went to press, buyers were lining up but no deals had yet been struck. Check *Time Out* magazine for the current situation.

Accommodation

London is notorious for its expensive hotels, but it is still possible to find a decent bed for the night without breaking the bank. And, as a bonus, you'll often get a belting British breakfast.

Finding a small, cheap but stylish, friendly hotel in the centre of the city can seem a Herculean task, and is especially difficult to contemplate after arriving from the airport in the early hours of the morning. But although prices in London have a high starting point compared to hotels in most of Europe, there are decent, inexpensive places to be found: if you know where. Below, we've sorted out the salubrious from the seedy.

If you do arrive very late and want to simply find a bed for the night, the best bet is to head for Ebury Street, in Victoria, SW1, as there is an entire road of hotels there, with several good ones, in particular **James House/Cartref House** (*see below* Hotels: Medium) and **Ebury House** (*below* Hotels: Budget). Earl's Court, though farther from central London, is another area replete with budget-priced hotels and is especially popular with Antipodean backpackers.

Youth hostelling is more basic and offers very little privacy. And it isn't always the cheapest option. However, some hostels are in great locations, none more impressive than **Holland House** (*see below* Youth Hostels: IYHF Hostels) which occupies a Jacobean mansion. The main YMCA and IYHF hostels have been listed below. If you're a student, it's also worth trying university residences that are vacant during the holidays. *See chapter* Students, or look in *Where to Stay in London* (£2.95), which is produced by the British Tourist Board and is on sale in tourist centres and large bookshops.

Hotels are rated through the star system or the crown system (smaller hotels often have a sign with their stars/crowns hanging outside). The highest rating is five-star. The more amenities offered, the higher the number of stars/crowns. (A five-star will always have 24-hour room service, valet, chauffeur, butler service, a comprehensive menu, and some access to health facilities). All the **Expensive** hotels listed, and most of the **Medium**s have an en suite bathroom and toilet.

We've classified hotels according to the price of a single room for one night. 'Expensive' is over £120 (usually well over); 'Medium' is from £120 down to £35; 'Budget' is below £35.

Hotels such as **Claridges** and **Browns** are out of most people's price range, but we have reviewed London's famous luxury establishments (*see* **Expensive**) which are often interesting to visit, if only for a drink or tea. Avoid the modern five-star hotels on the whole, unless someone else is paying and you are merely looking for something very functional, as they tend to be rather bland and do not give a feel of London, or a real taste of English-ness.

Lower down the price scale, we have tried to include some more unusual, quirky places where you might want to throw caution to the wind and live it up for a night. **11 Cadogan Gardens** is one such venue. It's a beautiful house more like a home than a hotel, buried in a wealthy residential area. **Hazlitt's Hotel** is where to go if it's genuine old-English charm you are looking for. Four-poster beds, rickety stairs and huge wooden chests make it unique. But for charm at a slightly more affordable price, head for the **Portobello Hotel**. The **Holland Park Hotel** is incredibly cheap considering how elegant it is and where it is, and the much-quoted **Edward Lear Hotel** also offers excellent value. For all these hotels, *see below* Hotels: Medium).

Visitors with disabilities should contact the Holiday Care Service, 2 Old Bank Chambers, Station Road, Horley Surrey RH6 9HW (0293 774 535/fax 0293 784647). It's a charitable advisory service which can help you find accommodation easily. Either ring the reservations helpline (0891 515494; calls are charged at 36p a minute off-peak, 48p a minute peak), or write or phone for the brochure listing accessible accommodation (50p).

Many of the hotels in the **Budget** section go by the name of 'guest house', or 'bed and breakfast'. Breakfast is often included in the price at these establishments. 'Continental breakfast' could be little more than a coffee and a slice of toast, or a croissant if you're lucky; 'full English breakfast' invariably involves egg and bacon, but could also include sausages, baked beans, tomatoes, mushrooms, fried bread, and sometimes even black pudding, in any combination.

If you're stuck for choice about where to stay, contact The London Tourist Board (071 730 3488)

which has hotel booking services at a number of its information centres (*see chapter* **Survival**). The LTB should also be contacted if you have any complaint to make about a hotel. If we've included the culprit in our selection, let us know.

Hotels

Expensive

Blakes

33 Roland Gardens, SW7 (071 370 6701/fax 071 373 0442). Gloucester Road or South Kensington underground. **Rates** *single* £138.50; *double* £185.50; *junior suites* £230; *deluxe double* £275. **Credit** A, AmEx, DC, £$TC, V.

Blakes is in its heyday and is the only younger hotel (opened 15 years ago) to have developed a 'scene' equal to that of Claridges or the Ritz. The fashion designer, Anouska Hempel, designed the hotel to provide glamorous surroundings, yet seclusion, for its star guests (Versace, Armani, Naomi Campbell and Richard Branson have stayed here). The 50 bedrooms and suites are lavish. Each room is crammed with old prints, antiques and tapestries. The restaurant offers food ranging from sushi to traditional British. Unashamedly expensive.

Hotel services *24-hour bar. All major languages spoken (excluding Japanese). Butler. Housekeeping. Nanny. Restaurant. Secretarial. Valet.* **Room services** *24-hour room service. Air-conditioned. Fax. Mini-bar. Telephone. Satellite TV; CNN.*

Browns

Albemarle Street (entrance in Dover Street), W1 (071 493 6020/fax 071 493 9381). Green Park underground. **Rates** *single* £194-£206; *double* £211-£252; *suites* £270-£470. **Credit** A, AmEx, DC, £$TC, V.

The quintessentially English hotel: discreet, old-fashioned, sober and understated. It was opened in 1837 by James Brown and has since served Theodore Roosevelt (who got married here) and Queen Victoria. The hotel consists of 12 town houses combined to make 120 rooms. Room and floor numbers do not follow a logical sequence, making it hard for unwanted visitors to track you down. Most guests are Americans on business, but Browns' famous afternoon teas (served on a three-tiered silver platter) appeal to all. The Wedgewood tea service clinks, the low lamps glow, and the lounge feels like that of a small country hotel (even though the establishment is owned by Forte).

Hotel services *Afternoon tea (£13.95). Restaurant.* **Room services** *24-hour room service. Buffets. Butler. Conferences. Private dinners. Mini-bar. Valet.*

Cadogan Hotel

Sloane Street (Knightsbridge end), SW1 (071 235 7141/fax 071 245 0994). Knightsbridge or Sloane Square underground. **Rates** *single* £147-£170; *double* £170-£194; *suite* from £323; *Fri-Sun* £76 per person per night. **Credit** A, AmEx, DC, £$TC, V.

Lilly Langtry, Edward VII's mistress, once lived in one of these Edwardian town houses which now form the Cadogan. It's a cosy 70-room hotel, very popular with honeymooners. Owners, Historic House Hotels, plan to modernise it, but at present it is extremely light, with delicate carved-oak panelling, pale salmon water-silk walls, and tasteful Chinese lamps. About 75 per cent of guests are European. The rooms have charm, but bathrooms are old-fashioned and there's no air-conditioning. Traffic noise is also a problem. The relaxed but refined dining room serves a mixture of modern and traditional British food and has a comprehensive wine list.

Hotel services *Gardens. Restaurant. Tennis courts.* **Room services** *Mini-bar. Radio. Safe. TV.*

Balconies, boats and Sunday brunch at the **Hotel Conrad**. See **review** page 17.

Claridges

Brook Street, W1 (071 629 8860/fax 071 499 2210).
Bond Street or Green Park underground. **Rates** *single*
£211-£252; *double* £270-£329; *suite* from £552. **Credit** A,
AmEx, DC, £$TC, V.
Claridges still has an air of excitement. It's a place where
old stars brush shoulders with star-struck secretaries.
Royals since Queen Victoria have stayed at this Mayfair
hotel. Sweeping stairways and marble floors lead to
rooms individually designed by the American Jessie
Kennedy (including the garish Hollywood Suite: all
green and white stripes). Only men can have free mem-
bership to the Bath and Racquets Club.
Hotel services *Florist. Free membership to Bath and*
Racquets Health Club and Wentworth Golf Club.
Hairdressing. Limousines. Three restaurants. **Room**
services *24-hour room service. Computer points. Fax.*
Maid. Satellite TV; CNN. Telephones. Valet.

The Connaught

Carlos Place, W1 (071 499 7070/071 495 3262).
Green Park underground. **Rates** *single* £208; *double*
£258-£276; *suites* £499. **Credit** A, AmEx, DC, £$TC, V.
Intent on maintaining a low profile, the Connaught does
not seem to welcome enquiries. However, 90 per cent of
its guests return, and it's in an excellent location in the
heart of Mayfair, walking distance from Bond Street's
exclusive shops. It has a wonderfully old-fashioned rich-
ness, with a heavily-carved mahogany stairway, salmon
carpets, and brocade drapes. The building has not
changed since 1897. The rooms are stylish and comfortable, with space to put a family in adjoining rooms. Both
restaurants serve classic French and British cuisine.
Hotel services *All European languages spoken. Two*
restaurants. Waiters on every floor. **Room services** *Air-*
conditioned. Direct dial phones. Fax lines. Mini-bars in
suites. TVs.

The Dorchester

Park Lane, W1 (071 629 8888/fax 071 409 0114).
Hyde Park Corner underground. **Rates** *single* £211;
double £252-£280. **Credit** A, AmEx, DC, JCB, £$TC, V.
This famous old hotel (opened in the 1930s), recently
received a major refurbishment, costing £100 million and
lasting two years. Work was completed in 1991 and the
result is dazzling, from the stunning entrance hallway
(all marble pillars and scalloped ceiling), to the sumptuous dining rooms (three, serving British, French and
Cantonese cuisine). Suites and bedrooms have triple-
glazing and look onto Hyde Park. Old-style grandeur per-
meates the place.
Hotel services *Dinner-dancing. Florist. Free*
membership to Dorchester Spa. Hairdressing.
Limousines. Theatre desk. Three restaurants. **Room**
services *24-hour room service. Computer points. Fax.*
Maid. Satellite TV; CNN. Three telephones. Valet.

Hotel Conrad

Chelsea Harbour, SW1 (071 823 3000/fax 071 351
6525). Fulham Broadway underground/11 bus/River
bus. **Rates** *single* £229; *double* £247; *penthouses* £470-
£1,410. **Credit** A, AmEx, DC, £$TC, V.
The three-year-old Hotel Conrad is a very popular retreat
for stressed-out businessmen, as it's surrounded by
water, bobbing boats and outdoor terraces. Many of the
spacious rooms have balconies with magnificent views
down the Thames, but the interior designs are rather
bland. The terraced restaurant is a great venue for
Sunday brunch.
Hotel services *Boat hire. Free parking. Health club*
(pool, gym, sauna, hair and beauty salon). Jazz
barbecues. Sunday brunch. **Room services** *24-hour*
room service. Air-conditioning. Books. Butler. Fax lines.
TV. Valet. Video.

The colonnade outside **The Ritz**. *See* **review**.

Mayfair Inter-Continental

Stratton Street, W1 (071 629 7777/fax 071 629 1459).
Green Park underground. **Rates** *single* £211; *double* £217-
£247; *suites* £352-£1,175. **Credit** A, AmEx, DC, £$TC, V.
Without a doubt, this is the most individual London
Intercontinental hotel. It has universal appeal: near the
sights and the shops and with a fully equipped health
club. The rooms are quiet, tasteful and spacious. Modern
British food is served in the restaurant, and there's also
a café and a pub.
Hotel services *Airport chauffeur service. Hair and*
Beauty salon. Health club (pool with aquajet, gym,
sauna, sunbed). Laundry. **Room services** *24-hour*
room service. Air-conditioning. Mini-bar. Satellite TV.

The Ritz

Piccadilly, W1 (071 493 8181/fax 071 493 2687). Green
Park underground. **Rates** *single* £190; *double* £220-£280;
suite £505-£640. **Credit** A, AmEx, DC, £$TC, V.
Sumptuous, glamorous, and elegant, the Ritz is still the
high-profile chateau hotel that Cesar Ritz intended it to
be in 1906, though it is now owned by Cunard. Despite
Louis XVI décor, gilded mirrors, and the extravagantly
sculptured Palm Court tea lounge, the hotel is unintimi-
dating, and caters for a mix of families and business people, as well as politicians and the odd pop star. The
famous teas need to be booked a week in advance. The
terrace overlooking Green Park and the magnificent
restaurant hall are popular for lunches (£26). Rooms are
decorated in understated colours with restored marble
fireplaces and many of Ritz's original bedsteads. More
people come to see the Ritz than to stay here, so it doesn't
have the cosy intimacy of the Ritz in Paris.
Hotel services *All major languages spoken. Bar.*
Afternoon teas. Chauffeur service. Laundry. Restaurant.
Room services *24-hour room service. Air-conditioning.*
Butler. Mini-bar. Nanny. Satellite TV. Valet.

The Savoy

The Strand, WC2 (071 836 4343/fax 071 872 8901).
Aldwych or Embankment underground/Charing Cross

underground/BR. **Rates** *single* £200; *double* £229; *deluxe double* £305; *suites* £329-£693. **Credit** A, AmEx, DC, £STC, V.

The celebrated Savoy has a hurly-burly bustle that appeals more to business folk, than tourists. However, the new fitness centre, with its elegant pool, gym and saunas is a major attraction, and a rarity in a central London hotel. The 152 rooms and 48 suites are uncompromisingly grand and individually furnished, from traditional to art-deco style. The French chateau-styled Lancaster ballroom has been used for opening parties of West End musicals. The three restaurants specialise in French, British and fish cooking. There is also the American bar (famous for inventing the White Russian cocktail) and a less formal champagne and oyster bar. **Hotel services** *24-hour garaging. Bar. Dinner dances (Mon-Sat). Florist. Hairdressers. Health centre (corporate membership available). Laundry. Messenger service. Three restaurants.* **Room services** *24-hour room service (full meal facilities). Butler. Computerpoints. Faxes. Maid. Mini-bar. TV. Valet.*

The Stafford

Stafford Street, James's Place, SW1 (071 493 0111/fax 071 493 7121). Green Park underground. **Rates** *single* £184; *double* £200-£215. **Credit** A, AmEx, DC, £STC, V.

The small sister of The Ritz has a slightly eccentric but warm atmosphere. It also has a 350-year-old wine cellar, which apart from holding 250,000 bottles, is the slightly surreal venue for Gothic-style, candle-lit banquets. The Stafford appeals to those in their thirties and forties. The most popular suites are in the stable block, overlooking a cobbled courtyard; each has its own front door. Some of the staff have been with the hotel 30 years, yet it is a relaxed place, and not stuffy (but over-expensive, considering the services on offer).

Hotel services *Bar. Chauffeur. Restaurant. Valet.* **Room services** *24-hour room service. TV; CNN.*

The Waldorf

Aldwych, WC2 (071 836 2400/fax 071 836 72544). Aldwych or Temple underground. **Rates** *single* from £130; *double* £150; *suites* £210-£250. **Credit** A, AmEx, DC, £STC, V.

The Waldorf oozes style, from the mahogany and chintz suites designed by Olga Polizzi, Lord Forte's daughter, right down to the airy Palm Court – a 24-hour drinks lounge – reminiscent of the Ritz. Its four-star status means there is no butler ready waiting; but the spacious rooms (all with bathroom en suite), friendly service, lavish modern-British restaurant, and its location just off Theatreland and near the City, make it an excellent place to stay. For guests and other visitors, the weekend tea dances (including five-course tea) are unmissable. **Hotel services** *Free membership to Canons sports club. Leisure break packages. No-smoking rooms. Theatre and tour booking. Tea dances £19.50.* **Room services** *24-hour room service. Air conditioning. Mini-bars. Satellite TV.*

Medium

11 Cadogan Gardens

11 Cadogan Gardens, off Sloane Street, SW3 (071 730 3426/fax 071 730 5217). Sloane Square underground/14 bus. **Rates** *single* £89-£119; *double* £132-£172; *suite* £200; *garden suite* £350.

Outside, little gives away the fact this is a hotel. Inside, the oak-panelled hallway filled with antiques and heavy nineteenth-century paintings, also looks more like an upper-class private home. The cosy bedrooms all have wooden furniture, large long windows and marble bathrooms. Guests can have breakfast in their rooms, in the drawing room, or in the small conservatory.

Hotel services *Car hire. Chauffeur and Limousine. Health Club (with pool, gym, sauna, solarium, beauty treatments). Laundry.* **Room services** *24-hour room service (includes simple meals). Telephone. TV.*

Amber Hotel

101 Lexham Gardens, W8 6JN (071 373 8666/fax 071 835 1194). Earl's Court underground. **Rates** *single* £50; *double* £60-£65. **Credit** A, AmEx, DC, £TC, V.

The Amber hotel is squeaky clean and new – unusually so for London. It is run by a Dutch company and has a modern but tasteful interior, music playing throughout the hotel, and an extremely laid-back atmosphere. All rooms have en suite baths. It's a far cry from the run-down Earl's Court hotels nearby.

Hotel services *Bar. Computer, photocopying and fax services. Continental/English breakfast.* **Room services** *Air-conditioning. Hairdryer. TV.*

Ebury House

102 Ebury Street, SW1 (071 730 1350/1059). Sloane Square underground or Victoria underground/BR. **Rates** *single* £40; *double* £50; *triple* £66; *four-bed room* £75. **Credit** A, AmEx, £STC, V.

Ebury House has a good location and is a lot cleaner and less basic than many of the hotels that line this street. **Hotel services** *Full English breakfast.* **Room services** *Hairdryer. TV.*

Edward Lear Hotel

28-30 Seymour Street, W1 (071 402 5401/fax 071 706 3766). Marble Arch underground. **Rates** *single* £37.50; *single with shower* £47.50; *single with bath* £55; *double* £49-£62.50; *triple* £59.75-£72.50. **Credit** A, £TC, V.

One of London's rare delights: clean and airy, in a perfect location, and moderately priced. The staff are mainly American, on the Bunac scheme; guests are mostly American or Australasian. The atmosphere is relaxed and friendly. Breakfast is served in a neatly wallpapered café-style room.

Hotel services *English breakfast. Baggage storeroom.* **Room services** *Radio. Tea/coffee. Telephones. TV; movie channel.*

La Gaffe

107 Heath Street, NW3 (071 435 8965/fax 071 794 7592). Hampstead underground. **Rates** *single* £40; *double* £60. **Credit** A, AmEx, DC, £TC, V.

The Bernados have been running the Italian restaurant downstairs together with this bed and breakfast for nearly 30 years. The Gaffe has a lot of character, not only because of the quaint building (once a shepherd's cottage), and the stylish rooms (two with four-poster beds), but also the ebulliency of the family that run it.

Hotel services *Continental breakfast. Terrace garden.* **Room services** *Showers and toilet. Telephone. TV.*

Hazlitt's

6 Frith Street, W1 (071 434 1771/fax 071 439 1524). Leicester Square or Tottenham Court Road underground. **Rates** *single* £112; *double* £135; *suite (with four-poster bed)* £177. **Credit** A, AmEx, DC, £TC, V.

This beautiful eighteenth-century hotel, in the heart of happening Soho, has been skilfully restored and the wooden panelling, crooked stairs, and poky dressing rooms still remain. Charm exudes out of the heavy mahogany pews, wooden bedposts and deep old-fashioned baths: all very popular with the film industry and with honeymooners. The staff look more like museum curators than hoteliers. For a quieter stay, plump for a double at the back. There are only five singles and they get booked up quickly. Breakfast is served in the bedrooms, or guests can eat with friends in the sinking leather sofas in the drawing room. The best room is the suite, with an elegant sitting room and amazing canopied four-poster bed – it has to be seen (and slept in). **Hotel services** *Continental breakfast. Fax.* **Room services** *Breakfast service. Telephone. TV.*

Holland Park Hotel

6 Ladbroke Terrace, W11 (071 792 0216/fax 071 727 8166) Notting Hill underground. **Rates** *single £37.60; single with bath £47; double £47; double with bath £63.45. extra single bed £11.75.* **Credit** A, AmEx, DC, £TC, V.

The Holland Park occupies an elegant Victorian townhouse in a leafy, quiet part of Notting Hill. It's near to Portobello Road market, some excellent pubs and plenty of good restaurants. The rooms at the back look over the garden and are more spacious. Downstairs there's a very civilised drawing room. Attentive, friendly service adds to the charm of this five-star budget hotel. Magnificent. **Hotel services** *Private garden.* **Room services** *Telephone. TV.*

Petersham Hotel

Nightingale Lane, Richmond, Surrey (081 940 7471/fax 081 940 9998). Richmond underground/BR/33, 37 bus. **Rates** *single £97-£115; double £130-£150.* **Credit** A, AmEx, DC, £STC. V.

Space and spectacular river views await visitors to the Petersham. The nineteenth-century hotel is privately owned, making it relaxed and friendly. And although only 8 miles (13km) from central London, it has the semblance of an English country retreat. Some of the back bedrooms have balconies looking over fields down to the Thames. They are tastefully attired, with fully modernised bathrooms; some have four-poster beds. The restaurant (traditional French/British cuisine) and lounges are popular with locals. Richmond itself has a lot to offer (*see chapter* **By Area: South**). **Hotel services** *Car park. Many European languages spoken.* **Room services** *24-hour room service and bar. TV.*

The Plough

42 Christchurch Road, SW14 (081 876 7833). Richmond underground/Mortlake BR. **Rates** *single £45; double £58.* **Credit** A, £TC, V.

This flower-decked pub feels as if it's buried deep in the country, with locals either sitting at the wooden benches in the front garden or under the low-beamed ceilings inside. The easy-going landlord, Brian O'Donovan has seven cottage-style bedrooms above the pub, with five looking out over the front garden. It is in a very quiet area, five minutes from Richmond Park, but the pub is busy. Pub lunches and dinners are available. All rooms have en suite bathrooms. **Hotel services** *Full English breakfast. Parking. Telephone.* **Room services** *Tea/coffee. TV.*

Portobello Hotel

22 Stanley Gardens, W11 (071 727 2777/fax 071 792 9641). Notting Hill underground. **Rates** *cabin £70; single £85; double £100-£120; special £170.*

This privately owned Victorian terrace hotel, with its potted palms, wooden blinds, languishing muslin drapes, and goose-down duvets, looks quite colonial. It's in a quiet residential road and has an idyllic back garden, but Notting Hill has plenty of life to offer those looking for it. The rooms are all different, some have four-poster beds. The Wedding Suite is quite something, with a round bed draped in a white canopy and an old-fashioned bath in the centre of the room. **Hotel services** *24-hour restaurant/bar/reception. Complimentary health facilities at Lambton Place Health Club. Fax service. Laundry. Limousine hire. Photocopying. Valet.* **Room services** *Bathroom en*

The **Petersham Hotel**. *See* **review**.

suite. Cable TV; CNN. Hairdryer. Mini-bar. Room service (8am-4pm daily). Tea/coffee. Telephone.

La Reserve

422-428 Fulham Road, SW6 (071 385 8561/fax 071 385 7662). Fulham Broadway underground. **Rates** *single £75; double £90; executive suite £110.* **Credit** A, AmEx, DC, £STC, V.

La Reserve is modern, but thankfully without frills and flounce. In fact, the reception hall looks more like a King's Road hairdresser's, with symmetrical glass tables, black leather sofas, stiff chrome chairs and dim spotlights. The rooms are as stylised, with arty bed headrests, and designer quilts. The cocktail bar and restaurant are also neat and black; a variety of food is available in the latter. **Hotel services** *24-hour bar.* **Room services** *Hairdryer. Mini-bar. Room service. Satellite TV. Tea/Coffee. Trouser press.*

South Kensington Guest House

13 Cranley Place, SW7 (071 589 0021/fax 071 723 0727). South Kensington underground. **Rates** *single £35-£45; double £50-£69; triple £60.* **Credit** A, £TC, V.

Rooms here are functional, basic, and have rather old showers and baths. The location in the heart of South Kensington, near the sights, museums, shops and restaurants is the main attraction. **Hotel services** *Breakfast.* **Room services** *TV.*

Budget

Abbeville Guesthouse

89 Abbeville Road, SW4 (071 622 5360). Clapham Common underground. **Rates** *single £15; double £26.* **Credit** £TC.

Mrs Coleman and her son run this spacious, detached house, situated in a quiet road. Clapham Common may seem far out of London, but the West End is only 15 minutes away by tube. **Hotel services** *Continental breakfast.* **Room services** *Tea/coffee. TV.*

Annandale House Hotel

39 Sloane Gardens, Sloane Square, W1 (071 730 6291/2). Sloane Square underground. **Rates** *single £33; double with bathroom £60-£75; extra bed £15.* **Credit** A, £TC, V.

Eddie and Estelle Morris have run the Annandale for 12 years and have an extremely loyal following, not solely due to their exuberance. The place is very clean, the rooms spacious, and breakfast is unique, with a different dish every day (from Welsh rarebit to potato pancakes, but all food is vegetarian). The excellent location close to the tube, and the mix of nationalities and ages, make this is a great place to stay.
Hotel services *Breakfast. Buffet. Parking.* **Room services** *Books. Hairdryers. Tea/coffee. Telephone. TV.*

Boka Hotel

33-35 Eardley Crescent, SW5 (071 373 2844). Earl's Court underground. **Rates** *single £15; double room £25; dormitory £10.* **Credit** A, AmEx, £TC, V.

Most of the rooms don't have a bathroom, but then this hotel is cheaper than most. It's in the heart of Earl's Court backpacker land, and tends to be full of Australians and South Africans.
Hotel services *Telephone. TV lounge.*

Curzon House Hotel

158 Courtfield Gardens, SW5 (071 581 2116). Gloucester Road underground. **Rates** *single £26; double £36-£38; triple £34-£38; dormitory £13.* **Credit** A, £TC, V.

The Curzon House Hotel is not specifically for tourists. Mostly young people stay here. Visitors can use the kitchen and are given their own front-door key. There are plenty of restaurants nearby.
Hotel services *Safe. TV lounge.*

Europa House Hotel

151 Sussex Gardens, W2 (071 723 7343/fax 071 224 9331). Paddington underground/BR. **Rates** *single £30; double £45; family £20 per person.* **Credit** A, £TC, V.

This friendly but quiet hotel is in a tree-lined road behind Hyde Park, close to Paddington Station. All rooms are clean and a good size. The long communal tables in the breakfast room are rather appalling, but functional.
Hotel services *Full English/Continental breakfast. TV lounge.* **Room services** *Shaver points. Tea/coffee. Telephone. TV.*

Gower House Hotel

57 Gower Street, WC1 (071 580 4892). Goodge Street underground. **Rates** *single £30; double £40; double with bathroom £55.* **Credit** A, £TC, V.

The manager here is very courteous and the rooms are clean and spacious. But Formica dominates the hard-seated lounge, and the breakfast room is like a workman's canteen. If you want a central location, and you'll be out a lot, the Gower is fine.
Hotel services *Breakfast.* **Room services** *Tea/coffee.*

Hampstead Village Guesthouse

2 Kemplay Road, NW3 (071 435 8679/fax 071 794 0254). Hampstead underground. **Rates** *single £21-£25; double £42-£59.* **Credit** A, AmEx, £TC, V.

All the rooms in this Victorian house are different: some vast, others cosy and small. They are not only very clean, but full of family clutter. Staff are friendly, and dogs and cats add to the homely feel of the place. Tourists and business people of all ages stay here. The location, off stylish Hampstead High Street, is only five minutes from Hampstead Heath. It's a non-smoking hotel: guests take their ciggies to the garden.
Hotel services *Continental breakfast (vegetarian option). Fax service. Meals served (with advanced*

warning). Private garden. **Room services** *Fridge. Tea/coffee. Telephone. TV.*

Hotel Saint Simeon

38 Harrington Gardens, SW7 (071 373 0505). Gloucester Road underground. **Rates** *single £8-£28; double £24-£40.* **Credit** A, AmEx, £TC, V.

Not far from the museums in civilised South Ken, the Saint Simon is especially good value because it has a kitchen available for guests. Basic, but for those on tight budgets, a great place to stay.
Hotel services *Continental breakfast. Telephone. TV lounge.* **Room services** *Tea/coffee. TV.*

Hyde Park House

48 St Petersbrugh Place, W2 (071 229 1687). Bayswater underground. **Rates** *single £20; double £30; twin with bathroom £30.* **No credit cards.**

A clean, cheap hotel, just to the west of central London and near to Hyde Park. It's often packed with Americans and Australians who take advantage of the kitchen facilities to cook their own meals. Some of the 18 rooms even have their own fridges; few have bathrooms.
Hotel services *Continental breakfast. Kitchen for guests.* **Room services** *Telephone. TV.*

James House/Cartref House

108/129 Ebury Street, SW1 (071 730 7338/071 730 6176). Sloane Square underground or Victoria underground/BR. **Rates** *single £45; family £65-£75; double with bathroom £55; family with bathroom £75-£85.* **Credit** A, AmEx, £TC, V.

James and Cartref House are situated in a very chic area, behind Eton Square, not far from Victoria Coach Station. They have been run by the James family for years. Not surprisingly, both houses are nearly always full – particularly with Americans. Commemorative plates and fussy frills may not be to everyone's taste, but the rooms are scrupulously clean, with neat new bed-covers.
Hotel services *Full English breakfast.* **Room services** *Tea. TV.*

The **Annandale House Hotel.** *See* **review.**

*Breakfast at the **Vicarage**. See **review**.*

Jesmond Hotel
63 Gower Street, WC1 071 636 3199). Goodge Street underground. **Rates** *single £22; double £32.* **Credit** A, £TC, V.
Run by an omnipresent husband and wife, the Jesmond is spotless, cheap but a little characterless. Gower Street is fearfully busy, but very handy for the British Museum and the West End.
Hotel services *Full English breakfast. TV lounge.* **Room services** *Tea/coffee.*

Nevern Hotel
31 Nevern Place, SW5 (071 370 4827/fax 071 370 1541). Earl's Court underground. **Rates** *single £20-£30; double £30-£40; triple £15 per person.* **Credit** A, AmEx, £TC, V.
Cheery receptionists welcome an assortment of people to the Nevern: teachers with young children, backpackers, Arabs, Malays, and pensioners. The hotel is a stone's throw from the tube, in cosmopolitan Earl's Court.
Hotel services *Continental/full English breakfast.* **Room services** *Direct-dial telephones. TV.*

Oak House
29 Hugh Street, SW1 (071 834 7151). Sloane Square or Victoria underground. **Rates** *double £25.50; family £10 per person.* **Credit** £TC.
Scottish Mr Symington and his Welsh wife run this hotel with great attention to detail. The six rooms are very popular with all ages, and are often all booked. However, there are several other good budget hotels in the area to choose from.
Room services *Hairdryer. Tea/coffee. TV.*

Ruskin Hotel
23-24 Montague Street, WC1 (071 636 7388/fax 071 323 1662). Tottenham Court Road underground. **Rates** *single £34; double £49.* **Credit** A, AmEx, DC, £TC, V.
The Ruskin looks onto the back of the British Museum and is in a superb location in Bloomsbury. Although inexpensive, the hotel is spotless and airy with decent-sized rooms. It also boasts a lift.
Hotel services *Breakfast. Cold drinks machine. Telephone. TV lounge.* **Room services** *Hairdryers. Tea/coffee.*
Branch: Haddon Hall Hotel, 39-40 Bedford Place, WC1 (071 636 0026).

Swiss House Hotel
171 Old Brompton Road, SW5 (071 373 2769/fax 071 373 4983). Gloucester Road underground. **Rates** *single £32; single with shower and toilet £45; double £48; double with shower and toilet £58; extra bed £8.50.* **Credit** A, AmEx, £STC, V.
The Maltese owner, Peter Vicinti and his European staff make this hotel a joy to stay in. It has trailing plants over the door, elegant russet-carpeted hallways, and a break-

fast room complete with wooden dresser. The bedrooms have the same attention to detail, with canopies over the beds, and neat bedcovers. Spacious, clean and quiet in a chic part of town.
Hotel services *Continental breakfast (English breakfast £3.50 extra). Parking. Telephone.* **Room services** *TV (plus satellite).*

Vicarage Private Hotel
10 Vicarage Gate, W8 (071 229 4030). High Street Kensington underground. **Rates** *single £30; double £52; triple £65; four-bed room £70.* **No credit cards.**
This family-run hotel has 19 rooms and very friendly staff. Visitors can arrive at any time of the day and leave their bags, or sit in the TV lounge. Single guests are all put on one large table for breakfast, so they don't feel lonely. Most clients are antiques dealers from the USA, who book at least three months in advance. The rooms are spacious and thoroughly cleaned.
Hotel services *Tea and coffee machines. Telephone.*

Children's Hotel

Pippa Pop-Ins
430 Fulham Road, SW6 (071 385 2458). Fulham Broadway underground. **Rates** *single or multiple £25-£30.* **Credit** A, AmEx, £TC, V,
Children (aged 2-14) can have their own dinner parties and rooms at Pippa's. If need be, they can be left here 24 hours a day, seven days a week. *See also chapter* **Children**.
Hotel services *Meals included.*

Youth Hostels

For a full list of all **YMCA** and **YWCA** hostels in London contact: the National Council for YMCAs at 640 Forest Road, E17 (081 520 5599). To stay at **IYHF** (International Youth Hostel Federation) hostels, you need to become a member of the organisation (the charge is £8). You can join at Covent Garden's **YHA Shop**, 14 Southampton Street, WC2 (071 836 8541); open 9.30am-6pm Mon, Wed, Fri, Sat; 10am-6pm Tue; 9.30am-7pm Thur.

IYHF

City of London Youth Hostel
36 Carter Lane, EC4 (071 236 4965/fax 071 236 7681). St Paul's underground. **Reception open** *7am-11.30pm daily.* **Rates** *£19.30 per person; £16 under-18s.* **Hotel services** *Bureau de change. Full canteen facilities. Public telephone. Shop. TV.*

Earl's Court Youth Hostel
38 Bolton Gardens, SW5 (071 373 7083/fax 071 835 2034). Earl's Court underground. **Reception open** *7am-11.30pm daily.* **Rates** *£16.10; £14.50 under-18s.* **Credit** A, £STC, V.
Hotel services *Bureau de change. Coach and hostel booking service. Full canteen and kitchen facilities.*

Hampstead Heath Youth Hostel
4 Wellgarth Road, NW11 (081 458 9054/fax 081 209 0546). Golders Green underground. **Reception open** *7am-11.30pm daily.* **Rates** *£13.90 per person; £11.80 under-18s.*
Breakfast, lunch and dinner are served in the canteen. **Hotel services** *Bureau de change. Kitchen facilities. Launderette. Public telephones. TV.*

Highgate Village Youth Hostel
84 Highgate West Hill, N6 (081 340 1831/fax 081 341 0376). Archway or Highgate underground. **Reception open** 8.45am-10am, 1-11.30pm, daily. **Rates** £11.40; £7.60 for under-18s.
Only breakfast is available here.
Hotel services *Kitchen facilities. Public telephone. TV.*

Holland House
Holland Park, W8 (071 937 0748/fax 071 376 0667). High Street Kensington or Holland Park underground. **Reception open** 7am-11.30pm daily. **Rates** £18.10; £16 under-18s. **Credit** A, £STC, V.
A 190-bed hostel that occupies the remains of a Jacobean mansion. It's basic, but its superb location in tranquil Holland Park ensures a regular full house. Meals are served in a canteen.
Hotel services *Bureau de change. Kitchen facilities. Launderette. Public telephone. TV.*

Oxford Street Youth Hostel
14-18 Noel Street, W1 (071 734 1618/fax 071 734 1657). Oxford Circus underground. **Reception open** 7am-11pm daily. **Rates** £16.70 per person; £13.50 under-18s. **Credit** A, TC, V.
Hotel services *Bureau de change. Kitchen facilities. Public telephones. TV.*

YMCA

Barbican YMCA
Fann Street, EC2 (071 628 0697). Barbican underground or Moorgate underground/BR. **Open** 24 hours daily. **Rates** *single* £22; *double* £20; long stay (over six months) £85.10 per week. **Credit** A, £TC, V.
Accommodates 250 people and is often packed. Book well in advance. Prices include breakfast and dinner during the week, three meals Saturday and Sunday.

Indian Students YMCA
41 Fitzroy Square, W1 (071 387 0411). Warren Street underground. **Open** 24 hours daily. **Rates** *single* £26.60; *double* £35. **Credit** £TC.
This hostel is specifically for Indian students, but is open to anyone else who wants to stay. Vegetarian breakfasts and dinners are included in the price; dinner is very good Indian food, breakfast is English. Discounts are given for bookings in advance of over a month.

London City YMCA
8 Errol Street, EC1 (071 628 8832). Barbican underground, Moorgate BR/underground. **Open** 24 hours daily. **Rates** *single* £24, £126 per week (includes breakfast and evening meal); £93.10 per week after three months, via a waiting list. **Credit** A, £TC, V.

Wimbledon YMCA
200 The Broadway, SW19 (081 542 9055). Wimbledon BR/93 bus. **Open** 24 hours daily. **Rates** *single* £19.50; *double* £34. **Credit** A, £TC, V.

YWCA

YWCA Central Club
Helen Graham House, 57 Great Russell Street, WC1 (071 636 7512). Tottenham Court Road underground. **Rates** *single* £34.75; *double* £64.50. **Credit** A, £TC, V.
Beds for women-only.

YWCA
Elizabeth House, 118 Warwick Way, SW1 (071 630 0741). Victoria underground/BR. **Credit** £TC.

Rates *single* £20; *dormitory* £15 (women-only).
Accommodation for both men and women; Continental breakfast is included.

Camping & Caravanning

Abbey Wood Caravan Club
Federation Road, SE2 (081 310 2233). Abbey Wood BR. **Open** *office* 8am-10pm daily. **Rates** £3.20 (off-peak £2.65); £1.30 children; *car and tent pitch* £5; *motorvan and pitch* £5; *electricity hook-up* £1. **Credit** A, £TC, V.
The site has a laundry, three shower blocks, a mini-market, and children's play area. The maximum length of time for a stay is two weeks.

Hackney Camping
Millfields Road, E5 (081 985 7656). Bus 38. **Open** mid-June to late Aug. **Rates** £2.50 per person. **Credit** £TC.
Only four miles (6.4km) from central London, this old East End park is right by a canal. It is also well-equipped with toilets, showers, baggage storage and a shop.

Lee Valley Campsite
Sewardstone Road, E4 (081 529 5689). Walthamstow underground/BR then 215 bus. **Open** *Apr-Oct* 8am-10pm daily. **Rates** £4.50 adults; £1.80 under-15s; *electrical hook-up* £1.60 per day. **Credit** A, £TC, V.
Mr Pegg runs this spacious campsite, off the A112 between Chingford and Waltham Abbey. It's 12 miles (20km) from central London, but very cheap, and has plenty of facilities (shop, showers, play-areas) on the 200-pitch site. No unaccompanied under-18s are admitted.

Lee Valley Park
Pickett's Lock Centre, Pickett's Lock Lane, N9 (081 345 6666/fax 081 884 4975). Ponders End BR/W8 bus. **Open** 8.30am-7.30pm Mon-Sat. **Rates** £4.20; £1.70 under-15s; *electrical hook-up* £2 per day. **Credit** £TC.
There is plenty of activity for the sporty at Pickett's Lock (a golf course is nearby). In addition, there are 125 touring caravan pitches, 75 tent pitches, and a nearby sewage works.

Tent City
Old Oak Common Lane, W3 (081 749 9074/081 743 5708). East Acton underground/7, 12, 52A bus. **Open** *May-Oct* 24-hours daily. **Rates** £5; £3 under-15s; under-5s free. **Credit** £TC.
Visitors can pitch their own tent or sleep in one of the dozen, large dormitory marquees. Tent City is a very relaxed, festive sort of place. Showers and a baggage store are provided. The site is about 10 minutes' walk from East Acton tube.

Emergency Accommodation

Even on a warm summer night, sleeping rough in London is not a good idea: it's not safe and you risk having your rucksack and belongings stolen. In an emergency, contact one of the agencies below.

Advisory Service for Squatters
2 St Paul's Road, N1 (071 359 8814). Highbury & Islington underground/BR. **Open** 2-6pm Mon-Fri.
Squatting in England is legal (though the government is trying to outlaw it). The ASS has details of empty properties and can inform you of squatters' rights. The service also produces *The Squatter's Handbook* (£1).

Shelter Nightline

(Freefone 0800 446 441). **Open** 6pm-9am Mon-Fri; 24-hours Sat, Sun.

Shelter, a voluntary organisation that helps the homeless, runs a number of help-lines. In addition to the Nightline, there is **Shack** (081 960 2532) and the **Piccadilly Advice Centre** (071 434 3773, after 2pm) both of which deal with emergency housing problems. **Alone in London** (071 278 4224) helps homeless under-21s.

The Tunbridge Club

80 Judd Street, WC1 (no phone). King's Cross underground/BR. **Rates** £2.50.

Emergency accommodation is offered to stranded tourists.

Women's Link

57 Great Russell Street, WC1 (071 430 1524). Tottenham Court Road underground. **Open** *personal calls* 11am-3pm Mon-Wed; 11am-7pm Thur; 1-3.30pm Fri; *telephone enquiries* 10am-4pm Mon-Wed; 10am-7pm Thur; 1-4pm Fri.

An information service that can provide a great deal of help in finding temporary, permanent or emergency accommodation for women. It produces a pamphlet, 'Hostels in London' (£2.50).

Accommodation Agencies

The agencies listed below can arrange bed and breakfast with a family in many areas of London and at a range of prices. Staying in someone's home can be good fun and is a great way of meeting Londoners.

Host and Guest Service

The Studio, 635 Kings Road, SW6 (071 731 5340/fax 071 736 7230). Fulham Broadway underground. **Open** 9.30am-5.30pm Mon-Fri. **Rates** *single* £12; *double* £20. **Credit** A, £TC, V.

This agency has 3,000 homes on its books. Its low rates reflect the outer-London location of the properties. A single room in a more central area will cost about £18 a night. Evening meal and packed lunch can be arranged. Minimum stay: three nights.

London Homestead Services

Coombe Road, Kingston-upon-Thames, Surrey (081 949 4455/fax 081 549 5492). Norbiton BR. **Open** 9am-5pm Mon-Fri. **Rates** *single* £16-£18; *double* £24. **Credit** A, £TC, V.

LHS can find you accommodation in a house in central or outer London. The minimum length of stay is three nights. Evening meals can be arranged on request. The company is extremely busy in peak season, so it's worth sending your requirements by fax two-to-three weeks in advance.

Self-Catering

It is often not, as popularly believed, cheaper to rent a flat than to stay in an hotel. Rented accommodation is expensive in London (more than most other European capital cities) and is difficult to find. But for a group of four or more people, hiring a flat can save money.

Aston's Budget and Designer Studios & Apartments

39 Rosary Gardens, SW7 (071 370 0737/fax 071 835 1419). Gloucester Road underground. **Open** 9am-5pm Mon-Fri. **Rates** *self-contained and non self-contained flats*

(max four people) £185-£900 per week. **No credit cards.**

All of Aston's accommodation, from budget to de luxe, is air-conditioned and situated in quiet Victorian town houses in South Kensington. There are 30 self-contained flats and 50 non-self-contained flats.

Butlers Wharf Residence

Gainsford Street, SE1 (071 407 7164). London Bridge underground/BR. **Open** 9am-5pm Mon-Fri. **Rates** *self-contained flats (maximum seven people)* £16.50 per person per night. **Credit** £TC.

There are 46 brand new flats for rent at Butlers Wharf, an eighties riverside development scheme that has yet to succeed in moving Londoners to this down-river spot. The problem is the lack of facilities: there are few restaurants, cinemas, theatres and shops in the vicinity. But the location is central (Tower Bridge is virtually visible), and the Thames almost looks picturesque from here in the early evening.

Luxury Holiday Short-Lets

14 Westpoint, 49 Putney Hill, SW15 (081 788 8735/fax 081 780 9529). East Putney underground/Putney BR. **Open** 9am-5pm Mon-Fri. **Rates** *one-bedroom apartments (up to two people)* £225 per week; *one-bedroom apartments (up to three people)* £275 per week; *two-bedroom apartments (up to four people)* £375 per week. **Credit** £TC.

An efficient agency that can provide flats in south-west and north London. Fax details of your arrival and departure (minimum 14-day stay), plus one week's deposit. More people can be squashed into the flats for an extra £4 per person per night.

Tennis London

24-25 New Row, WC2 (071 379 8029/fax 071 497 2486). Covent Garden underground. **Open** 9am-5pm Mon-Fri. **Rates** from £500 per week for a 2-3 bedroom house. **Credit** A, AmEx, £TC, V.

Renowned for organising digs for Wimbledon tennis players, this company also caters for visitors in general. Give two-to-three weeks' notice, especially in peak season. The minimum stay is two weeks. Apartments in central, as well as south-west, London are on the books.

Longer Stay

If you don't have the money for an apartment (*see above* **Self-Catering**) and are planning on staying longer than a month, you should try finding a bedsit, or a room in a flat. London accommodation prices are high and the competition can be fierce, though the recession has led to rooms being let by people burdened with crippling mortgages. You'll usually have to pay a month's rent in advance, but this is returned when you leave. Look in *Time Out* magazine every Tuesday; the 11am edition of the *Evening Standard; Dalton's Weekly* and the *London Weekly Advertiser* on Thursday, and *Loot,* daily; and *Capital Gay,* a free weekly magazine from gay clubs and bookstores. The Capital Radio flatshare list is available at 11am every Tuesday from the foyer of Capital Radio at Euston Tower, Euston Road, NW1 (Warren Street underground) or in *Midweek* magazine, free from major underground stations on Thursday. If you can find a room in a shared house for £200 a month, you're doing well.

London by Season

A year-round guide to festivities, from pancakes in spring to new year in Chinatown.

London seems to have more than its fair share of seasonal events. There are the major occasions, such as the Lord Mayor's Show, Wimbledon, the Proms and the London to Brighton Rally; but there is also a number of weird, lesser-known events: the vicar who conducts a service on horseback and the livery company officials who paddle about counting angry swans.

FESTIVAL TIME

London's own multi-ethnic culture has spawned the **Notting Hill Carnival** and **Chinese New Year** celebrations. Specialist festivals are often spread over several venues: the **Greenwich Festival** in June (081 317 8687); the July **City of London Festival** (071 606 3030); the **Soho Jazz Festival** (late Sept-early Oct, 071 434 3995); the **Capital Radio Music Festival** (mid June-mid July, 071 379 1066), which is Europe's biggest music festival; and the August **International Street Performers Festival**, which is held in the Covent Garden Piazza.

Frequent Events

Ceremony of the Keys
HM Tower of London, EC3 (071 709 0765). Tower Hill underground. **Date** 9.35-10.05pm daily (except Christmas Day). **Maximum** in party *Apr-Oct* 8; *Nov-Mar* 15. **Admission** free, by prior arrangement.
'Halt! Who comes there?' 'The keys.' 'Whose keys?' 'Queen Elizabeth II's keys' 'Pass the keys. All's well.' This laborious routine of locking-up the Tower of London has been going on every night for 700 years. Ticket holders should arrive by 9.35pm. The real business begins at 9.53pm exactly, when the Chief Warder leaves the Byward Tower and it's all over before the clock chimes 10 o'clock and the Last Post is sounded. Apply for tickets, giving alternative dates, at least two months in advance in writing with a stamped addressed envelope to: The Resident Governor, Queen's House, HM Tower of London, EC3N 4AB.

Changing the Guard
Buckingham Palace SW1. St James's Park or Victoria underground/BR. **Times** *May-July* 11.30am daily; *Aug-Apr* 11.30am alternate days.
Tower of London Tower Hill, EC3. Tower Hill underground. **Times** *Mar-Oct* 11.30am daily; *Nov-Feb* 11.30am alternate days.
Whitehall SW1. Charing Cross underground/BR. **Times** 11am, 4pm Mon-Sat; 10am, 4pm Sun.
These famous ceremonies derive from the days when the lifeguards directly protected the monarch's life. Now they entertain both tourists and British patriots, who just love the uniforms and royalist imagery. For full details *see chapter* **Sightseeing**. There's yet another ceremony at **Windsor Castle** (*see chapter* **Trips Out of Town**; phone 0753 868286 for details, 0753 831118 for recorded information).

Druid Ceremonies
(Druid Order 081 771 0684) .
Summer Solstice *Stonehenge, A303, Wiltshire or White Horse Stone, A229, 2 miles east of Aylesford, Kent.* **Date** Dawn (about 4.30am), 21 June 1994, 1995. **Autumn Equinox** *Primrose Hill, NW3.* **Date** 1pm 21 Sept 1994, 22 Sept 1995. **Spring Equinox** *Tower Hill, (west side of Tower) EC3.* **Date** noon 20 Mar 1994, 21 Mar 1995. **Admission** free.
By day the druids are probably bank clerks, but come a solstice or equinox, they don white, hooded gowns and worship the seasons. You can witness their rites at these symbolic sites (Primrose Hill and Aylesford are alleged-ly the burial barrows of, respectively, Boudicca and Horsa); for details on Stonehenge *see chapter* **Trips out of Town**. Don't expect to see any blood sacrifices – unless the hippies get set on by the police.

Funfairs
Alexandra Park *Muswell Hill, N22 (081 365 2121). Wood Green underground/Alexandra Palace BR/W3 bus.* **Battersea Park** *Albert Bridge Road, SW11 (081 871 7530). Sloane Square underground/Battersea Park or Queenstown Road BR/97, 137 bus.* **Hampstead Heath** *NW3 (071 485 4491 for a leaflet detailing events in the park throughout the year). Belsize Park or Hampstead underground/Gospel Oak or Hampstead Heath BR/24 bus.* **Dates** *Easter* Fri 1-Mon 4 April 1994. *Spring Bank Holiday* Fri 20-Mon 23 May 1994. *August Bank Holiday* Fri 26-Mon 29 Aug 1994. **Admission** free.
On the many rides at these fairgrounds you can regur-gitate your candyfloss and disorientate the goldfish you've just won. All the funfair works are here, from dodgems to merry-go-rounds.

Gun Salutes
Hyde Park, W2 and the Tower of London, EC3. **Dates** 2 June (Coronation Day); 10 June (Duke of Edinburgh's birthday); 16 June (Trooping the Colour, *see below* **Summer**); 4 Aug (Queen Mother's birthday); 6 Feb (Accession Day); 21 Apr (the Queen's birthday); the State Opening of Parliament (*see below* **Autumn**). If the date falls on a Sunday, salutes are fired on following Monday. **Admission** free.

The cannons are primed on important royal occasions for gun salutes. The King's Troop of the Royal Horse Artillery make a mounted charge through Hyde Park, set up the guns and fire a 41-gun salute (noon, except for Opening of Parliament); then, not to be outdone, at the Tower of London, the Honourable Artillery Company fires a 62-gun salute at 1pm.

Spring

Soho Pancake Day Race
Carnaby Street, W1 (071 375 0441). Oxford Circus underground. **Dates** Shrove Tuesday (last day before Lent) 22 Feb 1994, 7 Mar 1995. *Races start* from noon. **Admission** free.
Shrove Tuesday is the last day before the fasting of Lent begins and a day for scoffing all the stuff you aren't supposed to be eating for the following 40 days, hence the eggs, flour and milk of the pancakes. God knows how tradition decreed that races would be held of people tossing pancakes in a frying pan as they went. You can join them if you like; phone a few days in advance.

St Patrick's Day
Date 17 March.
London is the third largest Irish city, after New York and Dublin. You don't get any large-scale parades as you do in New York, but head for Kilburn, NW6 on St Patrick's day and you'll find the local pubs heaving with an enthu-

siastic clientele. There's plenty of music and a lot of drinking.

Oxford and Cambridge Race
On the Thames from Putney to Mortlake (071 730 3488). **Date** 26 Mar 1994. **Admission** free.
Oxford and Cambridge universities clash on the Thames in this annual sporting battle and social shindig. Starting from Putney, SW6, it finishes at Mortlake, SW14. Bridges and pubs, like the Swan Inn at Mortlake, are good but crowded vantage points from which to see the race and the earlier reserves' challenge between the Goldie (Cambridge) and Isis (Oxford) crews.

London Harness Horse Parade
Regent's Park, NW1 (0733 234451). Camden Town, Great Portland Street or Regent's Park underground. **Date** 9am-1.30pm Easter Monday (4 April 1994; 17 April 1995). **Admission** free.
Before the parade around the Inner Circle of Regent's Park gets under way at noon, you're welcome to inspect the horses.

Kite Festival
Blackheath, SE3 (081 808 1280). Blackheath BR. **Date** Easter Sunday and Monday, 3, 4 April 1994; 16, 17 April 1995. **Admission** free.
A spectacular event given a fine wind, the festival attracts hosts of international stunt kite flyers and a number of innovative new designs make their debut flights each year.

Festivals

City of London Festival
230 Bishopsgate, EC2 (071 377 0540). Liverpool Street underground/BR. **Dates** Sun 3-Wed 20 July 1994, similar dates 1995.
Classical music, poetry and theatre in the City of London's churches, livery halls and corporate buildings.

Edinburgh International and Fringe Festivals
International Festival, *21 Market Street, Edinburgh EH1 (031 226 4001).* **Festival Fringe**, *180 High Street, Edinburgh (031 226 5257).* **Jazz Festival**, *116 Canongate, Edinburgh EH8 8DD (031 557 1642).* **Dates** last three weeks of August and the first in September.
The capital of Scotland becomes the Athens of the North for the last three weeks of August each year, when the world's largest Arts festival is staged in the city. Officially, it divides into different parts: the International Festival, with prestigious visiting orchestras and opera, ballet and theatre companies; the Film Festival at cinemas all over town showing previews of blockbusters and art-house titles; the Jazz Festival, with visiting musicians from around the world; the ever-popular Scottish equivalent of the Royal Tournament, the Military Tattoo, performed in the dramatic setting of the Castle; and perhaps most impressively, the Fringe Festival, with literally hundreds of visiting companies occupying every available yard of performance space, from the grand Assembly Rooms to street corners.

Festival of Mind, Body, Spirit
The Royal Horticultural Halls, Greycoat Street, SW1 (071 938 3788). St James's Park underground. **Dates** last ten days of May 1994, similar dates 1995.

A New Age festival, entering its eighteenth year, where you can discover an astonishing variety of different approaches to health, healing and the environment. There's also music and dance.

Latin American Festival
The Calthorpe Project Community Garden, 258-274 Gray's Inn Road, WC1 (071 837 8019). King's Cross underground/BR. **Date** first weekend in August.
From noon to midnight there's a carnival of Latin American bands, foods and crafts.

Great British Beer Festival
Olympia, Hammersmith Road, W4 (0727 867201). Olympia Kensington underground. **Date** first week in August. **Admission** £1-£3; phone for details.
Organised by the Campaign for Real Ale (CAMRA), this is where you can become an instant expert on beer, with around 400 different types of the stuff available for tasting. The difficulty will be remembering them.

Glastonbury Festival
Worthy Farm, Pilton, Somerset (0749 890470). **Date** last weekend in June.
One of the largest rock music festivals in the country. For three days over the last weekend in June a valley in Somerset becomes a throbbing city of live music stages, alternative art performances and food stalls. You'll have to arrange your own temporary accommodation, which ranges from sleeping bags in the mud to mobile homes for the stars. Entrance fees are high (£55 in 1993).

Chaucer Festival
*Tower of London, Tower Hill, EC3 (information on
0227 470379/071 229 0635). Tower Hill underground.*
Date 9 April 1994; similar date 1995. **Admission** free.
A costumed cavalcade proceeds from Southwark
Cathedral to the Tower of London for this annual celebration of Chaucer's *Canterbury Tales*. The 'pilgrims'
then join a medieval fair at the Tower, with sideshows,
food-stalls and much merry-making.

London Marathon
*Greenwich Park, Blackheath to Westminster Bridge via
the Isle of Dogs, Victoria Embankment and St James's
Park (071 620 4117).* **Date** 17 April 1994, phone to
confirm 1995 date. **Admission** free to spectators.
The London Marathon is the world's biggest road race.
Over 90 per cent of the 35,000-odd starters (out of about
75,000 applicants) finish the route. It's a friendly spectacle, as the crowds lining the route urge on the more rub-
ber-legged athletes. The racers are a mixed bunch of
record breakers, celebrities, fancy dressers, joggers,
club runners and wheelchair racers. The atmosphere
and crowds are greatest at the start and finish (near
Admiralty Arch on The Mall) and at Tower Bridge and
the Cutty Sark in Greenwich.

May Fayre and Puppet Festival
*St Paul's Church Garden, Covent Garden, WC2 (071
375 0441). Covent Garden underground.* **Date** 8 May
1994; similar date 1995. **Admission** free.
A celebration of the first reported viewing of a Punch and
Judy show, by London diarist Samuel Pepys in 1662, with
a procession and other entertainments.

Summer

Chelsea Flower Show
*Royal Hospital, SW3 (071 834 4333). Sloane Square
underground.* **Dates** 24-29 May 1994; 1995 phone for
details. **Open** 8am-8pm Thur; 8am-5pm Fri.
Admission £10 Thur; £16 Fri.
The world-famous gardening extravaganza, laid on by
the Royal Horticultural Society, is a prime chance for the
green-fingered to turn the more horticulturally challenged green with envy.

Beating Retreat
*Horse Guards Parade, Whitehall, SW1 (071 930 4466).
Westminster underground or Charing Cross
underground/BR.* **Dates** 6-10 June 1994; 1995 phone
for details. **Admission** £3-£10.
The 'Retreat', beaten on drums with pomp by the
Household Division, refers to the setting of the sun, not
of the British Empire. The soldiers, on foot and on horseback, provide a great splash of colour and some rousing
band playing. The floodlit evening performances are very
atmospheric. The later 'Sounding Retreat' is similar, and
each year is performed by a different regimental band.
Tickets from Premier Box Office (071 930 0292). There
are often tickets left on the day of performance.

Kenwood Lakeside Concerts
*Kenwood House, Hampstead Lane, NW3 (081 348
1286). Archway, Hampstead or Highgate
underground/210 bus.* **Dates** every Sat June-Sept.
Tickets book on 071 379 4444, or on the night two
hours before the concert begins. **Admission** £4.50-
£30.
A picnic at one of these outdoor concerts of popular classics can make an idyllic summer evening (if the weather's kind). On 4 July Handel's fireworks music is played
to suitable pyrotechnic accompaniment in celebration of

The **Chelsea Flower Show**. *See* **review**.

American Independence day. *See chapter* **Music:
Classical & Opera**.

Derby Day
*Epsom Racecourse, Epsom, Surrey (03727 26311).
Epsom BR.* **Date** first Wed in June. **Open** 10am. **Race**
3.45pm. **Admission** £5-£24. **Credit** V.
This world-famous horse race over the flat is responsible for millions of bets and a few heart attacks. The poor-
er classes are herded into one enclosure; those with big
wallets, stripey blazers and braying voices strut about in
another.

Royal Academy Summer Exhibition
*Royal Academy, Burlington House, Piccadilly, W1 (071
439 7438). Green Park or Piccadilly Circus
underground.* **Open** 10am-6pm (last
admission 5.30pm) daily. **Admission** £3.60; £2.40
OAPs, students, UB40s; £1.80 under-18s.
Something of an artistic pick 'n' mix with loose criteria
for determining what's exhibited. It's an amateur event,
so would-be Bacons and Warhols rub canvasses with precise architectural elevations and tediously tasteful watercolour landscapes.

Trooping the Colour
*Horse Guards Parade, Whitehall, SW1 (information
071 930 4466). Westminster or Charing Cross
underground/BR.* **Date** 11 June 1994; 10 June 1995.
Rehearsals 28 May, 4 June 1994; 27 May, 3 June 1995.
Starts 10.40am Buckingham Palace. **Tickets** write by
end of Feb to *The Brigade Major (Trooping the
Colour), HQ, Household Division, Horse Guards,
Chelsea Barracks, SW3.* **Admission** about £12 – two
per person. **No credit cards.**
Trooping the Colour is the Queen's official birthday party
– her real one is in April. The ceremony originates in the

Notting Hill Carnival. *See* **review** page 29.

battlefield tradition of raising a regiment's colours for identification. If you can't get a ticket, there might be some left for the rehearsals, but after four decades' practice, the Queen does not rehearse. The royal party can be glimpsed during its procession down the Mall, leaving Buckingham Palace at 10.40am. The route to Horseguards Parade is always packed but you may find space on the Green Park side of the Mall. Back home in the Palace by 12.30pm, the Queen takes to the balcony to watch an air force jet zoom past at about 1pm.

Royal Ascot
Ascot Racecourse, Ascot, Berkshire (0344 22211). Ascot BR. **Dates** 14-17 June 1994; similar dates 1995, phone for details. **Open** 11am until last race. **Admission** *16 June* £24; *14, 15, 17 June* £22.
The Queen and her chums, plus assorted other royals travel down the racecourse in open pram-like carriages each day before the cup races are run. The fashionable headwear of the *belle monde* jockeys for attention with the racing results.

National Music Day
Trafalgar Square, WC1 (071 491 0044). Charing Cross underground/BR. **Dates** 25, 26 June 1994; similar dates in 1995. **Admission** free.
Massed steel bands, brass bands and youth orchestras around Nelson's Column are the highlight of this nationwide celebration of musicianship. Expect appearances from music business celebs and the odd sweetly-smiling tone-deaf politician.

Middlesex Show
Showground, Park Road, Uxbridge, Middlesex (081 866 1367). Uxbridge underground, then free bus to ground. **Dates** 25, 26 June 1994; 24, 25 June 1995. **Open** 9am-6.30pm. **Admission** £6; £2 under-16s, OAPs; free under-5s. **No credit cards.**

County shows are a British institution, harking back to when ye olde British yeomen chewed straw at farm gates. This major show is a great family day out for fans of Morris dancing, falconry, farmyard animals and dog agility trials.

Wimbledon Lawn Tennis Championships
All England Club, PO Box 98, Church Road, SW19 (081 944 1066/recorded information 081 946 2244). Southfields underground/Wimbledon BR/39, 93, 200 bus. **Dates** last week of June, first week of July. **Open** 11am; *play on outside courts* 12.30pm; *play on show courts* 2pm. **Admission** tickets by ballot of entries between Sept and Dec previous year; send SAE to above address for application form. **No credit cards.**
As much society event as ball-game, Wimbledon's international reputation cannot be disputed. If you haven't ordered tickets or blagged free seats at a company marquee, you'll have to queue from early morning. Go early evening, when you can usually get a seat for an evening match.

Horse of the Year Show
Wembley Arena, Wembley, Middlesex (081 900 1234). Wembley Central underground. **Date** early Oct. **Admission** £10-£30, bookable in advance.
An international horse show with dressage, show-jumping and pony club trials.

Royal Tournament
Earl's Court Exhibition Centre, Warwick Road, SW5 (tickets 071 373 8141/information 071 799 2323). Earl's Court underground. **Dates** 19-30 July 1994; similar dates in 1995, phone to confirm. **Admission** £8-£22. **Credit** A, AmEx, V.
Presented by the armed forces, this is a sanitised, family show with deafening military bands, pageantry and lots of running about with gun carriages. For the 1994 show it's the Army's turn to ride a motorbike as multi-handedly as possible.
Group discount. Wheelchair access.

Swan Upping on the Thames
from Sunbury, Surrey to Pangbourne, Berkshire, and back (071 236 1863). **Dates** Mon-Fri third week in July; 9.30am-5pm each day. **Admission** free.
Utterly eccentric, this tradition of marking swans is a tricky spectator event. All the swans on the Thames belong to either the Queen or to the Vintners' or Dyers' livery companies. For five days herdsmen paddle about attempting to record the birds by marking their beaks. The Dyers' swans get one nick, the Vintners' two and the Queen's remain unblemished. In theory, the fleet should reach Windsor, Marlow and Sonning Lock on respective nights, and then turn back at Pangbourne, but its exact whereabouts depends on how co-operative the swans are feeling.

BBC Henry Wood Promenade Concerts
Royal Albert Hall, Kensington Gore, SW7 (071 927 4296). South Kensington underground. **Dates** 15 July-10 Sept 1994; 21 July-16 Sept 1995. **Admission** £3-£15. **Credit** A, AmEx, V.
This is one of the world's greatest classical music festivals (*see chapter* **Music: Classical & Opera**) and 1994 is its centenary year. The Last Night of the Proms is famous for its overdose of patriotism, culminating in a tumultuous rendition of *Land of Hope and Glory*.

Cart Marking
Guildhall Yard, EC2 (071 489 8287 for details). Bank underground or Moorgate underground/BR. **Date** end of July to early Aug, phone to confirm. **Starts** 11am. **Admission** free.
Traffic jams in 1681 forced the city authorities to pass an

Act of Common Council limiting the number of carts on the road to 421. With traffic today back to horse-and-cart speeds, there's a lesson here. Many superb vintage vehicles assemble for this revived ceremony, lasting about three hours. The participants are from the Worshipful Company of Car Men.

Notting Hill Carnival

Around North Kensington (081 964 0544). Ladbroke Grove, Notting Hill or Westbourne Park underground. **Date** last Sun, Mon in Aug; noon-9pm Sun, Mon. **Admission** free.

Reputed to be Europe's biggest outdoor festival, the carnival is an open-air party, featuring live music (mostly at Portobello Green), dancing in the street, a procession of floats, Caribbean food sold from front gardens – and millions of people. Sunday is best for children, but Monday is the main day. Every year calypso and reggae sounds compete with louder and harder house and rap rhythms. It's best not to bring any valuables or linger too late into the evening.

Autumn

Chinatown Mid-Autumn Festival

Chinese Community Centre, Gerrard Street & Newport Place, WC1 (071 439 3822). Leicester Square or Piccadilly Circus underground. **Date** Sept (phone to confirm). **Admission** free.

A smaller, but similar festival to the Chinese New Year (*see below* **Winter**). Colourful lanterns of every shape and size are made by and for children, and there's plenty of entertainments and stalls. A stage is set up in Gerrard Street and dragons dance about outside Chinese restaurants and shops. Much of the food on sale is specially for this festival.

Horseman's Sunday

Church of St John & St Michael, Hyde Park Crescent, W2 (071 262 1732). Marble Arch underground or Paddington underground/BR. **Dates** third Sunday in Sept, phone to confirm. **Service** 11.30am. **Admission** free.

During a weird 30-minute religious service, the vicar sits in a saddle, rather than stands in a pulpit. From horseback he blesses over 100 horses. Afterwards, the blessed animals trot around the surrounding streets and then through Hyde Park. Later (1.30-5.30pm) you can watch show-jumping at nearby Kensington paddock, in the north of Kensington Gardens. Early arrivals can catch the Morris dancing at 11am.

Costermonger's Pearly Harvest Festival

St Martin-in-the-Fields, Trafalgar Square, WC2 (071 930 0089). Leicester Square underground or Charing Cross underground/BR. **Dates** first Sun in Oct. **Service** 2pm. **Admission** free.

Cockney clichés are for real at the Pearly Harvest Festival. Costermongers sell fruit and veg on the streets of London. Their representatives, the Pearly Kings and Queens, gather here for the harvest festival service. Over a hundred of this hardy breed will be wearing their pearl-button decorated garments and mouthing 'cor blimey'.

Punch and Judy Festival

Covent Garden Piazza, WC2 (071 240 0930). Covent Garden underground. **Date** first Sunday in Oct. **Admission** free.

Punch and Judy professors from all over the country gather to demonstrate the conjugal hell of the quarrelsome puppets.

Bonfire Night

All over England, Scotland and Wales (phone London Tourist Board 071 971 0026, 9am-6pm, Mon-Fri for details of major firework displays). **Date** 5 Nov; firework displays on nearest weekend.

In 1605 Guy Fawkes, one of the leaders of a group of Catholic conspirators, was caught beneath the Houses of Parliament with enough gunpowder to blow up James I and his Protestant Parliament. Since then Bonfire Night has been celebrated all over Britain. A bonfire is stacked high with the 'guy' (an effigy of Fawkes) on top and someone rushes about letting off fireworks. Organised firework displays are the best and the safest; check *Time Out* magazine or phone the LTB for details

London to Brighton Veteran Car Run

Starting point: Serpentine Road, Hyde Park, W2 (0753 681736 for details). Hyde Park Corner underground. **Date** first Sun in Nov. **Start** 8-9am. **Admission** free.

First held in 1896, the rally celebrates the abolition of the Act that forced cars to be heralded by a walker with a red flag at a 2mph (2.5kmh) speed limit. The motors, now limited to an average of 20mph (32kmh), aim to reach Brighton before 4pm. Only cars built before 1905 can be entered, so the sight of all the gleaming coachwork and distinctive radiator grilles is magnificent. The start at Hyde Park has a great sense of occasion, but crowds line the whole route (via Westminster Bridge and Croydon, along the A23), particularly outside pubs.

State Opening of Parliament

House of Lords, Palace of Westminster, SW1 (071 219 4272). Westminster underground. **Date** usually first week in Nov, phone for details. **Admission** free.

Members of Parliament are welcomed back from their summer hols by the Queen at the State Opening of Parliament; she then reads a speech outlining the Government's legislative plans. Although it's a private (if televised) affair, the public do get a good chance to see the Queen. In either the Irish or Australian State Coach, she leaves Buckingham Palace at 10.37am and passes down The Mall and Horse Guards Parade; on her entry to the House of Lords at 11.15am, a gun salute (*see above* **Frequent Events**) goes off in Hyde Park. Spectators should get into position early: a good place to watch the event is at the north side of The Mall where the crowds are slightly less dense.

Lord Mayor's Show

Various streets in the City of London (071 606 3030). **Date** usually second Sat in Nov. **Show** 9am-5pm. **Admission** free.

The Lord Mayor's Show banishes the usual severe, pin-striped face of the City for one day a year. The plume-hatted new Lord Mayor travels from Westminster, leaving at 9am. From 11.10am at the Guildhall, a procession of the 1756 State Coach and around 140 floats snake through the City to the Law Courts at 11.50am. There the new mayor swears solemn vows before heading back via the Embankment, returning to the Guildhall by 2.20pm. Fireworks are later launched from a barge moored on the Thames between Waterloo and Blackfriars bridges. Try to find a place at least 30 minutes before the procession starts.

Remembrance Sunday Ceremony

Cenotaph, Whitehall, SW1 (071 730 3488). Westminster underground or Charing Cross underground/BR. **Date** nearest Sun to Armistice Day (11 Nov); 10.30am-11.30am. **Admission** free.

For details of this ceremony to remember the dead of two World Wars, *see chapter* **The World Wars**.

Dragons in Gerrard Street at the **Chinese New Year Festival**. *See* **review**.

Winter

Christmas Lights

Covent Garden, WC2 (071 836 9136); Oxford Street, W1 (071 629 1234); Regent & Bond Streets, W1 (071 629 1682); Trafalgar Square, SW1. **Date** *lights on* early Nov; *Trafalgar Square Christmas Tree* early Dec.

Every year Norway thanks Britain for liberation from the Nazis by sending a fir tree to put up in Trafalgar Square. But acid rain damage to Norwegian firs by British pollution has put the tradition in doubt, perhaps even more so now the Norwegian Environment Minister has called his British opposite number, the ludicrous John Selwyn Gummer, a *drittsek* (shitbag). Regent Street has London's best decorations, putting Oxford Street's dreary effort to shame. Don't go to see them being switched on by a celebrity; the congestion is a nightmare. Go later. Other lights at which to gawp hang across St Christopher's Place, W1, Bond Street, W1, and Kensington High Street, W8. 'Alternative' lights twinkle around Carnaby Street, W1.

New Year's Eve Celebrations

Trafalgar Square, W1. Leicester Square or Charing Cross underground/BR. **Date** 31 Dec-1 Jan. **Admission** free.

The national centre for ringing-in the new year is Trafalgar Square, where thousands congregate to sway about, singing *Auld Lang Syne*. Apart from the discomfort, drunkenness, pickpocketing, occasional violence and absence of joy at this knees-up, the actual moment of midnight is infuriatingly unclear as Big Ben is drowned out by all the noise. Choose almost any pub or club and have a far better time there. In recent years, Lager companies have done the one thing to stop drunk driving the Government won't admit works: sponsoring free public transport all night. On new year's day a procession of bands marches through town from the West End to Hyde Park at lunchtime.

Chinese New Year Festival

Chinatown, around Gerrard Street, W1 (Chinatown Chinese Association 071 437 5256). Leicester Square, Piccadilly Circus or Tottenham Court Road underground. **Date** first Sun after Chinese New Year, phone to confirm; 11am-5pm. **Admission** free.

This is a garish, exuberant affair. Spilling out of the main Gerrard Street/Newport Place area are stalls selling crafts and delicacies, surrounded by performers and big crowds. Lions and dragons wade through the streets to 'eat' cabbages and coins donated by the Chinese restaurants. There's a stage for performers in Leicester Square and early Chinese history is told to anyone who'll listen. Afterwards, eat from the special dim sum menus offered by many local Chinese restaurants (*see chapter* **Eating & Drinking**).

Sightseeing

London's sights are famous around the world. Now's your chance to explore them. We separate the treats from the trite.

London's big sights – the palaces, parks, museums and landmarks – each attract between half a million and over six million visitors a year. This can make sightseeing murder in high summer and at Christmas. Below we advise on the best times to go, and how to make the most of your time there.

One way of getting to grips with London is to take a bus tour of the main sights (*see below* **Bus Tours**), although pre-packaged coach parties are the bane of the liberated tourist. Fewer tours operate on Mondays and many follow a daily pattern. About 20 coach-loads invade Westminster Abbey at 9.30am, then crowd out Buckingham Palace's Changing of the Guard ceremony at 11.15am. After blitzing St Paul's Cathedral, they end up, like many an historical pariah, at the Tower of London. Come evening, they dine at the Cockney Pride before being forced to watch an Andrew Lloyd Webber musical. So, now you can plan to avoid them.

If your stay in London falls during college term-time, sights that attract school parties are best visited after about 2.30pm. School holidays coincide with the main tourist seasons, so do your sightseeing as early in the day as possible, avoiding weekends, to miss the hordes of families and student groups.

Attractions

Guinness World of Records

The Trocadero, Piccadilly Circus, W1 (071 439 7331). Piccadilly Circus underground. **Open** 10am-10pm daily. **Admission** £5.40; £4.20 OAPs, students; £3.50 under-16s; under-4s free; £16 family ticket (two adults, two children). **Credit** A, AmEx, DC, £TC, V.
An exhibition of superlatives doesn't make a superlative exhibition, but the Guinness World of Records is reasonable as tourist-traps go; plus it's open (and quietest) in the evening. Trivia from the *Guinness Book of Records* (itself included as the best-selling copyright book) is well suited to this kind of display. The exhibits can often be effective – a popular one compares your vital statistics with the world's tallest and fattest people – but they're a bit tacky and tatty. There are few interactive exhibits and the entrance fees are hefty. There's also lots of reading to do, which is tiresome for children, who otherwise find it fun. Unsurprisingly, Guinness books are heavily promoted in the shop, and you can't avoid the whining voice of David Frost accompanying you around.
Group discounts. Shop. Toilets for the disabled. Tour by prior arrangement. Wheelchair access.

London Dungeon

28-34 Tooley Street, SE1 (071 403 0606). London Bridge underground/BR. **Open** *Apr-Sept* 10am-6.30pm daily; *Oct-Mar* 10am-5.30pm daily (last admission 1 hour before closing). **Admission** £6; £5 students; £4 OAPs, under-14s; disabled in wheelchairs and under-5s free. **Credit** A, AmEx, £TC, V.
Peer through corroded railings in a dank, dark, musty-smelling maze of towering arches and eerie nooks. You'll see medieval torture scenes and hear the screams as the rack tightens. The location, artefacts, atmosphere and basic idea of presenting the grizzliest moments of British history are successful and most people enjoy their visit. But why do the tortured models possess all the realism of shop dummies? A recent addition is the Jack the Ripper experience, which has provoked protests for its glorification of a rapist and murderer. Generally, the Dungeon is let down by a lack of surprise-shocks. Still, the coach parties pile through, overdosing on tat from the shop. The Dungeon is least busy before noon, Monday to Wednesday.
Café. Group discount. Shop. Toilets for the disabled. Wheelchair access.

London Planetarium

Marylebone Road, NW1 (071 486 1121). Baker Street underground. **Open** *June-Aug* 10.20am-5.20pm Mon-Fri; 10.40am-5pm Sat, Sun. *Sept-May* 12.20-4.40pm Mon-Fri; 10.40am-5pm Sat, Sun. **Admission** £4; £3.10 OAPs; £2.50 under-16s (no children under 5). *Combined ticket with Madame Tussaud's* £9.40; £7.05 OAPs; £6 under-16s; £21.80 family ticket (two adults, two children). **Credit** A, AmEx, £TC, V.
Wallow in an inclined padded seat (very welcome after shuffling around in queues at Madame Tussaud's), gaze up into the large dome-ful of stars, and prepare for a lesson in astronomy. The audio-visuals are enjoyable but presume you know nothing about the universe. The habits of planets, stars and time itself are demystified with sophisticated projections onto the inside of the dome. Sit on the immediate right as you enter.
Café. Group discount. Shop.

London Zoo

Regent's Park, NW1 (071 722 3333). Camden Town underground. **Open** *Apr-Oct* 10am-5.30pm daily; *Nov-Mar* 10am-dusk daily. **Admission** £6.50; £5 students, OAPs; £4 under-15s; under-4s free; £17 family ticket (two adults and two children). **Credit** A, AmEx, £TC, V.
Now that the storm over funding has blown over, the Zoo is embarking on a ten-year programme of development with 'conservation in action' as the main theme. The British obsession with pets also gets serious here, where you can adopt an octopus for £15 or an elephant for £6,000. The money goes towards looking after the beast for a year and your name will go on a plaque by its enclosure. Try to get into position for one of the feeding times. Of the 8,000-plus animals, the koalas and Rosie the Rhino (the first to be hand-reared in Europe) are favourites. It's a marvellous place for kids and there's even a Children's Zoo (*see chapter* **Children's London**). Zoo buildings include some gems of modern architecture; look for the

London's top ten sights

These sights are reviewed in this chapter, unless otherwise indicated.

1 **British Museum:** A massive museum in Bloomsbury that attracts almost as many visitors each year as it houses exhibits: 6.3 million culture vultures and 6.5 million artefacts, at the last count. *See chapter* **Museums**.

2 **National Gallery:** The large collection of Impressionist paintings is the main draw to this Trafalgar Square edifice, though the Gallery's hoard ranges from the thirteenth- to the nineteenth-century. *See chapter* **Art Galleries**.

3 **Madame Tussaud's:** The queue outside these waxworks is almost as famous as the exhibits. About 2.3 million visitors a year head here, most have to wait at least half an hour before gaining entrance.

4 **The Tower of London:** Expect to queue at least 15 minutes to enter the Tower, the best example of a medieval fortress in Britain. Inside are some of London's finest treasures, including the Crown Jewels.

5 **Tate Gallery:** The storehouse of the national collection of British paintings from the sixteenth century to the pre-

sent, the Tate also displays an international collection of modern masterpieces. *See chapter* **Art Galleries**.

6 **St Paul's Cathedral:** Wren's creation draws 1.4 million visitors a year, but you'll have to pay to get in: God is learning a thing or two about profit margins from the City.

7 **Natural History Museum:** A huge neo-Gothic edifice that is famous for its dinosaurs. It's likely to rise up the chart following the success of *Jurassic Park*. *See chapter* **Museums**.

8 **Science Museum:** Noisy and busy, the Science Museum attracts hordes of kids to its interactive displays. *See chapter* **Museums**.

9 **Victoria & Albert Museum:** Top attraction is the dress collection which includes exhibits from the early seventeenth century up until 1992. The museum is so large that queuing is never a problem. *See chapter* **Museums**.

10 **Royal Botanic Gardens:** London's prettiest and most peaceful tourist attraction. The Gardens are quiet and pollution-free: pick a sunny day to visit.

1934 Penguin Pool and the Aviary by Lord Snowden. Avoid the tacky shop and expensive café.
Education centre. Films. Group discount. Lectures. Restaurant. Shop. Toilets for the disabled. Wheelchair access.

Madame Tussaud's

Marylebone Road, NW1 (071 935 6861). Baker Street underground. **Open** *May-Sept* 9am-5.30pm daily; *Oct-Jun* 10am-5.30pm Mon-Fri; 9.30am-5.30pm Sat, Sun. **Admission** £7.40; £5.50 OAPs; £4.75 under-16s; £19.55 family (two adults, two children). *Combined ticket with Planetarium* £9.40; £7.05 OAPs; £6 under-16s; £21.80 family. **Credit** A, AmEx, £$TC, V.
To be measured up for a wax model here is proof of fame. Ideas for new figures come from a poll of visitors. Public heroes are a mixed bag: Bob Geldof, Joan Collins, even John Major. It emerges that British politician Edwina Currie is as hated as Charles Manson and that TV's Anneka Rice beats Jack the Ripper for inclusion in the Chamber of Horrors. While there are several eerie likenesses, the Royal Family makes convincing wax dummies. The 'Spirit of London' dark-ride takes you on a journey through London's history in a so-called 'time-taxi'. It's permanently crowded, attracting 2.3 million visitors a year, so there's a long wait to get in, unless you go early or late in the day. *Café. Group discount. Toilets for the disabled. Wheelchair access by prior arrangement.*

Rock Circus

London Pavilion, Piccadilly Circus, W1 (071 734 7203). Piccadilly Circus underground. **Open** 11am-9pm

Mon, Wed, Thur, Sun; noon-9pm Tue; 11am-10pm Fri, Sat. **Admission** £6.25; £5.25 OAPs, students; £4.25 under-16s; disabled and under-5s free; £16.75 family (two adults, two children). **Credit** £$TC.
Seeing a bionic wax model of Madonna or the Beatles in a revolving theatre is somewhat unnerving. There's no denying the eerie sensation when the lips and singing synchronise, or when Bruce Springsteen thrashes at his guitar and a drugged-up Janis Joplin stands up to sing. But when a video backing was used it rather undermined the whole concept. The spectre of a robotic middle-aged Tim Rice as compère raises the biggest laugh. Before this half-hour 'concert' (there's no re-entry after the show), you're free to wander past static tableaux of wax pop stars. The cleverest bit is the headphones, which pick up infra-red signals and play the song from whichever display you're looking at. It's all good fun. Prince, George Michael, Status Quo and the late Jim Morrison are all present. Sadly, there's only a tiny snippet of one song from each artist and the patronising commentary by DJ Paul Gambaccini is a big turn-off. The shop is stocked with books, T-shirts and souvenirs. *Group discount. Shop. Toilets for the disabled. Wheelchair access.*

Spitting Image Rubberworks

Cubitt's Yard, James Street, WC2 (071 240 0393/information line 071 240 0838). Covent Garden underground. **Open** 11am-5.30pm Mon-Fri; 11am-6.30pm Sat, Sun. **Admission** £3.95; £2.95 OAPs, students, under-12s; £11.50 family (two adults, two children). **No credit cards.**

No chance of missing the entrance to this attraction: you're likely to bump into John Major or Prince Charles hanging around outside – or rather their Fluck and Law rubber *dopplegängers*. Inside, you'll find all the regular *Spitting Image* players: Mrs Thatcher, the Queen and Phil the Greek taking part in the computerised panel game 'Lickety Lick', presided over by the oleaginous Alastair Burnett. Those familiar with the eponymous television series may well be interested in the tour of the workshop, which gives you an idea of what goes on behind the scenes: there's a video, a lecture and demonstrations of the technical difficulties involved. The souvenir shop offers the opportunity to have your photograph taken with the dummy of your choice, and have the result printed on a T-shirt.
Shop

Trocadero

Piccadilly Circus, W1 (071 439 1791/Food Street 071 287 2681). Piccadilly Circus underground. **Open** 10am-midnight daily; *Food Street* noon-midnight Mon-Thur, Sun; noon-12.30am Fri, Sat. **No credit cards.**
Most visitors end up in this tourist-trap because of where it is and because the **Guinness World of Records** (*see above*) is on the top floor. But apart from chainstores, there's nothing here but **Food Street**. This pseudo-Eastern food mall is more imaginative than most fast-food emporia – the dim sum and satay are palatable and inexpensive. But two minutes' walk away is the genuine Chinatown (*see chapter* **The West End**). Eat there instead.

Historic Interest

Royal Mews

Buckingham Palace Road, SW1 (071 930 4832). St James's Park or Victoria underground/BR. **Open** Oct-Dec noon-4pm Wed; Apr-Oct noon-4pm Tue-Thur (last admission 3.30pm). **Admission** £2.50; £1.80 OAPs, £1.20 under-16s; free for disabled. **Credit** A, AmEx, DC, £TC, V.
The best appointed garage in town, the Mews houses the Royals' splendid coaches and carriages, along with their livery. A recent addition, the first since 1910, is the Australian State Coach, donated on the Australian bicentennial. The gilt palm-wood of the Coronation Coach, the immaculately-groomed horses and the craftsmanship of the sleek black landaus make the Mews one of the capital's better value collections, but the exhibits are abysmally labelled, if at all.
Shop. Wheelchair access.

Spencer House

27 St James's Place, SW1 (071 499 8620). Green Park underground. **Open** 11.45am-4.45pm Sun (closed Aug and Jan). **Admission** £6; £5 OAPs, students, under-16s (no children under 10). **No credit cards.**
Recently restored at a cost of £1.6 million, Spencer House was built between 1756 and 1766 by John Vardy for the first Earl Spencer (ancestor of Princess Diana). The nine state rooms were the first in the neo-classical style to be designed in England. The original furniture of the Painted Room is back in place, as are the tables designed by Vardy for the dining room. Guided tours, for a maximum of 15 people, start at 11.45am and continue at 15-minute intervals. Tours for larger groups may be pre-booked.
Guided tours.

Major Sights

The changing of the Guards is listed in *chapter* **London by Season**.

Buckingham Palace

SW1 (071 930 4832). St James's Park underground or Victoria underground/BR. **Open** to be decided in spring 1994; phone to check.
In 1993 a total of 18 major rooms at Buckingham Palace were opened to the public for the first time (9.30am-5.30pm daily from 7 August to 1 October; tickets: £8). The rooms are chock-a-block with pictures of big-nosed Georgians who really went to town on red carpet. The Throne Room and the royal collection of paintings (including works by Van Dyck, Rembrandt and Rubens) are among the highlights. But in 1993, visitors only got to see the State Rooms. In other words, they could only see the boring parts where heads of state like to have their photos taken. No bedrooms, playrooms, kitchens, toilets or telly rooms where the Windsors like to be. It is likely that the Palace will again be open in 1994, but its officials won't make an announcement until the spring. It was John Nash who turned Buckingham House into a regal home for George IV, but unfortunately in 1913 his work was inelegantly refaced in the style of an insurance company office. The most flattering view is from the bridge over St James's Park lake. The Royal Standard flies when the Queen is at home and there are regular opportunities to royalty spot (*see chapter* **London by Season**). *See also* **Queen's Gallery** (*chapter* **Art Galleries**), and **Royal Mews** (*above*).

Houses of Parliament

Parliament Square, SW1 (Commons information 071 219 4272/Lords information 071 219 3107). Westminster underground. **Open** when the Houses of Parliament are in session. *House of Commons Visitors' Gallery* 2.30-10.30pm (or later) Mon-Thur; 9.30am-3pm Fri. *House of Lords Visitors' Gallery* 2.30pm until debating ends Mon-Wed; 3pm until debating ends Thur; 11am until debating ends (about 4pm) Fri. *Victoria Tower Gardens* 7am-dusk daily. **Admission** free for both houses.
When the Palace of Westminster, where the Houses of Parliament are housed, was cleaned recently, its architectural beauty was fully revealed. In 1834 all of the old Palace except Westminster Hall burnt down, to be replaced by this neo-Gothic edifice, designed by Charles Barry and Augustus Pugin: it was completed in 1852. There are 1,000 rooms, yet most politicians must share an office. Despite the televising of the House of Commons, it's still best to see the politicians – sometimes dozing off – from the Visitors' Galleries. If you haven't got an advance ticket and don't want a long wait, go after 5.30pm. Don't take noisy children, since the fancy-dressed warders take their job very seriously. For Westminster Hall, *see chapter* **The Middle Ages**.
Educational facilities/worksheets. Guided tour (Mon-Thur only) or a seat at Question Time (2.30pm Mon-Thur) by prior arrangement with your MP or embassy. Post Office. Shop. Toilets for the disabled. Wheelchair access.

Nelson's Column

Trafalgar Square, WC2. Charing Cross underground/BR.
This familiar landmark to Admiral Horatio Nelson has recently had a tonne of pigeon droppings cleaned off it. Erected in the 1840s, the 170-ft (51m) Corinthian column dominates the Square (named after Nelson's naval defeat of Napoleon). Clambering over Landseer's sentinel lions at the base is a great sport for children. The square is a focus for demonstrations and New Year celebrations around the Christmas Tree (*see chapter* **London By Season**).

Piccadilly Circus

SW1. Piccadilly Circus underground.

The Circus is *the* cliché place to be photographed to prove you've experienced London. Flower girls used to sell their blossoms 'down Dilly' until World War II, but later it became identified with the swinging sixties and then with punks charging to be photographed. The Circus's big draws are the huge neon advertisements and Alfred Gilbert's fountain statue, known as Eros. No longer isolated in Nash's traffic circus, the aluminium statue points its arrow at the tourists. *See also chapter* **London by Area: West End**.

St Paul's Cathedral

EC4 (071 248 2705). St Paul's underground. **Open** *doors open* 7.30am-6pm daily. *Galleries, crypt and ambulatory* 10am-4.15pm Mon-Fri; 11am-4.15pm Sat. **Admission** *cathedral and crypt* (except services) £2.50; £2 students; £1.50 under-16s. *Galleries* £2.50; £2 students; £1.50 under-16s. *Ambulatory* free. **Credit** (shop only) A, £TC, V.

Dominating London's skyline, St Paul's is Christopher Wren's masterpiece. His epitaph on the floor below the dome states, 'If you seek his monument, look around you', and looking up you'll spot people on the Whispering Gallery straining to hear reverberating voices above the muffled din of the crowds. Beyond that are the viewing galleries (*see below* **Bird's-Eye Views**). Some of the tower blocks that mar the setting of the Cathedral are to be demolished and Prince Charles has fought for the replacements to be classically inspired. Ironically, Wren's design was popularly hated when first built for having no spire.

Guided tours. Shop. Wheelchair access to main body and crypt.

Tower of London

Tower Hill, EC3 (071 709 0765). Tower Hill underground/Fenchurch Street BR/15, 42, 78 bus. **Open** *Start of British Summer Time (Mar)-May, Sept-end of BST (Oct)* 9am-6pm Mon-Sat; 10am-6pm Sun; *Jun-Aug* 9am-6.30pm Mon-Sat; 10am-6.30pm Sun; *Greenwich Mean Time (Oct-Mar)* 9.30am-5pm Mon-Sat; 10am-5pm Sun. **Admission** £6.70; £5.10 OAPs, students, UB40s, disabled; £4.40 under-15s; under-5s free; £19 family (two adults, three children). **Credit** A, £TC, V.

The Tower has been a castle, a palace and a prison during its long history and it remains one of the capital's most

Westminster Abbey

Westminster Abbey looks more French than English. But it has been the wedding, coronation and burial church of British royalty since the Saxon, Edward the Confessor. He built the first church on this site since the Normans invaded and his tomb's still here, along with scores of others.

In general, the bigger the tomb, the more insignificant the corpse inside it. You can walk amongst the dry bones of kings, queens, generals, politicians, scientists, writers, painters and musicians, but the really impressive memorials are to those forgotten rich gits that the multi-lingual tourist tape knows nothing about. Take Sir Cloudesley Shovell, prominently positioned half way down the south side of the nave. What did he ever do for the nation? Yet his memorial is more flamboyant than anybody's. He lies in perpetuity surrounded by marble clouds, recumbent on a *chaise longue*, his lips pursed, his shirt unbuttoned and his pubic hair showing – more of an old queen than the old queens. Or what about William Webb Follett (died 1735), alone on a plinth in the little-known but ridiculously camp Nightingale Chapel? Fossett posed for his twice life-size statue with a length of rubber tubing in his breeches. Come on, no one's got one that big.

Forget coronations, it is death which is revered, glorified, honoured and celebrated. In a vestibule next to Congreve's modest memorial, a wooden board records the number of World War I dead as if it were a high score in a game show. Total number enlisted: 9,291,526; total dead: 1,069,825. On the door of the chantry house in the far wall of St Faith's Chapel you can still see traces of the skin of Richard Podlicote, the man who tried to nick the crown jewels in the fourteenth century. They flogged him to death, emptied his carcass and hung it there forever.

As to the rest of the Abbey, the fan-vaulted ceiling of the Henry VII chapel is breathtaking. But everyone heads for Poets' Corner, Statesman's Aisle, the chapels and the Coronation Chair, the graffiti on which is by Georgians who despised anything Gothic. Visit after late morning midweek to avoid a crush. On Wednesday evenings you can take photographs. *See also chapter* **The Middle Ages**.

Westminster Abbey Dean's Yard, SW1 (071 222 5152). St James's Park or Westminster underground/3, 11, 12 bus. **Open** *nave* 7.30am-6pm Mon, Tue, Thur-Sat; 7.30am-7.45pm Wed; between services on Sunday. *Royal Chapels* 9.20am-4pm Mon, Tue, Thur, Fri; 9am-4pm, 6-7.45pm, Wed; 9am-2pm, 4-5pm, Sat. *Chapter House, Pyx Chamber, Abbey Museum* 10.30am-4pm daily. *College Garden Apr-Sept* 10am-6pm Thur; *Oct-Mar* 10am-4pm Thur. *Brass Rubbing Centre (071 222 2085)* 9am-5.30pm Mon-Sat. **Services** 7.30am, 8am, 12.30pm, 5pm (choral) Mon-Fri; 8am, 9.20am, 3pm (choral) Sat; 8am, 10am (choral), 11.15am (abbey Eucharist), 3pm (choral), 5.45pm (organ recital), 6.30pm Sun. **Admission** *nave* free; *Royal Chapels* £3; £1.50 OAPs, students, UB40s; £1 under-16s. *Abbey Museum* £2; £1.60 OAPs, students, UB40s; £1 under-16s. **Credit** (shop only) A, AmEx, £$TC, V. *Cassette tour, £5. Shop (9.30am-5pm Mon-Sat). Wheelchair access.*

The Penguin Pool at **London Zoo**. See **review** page 31.

important sights. It's expensive, but it's not a rip-off. It takes several hours to see it all, from William the Conqueror's White Tower, the ravens and polite Beefeaters, who give free tours, to the recently opened Medieval palace of Edward I. Traitor's Gate and the Bloody Tower allow a glimpse into Britain's macabre history, but the Bowyer Tower's torture display could be bigger and less static. Of the many armour museums, the remarkable oriental display is the one your tired body won't regret exploring. When ogling the Crown Jewels, it's best to go round the no-stopping, close-up route first, then linger on the balcony – or go late in the day when it's far quieter. Otherwise, Monday and weekday mornings are the best times to visit. A purpose-built Jewel House is under construction, expected to open by the summer of 1994.

Gift shops. Group discount. Guided tours (free, every half hour for one hour). Wheelchair access with assistance (one adult admitted free if assisting disabled person).

Westminster

The City of Westminster has had a long and chequered history. The Palace of Westminster, better known as **The Houses of Parliament** (*see above*), is where English governments have attempted to hold-back the tide since the days of Edward the Confessor (1042-66). **Whitehall** has been the principal corridor of power since medieval times, when Whitehall Palace stretched almost to Somerset House. All that remains today is the **Banqueting House** (*see chapter* **Tudors & Stuarts**). Among the great concentration of government buildings here is, of course, **No.10 Downing Street**, which, because of security measures, you can only see from afar. But you can visit the intriguing

Cabinet War Rooms (*see chapter* **The World Wars**) behind the Foreign Office.

Westminster hasn't always been a dignified place, however. Until the reign of Victoria, when massive slum clearance programmes established Victoria Street in 1851 and Parliament Square in 1868, much of the area was crowded with dangerous, filthy alleys. Aptly-named Thieving Lane ran from Little Sanctuary to Tothill Street, while modern-day Abingdon Street used to be referred to as Dirty Lane. The unusually high proportion of undesirables stemmed from the ancient practice of offering sanctuary to fugitives from justice in **Westminster Abbey** (*see* **Box**). Even the elegant eighteenth century-development of Queen Anne's Gate is adjacent to Cockpit Steps, a reminder of the local popularity of the bloody sport of cockfighting, not outlawed until 1849.

Downing Street
W1 Westminster underground.
Downing Street is named after a 'perfidious roge' from Dublin, Sir George Downing, ambassador to The Hague, who constructed four 'well-built houses, fit for persons of honour and quality' in 1681. No.10 has been at the centre of British political life ever since Sir Robert Walpole made it the Prime Ministerial residence in 1735. No.11, next door, is the home of the Chancellor of the Exchequer. Protective gates (commissioned by Margaret Thatcher) prevent the British electorate getting too close to its leader.

Little Sanctuary
SW1. Westminster underground.

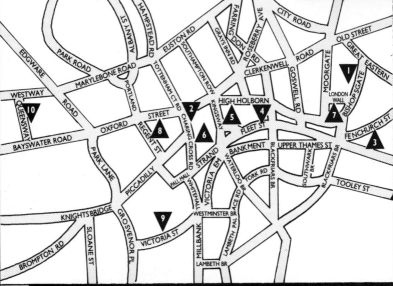

Across from the grounds of Westminster Abbey is a well-kept secret. The aptly-named Little Sanctuary, on the site of the old sanctuary of St Peter, is a grassed square secluded behind government buildings, including the offices of Hansard, the parliamentary record.

St Margaret's
Parliament Square, SW1 (071 222 6382). Westminster underground. **Open** 9.30am-5.15pm daily. **Services** 11am Sun.
Even Socialist politicians pray here to St Margaret (no, not that Conservative deity, Mrs Thatcher). This was adopted as the parish church of the House of Commons in 1614, when Protestant MPs suspected (wrongly) that Westminster Abbey was about to go Catholic. Samuel Pepys, John Milton and Winston Churchill got married at St Margaret's and Sir Walter Raleigh was apparently interred here in 1618, after losing his head just over the road in Old Palace Yard. The stained glass is among the best in London. The impressive 1501 east window pre-dates the present church by some 20 years. The Caxton window celebrates Britain's first printer, William Caxton, buried here in 1491. The south windows are a subtle work from 1967 by John Piper.
Wheelchair access.

Victoria Tower Gardens
Millbank, SW1. Westminster underground. **Open** 7am-dusk daily. **Admission** free.
A charming, quiet riverside garden with a beautiful view across the Thames to Lambeth Palace – and plenty of deckchairs to laze in. There's a Gothic-revival drinking fountain, a children's play area, a cast of Rodin's *Burghers of Calais* and a splendid bronze statue of the suffragette, Emmeline Pankhurst (*see chapter* **Women's London**).

Whitehall
SW1. Westminster underground or Charing Cross underground/BR.
This wide, elegant thoroughfare leads from Trafalgar Square to the Houses of Parliament. At the north end is the Admiralty and, behind Banqueting House (*see chapter* **Tudors & Stuarts**), the Ministry of Defence. At Horse Guards Parade (1753), adjoining the Victorian Treasury buildings, the mounted guard is changed (*see chapter* **London by Season**). Opposite Downing Street is the Cenotaph war memorial (*see chapter* **The World Wars**).

Military

HMS Belfast
Morgan's Lane, Tooley Street, SE1 (071 407 6434). London Bridge underground/BR/river boat from Tower Pier (Feb-Oct daily; Nov-Jan Sat, Sun; 40p adult, 30p under-16s). **Open** *Mar-Oct* 10am-6pm daily; *Nov-Mar* 10am-4.30pm daily. **Admission** £4; £3 OAPs, students; £2 under-16s; under-5s free; £10 family ticket (two adults and two children). **Credit** A, £TC, V.
Pose on the prow before the 6in (152.4mm) guns, or stand on the bridge and pretend that you're full-steaming ahead to sink the *Scharnhorst*. Restored to its wartime Arctic camouflage, this 1938 cruiser is an uncompromisingly physical tourist attraction: there is effort – and hence fun, unless you're wheelchair-bound – involved in getting round it. To see the cabins, gun turrets, sick-bay, brig and boiler-room with its gleaming instruments (polished daily), you must negotiate gangways, airlocks and near-vertical stairways. It's interesting to discover the problems of living in a battleship, and the technical ingenuity involved – the pipes carrying oil, water, sewage and so on are colour-coded. The exhibition on D-Day (in which the *Belfast* took part) is a reminder of why the ship was built. *See also chapter* **The World Wars**.

Café. Group discount. Shop. Wheelchair access on main deck only.

Parks & Gardens

Battersea Park
Albert Bridge Road, SW11 (081 871 7530). Sloane Square underground/Battersea Park or Queenstown Road BR/19, 39, 44, 45, 49, 130, 137, 170 bus. **Open** 8am to dusk daily.
This riverside park, opened in 1858 by Queen Victoria, is now one of London's liveliest open spaces. Its most famous feature, the Festival Gardens, were one of the main attractions of the 1951 Festival of Britain. There are excellent sports and children's facilities, a good boating lake, and many events take place through the year. Bank Holiday fun-fairs (*see chapter* **London by Season**) are held here. The graceful Buddhist Peace Pagoda overlooking the Thames was built by Japanese monks and nuns.
Adventure and conventional playgrounds. Boating lake. Garden for the disabled. Zoo.

Hampstead Heath
NW3 (Parliament Hill 071 485 4491/Kenwood House 081 340 5303/Golder's Hill 081 455 5183). Belsize Park or Hampstead underground/Gospel Oak or Hampstead Heath BR/24 bus. **Open** 24 hours daily.
A stroll around this huge semi-landscaped heath rejuvenates both the tired Londoner and the visitor. At weekends it's packed with everyone and their dog, granny, child and Frisbee. The 800 acres (320 hectares) of rolling, wooded hills have been popular with the literary set for close on 200 years – **Keats' House** (*see chapter* **Museums**) is near the southern end. It is also popular

The Serpentine lake at **Hyde Park**. See review page 38.

with homosexuals after dark. There are woodland bathing ponds (one reserved for women), the mansion **Kenwood House** (*see chapter* **Georgian London** and *chapter* **Music: Classical & Opera**), funfairs on Easter, May and August Bank Holidays and remarkable views from Parliament Hill (*see below* **Bird's-Eye Views**). Bring a kite and catch the Hampstead air. *See also chapter* **London by Area: North**.
Toilets for the disabled at the running track. Three swimming ponds.

Hyde Park

W2 (071 298 2100). Hyde Park Corner, Knightsbridge, Lancaster Gate, Marble Arch or Queensway underground. **Open** 5am-midnight daily.
Hyde Park is central London's largest park and its 340 acres (136 hectares) of greenery are a wonderful place to relax. You can row a boat on the Serpentine lake, trot a horse down Rotten Row, gaze at paintings in the **Serpentine Gallery** (*see chapter* **Art Galleries**) or simply collapse into a deckchair and, on summer Sundays, listen to military bands. But the park should be avoided after dark. Marble Arch, at the north-east corner, was once the entrance gate to Buckingham Palace. On Sundays, at **Speaker's Corner** near the Arch, ranting – and often hilarious – soapbox orators revive the flagging tradition of British free speech.
Playground. Toilets for the disabled.

Kensington Gardens

W8 (071 724 2826). Bayswater, High Street Kensington, Lancaster Gate or Queensway underground. **Open** dawn-dusk daily.
These royal gardens merge into Hyde Park, but have a distinct, more formal character. Kensington Palace is the London home of the Prince and Princess of Wales, and the State Apartments (*see chapter* **Tudors & Stuarts**) provide a good fix for royalty addicts: the Court Dress Collection includes Princess Di's wedding outfit. In the grounds you can wander through the sunken garden and the Orangery.

The statue of Peter Pan, near the modest Italian fountains, is modelled on a girl not a boy, and was erected to delight children, which it does. There are puppet shows in the summer and a playground near Black Lion Gate.
Toilets for the disabled.

Kew Gardens

See **Royal Botanic Gardens**.

Regent's Park

NW1 (071 486 7905). Baker Street, Camden Town, Great Portland Street or Regent's Park underground. **Open** *park and Queen Mary's Rose Garden* 5am-30 mins before dusk daily; *tennis courts* 7am to 30 mins before park closing time daily; *playgrounds* 10am to 30 mins before dusk daily.
The strikingly beautiful Regent's Park is a highlight of John Nash's master streetplan for the Prince Regent. It's bordered by Regent's Crescent, Palladian mansions and the Regent's Canal. A former hunting ground of Henry VIII, it's still a lively place in the summer with puppet shows, bandstand music, softball players and pantaloon-clad actors in the Open Air Theatre. *See also* **London by Area: North**.
Car park. Running track. Softball and football at weekends. Toilets for the disabled.

Richmond Park

Surrey (081 948 3209). Richmond underground/BR. **Open** *pedestrians* 24 hours daily; *traffic Mar-Sept* 7am to 30mins before dusk daily; *Nov-Feb* 7.30am to 30mins before dusk daily.
The best countryside-substitute in London, Richmond Park is the largest city park in Europe, with 2,500 acres (820 hectares) of land. It is ideal for rambling, cycling and riding, and is also a home to wildlife. You can spot foxes scurrying about at dusk, badgers barging through the undergrowth and herds of red and fallow deer in the enclosures. There are two culls a year, in August and November, each lasting between two and three weeks.

A Sunday soliloquy at Speaker's Corner in **Hyde Park**. *See* **review**.

Blissful blossoms at the **Royal Botanic Gardens, Kew.** *See* **review.**

During these periods, pedestrians are asked to leave the park at the same time as the traffic (ie 30 minutes before dusk). The Isabella Plantation is a particularly beautiful watery, woodland garden enclosed by Lord Sidmouth in 1831. A wide variety of birds can be seen among the azaleas and rhododendrons.
Two public golf courses by Roehampton Gate (081 876 3205) £9 Mon-Fri; £12.50 Sat, Sun. Horseriding facilities at Roehampton Riding Stable (081 876 7089).

Royal Botanic Gardens, Kew

Kew Road, Richmond, Surrey (081 940 1171). Kew Gardens underground/Kew Bridge BR/27, 65 bus. **Open** *Nov-Jan* 9.30am-4pm daily; *Feb* 9.30am-5pm daily; *Mar* 9.30am-6pm daily; *Apr-Aug* 9.30am-6.30pm Mon-Sat; 9.30am-8pm Sun, Bank Holidays; *Sept-mid-Oct* 9.30am-6pm daily (glasshouses close 30 mins before closing times, galleries 15 mins before closing times, subject to variation). **Admission** £3.50; £1.80 OAPs, students; £1.30 under-16s; under-5s free; £9 family day ticket; £33 family season ticket (two adults, three children); £17 single season tickets. **Credit** (shop only) A, £TC, V.

Best known as Kew Gardens, this is one of the most beautiful places in London and it attracts thousands of visitors, particularly on summer weekends. But it has a lot to offer in the winter, too. The climate is constant in Decimus Burton's glorious iron and glass Temperate House and the recently renovated Palm House. It's not a park, but a scientific institute. Important horticultural research is carried out here (it has the world's largest collection of orchids, for instance). The gardens were first laid out in 1751 by William Chambers, also responsible for the famous Pagoda. The Marianne North Gallery was designed by North to display her paintings of rare flora and this remains the Gardens' quietest corner. There's also a changing exhibition of botanical art. *Café, restaurant. Shop. Tour by prior arrangement. Wheelchairs for loan. Wheelchair access and toilets for the disabled.*

St James's Park

The Mall, SW1 (071 930 1793). St James's Park underground. **Open** dawn to dusk daily.
Compact, beautiful and convenient for the West End, St James's also has the best vistas of any central park. The buildings of Westminster and Horse Guards Parade peep above the trees, and along The Mall are Admiralty Arch, Nash's Carlton Terrace, the Duke of York's column and two palaces: Buckingham and St James's. The Park is ideal for a civilised stroll, particularly on late afternoons in summer, to see the wildfowl (the famous pelicans have been imprisoned in London Zoo, because they kept eating the pigeons). It's also a good place to glimpse the Queen's guards passing through for the **Changing of the Guard** (*see chapter* **London By Season**). But it's most special at night, when you can steal across to the bridge to see Buckingham Palace floodlit over the lake. *Playground. Restaurant. Toilet for the disabled at Marlborough Gate.*

Bird's-Eye Views

The beautiful London riverscape Canaletto painted may have been destroyed, but the city's skyline and panoramas are still magnificent. The river views are good, but there's nothing like climbing up above the rooftops for the sights suddenly to become obvious above the maze-like confusion at street-level. Here's how to put London into perspective.

Alexandra Park

Muswell Hill, N22 (park 081 444 7696/general information 081 365 2121). Wood Green underground/Alexandra Palace BR/84A, 144, 144A, W2, W3, W7 bus. **Open** 24 hours daily.
The 'Palace' (known universally as Ally Pally), at the top

of this steep north London park, once housed the BBC's first television studio, but it's now a multi-purpose entertainments centre. The view over London is impressive and clear. There are children's activities every day between June and September. Many events take place here; *see chapter* **London by Season** for the low-down on the funfairs on Easter, Whitsun and August Bank Holidays. A free firework display takes place here every 5 November, Guy Fawkes Night.

Cabair Helicopters

Elstree Aerodrome, Elstree, Herts (081 953 4411). Elstree Thameslink BR (will pick up free; phone from station). **Open** 11.30am alternate Sundays, by appointment only. **Fare** four people for one hour £500 inclusive; £99 per person for half an hour. **Credit** A, £TC, V.
Get your own back on those damned pigeons by invading their airspace to sample an exclusive view of London. You can choose your own hour-long helicopter route, but most favour the loop past Heathrow, then along the Thames past Hampton Court, Kew Gardens, Westminster, the City and Greenwich to the Flood Barrier; going back via north-east London. At 1,000ft (305m) the sights seem alarmingly close, and the ride's great for photography. You need to book a week or so ahead in summer and chance the weather, but there's only a refund if the flight's cancelled.

Constable Gallery, Victoria & Albert Museum

Henry Cole Wing, Victoria & Albert Museum, Exhibition Road, SW7 (071 938 8500/recorded information 071 938 8441). South Kensington underground/14, 30, 74, 503, C1 bus. **Open** noon-5.50pm Mon; 10am-5.50pm Tue-Sat; 2.30-5.50pm Sun. **Admission** free (donation requested: £3.50; £1.50 OAPs, students, UB40s). **Credit** (shop only) A, AmEx, £TC, V.
A similar vantage point to Queen's Tower (*see below*), but at roof-top level, looking from Harrods to Westminster. Inside the gallery, you're surrounded by Constable's paintings of a more rustic landscape. *See also chapter* **Museums**.

Golden Gallery, St Paul's Cathedral

EC4 (071 248 2705). St Paul's underground. **Open** *gallery* 9.45am-4.15pm Mon-Sat. **Admission** (in addition to the Cathedral entrance fees) £2.50 adults; £2 students; £1.50 under-16s.
The rickety steps up to the 281ft (85m) Golden Gallery of St Paul's Cathedral (*see above*) are not for those with vertigo; it's crowded and you can't turn back. But you'll see why the view was used for spotting fires all over the City during the Blitz in World War II (*see chapter* **The World Wars**).

Greenwich Hill

Greenwich Park, Charlton Way, SE10 (081 858 2608). Greenwich, Blackheath Village or Maze Hill BR/53, 177, 180, 286 bus/boat to Greenwich pier. **Open** *pedestrians* 5am-dusk daily; *traffic* 7am-dusk daily.
The symmetry of the view from the Wolfe Monument on top of this hill is stunning. The tall Canary Wharf development has now become centre (or rather, annoyingly off-centre) stage. *See also chapter* **London by Area: South**.

Hungerford Foot Bridge

between Victoria Embankment, WC2, and the South Bank, SE1. Embankment underground/Charing Cross or Waterloo underground/BR.
Brave the thunderous noise of the trains on Hungerford Bridge for a river panorama from Cleopatra's Needle past the City to the Festival Hall. It's unforgettable at night. The next span downstream, **Waterloo Bridge**, offers a more all-round view, taking in both Westminster and the City.

London Flightseeing Tours

36 Rostella Road, SW17 (081 767 9055/fax 081 767 9055). **Open** 9am-6pm daily. **Fare** £65 per person (for a party of four). **No credit cards.**
In a tour lasting about 30 minutes, LFT will pick you up from central London and whisk you off to an aerodrome in Essex. From there, a twin-engined Piper aircraft will take you on a 30-minute flight over central London, doing two circuits. Parties must be of four people (otherwise the price rises).

London Hilton

'Windows on the World' London Hilton, Park Lane, W1 (071 493 8000). Hyde Park underground. **Open** *bar* noon-3.30pm, 5.30pm-1.45am, Mon-Sat. *Restaurant* **lunch served** 12.30-2.30pm Mon-Fri; noon-2pm Sun. **Dinner served** 7pm-2am Mon-Sat. **Credit** A, AmEx, DC, £TC, V.
Get vertigo on a full stomach 28 floors up in London's highest restaurant and bar. Sadly, it's the only high-rise restaurant in town. Sip one of the hotel's 70 cocktails as you wander round to see London fanning out below. It's spectacular at night.
Booking advisable. Dress: jacket in bar; jacket and tie, no jeans, in restaurant. Wheelchair access.

Monument

Monument Street, EC2 (071 626 2717). Monument underground. **Open** *Apr-Sept* 9am-6pm Mon-Fri; 2-6pm Sat, Sun (last admission 20 mins before closing). *Oct-Mar* 9am-4pm Mon-Sat. **Admission** £1 adults; 25p under-16s.
The 202ft (60.6m)-high Monument is London's reminder of the Great Fire of 1666. The view from the top (though slightly obscured by office blocks) is worth the climb, if you don't mind 311 steps up a narrow spiral staircase. *See also chapter* **Tudors & Stuarts**.

Parliament Hill

Hampstead Heath, NW3 (071 485 4491). Kentish Town underground, then C2 bus/Hampstead Heath or Gospel Oak BR. **Open** 24 hours daily.
Dubbed Kite Hill because kite-fliers exploit its exposed position at the south end of Hampstead Heath, Parliament Hill offers a peach of a view. On a clear day you can take in the whole of central London (there are boards outlining landmarks), even to Crystal Palace in the south-east. The hill was to have had a beacon in 1605 to signal Guy Fawkes' attempt to blow up Parliament – hence the name.

Primrose Hill

NW3 (071 486 7905). Chalk Farm, Camden Town or St John's Wood underground/31, 74 bus. **Open** 24 hours daily.
Not a primrose in sight, but on a fine day a cluster of the central-London landmarks are visible from this hill, with London Zoo in the foreground and Crystal Palace in the distance. In icy winters, the park becomes a venue for scudding toboggans; there are fireworks on Bonfire Night and druids conduct pagan rites at the Autumn Equinox. *See chapter* **London by Season**.

Tower Bridge

SE1 (071 407 0922). Tower Hill or London Bridge underground/BR. **Open** *Apr-Oct* 10am-6.30pm daily; *Nov-Mar* 10am-4.45 pm daily (last admission 45 mins before closing). Closed Good Friday, Christmas Eve, Christmas Day, Boxing Day and New Year's Day. **Admission** £3.60 adults; £2.50 under-15s, OAPs. **Credit** (shop only, but shop sells tickets) A, £TC, V.
The up- and down-stream panoramas from the overhead walkways give about the best of the many views of the City, and they are unique for viewing the Thames's bridges and Docklands. The only hazard in the safe, glazed walkways is the running about of kids. There are useful platforms

and portholes for picture-taking and panels clearly indicate the landmarks. For the admission price, you also get interesting displays, a museum, and the new 'Celebration Story', which charts the history of the bridge with animatronic characters, including 'Harry' the guide.
Group discount. Shop. Wheelchair access.

St Edward's Tower, Westminster Cathedral
Victoria Street, SW1 (071 834 7452). St James' Park underground or Victoria underground/BR. **Open** *Apr-Oct* 9.30am-5.30pm daily. **Admission** £2; £1 children, OAPs, students. **No credit cards**.
For a superb perspective of the Palace and Abbey of Westminster, take the lift up the 273ft (83m) campanile (bell tower) of Westminster Cathedral. This striking, striped building is the headquarters of the British Catholic church (*see chapter* **Early Twentieth Century**). Unforgivably, Victoria Street's tower blocks obscure much of the West End and City, but the vistas south over the Thames and west across Kensington are impressive.
Shop. Wheelchair access.

Bus Tours

Bus tours vary from 90-minute drives through the City of London and the West End, passing all the main sights; to full-day tours which include lunch and visits to places such as the Tower of London. Guides can make or break a tour. Below we've listed tours whose guides have the London Tourist Board qualification, the Blue Badge; phone for details of pick-up points. Pre-recorded commentaries are often inaudible and get out of synch when you're stuck in traffic. Live guides are better and can answer questions, but are more expensive.

Can-Be-Done
9-11 Kensington High Street, W8 (081 907 2400). High Street Kensington underground. **Open** 9am-8pm Mon-Fri. **Credit** AmEx, £STC.
This flexible company can arrange anything within reason – from a tour of famous cemeteries to a visit to the Houses of Parliament. Tours are arranged and priced individually.

Cityrama
British Rail Yard, Silverthorne Road, SW8 (071 720 6663). **Open** 9am-5pm Mon-Sat. **Journey time** 90 mins. **Fares** £8 adults; £3 under-14s; under-4s free. **Credit** £TC.
This is only satisfactory if you want a very basic tour. The bus sets off from five different departure points every 30 minutes from 9am to 8.20pm daily in the summer and from 9.30am to 6pm in the winter.
Headsets with commentaries in eight languages.

Evan Evans
26 Cockspur Street, SW1 (24 hours 071 930 2377). Charing Cross underground/BR. **Open** 8am-5.30pm Mon-Fri; 8am-2pm Sat, Sun. **Fares** *half day* £12.50-£23 adults; £10.50-£17.50 under-18s; under-3s free; *full day (including lunch)* £45 adults; £42 under-18s; under-3s free. **Credit** A, AmEx, DC, £TC, V.
This company picks up from over 30 hotels each morning. It offers seven tours around London including all the big attractions, for a full or a half day. Cruises on the Thames are also available. The air-conditioned coaches are new and comfortable. It's essential to book in advance. Disabled visitors should phone to check suitability of tours.

Frames Rickards
Offices and main pick-up: 11 Herbrand Street, WC1 (071 837 3111/night service 071 936 9344). Russell Square underground. **Open** 7.30am-7.30pm daily. **Fares** £8-£44 adults; £3-£32 under-16s. **Credit** A, AmEx, £TC, JCB, V.
Frames Rickards runs both full- and half-day guided tours of major sights; lunch is included for the all-day outings. The half-day tours are run twice daily in summer and once a day in winter. Coaches are air-conditioned single-deckers and the trips take in all the major sights, from the West End to Tower Bridge, but with taped commentaries.

London Transport Sightseeing Tour
Victoria Station, SW1 (071 222 1234). **Open** 8.15am-7.30pm daily. **Meeting points** Victoria Station, SW1; Marble Arch, W1; Haymarket, SW1 (Piccadilly Circus underground); Baker Street underground, NW1. **Tours** 9.30am-5.30pm daily. **Journey time** 90 mins. **Fares** £8 adult; £4 under-16s; £2 reduction if in advance from a Travel Information Centre. **Credit** (Wilton Road offices only) A, AmEx, DC, £TC, V.
The tour sets off every 20-30 minutes and takes in all the main sights. Traditional red double-decker buses are used; in summer they are open-topped. The live commentary is full of interesting facts, but you'll have to sit underneath one of the loud speakers if you want to hear it clearly.
Language buses in French and German.

William Forrester
1 Belvedere Road, Guildford, Surrey (0483 575401).
William Forrester is a wheelchair user who in 1989 deservedly became the first ever winner of the London Tourist Board's award for the best London Guide of the year. Will's tours, booked in equal numbers by both 'able-bodied' and disabled people are informative, racy and always highly entertaining. Will's services include itinerary-planning, illustrated lectures on British Heritage, study tours, consultancy on access and minibus tours. For information and fees contact him on the above number, well in advance of the date you are interested in booking.

Walking Tours

Walking in London is often the fastest way to travel around and certainly the best method of getting to know the city. From a central point such as Leicester Square, you can walk to Piccadilly, Soho, Covent Garden, or Trafalgar Square in less than ten minutes.

Anecdotes about the hidden corners and lesser-known aspects of London are the speciality of the many walking tours available. The entertainment level depends upon the guide's personality and knowledge. Prepare yourself for a couple of hours' walking, and the likelihood of ending up in a pub. Tours are listed throughout this Guide, but for details consult the 'Around Town' section of *Time Out* magazine, or contact one of the companies listed below:

Citisights *(081 806 4325).*

Historical Tours *(081 668 4019).*

Original London Walks *(071 624 3978).*

History

From Julius Caesar to John Major: we chronicle the startling growth of
London, through conflicts and conflagration, plagues and planners,
Reformation and riots – to become one of the world's great cities.

Contents

Roman to Norman

Founded as a port by the Romans, London's fortunes are at first tied to those of the Empire. But during the Middle Ages the city gains wealth and independence.

The Roman Province

Julius Caesar invaded Britain in 55 BC, but the island's first major contact with the Roman Empire was short-lived, and the famous general left within a year. It was almost a century later, in AD 43, that an invasion under the Emperor Claudius led to the occupation of Britain and the establishment of the Roman province.

Over the next three centuries or more, various peoples were absorbed and admitted to the benefits of the Roman system. Roads were built and town life began. Latin became the language of business, of culture, of command: graffiti found scratched on cement from the period suggests that bricklayers were able to read and write Latin.

London (named Londinium by the Romans) started to develop as a trading settlement at the highest point up the Thames which could be reached by sea-going vessels, and yet as near to the mouth as it was feasible to build a bridge.

Although the architectural development of Londinium up to AD 60 is unclear, evidence suggests a street plan in accordance with the strict grid patterns typical of Roman towns. Excavations have revealed that **Fenchurch Street** and the east end of **Lombard Street**, EC3, lie more or less above Londinium's first main road.

This development was interrupted in AD 60, when Boudicca, the widow of the chieftain of an East Anglian tribe, reacted against harsh treatment at the hands of local imperial officials. She led her tribe, the Iceni, in a general insurrection. After the destruction of the Roman colony at Colchester, she attacked London which was unfortified and without a garrison: there was a massacre and the settlement was burnt down. There is a statue depicting Boudicca and her daughters on Victoria Embankment, SW1, at the side of the Thames. It was sculpted in the 1850s by Thomas Thorneycroft.

CREATION OF A CAPITAL

Eventually, order was restored, and London was rebuilt as the capital of the whole province. There was a forum with a temple, shops, arcades and a basilica (a large public hall for law courts and other business, which was located where **Leadenhall Market**, EC3, now stands). The remains of an amphitheatre, which could seat 35,000 spectators, was discovered near the **Guildhall**, EC3, in 1987. Vestiges of its changing-rooms have also been unearthed (the site is closed to the public).

A Governor's Palace was also built during the Roman period. It would have had private baths, lavish state rooms and ornamental gardens. Its location is thought to be somewhere under Cannon Street Station, EC4. The **London Stone**, set behind an iron grille in the outside wall of 111 Cannon Street, EC4, may have been placed at the Palace entrance.

The **Museum of London** (*see chapter* **Museums**) contains the most treasured artefacts to have been recovered from the remains of Londinium, including the celebrated sculptures discovered in the **Temple of Mithras**, Temple Court, Queen Victoria Street, EC4. The site was discovered in 1954, when excavations for a new building in Bucklersbury uncovered the remains of a small Roman temple. Buried underneath were fine marble sculptures, including a marble head of the Persian god Mithras, revered by the Roman legions for his qualities of virility, strength and courage. The foundations of the temple, built about AD 240-50, have been restored and can be seen on Queen Victoria Street, EC4.

The **British Museum** (*see chapter* **Museums**) also contains Roman artefacts from Londinium, including the decorative tomb of Julius Classicianus, procurator of the town in AD 61.

About AD 200, a substantial wall was built around the new city. This wall continued in use throughout the Middle Ages. Though London has never stood a siege, its Roman wall is of very great importance since, in most directions, it fixed the boundary of the City of London (now London's financial district). The area of the City has remained almost exactly as the Romans determined.

The Museum of London has a public gallery that overlooks a section of the wall; more of it can be seen on a one-and-a-half-mile (2.5-kilometre) trail which follows the wall from the Museum to the **Tower of London** (*see chapter* **Sightseeing**), with illustrated panels to guide you. The information is also published in a booklet 'The London Wall Walk', £1.95, sold at the Museum of London bookshop.

Substantial Roman remains can be seen outside of London at **Fishbourne** and **Bath**.

Fishbourne Palace and Museum

Salthill Road, Fishbourne, Chichester, West Sussex (0243 785859). **Getting there** *by train* from Victoria (change at Chichester), 2 hours; *by bus* National Express from Victoria, 3 hours then bus 266 or 700 Coastliner, 10 minutes; *by car* A3 to Portsmouth then A27 (or take the scenic A286 route via Midhurst). **Open** *Mar, Apr, Oct* 10am-5pm daily; *May-Sept* 10am-6pm daily; *Nov* 10am-4pm daily; *Dec-Feb* 10am-4pm Sun only. **Admission** £3.40; £2.70 OAPs, students; £1.50 under-16s; under-5s free; £8.50 family ticket. **Credit** A, £TC, V.

The provincial villa, which was unearthed in Fishbourne in 1960, is the largest Roman building of its type found in Britain. It's thought to have been built for Cogidubnus, a Celtic prince who became a client king, or legate, and who would have governed the region on behalf of Rome. The building was found to have an unparalleled series of geometric mosaic floors, dating from the first century AD. The tessellated corridors have survived the ravages of time virtually intact and give a unique insight into Roman interior design.

Roman Baths and Museum

Stall Street, Bath, BA1 (0225 461111 ext 2785). **Getting there** *by train* from Paddington 80 minutes (longer on Sun); *by bus* National Express from Victoria 3 hours; *by car* M4 to exit 18. **Open** *Nov-Feb* 9am-5pm Mon-Sat; 10am-5pm Sun; *Mar-Oct* 9am-6pm daily; *July* 9am-6.30pm daily; *Aug* 9am-6.30pm, 8-10pm, daily. **Admission** £4; £1.90 under-17s; under-8s free. **Credit** A, AmEx, DC, £TC, V.

The museum houses the celebrated Roman baths, created around AD 60 under Flavian rule, and in use until the fourth century. Though neglected for 1,400 years, the famous watering hole of Aqua Sulis (the Roman name for Bath) has been the subject of numerous excavations since the eighteenth century, the most recent exposing the temple precinct. Artefacts displayed in the museum include the Gorgon's head, an icon created specifically for Bath and which would have squatted on the temple roof. *See also chapter* **Trips out of Town**.

Group discount by prior arrangement. Guided tour. Restaurant (The Pump Room). Shop. Toilets for the disabled. Wheelchair access to balcony (free).

The Dark Ages

During the fourth century, barbarian invasions from without, and economic disasters within led to the decline of the Roman Empire. In Britain, towns ceased to be important and gave place to large, self-sufficient country villas. After AD 410 Britain, while remaining culturally Roman, was no longer garrisoned or administered by the Empire.

The history of England during the fifth and sixth centuries is exceedingly obscure. The Saxons, a Teutonic people, crossed the sea and established themselves in what is now England. They could not have been numerous, but they destroyed all that was Roman and imposed their own culture on the land which they had occupied. Though they had no written language, their Germanic speech replaced Latin and became the primary source of modern English.

In AD 594 Pope Gregory sent Augustine to convert the English to Christianity. The Saxons proved themselves enthusiastic converts, and in AD 601, Augustine was appointed the first Archbishop of Canterbury. During the seventh century, England became the great centre of Latin scholarship and source of remarkable missionary activities. But little is known of London during early Saxon times, except the fact that Augustine established Mellitus as the first bishop of a restored hierarchy, and Ethelbert, King of Kent, founded a church dedicated to St Paul in AD 604. All that remains of medieval St Paul's are the ruined cloisters and the chapter house in the gardens on the south side of Wren's cathedral.

VIOLATION BY VIKINGS

London was sacked by the Danes in AD 839, but the town seems to have recovered sufficiently to be worth another Danish visit in AD 895. Under Alfred the Great, Londoners defeated the Danes and enjoyed a period of prosperous tranquillity.

In the eleventh century, the Danes again harassed the town, though it retained its wealth during the reign of Canute (1016-1040), one-seventh of whose revenues came from London. From this time it disputed with Winchester the priority among English cities.

Two years after Canute died, in 1042, Edward the Confessor came to the throne. He established his capital at Westminster, two miles (3 kilometres) up-Thames from the City. Here he replaced the small timber church of St Peter's with **Westminster Abbey** (*see chapter* **Sightseeing**) intending it to be the place of coronation and of burial for the kings and queens of England. The abbey was largely rebuilt during the thirteenth and fourteenth centuries, but today's structure still contains Edward's tomb and his relics.

Edward also built a palace in the latest Norman style. The palace at Westminster has often been rebuilt, yet it still contains the seat of government, the **Houses of Parliament** (*see chapter* **Sightseeing**).

Although noted for his piety and personal virtue, Edward proved a weak king. But, aware of his own limitations, he seems to have intended that his successor should be the capable but ruthless William of Falaise, Duke of Normandy. Yet when Edward died, his brother-in-law, Harold, seized the throne and had himself crowned in Westminster Abbey on the very day of Edward's burial.

William gathered a large army and invaded England. On 4 October 1066, he defeated Harold and marched on London. As they had previously arranged, the citizens of the City of London welcomed William and he was crowned at Westminster on the Christmas Day of 1066.

The Middle Ages

Among William's first acts as king was the granting of a charter to the bishop and burgesses of London: 'I grant them all to be law-worthy as they were in the days of King Edward, and I grant that every child shall be his father's heir after his father's days, and I will not suffer any man to do you wrong.' But

Westminster Hall

The City of London has not been a political capital since Britain ceased to be a province of the Roman Empire. The later Saxon kings of England used Winchester as the principal royal town and when Edward the Confessor (king from 1042-1066) decided to establish a centre of government by the Thames, he chose Westminster.

William the Conqueror was the first king to be crowned at Westminster. This William was succeeded by his second son William, nicknamed, because of his ruddy complexion, Rufus. Rufus intended to enlarge the new royal palace at Westminster, but he built only the hall. The walls that remain are substantially those of his building. About 240 feet (73 metres) in length, it was one of the largest medieval halls in Europe. Alterations were made in 1291 and about 1399 the whole hall was spanned by a hammer-beam roof which needed no supporting pillars. This supreme example of medieval carpentry (the largest of its kind in the world) has been preserved.

Medieval social customs made few concessions to privacy. Only the highest in rank had chambers of their own. The hall of a palace or castle did service as living room, dining room, and business centre of the whole establishment. Everyone ate in the same hall and most of the unmarried men and boys would have slept there. After a coronation in the Abbey, a great feast was held in Westminster Hall. During this banquet, an armed and mounted knight, the 'King's Champion', was led into the hall where he

threw down a gauntlet challenging to mortal combat any who might dispute the rights of the newly crowned monarch. Though this ceremony continued until the eighteenth century, it is not recorded that the gauntlet was ever taken up.

Westminster Hall survived the destruction of most of the royal palace in the fire of 1512. After this date Westminster ceased to be a royal residence, but it remained the centre of the administrative life of the nation. Parliament often assembled in the hall and it was here that the House of Commons was in session when, in 1641, Charles I came in person to arrest the five members. Law courts were held in the hall until they were moved to a new building in the Strand in 1882 (*see chapter* **London by Area: The City**).

Westminster Hall has been the scene of many memorable events in the history of England. Here, in 1327, Edward II abdicated and in 1399, Richard II was deposed. Ironically, both Edward and Richard had made notable contributions towards the building of the hall. Perhaps it was even more ironic that, after St Thomas More had been condemned to death because of his opposition to Henry VIII's attempt to marry Anne Boleyn, Anne herself should have been sentenced to death in the same hall only a year later. The most notorious show trial to be staged in Westminster Hall was that of Charles I in 1649.

The hall is now used for the lying-in-state of deceased monarchs.

Westminster Hall, *Parliament Square, SW1 (071 219 4273). Westminster underground*. **Open** by appointment only. **Admission** free.

not entirely convinced of the loyalty of the Londoners, he built the White Tower immediately outside the City to the east – it now forms part of the **Tower of London** (*see chapter* **Sightseeing**) – and Baynard's Castle at the western extremity (this castle was rebuilt in the fifteenth century and Henry VIII used it to house all of his wives; it was destroyed in the Great Fire).

In 1176 the priest Peter of Colechurch, began the erection of the first stone London Bridge. Lasting until the nineteenth century, the bridge originally carried two rows of multi-storied houses, a chapel and the grave of its architect. The bridges linked the City with Southwark, London's first suburb, which developed on the south bank of the Thames.

Since Southwark was outside the jurisdiction of the City authorities, it became London's 'red-light' district. Here were the brothels and pits for cock-fighting and bear-baiting.

At the end of the twelfth century we have the first written account of contemporary London life from Fitzstephen of Canterbury. Describing a walled city with seven gates, he is impressed by the wealth and power of the citizens and the well-stocked markets. He found most Londoners to be pious, vivacious and sociable. The only drawbacks were 'immoderate drinking by fools and the frequency of fires'.

In 1189 the City authorities decreed that all houses were to be built of stone, but building in timber continued. The City then contained over a hundred parish churches in addition to 13 larger conventual churches (*see below* **Church**).

FILTH AND LUCRE

London's wealth increased greatly during the Middle Ages. Its population grew from about 18,000 in 1100 to 50,000 in the 1340s. The monarch at Westminster came to depend on City merchants for finance; power was exchanged for their gold. In 1197, Richard I gave them control of the Thames (including the lucrative fishing rights), and King John (1199-1216) recognised the right of Londoners to elect their own mayor and aldermen, effectively recognising the City's independence from Westminster.

A lack of hygiene was a serious problem in medieval London. Water was provided in cisterns at Cheapside and elsewhere, but the supply (which came more or less directly from the Thames) was limited and polluted. Houndsditch (EC3), was so called because Londoners threw their dead animals into the ditch that formed one of the City's boundaries. These unsanitary conditions provided the breeding ground for the greatest catastrophe of the Middle Ages, the Black Death of 1348-9.

The plague reached England from Europe, by way of London's port, carried by rats on a cargo ship. During this period, about 30 per cent of England's population died of the disease. When the plague abated, it was to recur in London on several occasions during the next three centuries.

The Jewel Tower

Abingdon Street, SW1 (071 222 2219). Westminster underground. **Open** *Apr-Jun* 10am-1pm, 2-6pm, daily; *Oct-Mar* 10am-1pm, 2-4pm, Tue-Sun. **Admission** £2; £1.50 OAPs, students; £1 under-15s. **Credit** A, £TC, V.

Along with **Westminster Hall** (*see* **Box**), the Jewel Tower is a survivor from the medieval Palace of Westminster. It was built (1365-6) to house Edward III's gold and jewels. From 1621 to 1864, the tower stored records of the House of Lords, but since 1992 a permanent exhibition on the history of Parliament has been displayed here.

Commerce

Many of London's markets date from the Middle Ages. **Smithfield** sold meat, **Leadenhall** sold poultry (for both *see chapter* **London by Area: The City**), **Billingsgate** (now moved to East London, *see chapter* **London by Area: East End & Docklands**) sold fish. Eastcheap (now known as Cheapside, EC2) was a general market area. Nearby were other streets specialising in certain goods, as their names still indicate – Fish Street Hill, Sea Coal Lane, Milk Street, Ironmonger Lane, Bread Street.

In a medieval town a shop was, quite literally, a workshop. All that was offered for sale was homemade. Not only were there no departmental stores, but there were no general stores either. Chairs came from the carpenter's, shoes from the shoemaker's and candles from the chandler's. There were no wholesaler's warehouses, no middle-men, and no shop assistants. There were only manufacturers (Latin for 'makers by hand'). Any item that was not in daily demand would have been made to order. If a knight wanted a shirt of mail from the armourer, it had to be ordered and therefore was made to measure. The customer dealt directly with the master craftsman who himself made what was sold. The master was assisted by youthful apprentices who, in return for their labour, were taught the craft so that eventually they would themselves become masters.

This method of trade and manufacture determined the form of the buildings in a medieval city. The ground floor was the place for making, selling and storing. Above the shop was a hall and one or two chambers where all the

hall and one or two chambers where all the members of the establishment ate and slept.

Medieval society readily accepted the natural instinct of the young to leave their family home and parents. A knight would send his son to serve as the squire of another knight, who would train the youth and expect, in return, service and friendship. Similarly, if the son of a master craftsman intended to learn a craft, he would be sent to join the household of another master, as an apprentice. Thus those who lived over a medieval shop would have included youths who were not related to the master of that household.

The **British Museum** has a permanent display of medieval crafts, including gold and silver work, jewellery, and glass. Many other medieval artefacts are displayed at the **Museum of London**, alongside maps and models of buildings from the period (for both museums, *see chapter* **Museums**).

During the Middle Ages, all the 'masters' were organised in craft guilds. Only members of guilds were permitted to conduct trade inside the City. It was the duty of each guild to ensure that its members were qualified, to fix 'just prices' and to oversee the instruction and welfare of apprentices. The guilds also took care of their members in times of distress, providing some measure of social security. As with all other medieval institutions, craft guilds established charity foundations in the parish churches, endowed chaplaincies and made donations to various charitable works. The guilds also had an important role in the election of City officers.

At the Reformation, the religious aspect of guild life provided an excuse for limiting their power, and eventually for destroying them. London seems the only city in which the guilds (called in London 'livery companies') still survive, but it is only a nominal survival. Today, the London livery company does little more than provide status for businessmen who justify their honours by various philanthropic activities. No present member of the Clothworker's Guild weaves cloth.

The City's government has been based at the **Guildhall** (*see chapter* **By Area: The City**) for over 800 years. The Gothic porch, finished in 1430, is still the ceremonial entrance to the hall from Guildhall Yard. It is also possible to visit the ceremonial halls of many of the City's livery companies; contact the **City**

of London Information Centre (*see chapter* **London by Area: The City**).

Crosby Hall
Cheyne Walk, SW3 (071 352 9663). Sloane Square underground.
The only surviving part of a medieval merchant's house in London, Crosby Hall is referred to by Shakespeare on three occasions. It was removed to Chelsea, from the City, in 1910 under threat of demolition. Sir Thomas More leased the Hall and Richard III is known to have stayed here. It is now privately owned and not open to the public.

Church

Like every other medieval city, London had a large number of parish churches, and in addition to St Paul's Cathedral, many monastic churches. Although there was ready access to the great churches, most Londoners preferred to worship in their own small parish churches, which they decorated with precious objects and maintained clerics who sang the full round of daily offices. **Westminster Abbey** (*see chapter* **Sightseeing**), though outside the walls of the City, provides some idea of what the larger churches were like. Adjacent to the Abbey's Chapter House (1250-53), there's the Pyx Chamber, built 1065-90 but subsequently much restored. Here were deposited standard weights and measures.

More medieval churches are listed in *chapter* **London by Area: The City**.

Southwark Cathedral
Montague Close, SE1 (071 407 2939). London Bridge underground/BR/Riverbus to London Bridge City Pier. **Open** 8am-6pm daily. Closing times vary on religious holidays. **Services** 12.45pm, 5.30pm, Mon-Fri; noon, 4pm, Sat; 9am, 11am, 3pm, Sun. **Admission** free. **Credit** (café only) A, AmEx, DC, £TC, V.
Southwark Cathedral was a monastic church which became an Anglican cathedral in 1905. Parts of the building date back to 1220, when the church was known as St Mary Overy. After the Reformation it fell into disrepair, and sections of it became a bakery and a pig-sty. It was much restored during the nineteenth century, when the nave was entirely rebuilt. The cathedral possesses a fascinating mixture of architecture, including a fine Gothic choir. As the church is off the tourist track, it makes a quiet retreat.
Café (071 378 6446; open 10am-4.30pm Mon-Fri). Crèche (Sun 11 am service only). Shop. Tour by prior arrangement. Wheelchair access.

Temple Church
Inner Temple, King's Bench Walk, EC4 (071 353 1736). Temple underground. **Open** 10am-4pm Mon-Sat. **Services** 8.30am Holy Communion, 11.15am morning service, Sun. **Admission** free.
Built by the Knights Templars between 1170 and 1240, the beautiful Temple Church is based on the Church of the Holy Sepulchre in Jerusalem. Although it has been rebuilt after bomb damage during World War II, it still has the ground plan of the original church. An underground chamber dating from the twelfth century has been excavated under the south aisle of the chancel. *Wheelchair access.*

Opposite: *The Guildhall. See above.*

Tudors & Stuarts

Despite plagues and conflagrations, and a series of wars (both civil and less so), London's population continues to increase.

Although it grew strongly in the Middle Ages, early Tudor London was a long way behind the great cities of Renaissance Europe in size, wealth and culture. The walled City of London was still separated from Westminster by fields and from Southwark by London Bridge. The Thames was much wider than it is today (about 1,900 feet/579 metres) and much more important in terms of transportation.

The first Tudor monarch, Henry VII, died in 1509 and was succeeded by his son Henry VIII. In 1512, much of the royal palace at Westminster was destroyed by fire. Henry VIII was left without a London residence until 1530, when he took possession of York Place, renaming it Whitehall Palace (the **Banqueting Hall** of which remains *see below* **The Stuarts**). The Palace had previously been owned by Henry's chancellor, Thomas Wolsey, who had also given the king **Hampton Court Palace**. In 1530, Henry began to build yet another residence for himself: **St James's Palace** (only the gatehouse and clock remain, *see chapter* **By Area: West End**).

Frustrated in his attempts to secure the annulment of his marriage with Catherine of Aragon so that he could make his mistress, Anne Boleyn, queen, Henry forced Parliament to declare that he was 'Supreme head of the church in England'. The monks of the London **Charterhouse** refused to take an oath accepting this and were among the first to suffer death by disembowelment. There followed the Dissolution of the Monasteries, where all property owned by the Catholic Church was confiscated. Even City guilds were robbed of most of their endowments which had been used for religious and charitable purposes.

The split from Rome made the two great European powers of France and Spain (both staunchly Catholic) religious, as well as political enemies of England. Henry therefore decided he needed to develop a full-time professional navy, leading to the foundation of the royal dockyards at Woolwich and Deptford.

Chapel of Henry VII

Westminster Abbey, SW1 (071 222 5152). Westminster or St James's Park underground. **Open** 9am-4pm Mon-Fri; 9am-2pm, 3.45-5pm, Sat. **Admission** £3; £1.50 OAPs, students; £1 children. **No credit cards.**
The tombs of Henry VII and his mother are among the earliest examples of Renaissance art in England. Other

inhabitants of this royal necropolis are Mary Queen of Scots, Elizabeth I and Mary Tudor. Look up at the early sixteenth-century pendant-vaulted roof and don't miss the remarkable collection of sculptured saints. The chapel is also open on Wednesday evenings (6-7.45pm) when admission is free and you're allowed to take photographs. *Guided tour. Shop.*

Charterhouse

Charterhouse Square, EC1 (071 253 9503). Barbican underground or Farringdon underground/BR. **Open** *guided tours Apr-Jul* 2.15pm Wed. **Admission** £2; £1.50 children, OAPs.
Charterhouse was established as a monastery in the fourteenth century. After the Dissolution it was owned by several Tudor aristocrats before being converted into a school in 1611 (past pupils include William Thackeray and John Wesley). The school moved to Surrey in the nineteenth century. The cloisters (much restored after wartime bomb damage) can be seen by appointment, or during the guided tour. The chapel can be seen during Sunday service (9.45am).

The Clink Exhibition

1 Clink Street, SE1 (071 403 6515). London Bridge underground/BR. **Open** *Jan-Nov* 10am-6pm daily. **Admission** £2; £1 OAPs, students, UB40s, under-16s. Under-16s must be accompanied by an adult. **No credit cards.**
In the fifteenth century, the Bishop of Winchester ran 22 brothels, and any prostitutes he wasn't pimping he incarcerated in Clink Prison. Thus 'Clink' became a byword for jail. The displays, in a warehouse on the site of the prison (which was destroyed in the Gordon Riots of 1780), has recreations of cells and torture implements, a fully functional working medieval armoury but few real artefacts from Southwark's ribald past. Many visitors head straight for the 'adults only' exhibition – a display of low life, including anti-masturbation devices. *Shop.*

Hampton Court Palace

East Molesey, Surrey (081 977 9500). Hampton Court BR/boat to Hampton Court Pier (Apr-Oct). **Open** *Apr-Oct* 10.15am-6pm Mon; 9.30am-6pm Tue-Sun; *Oct-Mar* 10.15am-4.30pm Mon; 9.30am-4.30pm Tue-Sun (last admission half an hour before closing). **Park open** dawn to dusk daily. **Admission** *inclusive ticket to palace, courtyard, cloister and maze* £6.50; £4.90 OAPs; £4.30 under-16s; under-5s free. *Maze only Mar-Oct* £1.50; £1 under-16s; 90p OAPs. **Credit** A, AmEx, £TC, V.
The grandest Tudor residence in England, Hampton Court Palace was built as a country residence by Cardinal Wolsey in 1514. Wolsey 'presented' the Palace to Henry in 1525 in an attempt to retain the King's favour after he'd failed to secure the longed-for divorce. It didn't work – Wolsey was arrested for high treason and died before his trial. Henry's additions to the Palace include the magnificent roof of the Chapel Royal, which took 100 men nine months to complete. The State Apartments, added by William and Mary, were designed by Sir Christopher Wren in the late seventeenth century. In 1986, a fire dev-

A sole survivor in central London: **Staple Inn**. *See* **review** page 54.

astated the King's Apartments, but they have since been painstakingly restored. Outside, the famous maze is fun to get lost in.
Car park (free). Group discount. Guided tours (Mar-Sept 11.15am, 2.15pm, Mon-Sat; free with full-price ticket). Shop. Toilets for the disabled. Wheelchair access.

The Royal Armouries
HM Tower of London, EC3 (071 480 6358). Tower Hill underground. **Open** *Mar-Oct* 9am-5.45pm Mon-Sat; 10am-5.45pm Sun. **Admission** £6.70; £4.50 disabled, OAPs, students, UB40s; £3.35 children. **Credit** (shop only) A, V.
London's oldest museum contains exhibits from the Dark Ages to the present day. Major attractions include a Tudor and Stuart gallery with the armours of Henry VIII and Charles I. There's an oriental armoury with the world's largest suit of armour, designed for an Indian elephant, plus a collection of eighteenth- and nineteenth-century British military weapons.
For **Tower of London** *see chapter* **Sightseeing**.
Group discount. Wheelchair access.

The Elizabethan Age

After Henry's death in 1547, The Reformation continued apace and Protestantism was imposed on the whole kingdom. In many parts of England, there had been strong resistance to religious change. The resistance had been suppressed with great ferocity. However, most Londoners seem to have been in sympathy with the new religion. The brief Catholic revival under Mary met with much opposition in the capital.
Elizabeth I came to the throne in 1558.

During her 45-year reign, British explorers sailed far and wide. In 1581 she knighted Sir Francis Drake at Woolwich Dockyard on his return from a three year circumnavigation of the globe. Drake's portrait, along with those of every Tudor and Stuart monarch, can be seen in the **National Portrait Gallery** (*see chapter* **Art Galleries**).
London became a major port for goods from America, Africa and the Far East – 90 per cent of England's overseas trade went through the city. As trade increased, so did London. By 1600 there were 200,000 people living in the capital, many in dirty and overcrowded conditions. For though the Tudor period saw a great increase in London's commercial prosperity, it was a prosperity not generally shared. During the next three centuries the difference between the rich and the poor was to become immense.

Hatfield House
Hatfield, Hertfordshire (07072 62823). Hatfield BR. **Open** *Mar-Oct* noon-4pm Tue-Sat; 1.30-5pm Sun (*Mar-Jul* gardens closed on Sundays); 11am-5pm Bank Holidays. **Admission** *house and gardens* £4.70; £3.90 OAPs; £3.20 under-16s. *Gardens only* £2.60; £2.40 OAPs; £2 under-16s. **Credit** (shop only) A, £$TC, V.
A splendid, fully-furnished Jacobean house with paintings (including the Rainbow Portrait of Elizabeth I), tapestries and armour, as well as exhibitions of model soldiers and Jacobean kitchens. Look round the late-fifteenth-century gardens and see the ruins of the Royal Palace of Hatfield where Elizabeth I spent much of her childhood.

Café. Children's playground. Elizabethan banquets (07072 62055). Garden festival (June). Group discount. Guided tours. Multi-lingual tours by prior arrangement. Restaurant. Shop. Toilets for the disabled. Wheelchair access.

Middle Temple Hall

Middle Temple Lane, EC4 (071 353 4355). Temple underground. **Open** 10am-noon, 3-4.30pm, Mon-Fri (the Hall is often in use in the afternoon, so phone first). **Admission** free.

The most impressive feature of the Hall, completed in 1573, is its oak, double hammerbeam roof. The 29-ft (9m) Bench Table, given to the Temple by Elizabeth I, was made from a single Windsor Park oak. The smaller table in front of the Bench Table, known as 'the Cupboard', was made from a piece of wood from Sir Francis Drake's *Golden Hind. See also* **London by Area: The City**.

Staple Inn

Holborn, WC1 (no phone). Chancery Lane underground. **Open** *courtyard only* 8am-8pm Mon-Fri. **Admission** free.

Staple Inn is the only surviving half-timbered Elizabethan terrace in central London. It was founded in 1378 as an Inn of Chancery, a type of prep school undertaken before joining the Inns of Court to train as a barrister. It became part of Gray's Inn (on the opposite side of Holborn) in 1529. The present splendid building dates from 1586. A silver dragon on a plinth in front of Staple Inn marks the boundary of the City of London.

Elizabethan Theatre

The great glory of the reign of Elizabeth I was the development of English drama. The first theatres, the Rose, the Globe and the Hope, were erected on the south bank of the Thames, as the City authorities forbade them to be established within the area of their jurisdiction. Since daylight was essential, the theatres had to be largely open-air. An open central area with a large stage was closely surrounded by galleries of timber built one over the other. Marlowe and Shakespeare wrote their plays specifically for performance in such theatres, adapting major roles to men and boys who were personally

Thomas More

Thomas More, the son of a judge, was born in Milk Street in the City of London in 1478. After studying law at **Lincoln's Inn** (*see chapter* **London by Area: The City**) he was called to the Bar and elected Member of Parliament. At 26 he married and eventually set up home in Chelsea, whence he became one of London's first commuters, travelling down the Thames to his work in Westminster.

His satire *Utopia* made an important contribution to the development of the English novel and added a new word to the language. He was an accomplished linguist and mathematician, and taught himself to play various musical instruments.

Noted for good humour, More was also deeply religious. He became Speaker of the House of Commons and, in 1529, Henry appointed him Lord Chancellor. But at the height of More's career, the king began his affair with Anne Boleyn and tried to force the Church to annul his marriage to Catherine of Aragon.

More was convinced that Henry was in the wrong. Aware that the king was headstrong and capable of great cruelty, he resigned the chancellorship and retired from public life.

In 1532, More refused to take an oath that the king was supreme head of the English Church. He was accused of treason and committed to the Tower of London. After 15 months in prison, he was taken to West-

minster Hall where he himself had so often sat in judgement. Refusing to save his life at the cost of his conscience, he was found guilty of high treason.

On 6 July, 1535 he was beheaded. Going merrily to the scaffold on Tower Hill, he told the crowd that he remained 'the King's good servant, but God's first'.

Though he died for the old religion, Thomas More – civil servant, novelist and commuter – belongs to the modern age. In 1935 Thomas was canonised by Pope Pius XI. A bronze statue of More, gazing across the river, near to where he lived, can be seen outside **Chelsea Old Church** (*see chapter* **London by Area: West**).

known to them. These early wooden theatres were built and owned by the actors. During the reign of Elizabeth, the theatre was popular with all social classes.

For information on the recent excavation of the Rose Theatre, together with details about the Globe Theatre Centre project, contact the **Shakespeare Museum** (*see chapter* **Museums**).

George Inn

77 Borough High Street, SE1 (071 407 2056). Borough underground or London Bridge underground/BR. **Open** 11am-11pm Mon-Sat; noon-3pm, 7-10.30pm, Sun. **Credit** (restaurant only) A, AmEx, DC, V.
This large, half-timbered pub is the only galleried coaching inn left in London. The present building dates from 1676 but the pub was mentioned by John Stow in his 1598 *Survey of London*. During the summer there are occasional Shakespeare productions in the yard – the way plays were performed before 1576, when the first purpose-built theatres appeared.

Historical Walks

(081 668 4019). **Cost** £4.50; £3.50 OAPs, students, UB40s; under-14s free, if accompanied by an adult. **No credit cards.**
The Inns of Court 11am Mon, Wed; meet at Temple underground. Takes in the Middle and Inner Temples, plus Lincoln's Inn.
Hidden interiors 11am Thur; meet at Temple underground. Includes the church of the Knights Templar, two sixteenth-century cottages.
The London of Dickens and Shakespeare 11am Sun; meet at Blackfriars underground, exit 1. This walk round Bankside includes the site of the Globe Theatre, Southwark Cathedral, and a couple of historic pubs.
Royal and Aristocratic Stuarts 2.30pm Sun; meet at Green Park underground for this tour of Mayfair and St James's.

The Stuarts

Elizabeth I died in 1603 and the Tudor dynasty died with her. Her successor, James VI of Scotland, also James I of England and Wales, united the two kingdoms for the first time.

On 5 November 1605, James narrowly escaped death when Guy Fawkes and his gunpowder were discovered in a cellar underneath the Palace of Westminster. The Gunpowder Plot to blow up the king and Parliament was in protest at the failure to improve conditions for the persecuted Catholics. The event is still commemorated on **Bonfire Night**, 5 November (*see chapter* **London By Season**).

The early Stuart period saw the first real flowering of Renaissance architecture in London. Inigo Jones, stage designer and architect, designed Covent Garden (completed in 1639) as the first planned square in London, *see chapter* **London by Area: Central London**). Immense profits were made by the developer, the Earl of Bedford, by selling 31-year leases.

Banqueting House

Whitehall, SW1 (071 930 4179). Westminster underground or Charing Cross underground/BR. **Open** 10am-5pm Mon-Sat (can be shut at short notice for

government receptions). **Admission** £2.75; £2.10 OAPs, students, UB40s; £1.90 under-16s. **Credit** (shop only) A, AmEx, £TC, V.
The Banqueting House is the only surviving part of Whitehall Palace. It was designed by Inigo Jones, completed in 1622, and was the first purely Renaissance building in London. Charles I commissioned Rubens to celebrate the divine right of the Stuarts. His 12 canvasses were put on the ceiling of the saloon room of the Banqueting House where they have remained for over 350 years. This is the only room open to the public and, unless you want to study the paintings in detail, can be seen in five minutes.
Shop. Group discount. Video tours.

Forty Hall Museum

Forty Hill, Enfield, Middlesex (081 363 8196). Enfield Chase or Enfield Town BR/191, 231 bus. **Open** 11am-5pm Thur-Sun. **Admission** free. **No credit cards.**
Forty Hall is a magnificent Caroline mansion built in 1629. On the ground floor are displays of seventeenth- and eighteenth-century furniture. Upstairs is devoted to a bizarre exhibition of the history of advertising and packaging, and a childhood gallery.
Café (11am–5pm Thur-Sun). Tour by prior arrangement. Wheelchair access to ground floor.

Ham House

Ham, Richmond, Surrey (081 940 1950). Richmond underground/BR then 71 bus. **Open** *house* 1-5pm Mon-Wed; 1-5.30pm Sat; 11.30am-5.30pm Sun. *Gardens* 10.30am-6pm (or dusk) daily. **Admission** *house* £4; £2 OAPs, under-16s. **No credit cards.**
Ham House will open after refurbishment in April 1994, but the restored Stuart garden is very much open. Surrounded by water meadows, the formal garden looks much as it did 300 years ago. The National Trust hopes to provide refreshments from Easter to September.

Civil War

In the Civil War (1642-52) between the Parliamentarians (representing landowners and the wealthy merchants) and the Royalists (those loyal to Charles I), London's influential men supported the Parliamentarians. During the course of the war, earthworks were built around the City, in prospect of a siege, but this never occurred.

At the end of the Civil War, Charles I became prisoner of Oliver Cromwell, the leading general of the Parliamentarian army. Charles was taken to **Westminster Hall** (*see chapter* **Middle Ages**) where he underwent a form of trial on charge of treason. He rejected the legitimacy of the court, refusing to plead. He was declared guilty and returned to the palace at Whitehall. A few days later he was beheaded on a scaffold erected in Whitehall outside the **Banqueting House**. There is a splendid equestrian statue of Charles I in Whitehall on a small island to the south of Trafalgar Square. It was made during his life-time in 1633, and, in the Civil War, was hidden in the crypt of St Paul's Covent Garden.

After Charles's execution, England was under the military dictatorship of Cromwell, an

Queen's House, *Greenwich: Inigo Jones's Palladian palace. See* **review**.

episode called the Commonwealth (lasting from 1653-60). During this period, London's theatres were closed and the liturgical worship of the Church of England proscribed. On the restoration of the monarchy, the theatres re-opened, although the tradition of the open-air theatre was not revived. The old conventions of the Tudor playhouse came to an end with the introduction of Continental-style drama. Restoration drama was presented in indoor theatres, and actresses were admitted to the stage for the first time.

Plague & Fire

After a brief return to normality, London was struck by the Great Plague of 1664-5, which killed at least 69,000 Londoners. Presumably those who survived had developed an immunity because, although various epidemics occurred during the following centuries, the bubonic plague did not return.

The Great Fire of London of 1666 was started on Pudding Lane. It was an unmitigated disaster for the City, and led the diarist John Evelyn, who witnessed the flames, to write: 'London was but is no more'. The entire City burned for three days. The vast St Paul's Cathedral was destroyed together with almost all that remained of medieval London.

After the fire, attempts at town planning were completely frustrated by the insistence of owners that they should retain the exact sites of their former property. Thus ancient topographical and historical associations were preserved, but at the cost of convenience and appearance. Even the plans for Christopher Wren's new **St Paul's Cathedral** (*see chapter* **Sightseeing**) were criticised because no provision was made for a spire. In his designs for some of the new parish churches, Wren made minimal concessions to public demand by the ingenious, but often incongruous,

arrangement of classical details to provide the semblance of a spire. Clearly then, as now, there was a clash between what the people wanted and what arrogant architects decided was good for the people to have.

Monument

Monument Street, EC2 (071 626 2717). Monument underground. **Open** *Apr-Sept* 9am-6pm Mon-Fri; 2-6pm Sat, Sun; *Oct-Mar* 9am-4pm Mon-Sat. **Admission** £1; 25p OAPs, under-16s.
London's reminder of the Great Fire of 1666 is 202ft (60.6m) high; equal to its distance from where the five-day blaze started in a Pudding Lane bakery. When built, it was the world's tallest isolated stone column. And isolated it is, amid faceless tower blocks, from Wren's other rebuilding works. Even St Paul's is obscured, but the river-scape and bits you can see make the climb worthwhile.

Prince Henry's Room

17 Fleet Street, EC4 (081 294 1158). Temple underground. **Open** 11am-2pm Mon-Sat. **Admission** free.
Built in 1611 and named in honour of James I's eldest son, this is one of the few City buildings to survive the Great Fire, with oak panelling and plaster ceiling intact. It now houses a collection of Samuel Pepys' memorabilia, which seems apt as much of what we know about the Fire was vividly described in his diary.

Expansion Continues

From the seventeenth century, London underwent a great and permanent change. The centre of social life passed from the City to the newly built-up area on the west side of the town. The City was left only as a centre of commercial life.

Meanwhile, the Royal Family contributed to the seventeenth-century building programme by commissioning works from the leading architects of the day. *See also chapter* **London by Area: South.**

Queen's House

Romney Road, SE10 (081 858 4422). Greenwich or Maze Hill BR/Island Gardens DLR then Greenwich foot tunnel/53, 54, 75, 89, 108, 177, 180, 188 bus. **Open** *May-Sept* 10am-6pm Mon-Sat; noon-6pm Sun. *Oct-Apr*

10.30am-3.30pm Mon-Sat; 2.15-4pm Sun. *Tours* every 15 mins. **Admission** £3.75; £2.75 under-16s. **Credit** A, AmEx, DC, JCB, £TC, V.
After six years of restoration and refurbishment, Queen Henrietta Maria's Palace at Greenwich re-opened in May 1990. Inigo Jones designed the house in 1616 as the first truly classical Palladian building in Britain and it is the architectural ancestor of the White House in Washington DC. The royal apartments have been restored as they were in 1660, when Charles II's dowager queen moved in.

The Old Royal Observatory

Romney Road, SE10 (081 858 4422). Greenwich or Maze Hill BR/Island Gardens DLR then Greenwich foot tunnel/1, 177, 188 bus/boat to Greenwich Pier. **Open** *Mar-Oct* noon-6pm Mon-Sat; 2-6pm Sun. *Nov-Feb* 10am-5pm Mon-Sat; 2-5pm Sun. **Admission** *passport to all sections* £6.95; £4.95 disabled, OAPs, students, UB40s, under-16s; £13.95 family ticket; under-7s free. *Any one of National Maritime Museum, Queen's House, East Wing Exhibition or Old Royal Observatory* £3.50; £2.50 disabled, OAPs, students, UB40s, under-16s. **Credit** A, AmEx, £TC, V.
The observatory commands a fine view across Greenwich Park to the **National Maritime Museum** (*see chapter* **Museums**), the Queen's House and beyond. The Observatory was founded by Charles II in 1675 to find a solution to the problem of determining longitude at sea. It's the home of Greenwich Mean Time and the zero meridian line, dividing the globe into East and West. *See also chapter* **London by Area: South.**
Café. Group discount. Shop.

Royal Hospital

Chelsea Royal Hospital Road, SW3 (071 730 5282). Sloane Square underground/11, 19, 22, 137 bus. **Open** *museum, chapel and great hall* 10am-noon, 2-4pm, Mon-Fri; 2-4pm Sat. **Services** (in chapel) *Communion* 8.30am Sun; *Parade Service* 11am Sun. **Admission** free.
This 1682 Wren building was founded by Charles II for veteran soldiers and is still home for 420 Chelsea Pensioners. See the famous painting of Charles II on horseback by Antonio Verrio and Van Dyck's Charles I and family.

Glorious Revolution

James II laid the basis for the Royal Navy to become a modern department of state, with Samuel Pepys (sometimes described as 'the first civil servant') as secretary to the admiralty. But James's religious affiliations aroused fears of a return to state-Catholicism and led to William of Orange being invited to take the throne jointly with his wife Mary, elder daughter of James II. James fled to France in what became known as the Glorious Revolution of 1688.

Mary died in 1694, and on William's death in 1702, the throne passed to Mary's sister Anne, the last of the Stuart monarchs. Anne's reign saw the Act of Union between England and Scotland (1707).

These changes at the top had no effect on London's growth, and by 1700 the capital's population stood at 500,000. London was now the biggest city in western Europe and the fourth largest in the world.

Fenton House

Hampstead Grove, NW3 (071 435 3471). Hampstead underground. **Open** *May-Oct* 1-5.30pm Mon-Wed; 11am-5.30pm Sat, Sun. **Admission** £2.80 adults; £1.50 children. **No credit cards.**
Built in 1693, Fenton House is one of the earliest William and Mary style houses, set in a walled garden. It boasts a collection of pictures, porcelain, furniture and keyboard instruments, including a 1612 harpsichord.
Wheelchair access to ground floor only.

Kensington Palace

Kensington Gardens, W8 (071 937 9561). Queensway or High Street Kensington underground. **Open** 9am-5.30pm Mon-Sat; 11am-5.30pm Sun. **Admission** £3.95; £2.95 OAPs, students, UB40s; £2.60 under-15s. **Credit** £TC.
William and Mary came to live here in 1689. The State Apartments have been open to the public since 1899. The Court Dress Collection dates from the mid-eighteenth century onward.
Café. Group discount. Shop. Wheelchair access to ground floor only.

Royal Naval College

King William Walk, SE10 (081 858 2154). Greenwich or Maze Hill BR. **Open** 2.30-5pm Mon-Wed, Fri-Sun. **Admission** free.
Walk through the Greenwich foot tunnel to Island Gardens for a superb view of the College (possibly the least altered view in London). It was founded by William III as a naval hospital, designed by Wren, and built on the site of Greenwich Palace. The College (which is a working naval college) is split in two because Queen Mary didn't want the view of the River obscured from the Queen's House. Inside, the Chapel ceiling is classically ornate and the Hall lavishly painted by Sir James Thornhill.
Shop. Wheelchair access by prior arrangement.

The **Fenton House** *harpsichord. See* **review.**

Georgian London

The wealthy held fashionable parties in beautiful houses in the eighteenth century. The poor had gin and little else.

During the eighteenth century, the total population of Britain began to increase with enormous rapidity. In 1740 some seven million people lived in Great Britain. By the end of that century, there were over ten million.

London, too, increased with astonishing acceleration, both in population and built-up area. After the Great Fire, fashionable life moved to the West End, where, for the most part, more expensive houses and their amenities are still to be found. Much of the building in west London at this time was due to speculative development by wealthy landowners. Large and fashionable houses were built around squares and leased to

equally fashionable courtiers and gentry. One of the first of these developments was Grosvenor Square in Mayfair, completed in 1737. Although slumps did occur through the century, such were the eventual profits that ensued to the Grosvenors (which helped to net the family the dukedom of Westminster), that other local landowners followed suite: Berkeley Square was completed in 1745, and Portman Square in 1763.

The **Museum of London** (*see chapter Museums*) provides a good general synopsis of life in Georgian London. Exhibits have been collated mainly from the lives and homes of the wealthy.

Monarchs & monuments

George I (reigned from 1714 to 1727). An unpopular man who spoke no English and made no effort to learn. He divorced and imprisoned his wife of 32 years for infidelity, left government to his fawning ministers and all but permanently disgraced the monarchy by being implicated in the infamous South Sea Bubble stock market collapse of 1720. Building legacies: all the Hawksmoor churches; much of Spitalfields; Hanover Square; Cavendish Square; St Martin-in-the-Fields; Church Row, NW3.

George II (reigned from 1727 to 1760). Famous both for his patronage of Handel and for being the last English king to take part in a battle. For government he relied heavily on Robert Walpole who was (unofficially) Britain's first Prime Minister. Building legacies: St Bartholomew's Hospital; Grosvenor Square; Berkeley Square; Mansion House; Horse Guards; Marylebone Road; Euston Road.

George III (reigned from 1760 to 1820). The king who is remembered for having lost Britain the American colonies and, later, his mind. His mental health deteriorated in the 1780s, and by 1811 he was completely insane. Building legacies: Bedford Square; Portland Place; Lord North Street; Somerset House;

Baker Street; Russell Square; The Docks; Dulwich Art Gallery.

George IV. Because of his father's insanity, he ruled as Regent from 1811 to 1820, and in his own right from 1820 to 1830. The duration of his reign was called The Regency. His first marriage – to a Catholic – was declared invalid, while his second to a Protestant ended in separation after only a few years. He was clever, even artistic, but given to such bouts of dissipation and extravagance that his behaviour seriously discredited the monarchy. His intimate friendship with the architect John Nash gave rise to many of London's more spectacular edifices, including Regent Street, Regent's Park Terraces and Buckingham Palace. Other building legacies: Eaton Square; British Museum; Belgrave Square.

William IV (reigned from 1830-1837). 'Silly Billy' had the reputation of an idle philanderer, siring ten illegitimate children by an Irish actress before marrying someone more suitable and fathering none. During his reign he created enough peers to ensure that the Great Reform Bill (which shifted political power from the upper to the middle classes) became law. He was succeeded by his niece, Victoria. Building legacies: the National Gallery; University College.

Chiswick House: *designed by its first owner, Lord Burlington. See* **review** *page 60.*

Architecture

By the time the area of **Spitalfields** in east London had been built in the first quarter of the eighteenth century, the Georgian town house had already achieved a more or less standard design. A stroll around this area is the quickest way of getting to know early Georgian architecture. Note the genuine Georgian shop-front (extremely rare in London), at 56 Artillery Lane, E1. And don't miss **Christ Church, Spitalfields** (*see below* **The Church**), one of Hawksmoor's masterpieces.

The Tower Hamlets Environment Trust (071 377 0481/2) is a store of information on the area. *See also chapter* **London by Area: East End & Docklands**).

The interior of a Georgian town house conformed to certain patterns. Pairs of oak- or pine-panelled rooms were situated at the front of each floor. A smaller room shared the rear of the house with a dog-leg staircase running up through the house. Attics and basement kitchens were for servants.

As the century wore on, new architectural ideas served to modify the Georgian terraced house, though none managed to change its basic, straightforward shape. Palladian and neo-classical styles (which widely influenced the architecture of larger mansions and country houses) added door arches, stucco façades, elegant interior plasterwork, reproduction carvings of figures and motifs from antiquity, and a mathematical precision and regularity of design that was readily associated with the ancients. Many Georgian terraces still stand in London but few have been left untouched by the intervening years. Only Bedford Square, WC1 and Lord North Street, SW1, off Smith Square, remain untarnished.

Dennis Severs' House

18 Folgate Street, E1 (071 247 4013). Liverpool Street underground/BR. **Open** 2-5pm first Sun of every month; three times per week for theatrical performances, played to an audience of eight people. Phone for details. **Performance** 7.30pm. **Admission** *Performance* (book) £30; *house* £5. **No credit cards**.
In a performance lasting three hours, Mr Severs' eight paying guests become ghosts of an imaginary family, which inhabits the various rooms of the house (built 1724) between the years 1685 and 1919. It's a great introduction to the flavours and feelings of eighteenth-century life. The house is also open occasionally for tours – phone for details. You should book about three weeks in advance for the shows; although it's always worth phoning to see if there's been a cancellation.

Great Architects

If buildings in the earlier part of the century had been erected largely by anonymous builders, in the latter half it became a matter of some social cachet to have a house built by a well-known architect. Property owners, speculators and the state all vied with each other to commission the likes of John Adam (Portland Place); his brother Robert Adam (the Courtauld Institute at 20 Portman Square); William Kent (Horse Guards; 44 Berkeley Square and its marvellous interior); John Soane (Dulwich Picture Gallery); William Chambers (Somerset House); Robert Smirke (British Museum); William Wilkins (National Gallery); and Decimus Burton (the Athenaeum).

And then there was John Nash, whose work is the apotheosis of late-Georgian architecture; his extravagant plans for London, including Regent Street and Buckingham Palace, were heartily supported by the Prince Regent, the future George IV.

Yet it is to the eternal discredit of the Victorians and later commercially-motivated twentieth century entrepreneurs that almost all of Nash's Regent Street has been pulled down. Only Suffolk Place and the eccentric church of All Soul's, Langham Place remain. Even the present façade of Buckingham Palace is a later, Victorian addition. The Marble Arch too, was moved in 1847 to its present site, at the northeast corner of Hyde Park, as a result of the redevelopment of the Palace.

Sir John Soane's Museum

13 Lincoln's Inn Fields, WC2 (071 405 2107). Holborn underground. **Open** 10am-5pm Tue-Sat; 6-9pm first Tue of month. **Admission** free.
Britain's smallest national museum is also its most unusual. Sir John (1753-1837), a contemporary rival of John Nash, was not only a superb architect but also an avid collector of knick-knacks and beautiful objects, from Hogarth's *The Rake's Progress* to the sarcophagus of Seti I, pharaoh of Egypt 1303-1290 BC. Soane had the good sense to leave his house and its contents for later generations to explore, sketch and gaze at in awe. The lanterned room, bristling with statues, is quite an experience. *Guided tour (2.30pm Sat).*

Country Seats

Chiswick House

Burlington Lane, W4 (081 995 0508). Turnham Green underground/Chiswick BR. **Open** *Apr-Sept* 10am-1pm, 2-6pm, daily; *Oct-Mar* 10am-1pm, 2-4pm, daily. **Admission** £2.20; £1.60 OAPs, students, UB40s; £1.10 under-16s. **Credit** A, V.
The Italian architect Andrea Palladio's architectural studies of ancient buildings influenced designers more than any other in the eighteenth century. Lord Burlington's 1729 design for this exquisite mansion is based on Palladio's Villa Rotunda in Vicenza and was realised by the architect William Kent (also responsible for Horse Guards Parade). The furniture and decoration include many fine period examples.
Group discount.

Kenwood House

Hampstead Lane, NW3 (081 348 1286). Archway, Golders Green or Highgate underground/210 bus. **Open** *Apr-Sept* 10am-6pm daily; *Oct-Mar* 10am-4pm daily. **Admission** free.
The Gainsboroughs and Rembrandts (including a

famous self-portrait) displayed here are worth visiting for their own sake. The house's present shabbiness is rather appealing and should not be renovated: no lived-in house was ever pristine. The Georgian painting and furniture are of the highest quality. There is no more life-enhancing way of accounting for a warm summer Saturday than a visit to the house and gardens followed by evening attendance at one of Kenwood's lakeside concerts *(see chapter* **London by Season***).*
Café. Gift shop. Wheelchair access.

Marble Hill House

Richmond Road, Twickenham, Middlesex (081 892 5115). Richmond underground/BR/33, 90B, 202, 270, 290 bus. **Open** *Apr-Sept* 10am-6pm, *Oct-Mar* 10am-4pm, daily. **Admission** free.
In line with other Georgian three-dimensional architectural experiments, Marble Hill House has the proportions of a cube – it's in fact slightly wider at the top than the bottom. This fine example of the Palladian style was commissioned by Henrietta Howard, the mistress of George II, and designed by Lord Herbert and the builder Roger Morris. The interior Cube Hall contains fine moulded decoration. Those interested in Georgian furniture and fine art could do worse than start here.
Café (Apr-Sept). Wheelchair access to ground floor only.

Osterley Park

Osterley, Isleworth, Middlesex (081 560 3918). Osterley underground. **Open** 11am-4.30pm Tue-Sun. **Admission** £2; £1 children, OAPs, students, UB40s. **No credit cards.**
There are only so many state rooms you can see before boredom sets in. The fascinating parts of Osterley are the rooms 'below stairs' – the kitchens, the housekeeper's rooms and the head butler's offices – where real life happened. Look for the list of wage payments on the wall. The gardens are extensive and magnificent with huge cedars, spreading oaks, and a very old mulberry tree. There's an artificial lake containing a small floating pagoda (a gift from an oriental financial corporation) as a mild visual joke.
Café (Apr-Oct). Group discount. Tour by prior arrangement.

Syon House

Syon Park, Brentford, Middx (081 560 0881). Gunnersbury underground/Syon Lane BR/237, 267 bus. **Open** *house Apr-Sept* 11am-5pm Wed-Sun; *Oct* 11am-5pm Sun. *Gardens* 10am-6pm daily. **Admission** *house* £3; £2.25 children, OAPs. *Gardens* £2; £1.50 children, OAPs. **Combined ticket** £4.50; £3.25 under-16s. **No credit cards.**
This house is arguably Robert Adam's masterpiece, built when the architect was at the height of his fame. His task was to remodel an existing house that had been the home of the Percy family (the Earls of Northumberland) since 1594. Nowadays all rooms on the ground floor (except the toilet) are accessible to both men and women, but in the eighteenth century the sex of the rooms was clearly defined and they were decorated accordingly. The long gallery leading to the circular bird-cage room was designed for use by women and is the essence of camp with its pastel purples, greens, delicate light grey, and sickly-sweet pinks. The dining room, anteroom, and hall, on the other hand, were bastions of masculinity and are adorned with classical heroes. The grounds were landscaped by Capability Brown.
Car Park. National Trust shop. Wheelchair access to gardens only.

Churches

In 1711, an Act was passed for the building of 50 churches in London. It was thought that this would help to bring law and order to the suburbs, and help staunch the flow of likely ministers into non-conformist sects. Although the scheme ran out of steam before 50 churches were built, it did give the greatest Georgian church-builder Nicholas Hawksmoor, the chance to show his brilliance.

Christchurch, Spitalfields
Commercial Street, E1 (071 247 7202). **Open** for concerts, otherwise apply at the crypt door.
This is the largest of Hawksmoor's churches. Its neat, triangular spire towers above the splendid Georgian houses in Spitalfields like a beacon. The crypt has been turned into a rehabilitation centre for alcoholics.

St Alfege with St Peter & St Paul
Greenwich High Road, SE10 (081 858 3458). Greenwich BR. **Open** 11am-3pm Tue-Fri; 2-4pm Sat, Sun.
Hawksmoor's Greenwich church is one of his best. Sadly the woodwork, by one of the century's finest craftsmen (Grinling Gibbons), was thrown out and destroyed by the Victorians, but the church is still a restful place to sit and think in the middle of Greenwich town. General Wolfe of Quebec is buried in the crypt.

St George
Bloomsbury Way, WC1 (071 405 3044). Holborn or Tottenham Court Road underground. **Open** 10am-3pm Mon-Fri. **Services** 1.10pm Wed, Fri; 10am, 6.30pm, Sun.
Another of Hawksmoor's churches and the only one he sited west of the City. With a nod to antiquity, the spire is obelisk-shaped. With another nod to royalty, the statue on top is of George I, masquerading as St George. The unpopular king's effigy was the target of some cruel practical jokes at the time.

St Martin-in-the-Fields
Trafalgar Square, WC2 (071 930 1862). Charing Cross underground/BR. **Open** 8am-6.30pm daily. **Services** 7pm Mon (taize prayers); 8am, 8.30am, 5.30pm, Mon-Fri; 6pm Wed; 1.05pm Thur; 9am Sat; 8am, 9.45am (choral), 11.30am, 12.30pm, 2.45pm (service in Cantonese), 6.30pm Sun.
There's no better way to enjoy the soaring magnificence of St Martin's than to attend one of the midday lunchtime concerts on Mondays and Tuesdays throughout the year. James Gibbs's beautiful church was one of the most influential of its time. The wide portico is topped with a spire built on a tower; the interior is plain, but embellished with dark woodwork and ornate Italian plasterwork.

The Poor

Not only did the indigenous population of London increase in the eighteenth century, but country people (who had lost their own land because of enclosures, and were faced with starvation wages or unemployment) drifted into the towns in large numbers. There was indescribable squalor and filth in many parts of the city. Dr Johnson's house off Fleet Street (*see below* **Artists & Writers**) was within a stone's throw of slums where 20 people a week died of starvation.

Worse still, the well-off seemed completely complacent. They regularly amused themselves with organised trips to Bedlam (Bethlehem Hospital) to mock the mental patients, and executions at Tyburn (close to where Marble Arch now stands) were among the most popular events on the social calendar.

Many Londoners attempted to escape the horrors of daily life by the consumption of excessive amounts of alcohol, which commerce made readily available at low but profitable prices in the form of gin – 'London Gin'. The average per capita consumption (children very much included) was two pints a week. This contributed to the appalling death rate: in the years 1725 to 1750, three out of four children aged one to five died. Hogarth's print, *Gin Lane*, gives some idea of the terrible squalor to which the great mass of Londoners was reduced.

The outrageous imbalance in the distribution of wealth encouraged crime. In the decade from 1770 to 1780, the Prince of Wales, the Prime Minister, and the Lord Chancellor were all robbed in broad daylight in the West End.

This was the age of the London Mob, when a large band of protesters could gather at short notice. Riots were usually directed against middle-men charging too high prices, or merchants adulterating their food. In 1780, London was hit by the Gordon Riots, the worst in its violent history. They started when Lord George Gordon, an MP, led a crowd of 50,000 to Parliament with a petition against the repeal of anti-Roman Catholic legislation. Gordon soon lost control of his mob which, apparently forgetting why it had assembled, spent the next five days looting and pillaging the capital. Prisons were burnt down and the inmates set free; a distillery was broken into; Downing Street and the Bank of England were unsuc-

St George's *Church. See* **review**.

cessfully stormed. The riots were eventually suppressed with the loss of 850 lives.

Spaniard's Inn
Spaniards Road, NW3 (081 455 3276). Hampstead underground/210, 268 bus. **Open** 11am-11pm Mon-Sat; noon-3pm, 7-10.30pm, Sun.
The registered ghost of a grey lady inhabits this low-ceilinged, oak-panelled pub, built 1585 when it was the home of the Spanish ambassador to James I. The Gordon rioters (1780) refuelled here but the landlord managed to keep them drinking for so long that the King's Guards were able to catch up with and apprehend them.

Reformers

Reformers were few and far between, though there were some notable exceptions. Henry Fielding, the satirical writer, critic of society's ills, and author of the picaresque novel *Tom Jones* was also an enlightened magistrate at Bow Street Court. In 1751, he established, with his blind brother John, a volunteer force of 'thief-takers' to back up the often ineffective efforts of the parish constables and watchmen who were the only law-keepers in the city. This group of early cops later became known as the Bow Street Runners, to whom the present day Metropolitan police force may trace its origins.

John Wesley, founder of Methodism, also did a great deal to help the eighteenth-century poor. His popularity was immense in London and his outdoor sermons could draw 10,000 people. An account of his conversion is written in stone outside the entrance to the **Museum of London** (*see chapter* **Museums**).

During the eighteenth century, some attempt to alleviate the grosser ills of poverty was made by the establishment of many of London's world-famous teaching hospitals. St Thomas's and St Bartholomew's had already been established as monastic institutions for the care of the sick, but Westminster (1720), Guy's (1725), St George's (1734), London (1740), and Middlesex (1745) Hospitals were all instituted in the eighteenth century.

Historic Barts & Smithfield
(071 837 0546). Farringdon underground. **Meet** Henry VIII Gateway, West Smithfield, EC1. **Tour** *Apr-Oct* 2pm Sun. **Cost** £4 adults; under-15s free.
The tours last between 90 minutes and two hours, taking in St Bartholomew the Less, the Hogarth murals in St Bart's Hospital, Smithfield Market, Cloth Fair and St Bartholomew the Great. The cost of the tour goes to Bart's Heritage Fund.

Museum of Methodism
Wesley Chapel, 49 City Road, EC1 (071 253 2262). Old Street underground/BR. **Open** 10am-4pm Mon-Sat. **Service** followed by lunch and guided tour, 11am Sun. **Admission** *Museum and house* £3; £1.50 children, OAPs, UB40s. **No credit cards.**
In both chapel and house, all artefacts and memorials of the great philanthrope's life are original. The crypt hous-

es a museum containing the most curious collection of oddments pertaining to the growth of Methodism. The wardens of the premises still maintain traditions that Wesley started.
Films. Shop. Tour by prior arrangement.

St Thomas's Old Operating Theatre
9A St Thomas Street, SE1 (081 806 4325/071 955 5000; ext 3182). London Bridge underground/BR. **Open** 10am-4pm Tue-Sun. **Admission** £2 adults; £1.50 under-15s. **No credit cards.**
Vistors climb a narrow, winding flight of 37 stairs to the belfry of an old church. In a well-lit adjoining room, ancient banks of viewing stands rise in semi-circles round a crude wooden bed (really no more than an adapted kitchen table). Close your eyes and you can almost hear the screams from an unanaesthetised, blindfolded patient, as the blood-stained surgeon carefully saws through his leg. This is one of the most vivid museums in London and it was discovered only by accident some 20 years ago. Many exhibits are labelled and explained with loving care.
Shop.

Artists & Writers

Hogarth's House
Hogarth Lane, Great West Road, W4 (081 994 6757). Turnham Green underground/Chiswick BR. **Open** *Apr-Sept* 11am-6pm Mon, Wed-Sat; 2-6pm Sun. *Oct-Mar* 11am-4pm Mon, Wed-Sat; 2-4pm Sun (closed first two weeks in Sept and last three weeks in Dec). **Admission** free.
Hogarth's modest domicile has been restored more or less faithfully to its eighteenth-century condition and now provides wall-space for some 200 of the great social commentator's prints, though his most famous work, *The Rake's Progress*, is present only in the form of photographic copies. An original is in **Sir John Soane's Museum** (*see above*).
Car park. Gift shop. Tour by prior arrangement. Wheelchair access.

Dr Johnson's House
17 Gough Square, Fleet Street, EC4 (071 353 3745). Chancery Lane or Temple underground or Blackfriars underground/BR. **Open** *May-Sept* 11am-5.30pm Mon-Sat; *Oct-Apr* 11am-5pm Mon-Sat. **Admission** £2.50; £1.50 children, OAPs, students. **No credit cards.**
A splendid example of a grand Georgian town house. The dog-leg staircase running up the rear of the building gives onto successive landings and pairs of rooms at the front of the house. The long top room is where Johnson compiled his famous dictionary, which includes the definition: 'Dull: to make dictionaries is dull work'. Furnishings are few and visitors who go to see the great man's possessions will be disappointed. Those who go for the atmosphere won't be.
Shop.

Keats' House
Keats Grove, NW3 (071 435 2062). Hampstead underground/Hampstead Heath BR. **Open** *Apr-Oct* 10am-1pm, 2-6pm, Mon-Fri; 2-5pm Sat; 1-5pm Sun. *Nov-Mar* 1-5pm Mon-Fri; 2-5pm Sat; 10am-1pm, 2-5pm, Sun. **Admission** free. **No credit cards.**
The tragic Romantic poet penned many of his most inspired compositions here. Relics of Keat's life tell a fascinating, if poignant, story. The library is much visited by students and connoisseurs of his works.
Library by prior arrangement. Shop. Tour by prior arrangement.

Victorian Times

The energy that made Britain the workshop of the world, also turned London into the capital of an immense empire.

Leadenhall Market: *Horace Jones's stylish Victorian arcade.*

London in Victorian times (strictly speaking 1837-1901) was a city of uncomfortable extremes. It was the capital of an empire that spanned one fifth of the globe and yet it was a city of squalor, poverty and prostitution. The growth of the metropolis in the century before Victoria came to the throne had been spectacular enough, but during her reign, thousands of acres of land were covered with housing, roads and railway lines. London had not seen the like of it before and has not since. Even today, if you pick any street at random within five miles (eight kilometres) of central London, the chances are that its houses will be mostly Victorian.

All over Britain this energy was shown. The small towns of Manchester, Leeds, Sheffield and Birmingham grew to mighty cities in the course of the nineteenth century.

A DASH OF DEMOCRACY

The Industrial Revolution led to a fundamental shift in economic power away from the land-owning gentry and towards the new class of merchants and industrialists. Pressure for political change grew and led to the passing of two Reform Acts (in 1832 and 1867) which gave the vote to the middle classes. The working class, meanwhile, began to become a cohesive force, forming movements such as the Chartists (who demanded a charter of rights, and who frequently held meetings on Clerkenwell Green, EC1). Yet the franchise wasn't widened to include working-class men until the end of the century; and women didn't get the vote until after World War I (*see chapter* **Early Twentieth Century**).

The dramatic increase in the inner-city population made acute the need for more effective government, more housing (particularly south of the river), a national education system, railways, cleaner water supplies, bigger docks, and safer factories. But in an age famed for its engineering miracles, it took a surprisingly long time before the link between disease and drinking water was established. Before Edwin Chadwick managed to carry the Public Health Act through Parliament, cholera was claiming the lives of over 2,000 people a week at its height in 1849. The problem was simply that independent suppliers pumped unfiltered water direct from the Thames to communal street fonts. But it wasn't until 1860 that Sir Joseph Bazalgette devised a system to direct sewage to the Thames Estuary via the Victoria and Albert Embankments.

Some idea of the ingenuity of the Victorians in solving London's fresh-water problems can be gained by watching the monstrous pumping engines 'in steam' at the **Kew Bridge Steam Museum** (*see chapter* **Museums**).

Architecture

There are several examples in the city that demonstrate the lavishness of Victorian design. Neo-Gothic, inspired by the medieval architecture of Europe, was the fashion at the beginning of Victoria's reign. One of the best examples is Pugin and Barry's **Houses of Parliament**, built 1837-52 (*see chapter* **Sightseeing**). **The Royal Exchange** (*see chapter* **The City**) is typical of the other favoured style – classical. It dominates Mansion House Place opposite the Bank of England.

The Gothic influence re-emerged in the substantial shape of the **Royal Courts of Justice**, designed by GE Street in the 1870s (*see chapter* **London by Area: The City**). The Law Courts are a cloistered, turreted stone counterpart to the brick work and glass-domed sheds of **St Pancras** railway station (*see below* **Railways**).

The abolition of the tax on glass allowed Joseph Paxton to build the Crystal Palace for the **Great Exhibition** (*see* **Box**). It also enabled ornate glass-fronted shopping arcades to flourish, notably in the **Royal Arcade** and **Leadenhall Market**. Both Leadenhall (1881), with its splendid curved arcades of iron and glass and **Smithfield Market** (1866), with its domed and turreted roof were designed by the prolific Horace Jones (for both *see chapter* **London by Area: The City**).

Athenaeum

107 Pall Mall, SW1. Piccadilly Circus underground.
Named after Emperor Hadrian's university in Rome, the classically-styled Athenaeum club was designed by Decimus Burton and has been used as a meeting place and home-from-home by (male) government ministers, bishops and writers since 1824. Although it's not open to the public, a visit may be arranged by writing to the Club Secretary.

Royal Arcade

Connects Albemarle Street with Old Bond Street, W1. Green Park or Piccadilly Circus underground.

This fashionable shopping promenade, built in 1879, used to count Queen Victoria amongst its regular customers. The Royal Arcade is similar in style to the nearby Piccadilly and Burlington Arcades.

Bridges

London's bridges, the majority of which were constructed during the Victorian era, are alternately ornate, functional, durable and historical. The housing boom south of the river made it expedient to provide a link for these new inhabitants with the business interests on the northern side. And these arteries cemented the two halves of London into a homogeneous, albeit sprawling, whole.

Incidentally, the **London Bridge** of the nursery rhyme, originally a wooden medieval structure, was replaced several times, penultimately in 1831 by a stone arched bridge. This was what, in 1967, was sold to an American millionaire, who re-erected it in the Arizona desert. *See also* **Tower Bridge** in *chapter* **Sightseeing**.

Albert Bridge

SW11. Sloane Square underground/19, 22 bus.
Built during the 1870s, this triple-arched, cast iron bridge is lit like a Christmas tree at night. Traditionally soldiers crossing Albert Bridge must break step because of the fear that their marching rhythm will weaken the structure.

Hammersmith Bridge

W6. Hammersmith underground.
The original Hammersmith Bridge, built in the 1820s, was the first suspension bridge across the Thames. It was replaced in 1887 by the present decorative structure.

Westminster Bridge

SW1. Westminster underground.
The present bridge, built by Thomas Page and Charles Barry in 1862, measures over 80ft (24m) wide. It has the best views of Parliament, the Victoria and Albert Embankments and the Edwardian façade of County Hall.

Churches

During the nineteenth century, hundreds of churches and other places of worship were erected in Greater London. Many of these were Anglican parish churches, built to serve the new parishes of the expanding suburbs. Almost all were designed in the Gothic style.

After the final Catholic Emancipation Act was passed in 1829, the Catholic population of London increased rapidly and new Catholic churches were built in every district.

All Saints

7 Margaret Street, W1 (071 636 1788). Oxford Circus underground. **Open** 7am-7pm daily. **Services** 7.30am, 8am, 1.10pm, 5.30pm, 6.30pm, Mon-Fri; 7.30am, 8am, 5.30pm, 6.30pm Sat; 8am, 10.20am, 11am, 5.15pm, 6pm Sun.
Designed by William Butterfield in the 1850s, All Saints has the novel feature of incorporating coloured bricks to decorative effect. The neo-Gothic exterior is complemented by an ornate interior, heavy with marble, alabaster and granite.

Brompton Oratory
Thurloe Place, Brompton Road, SW3 (071 589 4811).
South Kensington underground. **Open** 6.30am-8pm
daily. **Services** six masses daily Mon-Sat (phone to
check); 7am, 8am, 9am, 10am, 11am (Sung Latin
mass), 12.30pm, 4.30pm, 7pm Sun.
Brompton Oratory, built in 1884 by Herbert Gribble, was
the leading Catholic church in London until Westminster
Cathedral opened its doors in 1903. The most striking
feature about this wonderful church, apart from its
ornate, heavy Baroque exterior, is the dark atmosphere
of the interior, ribbed with marble.

St Augustine, Kilburn
Kilburn Park Road, NW6 (071 624 1637). Kilburn
Park underground. **Open** 9.30am-noon Sat. **Services**
8.30am and 5.45pm (prayers) Mon-Fri; 8am, 10.30am,
6pm Sun.
Architecturally, this is the most splendid parish church
in London. It was designed (1880) by John Pearson, who
made original use of the thirteenth-century French
Gothic idiom. It is cathedral-like in style, very large and
vaulted throughout. Inside are original paintings from
the Italian Renaissance.

St Cyprian's, Clarence Gate
Glentworth Street, NW1 (071 402 6979). Baker Street
underground/Marylebone underground/BR. **Open** by
arrangement only. **Services** 6.15pm Mon; 10.30am
Wed; 1.10pm Thur; 8.30am Fri; 11am Sun.
Although not finished until 1903, St Cyprian's illustrates
the final splendour of the Gothic Revival. The exterior is
modest, but inside it is gloriously spacious and light. The
screens are gilded and fan-vaulted, the chancel screen
surmounted with a Calvary and angels.

Houses & Housing
The type of houses built during the Victorian
era varied as widely as the division between
rich and poor. The success or failure of an area
depended to a large extent on whether the railway ran through or near it. At the bottom of the
pile were humble tenements, line after line of
bleak terraced houses adjacent to the tracks.
The areas intended for the rich, such as
Belgravia, SW1, were the most carefully
planned, with generous-sized houses and elegant frontages, often built around squares.

Apsley House
149 Piccadilly, W1 (071 499 5676). Hyde Park Corner
underground. **Open** 11am-4.50pm Tue-Sun (closed
until summer 1994, phone for details). **Admission** £2;
£1 OAPs, students, under-16s. **No credit cards.**
The extensive collection of paintings and memorabilia
belonging to the Duke of Wellington pays tribute to his
enormous military and social stature. The victor at
Waterloo later became one of the century's most reactionary Prime Ministers. He earned the nickname the
Iron Duke not for his prowess on the battle field, but for
the iron shutters he installed after rioters broke his windows. A modest man, he referred to his home as 'No 1
London'. Works of art abound, and there's a portrait of
Wellington by Goya. One of the more eccentric touches
is an 11ft (3.3m) statue of the diminutive Napoleon.

Brixton
SW9. Brixton underground/BR.
Row after row of typical Victorian workers' terraces are
found in the streets to the south and north of the Brixton

Road. Many houses were gentrified in the late 1980s as
Brixton began to be colonised by the wealthy young. *See*
also chapter **London by Area: South.**

Leighton House Museum
12 Holland Park, W14 (071 602 3316). High Street
Kensington underground/9, 93 bus. **Open** 11am-5.30pm
Mon-Sat. **Admission** free but donations appreciated.
Leighton House, designed by Lord Leighton in 1866 in
collaboration with George Aitchison, derives its inspiration directly from the East. Its most striking feature is
the exotic Arab Hall added in 1879. This domed structure, with its elaborate Persian tiles, mosaic floor and
square fountain, has a startling cupola of stained glass.
The unusual tiles were collected by Leighton and friends
from frequent trips to Damascus, Rhodes and Cairo.
Leighton, himself an artist of no mean repute, collected
a variety of works that are now on permanent display.
See also chapter **Art Galleries.**

Linley Sambourne House
18 Stafford Terrace, W8 (Victorian Society 081 994
1019). High Street Kensington underground. **Open**
Mar-Oct 10am-4pm Wed; 2-5pm Sun. **Admission** £3
adults; £1.50 under-16s. **No credit cards.**
Edward Linley Sambourne was a leading *Punch* car-
toonist and political illustrator of the late Victorian and
Edwardian period. His eccentric town house retains its
original fittings and decorations (the wallpaper, carpet
and textile designs are by William Morris). There is a
magnificent clutter of period furniture, prints, photographs and ceramics.

Monuments
The Victorians liked their monuments. All over
Britain they erected memorials to great inventors, local worthies, and above all, to their
queen, every time she reached another mile-

Brompton Oratory. *See* **review.**

stone in her reign. Tastes change: the **Albert Memorial** in Kensington Gardens was tenuously acclaimed when first unveiled, but universally snubbed ten years later. And when **Nelson's Column** was erected, many complained that Horatio's features were too crude.

Albert Memorial
Kensington Gardens, SW7. Knightsbridge or Kensington High Street underground, then 9, 33, 49, 52, 73 bus.
The most ostentatious memorial to an individual in Britain. It was built in the early 1870s to mourn the early death of the Prince Consort. A mere 175ft/52m high, it

is decorated with life-size marble friezes of artists, and crowned by an ornate Gothic canopy. The brooding, bronze figure of a much romanticised Albert sits in contemplation of his brainchild, the museums, institutes and educational facilities of South Kensington. Pollution has taken its toll on the Memorial and it is currently shrouded in sheeting and supported by scaffolding.

Cleopatra's Needle
Victoria Embankment, WC2. Embankment underground.
This 3,500-year-old monument was presented to the British in 1819 by the Turkish Viceroy in Egypt and was finally erected in 1878. Several Victorian items including a copy

The Great Exhibition

The Great Exhibition of 1851 was the largest single arts and sciences event that had ever been staged. It was held in what Londoners nicknamed the Crystal Palace, a massive iron and glass structure built in Hyde Park.

About 100,000 exhibits from all parts of the globe were assembled. These ranged from stuffed animals to recent inventions such as a steam-driven combine harvester. A staggering total of six million people visited the exhibition during the five months that it was open.

When the exhibition finally closed, the Crystal Palace was taken apart and re-assembled at Sydenham where it served as an

amusement park until destroyed by fire in 1936. You can learn about it and see the remains at the **Crystal Palace Museum** (*see chapter* **Museums**).

The profit made from the Great Exhibition of 1851 inspired the ambitious Prince Consort to establish a permanent centre, where the arts and sciences could be studied and applied. Though he never lived to see his vision fulfilled, he sowed the seeds for some of London's most famous museums and institutes.

The **Natural History Museum** (*see chapter* **Museums**) opened its impressive portals in 1881. Designed by Alfred Waterhouse in the Romanesque style (which developed in Central Europe from the tenth to the twelfth century), the building itself more resembles a cathedral, and is just as awe-inspiring as the formidable collection of dinosaurs within.

The **Victoria and Albert Museum** (*see chapter* **Museums**) was redesigned by Aston Webb in 1890 so that it could house the congested collections of treasures that had outgrown its original old corrugated structure. Of all London museums, it is undoubtedly the most ornate and lavish. The V&A has built up a magnificent collection of commercial art and design, and there is an excellent selection of Victorian plate, glass, porcelain, silver, costumes and furniture.

The famous oval concert venue, the **Royal Albert Hall**, was planned by Prince Albert and built as his memorial after his early death. See *chapter* **Music: Classical & Opera**.

But the museum that was most strongly influenced by the Great Exhibition is the **Science Museum** (*see chapter* **Museums**). Its collection of nineteenth-century machine tools, steam engines and mechanical instruments provides the most comprehensive explanation of why Britain was once the foremost industrial nation in the world.

The **Albert Memorial**: the worse for wear.
See **review** page 66.

of *The Times*, a portrait of Queen Victoria and a railway timetable are buried under the Needle in a time capsule.

Eros
Piccadilly Circus, W1. Piccadilly Circus underground.
London's unofficial mascot, this fountain statue is the memorial to the philanthropy of the seventh Earl of Shaftesbury. Erected in 1893, it was London's first aluminium statue. In fact it's not the God of Love, Eros, at all, but the Angel of Christian Charity.

Nelson's Column
Trafalgar Square, WC2. Charing Cross underground/BR.
London's best-known landmark, the 16-ton statue by Baily, the 168-ft (50m) pedestal by Railton and the enormous lions by Landseer were constructed to commemorate the famous admiral who defeated Napoleon in 1805. Today it's a rallying point for political demonstrations and New Year revellers. *See chapter* **London by Season**.

Victoria Memorial
Queen's Gardens, Buckingham Palace, SW1. St James's Park underground.
Thomas Brock, who designed this lavish piece of nonsense, won a knighthood for his trouble. It commemorates the life of England's longest-reigning monarch. Standing in front of Buckingham Palace, the 13-ft (3.9m)-high queen is surrounded by the female allegories of Victorian virtues – charity, truth and justice must share space with shipbuilding, war, manufacturing and progress. 'Victory' soars over all.

Railways
One of the greatest influences of the Industrial Revolution on Victorian London was the introduction of the railway and eventually the underground network. By the 1860s traffic congestion in the capital had reached a point where people were prepared to accept any schemes that relieved the situation. The railway companies spent enormous sums of money designing ostentatious train stations to impress the cynical public. Euston Station's classical portico (destroyed by British Rail in 1963 in order to expand the station) cost nearly £40,000, but it

fronted some very unspectacular railway sheds and platforms.

In 1863, the first underground line, between Paddington and Farringdon Street, proved an instant success, attracting over 30,000 travellers on the first day. The Metropolitan and Circle lines at Baker Street, NW1, and Great Portland Street, W1, are almost intact examples of mid-Victorian stations. The world's first electric track followed in 1890, opened between King William Street, EC4, and Stockwell, SW9.

In spite of the general enthusiasm for more underground railways, it was an American, Charles Tyson Yerkes, who exploited the idea and started building the Bakerloo, Piccadilly and Northern lines, which form the basis of today's system. Examples of the early underground trains are on view at the **Science Museum** (*see* **Box: The Great Exhibition**).

For a comprehensive view of Victorian travel, from horse-drawn trams and hackney carriages to the underground system, go to the **London Transport Museum**, 39 Wellington Street, WC2 (*see chapter* **Museums**).

St Pancras Station
Euston Road, NW1. King's Cross underground/BR.
The decorative exuberance of St Pancras symbolised the way Victorians justified the disruptive building of railways; they made catching a train an event. Giles Gilbert Scott's 1870s design for the luxury hotel frontage is inspired by Medieval High Gothic. But the train shed is pure engineering. A lofty 100ft (30m) high, with a 240ft (72m) span, the glass arch is supported solely by its huge iron ribs. Many times threatened, St Pancras is to be restored in the King's Cross redevelopment.

Cemeteries
Because of the massive increase in population, and subsequent problems of finding ground for burials, the government was forced to act. Public graveyards were hazardous and extremely unhealthy. After a public inquiry into the matter, seven enormous cemeteries were laid out, providing a much more agreeable resting place for those who could afford it. The cemeteries were operated by private companies, and one, **Kensal Green**, is still run by the original firm.

Brompton Cemetery
Finborough Road, SW10 (071 352 1201). West Brompton underground. **Open** 8.30am-dusk daily.
The main entrance to this graceful cemetery is surrounded by catacombs and is crowned by a triumphal arch. It holds some eminent corpses, including those of Emmeline Pankhurst, the suffragette (died 1928), and Frederick Leyland, patron of the pre-Raphaelites.

Highgate Cemetery
Swain's Lane, N6 (081 340 1834). Archway underground/271 bus. **Open** Apr-Oct 10am-5pm daily; Nov-Mar 10am-4pm daily. **Admission** £1 East Cemetery; £3 tour of West Cemetery, £2 students, OAPs, UB40s. **No credit cards.**

Opened in 1839, this is London's most famous and exotic graveyard. The latest addition, east of Swain's Lane, is the resting place of Karl Marx. But apart from this, the east side is rather crowded and drab. The west side is a romantic wilderness of tombs, catacombs and gravestones, with ornate stonework covered in ivy. Usually, this section can only be visited as part of a guided tour (phone for details), but on open days (held on three Sundays a year, phone to check) you can wander around by yourself. Eminent Victorians now residing here include Mrs Henry Wood, wife of the composer, and George Eliot, the female novelist.

Kensal Green Cemetery

Harrow Road, W10 (081 969 0152). Kensal Green underground. **Open** 8.30am-5.30pm Mon-Sat; 10am-5.30pm Sun.
This was very much an in-place to be buried during Victoria's reign. Famous bodies interred here include the novelists Anthony Trollope and William Thackeray, and engineer Sir Isambard Kingdom Brunel.

Discoveries

When the Victorians were not colonising the world by brute strength, they had the foresight to combine their conquests with scientific developments. **The Royal Geographical Society** sent navigators to chart unknown waters, botanists to bring back new species, and geologists to study the earth. Many of these specimens ended up in the **Royal Botanic Gardens** at Kew (*see chapter* **Sightseeing**); others found a home in the South Kensington museums (*see* **Box: The Great Exhibition**). The most influential RGS expedition was **Charles Darwin's** voyage on *HMS Beagle*. The very foundations of science and religion were rocked when the naturalist published his theory of evolution.

Charles Darwin Memorial

Down House, Luxted Road, Downe, Orpington, Kent (06898 59119). Bromley South BR, then 146 bus. **Open** 1-6pm Wed-Sun (last admission 5.30pm). **Admission** £2; £1.50 OAPs, students; £1 under-15s. **No credit cards.**
Charles Darwin's radical theory of evolution was partly thought-out and written in Down House, where he lived for 40 years. The large house has been restored as closely as possible to its state in Darwin's lifetime and contains the original drawing room and study where he wrote his *Origin of the Species*. A permanent Darwin exhibition is on display in the Western Gallery on the first floor of the **Natural History Museum** and some of the original manuscripts are in the library of the **British Museum** (for both *see chapter* **Museums**).
Shop. Wheelchair access.

Royal Geographical Society

Lowther Lane, Kensington Gore, SW7 (071 589 5466). South Kensington underground then 9, 33, 49, 52, 73 bus. **Open** *main hall and map room* 10am-1pm, 2-5pm, Mon-Fri. **Admission** free.
Lowther Lodge is the splendid red brick headquarters of this society dedicated to the exploration of the unknown. The map room has over 800,000 maps, including the African explorer Livingstone's manuscript papers and his cap, and the redoubtable Stanley's boots. There is a fine collection of paintings and nineteenth-century travel photography by fellows of the society.

Writers & Thinkers

The Victorian age had more than its fair share of intellectuals and artists and the closing years of the century witnessed a reaction against the Victorian moral certitude. Uppermost among the writers and thinkers of the period was **Charles Dickens**, much of whose work was concerned with social injustice. The designer, socialist and poet **William Morris** was also moved to write about the conditions of the working class. His house in Walthamstow now holds a collection of his wallpaper and textile designs, *see chapter* **Museums**). At the same time, **Karl Marx** used the British Museum Reading Room to write *Das Kapital*, the seminal work of left-wing economics and politics.

Café Royal

68 Regent Street, W1 (071 437 9090). Piccadilly Circus underground. **Open** *brasserie* noon-3pm, 6-11pm, Mon-Sat. *Grill room* noon-2.45pm, 6-10.45pm, Mon-Fri; 6-10.45pm Sat. *Cocktail bar* noon-11pm Mon-Sat; noon-3pm Sun. *Daniels: food* 11am-3pm Mon-Fri; *bar* noon-3.30pm Mon-Sat. **Credit** A, AmEx, DC, V.
This fashionable café-restaurant, decorated with huge mirrors and gilded caryatids, was founded by a Parisian wine merchant on a borrowed capital of £5. There will always be a faint taste of scandal and decadence in the air here, a lingering memory from the days when Oscar Wilde and Aubrey Beardsley frequented the café.
Wheelchair access.

Dickens's House

49 Doughty Street, WC1 (071 405 2127). Russell Square or Chancery Lane underground. **Open** 10am-5pm Mon-Sat. **Admission** £3; £2 OAPs, students, UB40s; £1 under-16s; £5 family ticket (two adults, three children). **Credit** (shop only) A, AmEx, V.
The house, a shrine to London's most famous novelist, has recently been fully renovated and restored. It holds an enormous collection of Dickens memorabilia, including portraits of the novelist and his family, personal effects and a comprehensive Dickens library. Although the novelist lived here for just two and a half years, this is where he wrote *Oliver Twist*, *Nicholas Nickleby* and the last five chapters of *The Pickwick Papers*.
Bookshop (sells first and early editions of Dickens). Research facilities.

Marx Memorial Library

37-38 Clerkenwell Green, EC1 (071 253 1485). Farringdon underground. **Open** 1-6pm Mon; 1-8pm Tue-Thur; 10am-1pm Sat (visitors are requested to come before 6pm Tue-Thur, phone on Sat). **Admission** free.
The Marx Memorial Library has an exceptional collection of political, social and philosophic literature. Lenin, the architect of the 1917 Russian Revolution, used an office in the building between 1901 and 1902. Only members may use the library. Marx is buried in **Highgate Cemetery** (*see above* **Cemeteries**).

Information

The Victorian Society

(081 994 1019). **Open** 9am-5pm Mon-Fri.
A very helpful bunch of enthusiasts who will try to answer enquiries about period architecture and interiors.

Early Twentieth Century

Every aspect of urban living, from transport to entertainment, is transformed in this tumultuous period.

Emmeline Pankhurst: suffragette.

The old order broke up in the early part of the twentieth century. New thinking, new inventions and modernist buildings all transformed ways of living. The Russian Revolution, two major wars, the Depression and, for Britain, the loss of the Empire, brought great political and social transformation.

Political change happened quickly after World War I. Lloyd George's government averted revolution in 1918-19 by promising (but not delivering) 'homes for heroes' for the embittered returning soldiers. But the Liberal Party's days in power were numbered. The Labour Party, which had gained its first seats in Parliament at the turn of the century, enjoyed rapid growth. By 1924, the party had enough MPs to form its first government, with Ramsay MacDonald as Prime Minister. Meanwhile the suffragettes, led by **Emmeline Pankhurst** (*see chapter* **Women**), put up a spirited fight to gain votes for women, finally achieved in 1928.

Civil disturbances made the headlines, caused by rising unemployment and an increased cost of living. As a result of the 1926 General Strike, when the working classes downed tools en masse in support of the miners, the streets were teeming with army-escorted food convoys, aristocrats running soup kitchens and office workers cycling to work. The *Daily Mail* demanded 'Clear out the Soviets'. But after nine days of chaos, the strike was called off by the Trades Union Congress, leaving the miners to fight alone.

Modernism was the intellectual driving force of the time; experimental literature flourished. The Bloomsbury Group was a renowned intellectual clique, boasting the novelist Virginia Woolf and the influential economist JM Keynes (*see chapter* **London by Area: Central London**). During the 1930s Aldous Huxley and George Orwell wrote angry books, *Brave New World* and *Down and Out in Paris and London* about poverty and society's dismal future.

Bloomsbury Workshop

12 Galen Place, off Bury Place, WC1 (071 405 0632). Holborn underground/19, 22, 25 bus. **Open** 10am-5.30pm Mon-Fri. **Admission** free. **Credit** A, £TC, V.
This small, fascinating bookshop-cum-gallery sells works by, and relating to, the Bloomsbury Group, including first editions, biographies, prints, drawings and paintings. Staff can supply details of organised walks around the Bloomsbury landmarks.
Mail order. Wheelchair access.

Fashion

As with political and intellectual movements, fashion underwent dramatic changes during the first three decades of the century. Edwardian fashion took Victorian values to an extreme. Corsetted women pinned enormous hats to their long hair and were swathed in long, bustled dresses, even when playing tennis – showing even a little ankle was considered racy. Inevitably there was a reaction. The 'roaring' twenties saw the arrival of the 'flapper', with her bobbed hair, skin-tight boyish shimmy dress and cloche hat. The Charleston became the rage and Schiaparelli, Coco Chanel, *Vogue*, *Vanity Fair* and *Harper's Bazaar* set the trends. For men, plus fours and diamond-patterned sweaters were casual-chic and a tuxedo *de rigueur*.

This period is well represented at the Dress Collection of the **Victoria & Albert Museum** (*see chapter* **Museums**). The array of gear includes flapper dresses, Edward VIII's checked suits and George Bernard Shaw's stetson. The V&A's Twentieth Century Primary Galleries on the second floor has an interesting display of furniture, sculpture and art deco frippery. And at the **Geffrye Museum** (*see chapter* **Museums**) a thirties living room has been recreated, complete with period three-piece suite, Bakelite wireless, tiled fireplace and other modest art deco features.

Entertainment

To the Edwardians, mass entertainment meant a night out at the music hall. Audiences cheered and jeered at the songs and jokes of Max Miller and Marie Lloyd right into the thirties. But, one by one, the variety shows fell victim to cinema, radio and eventually television. Most music halls were converted into movie theatres. About the only variety venues remaining are the **Hackney Empire** (*see below*) and the **London Palladium** (*see chapter* **Music: Rock, Folk & Jazz**).

After the trauma of World War I, a 'live for today' attitude prevailed among the young upper classes in the 1920s. A whole new social life opened up, particularly for women. 'Flappers' would gather in cocktail bars to drink, smoke and swap comments about sex, Freud and the latest jazz music and dances. The revellers expected dancing as accompaniment to their food and gossip. Thus evening and tea dances became all the rage at the luxurious hotels, particularly the **Ritz**, W1 and the **Savoy**, WC2.

The new medium of film became immensely popular, and a night at the flicks was soon regular entertainment for all social classes.

Cinema-going was turned into an event with the advent of the 1930s art deco picture palace. The **Odeon Leicester Square** (*see chapter* **Film**) retains its dramatic geometric black frontage and tower, but is not unusual in having lost its elaborate interior.

Radio also took off in a big way in the twenties and thirties. Families gathered round enormous Bakelite wireless sets, decorated with stylised sunbursts, to hear the latest sounds from the British Broadcasting Company (BBC). Television broadcasts started on 26 August 1936, when the first BBC telecast went out live from the Alexandra Palace studios in **Alexandra Park** (*see chapter* **Sightseeing**). The **Museum of the Moving Image** (*see chapter* **Museums**) has a fund of material from the early days of film and TV.

The Ritz
Piccadilly, W1 (071 493 8181). Green Park underground. **Tea served** 3pm, 4.30pm, daily. **Set tea** £13.50. **Credit** A, AmEx, DC, V.
To relive the day of a (very wealthy) socialite of the 1920s, drink a leisurely tea here in the afternoon (booking advised), then slip into a sequinned ball gown or a dapper dinner suit and tango in the Palm Court during the dinner dance (10pm-1am Fri, Sat).
Wheelchair access.

Broadcasting House
Langham Place, Regent Street, WC1 (071 580 4468). Oxford Circus underground.
Daily BBC radio programmes first emanated from Savoy Hill (next to the Savoy Hotel) on 14 November 1922, but by 1932 Broadcasting House was ready, complete with 22 sound-proofed studios. Vaguely reminiscent of an old Bakelite radio, it was designed by G Val Myers and is decorated with a notable sculpture of Shakespeare's *Prospero and Ariel* by Eric Gill. Close inspection of the statue will reveal that the figures represent God the Father sending forth the Son into the world. Gill originally gave Ariel a large penis, but was made to recline it before the unveiling.

Brick Lane Music Hall
152 Brick Lane, E1 (071 377 9797). Aldgate East or Shoreditch underground. **Open** *booking office* 10am-5pm Mon-Fri. **Shows** 7.15-11.30pm Wed-Sat. **Admission** £20 (incl 3-course meal). **House wine** £7.50 bottle, £1.90 glass. **Credit** A, £TC, V.
So long as you can forget that 'alternative' comedy ever happened, the full-scale re-enactments of the old-time East End music hall are well performed here. There's a jolly sing-along atmosphere, so expect to be made to feel guilty if you don't laugh at the jokes. Food is of the 'boiled beef and carrots' variety.

Hackney Empire
291 Mare Street, E8 (081 985 2424). Hackney Central BR/22B, 38, 55 bus. **Open** *booking office* noon-6pm Mon-Sat. **Credit** A, V.
When this theatre was built in 1901, the architects evidently had in mind a Turkish bazaar. The turreted exterior and heavily ornate proscenium arch have been beautifully restored. It was originally a variety theatre, where Marie Lloyd, local girl turned famous bawdy singer, made her name. It's now a venue for both mainstream and alternative performers.
Bar. Wheelchair access.

Metroland

London became Greater London between 1900 and World War II, as suburbs and villages were swallowed up by the metropolis. Its population rose from four and a half million to a peak of eight and a half million in 1939. Commuter towns which benefited from the new Metropolitan Line were described by poet John Betjeman, as 'Metroland'.

Road transport was revolutionised, too. From Edwardian times, motorcars started to 'put-put' around London's congested streets. The first motor bus was introduced in 1904, and by 1911 the use of horse-drawn buses had been abandoned. Electric trams (all double-deckers) started running in 1901 and didn't die out until the early 1950s (though they never ran through the West End or the City). The **London Transport Museum** (*see chapter* **Museums**) contains models (and some real examples) of public transport of the period.

Modernism

Although architecture was on the threshold of modernism during the early decades of the century, the British were slow to adopt the geometric styles of le Corbusier, or the Bauhaus. Grand-scale buildings continued to go up, but with cleaner forms and invariably in Portland stone. **County Hall**, SE1 (1905-33) is a good example. The main British contribution to the modern movement was the use of local materials. Significant arts and crafts buildings include Richard Norman Shaw's New Scotland Yard, SW1; and **Hampstead Garden Suburb**. Two rare examples of art nouveau are the **Horniman Museum** (*see chapter* **Museums**) and the **Whitechapel Art Gallery** (*see chapter* **Art Galleries**). The neo-Byzantine **Westminster Cathedral** is simply in a style of its own.

Transport is a fitting symbol of the age, and the motorcar was the inspiration for two exuberant buildings of the period, **Michelin House** and the Royal Automobile Club (RAC), Pall Mall, SW1 (1911). Of the many underground stations built before World War II, many were modernist gems. Charles Holden designed over 30, notably Bounds Green station (1930).

Modernism did have its moments, most impressively with the **Daily Express building**. The same architect, Owen Williams, was responsible for **Wembley Arena** (*see chapter* **Music: Rock, Folk & Jazz**). The **Penguin Pool** in **London Zoo** (*see chapter* **Sightseeing**) is a playful construction of interlocking concrete spirals, designed in 1934.

Freemasons' Hall, WC2, was loathed by half the population when it was opened in 1933 and kept the *Times* letters page filled for months (*see chapter* **Museums**). The University of London's bold **Senate House**, Malet Street, WC1, opened a year earlier as the tallest building in London at the time. Buildings of the thirties were built to be noticed and the massive **Battersea Power Station**, Kirtling Street, SW11 looks as if it's a left-over from the film set of Fritz Lang's *Metropolis*.

Daily Express Building
121–128 Fleet Street, EC4. Blackfriars underground/BR.
Owen Williams's Daily Express Building is the most dramatic piece of art deco in central London. Completed in 1932, the building is sheathed in a chrome and black glass curtain wall. Behind this stark exterior is an art deco foyer and staircase. This is all that the public can see of Robert Atkinson's interior of zig-zag geometry and stylised images in black marble, figured ebony, travertine and chrome.

Hampstead Garden Suburb
Hampstead, NW11. Golders Green underground, then H2 bus.
Begun in 1907, this tree-lined domestic development was a fine, but fairly dull exercise in the vernacular style. Possibly the last successful suburban scheme in London, it was originally intended to accommodate all types of people, regardless of age, class or income. The layout incorporates apartment buildings to the north, villas in the west and larger houses in the south. The central square is by Lutyens.

Michelin Building
Michelin House, Fulham Road, SW3 (071 589 7401/Bibendum restaurant 071 581 5817). South Kensington underground. **Open** 9.30am-6pm Mon, Wed-Sat; 10am-6pm Tue; noon-5pm Sun.
The Michelin Building, designed as an advertisement for the French tyre manufacturers, has often been threatened with demolition. Saved in 1985, the frontage has been restored, and is decorated with tiles depicting motorcars. Look for the exquisite mosaic Bibendum (tyre man) floor in the foyer. Lost original features, notably the glass cupolas, and Bibendum stained glass have been replaced. It's now home to a publishing company, the Conran shop, and the **Bibendum** restaurant (*see chapter* **Eating & Drinking**).
Wheelchair access.

Westminster Cathedral
Victoria Street, SW1 (071 834 7452). Victoria underground/BR. **Open** 7am-8pm daily. **Services** 7am, 8am, 8.30am, 9am, 10.30am, 12.30pm, 1.05pm, 5.30pm (sung Mass) Mon-Fri; 7am, 8am, 8.30am, 9am, 10.30am (sung Mass), 12.30pm, 6pm Sat; 7am, 8am, 9am, 10.30am (sung Mass), noon, 5.30pm, 7pm Sun.
Candy-like bands of red brick and stone in Christian Byzantine style make this 1903 cathedral an imposing sight. Inside, the decoration still isn't complete, and the domes are bare. But the columns and mosaics (made from over a hundred kinds of marble) are magnificent, the nave is the widest in Britain, Eric Gill's sculptures of the Stations of the Cross (1914-18) are especially fine, and the view from the campanile is superb. The cathedral is the headquarters of the Catholic Church in Britain.

The World Wars

Zapped by Zeppelins, then battered by the Blitz, London survives two world conflicts.

Twice in this century, Britain has fought in world wars. But although the conflict of 1914-18 was far the most costly in terms of British lives lost, its effect on the structure of London was limited. To grasp the enormity of the impact of World War I on the British people, examine some of London's **memorials** (*see below*), or visit any of Britain's parish churches. Even the smallest villages contain a Role of Honour, with a long list of war dead.

The impact of World War II on London is more obvious. Hitler's bombs did more to change the city than anything since the Great Fire. Londoners were in the front line for much of the war. Thousands died in their homes, at factories, in offices or in defence of the city.

The course of both world wars is thoroughly charted at the **Imperial War Museum**, while wartime London is examined at the **Museum of London** and the British Army's wartime role is explained at the **National Army Museum** (for all *see chapter* **Museums**).

Blunderbuss Antiques

29 Thayer Street, W1 (071 486 2444). Bond Street underground. **Open** 9.30am-4.30pm Mon-Fri; 9.30am-4pm Sat. **Credit** A, AmEx, £TC, V.
Wartime memorabilia is big business and Blunderbuss has a rapidly changing stock. You could spend anything from 50p for a badge, up to several thousands of pounds for a suit of armour.
Mail order. Wheelchair access.

World War I Memorials

It's easy to overlook the fact that the capital was bombed in World War I. You need to look hard to find the traces. Evidence of air-raids by German Zeppelin airships was largely obliterated by the bombs of World War II. But at **Cleopatra's Needle** on the Victoria Embankment, WC2, you can see where the first aircraft raid (on 17 December 1917) caused damage to the obelisk's plinth and one of its sphinxes.

At an early stage of World War I, the opposing armies 'dug-in', creating trenches across northern France and Belgium. Millions of men on both sides were killed in the conflict, or died of disease in the filthy conditions. The Trench Experience of the **Imperial War Museum** (*see chapter* **Museums**) tries to recreate some of the horrors of a trench in Flanders (Belgium).

In response to the carnage, people in virtually every British town and village mourned the loss of a generation of young men by erecting war memorials. The national monument is the **Cenotaph** in Whitehall, SW1, which is where the Remembrance Day Service for the dead of both world wars takes place (*see below* **The Home Front**). This geometric monolith was a bold piece of architecture in 1919-20. Timeless and devoid of religious symbolism, it is one of the best works by Edwin Lutyens.

There are many other memorials in the capital which are also important or unusual pieces of sculpture. Hyde Park Corner, SW1, has the **Royal Artillery Regiment** statue, the best of many such pieces by C Sergeant Jagger; and a bronze **Boy David** (by Francis Derwent Wood, 1925) representing the Machine Gun Corps. Ironically, this muscular figure is a traffic hazard, distracting drivers so that they prang the vehicle in front.

The statues are not all heroic; many reflect how the average man became cannon-fodder. Witness the ordinary **Tommy** (slang for a British soldier) at Paddington Station, W2, unarmed and reading a letter from home. You can also find oddities such as the **Submariners** (by Hatch and Tension, 1922), Victoria Embankment opposite Temple Gardens, WC2; and the **Imperial Camel Corps** bronze (by Cecil Brown, 1920), in Embankment Gardens, SW1, topped by a soldier astride a dromedary. Remembrances of a more personal nature can be seen at institutions from churches to colleges to businesses. Typical is the stone bench memorial in Lincoln's Inn, WC2, devoted to soldiers who had trained as barristers there.

Edith Cavell, the British matron of a Red Cross hospital in Brussels, is commemorated in a statue at St Martin's Place, WC2 (by George Frampton, 1920). Cavell helped Allied soldiers escape to the Dutch frontier during World War I. She is alleged to have been shot as a spy by the Germans in 1915 (though the story may have been 'modified' for the purposes of British propaganda). Her 'last words' have been inscribed below the statue: 'Patriotism is not enough. I must have no hatred or bitterness towards anyone.'

The Tomb of the Unknown Warrior at

Westminster Abbey (*see chapter* **Sightseeing**) commemorates the hundreds of thousands of World War I dead whose bodies could not be identified. The remains of an unidentified soldier were covered with French soil, and Belgian marble was used for the memorial stone.

World War II

Unlike much of Europe, Britain never had a strong nationalist movement in the 1930s. Though Oswald Mosley's British Union of Fascists (BUF) had some powerful friends among industrialists and the ruling classes, his party never gained mass support. When, in 1936, Mosley tried to organise an anti-Jewish march through the East End, a crowd of 500,000 locals packed Cable Street, E1, to prevent it.

But as the 1930s progressed, and the Nazi party in Germany grew in strength, another world conflict looked increasingly likely. During the Munich Crisis of 1938 there was a mass evacuation of London's children to the countryside, and the digging of slit trenches in London's parks. On Prime Minister Neville Chamberlain's proclamation of 'Peace in Our Time', these preparations for war temporarily ceased. But the appeasement stopped with Hitler's invasion of Poland; Britain declared war on 3 September 1939.

The government quickly gave itself dictatorial powers to implement precautionary measures. Night-time blackout was enforced immediately in London, leading to many traffic accidents. Thousands of Germans and Italians were victimised and the males were interned, even if they were shopkeepers who had lived here for years.

Battalions of Home Guard were made ready to fight an invasion, and London's factories stepped-up production of weapons. In Walthamstow, factories stopped making furniture and started building Mosquito aeroplanes out of balsa and plywood. Even in the Houses of Parliament, a cellar was converted into a submarine factory.

Kitted out with just a change of clothes and a gas mask, some 750,000 children became evacuees when they were sent away to families in the remote countryside. Some were even shipped off to Canada. But most Londoners decided to stay put, erecting Anderson air-raid shelters to provide some protection from the bombs. These tiny, damp, concrete boxes were installed in back yards and suburban gardens all over Britain. Many still remain, grassed over.

To everyone's surprise, during the autumn and winter of 1939/40, nothing happened. As the months drew on, Londoners became used to rationing and black-outs, but as the fighting remained far away, this period became dubbed the 'Phoney War'.

Blitz

The Phoney War came to an end abruptly in 1940 when the German army quickly overran most of northern Europe. By June, France had surrendered and the beleaguered British forces had had to be rescued from the beaches at Dunkirk. The German army was just 100 miles (160 kilometres) from London.

The spring of 1940 also saw a change at the top of Britain's government. The unpopular Chamberlain resigned in May, to be replaced as Prime Minister by the 66-year-old Winston Churchill.

In the late summer of 1940, the first few incendiary bombs fell on the West End. These were quite light, and it was found that they could be rendered harmless if put quickly in a bucket of water. They did little to prepare Londoners for what was to happen on 7 September.

It was a hot, sunny Saturday afternoon which brought the first huge wave of German bombers. Hundreds of aircraft dumped their load of high explosives on east London and the docks. Whole streets were left burning and the dead and injured numbered over 2,000. That evening, Londoners in the West End saw two sunsets, one in the west and a fierce red glow in the east. The Blitz had begun.

There was no relief; the Germans returned on 56 consecutive nights before picking on the car-manufacturing city of Coventry. As the air-raid klaxon sounded and giant searchlights scoured the skies above the blackened city, East Enders poured underground. Huge but cramped communal shelters were built; the largest, by Tilbury docks, held 16,000 people. Underground stations proved to be ideal shelters. As the raids became nightly, people took to living in them. The sketches by war-artist Henry Moore of war-weary Londoners huddled on the platforms can be seen in the Imperial War Museum. Less well known are the rare surviving public air-raid shelter signs on house numbers 7-10 and 13-17 Lord North Street, Westminster, SW1 (just behind Westminster Abbey).

Londoners reacted with tremendous bravery and stoicism. Because of the way communities pulled together, you'll still hear the nostalgic refer to the period as 'Britain's finest hour'. Most people attempted to work as normally as possible, often after interrupted sleep in a shelter. Others, like the poet Louis MacNeice, spent their nights up in the dome of St Paul's Cathedral fire-watching, so the wardens could assist the injured and so the

Bed-time for Winston at the **Cabinet War Rooms**. *See* **review**.

firemen – popular heroes of the time – could fight the continuous blazes.

The government had to dodge Hitler's bombs, too. Winston Churchill, the War Cabinet and the Defence Committee planned the Allies' moves from an underground warren near Whitehall known as the **Cabinet War Rooms**. Their secretaries got so little daylight that they needed sun-lamp treatment. You can visit the Cabinet War Rooms, which were so Spartan that Churchill preferred to kip at the Savoy Hotel, WC2. The hotel was often bombed; but nowhere in central London was safe. Buckingham Palace, Westminster Abbey and St Paul's were all hit. BBC Radio's Broadcasting House – a prime target because of its propaganda role – was painted grey to elude the bombers' sight. It was eventually hit on 15 October 1940, during the Nine o'Clock News. Newscaster Bruce Belfrage continued to read the day's headlines.

By the end of the war much of the City and East End was in ruins – two out of every five houses in Stepney, east London, were lost.

Cabinet War Rooms
Clive Steps, King Charles Street, SW1 (071 930 6961). Westminster or St James's Park underground/24, 29, 53, 88 bus. **Open** 10am-5.15pm daily. **Admission** £3.80; £2.80 OAPs, students, UB40s; £1.90 under-16s. **Credit** A, AmEx, £TC, V.

The British Government's wartime headquarters lies underground near Downing Street and has been restored to its 1940 state. It must have been a grim life in this bunker: behind the heavy security doors are tiny rooms with Spartan utility furniture. The appeal of the place lies in how realistic it is, but there's not much you can actually do but look at the room sets. Most interesting are the map rooms and Winston Churchill's bedroom. As there were no toilets, you also have the privilege of viewing the Prime Ministerial chamber pot. *Cassette-guided tour. Group discount. Shop. Toilets for the disabled. Wheelchair access.*

Christ Church, Greyfriars
Newgate Street, EC1. St Paul's underground.
Wren's Christ Church (1691) was a victim of the incendiary devices that destroyed many of the great City churches. The tower and vestry have been restored, but the bare walls are left to commemorate the destruction.

Battle of Britain

In 1940 the threat of invasion was very real and London's defences were sorely stretched. Pillboxes (machine gun emplacements) sprang up everywhere. Some of them still survive: there's one by Putney Bridge underground station, overlooking the river. In July 1940, the first German operations in preparation for an invasion took place. Luftwaffe bombers were employed to destroy the British airfields, while fighter planes accompanied them to take on the Royal Air Force (RAF). Air battles continued over the fields of southern England until October. But though the RAF's Hurricanes and Spitfires were greatly out-numbered, it was the Luftwaffe that suffered heaviest casualties. The Germans eventually stopped this line of attack; what became known as the Battle of Britain was over. You can see some of the planes that defended London – as well as some of the bombs that fell – in the Imperial War Museum, the Royal Air Force Museum (for both *see chapter* **Museums**) and at **Duxford Airfield** near Cambridge.

Duxford Airfield

Duxford, Cambridgeshire (0223 835000). **Getting there** *by car* M11 to Junction 10, then A505/Cambridge; *by train* to Whittlesford, Royston BR, then taxi; *by bus* daily from Victoria Station. **Open** *Mar-Oct* 10am-6pm daily; *Oct-Mar* 10am-4pm daily. **Admission** £5.80; £4 OAPs; £2.90 students, UB40s, under-16s; £15 family (two adults, three children). **Credit** A, AmEx, £TC, V.
Duxford aerodrome, a wartime RAF base, now has a large collection of civil and wartime aircraft from bi-planes to Concorde to the U2 spy-plane. There's also a 1940s pre-fab house furnished with original utility (frugal wartime) furniture. You can also experience either a World War II dog-fight or a space flight in a flight simulator.
Café. Group discount. Shop. Toilets for the disabled. Tour by prior arrangement. Wheelchair access.

The Home Front

Life in London during the war became increasingly austere. Rationing was tight because German U-boats were sinking so many ships in the Atlantic. People were allowed just four ounces (100 grammes) of bacon and cheese a week and a packet of dried eggs. The make-do-and-mend philosophy extended to wartime clothes, which were also strictly rationed. You can see an example of a 'utility' dress in the **Victoria & Albert Museum** (*see chapter* **Museums**). Slogans such as 'Dig for Victory' were taken to heart: even the swimming pool of the prestigious Ladies' Carlton Club in Pall Mall was turned into a pigsty.

D-Day

From 1942 the tide of the war slowly began to turn. The Germans were suffering huge losses on the Eastern Front, and the USA had joined the war on the side of the Allies. A cosmopolitan mix of soldiers was based in Britain. American GIs joined representatives of diverse nations of the British Empire, and expatriate resistance fighters from throughout Europe. General de Gaulle and other members of the French government-in-exile met at the French House pub (*see chapter* **London by Area: West End**) to co-ordinate the French resistance.
By 1944 the Allies were preparing for the D-Day invasion of Europe, which began on 6 June. The London Underground workers in Acton had discovered a method of waterproofing tanks, invaluable during the D-Day beach landings. Perhaps the most dramatic reminder of World War II is **HMS Belfast** (*see chapter* **Sightseeing**). This landmark in the Thames is the last of Britain's great cruisers that protected the vital convoys in the Atlantic, and took part in D-Day.

Doodlebugs

As the Germans retreated, they resorted to desperate measures, using weapons that could not be aimed accurately, but were designed to cause indiscriminate destruction. The V-1 was a pilot-less plane, packed with explosives and with an engine programmed to shut down over London, crashing into the city. During the summer of 1944, these 'Doodlebugs' (as they were soon nicknamed) fell at the rate of 73 a day, mostly on south London. You can see some examples in the Imperial War Museum (*see chapter* **Museums**).
After D-Day, the Allies eventually over-ran the launch pads of the V-1s. The Germans then began firing V-2s at London. These were ground-to-ground rockets carrying a considerable charge of high explosives. They gave no warning of approach and made a large crater. Whole rows of houses could be destroyed by one rocket. But because the Germans were able to produce only a small number of the rockets, their effect was minimal.

Victory at Last

London was the scene of one big party on 8 May 1945 – VE Day. Hundreds of thousands of people took to the streets after victory was announced. They went wild, dancing in the Trafalgar Square fountains, and doing the conga in Leicester Square. At Piccadilly Circus, a naked sailor climbed on to Eros's pedestal and draped himself in a Union Jack.
Today, most Londoners have had no experience of war, but every year, in the week before Remembrance Sunday, many don red poppies and donate to soldiers' charities. Remembrance Day services are held at churches throughout the land, but the national ceremony is at the Cenotaph in Whitehall.

Remembrance Service at the Cenotaph

Whitehall, SW1. Westminster underground. **Date** Sunday closest to 11 November. **Admission** free.
The Cenotaph is the scene of the annual Remembrance Day service. The Queen, Prime Minister and other dignitaries lay wreaths and observe one minute's silence to commemorate the British and Commonwealth citizens who died in both World Wars. It's held here on the nearest Sunday to the anniversary of the World War I armistice. Unless you're in the front row at dawn, all you'll get to see is the parade of old soldiers as they go through Parliament Square at the end.

Post-War London

Saddled with a stop-start economy, unscrupulous developers, and hostile governments, London is still thriving.

World War II left Britain almost as shattered as Germany. Soon after VE day a General Election was held and Churchill was heavily defeated by the Labour Party. People wanted a change. A better Britain, the politicians promised, would be built from the rubble.

Planners were seen as the people who would construct a better life for everyone. This included removing London's slums, providing free health care for everyone and a better education system available to all. But for all the planned changes, life was drab, regimented and austere. Visitors to London in 1950 were appalled to find that they couldn't buy a steak in the better hotels; and it was only in February 1953 that chocolate rationing ceased.

In the midst of this austerity, London hosted the Olympic Games in 1948 and then the Festival of Britain in 1951, in an attempt to inject colour and life into the city. The temporary fairs and exhibitions that took over derelict land on the South Bank for the Festival provided the incentive to build what is now the largest arts centre in western Europe. The only permanent structure designed specifically for the Festival was Robert Matthew and JL Martin's Royal Festival Hall (*see chapter* **Music: Classical & Opera**).

The Fifties

'Let's be frank about it; most of our people have never had it so good' proclaimed Prime Minister Harold Macmillan in 1957. And perhaps he was right: the Welfare State was in operation, unemployment was low, prosperity was growing. The coronation of Queen Elizabeth II in 1953 had been the biggest television broadcast in history and there was the feeling of a new age dawning.

The craze for consumer durables and labour-saving devices came via the USA. Many were British made, like Belling fridges and New World cookers. The annual **Ideal Home Exhibition** (*see chapter* **London by Season**) displayed what people had to buy to 'keep up with the Jones's'. Many of these 1950s household goods can be seen at the Design Museum, while the Geffrye Museum contains an entire exhibition on life in the fifties, with mock-ups of prefabs and council houses. For both, *see chapter* **Museums**.

Fashion-conscious, youthful rebellion arrived

in the 1950s with rock 'n' roll. Elvis Presley replaced sentimental crooners, working-class lads adopted gravity-defying quiffs and fashionable neo-Edwardian clothes. Teenage girls copied the American high-school look: skimpy polkadot dresses, pony-tails and bizarrely framed sunglasses. The Saturday night 'hop' became a teen institution.

London's hippest district, Soho, was a centre for Bohemians, beatniks and jazz. By the mid-fifties, international attention focused on Soho's jazz clubs. **Ronnie Scott's** (*see chapter* **Music: Rock, Folk & Jazz**) dates from 1959.

The Sixties

Enthusiasm to improve society led to the sweeping away not only of slums but also of Georgian squares. Nothing was sacred in the 1960s. London councils erected more than 400 'streets in the sky' tower blocks and vast City office developments were of the same insensitive, uniform style. Quality standards succumbed to corruption and an orgy of property speculation. Some of London's ugliest buildings date from this period.

When Ronan Point, a new block in Newham, east London, partially collapsed in 1968, so did the boom. By then, logistical problems – lifts not working, nowhere for children to play, lack of neighbourhood focus – had turned the high-rise dream into a nightmare for the residents.

Conversely, the new immigrant communities that arrived from former British colonies, rejuvenated many remaining slums and started enterprises such as late-opening corner shops. The **Commonwealth Institute** (*see chapter* **Museums**) with its hyperboloid roof of Zambian copper (Robert Matthew and Johnson-Marshall, 1962) reflects official attempts to integrate Commonwealth immigrants into a multi-racial society.

Another 1960s London landmark is the British Telecom Tower (Eric Bedford, 1964) on Maple Street, W1. Formerly called the Post Office Tower, this *Thunderbirds*-like structure was Britain's tallest building until Canary Wharf was built in Docklands.

Liberation was the buzzword of the sixties. The decade started with the censorship trial of

Carnaby Street: *the fulcrum of Swinging London in the 1960s. See below.*

DH Lawrence's *Lady Chatterley's Lover*. Banned for 32 years as too erotic 'for your wife or servants to read', it sold two million copies in six weeks after Penguin was allowed to publish it. Another easing of restrictions occurred when homosexuality was legalised in 1968. Feminism also made some advances, though the contraceptive pill (1961) turned out to be a mixed blessing in the fight for women's rights.

Fashion achieved vast importance in London, and innovative mod styles by designers like Mary Quant broke the stranglehold of Paris on couture. Boutiques blossomed all along the King's Road (*see chapter* **London by Area: West**) and Soho's **Carnaby Street** sold an ever wider range of clothes. Early sixties London was seen as the fashion and music capital of the world.

Pillorying the Establishment became one of the great occupations of the 1960s. The TV show *That Was the Week That Was* led the way in highlighting hypocrisy and cant in the British ruling classes.

In 1964 off-shore 'pirate radio' stations revolutionised the music scene. The most famous was Radio Caroline, which played hits considered too racy for the BBC's mainstream radio stations and (still-running) *Top of the Pops* TV programme. Meanwhile, London's live music scene exploded, with bands like The Who, Manfred Mann, Spencer Davis and the Rolling Stones playing at venues such as the **Marquee** (*see chapter* **Music: Rock, Folk & Jazz**).

The decade ended with the Beatles naming their final album *Abbey Road* after the recording studios in London NW8, and the Stones playing a free gig in Hyde Park which attracted half a million people.

The Seventies

Too many Londoners remember the 1970s as a decade of economic strife. Inflation, the Oil Crisis and international debt finally flushed the British economy down the toilet. During 1974, Britain was put on a three-day working week, and a miner's strike brought down the government. This was also the period when the IRA started its bombing campaign in mainland Britain.

Against this background of strife and disunity, several important social and economic changes took place: Britain's idiosyncratic currency was replaced on 15 February 1971 with a decimal system (that worked on units of ten rather than the traditional 12); the UK joined the European Community in 1973; and racial discrimination was outlawed, as were practises that discriminated against women in the workplace. However, after almost two decades, society still has a long way to go before these last two laws prove effective.

And at long last in the 1970s, Londoners began to stand up against the planners, who had uglified much of their city since the end of the war. When **Covent Garden** market moved out of central London, the Greater London Council (GLC) wanted the handsome buildings replaced by office blocks. The local community – a motley band of actors, craftsmen, printers and traders – wanted to stay put. Vast meetings and candle-lit demonstrations finally caused the council to back down (*see chapter* **London by Area: Central London**).

For years, people sneered at the seventies, decade of the Bee Gees, flared trousers and soul singers with a lurv thang. Excess was the by-word of seventies fashion. Music veered between over-produced pap-pop and anarchic punk. The corridors of **Kensington Market** remain a popular hang-out for safety-pinned punk purists with the obligatory Mohican topping, whereas **World's End**, originally set up by Malcolm McLaren (manager of the Sex Pistols) and Vivienne Westwood, continues to sell Westwood's uncompromising collection of clothing design (for both *see chapter* **Shopping**). These days, early seventies' fashions are enjoying an unlikely revival, and flares are once-again flapping down the King's Road.

The Eighties

History will regard the eighties as the Thatcher era. Britain's first woman Prime Minister – the propagandist for the consumer society and little Englander morality – set out to expunge socialism and the influence of the sixties and seventies. A monetarist policy and cuts in public services savagely exacerbated the north-south divide, and the divide between the rich and poor. Unemployment soared. In London, riots erupted in Brixton in 1981 and Tottenham in 1985; mass unemployment and bad policing methods were seen as contributing factors.

The Greater London Council mounted spirited opposition to the Thatcher Government. This included lowering the price of tickets on the underground and buses. However, Margaret Thatcher responded by abolishing the GLC and since 1985 London has been without a single governing body.

Cash dispensers and wallets full of credit cards heralded the consumer-goods orgy of the eighties. In the money decade your bank account could now be a status symbol. Property prices – the biggest, and in the end the most boring, talking point of dinner parties in the eighties – rocketed. A spectacular boom in house prices at the end of the eighties was followed by an equally alarming slump at the outset of the nineties.

'Lifestyle' became a buzz word in the eighties. If you weren't in a social category, you didn't belong. Style magazines – *The Face, i-D, Blitz, Arena* – dictated distinct social types: yuppies, dinkies, Sloanes. Of course no one actually admitted to being one. Café Freud (198 Shaftesbury Avenue, WC2; 071 240 9933) epitomises the chic, starkly minimalist yuppy hang-outs of the era.

One of the biggest success stories of the decade was the growth of **Camden Market** (*see chapter* **Shopping: Markets**) which continues to draw thousands of visitors every weekend.

In 1986, Prince Charles described the proposed National Gallery extension as 'A monstrous carbuncle on the face of a much-loved friend'. This remark sparked off heated discussion amongst architects and the public. With whole areas of London being redeveloped – Broadgate, King's Cross, Docklands – Charles has become a major influence on what gets built. Both the National Gallery plan and the development of Paternoster Square near St Paul's Cathedral have been redesigned according to the Prince's populist, classical tastes. **Richmond Riverside** (by Richmond Bridge, Richmond, Surrey) is a typical 1980s office development in the post-modern style. Designed by architect Quinlan Terry, this classical edifice certainly pleases the eye. But, as with much that happened in the 1980s, it's all style, no content: its exterior is, quite literally, a façade.

The Nineties

At the beginning of the nineties, there was an upsurge of hope in London. The Berlin Wall had crumbled and (of more immediate relief to most Londoners) so too had Margaret Thatcher's leadership. A riot in Trafalgar Square had helped to see off both Margaret and her inequitable Poll Tax (a local-government financing scam where road-sweepers had to pay as much tax as millionaires).

Yet just as the 1990s got underway, Britain's economy slumped into its worst recession since the 1930s. In London, the yuppy accessory businesses of the 1980s have been among the worst hit: designer boutiques and restaurants have closed by the score. Much of the office space in Docklands remains empty, and the owners of the Canary Wharf development have gone into receivership (*see chapter* **London by Area: East End & Docklands**). To cap it all, the British people, in an extraordinary act of masochism, voted in yet another Conservative Government (the fourth in succession) in 1992.

But all is not gloom. The recession has meant that bargain shops and traditional street markets are thriving. And after overdosing on style in the eighties, London's myriad restaurants are now concentrating on giving good value. But perhaps the most cheering development has been the British Royal Family's descent into farce, giving many Londoners the best laugh they've had in years.

London Today

Steve Grant surveys the contours of the capital as it careers towards the twenty-first century.

I've lived in London for most of my life, and I'd be hard-pressed to find a city to compare; it doesn't have the breathtaking backdrops of Rio or Hong Kong; it has no Gaudí magnificence or landscaped Louis Quatorze elegance like Barcelona or Paris; there's no sand 'n' surf nearby like Los Angeles and Sydney. And though Wren's St Paul's Cathedral is a favourite with visitors, it doesn't have the Pope in residence, or the works of Michelangelo hanging on the walls. There are bomb-scares and tailbacks almost daily, road-works and building-schemes that seem to take longer than the pyramids; long distances to travel between east and west, north and south; buses that don't run on anything but psychedelic time, tubes that can be smelly and sweaty in summer and dank and depressing in winter, and sometimes so intimidating that even Freddie Kreuger would think twice about entering a compartment. And then there's the famous weather. As mid-summer visitors huddle under stylish umbrellas or in all sorts of protective clothing, on Birdcage Walk or Shaftesbury Avenue, one is reminded of Mark Twain's famous assertion that the worst winter he ever spent was summer in San Francisco — for the Dock of the Bay, just substitute the Docklands.

But now for the good news – and what compensations. London's sprawl has given it a tube system which is the envy of most of the urban world and a colour-coded map which is not only a monument to mathematical logic and organisation, but a post-modernist artefact to sit alongside the Zippo lighter, the Coca-Cola bottle or the Nintendo Gameboy. While all of London's public transport infrastructure has been affected by the creeping menace of privatisation and redundancy, there are few world cities which can boast such a mix of underground trains, all-night buses and trains. Together, these reach every part of the sprawl that is Greater London. By the end of the century, there should be three new tube lines, comprehensive modernisations of two more, an extension of the Jubilee Line into Docklands and a link from Paddington in the west to Liverpool Street and Bethnal Green in the east.

When Charles Dickens came to London in the early 1830s he could walk to the city through fields and past hedgerows, when bustling urban enclaves like Notting Hill, Camden and Maida Vale were little more than hamlets. If America is a country of great and various cities, then London, despite the concentration around the Mall and Shaftesbury Avenue, Marble Arch and Covent Garden, is still a collection of fine and bustling villages: they can be tough and salty like Hackney and Brixton; busy and lurid like Soho; exotic and cosmopolitan like Earl's Court and Camden, the two favourite successors to Notting Hill as London's Greenwich Village; posh, media-friendly and leafy, like Hampstead or Richmond; or watery, spacious, self-contained gems like Greenwich or Twickenham.

But the Conservative Government has been responsible for splitting London's politics asunder: not merely by its abolition of the Greater London Council in 1985, but by the introduction of the profoundly unpopular Community Charge (Poll Tax) in 1987 (*see chapter* **Post-War London**). This system has at least been replaced by the less controversial Council Tax, but even this – with its sometimes casual and inconsistent valuation of property – seems to combine the worst elements of the buried head-count Poll Tax and the old rates system.

GIVE US A BODY

Out of all this division there has been a call from former environment minister Hugh Rossi (a veteran north London Tory MP) for the re-creation of a single body to co-ordinate the mounting traffic, housing and environmental needs of the capital. The opposition Labour Party have even talked of the election of a strong American-style mayor in the tradition of Ed Koch or David Dinkins, although Rossi has knocked on the head any idea of a return to the days when 'Red Ken' Livingstone ruled the GLC, preferring to put his faith in the City of London with its links at diplomatic and international level. Sadly, even if the investment comes, the City couldn't be facing a bigger crisis than its own in the wake of several high-level financial scandals, a recession and the recent decision by the Irish Republican Army to squeeze the commercial life out of the City by a concerted bombing campaign. This has itself led to a massively-increased security presence in the area, which can have only limited success with such a seemingly ruthless and tenacious enemy.

But London lives on. Though such comparisons are misleading (after all John Major is no Winston Churchill), the indomitable spirit of the Blitz which touched and awed the free-world during the last war does continue. Londoners get thoroughly pissed off with white tape around streets and buildings, delayed journeys and warnings on the tube, but life goes on and when it comes to life then my city still leads the field: the best theatre; the best music; some of the finest restaurants; the uniqueness of the London pub (still alive despite the ravages of the big breweries and the hideousness of the theme-brigade with their cocktail-umbrellas, saddle-seats and flock wallpaper); the vast array of football grounds in the winter; the wide-open spaces of the Oval, south of the river, and Lords in St John's Wood; the thrill of Wimbledon; even a day at the Sobell Leisure Centre or watching an athletics meet at Crystal Palace. And to be fair and accurate, London is still one of the safest major cities on earth, provided you don't walk around Tooting Broadway or the Seven Sisters Road at three in the morning with a 'Please Mug Me' sign.

But what denotes London most is Benjamin Disraeli's maxim that it wasn't a city but a nation. Now that nation has become a world. Take a bus down the Edgware or Warwick Roads, Lavender Hill or the Strand any evening, any day, and you'll hear a veritable United Nations of accents and gestures: a still-potent tribute to Britain and London's ability to absorb refugees and seekers after betterment. Voices from the deserts of Africa, the slums of Eastern Europe, the battered alleys of the Middle East, the shanty-towns of the Caribbean, the villages of Central Asia, the chic boulevards of Paris, Vienna, or Berne, all co-mingling in a curiously interdependent isolation. But, yes, London is threatened like the rest of the Western world by unemployment and its bitter seeds; racist attacks have increased, an ultra-vicious element has been targeting immigrant families, notably in areas of south and east London where bad-housing, diminishing social services, and drug-trafficking have hardly helped community stability.

London's future is in its own hands but ultimately it has to sell itself to investors as well as visitors. Is there an argument for winding down a city which has seen its population decrease in the last decade? With the seat of government in Westminster, and with all the focus, from a premier at the Royal Shakespeare Company's Barbican Centre to the FA Cup Final at Wembley, stuck down in the south of England, then London may suffer at the hands of the devolvers and the regionalists. But then

London's power *is* likely to continue, notably with our increased participation in Europe, not only because of the obvious proximity to Heathrow Airport and its new fifth terminal, and to Stanstead, but because of the new Channel Tunnel. But though London is likely to maintain its position despite a predicted slow economic growth of two per cent a year throughout the nineties, it will have to fight hard on the financial front against the likes of Paris and Frankfurt to maintain its position as part of the golden triangle of finance that links it with New York and Tokyo.

Some years ago, the *New Statesman* magazine ran a competition asking for unhelpful tips to London visitors. Answers included the following gems: tell a tourist that yellow lines by the kerb indicate the number of cars which can be parked side-by-side; rush into the British Museum Library (where Karl Marx worked on *Das Kapital*) and shout a loud greeting to all fellow readers; or stand behind the goal at Chelsea FC's popular 'Shed' end waving a copy of *Gay News* and screaming 'Quiche at my place after, boys!'. They were misleading tips, but I hope this book will see you right.

Steve Grant, Executive Editor,
Time Out magazine

London by Area

You've seen the sights; now it's time to discover the London that Londoners know and love. Here we highlight the most fascinating districts, giving the inside information on the history and the famous residents, the backstreets as well as the high streets, and where to find the locals at play.

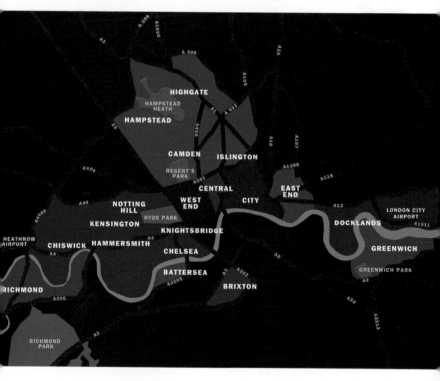

Contents

London Docklands.
(Don't go home without seeing it.)

PORTICO LIMEHOUSE LINK

London Docklands is a unique experience.

And the place to start the experience is the London Docklands Visitor Centre on the Isle of Dogs (get here by taking the scenic Docklands Light Railway to Crossharbour).

You'll watch our entertaining video. See our fascinating exhibition. Discover our seafaring history.

Then how about a guided Docklands coach tour? Startling modern architecture, beautiful old warehouses, breathtaking waterside vistas, an urban farm, historic locations associated with names like Nelson and ships like the Mayflower – all that and more in two hours.

After that, maybe tour Canary Wharf. Or walk below the Thames to Greenwich via the pedestrian tunnel.

To reserve your seat on a coach tour, simply call the London Docklands Visitor Centre on 071-512 1111. See you soon.

London Docklands

Central London

Like the eye of the storm, Bloomsbury is one of central London's most peaceful districts, but nearby is the exhilarating streetlife of Covent Garden.

For the purposes of this Guide, we have called that strip of land which lies east of the West End, yet west of Holborn and the City, Central London (*see* **Map**, page 83). Within its boundaries lie both the burgeoning entertainment and shopping district of **Covent Garden** and the quieter, bookish neighbourhood of **Bloomsbury**.

The busy, sometimes grimy **Charing Cross Road** separates Soho from Covent Garden. It runs from Trafalgar Square to St Giles Circus (the junction with Tottenham Court Road and Oxford Street). For decades this road has been famous for its bookshops, as recorded in Helen Hanff's novel *84 Charing Cross Road* (this is now a classical music shop). Of the 18 bookshops here, **Foyle's** (119) is the biggest and the most infuriating – its stock is chaotic and its system of purchase ludicrously antiquated. The **Waterstone's** branch next door (121-131) is a contrasting exercise in logic and clarity. The friendly **Silver Moon** (68) has recently been expanded, and has added to its superb range of feminist literature, while **Henry Pordes** (58-60) is the place to pick up good quality bargain books. **Zwemmers**, 24 Litchfield Street, WC2, is the Mecca for art book fans and **Sportspages** (Caxton Walk, 94-96) speaks for itself. But if you want to browse in peace, head for **Cecil Court**, off the main road. It is lined with antiquarian and specialist bookshops covering diverse subjects: cookery, travel, theatre and Victorian postcards. Prices start at 50p and rise to several hundred pounds for a rare first edition. (For more of London's best bookshops, *see chapter* **Shopping**.)

At the St Giles Circus end of Charing Cross Road is Denmark Street, London's Tin Pan Alley. Hopeless heavy rockers can be heard strumming *Stairway to Heaven* from any (sometimes all) of the several musical instrument shops in the area (*see chapter* **Shopping**).

A useful meeting place in the area is **The Spice of Life** pub, near the junction of the Charing Cross Road with Shaftesbury Avenue (*see chapter* **Eating & Drinking**).

Bloomsbury

Bloomsbury was named after Blemund, owner of the land at the time of King John (1199-1216). Its boundaries are Euston Road in the north, High Holborn in the south, Tottenham Court Road in the west, and Southampton Row in the East. It is now home to the University of London and the British Museum. Gower Street runs through its centre.

The great and good of Bloomsbury are almost too numerous to mention. Two of the greatest figures of the Victorian age lived in the area. Charles Darwin occupied 110 Gower Street, from 1838 until 1842 after his first trip on the *HMS Beagle*; and Charles Dickens wrote three of his novels while living in Doughty Street (*see chapter* **Victorian Times**).

Christina Rossetti, who is increasingly being seen as one of the finest poets of the age, lived at 30 Torrington Square from 1876 to 1894. And Bertrand Russell the philosopher and peace campaigner lived at 57 Gordon Square from 1918 to 1919. Russell was a member of the powerful

Bedford Square: *one of Bloomsbury's (and London's) finest squares.*

family that once owned much of Bloomsbury; there is a bronze statue of him by Marcelle Quinton in Red Lion Square.

The area is also a centre of the book trade, with many of the old publishing companies having offices around Bedford Square. The streets around the **British Museum** (*see chapter* **Museums**), particularly Great Russell Street and Museum Street, contain many antiquarian and specialist bookshops.

In the summer, Bloomsbury's many squares are ideal places for a picnic lunch. Russell Square, once part of the Duke of Bedford's estate, is one of London's biggest squares, and the gardens are open to the public. Emmeline Pankhurst the great campaigner for women's suffrage lived on the square (at No.8) from 1889 to 1893. Gordon Square is smaller and quieter – buy a book in the enormous four-storey Dillon's bookshop that's nearby and settle down to read it on the grass.

Just outside the north-western boundaries of Bloomsbury lies a smaller area sometimes called Fitzrovia. Together with Bloomsbury, this district provided the homes and the meeting places of a circle of intellectuals who became known as the Bloomsbury Group which flourished in the years between the two world wars. It centred on the house of the publisher, Leonard Woolf and his wife, the novelist Virginia Woolf at 52 Tavistock Square. The painters Duncan Grant and Vanessa Bell (Virginia Woolf's sister), John Maynard Keynes the economist and Lytton Strachey the biographer and critic were core members. EM Forster, author of *A Passage to India* and *A Room With a View* was also associated with the group. He lived at 26 Brunswick Square from 1929 to 1939. A plaque commemorating the group can be seen on Bloomsbury Square.

Bloomsbury has a number of local festivals held in the summer. Contact Camden Council (071 278 4444) for details.

Transport

Goodge Street, Holborn, Russell Square, Tottenham Court Road or Warren Street underground.

Museum Tavern

Great Russell Street, WC1 (no phone). Tottenham Court Road or Holborn underground. **Open** 11am-11pm Mon-Sat; noon-3pm, 7-10.30pm, Sun.
Karl Marx used to drink here after a hard day's work on *Capital* in the British Museum Library. These days you can contemplate dialectical materialism while sampling one of the good selection of draught beers or munching on above average pub grub.

Patisserie Deux Amis

63 Judd Street, WC1 (071 383 7029). Russell Square underground. **Open** 8.30am-5.30pm Mon-Sat; 8.30am-1.30pm Sun. **Credit** £TC.

An adorable patisserie and boulangerie in true French style. Try the succulent apricot tart and, in summer, eat it at one of the outside tables.

University of London

Gower Street, Malet Street, WC1.
London's first university was opened in 1828 (though it didn't receive a charter until 1836). Its aim was to provide a literary and scientific education to students of all religious denominations. In 1878 London became the first university to allow women to take examinations. **University College** in Gower Street is its oldest building, designed in a classical style by William Wilkins (who was also the architect of the National Gallery). The philosopher Jeremy Bentham was one of the founders of the college. In his will, he stipulated that his body be kept in the University so that he should appear to be still presiding over meetings of the council. The skeleton is now kept in a large wooden wardrobe. **Senate House** on Malet Street is the administrative headquarters of the University. Built in 1933 by Charles Holden, it resembles New York skyscrapers of the period. For amenities offered to students by the University, *see chapter* **Students**.

Covent Garden

Medieval monks from Westminster Abbey once grew vegetables and buried bodies at the convent gardens where today shoppers peruse bric-à-brac. Following Henry VIII's confiscation of church property in the Reformation, this promising site just outside the City walls passed to the Russell family in 1533, who were later granted the title, Earls of Bedford. An enterprising descendant employed the architect Inigo Jones to create London's first planned square in the 1630s. Jones's Palladian houses were much sought after. The spacious square rapidly became the most convenient centre for fruit and vegetable traders from outlying villages. The Earl built permanent sheds for the makeshift market, and by 1671, Charles II had granted a charter and official market rights, which remained with the Russell family until 1910.

The market was a most lively affair, with puppet shows, snails, parrots and love birds on sale to 'people of quality'. Samuel Pepys, Henry Fielding and Benjamin Franklin were all once residents of the Covent Garden area, and Dr Johnson first met his biographer James Boswell at an address on Russell Street (now a coffee house called Boswell's).

Coffee houses and taverns proliferated around the Piazza, and during the eighteenth century Covent Garden became the stamping ground for fashionable young ruffians known as Mohocks, who had a penchant for overturning coaches and their contents on to rubbish tips. Affronted aristocratic residents moved out, and market traders, publicans and pimps came to dominate the area. It is perhaps not a coincidence that London's first police

A craft stall in Covent Garden's **Apple Market**.

force established its headquarters on nearby Bow Street in 1748; the force became known as the Bow Street Runners.

Eventually, energetic Victorian developers cleared the slums, carved out the Charing Cross Road and built the iron and stone market buildings in the centre of the Piazza in 1850. After centuries of residency the thriving fruit and veg trade became too cramped, and in 1974 moved south of the river to Nine Elms. After demolition plans were scuppered by popular protest (*see chapter* **Post-War London**), the Greater London Council developed the area with an exemplary mix of conservation and innovation to create a very different kind of Covent Garden Market.

The tweely named Apple Market occupies the refurbished arcades of the Piazza that once housed fruit 'n' veg traders. High-quality antiques, crafts, knitwear and jewellery are sold at inflated prices. The Jubilee Market is sited near the Piazza's junction with Southampton Street. Behind its uninspiring edifice at weekends you'll find a crafts market of toys, clothes, gifts and pictures – but you won't find any bargains. Weekdays offer a more prosaic range of budget fashion, shoes and household goods, while Monday is antiques day. Go well before lunchtime, when traders are good-tempered and crowds are thin.

Cafés, restaurants, boutiques and market stalls cater for the large number of visitors and local workers that crowd into and around the Piazza from morning until late into the night. London's best buskers and street entertainers (all must be licensed) help to make Covent

Garden today one of the city's most lively places. Sadly, astronomical rent rises have forced out many unique small shops, to be replaced by conformist chainstores and offices. However, nearby Neal Street and **Neal's Yard** do harbour a variety of interesting (albeit expensive) specialist shops and designer fashion stores, as does Floral Street (*see chapter* **Shopping**).

Famous as a theatre district, Covent Garden is known internationally as the home of the **Royal Opera House** (*see chapter* **Music: Classical & Opera**). The **Theatre Museum** is appropriately located on the Piazza (*see chapter* **Museums**).

Transport
Covent Garden underground.

Africa Centre
38 King Street, WC2 (071 836 1973/restaurant 071 836 1976/shop 071 240 6098). Covent Garden underground. **Open** *Kikapu shop* 10am-7pm Mon-Fri; 10am-5pm Sat; 10am-6pm Sun; *Calabash restaurant* 12.30pm-3.30pm Mon-Fri; 6pm-midnight Sat. **Admission** free; phone for ticket prices for special events. **Credit** (restaurant and shop only) A, AmEx, V.
The umbrella for London-based African organisations, this centre is an unbeatable resource for information about culture, politics and travel in that continent. Regular club nights are hosted and the centre is a favourite venue for visiting African bands. The ground floor crafts shop sells handmade jewellery, and the basement restaurant offers an imaginative, changing menu of pan-African food at reasonable prices.

Ecology Centre
45 Shelton Street, WC2 (information centre and café 071 379 4324/shop 071 379 8208). Covent Garden underground. **Open** 10am-6pm Mon-Fri; *shop and café* 10am-6pm Mon-Sat. **Admission** free. **Credit** A, AmEx, V.

This multi-purpose building is London's best source of information on all things green. Its small, well-stocked shop sells third-world goods, and a variety of T-shirts, cards and books. The exhibition space has changing displays of art with a green theme, and the Yours Naturally Café is busy and friendly, although the quality of the food is variable. Stick to the spicy toasties and delicious cakes. Prices are low and portions large. The Centre is also the home of the Café Theatre (*see chapter* **Theatre**).

Neal's Yard
Neal's Yard, Shorts Gardens, WC2. Covent Garden underground.
There's a relaxed, 'alternative' feel to the cosy Neal's Yard courtyard. The colony includes health food shops, a bakery co-operative, and good vegetarian cafés (closed in the evenings). The excellent (but expensive) Neal's Yard Dairy now sells its cheeses from around the corner on Shorts Gardens (*see chapter* **Shopping**). A clock above Neal's Yard Wholefood Warehouse owes its design to the ever inventive Tim Hunkin. The minute tube fills with water until, on the hour, water passes through the system, ringing bells and tipping watering cans to nourish flowers, which appear to grow as they are mounted on floats. Unsuspecting people underneath used to get a soaking, but spoilsports have erected a guttered awning.

Penguin Bookshop
10 The Market, The Piazza, Covent Garden, WC2 (071 379 7650). Covent Garden underground. **Open** 10am-8pm Mon-Sat; 11am-5pm Sun. **Credit** A, AmEx, DC, £TC, V.
Like an iceberg, most of this popular bookshop is hidden below the surface. Every spare inch of the cavern-like basement is stocked with the full range of Penguin titles and books on every subject. The shop is a frequent venue for author-signing sessions; dates are listed in *Time Out* magazine. At 1 The Market is the **Puffin Bookshop** (*see chapter* **Children's London**), which caters for younger readers.

Seven Dials

The Seven Dials area of Covent Garden was developed by Thomas Neale, a speculative builder, about 300 years ago. Seven small streets converge on a roundabout that is barely large enough to cope with the traffic careering round its base. The monument in the centre was removed from the junction in 1773, reputedly because it was thought that there was treasure hidden beneath. If you're wondering why it's called Seven Dials when there are only six sundials on the column, the answer is that the column itself is the seventh gnomon (the pillar showing the time by its shadow).

The neighbourhood was notorious for its poverty during the Victorian age, but it was improved by the building of the Charing Cross Road. Recently, following the regeneration of Covent Garden, new fashion shops have opened in the area, alongside old-established stores. The best of the oldies are **Portwine** (24 Earlham Street), which continues to supply the area with fresh meat, as it has done for over 200 years; and the hardware store **FW Collins** (14 Earlham Street), which looks much as it must have done when first opened in 1835. Earlham Street also has a small general market with stalls selling second-hand books, seafood and some of the best flowers in London.

On Monmouth Street, The fashion boutiques **Distractions** and **Ritzy** lie each side of an undertakers. The **Crown** pub, overlooking the monument, has been on its present site for nigh-on 300 years and is more popular than ever. Opposite the pub is **Obsessions** a trendy gifts and accessories store selling chrome clocks and Bakelite phones.

At the moment, while old manages to co-exist with new at Seven Dials, the area provides a fascinating view of London in flux. But should Covent Garden's gentrification spread further, the older shops with lower profit margins will be in peril.

St Paul's ('The Actors') Church

Bedford Street, WC2 (071 836 5221). Covent Garden underground. **Services** 1.10pm Wed; 8.30am Mon, Tue, Wed; 11am Sun.

In 1633 the Earl of Bedford commissioned Inigo Jones to build St Paul's on the cheap, to be 'little more than a barn'. Jones called his work 'the handsomest barn in England'. It has since been rebuilt and altered a number of times. Its splendid portico on the Piazza, famously featured in *My Fair Lady*, is in fact at the back. There's a secluded churchyard at the front where you can relax, reached through King Street, Henrietta Street or Inigo Place. Theatrical memorials, including the casket containing Ellen Terry's ashes, adorn the interior – this theatreland church is dedicated to actors.

Trafalgar Square

Trafalgar Square, planned by John Nash but executed by Charles Barry among others, is an exercise in triumphalism uncommon in London. With its size, its crowds, the pigeons and punks (both sets trying to exploit tourists) and the endless traffic circling like sharks, it can be quite disorientating for a newcomer to the city. There is so much to see within such a short distance of Nelson's Column.

To get your bearings, the first thing to do is to have a walk round, looking at the streets leading out of the square. Westminster Clocktower (known to all as 'Big Ben') is clearly visible along Whitehall. This road runs past **Downing Street** and leads to the **Palace of Westminster** and **Westminster Abbey**. Face this direction, and at 2 o' clock to you will be **Admiralty Arch** through which is **The Mall** leading to **Buckingham Palace**. (For more information on these sights, *see chapter* **Sightseeing**). At 3 o' clock will be Cockspur Street, which leads up towards Pall Mall and **St James's** (*see chapter* **West End**) while directly behind you will be the porticoed entrance of the **National Gallery** (*see chapter* **Art Galleries**). At 7 o' clock lies the start of the Charing Cross Road (take this and turn left for **Soho**) and at its mouth on St Martin's Place is the church of **St Martin-in-the-Fields** (*see chapter* **Georgian London**). The major road at 9 o' clock is the Strand, which leads to Charing Cross Station and the **Savoy Hotel** (*see chapter* **Accommodation**). The Strand also provides the easiest route to **Covent Garden** (*see above*), though you'll eventually need to turn left up Southampton Street to reach the Piazza. Finally, at 11 o' clock is Northumberland Avenue which is the fastest route to the Thames. To escape the madness, follow this road and turn left at the Embankment to reach the relative peace of Victoria Embankment Gardens, where poetry readings and concerts are sometimes held at lunchtimes.

Transport

Embankment underground/Charing Cross underground/BR.

Café in the Crypt

Crypt of St Martin-in-the-Fields, Duncannon Street, WC2 (071 839 4342). Charing Cross underground/BR. **Coffee bar Meals served** 10am-8pm Mon-Sat; noon-6pm Sun. *Buffet counter* **Lunch served** noon-3.15pm daily. **Dinner served** 5.30-7.30pm Mon-Sat. *Both* **Average** £9. **House wine** £6.50 bottle, £1.25 glass. **Credit** A, LV, £TC, V.

Beneath James Gibbs' church off Trafalgar Square, black steel tables and chairs, bare brick vaulting and wrought-iron uplighters make a theatrical setting for this café. The two hot dishes from the canteen servery are usually fairly inspiring and inexpensive, and one of them is always vegetarian. Enthusiastic staff and the activity generated by the brass-rubbing centre, bookshop and gallery also housed in the crypt make this place lively and enjoyable. *No-smoking area. Wheelchair access* **Branch: The Place Theatre** 17 Dukes Road, WC1 (071 383 5469).

Chandos

29 St Martin's Lane, WC2 (071 836 1401). Charing Cross underground/BR. **Open** 11am-11pm Mon-Sat; noon-3pm, 7-10.30pm, Sun.

This large, two-floor pub is one of the nearest boozers to Trafalgar Square. It is consequently crowded with a mix of office workers and tourists. Prices are high, but the selection of real ales includes the estimable Sam Smith's brew. The Chandos has been known to stop serving well before 11pm.

St Martin-in-the-Fields Market

St Martin-in-the-Fields Churchyard, WC2. Charing Cross underground. **Open** 11am-5pm Mon-Sat; noon-5pm Sun.

A small crafts market has been operating from St Martin's Churchyard since the late eighties. Persist through the souvenirs (football scarves, London T-shirts) and you'll find some interesting handicrafts from around the world.

The **Café in the Crypt**. *See* **review**.

West End

Packed with pubs, clubs, shops and restaurants, the West End throbs with vitality. This is where London parties.

Although London as a whole is a sprawling giant of a city, the West End, its vibrant entertainments centre, is reasonably compact. A stroll from Oxford Street, through Soho to Piccadilly Circus and Leicester Square need only take 45 minutes. Trouble is, there's so much to see in between that you could easily lose an afternoon wandering around the backstreets.

Walk through the West End on a Friday evening, when office drones breathe a collective sigh of relief after work, queues fidget outside the cin-

emas, pubs spill their customers on to the pavements and hungry gourmands drool over the choice of restaurants. The weekend starts here.

Piccadilly Circus & Leicester Sq

It used to be said that if you hung around Piccadilly Circus for long enough, you would meet everyone you knew. Nowadays you would be poisoned by fumes from the endless traffic first. But big, brash and bustling Piccadilly Circus remains

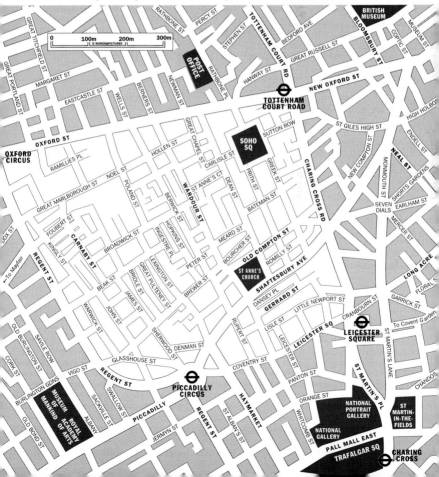

one of London's most important meeting-points. The famous statue in the Circus is a memorial to the philanthropy of Anthony Cooper, seventh Earl of Shaftesbury. The correct title of the figure portrayed is *The Angel of Christian Charity*, but it has become known universally as *Eros*, the Greek boy-god of love. In 1990, gay rights campaigners had a 'kiss in' around *Eros* to protest at the Government's repressive Section 28 which, among other things, bans local authorities 'promoting homosexuality'.

The neon-lit circus of today is a far cry from the elegant design envisaged by the Prince Regent. He commissioned John Nash to design a sweeping thoroughfare to link Regent's Park to his home at Carlton House on Pall Mall. The grandeur of the original plan, completed in 1812, lingers on in the high quality stores which line Piccadilly and Regent Street. *See chapter* **Shopping**.

Shaftesbury Avenue is one of the major thoroughfares off the Circus; it contains some of London's best-known West End theatres. To the left of it lies Soho, with Chinatown to its right.

Take Coventry Street from Piccadilly Circus and you soon reach Leicester (pronounced 'Lester') Square. The central gardens of this large, pedestrianised area have recently been re-opened and provide a much-needed lunchtime resting spot during good weather. At various times of the year, a fun-fair takes over a portion of the gardens.

Former residents of the square include the painters Sir Joshua Reynolds and William Hogarth; their busts can be seen in the gardens, as can a bust of Sir Isaac Newton (he lived in nearby St Martin's Street in a house later occupied by Fanny Burney), and statues of Charlie Chaplin and Shakespeare. But today Leicester Square is famous as London's epicentre of glitzy entertainment. In addition to nightclubs, pubs and restaurants, it is the home of four monster cinemas: the Warner, the Empire and the Odeons Leicester Square and West End (*see chapter* **Film**), and of the SWET cut-price theatre ticket booth (*see chapter* **Theatre**).

Transport
Leicester Square or Piccadilly Circus underground.

New Piccadilly
8 Denman Street, W1 (071 437 8530). Piccadilly Circus underground. **Meals served** 11am-9.30pm daily. **Credit** LV.
A large café on a quiet backstreet near Piccadilly Circus. The furnishings have hardly changed since the fifties, but the waiters are smartly turned-out and there are plenty of fry-ups and pasta dishes at low prices.

Soho

There's a couple of things to get straight about Soho. First, there's no underground station of

that name: you need to go to Oxford Circus, Tottenham Court Road, Leicester Square or Piccadilly Circus, which lie at the four corners of the district. Second, Soho Square is not the heart of Soho. Go there at night and it will be virtually deserted. The main artery of the district is Old Compton Street, which runs from Charing Cross Road to Wardour Street. Walk down this road at night and you'll see why Soho is London's most cosmopolitan and exciting quarter.

The district was first developed towards the end of the seventeenth century. Before that time the land from Greek Street to Regent Street was a sporting ground. The old hunting cry, 'So Ho!', to draw off the hounds, was frequently heard, and led to the area gaining its name.

Successive waves of immigrants and refugees have found a home in Soho. A colony of Greeks was among the first to inhabit the area, building a church (now demolished) in the Charing Cross Road in 1677. Huguenots followed soon after, coming to Soho in the 1680s to escape persecution in France. Services are still held at the French Protestant church (built 1893) in Soho Square.

Germans and Italians, Russians and Poles followed in the 1860s. Jewish people also found a refuge here, both from Eastern European pogroms and from textile bosses in London's East End (where many lost their jobs following a strike in the 1890s). Since World War II, the Cantonese Chinese came to work in the catering trades and have made the area between Leicester Square and Shaftesbury Avenue the capital's **Chinatown** (*see below*).

Many of these communities have left their distinctive cultural and gastronomic mark on Soho – this is London's major eating-out district. Below we have listed a small selection of restaurants; more can be found in *chapter* **Eating & Drinking**. But a wander around the area will reveal an extraordinary diversity of eating establishments, from cheap Italians to expensive Japanese and vice versa.

POETS ON POLAND STREET

For much of the past three centuries, the area was a hub of London's intellectual life. The poet and playwright John Dryden was one of the first literary stars to move to the area, living on Gerrard Street from 1687 until his death in 1700. A century later, William Blake wrote his *Songs of Innocence* while living at 28 Poland Street (from 1785 to 1791). In 1811, P B Shelley also lived on Poland Street (at No.15) after being sent down from Oxford.

Mozart stayed with his father in rooms at 20 Frith Street, giving recitals for the local gentry. At about the same time (1764) Casanova was lodging in Greek Street.

Berwick Street Market: *Soho's liveliest (and spiciest) day-time quarter.*

Political radicals have also had a long association with Soho, the most famous being Karl Marx, who lived at 28 Dean Street from 1850 to 1856 after being thrown out of his first London home by the bailiffs (*see below* **Leoni's Quo Vadis**). Later in the century, Rimbaud and Verlaine found sustenance in a bar on Old Compton Street after the fall of the Paris Commune.

In recent decades, Soho has enhanced its reputation for bohemianism. In the fifties it became a centre for jazz, and in the sixties bands such as the Kinks, the Who and the Rolling Stones played in Soho venues.

Soho's drift into pornography during the seventies has been curtailed by a clean-up campaign. Some strip joints and 'hostess' bars remain but, more typical of the current trend, the wholefood restaurant **Mildred's** on Greek Street (*see chapter* **Eating & Drinking**) occupies premises vacated by a sex cinema.

The eighties influx of rich, trendier-than-thou advertising and design agencies, with attendant boutiques, style-bars and eateries, has sent the original community scuttling into fragmented pockets. But old Soho is still there, and indeed has staged something of a comeback during the recession, which has cut down many ad agencies. **Berwick Street Market** (open Mon-Sat 9am-5pm) is the antidote to pretension, still thriving after more than a century. Its raucous traders sell some of the cheapest and most varied fruit and vegetables in London. Unique and long-established food shops, fabric shops, and

delis, can still be found along Berwick Street and Brewer Street. However, many have been forced out by rocketing rents.

During the fag end of the eighties, in the last wheezes of yuppiedom, boutiques started opening in West Soho, the network of streets just east of Regent Street. This area had been on the decline since Carnaby Street's descent into tackiness in the seventies (*see chapter* **Post-War**). Although the nineties recession has dealt a body blow to the latest regeneration, some London designers still operate from the area, including **John Richmond** (at 2 Newburgh Street) and **Pam Hogg** (at 5 Newburgh Street), while Jean Paul Gaultier has opened a shop at 28 Foubert's Place (*see chapter* **Shopping: Fashion**).

The nineties have also seen Soho enhancing its reputation as a centre for the gay community, with a number of sophisticated bars and clubs opening (*see chapter* **Gay**).

Should you want peace or somewhere to eat sandwiches in Soho, go to Golden Square Gardens, a quiet square lined with publishing houses near Regent Street. St Anne's Gardens, off Wardour Street, have recently been spruced up (though they're still popular with winos). On one Sunday in mid-July they are the venue for the small Soho festival, a village fete-style event where local restaurants provide food at stalls, local bands play on a makeshift stage, and waiters have a race around through the streets, finishing on Old Compton Street. The **Soho Society** (*see below*) helps run the event.

Transport
Leicester Square, Oxford Circus, Piccadilly Circus or Tottenham Court Road underground.

Bar Italia
22 Frith Street, W1 (071 437 4520). Tottenham Court Road underground. **Open** 7am-very late (at least 4am) Mon-Fri; 24 hours Sat, Sun. **Credit** LV, £TC.
An Italian snack bar with London's best cappuccino. During the early hours it's full of Soho bohos; during screenings of Italian football matches (on the video screen at the back of the bar) it's packed with ex-pats. Expensive but authentic.

Ben Uri Art Gallery
21 Dean Street, W1 (071 437 2852). Tottenham Court Road underground. **Open** 10am-5pm Mon-Thur; 3-6pm Sun. **Admission** free.
A variety of works of Jewish interest from both Jewish and non-Jewish artists are displayed here. Exhibitions change regularly.

Fratelli Camisa
1A Berwick Street, W1 (071 437 7120). Piccadilly Circus or Tottenham Court Road underground. **Open** 8.30am-6pm Mon-Sat. **No credit cards.**
A small delicatessen packed with Italian cheeses, breads and salamis, as well as tinned and bottled imported goods. High-prices, heavenly aromas.

Jimmy's
23 Frith Street, W1 (071 437 9521). Leicester Square underground. **Lunch served** 12.30-3pm, **dinner served** 5.30-11.30pm, Mon-Sat. **Average** £7. **House wine** £5.60 bottle, £1 glass. **Credit** £TC.
Greek Cypriot staples such as kleftiko, stifado and moussaka come in large portions at this bargain basement restaurant. The diabolical house red wine has caused

Soho pubs

The high point for Soho's low-life was the fifties. This was the decade when jazz burst upon the area, with British musicians such as Ronnie Scott and Humphrey Lyttelton playing in the coffee bars and clubs that sprang up everywhere. Scott went on to found his own jazz club on Frith Street that is still thriving, *see chapter* **Music: Rock, Folk & Jazz**).

Itinerant musicians used to gather in Archer Street to be hired by West End theatres and clubs. The **White Horse** pub, on the corner of Archer Street and Brewer Street, still retains some of this atmosphere. Bands often perform and there's usually blues or jazz playing on the jukebox.

The **French House** was formerly called the York Minster, but for most of this century was owned by the French Berlement family. During World War II members of the Free French armed forces used to drink there, while in the late forties, those stupendous drinkers (and writers) Brendan Behan and Dylan Thomas were regulars. Gaston Berlement finally retired in 1989 (in an explosion of fireworks on Bastille night), but although the French House is under new ownership, mercifully little has changed (apart from the opening of a good new Modern British restaurant upstairs). You still won't be able to buy a pint there (only halves are served), and you're still better off drinking one of the good selection of wines. The tiny interior remains the home of some of the best old-school Soho eccentrics.

The **Coach & Horses** is notorious both for its sozzled regulars such as Jeffrey Bernard,

and its rude landlord, Norman Balon. An entertaining collection of cartoons by Michael Heath, which first appeared in *The Times* and *Private Eye* now hangs on the bar walls. Stylish bar staff and good food also ensure that the pub is crowded.

Soho's hunting-ground ancestry is recalled in the name of one of its oldest pubs, the **Dog & Duck**. This popular drinking place has a beautiful exterior and Victorian mirrored and tiled fittings. George Orwell came here to celebrate the selection of *Animal Farm* by the American Book of the Month Club. These days Soho advertising types have taken it over, and it has recently been spruced up.

Because of England's ridiculous licensing laws, all the pubs mentioned here close at 11pm. However, Soho has more than its fair share of clubs, where drinks are served until 3am. For the best of these *see chapter* **Clubs**.

Coach & Horses
29 Greek Street, W1 (071 437 5920). Leicester Square underground. **Open** 11am-11pm Mon-Sat; noon-3pm, 7-10.30pm, Sun. **No credit cards.**

Dog & Duck
18 Bateman Street, W1 (071 437 3478). Tottenham Court Road underground. **Open** 11am-11pm Mon-Sat; noon-3pm, 7-10.30pm, Sun. **No credit cards.**

The French House
49 Dean Street, W1 (071 437 2799). Leicester Square underground. **Open** noon-11pm Mon-Sat; noon-3pm, 7-10.30pm, Sun. **Credit** (restaurant only) A, AmEx, DC, £$TC, V.

White Horse
45 Rupert Street, W1 (071 437 5745). Piccadilly Circus underground. **Open** 11am-11pm Mon-Sat; noon-2pm, 7-10.30pm, Sun. **No credit cards.**

many a hangover, but, together with the cheerful waiters, it gets Jimmy's buzzing.

Leoni's Quo Vadis

26-29 Dean Street, W1 (071 437 4809/9585). Leicester Square or Tottenham Court Road underground. **Lunch served** noon-2.30pm Mon-Fri. **Dinner served** 6-11.15pm Mon-Sat; 7-10.30pm Sun. **Average** £22. **Credit** A, AmEx, DC, £TC, V.
This rather expensive and classy Italian restaurant has been here since 1926, but the building is one of Soho's oldest, dating from 1692. Karl Marx lived on the top floor between 1850 and 1856, when he was working on *Das Kapital*. Waiters are pleased to show diners his lodgings.

Maison Bertaux

28 Greek Street, W1 (071 437 6007). Leicester Square underground. **Open** 9am-7.30pm Mon-Sat; 9am-1pm, 3-8pm, Sun. **No credit cards.**
A French patisserie that has become a Soho institution since opening in 1871. The upstairs tea room is a little too cosy during the crush for afternoon tea; arrive before 4pm to get a seat. The Mont Blancs are irresistible.

The Soho Society

St Anne's Tower, 57 Dean Street, W1 (071 439 4303). Leicester Square or Piccadilly Circus underground. **Open** 2-4pm Mon-Fri.
Housed in the tower of St Anne's Church, this information office is staffed by an eccentric and amiable band of volunteers, who possess an encyclopaedic knowledge of the area. You can also reach the office from Wardour Street, through St Anne's Gardens.

Chinatown

London's original Chinatown was situated near the Docks, in Limehouse E14, and was populated by Chinese merchant seamen and their descendants. During World War II the area was virtually destroyed by bombing, so in the late forties, Chinese Londoners began buying properties in the then cheap and down-at-heel area centred on Gerrard Street, W1. By that time, Soho had forged its reputation as London's most cosmopolitan restaurant district.

During the fifties and sixties, following the Communist revolution in China, more people arrived in the area from British-owned Hong Kong. Chinese restaurants began to be joined by shops that catered for the local Cantonese.

Cantonese are continuing to leave Hong Kong before it reverts to Chinese rule in 1997, and fortunately for London, some of the best chefs from the colony have settled in Soho. Their cooking can be sampled at any of dozens of restaurants along Gerrard Street, Lisle Street and the surrounding area. Dim sum, the lunchtime snack of various dumplings, is particularly good. Each snack costs less than £2; eight should be enough for two people. On Sundays, many Chinese families from London's suburbs travel to Soho to indulge in this leisurely repast, making Chinatown one of the liveliest districts to be on that day. *See chapter*

Eating & Drinking for more Chinese restaurants in the area.

Gerrard Street remains the heart of Chinatown. In the eighties it was given ornamental gateways and benches, and even pagoda-style telephone boxes. But the lurch into oriental clichés thankfully hasn't altered the chaotic, lively nature of this network of streets.

Chinese New Year and, to a lesser extent, the autumn **Moon Festival** are the highlights of Chinatown's year (*see chapter* **London in Season**). At these times, the streets come alive with lion and dragon dancers, Chinese musicians, and martial arts demonstrations.

Transport

Leicester Square or Piccadilly Circus underground.

Chinese Medicine Centre

7 Little Newport Street, WC2 (071 287 1095/071 287 1086/fax 071 287 5509). Leicester Square underground. **Open** 11am-6pm daily. **No credit cards.**
Traditional Chinese medicine makes use of a multitude of herbs and roots, which are stored in old wooden drawers on the ground floor of this building. Chinese massage and acupuncture are offered on other floors.

Kowloon

21 Gerrard Street, W1 (071 437 0148). Leicester Square underground. **Meals served** noon-11.30pm daily. **Credit** A, AmEx, DC, LV (lunchtime only), £TC, V.
Although there's a restaurant here, Kowloon is most popular for its sweet Chinese buns with savoury fillings (char siu, barbecued pork, is a particularly good choice and costs about 70p). Go at lunchtime (1pm) and they'll be hot.

New World

1 Gerrard Place, W1 (071 734 0677). Leicester Square underground. **Meals served** 11am-11.45am daily. **Average** £7 dim sum, £14 full menu. **Credit** A, AmEx, DC, £TC, V.
Dim sum is served (noon until 6pm) in the traditional manner, from trolleys, at this huge restaurant. The choice is large, the prices low.

See Woo Supermarket

18-20 Lisle Street, WC2 (071 439 8325). Leicester Square underground. **Open** 10am-8pm daily, incl Bank Holidays. **No credit cards.**
As well as a wealth of Chinese food (fresh, bottled and tinned), See Woo sells some of the cheapest Far Eastern cookery implements and tableware in town.

One of **Chinatown***'s many food shops.*

Shaolin Way
10 Little Newport Street, WC2 (071 734 6391).
Leicester Square underground. **Open** 11am-7pm daily.
Credit A, AmEx, V.
Authentic martial arts equipment, clothes and magazines
are sold at knock-down prices in this tiny shop on the
fringes of Chinatown.

The Sound of China
6 Gerrard Street, W1 (071 734 1970). Leicester Square
underground. **Open** noon-8pm daily. **No credit cards.**
A small, cramped shop with stocks of books, cards and
glossy magazines from Hong Kong, plus cassettes of
Chinese music, both popular and traditional.

Around Oxford Street

London's most famous shopping street has for
years been the preserve of the chain store. For
unique, family-run enterprises you must look
elsewhere (*see above* **Soho**, or, if you're feeling
rich, *below* **St James's**), but if you yearn for
acres of shelf-space and a jostling crowd, head
for this mile-long thoroughfare that runs from
Marble Arch to the junction with Tottenham
Court Road. Below we mention some of the
major stores to be found in the area; for more
information *see chapter* **Shopping**.

Oxford Street was formerly called the Tyburn
Road, after a river which now runs underground.
Today the only reference to Tyburn on the local
map is Tyburn Way, a concrete passage within
the Marble Arch traffic merry-go-round. Perhaps
the name has been almost expunged because of
the notorious 'Tyburn tree', a gallows where public hangings took place until 1783. You can see
the exact spot of the gallows, marked by a brass
plaque, on a small traffic island at the junction of
Bayswater Road and Edgware Road, next to the
huge Odeon Cinema.

Marks & Spencer (celebrated for its underwear) is the first major store you reach at the
Marble Arch end of Oxford Street, but it is the
classical frontage of **Selfridges** department
store that dominates the area. Selfridges food
hall is a treasure-house of high-class provisions.

Near the junction with Bond Street is the first
of Oxford Street's music megastores, **HMV**,
while across the road is **Debenhams**, yet
another department store.

Oxford Circus is a devilishly difficult junction
to cross when there are huge crowds at large
(the lead-up to Christmas is worst); best take
the underpass. A short detour down Regent
Street will take you to **Liberty** (the 'Arts and
Crafts' department store with its distinctive
printed fabrics) and **Hamleys**, the enormous
toy shop. For a half-time break from shopping,
stop for a drink at the **Argyll Arms** on Argyll
Street (*see chapter* **Eating & Drinking**).

Continue east along Oxford Street and among
a myriad high-street fashion stores, shoe shops

and tacky souvenir vendors, you'll pass the
entrance to the basement rock and jazz venue
the **100 Club** (*see chapter* **Rock, Roots &**
Jazz). Towards the junction with Tottenham
Court Road is the **Virgin Megastore** with
hordes of records, tapes, CDs and video games.
See chapter **Shopping**.

Transport
Bond Street, Marble Arch, Oxford Circus or Tottenham
Court Road underground.

Bonbonniere
36 Great Marlborough Street, W1 (071 437 2562).
Oxford Circus underground. **Meals served** 7.30am-7pm
Mon-Sat.
An old-fashioned dining room concealed behind a sandwich bar. Mixed grill, omelettes and fish and chips are
served; prices rarely exceed £6.

North of Oxford Street

The area to the north of Oxford Street is relatively unexplored by visitors, yet it contains
some fine squares and buildings, and offers
sanctuary from the crowds. Hertford House, in
Manchester Square, now houses the **Wallace**
Collection (*see chapter* **Art Galleries**), but in
the early nineteenth century it was the residence of Lady Hertford, mistress of the Prince
Regent.

Margaret Street (parallel to Oxford Street,
north of Oxford Circus) is the site of William
Butterfield's Church, **All Saints** (*see chapter*
Victorian Times). It was here that Laurence
Olivier started his career, performing Shakespeare at his choir school. One of the area's best
pubs is the **George** on Great Portland Street (*see*
chapter **Eating & Drinking**).

Marylebone, the area leading up to Regent's
Park, was once a fashionable village. Jonathan
Swift and (over a century later) Charles
Dickens were among the residents. In 1788,
George Gordon, Lord Byron was born in
Hollies Street. Today the area around Maryle-
bone Lane and Marylebone High Street still has
small shops, pubs and cafés that cater for local
workers. Take tea at the wonderful **Patisserie**
Valerie at Maison Sagne (*see chapter* **Eating**
& Drinking).

Transport
Bond Street, Baker Street, or Regent's Park
underground.

Mayfair

It's hardly surprising that Gerald Cavendish
Grosvenor, sixth Duke of Westminster, is the
richest man in Britain, if you consider that his
family owns much of London's most opulent
districts. The names of his ancestors have been
given to many of the streets and squares

around Mayfair, the district that lies to the east of Park Lane and the north of Piccadilly.

But this area hasn't always been the preserve of the wealthy. It gained its name from the seventeenth-century May Fair, 'that most pestilent nursery of impiety and vice'. From 1686 until the 1750s, for a fortnight each spring, the streets of what is now London's most sophisticated 'village' seethed with drunken revellers, prostitutes and shrewd traders like Tiddy Dols, the gingerbread man. The current (expensive, touristy) restaurant bearing his name at 55 Shepherd's Market was established on the site of his stall.

Once the annual junketing of the Fair was shut down, Mayfair began its upward spiral to respectability. Yet even today, reminders of the area's risqué history still exist in the shape of the 'hostesses', who ply their trade around Shepherd Market. The pedestrianised streets around this quaint area also contain antique dealers, a good sprinkling of wine bars and restaurants catering for both visitors and locals.

To the north of Shepherd Market, Grosvenor Square became famous in the sixties as the site of violent anti-Vietnam War demonstrations directed at the US Embassy which dominates the square. Today the spacious gardens (open 10am-5pm Mon-Sat) are ideal for an afternoon rest. As you put your feet up, it's worth pondering that even the site of the US Embassy is owned by the Grosvenor family – in the fifties, the Duke of Westminster announced he would sell the freehold to the Americans if they returned 12,000 acres of land in Florida (including Cape Kennedy) supposedly confiscated from the Grosvenors at the time of the war of independence. No deal was done.

Chic designer-fashion stores line South Molton Street and Avery Row, and the cosmopolitan shoppers they attract stray across Oxford Street into St Christopher's Place, and down to Maddox Street and Lancashire Court, from where more top designers operate. The area is well served by trendy cafés.

But London's Madison Avenue can be found along New and Old Bond Streets, which link Oxford Street to Piccadilly with a string of international couture stores. **Asprey's**, at 165-169 New Bond Street, takes the biscuit for ostentatious opulence. Queue here for essentials such as gold toothpicks. The auction house **Sotheby's** is at 34-35 New Bond Street. *See chapter* **Shopping** for both.

More fabulously-priced goods can be found on Cork Street, home to one of the most concentrated collections of commercial art galleries in town. *See chapter* **Art Galleries**.

Mayfair remained essentially residential until quite recently. The balance between high-class

Opulence at **Asprey's**.

homes, hotels, shops and clubs was upset by an invasion of solicitors, financiers and media folk, who have converted an enormous number of properties into office space. But the nobs and debs of London Society haven't quite deserted the district, and it's quite possible to spot an aristocrat around Berkeley Square (which, was once used as a cattle and hog pound). Though heavy traffic makes it difficult to imagine how, as the song goes, 'a nightingale sang in Berkeley Square'. At No.50 is London's best antiquarian bookshop, **Maggs Brothers**, and just off the square on Bruton Place is a fine old pub and restaurant, the **Guinea** (*see chapter* **Eating & Drinking**).

Mount Street Gardens (open 8am-7pm daily) make a tranquil spot to rest, except during playtimes at the neighbouring school. Close by is the Mayfair Library, at 25 South Audley Street (071 798 1391), which has books on the locality.

Transport
Bond Street or Green Park underground.

Church of the Immaculate Conception
Farm Street, W1 (071 493 7811). Green Park or Bond Street underground. **Services** 7.30am, 8.30am, 12.05pm, 1.05pm, 6pm Mon-Fri; 7.30am, 8.30am, 11am, 6pm Sat; 7.30am, 8.30am, 10am, 11am (sung Latin), 12.15pm, 4.15pm, 6.15pm Sun.
This splendid Gothic Revival building, beside Mount Street Gardens, is the British Province headquarters of the Jesuit Fathers. It's one of the very few Catholic churches in the city where a sung Latin mass is celebrated.

St James's

Piccadilly gets its name from the pickadill, an expansive collar or ruff fashionable in the early sixteenth century. Today, the swanky gents that inhabit this area are more likely to wear suits made in nearby Savile Row or Jermyn Street. St James's is where London's aristocrats and top business people (nearly all men) have their clubs. You'll be able to spot a few of these establishments along Pall Mall, but exclusivity is their attraction, so unless you cultivate a receding chin, a bulbous wallet or a string of titles, you won't be able to see inside.

The **Ritz Hotel** (*see chapter* **Accommodation**) exemplifies the sophistication and luxury to be found around St James's. But if the splendours of its restaurant are beyond your pocket, walk a little further down Piccadilly to the famed food hall of **Fortnum & Mason** (*see chapter* **Shopping**). Although it's also easy to spend a fortune there, a few luxuries (such as petits fours) are more modestly priced, and the store's Fountain Restaurant is great value and open late (until 11pm Monday to Saturday).

Some exceptionally good taste is also on show at the **Royal Academy of Art** (*see chapter* **Art Galleries**), also on Piccadilly. It occupies Burlington House, one of the West End's few surviving mansions from the early eighteenth century.

King Henry VIII had to move an ancient leper hospital when he began building St James's Palace. Only the gatehouse of the original building survives (it is not open to the public, but can be seen best from St James's Street), yet the royal tone of the neighbourhood prevails: many of the houses contain grace-and-favour apartments occupied by people who have been granted the right to residence by the sovereign.

The ideal place for a quiet stroll away from the mêlée is the wonderfully deserted network of streets at the end of Pall Mall, between Green Park and The Mall. Stable Yard, Cleveland Row and Catherine Wheel Yard are neglected by visitors and Londoners alike, but they still feel very much like Royal St James. Carlton Gardens, linked to the north side of the Mall by several flights of steps, is a captivating spot in which to pause and take in the view over the park and Westminster. Nearby, the small formal garden in the centre of St James's Square (open 10am-4.30pm Monday to Friday) provides a restful place to eat a sandwich.

The lively and controversial Institute of Contemporary Arts (ICA) on the Mall will bring you back up to date. Art, film, theatre and dance shows, many of them non-conformist and radical, are staged here (*see chapter* **Art Galleries**).

On the other side of The Mall, **St James's Park** is one of London's loveliest spots and a good place to retreat to after seeing the **Changing of the Guard** at **Buckingham Palace**, or visiting the **Queen's Gallery** or the **Royal Mews** (*see chapters* **Art Galleries** and **London by Season**). To the west of St James's Park is Green Park, covering the area between Piccadilly and Buckingham Palace. In fine weather, it becomes a magnet for sunbathers escaping the Piccadilly maelstrom, but in the eighteenth century the area was a favourite duelling site.

Transport
Green Park or Piccadilly Circus underground.

Burlington Arcade
off Piccadilly and Old Bond Street, W1. Green Park or Piccadilly Circus underground.
Named after the Earls of Burlington, this is the most celebrated of London's shopping arcades and a beautifully preserved monument to Regency refinement. The uniformed beadles (these days carrying walkie-talkies) help maintain the restrained atmosphere, ensuring that nobody runs, sings, whistles, carries large parcels, or opens an umbrella in the Arcade. The oldest shop in here is Lords, which has high-quality, British-made goods, including velvet smoking jackets. Crusty old gents, who rarely stray outside St James's and Mayfair, can be spotted here, waggling their walking-sticks.

St James's Church & Wren Café
197 Piccadilly, W1 (071 734 4511). Piccadilly Circus underground. **Open** 8.30am-8pm daily (phone for details of evening events). *Café* 8am-7pm Mon-Fri; 10am-7pm Sat; 10am-4pm Sun. **Services** 8.30am, 5.45pm Tue; 8.30am Wed-Fri; 8.30am, 11am, 5.45pm Sun.
St James's is the only church in London that Christopher Wren designed on a new site. He is quoted as saying it best embodied his idea of what a parish church should be. Regular concerts are performed here, and on Fridays and Saturdays there's a busy crafts market in its courtyard. The Wren Café, adjoining the church, has delicious and inexpensive food, mostly vegetarian.

Green Park: *a magnet for sunbathers.*

West London

With both deluxe and dynamic districts, west London is never out of fashion. We escort you from bustling Bayswater out to charming Chiswick.

Bayswater & Notting Hill

In 1752, Henry Fielding noted how developers were forever establishing new frontiers to the west of London: 'had they not been stopped by the walls of Hyde Park, they would by this time have arrived at Kensington'.

Seventy years later Hyde Park remained, but London was spreading either side of it. To the north, in **Bayswater**, the land belonged to the Bishop of London and was developed in grand style from the 1820s. When the gallows were removed from Tyburn (now Marble Arch, *see chapter* **West End**), in 1825, respectability took their place. By 1879 Westbourne Grove was being described as 'the centre of a new, prosperous and refined district'.

However, by the turn of the twentieth century, fashion had deserted the area and eventually many of the houses built for the bourgeoisie were divided into flats for the less wealthy or became hotels. Prostitutes discreetly moved in, and in 1963, Bayswater was at the centre of the Profumo sex scandal that caused a rumpus for the Conservative Government of the time.

Then, during the eighties, Bayswater's high streets, Queensway and Westbourne Grove, prospered again, partly thanks to wealthy Arabs settling in the area. Walk along these roads at 10pm and you'll still find clothes shops, newsagents (selling papers from around the world) and supermarkets open, along with a multitude of restaurants. Queensway is home to the greatest concentration of Chinese restaurants outside Soho's Chinatown, while nearby Westbourne Grove is famous for its curry houses. Queensway also contains **Whiteley's**, one of the world's first department stores. The building has now lost its turn-of-the-century glory, and has been converted into an up-market mall with a lively jumble of cafés, restaurants and boutiques, and an eight-screen cinema (*see chapter* **Film**). Further down the road is the **Queen's Ice-Skating Club** (*see chapter* **Sport & Fitness**).

The busy Bayswater Road runs from Marble Arch, alongside Hyde Park and Kensington Gardens, to Notting Hill Gate. Away from the main roads of Bayswater are quieter streets with stucco terraces. Many mid-price hotels remain in this area.

Notting Hill was a village on the Roman road west out of London until the nineteenth century. From its main road, a track ran north to a farm which had been named Porto Bello after Admiral Vernon had captured that Caribbean town from the Spanish in 1739. The track is now the **Portobello Road** and every week it plays host to one of London's most famous markets (*see chapter* **Shopping: Markets**). The best day to visit is Saturday, when a mass of antiques traders join the fruit and veg, junk and clothing stall-holders. But all through the week there are dozens of antiques shops trading in the neighbourhood.

During the fifties and sixties, many people from the West Indies moved into the area, and in 1966 they started the **Notting Hill Carnival** (*see chapter* **London By Season**). Taking place in the streets around Portobello Road and Ladbroke Grove on the last weekend in August, it's Europe's biggest street party.

West of Notting Hill is **Holland Park**, the result of speculative building in the nineteenth century. The curving crescents that run down from the church on Ladbroke Grove are a reminder of the Hippodrome Racecourse, which was built here in 1837. It closed five years later because no horse could run on the waterlogged clay soil.

Further north, a brick kiln built into one of the houses at Hippodrome Mews is all that is left of the notorious Piggeries and Potteries, a Victorian slum, infamous for crime and cholera epidemics. To the south, Holland Park Avenue boasts a very grand row of large porticoed houses. Holland Park itself is off Abbotsbury Road.

East of the park on Aubrey Walk lies the last of the country houses which once stood around Notting Hill village. You can peer through the gates of **Aubrey House** but cannot go in: it is still privately owned. Nearby on attractive Campden Hill Square, the residents all light candles in their windows on Christmas Eve. And on Campden Hill Road (at No.114) is one of the area's best pubs, the **Windsor Castle** (*see chapter* **Eating & Drinking**).

Transport

Bayswater, Holland Park, Notting Hill Gate or Queensway underground.

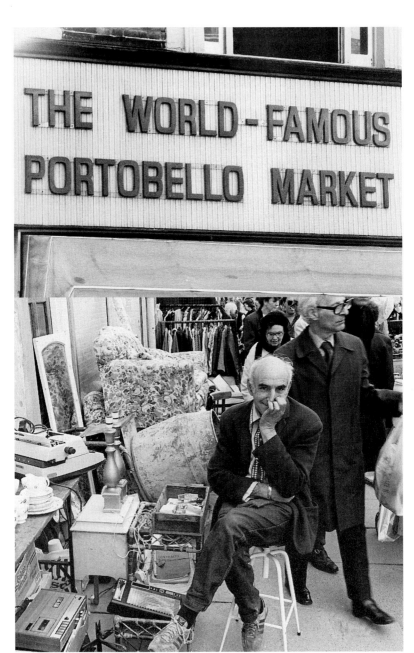

Portobello Road Market: world-famous and proud of it. *See* page 97.

Books for Cooks
*4 Blenheim Crescent, W11 (071 221 1992). Ladbroke
Grove or Notting Hill Gate underground.* **Open** *9.30am-
6pm Mon-Sat.* **Credit** A, AmEx, DC, £$TC, V.
An unparalleled collection of food books is kept in this
small shop. Every cuisine imaginable is dealt with, and
all the great cookery writers and chefs are represented.
Altogether there are over 5,000 volumes, both new and
second-hand, in ten different languages.

Holland House & Park
*Entrances in Holland Park, Abbotsbury Road, Holland
Walk and Kensington High Street, W8. High Street
Kensington or Holland Park underground.* **Open**
7.30am-30 minutes before dusk daily.
Built in 1606 as a country mansion, Holland House was
bombed in World War II and only one wing, now part of
the Youth Hostel (071 937 0748), remains. The park was
opened to the public in 1952, and has beautiful woods
and formal gardens. Open-air theatre is staged here in
the summer. For children, there's a splendid adventure
playground, with tree walks and rope-swings. You might
even spot a peacock or two. The house's summer ballroom has been converted into a stylish modern British
restaurant, the Belvedere (071 602 1238).

Magic Wok
*100 Queensway, W2 (071 792 9767). Bayswater
underground.* **Meals served** *noon-11.20pm daily.*
Average £15. **Credit** A, AmEx, DC, TC, V.
One of the best Chinese restaurants out of the many on
Queensway. The menu is long, but the finest food is
found on the specials list. Furnishings are cool and light
green. Service is friendly and enthusiastic.

Standard Tandoori
*21-23 Westbourne Grove, W2 (071 727 4818/071 229
0600). Bayswater, Royal Oak or Queensway
underground.* **Open** *noon-3pm, 6pm-midnight, daily.*
Average £11 incl 40p cover. **Credit** A, AmEx, £TC, V.
Among the oldest restaurants on west London's Curry
Corridor, the Standard is ever popular with locals and
visitors. The interior is large and relaxing, the curries
are formulaic, but good.

Kensington & Earl's Court

The Domesday Book of 1086 mentions a village
called Chenesitun to the west of London, but it
wasn't until 1689 that **Kensington** became a
residence of royalty. It was in this year that
King William III left Whitehall Palace for the
clearer air of his newly acquired country mansion, Nottingham House, situated at the edge
of Hyde Park.

Almost immediately, Christopher Wren and
Nicholas Hawksmoor were brought in to
embellish and enlarge the building, which was
renamed **Kensington Palace** (*see chapter*
Tudors & Stuarts). Royalty has lived here
ever since, and the Palace has witnessed Queen
Anne's death (in 1714), Queen Victoria's birth
(in 1819) and many twentieth-century shenani-
gans (both Prince Charles and Princess
Margaret have apartments in the building).

These days, the centre of Kensington is dominated by its High Street, one of London's major
shopping thoroughfares. Lacklustre chain-

stores are much in evidence, but there's also an
old department store, Barkers of Kensington
(63 Kensington High Street) and some of
London's most innovative street fashion is sold
by young designers and traders at **Kensington
Market** and **Hyper Hyper** (for both *see chapter* **Shopping**).

Away from the High Street, upper-crust
Kensington is thriving in the inequitable nineties.
Nannies can still be seen wheeling tiny aristocrats in prams around **Kensington Gardens** (*see
chapter* **Sightseeing**), and the gilded youth drink
in pubs such as the **Scarsdale** in Edwardes
Square. The original inhabitants of this pretty
square had to promise not to beat carpets outside, exercise a horse in the garden or allow pigs
to roam free. Another quaint area to explore is
the network of small streets off to the west of
Kensington Church Street.

Kensington Square, to the south of the High
Street, contains handsome eighteenth-century
houses, once occupied by such luminaries as
novelist William Thackeray, philosopher John
Stuart Mill and painter Edward Burne-Jones.
Thackeray also lived at No.2 Palace Green (to
the west of Kensington Gardens), which is the
site of some of Kensington's grandest Victorian
and Edwardian houses.

Earl's Court is so named because the Earls
of Oxford once lived in a manor court house in
the district (near the site of the underground
station). More recently, Earl's Court has
become a vibrant, multi-ethnic community,
famously a magnet for Australasian back-pack-
ers. This antipodean community is found on
both sides of the bar in the local pubs. There
are also a number of relatively cheap hotels in
the area (*see chapter* **Accommodation**).

This is very much a 24-hour zone – shops and
cafés open round the clock. In the seventies,
Earl's Court was the centre of London's gay
community, and it is currently the site of one of
London's best gay restaurants, **Wilde About
Oscar** (*see chapter* **Gay London**). The Earl's
Court Road, Hogarth Road and the tiny
Hogarth Place are the best streets to explore
for more restaurants.

North of the Old Brompton Road in Earl's
Court, is Bolton Gardens, where Beatrix Potter
lived from 1866 to 1913 (at No.2). Mrs Tiggy
Winkle, her pet hedgehog, is rumoured to be
buried in the back garden. South of here, The
Boltons consists of two picturesque crescents,
designed by architect George Godwin between
1850 and 1860. There's a Gothic church (St
Mary's) in the central gardens.

Earl's Court is also home to two of London's
largest exhibition halls, the Earl's Court Exhibition Centre (071 385 1200) and the Olympia
Exhibition Centre (071 603 3344).

Transport
Earl's Court, High Street Kensington or Kensington Olympia underground.

Church's
20 Kensington Church Street, W8 (071 938 2336). Kensington High Street or Notting Hill Gate underground. **Open** 11.30am-10pm Mon-Fri. **Average** £15. **Credit** A, AmEx, £TC, V.
A basement bar and restaurant which serves very fine, modern British food with a Mediterranean influence. Spanish wines are the best bet from the bar.

Kramps
6 Kenway Road, SW5 (071 244 8759). Earl's Court underground. **Meals served** noon-11pm daily. **Average** £8. **Credit** A, V.
A fair choice of galettes and crèpes can be ordered at this small wine bar. Space is limited and the décor is basic French-style.

The Muffin Man
12 Wright's Lane, W8 (071 937 6652). High Street Kensington underground. **Open** 8am-6pm Mon-Sat. **Credit** LV, £TC.
The frilly-uniformed staff at this twee tea shop serve breakfasts all day and traditional teas in the afternoon. Hot dishes and salads are on the lunch menu. Prices are reasonable for the area.

South Kensington & Knightsbridge

Much of **South Kensington** was conceived after the triumph of the **Great Exhibition** of 1851 (*see chapter* **Victorian Times**). Before that date, the area was semi rural, with market gardening being the main industry. But with the £200,000 profits obtained from the exhibition, Prince Albert set about building a more permanent showcase for the Arts, Science and Industry.

The 'museum village' of the **Victoria & Albert Museum**, the **Science Museum** and the **Natural History Museum** (for all, *see chapter* **Museums**) still dominates the area, along with the **Royal Albert Hall** (*see chapter* **Music: Classical & Opera**), but South Kensington is also a residential district. Its smart stuccoed terraces have accommodated the likes of Sir Winston Churchill (who lived at 28 Hyde Park Gate, SW7, just west of the Albert Hall, from 1945 until his death in 1965) and John F Kennedy (who, when his father was US Ambassador to Britain in 1939, stayed at 14 Princes Gate, SW7).

South Kensington's high street is the Old Brompton Road, and this, together with Bute Street and the district around Gloucester Road underground station, is where to find many of the area's local food shops, bars and wide variety of restaurants.

The name **Knightsbridge** recalls the legend that two knights once fought a battle on a bridge over the Westbourne River. In the eighteenth century, the Westbourne was dammed to fill the Serpentine Lake in Hyde Park, and Knightsbridge was gobbled up by London.

During the mid-nineteenth century, Knightsbridge prospered from the museum developments at nearby South Kensington and found itself fashionable. Its modest cottages were transformed into *pieds-à-terre* for the wealthy, and one of its traders, Charles Harrod, decided to expand his father's grocery shop.

Nowadays, most visitors flock to the area to visit **Harrods** (*see chapter* **Shopping**) or one of the many other expensive stores that line Knightsbridge and the Brompton Road. But there are plenty of interesting mews and small streets to wander round, away from the traffic-clogged main thoroughfares. Try to the west of Knightsbridge Green (site of the original village), or to the east of Sloane Street. The **Star Tavern** (*see chapter* **Eating & Drinking**) on Belgrave Mews West is one of the best pubs in this area.

Transport
Knightsbridge or South Kensington underground.

Bar Escoba
102 Old Brompton Road, SW7 (071 373 2403). Gloucester Road or South Kensington underground. **Open** 11am-11pm Mon-Sat; 11am-10.30pm Sun. **Average** £14. **Credit** A, TC, V.
Food is served throughout the day and evening at the lively Escoba, either in the form of tapas at the bar, or more substantial Spanish meals in the restaurant at the back. A young international crowd comes here to join in the fun, which is often boosted by live music.

Hyde Park Barracks
Knightsbridge, SW1. Knightsbridge underground.
Every day at 10.30am the Household Cavalry can be seen riding through Hyde Park from the barracks to Buckingham Palace. The Life Guards wear red tunics and white helmet plumes; the Blues and Royals sport blue tunics and red plumes. Basil Spence's brutal 1959 building design has been popularly (and properly) barracked as an eyesore.

Chelsea & Fulham

Quentin Crisp, who relishes his nickname, 'the stately homo of England', once said of Chelsea that it was the one area of London '... in which you can behave so badly with so little risk'. But this reputation for bohemian excess has only been built up over the past century.

Chelsea began life as a quiet fishing village, and in Tudor times it became fashionable to have an out-of-town riverside residence here, with Henry VIII and Sir Thomas More starting the trend (*see chapter* **Tudors & Stuarts**). Much of the area was once owned by Sir Hans Sloane 1660-1753 who became Lord of the Manor of Chelsea. He was a physician and botanist, and his collection of objects of natural history and manuscripts formed the basis of what is today the British Museum.

Pre-Raphaelite painter Dante Gabriel Rossetti

did more than most to establish Chelsea's arty credentials when he moved in to **Cheyne Walk** with his menagerie of peacocks, a kangaroo and a wombat. Today Cheyne Walk overlooks busy Chelsea Embankment, but until the 1870s, it was a peaceful riverside promenade. The walls of its buildings are peppered with blue plaques. JMW Turner (No.119), Mary Ann Evans 'George Eliot' (No.4), and Hilaire Belloc (No.103) are just some of the former residents. A more recent inhabitant was Rolling Stone Mick Jagger. Nos. 19 to 26 are on the site of Chelsea Manor, where Queen Elizabeth I lived as a child. **Crosby Hall** (*see chapter* **Roman to Norman**) also occupies the Walk, and there's a good pub, The King's Head & Eight Bells at No.50. **Carlyle's House** is in nearby Cheyne Row (*see chapter*

Museums). A short distance further west along the river lies Chelsea Harbour, a modern 'village' with a few shops and restaurants around a yacht-festooned marina.

Oscar Wilde also came to live in Chelsea, at 34 Tite Street (a rather ugly red-brick building, that Wilde insisted – wrongly – had been the home of Keats). In 1895, Wilde stayed at the Cadogan Hotel at 75 Sloane Street, SW1 (off Sloane Square). It was here that he was arrested, eventually being sentenced to two years' hard labour for acts of gross indecency.

Modern Chelsea begins at Sloane Square, close to the site of the Chelsea Bun House, which stood on Pimlico Road until 1839. This shop sold the original Chelsea bun, a rather delicious sticky and spicy confection filled with

King's Road

Once used by Charles II as his private road from Whitehall Palace to Hampton Court, the King's Road leapt to fame as the epicentre of 'swinging London' in the sixties. Grocers, bakers and butchers that once served the locals gave way to fashion shops and antiques galleries.

The road managed to maintain its popularity through the seventies, when the safety pins and Mohican haircuts of punk rockers, took over from the mini skirts and bell-bottoms of the hippy era, and Vivienne Westwood and Malcolm McLaren opened the now legendary Sex, later Seditionaries. The latest manifestation of the shop, **World's End** (at No.430), continues to showcase Westwood's bizarre clothing designs.

Many other fashion and antiques shops remain today (*see chapter* **Shopping**), albeit depleted by the recession. **Bluebird Garage** at No.350 contains dozens of stalls with street fashions from established names and newer talent; **Antiquarious** (No.137), the **Chenil Galleries** (No.181-3), and the **Chelsea Antiques Market** (No.253) each house a bunch of antiques dealers. There's also plenty of restaurants along the road's two miles (3km) stretch before it becomes the New King's Road in Fulham. Near Sloane Square are the chainstores; the middle third of it is where to look for the best bars and boutiques.

A number of handsome squares open onto the King's Road; Wellington Square with its stuccoed terraces is one of the grandest. Contrast it with the quaint artisan dwellings

(now trendy town houses) found on Bywater Street, opposite.

Although the King's Road Saturday parade of the painfully trendy has lapsed somewhat in recent years, it is still discernible: dress up to come here and watch the free spectacle.
King's Road, *SW3, SW10. Sloane Square underground/11, 22, 211 bus.*

raisins. The square also gave rise to the term Sloane Ranger which was coined to describe the young upper-class socialites who frequent the bars and restaurants of this area.

Chelsea begins to unfold as you travel down its long central artery, the **King's Road** (*see* **Box**). Nip down Lower Sloane Street for a sight of red-coated Chelsea pensioners and the **Royal Hospital** (*see chapter* **Tudors & Stuarts**).

One of the finest night-time views of the Thames can be seen by looking from Battersea Bridge, off Cheyne Walk, towards Albert Bridge, a stately Victorian structure that is illuminated by hundreds of light bulbs.

Fulham possesses the longest river frontage of any of London's boroughs. It was the site of a manor as early as AD 691, but came to prominence in the eighth century as the site of **Fulham Palace**. Country houses and market gardens accounted for most of the area until the nineteenth century. One of them, built in 1797, now houses the **Hurlingham Club**, home of croquet (*see chapter* **Sport & Fitness**).

Fulham today is a largely residential borough, one which has become noticeably gentrified in the past 20 years. The Brompton Cross end of Fulham Road forms a tight-knit community of high-fashion shops and restaurants, dominated by **Michelin House** (*see chapter* **Early Twentieth Century**). For a more peaceful time, take a stroll through **Brompton Cemetery** (*see chapter* **Victorian Times**).

Transport

Fulham Broadway, Sloane Square or West Brompton underground/11, 22, 211 bus.

Chelsea Kitchen

98 King's Road, SW3 (071 589 1330). Sloane Square underground/11, 19 bus. **Meals served** 8am-11.45pm Mon-Sat; noon-11.30pm Sun. **Average** £5. **Credit** LV, £TC.
One of the best low-price restaurants in town. A lively throng comes to enjoy the eclectic mix of food (from curries to pasta), to drink the house wine (only £4.60 a bottle), and in summer, to sit at tables outside.

Chelsea Old Church

Cheyne Walk, SW3 (071 352 5627). Sloane Square underground/19, 39, 45, 49, 219 bus. **Services** 8am Thur; noon Fri; 8am, 10am, 11am (matins), noon, 6pm Sun.
Most of this riverside church was destroyed in World War II, but the original structure dated back to 1157. Henry VIII reputedly married his third wife Jane Seymour here before their state wedding, and Sir Thomas More had a private chapel built on to the church in 1528. The church has now been rebuilt, but the monuments within are the most interesting aspect. Look for the memorials to Henry James and the architect Sir Hans Sloane – after whom Sloane Square and Sloane Street are named.

Fulham Palace

Bishop's Avenue, Fulham Palace Road, SW6 (071 736 3233). Putney Bridge underground/220 bus. **Open** 2-5pm Wed-Sun. **Admission** 50p adults; 25p children, OAPs, students, UB40s.

From the eighth century right up to 1973, Fulham Palace was the official residence of the Bishops of London. The present building dates from Tudor times and part of it is now open as a museum, detailing the history of the palace, the bishopric and the archaeology of the site. Displays are based in Bishop Howley's dining room and the Porteus Library. There are free tours of the palace and its grounds once a month (phone for details). You can also stroll through the surrounding **Bishop's Park** (open daily from dawn to dusk) which contains many plants that were brought back from the Americas in the seventeenth century.

Henry J Bean's Bar & Grill

195-197 King's Road, SW3 (071 352 9255). Sloane Square underground, then 11, 14, 19, 22, 49 bus. **Open** 11.45am-11pm Mon-Sat; noon-10.30pm Sun. **Credit** A, AmEx, £$TC, V.
Students, trendies, visitors and locals crowd into this big barn of a bar to drink cocktails, perhaps a tequila or two, or one of the bottled beers. Burgers and hot dogs are served daily until half an hour before closing.

North End Road Market

SW6. Fulham Broadway or West Kensington underground/11, 14, 28, 91, 283 bus. **Open** 8.30am-6pm Mon-Wed, Fri, Sat; 8.30am-1pm Thur.
A thriving market notable for the sheer diversity of goods on sale. Among the highlights are exotic fruit, fresh salmon and eels, an excellent plant stall, crockery and hardware. North End Road also has a treasured stock of local shops. At No.308 is the Jolly Brewer, a busy local boozer.

The Pie & Mash Shop

140 Wandsworth Bridge Road, SW6 (071 731 1232). Fulham Broadway or Parsons Green underground/28, 44, 295 bus. **Open** 11.45am-6pm Mon-Wed; 11.45am-8pm Thur, Fri; 11am-6pm Sat. **No credit cards.**
When in Fulham, stop off for a cheap lunch at this traditional pie and mash caff with beautiful original tiled walls and bench seating. Jellied eels, mashed potato, meat pies and liquor (green sauce made of parsley), plus a pie and custard for pudding, can all be had for under £5.

Ranelagh Gardens

Entrance on Royal Hospital Road, SW3, or Chelsea Embankment, SW3. Sloane Square underground. **Open** 10am-1pm, 2pm-sunset, Mon-Sat; 2pm-sunset Sun.
In the eighteenth century Ranelagh Gardens attracted the elite of London society, who promenaded around it on summer evenings. The eight year old Mozart gave a concert here in 1764. Canaletto's painting of the gardens can be seen in the National Gallery. The **Chelsea Flower Show** (*see chapter* **London By Season**) is held in the grounds every May, but on any fine day, the gardens provide a beautiful setting for a walk, or for views of the **Royal Hospital** (*see chapter* **Tudors & Stuarts**) contained within them.

Hammersmith & Chiswick

With both the Roman-built Bath Road and the River Thames passing through it, **Hammersmith** had long been a prosperous village when London claimed it as a suburb over a hundred years ago.

Queen Caroline Street, which runs from Hammersmith Broadway to the river, commemorates the fact that Caroline of Brunswick, estranged wife of George IV, once lived nearby. On George's accession to the throne in 1820, he tried unsuccessfully to divorce Caroline. The would-be queen wanted to be crowned, but she was refused entry to Westminster Abbey when she tried to gatecrash the coronation. The House of Windsor is now hoping that this unseemly episode in the Royal Family's history won't be repeated.

Modern Hammersmith is an extremely busy part of west London, with the main A4 route to the centre of town roaring through it (or over it in the case of the vast concrete flyover). Its high street, King Street, contains chainstores, a small fruit and veg market and the Lyric theatre, from which many productions transfer to West End theatres (*see chapter* **Theatre**). Hammersmith also boasts a first-rate arts centre, the **Riverside Studios** (*see chapter* **Art Galleries**), with its own café and restaurant.

Yet it's easy to escape the traffic: just head for the river. The path from Hammersmith Bridge to Chiswick is one of the most attractive riverside walks in London. A succession of beautiful eighteenth-century houses look out on to the Thames. One of them, Kelmscott House on Upper Mall, was once owned by William Morris, and was the point whence the hero in his socialist Utopian novel *News From Nowhere* started out for a trip up-river.

A splendid way of finishing an hour's stroll along the river from Hammersmith Bridge (perhaps via the Dove pub, *see chapter* **Eating & Drinking**) is to visit Hogarth's House (*see chapter* **Georgian London**) in Chiswick. Simply continue along the river until Church Street, walk to the end of this short road and take the subway (underpass) at the Hogarth Roundabout under the Great West Road to Hogarth Lane.

From this point, the Thames loops and becomes difficult to follow. Take Burlington Lane from the Hogarth Roundabout and you will pass the walled grounds of **Chiswick House** (*see chapter* **Georgian London**). After half a mile (1km) you will reach Chiswick BR station.

If you wish to continue the walk, head along Grove Park Road and back to the river at Strand-on-the-Green. This pathway is exceptionally pleasing on a summer's day, with willows lining the riverbank, and diminutive Georgian houses backing on to the river. Some (see Nos. 47 and 49) have tiny doors as a safeguard against flooding.

There are three pubs in close proximity on the Strand-on-the-Green. The Bell & Crown (72 Strand-on-the-Green, W4, 081 994 4164) has the best beer, brewed locally by Fullers; but the City Barge (27 Strand-on-the-Green, 081 994 2148), which dates from 1484, has the best food (served at lunchtimes and early evenings daily).

The Strand-on-the-Green, **Chiswick.**

From both of these pubs, there's a view across the Thames to Oliver's Island, where Cromwell supposedly hid from the Cavalier army during the English Civil War. The **Royal Botanic Gardens, Kew** (*see chapter* **Sightseeing**) are less than a mile across the river from here.

All along this stretch of the Thames, rowing teams can often be seen practising. And every spring, the crews taking part in the **Oxford and Cambridge Boat Race** (*see chapter* **London By Season**) steam through both Chiswick and Hammersmith on their way from Mortlake to Putney.

Transport
Gunnersbury, Hammersmith or Kew Gardens underground/Chiswick or Kew Bridge BR.

Fuller Smith & Turner Brewery
Griffin Brewery, Chiswick Lane South, W4 (081 994 3691). Hammersmith or Turnham Green underground. **Open** 10am-4pm Mon-Fri. **Tours** 1pm Mon, Wed, Thur; 4pm Thur. **Price** £41 per group (max 15), £2.50 per extra person by appointment.
Fuller's, one of London's two surviving independent brewers, has been making ale here since 1845, though the Griffin Brewery has operated for more than 300 years. Tours are booked up for months in advance (write for information), but beer can be bought direct from the brewery (the minimum amount sold is 14 pt/10.25 litres for about £13).

The Gate
51 Queen Caroline Street, W6 (081 748 6932). Hammersmith underground. **Lunch served** noon-3pm Tue-Fri; noon-5pm Sat. **Dinner served** 6-10.45pm Mon-Sat. **Average** £12. **Credit** A, LV, V.
High-quality vegetarian food is served in rather basic surroundings at this first-floor restaurant above a Christian Community Centre.

South London

Grandiose Greenwich and regal Richmond may grab the limelight, but there's plenty of local streetlife at Battersea and Brixton.

Battersea

Until the eighteenth century, Battersea was a small village whose boundaries were the Thames to the north and marshes to the south. The district was known for its market gardening, particularly for lavender. One of its main streets is still called Lavender Hill.

The first Battersea Bridge was built in 1771, and from that date manufacturing grew rapidly. The pace of industrialisation was stepped up with the opening of Clapham Junction Station in 1863. Much of the area remained solidly working class until the 1980s, when there was an influx of upwardly mobile professionals who found the Victorian housing and the area's proximity to central London to their taste. The *nouveaux arrivistes* pompously christened the area 'South Chelsea'.

Today, the skyline is still dominated by Battersea Power Station, the largest brick building in Europe. Resembling an upturned table, Giles Gilbert Scott's 1926 art deco design is officially protected, yet this much-loved landmark now faces possible demolition. An incompetent attempt to turn it into a theme park has tragically left it a semi-ruin. It's now destined to remain in a state of neglect until someone finds enough money to restart the grandiose plans for its revival.

Lavender Hill is the main shopping and entertainment area of the district, with **Jongleurs at the Cornet** (*see chapter* **Comedy**) and **Battersea Arts Centre (BAC)** along its route; the **Grand** is on nearby St John's Hill (*see chapter* **Music: Rock, Folk & Jazz**). Battersea's oldest part is around **St Mary's Church**, built by the river in 1775. One of the most notable buildings here is Old Battersea House in Vicarage Crescent, dated 1699.

You'll never be far from a park in Battersea. To the south-west lies Wandsworth Common, where cricket is played on summer Sundays. To the south-east is Clapham Common, a popular sunbathing spot. And to the north is **Battersea Park** which stretches to the banks of the Thames. The **Ship** on Jews Row (*see chapter* **Eating & Drinking**) is one of the area's most popular pubs, overlooking the river.

Transport
Clapham Junction or Battersea Park BR/45, 77, 156 bus.

Arding & Hobbs
Lavender Hill, SW11 (071 228 8877). Clapham Junction BR/45, 77, 137 bus. **Open** 9am-5.30pm Mon-Wed; 9am-8pm Thur; 9am-6pm Fri, Sat. **Credit** A, AmEx, DC, V.
A large, old-fashioned, shabby department store, where you can buy household goods, clothing and furniture at fairly cheap prices. It doesn't have a food hall, but there is a restaurant.

Battersea Arts Centre (BAC)
Old Town Hall, Lavender Hill, SW11 (box office 071 223 8413). Clapham South underground/Clapham Junction BR/45, 77, 156 bus. **Membership** £15.
Battersea's acclaimed arts centre has three theatre spaces where regular productions are staged; the emphasis is on new writing. Children's theatre takes over on Saturday afternoons at 2.30pm – admission is only £1.50 for children. A jazz and comedy club is run every Friday night.

Battersea Park
Albert Bridge Road, SW11 (081 871 7530). Sloane Square underground/Battersea Park or Queenstown Road BR/19, 39, 44, 45, 49, 130, 131, 170 bus. **Open** dawn to dusk daily.
The Duke of Wellington fought a duel on land that became Battersea Park, with a Lord Winchelsea over the Catholic Emancipation Bill in 1829. It's less dangerous territory now, and is a good place to watch the river go by. The land was turned into a park in 1858 and opened by Queen Victoria, but it's most famous for its Festival Gardens, a major attraction of the 1951 Festival of Britain (*see chapter* **Post-War London**). Events held here include Buddhist contemplation on Hiroshima Day (8

St Mary's, Battersea. *See* **review** *page 105.*

Aug) at the ornate riverside pagoda. For sporty types, there are 19 tennis courts to choose from.
Boating lake. Garden for the disabled. Zoo.

Northcote Road Markets
Northcote Road, SW11 (antiques market 071 228 6850). Clapham Junction BR/49 bus. **Open** *antiques market* 10am-6pm Mon-Sat; noon-5pm Sun. *General market* 9am-5pm Mon, Tue, Thur-Sat; 9am-1pm Wed.
The Northcote Road is a bustling mix of nationalities and classes – Halal butchers, Italian delicatessens and West Indian greengrocers. The general market has a wealth of good-quality fruit and veg, plus women's clothing. At No.155A, you'll find a small covered antiques market where 30 traders sell jewellery, china and furniture, specialising in Victoriana and art deco. There's a café upstairs.

St Mary's, Battersea
Battersea Church Road, SW11 (071 228 9648). Bus 19, 219. **Open** Fri afternoons, phone first. **Services** 11am Sun.
There has been a church on this site since Norman times, but the present simple edifice was built in the eighteenth century. One of the more startling monuments here is to Sir Edward Wynter, an East India merchant whose exploits, recorded in verse, included crushing a tiger to death in his arms, and routing 40 mounted Moors single-handed. In this church in 1782, William Blake, the great mystic poet and painter, married the daughter of a local market gardener. And in 1801, the American traitor of the War of Independence, General Benedict Arnold, was buried in the crypt. Later in the nineteenth century, J M W Turner came regularly to the church to paint the view here. His work can be seen in the **Tate Gallery** *(see chapter* **Art Galleries**).

Gallery Tea Rooms
103 Lavender Hill, SW11 (071 350 2564). Clapham Junction BR/45, 77 bus. **Open** 11am-midnight Mon-Sat; 11am-7pm Sun. **Credit** £TC.
A tearoom that looks like a tearoom should, in a *fin de siècle*, bric-à-brac stuffed sort of way. Traditional teas are served with aplomb, buttered scones and the occasional cucumber sandwich. There's a drinks licence, and Saturday and Sunday brunch is served from 11am-2pm.

Brixton

Little of Brixton existed before the 1870s. But from this decade until the beginning of World War I, its growth was explosive. Streets were laid on former fields and thousands of modest terraced dwellings were built to house local workers. **Brixton Market** *(see* **Box**) also dates from the end of the last century.

After World War II, thousands of people from the West Indies came to Britain to help solve its post-war labour shortage. Many of them settled in Brixton which could offer a choice of inexpensive housing.

The riots of 1981 and 1985 gave Brixton its reputation as a recalcitrant ghetto, and it became the subject of a myriad government initiatives. The local community has since built the district back into a busy commercial centre, but many of its problems remain unresolved.

You'll need to keep your wits about you in Brixton, but outside of the **Notting Hill**

Carnival *(see chapter* **London by Season**), this is the best place to sample the vibrant culture of London's West Indian community. For African and West Indian restaurants, *see chapter* **Eating & Drinking.**

Transport
Brixton underground.

Black Cultural Archives Museum
378 Coldharbour Lane, SW9 (071 738 4591). Brixton underground/BR. **Open** *office* 9am-5pm Mon-Fri; *archives* 9am-4pm Mon-Fri (appointment only); *museum* 10am-6pm Mon-Fri. **Admission** free.
The permanent collection in the museum charts the achievements of black people in Britain from Roman times to the present day. There are also regular changing exhibitions of artists' work or on specific themes. Timbuktu Books at the museum sells literature on related subjects.

Brixtonian
11 Dorrell Place, SW9 (071 978 8870). Brixton underground/BR. **Open** 5.30-11pm Mon; 11am-midnight Tue-Sat; noon-11pm Sun. **Happy hour** 5.30-7.30pm Mon-Fri. **Credit** A, £TC, V.
A middle-class enclave off busy Brixton Road, the Brixtonian is a very popular smart bar with a pricey Afro-Caribbean restaurant upstairs. Come here for designer beers, cocktails and, sometimes, live jazz and blues.

Pizzeria Franco
4 Market Row, Brixton Market, Electric Lane, SW9 (071 738 3021). Brixton underground/BR. **Meals** served 11.30am-5pm Mon, Tue, Thur-Sat. **Average** £7. **No credit cards.**
Try to sample Franco's excellent traditional pizza and calzone in mid-afternoon. It's a tiny café and gets impossibly crowded at lunch, with market-goers milling past.

Brixton Market

The influx of a large number of mostly working-class, mostly West Indian immigrants has, paradoxically, tended to preserve the essence of pre-sixties London life at Brixton Market. Although the range of commodities is startlingly different to what went before, the structure of the shops has remained the same. Away from the main Brixton Road, chainstores are few, lock-up shops are many, and the arcades are full of individual food stalls, rather than the same old boutiques.

Wander down **Electric Avenue** and you are eased into the market by a few nondescript stalls where fruit and veg, haberdashery, toys and women's shoes are sold. Past the junction with Electric Lane, the Avenue curves smoothly round to the left, showing the Victorian housing off to good effect. It is here that the first of many lock-up shops featuring the raw materials of Caribbean cooking makes an appearance. Brixton Market has the largest selection of African and Caribbean food in Europe. Yam, long black plantain, mangos and okra are everywhere. West Indian butchers' shops are also much in evidence, with unbleached tripe hung like dish-rags on meat hooks. Goat meat for currying is another popular line, as are trotters and calfheads.

Electric Avenue stops at the junction with Atlantic Road, the street that runs through the centre of the Brixton market area. Atlantic Road is where the market started, in the 1870s, but stalls were banned from here some 70 years ago because of the obstruction to traffic. So there is now an incongruous hiatus to the proceedings.

However, both the main indoor arcades, **Market Row** and **Granville Arcade**, have entrances on Atlantic Road. They are tatty and peeling, but both are great places for African and Caribbean food. Market Row has an excellent fish store with stocks of silver pollock, jackfish, talapias and yellow snappers. There are also butchers' shops, a DIY store, a collection of caffs and a smelly store selling strange vegetables, pulses, flours, saltfish and pigtails.

Granville Arcade is even better. Built in 1937, it has had few coats of paint since. Yet the yellow peeling walls, the cacophony of exotic languages, the thumping reggae and the alluring aromas make the arcade one of the most exciting shopping places in London. Stores are arranged in avenues but are otherwise in no particular order. The **Wig Bazaar**, with its selection of glossy black, red, yellow, brown and orange hair extensions, is on 3rd Avenue. Further along, you're likely to encounter a herd of cows' feet crammed into cardboard boxes.

Back outside and across Atlantic Road, the market continues on **Popes Road**, which goes underneath one of the many railway bridges in Brixton. Stalls seem to cling to the Victorian redbrick arches that bisect the district, and blaring music competes with the rumbling trains. A herb and tonic stallholder usually occupies a pitch under the first bridge on Popes Road, selling what at first appears to be bags of humus. Closer inspection reveals a collection of bitterwood, Jamaican sorrel and a hotchpotch of potions.

Popes Road ends at a T-junction with Brixton Station Road. To the right are about a dozen junk stalls, including many crammed with good-quality, cheap second-hand clothes. To the left, there's more fruit and veg, and some cheap jewellery. Pungent sweet smoke often floats down the street, emanating from one of the small group of quasi-religious stalls near the Brixton Road. Clumps of incense sticks are set alight and Islamic tracts are offered in print or on tape. Opposite this store, striking Rastafarian priests sell similar goods promulgating their religion. Tall, black and gracile in white robes, they bring a certain elegance to the area.

As if to counteract this refinement, a tatty speaker belts out the belching bass of raw reg-

gae from **Bob's Jamaican Food** takeaway nearby. Hardware soup is the evocatively-named speciality here: cowfoot, cowtail, goat and yam are among the ingredients.

Expect the unexpected at Brixton Market. On our last visit we encountered a large, muscular man parading around the stalls with a large and lively boa constrictor. Across the street, Jimi Hendrix's *Stone Free* was throbbing out of a butcher's shop: Brixton was grooving.

Brixton Market *Brixton Station Road, Electric Avenue and Popes Road SW9. Brixton underground/BR.* **Open** 8am-6pm Mon, Tue, Thur; 8am-1pm Wed; 8am-7pm Fri; 8am-6pm Sat.

Greenwich

The Thames runs deep and wide at Greenwich; for centuries, large ships have travelled up the Thames from the sea to dock here. In 1012, one such vessel belonged to Vikings who took hostage and executed Alphege, the Archbishop of Canterbury. A church dedicated to the canonised Archbishop was built on the site of the murder. (The present church, by Hawksmoor, was built in 1714 after the original had fallen down, *see chapter* **Georgian London**.)

But as well as its maritime history, Greenwich has long been associated with royalty. King Henry VIII and both his daughters who were to become queens, Mary and Elizabeth, were born here. Their home (known as the Palace of Placentia) was built by Humphrey Duke of Gloucester in the early fifteenth century.

England's greatest architects of the seventeenth and eighteenth centuries all designed buildings in Greenwich. Inigo Jones was the first, attaching the **Queen's House** (*see chapter* **Tudors & Stuarts**) to the original palace. Then, when Charles II came to the throne, he commissioned Christopher Wren to build the **Old Royal Observatory** (*see chapter* **Tudors & Stuarts**) in Greenwich Park. Charles also had the original Tudor palace pulled down and appointed Inigo Jones's nephew and pupil, John Webb, to build a new one, to be known as the King's House. Only the western part was completed before the king died.

In 1694, the palace ceased to be a royal home and work began to transform it into a hospital dedicated to the support of naval pensioners. Wren built the south-west wing (1698-1703) and the west front was finished in 1726 by Sir John Vanbrugh. Since 1873, the building has been the headquarters for the **Royal Naval College** (*see chapter* **Tudors & Stuarts**).

The site also contains the **National Maritime Museum** (*see chapter* **Museums**) designed by Jones and added to by Wren. Together, these buildings make up the most magnificent organ-

Greenwich Park: *wide-open spaces, topped by the Old Royal Observatory. See* **review**.

ised display of classical and baroque architecture to be seen in Britain.

Greenwich today is best reached by boat from Charing Cross or Tower Pier (*see chapter* **Getting Around**). On landing, you'll first see the masts of the **Cutty Sark** and **Gipsy Moth IV**. As well as its famous sights, Greenwich contains many restaurants, pubs and tea rooms; it's a bit touristy, but still makes an excellent day's excursion. Trips are also run from Greenwich Pier to the **Thames Barrier** (*see chapter* **East End & Docklands**).

One of the most impressive views of Greenwich can be seen by taking the Greenwich Foot Tunnel under the Thames (open 24 hours daily, lift open 5am-9pm daily) and looking across the river. The tunnel links Greenwich Pier and the Isle of Dogs in Docklands, from where it is possible to take the Docklands Light Railway back to Tower Hill (*see chapter* **Getting Around**).

Transport
Greenwich BR/Island Gardens DLR/177, 180, 286 bus.

Cutty Sark
King William Walk, SE10 (081 858 3445). Greenwich or Maze Hill BR/Island Gardens DLR/177, 180, 286 bus/boat to Greenwich Pier. **Open** *Apr-Sept* 10am-6pm Mon-Sat; noon-6pm Sun. *Oct-Mar* 10am-5pm Mon-Sat; noon-5pm Sun. (Last admission 30 mins before closing). **Admission** £3.25 adults; £2.25 under-15s, OAPs; £7.50 family ticket. Children must be accompanied by an adult. **Credit** (shop only) A, V.
The *Cutty Sark* is the closest to perfection that a sailing ship could be. The world's only surviving tea and wool clipper, this 1869 vessel was a wonder of its times, smashing speed records. You're free to roam about the beautifully-restored decks and crew's quarters and gaze up at the masts and rigging. Inside are collections of prints and naval relics, plus the world's largest collection of carved and painted figureheads.
English, French & German information point. Shop. Underground car park. Wheelchair access to one deck only.

Gipsy Moth IV
King William Walk, Greenwich, SE10 (081 853 3589).

Greenwich or Maze Hill BR/1, 177, 188 bus/boat to Greenwich Pier. **Open** *Easter-Oct* 10am-6pm Mon-Sat; noon-6pm Sun (last admission 5.30pm). **Admission** 50p adults; 30p under-16s, OAPs.
Beside the *Cutty Sark*, *Gipsy Moth IV* looks like a toy, but it's a record-breaking boat. Francis Chichester deserved his knighthood just for staying on it for 226 days at the age of 66, let alone for using the 54ft (16m) craft to make the first English solo circumnavigation of the world in 1966-67. Only enthusiasts need pay the admission fee: circumnavigating its exterior is free.

Greenwich Market
College Approach, Stockwell Street and corner of High Road and Royal Hill SE10. Greenwich BR/108, 177, 188 bus. **Open** 9am-6pm Sat, Sun.
The antiques and crafts market at Greenwich has enjoyed tremendous growth over the past decade. Dozens of trestle tables materialise here every weekend, stacked with banknotes, medals, old books, art deco furniture and assorted bric-à-brac. There is also a covered crafts market held on the site of a fruit and veg market built in 1737. Look for the inscription over the exit: 'A false balance is abomination to the Lord, but a just weight is his delight'. Today the market has clothes made by young designers, handmade jewellery and accessories. There are pubs and a café nearby.

Greenwich Park
Charlton Way, SE10 (081 858 2608). Greenwich or Maze Hill BR/177, 180, 286 bus/boat to Greenwich Pier. **Open** *Pedestrians* 5am-dusk daily; *Traffic* 7am-dusk daily.
The remains of a Roman temple and some 20 Saxon grave-mounds have been identified in Greenwich Park, but this beautiful spot is more famous for its Tudor and Stuart history. Both Henry VIII and Elizabeth I threw lavish parties here during their reigns. The area was first enclosed by the Duke of Gloucester in 1433, then tastefully re-designed in the 1660s for Charles II by Le Nôtre, who landscaped Versailles. Crowning Greenwich Hill is the Old Royal Observatory and the Wolfe Monument (which commemorates General James Wolfe who helped win Canada for Britain: he once lived in Macartney House, to the west of the park, now converted into flats). The view from here, over the Queen's House, Royal Hospital and the river, is one of the best in London. Further back is a deer enclosure and Blackheath. In summer, brass bands perform (Whit Sunday to end September; 3-4.30pm and 6-7.30pm Sun) and there are puppet shows in the children's play-

ground during August. The park also has an attractive café, the **Bosun's Whistle**, with hot dishes for lunch and teas in the afternoon.

Greenwich Theatre

Crooms Hill, Greenwich, SE10 (081 858 7755).
Greenwich BR/1, 177, 180 bus. **Open** *box office* 10am-8.30pm Mon-Sat. **Performances** 7.45pm Mon-Sat; *Matinées* 2.30pm Sat. **Tickets** £9.50-£12.75. **Credit** A, AmEx, DC, £TC, V.
Once a music hall, Greenwich Theatre now stages an eclectic programme of good, solid drama, with occasional gems that transfer to the West End. It has a picture gallery and a restaurant where there's live jazz on Sunday lunchtimes.

Greenwich Tourist Information Centre

46 Greenwich Church Street, SE10 (081 858 6376).
Open 10.15am-4.45pm daily.
Staff here will provide information about all aspects of Greenwich past and present. The centre is also used as a starting point for walking tours of the area (phone 081 858 6169 for details).

Richmond & Kew

Both Richmond and Kew are within easy reach of central London, but situated on its outskirts, they still have something of the country town about them. Kew's main attraction is undoubtedly the **Royal Botanic Gardens** *(see chapter* **Sightseeing**), but **Kew Palace** and Kew Green, with its charming seventeenth- and eighteenth-century houses should also not be missed. After crossing Kew Bridge, an energetic walk in either direction will take you to **Syon House** and Park *(see chapter* **Georgian London**), or **Strand-on-the-Green** *(see chapter* **West: Chiswick**) with its three old pubs.

Richmond is a long walk (down busy Kew Road) or a short bus journey (bus 65) from Kew. It has long been a privileged town, patronised by monarchs since the twelfth century. The district belonged to the Anglo-Saxon manor of Shene until 1499, when Henry VII named his new palace (the remains are by the river) after his Yorkshire estate of Rychemonde. Henry VIII came here to hunt; Elizabeth I came here to die. Up the steep hill is the nearest gate to **Richmond Park**, the largest city park in Europe *(see chapter* **Sightseeing**). One of London's best views of the Thames can be seen looking down from Howson Terrace, just off Richmond Hill.

There are several small shops to be explored around the beautiful Richmond Green area – some are shamelessly twee – and the town has two good theatres. **Richmond Theatre** (The Green, 081 940 0088) puts on mainstream touring productions, often featuring famous actors. The **Orange Tree Theatre** (1 Clarence Street, 081 940 3633) has two stages: downstairs is an Off-West End venue, upstairs is for fringe theatre.

Surrounded as it is by parkland, the Kew and Richmond area is the venue for much sporting activity. In winter, rugby is the major sport, with most of London's top teams having their grounds in the district *(see chapter* **Sport & Fitness**). In summer, cricket matches can be seen on Kew Green. And all year round, Richmond Park is a major destination for London's cycle-racing poseurs.

Both Kew and Richmond are best reached in summer by boat from **Westminster Pier**. You can also get to the area by tube or by overground train *(see chapter* **Getting Around**).

Transport

Kew Gardens or Richmond underground/Kew Bridge, Kew Gardens or Richmond BR.

Kew Palace

Kew Gardens, Richmond (081 940 3321). Kew Gardens underground/Kew Gardens or Kew Bridge BR/boat to Kew Pier/7, 22, 65, 90B, 237, 267 bus. **Open** *Apr-Sept* 11am-5.30pm daily (last admission 5.15pm). **Admission** £1.10 adults; 60p under-16s; 80p OAPs, students. **Credit** £TC.
The former name for this Jacobean mansion was the Dutch House, due to its distinctive gables. Built in 1631, it was purchased by George III in 1781 and used as a country retreat by the royal family until about 1820. It's the smallest and most intimate of the royal homes, but was modernised several times by its Georgian residents. Two floors are open to the public, decorated in eighteenth-century style. There's also a small museum. *Cafés in gardens. Group discount. Shop. Wheelchair access to ground floor only.*

Maids of Honour

288 Kew Road, Richmond (081 940 2752). Kew Gardens underground/Kew Gardens or Kew Bridge BR/boat to Kew Pier/27, 65 bus. **Open** 9.30am-1pm Mon; 10am-6pm Tue-Fri; 9am-6pm Sat. *Lunch* 12.30-1.30pm Tue-Sat. *Set tea* 2.30-5.30pm Tue-Sat. **Average** *lunch* £7; *set tea* £3.95. **No credit cards.**
This famous old tea room is named after the tarts that Henry VIII liked so much – they were baked by a Maid of Honour he imprisoned in Richmond Palace to keep him supplied with the pastries. It would be a great place to visit for a few home-baked Maids of Honour after a stroll in Kew Gardens, if only it wasn't for the queues: more than 1,000 people are served per day on an average summer Saturday. Maddeningly, it is closed on Sundays. *Alcohol licence. Babies, children welcome; high chairs for babies; children's portions. Takeaway service.*

Museum of Richmond

Old Town Hall, Whittaker Avenue, Richmond (081 332 1141). Richmond underground/BR/boat to Richmond Pier/27, 33, 37, 65, 71, 202, 270 bus. **Open** 11am-5pm Tue-Sat (throughout the year); 2-5pm Sun (May-Oct only). **Admission** £1 adults; 50p under-16s, OAPs, students, UB40s. **No credit cards.**
The Victorian Old Town Hall, close to the river, now houses one of London's best local museums. Naturally it dwells on Richmond's popularity as a royal resort, although it doesn't ignore its newer commuterland role. The regularly changing exhibitions often focus on one of Richmond's famous former inhabitants (this illustrious group includes actor Edmund Kean, painters Gainsborough, Reynolds and Pissaro, and writers George Eliot, Virginia Woolf and Bertrand Russell). *Café (10am-5pm Mon-Sat; 2-5pm Sun). Shop. Wheelchair access.*

The City

Ancient and modern co-exist in London's financial district, with medieval churches nestling next to shiny new office blocks.

Known to Londoners simply as the City (note the capital C), the City of London is unique – an area of just one square mile (259 hectares) that dates back to Roman times, yet today rivals New York and Tokyo as the world's most important financial centre.

The key to the City's success was trade. Even in the first century AD it was described by the

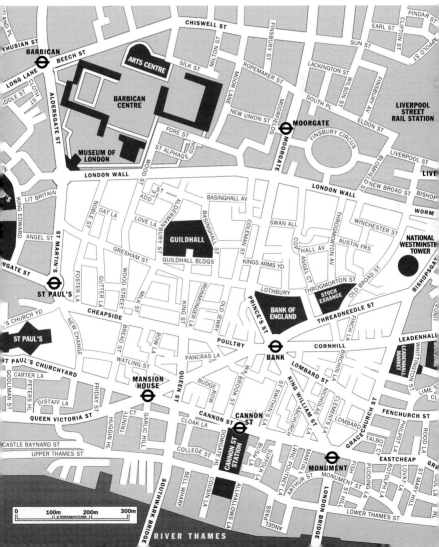

Roman historian Tacitus as 'a busy emporium for trade and traders'. But its unique status dates back to the Norman conquest of 1066, when William I granted the citizens of London a charter confirming their independence in return for recognising him as king. The king ruled at Westminster, but the merchants ruled in the City.

In 1215, King John confirmed the City's right to elect a mayor annually. The Lord Mayor of London still heads the Corporation of London, which is responsible for the area within the City boundaries. He (or, in one case, she) follows a tradition which extends back over 800 years, representing the City abroad and entertaining royalty and visiting VIPs. The annual Lord Mayor's Show (*see chapter* **London by Season**), when the new Lord Mayor is sworn in, is a great excuse for pageantry. Thousands of people line the City streets as the great procession of decorated floats and the Lord Mayor's golden coach pass by.

By the sixteenth century the City was the most prosperous port in the world, with a population of 200,000 crammed inside a city wall. But in the nineteenth century, as London expanded ever outwards and the docks moved further to the east, the area became the focus for banking, insurance and commodity exchanges, a role which continues today.

Barely 5,000 people now live within the Square Mile. But on working days, the influx of 300,000 City workers is a sight to behold at rush hour or during the lunch hour when pubs, wine bars and every available open space is full to bursting.

The artistic needs of the City's inhabitants are largely catered for by the Barbican Centre (*see chapter* **Music: Classical & Opera**). This vast brick conglomerate contains an assortment of exhibition halls, concert auditoria, an art gallery and three cinemas. It's the largest complex of its kind in Western Europe, and serves as home to the London Symphony Orchestra and is the London base of the Royal Shakespeare Company, both of which stage regular events. There's also an extensive library and various shops and refreshment areas, including a waterside terrace café and bars, and a conservatory. Sadly, though, it is an architectural mess, where an unsightly jumble of corridors ensures that all visitors manage to lose their way at least once.

The July **City of London Festival** is the Square Mile's biggest annual cultural event (for details, phone 071 377 0540). Its classical and jazz concerts are not confined to the Barbican and **Broadgate Arena** (*listed under* **Business**), but also test the acoustics of many City churches (*under* **Churches**).

Transport
Bank, Mansion House, Monument, Moorgate or St

Paul's underground/Cannon Street or Liverpool Street underground/BR.

The Old City

Two major fires devastated large areas of the City, in 1666 and 1940, destroying many of the old churches and historic buildings. Even so, much of the narrow medieval street plan has been retained in this small area. Hidden among the new skyscrapers, incongruous nuggets of the old city survive: the Roman wall (*see chapter* **Roman & Saxon London**); the ancient **Guildhall**; the spires and towers of the Wren churches; and the magnificent **St Paul's Cathedral** (*see chapter* **Sightseeing**).

Under the vigilant care of the Corporation, the City's streets are noticeably cleaner than the rest of London, and many small courts and former churchyards have been filled with trees and flowers, statues and fountains. These peaceful, secluded gardens provide a welcome respite for City workers and footsore visitors.

The story of London from its Roman beginnings, through the Plague, the Great Fire, Civil War, the Blitz to the present day financial metropolis is told at the **Museum of London** (*see chapter* **Museums**).

Bunhill Fields
City Road, EC1 (081 472 3584). Old Street underground. **Open** *Apr-Sept 7.30am-7pm Mon-Fri; Oct-Mar 7.30am-4pm Mon-Fri; 9.30am-4pm Sat, Sun.*
Bunhill probably got its name in 1549 when bones from the charnel chapel of St Paul's were deposited here. From 1665 until 1855 it was used as a graveyard. Daniel Defoe, William Blake and John Bunyan are all buried in the peaceful, shaded gardens.

City of London Information Centre
St Paul's Churchyard (on the south side of the Cathedral), EC4 (071 606 3030). **Open** *9.30am-5pm daily.*
Contact the centre for information on walks and events within the Square Mile.

College of Arms
Queen Victoria Street, EC4 (071 248 2762). Blackfriars underground/BR. **Open** *10am-4pm Mon-Fri.* **Admission** *free.*
Since 1484, the College of Arms has been the home of heraldry. Its seventeenth-century building has recently been restored and it is from here that the college grants coats of arms to those who think they are worthy having and can afford them. If you want to trace your roots, write for an appointment to the Officer in Waiting, College of Arms, Queen Victoria Street, EC4 (071 248 0893). The college is linked with the **Heralds' Museum** at the Tower of London (*see chapter* **Sightseeing**). *Tour by prior arrangement.*

Guildhall
off Gresham Street, EC2 (071 606 3030). Bank underground. **Open** *Guildhall 10am-5pm daily; clock museum 9.30am-4.30pm Mon-Fri.* **Admission** *free.*
Guildhall has been the centre of the City's local government for over 800 years. The fifteenth-century Great Hall, twice gutted by fire, has been beautifully restored. Meetings of the Court of Common Council (the govern-

ing body for the Corporation of London), presided over by the Lord Mayor, are held here every third Thursday, except during August (visitors are welcome; phone for dates). It's also used for magnificent banquets and ceremonial events, as well as the City's annual Flower Show. The modern buildings alongside house the Corporation offices, the Guildhall Library and a Clock Museum containing Mary Queen of Scot's skull-shaped watch, among some 600 watches and 30 clocks.

Free guided tours (write in advance to: The Keeper of Guildhall, Guildhall, EC2). Shop. Toilets for the disabled. Wheelchair access.

Leadenhall Market

Whittington Avenue, off Gracechurch Street, EC3. Bank underground. **Open** 7am-3pm Mon-Fri.
Leadenhall Market started in 1309, taking its name from a lead-roofed mansion that stood here. Dick Whittington, Lord Mayor in the early fifteenth century, acquired the market for the Corporation of London. The outstanding Victorian iron and glass arcades that stand today were designed in 1881 by Horace Jones (who was also responsible for Tower Bridge). It's best to wander through the market at lunch time, when the stalls (more like shops, these days) overflow with fish and vegetables and City workers unwind at the local bars and restaurants. Prices aren't low, but the variety is awesome: exotic fruits, seafood, game, gulls' eggs, caviar and vintage champagne. The market is on the site of a Roman forum (*see chapter* **Roman London**).

Livery Companies' Halls

All over City. **Admission** free, by ticket only.
Livery companies were guilds of craftsmen that were established in medieval times and acquired political strength, as well as huge amounts of money and possessions. Nowadays, their trade connections are minimal and they function more as private clubs, with charitable and ceremonial duties. Some halls hold open days, for example the **Fishmongers' Hall** (London Bridge, EC4), the **Ironmongers' Hall** (Barbican, EC2) and the **Vintners' Hall** (Kennet Wharf Lane, EC4). Only a certain number of tickets are allocated to view them, but they are free. Contact the City of London Information Centre (*listed above*).

Smithfield Market

London Central Markets, West Smithfield, EC1. Farringdon underground/N21, N76, N85, N89, N98. **Open** 5-10.30am Mon-Fri.
From 1150 to 1850 there was a livestock market on this site. Today only deadstock is sold and Smithfield is Europe's largest wholesale meat market. The pre-dawn bustle is something to behold; local pubs open from 7am (the Fox & Anchor on Charterhouse Street is famed for its breakfasts) and are full of meat-packers. Smithfield was also where the medieval Bartholomew Fair took place (it is described by Ben Jonson in the play of the same name) – a riotous jamboree that was finally suppressed by puritanical Victorians in 1855. *See also chapter* **Victorian London**.

Churches

Before the Great Fire of 1666, the City of London had an incredible 109 churches. A total of 84 were destroyed in the conflagration. The fire gave England's greatest architect, Sir Christopher Wren, the perfect opportunity to exercise his genius. He was responsible for 51 of the 54 churches that were rebuilt.

World War II saw almost all the churches bombed and 11 were totally destroyed. Today

they number only 48, or perhaps 47 following the virtual destruction of St Ethelburga's in Bishopsgate by an IRA bomb in 1993. But there's still a church virtually around every corner, providing a spiritual and aesthetic haven in a city dedicated to Mammon. Most are open between 10am and 4pm on weekdays, and on Sundays during services. Admission to the City's churches is free unless otherwise stated. For **St Paul's Cathedral** *see chapter* **Sightseeing**.

St Bartholomew-the-Great

West Smithfield, EC1 (071 606 5171). Barbican (closed Sun) or Farringdon underground. **Open** 8.30am-4.30pm Mon-Fri; 10am-4.30pm Sat; noon-6pm Sun. **Services** 12.30pm Tue; 8.30am Thur; 9am, 11am (choral) and 6.30pm (choral) Sun.
Part of an enormous twelfth-century priory, St Bart's is the City's only surviving Norman church (*see chapter* **The Middle Ages**). It was built by Rahere, a courtier of Henry I who also founded St Bartholomew's hospital (which still operates on the same site, but is currently under threat from government cuts). The oldest bells in the City (pre-Reformation) are rung here. William Hogarth was baptised in the church in 1697, and in 1725 Benjamin Franklin worked for a printer in the Lady Chapel. Enter the churchyard through the thirteenth-century gateway (opposite the east corner of Smithfield Market).
Bookshop. Tour by prior arrangement. Disabled toilets and wheelchair access.

St Bride's Church

Fleet Street, EC4 (071 353 1301). Blackfriars underground/BR. **Open** 8.30am-5pm Mon-Sat; 9am-7.30pm Sun. **Services** 8.30am (recitals at 1.15pm; not during Lent, Advent or August) Mon-Fri; 1.15am Thur; 11am (choral) and 6.30pm (choral) Sun.
Christopher Wren completed St Bride's in 1703. The spire – Wren's tallest at 226 feet/69 metres – became the model for English wedding cakes when it was copied by a local baker. The church was gutted in the Blitz, and during excavations afterwards, the remains of a Roman building were discovered. This can be seen in the crypt, along with the foundations of seven churches. There's also a museum and an exhibition of printing history. St Bride's now boasts one of London's finest church choirs (which sings at 11am and 6.30pm every Sunday). Though the national press has more or less deserted Fleet Street, this is still known as the Journalist' Church, and commemorative services are held here.
Wheelchair access to ground floor only.

St Etheldreda's

Ely Place, EC1 (071 405 1061). Chancery Lane underground. **Open** 8.30am-5.30pm daily. **Services** 8am and 1pm Mon-Fri; 9am and 11am (choral) Sun.
A fine example of Decorated Gothic architecture, the thirteenth-century St Etheldreda's is (with the exception of part of Westminster Abbey) London's only surviving edifice from the reign of Edward I (*see chapter* **The Middle Ages**). It's also Britain's oldest Catholic church, originating from the time when provincial bishops (in this case from the Cambridgeshire town of Ely) had their episcopal houses in London. At the height of the Tudor religious persecution, Catholic martyrs were paraded down Holborn to their place of execution at Tyburn. The statues on the walls in the church commemorate the martyrs. Ely Place, with its wonderful Dickensian atmosphere (Bleeding Heart Yard, where you can eat, was mentioned in *Little Dorrit*) is still famous for its straw-

berries (referred to in Shakespeare's *Richard III*) and hosts an annual 'Strawberrie Fayre'.

St Mary-le-Bow

Cheapside, EC2 (071 248 5139). Bank, Mansion House or St Paul's underground. **Open** 6.30am-6pm Mon-Wed; 6.30am-4pm Thur, Fri. **Services** 8.15am and 5.45pm Mon; 7.30am and 5.45pm Tue; 8.15am, 12.30pm and 5.45pm Wed; 8.15am and 5.30pm (choral) Thur; 8.15am and 8.30am Fri.

The elegant white tower of this renovated Wren church rises incongruously above busy, modern Cheapside. Traditionally, true Londoners, or 'cockneys', had to be born within the sound of Bow bells. The Great Fire of 1666 and the Blitz during World War II destroyed, in turn, the first two sets of bells; a small model inside the church gives you an impression of what was left after the Great Fire. On Tuesdays during University term-times at 1.05pm there's a 'dialogue' between the rector and an invited guest. On Thursdays at the same time there's a music recital. The crypt is occupied by **The Place Below** (071 329 0789; open 7.30am-3pm Mon-Fri; dinner served 6-10.30pm Thur, Fri), one of London's best vegetarian restaurants.

Walk

Historical Tours

(081 668 4019). **Meeting point** Monument underground (Fish Street Hill exit), Sat 2.30pm. **Duration** 2 hours. **Cost** £4.50 adults; £3.50 OAPs, students; free under-14s if accompanied by adult. **No credit cards.**

A comprehensive tour covering 2,000 years of City history, exploring the lesser known nooks and alleys, with plenty of juicy anecdotes.

Legal London

To look at them, you'd think that English High Court Judges had stepped out of another age. Unfortunately, this is often the case. Many of them pass from public school, to Oxbridge and thence to the **Inns of Court** (*see* **Box**), spending their social hours in clubs in **St James's** (*see chapter* **West End**). Having led this supremely closeted life, they must then pass judgement on people from the modern world. It is scarcely surprising that some decisions are eccentric in the extreme.

You can witness these bombastic, but occasionally eloquent, judgements by visiting the **Old Bailey**. The Courts provide a fascinating insight into how this old-fashioned world deals with twentieth-century criminals.

The legal system has come in for plenty of criticism lately. High-profile cases such as the Guildford Four and Birmingham Six, where people spent more than 15 years in prison for crimes they did not commit, have highlighted its shortcomings. And there has been a public outcry at the increasing cost of litigation and the time it takes to get a case to court.

Old Bailey

on the corner of Newgate Street and Old Bailey, EC4 (071 248 3277). St Paul's underground. **Open** 10.30am-1pm, 2-4pm, Mon-Fri. **Admission** free (no under-14s admitted, 14-16s accompanied by adults only).

The Old Bailey (its proper name is the Central Criminal Court) has dealt with some of the goriest and most publicised criminal cases in London's history. Past defendants include Oscar Wilde in 1895, and the murderous Dr Crippen in 1910. The court was built on the site of the notorious Newgate prison, and the gilded figure of Justice, up on the domed roof, overlooks the area where convicts were once executed. The tradition of judges carrying bouquets of flowers into court was originally designed to counteract the foul smells emanating from the prison. The public are admitted to watch any of the trials that are proceeding. The most important cases are heard in No.1 Court.

Royal Courts of Justice

Strand, WC2 (071 936 6000). Aldwych or Temple underground. **Open** 10am-4pm Mon-Fri; during August the building is open to the public, although court cases are suspended for the summer recess. **Admission** free. For centuries these courts, the civil equivalent of the Old Bailey, were housed in the Palace of Westminster. The current premises were opened by Queen Victoria in 1882. The neo-Gothic building, designed by G E Street, is a fine example of Victorian architecture, with its towers, pillars and great entrance hall. Cases held here range from divorce and libel hearings to company and bankruptcy actions. Visitors can walk into any of the public galleries at the back of the 58 courts to watch the proceedings. *Wheelchair access to main hall only.*

Business

Lombard Street, named after the Italian moneylenders from that region who lived here through the Middle Ages, has been the banking centre of London for hundreds of years. In the sixteenth century, the **Royal Exchange** became the focus for business deals and, later on, coffee houses (such as **Lloyd's**) became centres for shipping news and marine insurance. Nowadays, most of the important business institutions are clustered round the **Bank of England**, which will be celebrating the 300th anniversary of its foundation in 1994.

The eighties was a time of rapid change. The technological revolution in computers and communications led to 'Big Bang', the computerisation of trading. The tradition of face-to-face trading on the floor of the Stock Exchange ('my word is my bond') was over. Commodity exchanges and foreign exchange markets continue, but very few are open to visitors.

During the nineties, the City has had to contend with major problems. IRA bombs have caused hundreds of millions of pounds worth of damage: the visitors' gallery of the Stock Exchange on Old Broad Street was closed to visitors after a bomb went off in 1990. Paying for this destruction has been an added burden for an insurance market which already seemed close to breaking point.

In the summer of 1993, new security measures were taken to counter terrorism. Many City streets have been blocked to traffic, and

The Inns of Court

The Inns of Court are a part of London that few get to see, yet they encapsulate much that is traditional and eccentric about the British. All London barristers work from within their walls, and all students hoping to become London barristers must dine 24 times in the imposing halls before being eligible to be called to the Bar.

There are four Inns, or Honourable Societies of Barristers – Gray's Inn, Lincoln's Inn, Middle Temple and Inner Temple – all of them sited around Holborn, just west of the City. A stroll around these tranquil institutions is a spellbinding and eye-opening experience. You'll not only see dark Jermyn Street suits topped with the occasional bowler hat, but lawyers in wigs and gowns carrying paperwork tied with the traditional red ribbon.

The history of the Inns can be traced back to the thirteenth century, and some of the existing buildings (such as the Middle Temple Hall) date back to medieval times, though many were badly damaged in the Blitz.

Both the rich and famous have studied in and passed through the Inns, including Oliver Cromwell, William Penn, Thomas More, Sir Francis Bacon, Mohandas Gandhi and Margaret Thatcher.

Each Inn is very different in style and atmosphere. **Lincoln's Inn** is the best preserved. The chapel was built between 1620 and 1623 under the supervision of Inigo Jones. It occupies the first floor of a building; below are cloisters (Pepys records having walked along them in 1663). In the chapel's vestibule is a tablet to the memory of Spencer Perceval, the Prime Minister who was murdered in the House of Commons in 1812.

Particularly worthy of mention are the immaculate lawns of Lincoln's Inn Fields. The area once served as a jousting ground, but at the time of the Reformation, it was used for executions. Many Catholic martyrs met their end here.

Charles Dickens was a clerk at **Gray's Inn** (1827). By then it was already a venerable establishment, dating from the fourteenth century. Part of the hall's sixteenth-century interior screen has survived, and the gardens (described by Charles Lamb as 'altogether reverend and law-breathing') are particularly peaceful.

It seems that **Middle Temple** and **Inner Temple** have always been separate Inns. Lawyers first came to the Temple in 1320 when the land was leased by the Knights Hospitaller of St John to members of the profession who were working in Holborn. Prior to that, the area belonged to the Knights Templar (an order of monastic knights originally founded to protect pilgrims travelling to the Holy Land) who settled in the Temple in 1162. The **Middle Temple Hall** (*see chapter* **Tudors & Stuarts**), was the venue for a production of *Twelfth Night* in 1602. Shakespeare is likely to have acted in it. The hall also contains a wooden serving table reputedly made from the hatch of Sir Francis Drake's ship *The Golden Hind*.

The **Temple Church** is the only circular church in London. It was constructed by the Knights Templar in 1185, as a model of either the Dome of the Rock or the Church of the Holy Sepulchre in Jerusalem.

Lincoln's Inn *Lincoln's Inn Fields, WC2 (071 405 1393). Chancery Lane or Holborn underground.* **Open** *grounds* 9am-6pm Mon-Fri; *chapel* noon-2.30pm Mon-Fri.

Gray's Inn *Gray's Inn Road, WC1 (071 405 8164). Chancery Lane or Holborn underground.* **Open** 10am-4pm Mon-Fri.

Inner Temple *King's Bench Walk, EC4 (071 353 8462). Temple underground.* **Open** 10am-4pm Mon-Sat; 12.45-4pm Sun.

Middle Temple *Middle Temple Lane, EC4 (071 353 4355). Temple underground.* **Open** 10am-11.30am, 3-4pm, Mon-Fri. **Admission** free.

private vehicles entering the square mile are liable to be searched. Whether these measures are continued past the six-month trial period remains to be seen.

The worst recession in Britain since the thirties has added to the City's problems. Banks have shed huge numbers of staff because of technological advances and the reduction in trade. Yet parts of the City have continued to thrive. The recession put only a minor check on the viral growth of the Stock Market. Its index has reached record levels even while quoted companies are making thousands unemployed.

Bank of England Museum

Bartholomew Lane, EC2 (071 601 5545). Bank underground. **Open** *10am-5pm Mon-Fri; weekends and Bank Holidays subject to variation, phone for details.* **Admission** *free.*
Sir John Soane's design for the Bank of England was mostly demolished in an enlargement carried out between the wars, but this well thought-out museum contains a faithful restoration of the Bank Stock Office designed by Soane in 1793. Original artwork for banknotes is also displayed, kept inside closely monitored cabinets that check humidity and thieving hands. The Bank Today section has interactive videos and a dealing desk.
Educational films. Lectures by prior arrangement. Shop. Tour and touch sessions for the visually impaired by prior arrangement. Wheelchair access by prior arrangement.

Broadgate Centre

Eldon Street, EC2 (071 588 6565). Liverpool Street underground/BR.

This modern London square has been a success not only because everything was developed at the same time (so the buildings complement each other), but also because rents here are low by City standards. Bars, shops and restaurants could therefore get established and they now keep visitors and the resident bankers entertained. Vast glass atriums surround the central arena, which becomes a performance space on summer lunchtimes, and an open-air ice-skating rink in winter.

Lloyd's of London

Lime Street, EC3 (071 327 6210). Bank or Monument underground. **Open** *9.30am-12.30pm, 2-4pm, Mon-Fri (groups of at least four people from recognised organisations; book at least one week in advance).* **Admission** *free.*
The world's most famous insurance market operates in one of the City's most controversial, high-tech buildings, designed in 1986 by Richard Rogers (who was also responsible for the Pompidou Centre in Paris). After examining Mr Rogers' building, some say that Lloyd's began life in a coffee shop (a seventeenth-century coffee shop owned by Edward Lloyd, to be precise) and ended in a coffee percolator. Others consider it to be one of London's finest architectural landmarks. Lloyd's is a society of underwriters (called Names) who pledge their personal fortunes to insure everything from oil rigs and tankers to Rudolf Nureyev's legs. Marine insurance forms the bulk of the business. The bell of *HMS Lutine*, on the ground floor, is tolled once for bad news, twice for good. In the early nineties, most of the news was bad, and many Names are now on the brink of bankruptcy.
Exhibitions. Shop. Wheelchair access.

Royal Exchange

Cornhill, EC4 (071 623 0444). Bank underground. **Open** *group visits by appointment only.* **Admission** *free.*
The original Exchange, opened in 1567, was the first covered marketplace for traders in London and contributed

Fair exchange is no robbery? The **Royal Exchange***. See* **review***.*

Say 'cheese'. **Ye Olde Cheshire Cheese** *is a most venerable City pub. See* **review**.

enormously to London's prosperity. It was twice destroyed by fire but the present building by William Tite, opened in 1844, still honours its Elizabethan founder, Sir Thomas Gresham, with a statue over the entrance in Exchange Buildings and his emblem, a golden grasshopper, high on the bell tower. Recently renovated, the pediment sculptures, by Richard Westmacott, show the central figure of Commerce with the Lord Mayor and groups of merchants from all over the world. Underneath the Exchange is **The Imperial City** (071 626 3437), one of London's finest Chinese restaurants.

The Story of Telecommunication
145 Queen Victoria Street, EC4 (071 248 7444). St Paul's underground or Blackfriars underground/BR. **Open** 10am-5pm Mon-Fri (including Saturday of Lord Mayor's Show). **Admission** free.
Photos, old films and videos are used to relate the history of telecommunication (from before the Bell Era to the possible future) at this museum run by British Telecom. There are lots of snazzy buttons to press and you even get to send a fax (via satellite) from one side of a room to another and watch your voice in the form of sound waves.
Videos by prior arrangement. Parking. Shop. Wheelchair access by prior arrangement.

Pubs & Wine Bars

The City of London is famous for its watering holes which fill to bursting point at lunchtimes. The Fleet Street area is particularly well endowed – a legacy from the time when the street was the centre of national newspaper journalism.

Such is the exodus from the City after work, that most pubs and bars close before the usual 11pm watershed. Make sure you book if you're eating at a restaurant; if you just want to drink, you'll simply have to shove like all the rest. For restaurants and more wine bars, *see chapter* **Eating & Drinking**.

Bow Wine Vaults
10 Bow Church Yard, EC4 (071 248 1121). Mansion House or St Paul's underground. **Open** 11am-10pm Mon-Fri. **Credit** A, AmEx, DC, £TC, V.
The large rambling bar here becomes packed with City folk during their extended lunch breaks; in the evenings the atmosphere is less hectic. The basement restaurant serves unpretentious food – booking is advisable.

Ye Olde Cheshire Cheese
Wine Office Court, 145 Fleet Street, EC4 (071 353 6170). Blackfriars underground. **Open** 11.30am-11pm Mon-Sat; noon-3pm Sun.
A long time was recently spent enlarging this historic pub, but mercifully, the old small, low ceilinged rooms have been kept. Here writers from Pepys to Dickens have imbibed; Samuel Johnson used it as his local (his house nearby is open to the public *see chapter* **Georgian London**). The restaurant has a traditional menu of pies and steaks.

El Vino
47 Fleet Street, EC4 (071 353 6786). Temple underground. **Open** 11.30am-3pm, 5-8pm, Mon-Fri. **Credit** A, £TC, V.
From 1923, this legendary wine bar has been providing snifters for the legal profession, journalists and anyone wanting to enjoy its traditional, sedate atmosphere (though incredibly, women weren't served at the bar until 1982). It can get crowded, so expect to stand unless you book one of the small circular tables. A dress code is strictly enforced: women must wear skirts or 'City trouser-suits', men a jacket, collar and tie.

East End & Docklands

Stupendous street markets, classic curry houses and an exciting mix of cultures inhabit the East End, but the astonishing Docklands development remains half empty.

The East End

For much of the past two hundred years, the East End has been seen as the poor relation of London. Although the title has not always been deserved, the area was the site of some of the worst Victorian slums in the country, and today it still includes some of the most deprived districts in Britain. Even in the old nursery rhyme 'Oranges and Lemons' it is clear where the balance of wealth lies:

"When will you pay me?" say the bells of Old Bailey.

"When I grow rich," say the bells of Shoreditch.'

The East End is the home of the cockney. Genuine cockneys must be born within the sound of Bow Bells, pealed at **St Mary le Bow** Church (*see chapter* **The City**) – which means that the pearly kings and queens of Stepney need to be blessed with excellent hearing. Every autumn, these representatives of East London's costermongers dress in all their finery and attend a harvest festival celebration at St Martin-in-the-Fields church off Trafalgar Square (*see chapter* **London by Season**).

Throughout the centuries, the East End has provided a haven for refugees of diverse nationalities. French Huguenots were among the first, settling in **Spitalfields** in the late seventeenth century. At that time, the area was already known for its silk weaving, but the French master weavers and dyers helped the industry prosper and built themselves attractive Georgian houses in the area. Some of these have been renovated and can still be seen along Nantes Street, Fournier Street and Folgate Street. Part of **Dennis Severs' House** on Folgate Street recreates the interior as it might have been in the late seventeenth century. There are tours of the building (*see chapter* **Georgian London**).

The splendid **Christ Church** in Spitalfields (*see chapter* **Georgian London**) remains as a testament to the prosperity the Huguenot weavers brought to the area: nearly half the gravestones in its churchyard are in French. Although one of Hawksmoor's greatest buildings, it only narrowly escaped demolition in the sixties as, like much of the surrounding district, it had then fallen into disrepair. Now the church provides a venue for the Spitalfields Festival, a series of classical music concerts held in the first three weeks of June (contact **Tower Hamlets Environment Trust** for information, *see below*).

Spitalfields' wholesale fruit and vegetable market also dated from the Georgian period, but was moved from Brushfield Street to Leyton in north-east London in 1991. Today a small organic food market is run on the site (it's best on Sundays from 9am-3pm) and the rest of the area is being redeveloped for yet more office space.

The area's descent into poverty began in the mid-eighteenth century when the silk trade stagnated. Later the industrial revolution brought in the power loom which ended large-scale hand silk weaving. In 1832 there were 50,000 weavers unemployed. Entire families moved into single rooms of houses vacated by the rich.

Following the Russian pogroms of the 1880s, Spitalfields became the refuge for thousands of Jewish immigrants. The new residents continued to work in the clothing industry, specialising in tailoring and leather goods. These trades continue in the area today, run by Bangladeshis as well as Jews. Unfortunately, sweated labour persists.

In the late 1880s, Spitalfields was the scene of a series of five brutal murders; the perpetrator was never found. But thankfully, the area doesn't seek to benefit from its grisly association with Jack the Ripper. The exception is the Ten Bells pub, opposite the old market area, which has an engraved window listing the victims and where they were found.

Spitalfields is now home to a large number of Bangladeshis, who, as well as running curry restaurants (*see* **Box**), have opened many shops in the district selling leather goods, spices and saris.

On Sunday mornings, the northern part of Brick Lane and the surrounding area is taken over by one of the best jamborees around. **Brick Lane Market** (*see chapter* **Shopping: Markets**) shows the East End at its irreverent best. All manner of goods (some new, some second-hand, some stolen, some hopeless junk) are sold from a collection of stalls, yards and lock-ups that flower briefly from dawn until 2pm. The market is so huge that there are only a few empty streets to the north before you come across the glorious **Columbia Road Flower Market** (*see chapter* **Shopping: Markets**) in Shoreditch.

Some of the pubs round this area are sleazy strip joints, but if you fancy a break from the curry houses, or the hubbub of the market, try the Pride of Spitalfields (071 247 8933), just off Brick Lane on cobbled Heneage Street. The beer is good (it's a freehouse) and the regulars are friendly. Unfortunately, none of the Spitalfields pubs now sell locally brewed beer. The Truman Brewery (65-79 Brick Lane) was built in 1706, but although its fine building still houses the head office of one of Britain's biggest brewers, beer production ended here a few years ago.

Whitechapel is a rather unlovely and fume-laden area to explore, yet it harbours some fascinating revelations of London past and present. By far the most famous attraction is the **Petticoat Lane Market**, held on Middlesex Street, E1, on Sunday mornings (*see chapter* **Shopping**). Thousands of tourists and Londoners pack the narrow streets, while stall-holders proffer leather jackets, cheap watches and cart-loads of tacky souvenirs.

From Middlesex Street, turn left into Aldgate High Street. This traces one of London's oldest routes, the Roman road between London and Colchester. After a short walk you'll reach Whitechapel High Street. On the left is one of London's best small exhibition spaces, the **Whitechapel Gallery** (*see chapter* **Art Galleries**). Near to the gallery, at 90 Whitechapel High Street, is London's most famous Jewish restaurant, **Blooms** (*see chapter* **Eating & Drinking**). You'll probably need to book for a meal on Sunday lunchtimes as this is the traditional time for Jewish families to meet and feast here. If it's full, try a takeaway salt-beef sandwich.

Continue along Whitechapel High Street and it soon becomes Whitechapel Road. The major building that dominates the south side of the road is the **East London Mosque**, one of London's first purpose-built mosques. Some

3,000 of the local Bangladeshi community congregate here for Friday's Jumma ceremony.

Should you find yourself in Whitechapel during the week, try to take a glimpse at a couple of London's most unusual businesses. The **Freedom Press Bookshop** is difficult to find, hidden in a tiny alley not far from Blooms. Established in 1886 by Prince Peter Kropotkin, the press produces anarchist books and pamphlets from these cramped premises. The first-floor bookshop, run by laid-back revolutionaries, contains a wealth of left-wing literature. The **Whitechapel Bell Foundry** (32-34 Whitechapel Road, E1, 071 247 2599) has an even longer pedigree. Its history has been traced back to 1420 and it can lay claim to being the oldest British manufacturing industry still in existence. Both Big Ben and the USA's Liberty Bell were cast by the firm. No tours of the factory are run, but staff are happy to take orders for town-crier bells.

Transport
Aldgate East, Shoreditch (peak hours only) or Whitechapel underground.

Aukland Leather
151 Brick Lane, E1 (071 729 9859). Aldgate East underground. **Open** 10.30am-7pm Mon-Fri, Sun. **No credit cards.**
In addition to entering the restaurant business, Brick Lane's Bangladeshi community has also opened a number of shops in the area selling cheap leather clothing. Motorcycle jackets can be bought here for as little as £60, but you might have to haggle.

Brick Lane Beigel Bake
159 Brick Lane, E1 (071 729 0616). Aldgate East underground. **Open** 24 hours daily. **No credit cards.**
Jewish institutions in this district are now few and far between, following the Diaspora to wealthier suburbs in north London. The Beigel Bake resolutely remains: open all hours for freshly baked bagels with delicious fillings.

Brick Lane Music Hall
152 Brick Lane, E1 (enquiries 071 377 9797/bookings 071 377 8787). Aldgate East underground. **Shows** 7.15pm Wed-Sat. **Admission** £20 dinner and show; £10 show-only (not bookable in advance). **Meals served** 7.30pm Wed-Sat; noon-3pm Sun. **Credit** A, £TC, V, .
Though it's packed with cockney clichés, this recreated music hall isn't far from what the East End knees-ups must have been like, except that food (boiled beef and carrots, and the like) is provided. Come along for a sing-song.

East London Mosque
84-86 Whitechapel Road, E1 (071 247 1357). Aldgate East or Whitechapel underground. **Open** 9am-9pm daily. **Service** 1.25pm Fri.

Freedom Press Bookshop
Angel Alley, 84B Whitechapel High Street, E1 (071 247 9249). Aldgate East underground. **Open** 10am-6pm Mon-Fri; 10.30am-5pm Sat (phone to check). **No credit cards.**

Passmore Edwards Museum
Romford Road (near junction with Water Lane), E15 (081 534 2274/0276/fax 081 519 4296). Stratford underground/BR/DLR. **Open** 11am-5pm Wed-Fri; 1-

5pm Sat; 2-5pm Sun, Bank Holidays. **Admission** free. **No credit cards.**
The geology, archaeology, and social history of the East-End district of Newham and its surrounding areas can be explored at this local museum. Highlights include eighteenth-century Bow porcelain, and a set of mammoth's tusks.
Wheelchair access to 60% of museum; toilets for people with disabilities.

Ragged School Museum
46-48 Copperfield Road, E3 (081 980 6405). Mile End underground/25, 277, D4, D5, D6, D7 bus. **Open** 10am-5pm Wed, Thur; 2-5pm first Sun of month. **Admission** free. **No credit cards.**
The ragged schools were founded by Dr Barnardo to educate and feed poor kids. This canal-side warehouse was once the largest of the ragged schools and has changed little. As well as varied temporary exhibitions related to East End history, the museum contains a reconstructed Victorian classroom complete with (role-playing) pupils.
Café. Guided tours. Shop.

Tower Hamlets Environment Trust
150 Brick Lane, E1 (071 377 0481/2). Aldgate East underground. **Open** 9am-6pm Mon-Fri.
Provides information about Spitalfields and its environs, including advice on walks, and maps.

Docklands

As Britain's empire grew through the nineteenth and early twentieth centuries, so too did the network of docks to the east of London. Fleets of vessels loaded with raw materials from around the world ended their journeys here; others departed packed with manufactured goods from Britain, 'the workshop of the world'.

Yet despite the tremendous wealth flowing through the area, poverty was widespread among local workers. Dockers were hired by the day: no ships meant no work, and hence no money. Victorian charities and missions (including the Salvation Army) were started in an attempt to alleviate the misery, but many local people found more comfort in the creed of socialism.

The docks continued expanding until World War II when they became a prime target for the bombs of the Luftwaffe. The area was devastated. A massive rebuilding programme lasted until the fifties, but the final blow came with the advent of container ships, which allowed cargo to be loaded directly on to Juggernauts or railway. Tilbury, near the Thames Estuary, was better suited for this work, so the Port moved there from London. Between 1967 and 1982, all of London's docks between Tower Bridge and Barking Creek closed.

In 1981 the government gave an unelected quango, the **London Docklands Development Corporation (LDDC)**, almost unrestricted powers to revive the vast area from the Tower of London to Beckton. During the eighties,

Docklands became the biggest inner-city building site in Europe. Huge amounts of money and an unparalleled amount of greed were unleashed on the area. Thousands of offices and hundreds of homes for City professionals were built, while local Docklanders saw minimal benefits.

Ironically, the restraining factor was the recession of the early nineties, which brought much development to an abrupt halt, and many developers into the bankruptcy courts. **Tobacco Dock** (*see below*), the new Covent Garden-style 'shopping village', went into receivership in 1990; its new owners seem to be biding their time, hoping for a revival in the economy. **Canary Wharf**, with its vast 50-storey tower, also had problems when its owners, Olympia and York, went into receivership.

Acres of office-space remain empty here. Londoners who do work in the area regard it as an outpost, rather than 'London's Third City'. Yet the Docklands are still well worth visiting, whether you view them as a parable of Margaret Thatcher's economic folly, or as a site of future prosperity and architectural glory.

As most of the area's attractions are close to the river, on both the north and south banks, the best way of viewing them is to take a riverboat east along the Thames to Greenwich (for details of river transport, *see chapter* **Getting Around**). Below we list the sights in the order they will come into view. At **Greenwich** (*see chapter* **South London**), you can take the foottunnel under the Thames to reach the Island Gardens station of the **Docklands Light Railway (DLR)**. Although the DLR service back to Tower Gateway only runs from Monday to Friday – and pretty erratically at that – (*see chapter* **Getting Around**), it provides the most graphic way of witnessing the astounding contrast between the high-rise slums where the original Docklanders still live, and the postmodern blocks occupied by City brokers.

London Bridge to Tower Bridge

For **Tower Bridge**, *see chapter* **Sightseeing**.

Transport
Tower Hill underground/London Bridge underground/BR.

Hay's Galleria
Tooley Street, SE1 (071 403 4758). London Bridge underground/BR/47, 70, 7A bus/boat to London Bridge Pier. **Open** 6am-11.30pm daily.
The focal point of a development named London Bridge City, Hay's Galleria was created by filling Hays Dock, giving it a Victorianesque barrel-vaulted glass roof and fitting its warehouses to form an elegant arcade. The ground floor is lined with a few shops and eating places; upper floors contain offices. Much more fun is the fantastic fountain sculpture, *The Navigators*, by David Kemp.

Warehouses have become offices, boats are now tourist attractions in **Docklands**.

Wapping & Rotherhithe

Immediately by Tower Bridge on the north bank of the Thames is **St Katherine's Dock** yacht haven. Next are the warehouses of Wapping High Street, now converted into flats. After about half a mile are two old riverside pubs, the **Town of Ramsgate** and the **Prospect of Whitby**; for details *see chapter* **Eating & Drinking**.

Facing Wapping on the south bank is **Rotherhithe**, a maritime district retaining many of its Dickensian streets and the Georgian Nelson Dock House. It was from Rotherhithe in 1620 that Captain Jones set sail for America in the Pilgrim Fathers' boat, *The Mayflower*. Today its main feature is **Butler's Wharf**, a very expensive mixed development, which includes the **Design Museum** (*see chapter* **Museums**), some excellent restaurants, and the handsome **St Saviour's Dock**.

Past Wapping on the left (the north bank), behind a bright red iron bridge is Shadwell Basin, lined by classic examples of the new Docklands architecture: little Lego-land houses with garishly coloured balconies. Passing

between the two ventilation towers of the **Rotherhithe Tunnel** and the new development of Free Trade Wharf, you reach Limehouse Basin. This was the business end of Britain's canal network, where cargo travelling down the Regent's Canal arrived for shipping abroad. The basin is to become a yacht marina lined with up-market shops and flats. Some of the Georgian houses around Newell Street and Narrow Street survived the Luftwaffe, but little else remains of what was London's Victorian Chinatown, apart from a few street names (Ming Street, Canton Street, Mandarin Street).

Transport
Rotherhithe or Wapping underground/Shadwell DLR/underground.

Brunel Engine House
St Marychurch Street, SE16 (081 318 2489). Rotherhithe underground/95 bus/boat to Cherry Garden Pier. **Open** noon-4pm first Sunday in every month or by appointment. **Admission** £1.50 adults; 50p students, OAPs, UB40s.
This small museum of local history is housed in a building originally constructed for the steam engines that

Brick Lane curry houses

Not only is Brick Lane the venue for one of London's most colourful street markets, it is also the focal point for the city's large Bangladeshi population. Consequently the area boasts some of the best curry houses in the capital: there are over 20 in the immediate vicinity.

Many ex-patriot Bangladeshis moved into the area in the seventies, settling in the low-cost housing around Brick Lane. The first eating establishments they opened were basic caffs attracting an almost entirely Asian clientele. A few of these have remained largely unchanged. **Sweet and Spicy** is actually run by Punjabis, and its dhals (lentil), mixed vegetable, and roghan josh (lamb) curries, displayed in pots near the window, attracts punters from both inside and outside the Asian community. Simply go to the counter and point at what takes your fancy, tray in hand. Furnishings are tatty, but prices are low.

Nazrul is one of the oldest established restaurants on the Lane, but for the past ten years at least, its custom has come mainly from non-Asians. Students in particular are devoted to its large, inexpensive menu, and its policy of allowing diners to bring their own alcohol (there's a mediocre off-licence down the road). Near to Nazrul, **Aladin** also has a long menu of cheap curries; as more Bangladeshis eat here the spicing tends to be more authentic.

Although Bangladeshis are still the most impoverished ethnic group in Britain, a measure of prosperity has come to Brick Lane thanks to the success of the curry houses. New, sleek Bangla restaurants are popping up like bubbles on a popadom, and an increasing number of existing establishments now proudly proclaim that they are Bangladeshi, instead of using the blanket term 'Indian' to describe their food. The **Shampan** has been at the forefront of this move – its menu features a number of dishes that hail from the Sylhet region of Bangladesh, from where most of the local population originates. Yet the Shampan's smart interior is designed to appeal to a wide range of customers.

The **Clifton**, although it has been around for a long time, underwent a transformation a couple of years ago and now also has elegant furnishings. Prices were raised as a result, but local specialities (such as brain masala, or batera – quail – still appear on the menu).

But the relentless march up-market has also brought problems. Some of the newer Brick Lane restaurants are serving standard tandoori and curry dishes of the sort available all over London. The watering down of authentic flavours is a shame, and also means that the old curry caffs that cater for the local Bangladeshi community are likely to be forced out of the Lane to make way for more profitable concerns.

Nevertheless, Spitalfields is still a run-down area – a far cry from the West End – and Brick Lane can appear dingy and intimidating at night. Also, if you want the widest choice of food, it's wise to come to the area for lunch, as some of the caffs that cater mainly for Asians are only open during the day. Sunday lunch is particularly popular, and the area is swamped with crowds visiting Brick Lane's famous market.

Aladin
132 Brick Lane, E1 (071 247 8210). Aldgate East underground/8, 15, 25 bus. **Meals served** 11am-11pm daily. **Average** £5. **Unlicensed. No credit cards.**

Clifton
126 Brick Lane, E1 (071 247 2364/3108/fax 071 247 2364). Aldgate East underground. **Meals served** noon-midnight daily. **Average** £12. **Credit** A, AmEx, DC, LV, Switch, £TC, V.

Nazrul
130 Brick Lane E1 (071 247 2505). Aldgate East underground. **Lunch served** noon-3pm Mon-Sat. **Dinner served** 5.30pm-midnight Mon-Thur; 5.30pm-midnight Fri, Sat. **Meals served** noon-midnight Sun. **Average** £7. **Unlicensed. Credit** LV, £TC.

Shampan
79 Brick Lane E1 (071 375 0475). Aldgate East underground. **Lunch served** noon-3pm, **dinner served** 6pm-12.30am, daily. **Average** £13. **Credit** A, AmEx, DC, LV, £TC, V.

Sweet and Spicy
42 Brick Lane, E1 (071 247 1081). Aldgate East underground. **Open** 8am-10pm Mon-Sat; 8am-6pm Sun. **Average** £6. **Unlicensed. Credit** LV.

pumped water from Marc Brunel's Thames Tunnel completed in 1843, the world's first under-river public thoroughfare. The tunnel is now used by the East London Line of the Underground, connecting Wapping and Rotherhithe tube stations.
Guided tours. Shop. Wheelchair access.

St Anne's, Limehouse
Three Colt Street, E14 (071 987 1502). Westferry DLR. **Open** 3-4pm Sun or call in at rectory during office hours. **Services** 10.30am, 6pm, Sun.
Nicholas Hawksmoor built this gigantic white church between 1712 and 1724. The interior was rebuilt in 1851 after a fire. Outside is a large pyramidal tomb, thought to commemorate a number of sea captains.

St George-in-the-East
The Highway, E1 (071 481 1345). Shadwell underground/DLR. **Open** 8am-5pm Tue-Sun. **Service** 10.15am Sun.
Hawksmoor's 'trademark' tower, broad-based and massive with pepperpot turrets, is visible from the river. World War II fire bombs put paid to the interior; in 1963 a modest new church designed by Arthur Bailey was opened inside the great ruin.

St Katherine's Dock
E1 (071 488 2400). Tower Hill underground/Tower Gateway DLR/23, 42, 78 bus. **Open** 24 hours daily. **Admission** free.
Thomas Telford's only complete London project (1828) was originally the unloading point for rum, sugar and wool. In 1973 it became the first of the Docklands redevelopments. The network of warehouse conversions provides somewhere to relax and eat once you've trudged around the Tower of London over the road. The dock is full of bobbing yachts and vessels, including a bright red lighthouse ship, the *Nore*, and barges that once worked around the London docks. The Dickens Inn pub is a popular refuelling stop.

Tobacco Dock
The Highway, E1 (071 702 9681). Wapping underground/Shadwell underground/DLR. **Open** *shops* 10am-6pm daily.
This much-trumpeted Docklands shopping centre is still languishing from the recession. The listed warehouses are as beautiful as ever, but they're bereft of the chainstores they had hoped to attract. A few independent shops remain, lured in by very low rents, but many have left. We are told that the new owners of the development are planning to 'relaunch' it in late 1993 or 1994, but phone first to check what's happening. Moored by the dockside are replicas of two ships of the type that once delivered tobacco and wine to the dock. Their future too is uncertain.
Wheelchair access.

Isle of Dogs

As you skirt the horseshoe bend of the Isle of Dogs, evidence of the changing riverside now emerges with Cascades, an apartment block shaped like a ship's funnel. Further back there are a few impressive old structures such as Warehouses 1 & 2, by West India Quay station, and a couple of interesting new ones, like the **Daily Telegraph Building** (*see chapter* **Media**) on South Quay.

Transport
Crossharbour, Island Gardens, Mudchute or West India Quay DLR.

Billingsgate Fish Market
87 West India Dock Road, E14 (071 987 1118). West India Quay DLR/N95, N723 bus. **Open** 5-8.30am Tue-Sat. **Admission** free. **No credit cards.**
In 1982, Billingsgate wholesale fish market moved to its new Docklands premises after 900 years of trading in the City. From shark to cod, all things piscatory are sold here. Unless you're buying the more exotic and expensive varieties, the traders don't like to sell in small quantities. One of the market constables might show you round if asked.

London Docklands Visitor's Centre
3 Limeharbour, E14 (071 512 1111). Crossharbour DLR. **Open** 9am-6pm Mon-Fri; 10am-4.30pm Sat; 9am-4.30pm Sun. **Admission** free.
The Visitor's Centre gives away free maps and other information about the Docklands. There's a very useful audio-visual presentation of the goings-on.
Guided tours (by arrangement). Shop. Wheelchair access.

Mudchute City Farm
Pier Street, E14 (071 515 5901). Mudchute or Island Gardens DLR/277, D7 bus. **Open** 9am-5pm daily. **Admission** free.
City farms are an unusual, but valuable, British phenomenon, devised to offer inner-city children a taste of the rural life. On these 35 acres (14 hectares) you'll find all kinds of farm animals and an orchard. A new study centre is opening in 1994. Riding lessons are available for anyone over the age of seven. Phone 071 515 0749 for details.
Café (open 10am-5pm daily).

Royal Docks

With south-east England slowly sinking and global warming raising the sea level, the **Thames Flood Barrier** was built a few years ago to protect London from freak tides. But nobody expected the tidal wave of corporate offices that has engulfed the Royal Docks. Together, the Victoria, Albert and George VI Docks, covering seven miles (11 kilometres) of quay, were the largest in the world. Today, the central area has become the **London City Airport** (*see chapter* **Getting Around**).

Transport
City Airport, North Woolwich or Silvertown BR/D11, 69, 276 bus.

Thames Barrier Visitor's Centre
Unity Way, Woolwich, SE18 (081 854 1373). Charlton BR/boat to Thames Barrier Pier/180 bus. **Open** 10.30am-5pm Mon-Fri; 10.30am-5.30pm Sat, Sun. **Admission** £2.25; £1.40 OAPs, under-16s; £6.10 family ticket (two adults, three children). **Credit** (shop only) A, V.
The Thames Flood Barrier is the largest of its type in the world. A prudent piece of architecture, it guards against the Thames flooding the capital, as it did in 1928 when 14 people drowned in waves of 20ft (6m). Nine metal-capped concrete piers support the giant steel floodgates. The Visitor's Centre has scale working models of the construction, plus audio displays which explain the entire Thames flood protection system. The Centre gets busy during the week, as it's popular with school parties.
Café. Cruises around the barrier (£1.50 adults, £1 under-16s, 10% discount for groups of 20 or more; information 081 854 5555). Shop. Toilets for the disabled. Wheelchair access.

North London

Camden is cooking and Islington's fizzing, while Hampstead and Highgate are havens for highbrows.

Islington

There has been a settlement at Islington for at least 1,000 years. As the first village on the main road out of the City of London, it was the final stopping off point for all trade coming down from the north of the country, in particular farmers and their cattle travelling to **Smithfield Market** (*see chapter* **The City**). The raised pavement on Upper Street was built to stop pedestrians being splashed by the animals and carts.

In the time of Henry VIII, the rural area between Finsbury (in the City) and the village of Islington was used by the king and his entourage to practise archery. Henry even granted titles to distinguished archers: the Duke of Shoreditch, the Marquis of Islington, and the Earl of Pancras.

But it was in the late seventeenth century that Islington first became fashionable. A spa to the south of the village was said to work wonders on 'Hysterics, Vapours, Dropsies, and Swellings of the Legs'. Gentry came to take the waters until well into the eighteenth century.

Residents of Islington have included a varied mix of artists, writers, philosophers and political leaders: Tom Paine wrote the first section of *The Rights of Man*, Lenin edited the journal *Iskra* and Trotsky studied books in what is now the **Marx Memorial Library** (*see chapter* **Victorian Times**). Literary residents have included Evelyn Waugh, George Orwell, Charles and Mary Lamb and Kate Greenaway. Playwright Joe Orton was living at 25 Noel Road (an attractive street with a popular pub, the **Island Queen**, at No.87), until 1967 when he was murdered there by his lover.

During the seventies, Islington became the home of affluent liberals, usurping Hampstead's traditional role. The 'trendy leftie' was born here. In the eighties, City yuppies arrived, making use of the area's proximity to their workplace. The Agricultural Hall, built in 1862 to house cattle shows, became the **Business Design Centre** (*see chapter* **Business**), house prices soared and Islington's beautiful Georgian and Victorian squares (often described in Charles Dickens' works) were once again highly desirable addresses. Worth visiting are Thornhill, Canonbury, Barnsbury, Cloudesley, Lonsdale, Milner and Gibson Squares.

Islington today is Londoners' London, where the best of the East End and West End have combined. It's truly cosmopolitan – you can eat Lebanese, drink Central American, then watch an African band within a few hundred metres. But even though the area is largely gentrified, there are still spirited outcrops of older, working class culture, no more vibrant than at **Chapel Market**.

Islington's main thoroughfare, Upper Street, is now lined with restaurants and a sprinkling of designer shops. At No.60 there's the **Glorious Clothing Co**, a first-rate second-hand clothes shop that's a hunting ground for many fashion stylists, and opposite Islington Green is the beginning of the antique-filled **Camden Passage** (the street itself was built in 1776). The open-air market, specialising in old silver, jewellery and prints, happens on Wednesday and Saturday; the surrounding shops are open all week. Prices tend to be high, but relentless bargaining is worth a try.

Every night of the week there's usually a band playing somewhere in Islington, sometimes for free. And the district also has some

The **Tower Theatre**. *See* **review** *page 123.*

of the best pub theatres in town. Yet compared to much of central and west London, the area attracts few tourists.

Transport
Angel underground/Highbury & Islington BR.

Alfredo's
4-6 Essex Road, N1 (071 226 3496). Angel underground/38, 73 bus. **Meals served** 7am-2.30pm Mon-Fri; 7.30am-3.30pm Sat; 8.30am-4pm Sun. **Average £4. No credit cards.**
A cherished caff which has been serving cheap British food – pies, fry-ups and puddings drowned in custard – since its art deco fittings were new in the 1920s.

Chapel Market
Chapel Street, N1. Angel underground. **Open** 9am-3.30pm Tue, Wed, Fri, Sat; 9am-1pm Thur, Sun.
One of the best local street markets in London. Islingtonians have bought their fresh fruit and veg here for over a century. Fish, meat, clothes, crockery and household goods are also sold; the market reaches its climax at weekends.

Discover Islington Visitors' Information Centre
44 Duncan Street, N1 (071 278 8787). Angel underground. **Open** 10am-5pm Mon-Sat.
Staff at the Centre have a wealth of information about Islington's history at their fingertips, as well as tourist information on the rest of the UK.

Islington Green
Islington Green, N1. Angel underground.
These small gardens at the junction of Essex Road and Upper Street contain a statue of Sir Hugh Myddleton. During the reign of King James I, Sir Hugh sank all his fortune into building the New River, a channel carrying drinking water from springs in Hertfordshire a distance of 38 miles (60km) to a reservoir near his home in Islington. The river mostly flows underground these days, but it can still be seen along New River Walk, near Canonbury House (by the **Tower Theatre**, *see below*).

King's Head
115 Upper Street, N1 (theatre box office 071 226 1916/pub 071 226 0364). Angel underground. **Open** 11am-midnight Mon-Sat; noon-3pm, 7-11.30pm, Sun.
Customers are still charged in shillings and pence for drinks at this polished Victorian pub (for those too young to remember, 10p equals two shillings). Free performances of jazz, rock or pop are given (at lunchtimes and evenings). The back-room theatre puts on enterprising plays, which often move on to the West End. Alcohol can be served after 11pm to customers who have bought food.

Patisserie Bliss
428 St John Street, EC1 9071 837 3720). Angel underground/19, 38, 43, 56, 73, 171A, 214, 279 bus. **Open** 8.30am-8pm Mon-Fri; 9am-6pm Sat, Sun. **Unlicensed. Credit** LV, £TC.
Locals cram into the tiny ground floor café at weekends to sample the delicious cakes and pastries that appear from the downstairs kitchen, so it's a lot more comfortable to come here in the week. Try an almond croissant, the most popular choice, washed down with a good caffè latte.

Tower Theatre
Canonbury Place, N1 (071 226 5111). Highbury & Islington underground/4, 19, 30, 43, 271, 279 bus. **Open** *Booking hall* 10am-5pm Mon-Fri; *shows* 7.30pm Mon-Sat (closed August); *matinées* 3pm every first Sun

Nash's York Terrace, near **Regent's Park**.

of the month. **Admission** £7; £4 OAPs (standby), students, UB40s. **Credit** A, V.
The Tavistock Repertory Theatre has been staging productions varying from Shakespeare to *Cabaret* here since the 1950s. The Theatre adjoins what remains of the sixteenth-century Canonbury House; Thomas Cromwell, Sir Francis Bacon, and Oliver Goldsmith once resided there. Visitors are admitted by appointment to see the house (contact **Canonbury Academy** on 071 359 6888). Two upper rooms retain their Elizabethan panelling, plaster ceilings and chimney pieces.

Union Chapel
Compton Terrace, N1 (071 354 3631). Highbury & Islington underground/BR. **Open** 9am-5pm Mon-Fri (vestry entrance). **Services** 12.45pm Wed, 11am Sun.
The Chapel bills itself as 'London's funkiest church' and often stages world music and jazz concerts. Built by a group of Nonconformists and Anglicans, it is an impressive edifice designed by Cubitt, who was inspired by the church of Santa Fosca, Torcello, near Venice. Inside is a piece of the Plymouth Rock (upon which the Pilgrim Fathers first landed in 1620) donated by the Pilgrim Society in 1883.

Camden Town & Regent's Park

Henry VIII used what is now **Regent's Park** as a hunting ground, and had a lodge nearby. The land became known as Marylebone Park, but during the Civil War, it was mortgaged by cash-strapped Charles I and was then farmed for over 100 years.

In the eighteenth century, the area (then called Marylebone Gardens) became a fashionable place for the gentry to take summer breakfasts, or to watch firework displays (Dr Johnson is recorded as having attended one such event, and Fanny Burney mentions the Gardens in her novel *Evelina*). Nowadays, there are still firework displays every year on Bonfire Night (5 November), but in the northern part of the park, called Primrose Hill.

When the farming leases ran out in 1811, the Prince Regent employed the architect John Nash to design Regent's Park. Most of the Nash terraces are still standing and streets such as **York Terrace** (1824-6), around the park, retain their pristine stucco frontages and have frequently been used for filming period dramas.

An extraordinary variety of people have lived in the Regent's Park area: Friedrich Engels spent 24 years at 121 Regent's Park Road (from 1870 to 1894); Cecil Sharpe, the collector of folk songs, lived at 2 Regent's Park Road (his house is now used as a centre for folk music, *see chapter* **Music: Rock, Folk & Jazz**); WB Yeats, the Irish poet, spent much of his boyhood at 23 Fitzroy Road between 1867 and 1873; Sylvia Plath, the American poet, committed suicide later at the same address in 1963; and in 1935, Wallis Simpson lived at 16 Cumberland Terrace, NW1, shortly before her affair with Edward VIII caused him to renounce the throne.

Regent's Park, with its rose garden, willow trees and waterways is today one of the most beautiful parts of central London. To its north is the **Regent's Canal**, (which runs east to Camden and Islington, and west to Little Venice and Westbourne Park), and **London Zoo** (*see chapter* **Sightseeing**) which seems to have survived the threat of closure. To the south west is a boating lake, where boats may be hired from 10am to dusk. And in summer, plays are staged within the Inner Circle (phone 071 486 2431 for details). The principal mosque in Britain, **London Central Mosque** (built 1978), occupies a site off Hanover Gate, NW1.

The canal that runs along the park's northern borders was built to bring transport and industry to the area, and hot on its heels grew the working-class district of **Camden Town**.

In the seventies and eighties, Camden, like its near neighbour Islington, became partially gentrified. The Kentish Town Road has kept its local shops and pubs, however, and Camden High Street still has busy a fruit and vegetable market (on Inverness Street), splendid fish shops, and Greek restaurants, bakeries and food stores run by the numerous local Cypriots. But **Chalk Farm Road** now has multifarious small shops selling crafts from around the world, brasseries are sprouting on the High Street, and the cottage-like terraces away from the main roads have BMWs parked outside.

Since the eighties, the streets around **Camden Lock**, on the canal, have been filled every weekend with trendy shoppers and browsers. They come to visit the **Camden Markets** (*see chapters* **Post War** *and* **Shopping**) that are crammed with stalls stocking all manner of clothing, post-hippy accessories, crafts and second-hand goods. The Lock area was extensively redesigned and revamped in 1991 and the project has been widely acclaimed a success. It's still horribly crowded at weekends, though.

Camden's choice of restaurants is one of the best outside the West End (Camden High Street and Parkway are good places to look), and the area has some of the top venues in London for live music, including the **Jazz Café**, the **Forum** and **Camden Palace** (*see chapter* **Music: Rock, Folk & Jazz**). Camden Town's large Irish population means the music on the pub juke-box is as likely to be The Dubliners as Madonna.

Every March, Camden has a three-week festival of music and dance (phone Camden Council on 071 278 4444 for details).

Transport
Camden Town, Chalk Farm or Regent's Park underground.

Arizona
2-2A Jamestown Road, NW1 (071 284 4730). Camden Town underground. **Open** noon-midnight Mon-Sat; noon-10.30pm Sun. **Average** £12. **Credit** A, AmEx, £TC, V.
A Tex-Mex joint that has become a prime meeting place for local young trendsters. Cocktails and bottled beers are sipped outside on the roof terrace in summer, there's an undistinguished nachos and ribs menu, and MTV provides the accompaniment.

Compendium Books
234 Camden High Street, NW1 (071 485 8944/071 267 1525). Camden Town underground/24, 29, 31, 134, 253 bus. **Open** 10am-6pm Mon-Sat; noon-6pm Sun. **Credit** A, £TC, V.
An excellent bookshop on two floors. Both fiction and non-fiction are covered well; the green issues and feminism sections are first rate. Staff are unusually knowledgeable, and it's one of the very few British bookshops stocking the latest North American imports, as well as a great selection of arty magazines and weird fanzines.

Regent's Canal Information Centre
Camden Lock, NW1 (071 482 0523). Camden Town or Chalk Farm underground/Camden Road BR/24, 29, 168, 253 bus. **Open** daily, phone for details.
The castellated former lock-keeper's cottage of Camden Lock has become an outlet for maps, books and information related to the canal. This is the ideal place to start a tow-path walk or narrowboat trip, particularly if you want to get away from the weekend market crowds. One of the best journeys is to Little Venice, with its attractive houseboats, and expensive stucco houses.
Shop. Wheelchair access.

St Pancras Old Church
Pancras Road, NW1 (071 387 7301). Camden Town underground. **Services** 7pm Tue-Thur; 10pm Sat; 10am Sun.
Dedicated to St Pancras, the avenger of broken oaths, this church was built in 1848 on the site of a thirteenth-century place of worship. It has a marvellously gloomy churchyard, where Shelley courted Mary Godwin, author of the Gothic novel *Frankenstein*, over the grave of her mother, Mary Wollstonecraft (the body was

removed when the railways from St Pancras Station cut through the site). The architect Sir John Soane's magnificent grave (designed by himself) remains.

Hampstead & Highgate

Of all the districts near to central London, Hampstead and Highgate have retained the feel of small country towns, despite being surrounded by the urban sprawl. Both are easily reached by underground and both can be seen in a day. A walk through **Hampstead Heath** will provide an enjoyable bucolic interlude between the two in fine weather.

Hampstead stands upon one of the highest hills around London, four miles (6.4 kilometres) north-west of the City. The village remained small until, in 1698, an advertisement was published claiming that the Hampstead chalybeate waters were 'of the same nature and equal in virtue with Tunbridge Wells'. It was a PR triumph: within a few years Hampstead had been rechristened Hampstead Wells, and become a fashionable health resort with a spa.

This was also the period when literary society discovered Hampstead. Alexander Pope came here regularly to take the waters, along with his friend John Gay, author of *The Beggar's Opera*. Sir Joshua Reynolds and Samuel Johnson also attended dances and assemblies in the area.

Ever since, Hampstead has been the chosen home of writers and artists (although it is some time since impoverished ones could afford to live here). **Keats** is inextricably linked with the district, and his house (*see chapter* **Museums**) is open to the public. July 1995 will be the 200th anniversary of his birth.

John Constable was a particularly enthusiastic resident: 'I love every stile and stump and lane in the village'. He worked on many paintings of the area during time spent at 40 Well Walk, NW3; they can be seen at the **Tate** (*see chapter* **Art Galleries**). Other local celebrities include General de Gaulle, who lived at No 99 Frognal during World War II; and Sigmund **Freud**, whose house is open to the public (*see chapter* **Museums**).

Hampstead today still has innumerable old houses and cottages in the narrow streets that wind around the hill to the Heath. Well, Walk, Holly Bush Hill, Church Row, and Flask Walk are particularly picturesque. If you prefer something on a grander scale, visit the local sixteenth-century mansion, **Fenton House** (*see chapter* **Tudors & Stuarts**). Or take a trip down **Bishop's Avenue**, known as Millionaire's Row, where today's *nouveaux tres, tres riche* live in vast over-adorned twentieth-century piles that seem clumsily crowded together.

Restaurants tend to be pricey, but there's a fair choice, and many of the area's splendid old pubs have decent food. One of the most famous pubs is the **Spaniard's** a sixteenth-century hostelry on Spaniard's Road near the Heath (*see chapter* **Eating & Drinking**). If you want celluloid entertainment, Hampstead has one of London's best repertory cinemas, the **Everyman** (*see chapter* **Film**). And if you want fashion, Hampstead is full of chic shops, many of which are open on Sundays.

Highgate, with its position on a main route between London and the North, about five miles (8 kilometres) from the City, became (along with Islington) a stop-over point for stage-coaches. In the eighteenth century there were up to 19 licensed taverns in the village. One of Highgate's best pubs, the **Flask** on Highgate West Hill (*see chapter* **Eating & Drinking**) was popular with the eighteenth-century chronicler of low life, William Hogarth, who used to sketch scenes of drunken revelry there. The pub got its name from the containers in which the salubrious spa water of the area was sold.

Like Hampstead, Highgate rests near the top of a hill. In 1837, Queen Victoria almost came to grief on the slope when the horses towing her carriage bolted down Highgate West Hill. A local landlord came to her assistance, and his swift action led to his pub being granted a royal coat of arms.

Lauderdale House, half-way up Highgate Hill, is said to be where King Charles II kept trysts with his mistress, Nell Gwyn. Lauderdale House is now open to the public, and has frequent recitals and exhibitions *(see chapter* **Music: Classical & Opera**).

Kenwood House (*see chapter* **Georgian London**), set on the edge of Hampstead Heath is another local mansion open to the public. Classical concerts are staged in its grounds during the summer (*see chapter* **London By Season**). More of Highgate's handsome houses can be seen on The Grove, an avenue lined with seventeenth- and eighteenth-century dwellings. The nineteenth-century poet Samuel Taylor Coleridge lived at No.3 from 1816 to 1834 with his friend Dr Gillman, who tried to rid the poet of his drug addiction. More recently the house was owned by the playwright and novelist, JB Priestley.

The most attractive part of Highgate can be reached from Hampstead by walking across Parliament Hill. If you travel to Highgate station, your first view of the area will be Archway Road, the main A1 rat-run into the City. Cross this sharpish, and walk down Southwood Road to reach Highgate High Street, which is lined with local shops (not a chain store or supermarket in sight) and dignified Georgian houses. As you walk down the hill, Waterlow Park is to the right (open dawn to dusk daily), with about 29 acres (12 hectares) of hillside, stately beech and yew trees. A stroll across it to Swains Lane will lead you to the entrance of Highgate Cemetery (*see chapter* Victorian Times), where, for over 110 years, Karl Marx has been a famous resident.

Transport
Archway, Hampstead or Highgate underground.

Burgh House (Hampstead Museum)
New End Square, NW3 (071 431 0144). Hampstead underground/Hampstead Heath BR/24, 46, 168, 210, 268 bus. **Open** noon-5pm Wed-Sun; 2-5pm Bank Holidays. **Admission** free.
Hampstead's local history museum is housed in a finely proportioned Queen Anne building constructed in 1703. Its interior features an intricately carved staircase, wood-panelled rooms and a basement café with a terrace over-looking the garden. One of the early inhabitants was a Dr William Gibbons, who grew rich prescribing the foul-tasting waters of Hampstead Wells. The museum includes a display of prints (but no paintings) of John Constable. Other local residents covered include D H Lawrence, Keats and the artist Stanley Spencer.
Café (11am-5.30pm). Shop.

Hampstead & Highgate Bathing Ponds
Hampstead Mixed Bathing Pond *East Heath Road, NW3 Hampstead underground.* **Open** *May-Sept* 10am-6pm daily; *Oct-Feb* 10am-3pm daily.
Highgate Pond *Millfield Lane, N6 (081 340 4044). Kentish Town underground/210, C2 bus.* **Open** 7am-dusk daily.
Competent male swimmers only.
Kenwood Pond *Millfield Lane, N6 (081 348 1033). Kentish Town underground/210, C2 bus.* **Open** 7am-dusk daily.
Females over eight years old.
Admission all free.
Free, fresh-water bathing can be shivered through at these three ponds. The Hampstead mixed bathing pond is rather more seedy than the single-sex ponds but pleasant nonetheless, and it has an indomitably British feel. The Highgate men-only pond, in a delightful wooded setting, is popular with naturists and gays. The women-only pond, a little further north, has few facilities, but is in a beautiful secluded spot surrounded by trees and banks for sunbathing. Take along a picnic for those after-swim hunger pangs (*see chapter* **Sport & Fitness**).

Hampstead Heath
NW3 (Parliament Hill 071 485 4491/Kenwood 081 340 5303/Golder's Hill 081 455 5183). Belsize Park or Hampstead underground/Gospel Oak or Hampstead Heath BR. **Open** 24 hours daily.
When Hampstead became a fashionable spa town in the late seventeenth century, its heath was still a notorious spot for highwaymen. Nowadays, the 800 acres (320 hectares) of wonderful, wild parkland is the place to go if you want a bit of exercise, or to fly your kite (from the top of Parliament Hill). Alternatively, sit and admire the splendid views over London and count how many of the hundred or so resident species of birds you can spot. Funfairs are held here on the Easter, Whitsun and August Bank Holiday weekends (*see chapter* **London by Season**).
Fishing. Three swimming ponds. Toilets for the disabled.

Louis Patisserie
42 Heath Street, NW3 (071 435 9908). Hampstead underground. **Open** 9.30am-6pm daily. **No credit cards.**

Louis just has to be in Hampstead. Tea comes in a silver pot, waitresses disappear behind swishing curtains and spectacular selections of cream cakes are waltzed through the room on large trays. Don't miss the Louis cake, a completely wonderful chocolatey triangle that's worth crossing London for.

Village Bistro
38 Highgate High Street, N6 (081 340 0275/5165). Archway or Highgate underground. **Lunch served** noon-2.45pm daily. **Dinner served** 6-11.30pm Mon-Sat; 6-11pm Sun. **Average** £20. **Credit** A, AmEx, DC, £TC, V.
Old beams, pretty table-cloths and lacy knick-knacks suggest a twee tea shop, but the Village Bistro is, in fact, a tiny restaurant. Food is French, but with British influences. Just right for a romantic dinner in Highgate village.

Whitestone Pond Open Air Art Exhibition
Whitestone Pond, Heath Street, NW3. Hampstead underground. **Open** *May-Aug* 11am-7pm Sat, Sun, Bank Holidays.
Pottery, paintings, prints and jewellery are on sale around Whitestone Pond at the top of Heath Street on summer weekends.

Whittington Stone
Highgate Hill. Archway underground.
Dick Whittington came to London to seek his fortune and became the city's mayor four times between 1397 and 1419; he served one interim term (on the death of the previous incumbent) and three full terms. This block of stone was placed here in 1821 to mark the spot where he is said to have heard the bells of London summoning him: 'Turn again Whittington, thrice Mayor of London'. The cat which sits on the stone was added in 1964 to commemorate the animal whose skill in rat-catching was (according to the legend enacted in pantomimes across the land every Christmas-time) the foundation of Whittington's fortune.

The **Hampstead Bathing Ponds**. *See* **review**.

Eating
& Drinking

The past 20 years have seen an astonishing improvement in both the quality and variety of London's restaurants. Bars and cafés have also diversified, but the peerless London pub has more than held its own. The choice is fantastic, and it begins here.

Contents

Restaurant Area Index

Dumpling delicacies at **China Court**. *See* **review** *page 135.*

Restaurants

Eat your way round the world in a city where an African lunch can be followed by a Vietnamese supper.

For diversity of cuisines, London can match anywhere in the world. The quality isn't bad either, and is getting better all the time. It's one of the best cities in which to eat Indian food; Chinatown can lay claim to serving the best dim sum in the world; and inventive Modern British chefs are constantly pushing the boundaries of their cuisine forward. The other joy is that experimentation and culinary satisfaction don't depend on money alone. Here, alongside celebrity chefs and top rank restaurants, we've included Japanese diners, fish and chip shops, pizza parlours and burger joints – united by the fact that they are among the best of their type.

Many of London's drinking establishments also serve good, inexpensive food; the best are listed in *chapter* **Cafés, Pubs & Bars**. And if you fall victim to the midnight munchies, *see* *chapter* **Early Hours**, which lists a selection of restaurants that stay open late.

If you want to investigate London's restaurant scene further, the *Time Out Guide to Eating and Drinking* (updated annually, it costs £6.99) lists over 1,500 restaurants, cafés and bars. The **average prices** quoted below are based on the cost of a three-course meal (or the ethnic equivalent) for one person. They do not include alcohol.

Celebrated Chefs

Alastair Little
49 Frith Street, W1 (071-734 5183). Leicester Square or Tottenham Court Road underground. **Lunch served** noon-3pm Mon-Fri. **Dinner served** 6-11.30pm Mon-Sat. **Average** £45. **Set lunches** £10 two courses (basement); £20 three courses. **House wine** from £12 bottle, £3 glass. **Mineral water** £2.75 bottle, £1.25 glass. **Credit** A, AmEx, £TC, V.
Prices are high (try the no-choice set lunch) and the décor shabby, but Alastair Little's cooking rarely gives cause for complaint. His dishes are always innovative as his repertoire constantly evolves.

Slip between the suits to sample **Imperial City's** *Chinese cooking. See* **review** *page 137.*

Canteen

Unit 4G, Harbour Yard, Chelsea Harbour, SW10 (071 351 7330). Fulham Broadway underground then C3 bus. **Lunch served** noon-3pm Mon-Sat; 12.30-3.30pm Sun. **Dinner served** 6.30pm-midnight Mon-Sat; 7-11pm Sun. **Average** £26 incl £1 cover. **House wine** £12 bottle, £3 glass. **Mineral water** £3 bottle, £1 glass. **Credit** A, £TC, V.

Marco Pierre White's new venture with actor Michael Caine offers grandish French food at reasonably accessible prices. The place is smooth and a bit flashy. Service can be offhand.

The Capital

22-24 Basil Street, SW3 (071 589 5171/fax 071 225 0011). Knightsbridge underground. **Lunch served** noon-2.30pm, **dinner served** 7-11pm, daily. **Average** £25. **Set lunches** £21.50, £25, three courses incl coffee, service. **Set dinner** £25 three courses incl coffee, service. **Service** 12½%. **House wine** £10.50 bottle, £3.75 glass. **Mineral water** £2.50 bottle, £1.50 glass. **Credit** A, AmEx, DC, TC, V.

A small but perfectly formed hotel restaurant. Philip Britten's superb, unshowy cooking is French in principle, but his dishes take note of the English seasons, as in a summery dish like salmon mille feuille with asparagus. The daunting wine list has a helpful page of selections, often priced at less than £15. Dress: smart

Chez Nico at Ninety Park Lane

90 Park Lane, W1 (071 409 1290/fax 071 355 4877). Hyde Park Corner or Marble Arch underground. **Lunch served** noon-2pm Mon-Fri. **Dinner served** 7-11pm Mon-Sat. **Average** £60. **Set lunch** £25 three courses incl service. **Service** 12½%. **Wines** from £18 bottle, £5 glass. **Mineral water** £3.50 bottle, £1.25 glass. **Credit** A, AmEx, DC, £TC, V.

Nico Ladenis operates here under the wing of Forte, cooking sumptuous dishes such as salad of warm foie gras on toasted brioche with caramelised orange. The atmosphere remains that of a hotel-dining room. The long wine list includes a selection of just-about affordable bottles. Chefs trained the Nico way cook at the branches listed below (where the average is £25 a head). Dress: jacket and tie.

Branches: Nico Central 35 Great Portland Street, W1 (071 436 8846); **Simply Nico** 48A Rochester Row, SW1 (071 630 8061).

Fish and chips

Okay, so Britain is the constant butt of jokes concerning its people's fondness for chips drenched in vinegar, and fish caked in batter. But at its best, fish and chips is a gloriously appetising and inexpensive meal. Ideally the fish should be cooked to order, its batter crisp and crumbly; the chips should come straight out of the fryer, and the accompaniment should be a blob of mushy peas. Unfortunately, most London chip shops serve pretty mediocre food, compared to the ambrosia produced by chippies in the north of England. All too often, the chips you'll get here are like cardboard, the fish like rubber, the batter like leather encasing custard. But good chip shops do exist in the capital. As a rule, avoid anywhere festooned with a Union Jack flag, and you've made a start. The establishments listed below all cook excellent fish and chips, available in the restaurant, or as a takeaway.

Geales

2 Farmer Street, W8 (071 727 7969). Notting Hill Gate underground. **Meals served** noon-3pm, 6-11pm, Tue-Sat. **Average** £9.50 incl 15p cover. **Set lunch** (Tue-Fri) £6.95 three courses. **House wine** £5.75 bottle, £1.70 glass. **Mineral water** 80p glass. **Credit** A, LV, £TC, V.

A notable chippie where the frying is done in beef dripping, producing a gorgeous, dark, crunchy and grease-free coating. The fish here is outstandingly fresh, the chips good, the portions generous. Décor is cottage-like.

Rock & Sole Plaice

47 Endell Street, WC2 (071 836 3785). Covent

Garden underground. **Meals served** 11.30am-10.30pm Mon-Sat. **Average** £7. **Minimum** £1 (12.30-2.45pm). **Unlicensed. Corkage** no charge. **Mineral water** 50p glass. **Credit** LV, £TC.

There are no fancy decorations, the tables are Formica and it's all a bit of a squash, but the quality of the limited range of fish (cod, rock salmon, haddock, plaice and skate), served here belies the humble surroundings. The mushy peas are good too.

Sea Shell Fish Restaurant and Takeaway

49-51 Lisson Grove, NW1 (071 723 8703/071 724 1063). Marylebone underground/BR. **Lunch served** noon-2.15pm, **dinner served** 5.15-10.30pm, Mon-Fri. **Meals served** noon-10.30pm Sat. **Average** £13. **Minimum** £3.50. **Set meal** (noon-2.15pm, 5.15-7pm) £8.95 three courses incl coffee. **House wine** £8.95 bottle, £1.95 glass. **Mineral water** £3 bottle, £1 glass. **Credit** A, AmEx, DC, LV, £TC, V.

Contender for the title of best fish and chip restaurant in London. The fish (the very freshest) and chips are cooked to a T. Prices are higher than usual, but worth it. Décor is typical.

Branch: Gutter Lane, Gresham Street, EC2 (071 606 6961).

Upper Street Fish Shop

324 Upper Street, N1 (071 359 1401). Angel underground. **Lunch served** noon-2pm Tue-Fri; noon-3pm Sat. **Dinner served** 5.30-10pm Mon-Sat. **Average** £11. **Minimum** £5. **Unlicensed. Corkage** no charge. **Mineral water** 75p glass. **Credit** £TC.

A small, French bistro-style room with a jolly atmosphere. First-rate fish comes fried, grilled or poached and is followed by enticing desserts, such as bread and butter pudding or rhubarb tart, with custard or ice-cream.

Clarke's
*124 Kensington Church Street, W8 (071 221 9225).
Notting Hill Gate underground/12, 27, 28, 31, 52 bus.*
Lunch served 12.30-2pm, **dinner served** 7-10pm,
Mon-Fri. **Set lunch** £22 two courses, £26 three
courses, incl coffee, service. **Set dinner** £37 four
courses incl coffee, service. **House wine** £8 bottle, £2
glass. **Mineral water** £1.50 large bottle, 75p small
bottle. **Credit** A, £TC, V.
An intimate, discreet dining room, driven by the talents
of chef Sally Clarke. The style is Californian, with French
and Italian influences. There's a limited choice of dishes at lunch, no choice in the evening, so check what's on
when you book.

La Tante Claire
*68 Royal Hospital Road, SW3 (071 352 6045/071 351
0227/fax 071 352 3257). Sloane Square underground.*
Lunch served 12.30-2pm, **dinner served** 7-11pm,
Mon-Fri. **Average** £55 dinner. **Minimum** £45 dinner.
Set lunch £24.50 three courses incl coffee, service.
House wine £11.90 bottle, £3 glass. **Mineral water**
£2.50 bottle. **Credit** A, AmEx, DC, TC, V.
Pierre Koffman now has three Michelin stars, but this
temple of gastronomy has a pleasant atmosphere and a
pretty, unfussy dining room. You can expect daring combinations and sensational flavours with an underlying
gutsiness. The wine list is massive and has some French
country wines for everyday consolation. Dress: jacket
and tie.

African

Calabash
*The Africa Centre, 38 King Street, WC2 (071 836
1976). Covent Garden underground.* **Lunch served**
12.30-3pm Mon-Fri. **Dinner served** 6-10.30pm Mon-
Sat. **Average** £15 incl 25p cover. **Service** 10%.
House wine £6.50 bottle, £4.25 carafe, £1.60 glass.
Mineral water £2.70 bottle, 80p glass. **Credit** A,
AmEx, DC, £TC, V.
Dishes from all parts of Africa are served in this sur-
prisingly large restaurant. The menu carries clear expla-
nations to help newcomers. A typical dish is yassa, a
Senegalese dish of chicken marinated with lemon juice
and peppers. Wines are from Algeria and Zimbabwe,
beers from all over Africa.

The Americas

Café Pacifico
*5 Langley Street, WC2 (071 379 7728). Covent Garden
underground.* **Meals served** noon-11.45pm Mon-Sat;
noon-10.45pm Sun. **Average** £14. **Set lunches** (Mon-
Fri) £5 one course incl glass of beer or wine, coffee.
Service 12½%. **House wine** £7.95 bottle, £1.95 glass.
Mineral water £2.50 bottle, £1 glass. **Credit** A,
AmEx, £TC, V.
A large restaurant with huge windows and a wooden interior, Café Pacifico is the most attractive Mexican in town.
Dishes employ the usual permutations of tacos, tortillas,
beans and sour cream: presentation is good and portions
are ample. The margaritas are worth sampling.

Christopher's
*18 Wellington Street, WC2 (071 240 4222). Covent
Garden underground.* **Brunch served** 11.30am-3pm
Sun. **Lunch served** noon-3pm Mon-Fri. **Dinner
served** 6-11.30pm Mon-Sat. **Average** £30. **Set
brunch** (Sun) £19.95 three courses incl ½ bottle
champagne. **Pre-theatre menus** (6-7pm) £15, £17,

F Cooke & Sons. *See* **review** page 133.

£19, three courses. **Service** 12½% for parties of seven
or more. **House wine** from £10 bottle; £2.50 glass.
Mineral water £2.95 bottle, £1.25 glass. **Credit** A,
AmEx, DC, £TC, V.
The impressive indoor decoration contrasts with the sim-
plicity of the food at this formal American restaurant.
Prices are high, but the quality of the ingredients is excellent and the cooking accomplished. The lengthy wine list
includes a good selection of American wines. Shame
about the two-sittings-a-night policy.

Ed's Easy Diner
*12 Moor Street, W1 (071 439 1955). Leicester Square
or Tottenham Court Road underground.* **Meals served**
11.30am-midnight Mon-Thur; 11.30am-12.30am Fri,
Sat; 9am-11pm Sun. **Average** £6. **Minimum** £3.95
when busy. **House wine** £3.50 carafe. **Mineral water**
£1 small bottle. **Credit** LV, TC.
Ed's looks just like a 1950s diner, until you reach the
menu, which lists but a small selection of diner staples.
Everything is cooked to order behind the diner counter
where you sit. The music is great, and the service is
speedy and attentive.
Branches: 362 King's Road, SW3 (071 352 1956); 16
Hampstead High Street, NW3 (071 431 1958); 333-337
Fulham Road, SW10 (071 352 1952).

Hard Rock Café
*150 Old Park Lane, W1 (071 629 0382). Hyde Park
Corner underground.* **Meals served** 11.30am-12.30am
Mon-Thur; 11.30am-1am Fri, Sat; 11.30am-midnight
Sun. **Average** £14. **Minimum** main course when
busy. **Service** 12½%. **House wine** £8.95 bottle, £2.45
glass. **Mineral water** £1.15 small bottle. **Credit** A,
AmEx, £STC, V.
The queue is the talking point, rather than the food or
the rock 'n' roll artefacts, but once you're inside this
object of pilgrimage, the burgers are fine. Portions,
especially the puddings, are large. Bookings not
accepted.

Joe Allen
*13 Exeter Street, WC2 (071 836 0651). Aldwych or
Covent Garden underground.* **Meals served** noon-
12.45am Mon-Sat; noon-11.30pm Sun. **Average** £20.
House wine £7 bottle, £2 glass. **Mineral water** £2.50
bottle, £1 small bottle. **Credit** TC.
This blackened basement, relieved by theatrical posters
and red and white checked tablecloths, has a reputation
as a media haunt. The menu mixes American classics
with modish dishes, to generally good effect. Service is
not all it could be.

SPAGHETTI HOUSE

A Group of Individuals

Jermyn Street
Well suited to everyone
16-17 Jermyn Street SW1. Tel: 734 7334

Haymarket
Opposite Burberry's
66 Haymarket SW1. Tel: 839 3642

◆ TRATT ◆
Close to the British Museum
4 Victoria House, Southampton Row WC1.
Tel: 405 6658

Vecchia Milano
Elegant Old Milan
74 Welbeck Street W1. Tel: 935 2371

Zia Teresa
Neighbour to Harrods
6 Hans Road SW3. Tel: 589 7634

Villa Carlotta
The freshness of a garden setting
Private banqueting suite for
120 people is available Tel: 637 9941
33/37 Charlotte Street W1. Tel: 636 60

Head Office: 39 Charlotte Street, London W1.
Tel: 637 9941

Planet Hollywood

Trocadero, Piccadilly, W1 (071 287 1000). Piccadilly Circus underground. **Meals served** 11am-11pm daily. **Average** £17. **Service** 12½%. **House wine** £8.95 bottle, £2.50 glass. **Mineral water** £2.95 bottle, £1.50 glass. **Credit** A, AmEx, DC, £TC, V.
Admire film ephemera while queuing at the much-hyped Planet Hollywood. The food comes in sizable amounts – a big burger is accompanied by chips, half a pickled cucumber, a large, slightly crispy bun, tomatoes, onion, sweet coleslaw and a mustard dip – at fairly hefty prices. Bookings not accepted.

Belgian

Belgo

72 Chalk Farm Road, NW1 (071 267 0718). Chalk Farm underground. **Lunch served** noon-3pm, **dinner served** 6-11pm, Mon-Fri. **Meals served** noon-midnight Sat; noon-10.30pm Sun. **Average** £20. **Set meal** £8.95 two courses incl one beer. **Service** 15%. **House wine** £8.50 bottle, £1.75 glass. **Mineral water** £2 bottle, £1 glass. **Credit** A, AmEx, LV, £TC, V.
One of the most fashionable joints around, Belgo boasts a stark interior, connoisseur Belgian beers and waiters in monk's garb. Food revolves around mussels and frites. The seats are a little too austere.

British

See also **Box: Fish & chips**.

Bentley's

11-15 Swallow Street, W1 (071 734 4756/fax 071 287 2972). Piccadilly Circus underground.
Restaurant & oyster bar **Lunch served** noon-2.30pm, **dinner served** 6-10.30pm, Mon-Sat. **Average** £30. **Set lunches** £16.50 two courses, £19.50 three courses. *Wine bar* **Open** noon-11pm Mon-Sat. **Average** £10. *Both* **House wine** £11 bottle, £2.50 glass. **Mineral water** £3 bottle, £1 glass. **Credit** A, AmEx, DC, JCB, £TC, V.
Chef Richard Corrigan's arrival has ensured that the standard of the cooking now matches the opulence of the surroundings. Cornish crab salad, sautéed calf's liver and sweetbreads and summer pudding are typical dishes. Dress: smart.
Branch: 11 Queen Victoria Street, EC4 (071 489 8067).

F Cooke & Sons

41 Kingsland High Street, E8 (071 254 2878). Dalston Kingsland BR/22A, 22B, 38, 67, 149, 243 bus. **Open** 10am-7pm Mon-Wed; 10am-8pm Thur; 10am-10pm Fri, Sat. **Average** £4. **Unlicensed**. **No credit cards.**
London's traditional pie and mash shops are dotted around working-class areas of south and east London. Sit on hard wooden benches and tuck into minced beef pie, jellied eels, liquor (parsley sauce) and a wedge of mashed potato. Follow it with cherry pie and custard. At Cooke's, you can also admire beautiful, but basic Victorian tiles and furnishings.

The Goring Hotel

15 Beeston Place, Grosvenor Gardens, SW1 (071 396 9000). Victoria underground/BR. **Breakfast served** 7am-10am daily. **Lunch served** 12.30-2.30pm Mon-Fri, Sun. **Afternoon tea served** 3.30-5pm, **dinner served** 6-10pm, daily. **Set lunches** £16.50 two courses, £19.50 three courses. **Set dinner** £25 three courses. **Service** 10%. **House wine** £13.50 bottle,

The Square. *See* **review** page 137.

£3.50 glass. **Mineral water** £2 bottle, 85p glass. **Credit** A, AmEx, DC, £TC, V.
An old-style, family-run business. The stately, classical dining hall is the setting for many an impressive meal. Dishes range from traditional to slightly more modern; the wine list is long and serious. Staff, like the place, are friendly in a formal sort of way. Dress: smart.

The Guinea

30 Bruton Place, W1 (071 499 1210). Green Park or Oxford Circus underground. **Lunch served** 12.30-2.30pm Mon-Fri. **Dinner served** 6.30-11pm Mon-Sat. **Alcoholic drinks served** 11am-11pm Mon-Sat. **Average** £30 incl £1.25 cover (dinner). **Set lunch** £15.50 two courses, £21.45 three courses, incl coffee. **Service** 12½%. **House wine** £9.85 bottle, £2.45 glass. **Mineral water** £3 bottle, £1.10 glass. **Credit** A, AmEx, DC, JCB, £$TC, V.
A staidly decorated restaurant at the back of a Young's boozer, where the food is best of British. Pies (steak and kidney) and grills (steak, and wild salmon) are top-notch and the wine cellar bounteous. Service is impeccable. The lighter set-lunch menu is excellent.

Quality Chop House

94 Farringdon Road, EC1 (071 837 5093). Farringdon underground/BR/19, 38 bus. **Lunch served** noon-3pm Mon-Sat; noon-4pm Sun. **Dinner served** 6.30pm-midnight Mon-Sat; 7-11.30pm Sun. **Average** £18. **House wine** £8.75 bottle, £2.25 glass. **Mineral water** £2 bottle, 75p glass. **Credit** £TC.
The tiny, 120 year-old interior – tiled floor, ornate yellowing plasterwork, wooden booths – is usually packed with fans of Charles Fontaine's updated British tuck. Fishcakes are salmon, and come with sorrel sauce; black pudding is accompanied by apple compote.

Simpson's-in-the-Strand Grand Divan Tavern

100 Strand, WC2 (071 836 9112). Charing Cross underground/BR. **Lunch served** noon-2.30pm daily. **Dinner served** 6-11pm Mon-Sat; 6-9pm Sun. **Average**

£25. **Set meal** £10 two courses incl coffee. **House wine** £12 bottle, £8.95 pint carafe, £2.25 glass. **Mineral water** £2.95 bottle, £1.60 half bottle. **Credit** A, AmEx, DC, JCB, £$TC, V.
The best roast beef in town in suitably fusty surroundings. Yorkshire puddings are dryish, but afters include such delights as treacle roll (£3.25) and vintage port (£4.50 a glass). The atmosphere is masculine; dress: jacket and tie.

Sweetings
39 Queen Victoria Street, EC4 (071 248 3062). Cannon Street underground/BR. **Lunch served** 11.30am-3pm Mon-Fri. **Average** £19. **House wine** £10.50 bottle, £3.15 glass. **Mineral water** £3.50 bottle, 90p glass. **Credit** £TC.

A hugely popular City fish restaurant where space is tight and service unpredictable. The old-fashioned surroundings are scenic though, and the fish and seafood very fresh. Puddings are the best of British.

Modern British

The Modern British restaurant was an innovation of the 1980s, when talented chefs began experimenting with ingredients from around the world to create a palpably new cuisine. The result is often exciting, and unfailingly fashionable. *See also above* **Celebrated Chefs**.

Dim sum

As a result of the exodus of top chefs from Hong Kong (before the colony reverts to Chinese rule in 1997), London has garnered together some of the world's finest Cantonese culinary talent. Perhaps the most distinctive manifestations of Cantonese cuisine is dim sum: delicious snacks and dumplings, deep-fried or steamed, that are served every lunchtime and afternoon (never after 6pm). Soho's Chinatown has numerous restaurants that serve these snacks; we list the best below. Sunday lunchtime is the most popular time to partake of the meal. From noon, tables quickly become full of chattering throngs of local Cantonese.

Whether you order from a menu, or (the traditional way) choose from a trolley, dim sum should cost only about £1.60 a portion. Seven or eight portions will provide a large lunch for two – bestowing both excellent food and great fun.

China Court
Swiss Centre, 10 Wardour Street, W1 (071 434 0108/0109). Piccadilly Circus underground. **Meals served** 11.45am-11.30pm Mon-Sat; 11am-11.30pm Sun. **Dim sum** 11.45am-4.45pm Mon-Sat; 11am-4.45pm Sun. **Average** £8 dim sum, £15 full menu. **Set dinners** £6.50-£7.90 per person (minimum two). **House wine** £6.90 bottle, £2 glass. **Mineral water** £3 bottle, £1 glass. **Credit** A, AmEx, £TC, V.
Some of the best dim sum dishes are listed on the Chinese menu only, but it's worth persisting as many Cantonese eat here regularly. The quality drops when the dim sum chefs go home.
Branch: London Chinatown Gerrard Street, W1 (071 437 3186).

Chuen Cheng Ku
17 Wardour Street, W1 (071 437 1398). Leicester Square or Piccadilly Circus underground. **Meals served** 11am-11.30pm daily. **Dim sum** 11am-5.30pm daily. **Average** £7 dim sum, £13 full menu. **Set meals** from £9 per person (minimum two).

House wine £7.30 bottle, £1.90 glass. **Mineral water** £2.80 bottle, 95p glass. **Credit** A, AmEx, DC, £TC, V.
Trolleys trundle around CCK's ornate, vast dining area, laden with dumplings, buns and unusual titbits. Just point at what you want – it's likely to be an appetising treat.

Harbour City
46 Gerrard Street, W1 (071 439 7859/071 287 1526). Leicester Square or Piccadilly Circus underground. **Meals served** noon-11.30pm Mon-Sat; 11am-11pm Sun. **Dim sum** noon-5pm daily. **Average** £7 dim sum, £15 full menu. **Set dinners** £10.50-£25 per person (minimum two). **Service** 10%. **House wine** £7.50 bottle, £1.90 glass. **Mineral water** £1.50 small bottle. **Credit** A, AmEx, DC, £TC, V.
Here the entire dim sum menu has been translated into English – a rare occurrence. The 'exotic' list contains the delicacies. All three floors have light, modern décor, and service is usually gracious.

Hong Kong
6-7 Lisle Street, WC2 (071 287 0324/0352). Leicester Square or Piccadilly Circus underground. **Meals served** noon-11.30pm daily. **Dim sum** noon-5pm daily. **Average** £8 dim sum, £15 full menu. **Set dinners** £9-£15 per person (minimum two). **House wine** £7.50 bottle, £1.70 glass. **Mineral water** £2 bottle, £1 glass. **Credit** A, AmEx, TC, V.
The quality of the dim sum is supreme at this large ground floor restaurant. A few vegetarian (*zhai*) dishes are available – ask for them, as they appear only on the Chinese menu.

Tai Wing Wah
7-9 Newport Place, WC2 (071 287 2702). Leicester Square underground. **Meals served** noon-11.30pm Mon-Thur; noon-midnight Fri, Sat; 11am-10.30pm Sun. **Dim sum** noon-5pm Mon-Sat; 11am-5pm Sun. **Average** £8 dim sum, £15 full menu. **Set meal** £7.90 per person (minimum two). **House wine** £6.90 bottle, £1.80 glass. **Mineral water** £3 bottle, 90p glass. **Credit** A, AmEx, DC, £TC, V.
Even if you stick with the English-translation menu, the standard of the dim sum is generally high. Try the delicate chicken and mushroom pastries, or the roast pork crispy buns. Furnishings are light and the place is pristine.

"WHAT D'YA MEAN WE CAN'T BRING OUR HORSES?"

LOOKING FOR A GREAT NIGHT OUT AND YOU'VE NOT TRIED BREAK FOR THE BORDER? WITH ITS LEGENDARY TEX-MEX MENU, ONE OF THE MOST IMPRESSIVE BOOZE LISTS IN TOWN AND THE HOTTEST LIVE MUSIC THIS SIDE OF THE RIO GRANDE,

BREAK FOR THE BORDER IS THE BEST PARTY VENUE IN LONDON. THERE'S A BRAND NEW MENU - MEAT AND VEGETARIAN, YOU CAN FEAST, YOU CAN BOOGIE, YOU CAN SLAM!, AND YOU'LL HAVE SUCH A GREAT TIME YOU WON'T REMEMBER WHERE YOU TIED UP TRIGGER.

BREAK FOR THE BORDER - IT'S TEXAN FOR PARTY.

HAPPY HOUR 5.30 TO 7.30 7 NIGHTS A WEEK
HALF PRICE COCKTAILS

5 GOSLETT YARD
(OFF CHARING CROSS ROAD)
NEAREST TUBE TOTTEHAM COURT RD
071 437 8595
OPEN 5.30PM - 3AM MONDAY-SATURDAY
5.30PM - 11PM SUNDAY

7-8 ARGYLL STREET
(OFF OXFORD CIRCUS)
NEAREST TUBE OXFORD CIRCUS
071 734 5776
OPEN 12 NOON - 1AM MONDAY-SATURDAY
5.30PM - 11PM SUNDAY

The Ivy

1 West Street, WC2 (071 836 4751). Leicester Square underground. **Lunch served** noon-3pm, **dinner served** 5.30pm-midnight, daily. **Average** £30 incl £1.50 cover. **Set lunch** (Sat, Sun) £12.50 three courses. **House wine** £8.50 bottle, £2.25 glass. **Mineral water** £3 bottle, £1.75 glass. **Credit** A, AmEx, DC, £TC, V.
A place to see and be seen. The convivial, clubby setting is enlivened by stained glass and murals. The food is good; the menu moderately modish.
Branch: Le Caprice Arlington House, Arlington Street, SW1 (071 629 2239).

Kensington Place

201 Kensington Church Street, W8 (071 727 3184/fax 229 2025). Notting Hill Gate underground/12, 27, 28, 31, 52 bus. **Lunch served** noon-3pm Mon-Fri; noon-3.30pm Sat, Sun. **Dinner served** 6.30-11.45pm Mon-Sat; 6.30-10.15pm Sun. **Average** £20. **Set lunch** (Mon-Fri) £12.50. **House wine** £8.15 bottle, £1.95 glass. **Mineral water** £2.25 bottle, 65p glass. **Credit** A, TC, V.
A slick canteen that remains one of the most fashionable restaurants in town. The near-faultless kitchen and polished service give the place a head start; the austere goldfish-bowl interior does the rest. Noisy but fun.

Museum Street Café

47 Museum Street, WC1 (071 405 3211). Holborn or Tottenham Court Road underground. **Lunch served** 12.30-2.30pm, **dinner served** 7.15-9.15pm, Mon-Fri. **Set lunches** £11 two courses, £14 three courses. **Set dinner** £19.50 three courses. **Unlicensed. Corkage** no charge. **Mineral water** £2 bottle, 65p glass. **No credit cards.**
A tiny room, crammed with wooden tables, where the short menu is chalked on a blackboard. Cooking is simple and successful: meat or fish is char-grilled; excellent bread is freshly-baked. The Spartan formula works best at lunch-time.

Sonny's

94 Church Road, SW13 (081 748 0393). Hammersmith underground then 9, 33, 72 bus/Barnes BR. **Lunch served** 12.30-2.30pm Mon-Sat; 12.30-3pm Sun. **Dinner served** 7.30-11pm Mon-Sat. **Average** £20. **Set meal** £12.50 two courses incl coffee. **Set Sunday lunch** £14.50 three courses. **House wine** £7.95 bottle, £1.75 glass. **Mineral water** £2.50 bottle, £1 glass. **Credit** A, £TC, V.
A stylish local where charming staff ply diners with dishes from a short, keenly-priced menu. Vogueish dishes combine Mediterranean ingredients and oriental influences. The wine list is equally affordable. There's now a café on the same premises.

The Square

32 King Street, SW1 (071 839 8787/fax 071 321 2124). Green Park or Piccadilly Circus underground. **Lunch served** noon-3pm Mon-Fri. **Dinner served** 6-11.45pm Mon-Sat; 7-10pm Sun. **Average** £30. **House wine** £10.50 bottle, £3.50 glass. **Mineral water** £3.50 bottle, £1.50 glass. **Credit** A, AmEx, £TC, V.
Glamorous and gilded, The Square offers sublime cooking in elegant surroundings – a price. As a consequence the clientele tends to be an older, more sedate bunch. The wine list is a serious document. Winner of the 1993 *Time Out* Eating and Drinking Award for Best Modern British Restaurant.

Stephen Bull's Bistro & Bar

71 St John Street, EC1 (071 490 1750). Barbican underground/Farringdon underground/BR. **Lunch served** noon-2.30pm Mon-Fri. **Dinner served** 6-10.45pm Mon-Sat. **Average** £20. **Wines** from £8.95

bottle, £2.20 glass. **Mineral water** £2.85 bottle, £1 glass. **Credit** A, £TC, V.
Bare white walls off-set by black furniture and the odd blast of sun-bleached colour form the décor at this trendy City bistro. A short, daily-changing menu keeps prices to a minimum; there's always a tart, a pasta and a risotto plus heartier dishes. The branch is more serious, with prices to match.
Branch: Stephen Bull 5-7 Blandford Street, W1 (071 486 9696).

Caribbean

Brixtonian

11 Dorrell Place, off Nursery Road, SW9 (071 978 8870/fax 071 737 5521). Brixton underground/BR. **Bar open** 5.30pm-midnight Mon; noon-midnight Tue, Wed; noon-1am Thur-Sat. **Dinner served** 7-11.30pm Tue-Thur; 7-11.30pm Fri, Sat. **Set dinners** £14.95 two courses, £18.95 three courses. **Service** 12½%. **House wine** £7.95 bottle, £2 glass. **Mineral water** £3 bottle, £1 glass. **Credit** A, £TC, V.
Reliable, French-influenced cooking from the islands of the Caribbean is served in a coolly elegant, sparingly furnished room. The bar downstairs is altogether more lively. *See chapter* **Cafés, Pubs & Bars.**
Branch: Brixtonian Backayard 4 Neal's Yard, WC2 (071 240 2769).

Chinese

See also page 135 **Dim sum** *and chapters* **London by Area: West End** *and* **West.**

Fung Shing

15 Lisle Street, WC2 (071 437 1539). Leicester Square underground. **Meals served** noon-11.30pm daily. **Average** £18. **Minimum** £8.50 (after 6.30pm). **Set meals** £11, £12, per person (minimum two). **House wine** £8.50 bottle, £2.20 glass. **Mineral water** £4 bottle, £1.10 glass. **Credit** A, AmEx, DC, £TC, V.
Both traditional and innovative dishes appear on the long menu at this reputable Chinatown restaurant. Further pluses are the cool green décor, attentive service and an eclectic wine list.

Imperial City

Royal Exchange, Cornhill, EC3 (071 626 3437). Bank underground. **Meals served** 11.30am-8.30pm Mon-Fri. **Average** £20. **Set meals** £13.50-£24.50. **Service** 12½%. **House wine** £8.50 bottle, £2.20 glass. **Mineral water** £2.80 bottle, £1.35 glass. **Credit** A, AmEx, DC, £TC, V.
Impressive MSG-free, Hong Kong style dishes are the attraction at this designer, City Chinese restaurant. The service is uninspiring.

French

See also above **Celebrated Chefs.**

Bistrot Bruno

63 Frith Street, W1 (071 734 4545/fax 071 287 1027). Leicester Square or Tottenham Court Road underground. **Lunch served** 12.15-2.30pm Mon-Fri. **Dinner served** 6.15-11.30pm Mon-Sat. **Average** £20. **House wine** £8.75 bottle, £2.50 glass. **Mineral water** £2.80 bottle, 75p glass. **Credit** A, AmEx, DC, TC, V.
Bruno Loubet's so-called bistro has a frequently changing menu and a minimalist interior, and is best known for startling combinations that work most of the time. Past

examples are salmon carpaccio and samphire pickle, and brawn pâté with cucumber and mushroom dressing.'

Chez Gérard

8 Charlotte Street, W1 (071 636 4975). Goodge Street or Tottenham Court Road underground. **Lunch served** noon-3pm Mon-Fri, Sun. **Dinner served** 6-11pm daily. **Average** £20 incl £1 cover. **Set meal** £15 four courses. **Service** 12½%. **House wine** £7.95 bottle, £2.10 glass. **Mineral water** £2.95 bottle, £1 glass. **Credit** A, AmEx, DC, £TC, V.
A radical new 'dining car' look – cream paint, art deco light fittings and chrome luggage racks – is complemented by a new menu at this respected restaurant. French classics now come with a novel twist, but the steaks remain as good as ever.
Branches: 31 Dover Street, W1 (071 499 8171); 119 Chancery Lane, WC2 (071 405 0290).

L'Escargot

48 Greek Street, W1 (071 437 2679). Leicester Square or Tottenham Court Road underground. Brasserie **Lunch served** 12.15-2.30pm, Mon-Fri. **Dinner served** 6-11.30pm Mon-Sat. **Average** £18. **Pre-theatre menu** (6-7.30pm) £14 two courses, incl coffee. *Restaurant* **Lunch served** 12.15-2.30pm Mon-Fri. **Dinner served** 7.30-11pm Mon-Sat. **Average** £25. *Both* **House wine** £8.95 bottle, £1.50 glass. **Mineral water** £2.50 bottle, £1 glass. **Credit** A, AmEx, DC, TC, V.
Michelin-starred chefs Garry Hollihead and David Cavalier grace the relaunched L'Escargot with their splendid French cooking. The sleek new furnishings add to the air of assurance at this Soho establishment.

Mon Plaisir

21 Monmouth Street, WC2 (071 836 7243/071 240 3757). Covent Garden or Leicester Square underground. **Lunch served** noon-2.15pm Mon-Fri. **Dinner served** 6-11.15pm Mon-Sat. **Average** £20. **Set lunch and pre-theatre dinner** (6-8pm) £13.95 three courses. **Service** 12½%. **House wine** £8.50 bottle, £2.50 glass. **Mineral water** £1.50 bottle, 80p glass. **Credit** A, AmEx, DC, £TC, V.
The three rooms at this Monmouth Street institution fill up quickly with devotees of the bistro experience. Classic dishes are competently executed and served; the set meal is a snip.

Spread Eagle

1-2 Stockwell Street, SE10 (081 853 2333). Greenwich

Japanese diners

Only five years ago, Japanese food was enormously expensive in London. But as the number of business visitors from the Far East has grown, and the cuisine has become increasingly popular with Londoners, there has been an emergence and proliferation of several cheap noodle bars and diners in the West End and the City. Furnishings tend to be functional rather than comfortable, and lingering is neither encouraged nor desirable, but the food is usually astonishingly good.

Hamine

84 Brewer Street, W1 (071 439 0785/071 287 1318). Piccadilly Circus underground. **Meals served** noon-3am Mon-Fri; noon-2am Sat; noon-midnight Sun. **Average** £7. **Beer** Kirin £3.50 large, £2.50 small; Suntory £2 glass. **Mineral water** £1 glass. **No credit cards.**
Britain's first Japanese noodle bar, serving huge bowls of ramen (noodle soup), plus a few rice dishes. You order from the counter, pay, then sit down. Japanese satellite TV and Japanese comic books are provided.

Jin Kichi

73 Heath Street, NW3 (071 794 6158). Hampstead underground. **Lunch served** noon-2.30pm Sat, Sun. **Dinner served** 6-11.30pm Mon, Wed-Sun. **Average** £7 lunch, £15 dinner. **Set meals** £5.50-£8.50 incl green tea, dessert. **Service** 12%. **Beer** Kirin £1.90. **Saké** £4.80 large tokkuri, £2.40 small tokkuri. **Mineral water** 90p small bottle. **Credit** A, AmEx, DC, £TC, V.
A yakitori bar with authentically basic décor: honey-coloured wood panelling and plain tables clustered around a sushi bar. The menu lists more than two dozen dishes, each consisting of one or two skewers of grilled meat costing under £2.

Noto

Bow Bells House, 7 Bread Street, EC4 (071 329 8056/fax 071 253 0669). Bank or Mansion House or St Paul's underground. **Meals served** 11.30am-9pm Mon-Fri; 11.30am-6pm Sat. **Average** £8. **Unlicensed. Mineral water** £1 can. **Credit** £TC.
A tiny noodle bar where diners perch on high stools round a horseshoe bar to enjoy good-sized ramen dishes and gyoza (dumplings). The salty sansai ramen contains egg noodles, sweetcorn, spinach, bamboo shoots, spring onions, seaweed and mushrooms.
Branch: 2-3 Bassishaw High Walk, London Wall, EC2 (no phone).

Tokyo Diner

2 Newport Place, WC2 (071 287 8777). Leicester Square underground. **Meals served** noon-midnight daily. **Average** £7. **Beer** Kirin £1.90, Sapporo £2. **House wine** £6.50 bottle. **Mineral water** 90p small bottle. **Credit** A, LV, V.
A pleasant ground floor and basement diner that's amazingly cheap for the area. The carefully annotated menu covers a wide range of the most popular Japanese dishes: bento boxes, katsu curry, noodles, sashimi (raw fish) and sushi.

Wagamama

4 Streatham Street, off Coptic Street, WC1 (071 323 9223/fax 071 323 9224). Tottenham Court Road underground. **Lunch served** noon-2.30pm Mon-Fri; 1-3pm Sat. **Dinner served** 6-11pm Mon-Sat. **Average** £6. **Beer** Kirin £2.30 large, £1.60 regular; Sapporo £2.10. **Saké** £1.90 large tokkuri. **Mineral water** £1 small bottle. **Credit** LV, £STC.
This large, stunningly designed noodle bar is phenomenally successful, and queues are commonplace. Ramen (egg noodles) come stir-fried or in soup; there are also domburi dishes (rice with stir-fried topping) and several vegetarian choices. It's fashionable and deserves to be. No smoking.

Mega-Kalamaras. *See* **review.**

BR. **Lunch served** noon-3pm daily. **Dinner served** 6.30-10.30pm Mon-Sat. **Average** £25. **Set meal** £13.50 three courses. **House wine** £8.25 bottle, £2 glass. **Mineral water** £2.50 bottle, £1 glass. **Credit** A, AmEx, DC, £TC, V.
An appealing warren of rooms, all decorated in a different, old-fashioned style. Dishes are sometimes unnecessarily complicated, but on the whole pleasing; portions are generous.

Villandry Dining Room
89 Marylebone High Street, W1 (071 224 3799). Baker Street underground. **Open** 8.30am-5.30pm, **lunch served** 12.30-2.30pm, Mon-Sat. **Dinner** **served** once a month, or for parties of 15 or more. **Average** £20. **Minimum** £6.90. **House wine** £10 bottle, £2.50 glass. **Mineral water** £3.50 bottle, £1.50 glass. **Credit** A, LV, V.
A tiny, noisy café furnished with wobbly wooden furniture, behind an *épicerie*. Simple dishes – saffron soup or Toulouse sausages with mash and mustard sauce, say – are expertly cooked. The drinks list is brief.

Greek

Greek Valley
130 Boundary Road, NW8 (071 624 3217). St John's Wood underground/16, 98, 139 bus. **Lunch served** noon-2.30pm Mon-Fri. **Dinner served** 6pm-midnight Mon-Sat. **Average** £15. **Set meal** £7.95 three courses. **Meze** £8.50, £10.95. **House wine** £6.50 bottle, £1.75 glass. **Mineral water** £2.50 bottle, £1 glass. **Credit** A, £TC, V.
A husband and wife team run this reliable, pleasantly decorated local. The menu offers all the standard Cypriot fare, and has a good selection for vegetarians together with some more unusual dishes, such as prawns baked with feta cheese (£8.50).

Lemonia
89 Regent's Park Road, NW1 (071 586 7454). Chalk Farm underground/31, 168 bus. **Lunch served** noon-3pm Mon-Fri, Sun. **Dinner served** 6-11.30pm Mon-Sat. **Average** £13. **Meze** £9.50 per person (minimum two). **House wine** £9 litre, £1.70 glass. **Mineral water** £2.50 bottle; £1.25 glass. **Credit** A, £TC, V.
Booking is essential at this large, brasserie-like restaurant. The Greek-Cypriot cooking is way above average and very good value. The meat and vegetarian moussakas and the succulent charcoal grills are worth having.

Mega-Kalamaras
76-78 Inverness Mews, W2 (071 727 9122/2564). Bayswater or Queensway underground. **Dinner served** 7pm-midnight Mon-Sat. **Average** £22. **Set dinner** £15.50 incl coffee. **Service** 10%. **House wine** £7.95 bottle, £2 glass. **Mineral water** £2.20 bottle, 80p glass. **Credit** A, AmEx, DC, £TC, V.
Greek, rather than Greek-Cypriot, food is served in this cavern-like interior. The menu includes dishes unheard of in more run-of-the-mill establishments, and the quality is high.
Branch: Micro-Kalamaras 66 Inverness Mews, W2 (071 727 5082).

Hungarian

The Gay Hussar
2 Greek Street, W1 (071 437 0973). Tottenham Court Road underground. **Lunch served** 12.30-2.30pm, **dinner served** 5.30-11pm, Mon-Sat. **Average** £20. **Set lunch** £15.50 three courses. **Service** 12½%. **House wine** £9 bottle, £6.80 carafe, £2.50 glass. **Mineral water** £3 bottle. **Credit** A, AmEx, DC, £TC, V.
Looks- and atmosphere-wise this place resembles a men's club; the food consists of meat-laden dishes from around the old Hapsburg Empire, not forgetting the famous cherry soup. The wine list is hugely tempting, with fine bottles from France, Hungary and Bulgaria. An experience.

Indian
See also chapters **London by Area: East End & Docklands** *and* **West.**

Bombay Brasserie
Courtfield Close, Courtfield Road, SW7 (071 370 4040/fax 071 835 1669). Gloucester Road underground. **Lunch served** 12.30-3pm, **dinner served** 7.30pm-midnight, daily. **Average** £30. **Minimum** £20 dinner. **Set buffet lunch** £13.95 incl coffee. **House wine** £9.75 bottle, £2.50 glass. **Mineral water** £1.50 bottle. **Credit** A, DC, TC, V.
The Brasserie tries to elevate Indian food to the levels of haute cuisine. Starters and vegetable side dishes display the most imagination; meat and fish dishes are generally mildly spiced. Furnishings are imposing.

Chutney Mary
535 King's Road, SW10 (071 351 3113/fax 071 351 7694). Fulham Broadway underground. **Lunch served** 12.30-2.30pm Mon-Sat; 12.30-3pm Sun. **Dinner served** 7-11.30pm Mon-Sat; 7-10.30pm Sun. **Average** £28 incl £1.50 cover. **Set meal** (lunch and after 10pm) £10 two courses, £12.95 three courses. **Set buffet lunch** (Sun) £12.95. **Service** 12½%. **House wine** £8.50 bottle, £2.10 glass. **Mineral water** £3.50 bottle, £1.25 glass. **Credit** A, AmEx, DC, JCB, £TC, V.
Four years old, but famous from the start, Chutney Mary has an exciting menu that harks back to the hybrid cooking of the British Raj, with dishes such as Bangalore bangers and mash. Décor is expensive but bland.

Diwana Bhel Poori House
121 Drummond Street, NW1 (071 387 5556/fax 071 383 0560). Euston Square underground or Euston underground/BR. **Meals served** noon-11.30pm daily. **Average** £8. **Set buffet lunch** (noon-2.30pm) £4.95.

JD WETHERSPOON PUBS - GREAT BEER, ALL DAY FOOD, NON - SMOKING AREAS, NO DISTRACTIVE MUSIC AND PRICES TO SUIT YOUR POCKET - WHAT MORE COULD YOU WANT?

LEICESTER SQUARE –	**THE MOON UNDER WATER** 28 LEICESTER SQUARE, WC2
VICTORIA STATION –	**WETHERSPOONS FREEHOUSE** MEZZANINE LEVEL, VICTORIA ISLAND, VICTORIA STATION, SW1
CAMDEN TOWN –	**THE MAN IN THE MOON** 40-42 CHALK FARM ROAD, NW1
ISLINGTON –	179 UPPER STREET 179 UPPER STREET, N1
THE CITY –	HAMILTON HALL BROADGATE CENTRE (*OFF BISHOPSGATE*) LIVERPOOL ST. STATION, EC2
HEATHROW AIRPORT –	**WETHERSPOONS BAR** & **JJ MOON'S BAR** TERMINAL 4 MEZZANINE LEVEL (*LANDSIDE*) & TERMINAL 4 DEPARTURES LOUNGE

AND OVER 70 OTHER PLACES ACROSS LONDON. RING 081-446 9099 FOR YOUR NEAREST JD WETHERSPOON FREEHOUSE.

Unlicensed. Corkage no charge. **Mineral water** 70p glass. **Credit** A, AmEx, DC, LV, £TC, V.
A cheap, functionally-decorated café, where benches and tables are bolted to the floor, and water comes in jugs and steel beakers. The vegetarian food is generally good. Bhel poori consists of small puffed bread served with chopped vegetables and chutney.
Branch: 50 Westbourne Grove, W2 (071 221 0721).

Gopal's of Soho
12 Bateman Street, W1 (071 434 1621/0840).
Piccadilly Circus or Tottenham Court Road
underground. **Lunch served** noon-3pm daily. **Dinner served** 6-11.30pm Mon-Sat; 6-11pm Sun. **Average** £20 incl £1 cover. **Thalis** (set meals) £10.50 vegetarian, £11.50 meat. **House wine** £7.90 bottle, £2.25 glass. **Mineral water** £3.10 large bottle, £1.30 small bottle. **Credit** A, AmEx, DC, £TC, V.
Gopal's freshly cooked, delicately spiced food is among the best to be found in this price range. Old favourites appear on the menu alongside more adventurous dishes. The interior is smart, if a little cramped.

Ragam
57 Cleveland Street, W1 (071 636 9098). Goodge Street
or Warren Street underground. **Lunch served** noon-3pm daily. **Dinner served** 6-11.15pm Mon-Thur, Sat; 6-11.45pm Fri; 6-10.45pm Sun. **Average** £10. **Minimum** £5.50. **Service** 10%. **House wine** £8 bottle, £1.30 glass. **Mineral water** 90p glass. **Credit** A, AmEx, DC, LV, £TC, V.
A small, unassuming and enduringly popular restaurant. The cooking is of a high standard; dishes include curry-house regulars, and excellent South Indian vegetarian dishes.
Branch: Sree Krishna 192-194 Tooting High Street, SW17 (081 672 4250).

Irish

Mulligans
13-14 Cork Street, W1 (071 409 1370). Oxford Circus
or Piccadilly Circus underground.
Bar **Open** noon-11pm Mon-Sat. **Average** £8.
Restaurant **Lunch served** 12.30-2.15pm Mon-Fri.
Dinner served 6.15-11.15pm Mon-Sat. **Average** £28.
Service 12½%.
Both **House wine** £8.50-£10.25 bottle, £1.95-£2.20 glass. **Mineral water** £2.75 bottle, 90p glass. **Credit** A, AmEx, £TC, V.
Decorated in shades of brown, beige and cream, and staffed by motherly but efficient Irish waitresses, Mulligans is supremely comforting. Roast loin of pork with glazed onions, mushrooms and colcannon (cabbage and mashed potato) is typical of the modern Irish cooking on display. There's an oyster bar on the ground floor.

Italian

Al San Vincenzo
30 Connaught Street, W2 (071 262 9623). Marble Arch
underground. **Lunch served** 12.30-2.15pm Mon-Fri.
Dinner served 7-10.30pm Mon-Sat. **House wine** £9 bottle, £2.75 glass. **Mineral water** £1.95 small bottle, £1.50 glass. **Credit** A, £TC, V.
Intimacy and comfort are combined with a lean and modern look here. The rustic Italian cooking is brilliant, and the attention to detail extends to the wine list.

Bertorelli's
44A Floral Street, WC2 (071 836 3969). Covent
Garden underground.
Café **Lunch served** noon-3pm, **dinner served** 5.45-11.30pm, Mon-Sat. **Average** £15. **House wine** £7.60 bottle, £1.75 glass.
Restaurant **Lunch served** noon-3pm Mon-Fri. **Dinner served** 5.45-11.30pm Mon-Sat. **Average** £20 incl £1.50 cover. **House wine** £7.95 bottle, £1.95 glass.
Both **Service** 12½%. **Mineral water** £2.95 bottle, £1.25 glass. **Credit** A, AmEx, DC, £TC, V.
Chef Maddalena Bonino produces winning meals at this buzzy Covent Garden restaurant. Current food fashions are noted, but none has been followed too slavishly. Service is friendly.

Del Buongustaio
283 Putney Bridge Road, SW15 (081 780 9361). East
Putney or Putney Bridge BR/14, 22, 220 bus. **Lunch served** noon-3pm Mon-Fri; 12.30-4pm Sun. **Dinner served** 6.30-11.30pm Mon-Sat. **Average** £18. **Set lunch** (Mon-Fri) £9.50 two courses. **Set dinner** £19.50 five courses. **House wine** £8.50 bottle, £6.90 carafe, £2.30 glass. **Mineral water** £2.40 bottle. **Credit** A, AmEx, V.
A daily-changing menu of regional specialities is served in a room that resembles a modish version of an Italian front parlour. Flavours are satisfying, portions large. The wine list is, like the management, a mix of Australian and Italian.
Branch: Osteria Antica Bologna 23 Northcote Road, SW11 (071 978 4771).

La Delizia
Chelsea Farmers' Market, Sydney Street, SW3 (071 351
6701). Sloane Square underground then 11, 19, 22, 49
bus. **Meals served** noon-midnight daily. **Average** £10. **Minimum** £7 when busy. **Unlicensed. Mineral water** £1 bottle. **No credit cards.**
Bona fide Italian pizzas, ices and coffees at very reasonable prices. This branch is a sort-of log cabin with a lot of tables outdoors.
Branches: 63-65 Chelsea Manor Street, SW3 (071 376 4111); 246 Brompton Road, SW5 (071 373 6085).

Lorelei
21 Bateman Street, W1 (071 734 0954). Leicester
Square or Tottenham Court Road underground. **Meals served** noon-11pm Mon-Sat. **Average** £8. **Unlicensed. Corkage** 80p per person. **Mineral water** £1 bottle. **Credit** LV, TC.
A minute pizzeria with few fancy touches in decoration or service but the pizzas aren't bad and the prices are modest (£4 at most). Very much part of the old-style Soho.

Orso
27 Wellington Street, WC2 (071 240 5269/fax 071 497
2148). Covent Garden underground. **Meals served** noon-midnight daily. **Average** £25. **House wine** £9 litre, £3 ¼-litre. **Mineral water** £2.50 bottle, £1.50 glass. **Credit** £TC.
A noisy, stylish basement restaurant where two sittings a night are the norm. Contemporary Italian food is served on brightly patterned plates; Italian wine comes in squat glasses.

Pollo
20 Old Compton Street, W1 (071 734 5917). Leicester
Square underground. **Meals served** 11.30am-11pm Mon-Sat. **Average** £7. **House wine** £5.30 bottle, £1.50 glass. **Credit** LV, £TC.
Pollo's popularity (with everyone from tourists to poseurs) means there's often a queue, but it's a fast-moving one. Efficient but polite staff deliver a combination of familiar Italian pasta and meat dishes, customised to suit the fast turnover.

The River Café

Thames Wharf, Rainville Road, W6 (071 381 8824). Hammersmith underground/11 bus. **Lunch served** 12.30-3pm Mon-Sat; 1-3pm Sun. **Dinner served** 7.30-9.15pm Mon-Sat. **Average** £28. **Service** 12½%. **House wine** £9.50 bottle, £2.80 glass. **Mineral water** £3 bottle, 75p glass. **Credit** A, £TC, V.

The River Café is pricey and off the beaten track, but worth seeking out. It looks like an upmarket canteen, but the food is a revelation (char-grilling and searing feature heavily). The wine list makes good reading.

Japanese

See also **Box: Japanese diners.**

Miyama

38 Clarges Street, W1 (071 499 2443). Green Park underground. **Lunch served** noon-2.30pm Mon-Fri. **Dinner served** 6-10.30pm daily. **Average** £20 lunch, £40 dinner. **Set lunches** £12-£18 incl green tea, miso soup, rice & pickles. **Set dinners** £32-£40 incl green tea, miso soup, rice & pickles. **Service** 15%. **Beer** Kirin £2.80. **Saké** £2.80 small tokkuri. **Mineral water** £2.50 small bottle. **Credit** A, AmEx, DC, JCB, £TC, V.

One of the best Japanese restaurants in London. The menu is clearly annotated and the set lunches are a must. There's a teppan grill downstairs, along with the sushi bar and private rooms. The City branch is a slightly flashier place and also has a sushi bar

Branch: City Miyama 17 Godliman Street, EC4 (071 489 1937).

Suntory

72-73 St James's Street, SW1 (071 409 0201). Green Park underground. **Lunch served** noon-1.30pm, **dinner served** 7-9.30pm, Mon-Sat. **Average** £30 lunch, £50 dinner. **Set lunches** £15-£60 incl green tea, dessert, service. **Set dinners** £48-£90 incl green tea, miso soup, rice & pickles, dessert, service. **Beer**

Sir Terence Conran

Sir Terence Conran is a one-man London restaurant boom. The golden touch hasn't deserted him so far, and all the restaurants listed below are very successful, particularly Quaglino's (where you have to book weeks ahead for a weekend table). Yet another Conran restaurant, a Chop House serving traditional British food, opened in October 1993 at his Butlers Wharf 'gastrodrome'.

Bibendum

Michelin House, 81 Fulham Road, SW3 (071 581 5817/fax 071 823 7925). South Kensington underground. **Lunch served** 12.30-2.30pm Mon-Fri; 12.30-3pm Sat, Sun. **Dinner served** 7-11.30pm Mon-Sat; 7-10.30pm Sun. **Average** £45. **Set lunch** £25 three courses. **Service** 15%. **House wine** £9.50 bottle, £2.99 glass. **Mineral water** £1.75. **Credit** A, AmEx, £TC, V.

Simon Hopkinson's fabulous cooking combines bold innovation with dyed-in-the-wool traditionalism. The food is deceptively simple, but intensely flavoured. The surroundings (the spectacular, restored Michelin building) are sublime, the service excellent. Dress: smart.

Blueprint Café

Design Museum, Butlers Wharf, SE1 (071 378 7031/fax 071 378 6540). Tower Hill underground/Tower Gateway DLR/London Bridge underground/BR/47, 78 bus. **Lunch served** noon-3pm Mon-Sat; noon-3.30pm Sun. **Dinner served** 7-11pm Mon-Sat. **Average** £20. **Service** 15%. **House wine** £9.50 bottle, £2.25 glass. **Mineral water** £2.95 bottle, 95p glass. **Credit** A, AmEx, DC, £TC, V.

A stylish white room atop the **Design Museum** (*see chapter* **Museums**) with great river views. Reliable Cal-Ital food and a slick crew of uniformed waiting staff mean that satisfaction is guaranteed.

Cantina del Ponte

Butlers Wharf Building, 36C Shad Thames, SE1 (071 403 5403/fax 071 403 0267). Tower Hill underground/Tower Gateway DLR/London Bridge underground/BR/47, 78, P11 bus. **Lunch served** noon-3pm daily. **Dinner served** 6-11pm Mon-Sat. **Average** £30. **Service** 15%. **House wine** £8.75 bottle, £1.95 glass. **Mineral water** £2.50 bottle, 85p glass. **Credit** A, AmEx, DC, TC, V.

A bare but beautifully designed restaurant that specialises in Mediterranean food. Prices are high, but flavours are rewarding, and portions generous – hunks of tuna on thin green beans, tomatoes and olives might be followed by panna cotta with pineapple and passion fruit.

Le Pont de la Tour

Butlers Wharf Building, 36D Shad Thames, Butlers Wharf, SE1 (restaurant 071 403 8403/bar and grill 071 403 9403/fax 071 403 0267). Tower Hill underground/Tower Gateway DLR/London Bridge underground/BR/47, 78 bus. **Brunch served** 11.30am-3pm Sat. **Lunch served** noon-3pm Mon-Fri, Sun. **Dinner served** 6pm-midnight Mon-Sat; 6-11pm Sun. **Average** £45. **Set lunch** £25 three courses. **Service** 15%. **House wine** £9.50 bottle, £2.95 glass. **Mineral water** £2.50 bottle, 85p glass. **Credit** A, AmEx, DC, £TC, V.

A large, sumptuous dining room overlooking the river. Expertly produced meals are served with a certain amount of formality. The bar area is more relaxed, and majors in shellfish.

Quaglino's

16 Bury Street, SW1 (071 930 6767/fax 071 839 2866). Green Park or Piccadilly Circus underground. **Restaurant Lunch served** noon-2.45pm daily. **Dinner served** 5.45-11.45pm Mon-Thur; 5.45pm-12.30am Fri, Sat; 6-10.45pm Sun. **Average** £20. **Bar Open** 11am-midnight daily. **Average** £10. *Both* **House wine** £9.50 bottle, £2.25 glass. **Mineral water** £2.50 bottle, 85p glass. **Service** 15%. **Credit** A, AmEx, DC, £TC, V.

A resoundingly successful metropolitan restaurant – eating here will always feel like an event. As is often the case, fish and seafood are particular strengths. The balcony bar offers a shorter, cheaper menu.

Del Buongustaio *excels at regional Italian cooking. See* **review** *page 141.*

Suntory £3.50. **Saké** £5 small tokkuri. **Mineral water** £5 bottle. **Credit** A, AmEx, DC, JCB, £$YTC, V.
An elegant, spacious establishment, with correspondingly high prices. The food and service are unbeatable – the set lunches offer an affordable way of experiencing them. Dress: smart.

Jewish

Bloom's
90 Whitechapel High Street, E1 (071 247 6001/6835). Aldgate East underground. **Meals served** 11am-9.30pm Mon-Thur, Sun; 11am-2pm Fri. **Average** £15. **House wine** £8.90 bottle, £2.40 glass. **Mineral water** £1.20 glass. **Credit** A, AmEx, DC, £TC, V.
An institution founded on East End charm and traditional fare. The likes of borscht (beetroot soup), potato latkes (pancakes), carrot tzimmes (casseroles) and dumplings, and apple strudel will set you up for the next 24 hours. Kosher supervised (Beth Din).
Branch: 130 Golders Green Road, NW11 (081 455 1338/3033).

Korean

Seoul
89A Aldgate High Street, EC3 (071 480 5770). Aldgate or Aldgate East underground. **Lunch served** noon-3pm, **dinner served** 6-10pm, Mon-Fri. **Average** £12. **Service** 10%. **House wine** £7 bottle, £1.60 glass. **Mineral water** £2.50 bottle, 90p glass. **Credit** A, LV, V.
A small, Spartan restaurant offering a decent array of dishes at an attractive price – kim chee (pickled vegeta-

bles) costs just over £1. The polite service is exceptionally fast, but they will slow down if you ask them to.

Malaysian & Indonesian

Melati
21 Great Windmill Street, W1 (071 437 2745). Piccadilly Circus underground. **Meals served** noon-11.30pm Mon-Thur, Sun; noon-12.30am Fri, Sat. **Average** £15. **Set meals** £19.75 per head (minimum two), incl beer, coffee. **Service** 10%. **House wine** £7.85 bottle, £2.10 glass. **Mineral water** £2.45 bottle, £1.15 glass. **Credit** A, AmEx, DC, LV, £TC, V.
Great food for a fair price, right in the heart of town. The Singapore laksa (noodles in sour fish soup) for around a fiver is one of the best options on the menu. The interior is simply decorated. Service can get overstretched.
Branch: Minang 11 Greek Street, W1 (071 287 1408).

Rasa Sayang
38 Queensway, W2 (071 229 8417). Bayswater or Queensway underground. **Meals served** noon-11.15pm daily. **Average** £15. **Set buffet meal** (noon-7pm daily) £5.90 incl soup and choice of ten dishes. **Set dinners** £28 for two, £53.50 for three, £70 for four, all three courses incl wine, liquor, coffee. **House wine** £6.90 bottle, £1.80 glass. **Mineral water** £2 bottle, £1 glass. **Credit** A, AmEx, DC, £TC, V.
Ignore the décor, which resembles a glitzy eighties nightclub and head straight for the buffet. It's superb value. Dishes are fresh, well-presented and cooked: peppery chicken soup, chicken wings with sambal sauce, fish curry on the bone – all splendid.

Branches: 10 Frith Street, W1 (071 734 8720); 3 Leicester Place, W1 (071 437 4556).

Singapore Garden
154-156 Gloucester Place, NW1 (071 723 8233). Baker Street underground/Marylebone underground/BR. **Lunch served** noon-2.45pm daily. **Dinner served** 6-10.45pm Mon-Thur, Sun; 6-11.15pm Fri, Sat. **Average** £20. **Minimum** £9 dinner. **Set meal** £14.85 four courses incl service. **Service** 12½%. **House wine** £7.65 bottle, £2.05 glass. **Mineral water** £2.95 bottle, £1.50 glass. **Credit** A, AmEx, DC, £TC, V.
A plush, understated Chinese-Singaporean restaurant where the cooking is second to none. Service is charming.
Branch: 83-83A Fairfax Road, NW6 (071 328 5314/071 624 8233).

Mediterranean

est
54 Frith Street, W1 (071 437 0666/0777). Leicester Square underground. **Lunch served** noon-3pm Mon-Fri. **Dinner served** 6-11pm Mon-Thur; 6-11.30pm Fri, Sat. **Average** £15. **Service** 12½%. **House wine** £8.50 bottle, £2.50 glass. **Mineral water** £2.50 bottle, 95p glass. **Credit** A, AmEx, £TC, V.
A blond wood and glass bar that's young, loud and crowded. The menu covers Mediterranean standards like crostini (toasted bread with savoury topping), squid, rocket, risotto and includes a pasta of the day. A laid-back place where the bill is often higher than anticipated.

O'Keefe's
19 Dering Street, W1 (071 495 0878/fax 071 629 7082). Oxford Circus or Bond Street underground. **Open** 8am-5pm Mon-Fri; 10am-5pm Sat. **Lunch served** noon-3pm Mon-Sat. **Dinner served** 7.30-9.30pm Thur. **Average** £12. **Minimum** £6 (12.30-2.30pm). **House wine** £7.50 bottle, £1.75 glass. **Mineral water** £2 bottle, £1 glass. **Credit** LV, £TC.
A simply decorated room – white walls and brown paper-covered tables – where the colour is provided by the food. Dishes – a plate of antipasti, asparagus risotto – are intensely flavoured. There's a delicatessen counter too.

Middle Eastern

Al Basha
222 Kensington High Street, W8 (071 937 1030/071 938 1794). High Street Kensington underground/9, 10, 27, 28, 33, 49 bus. **Meals served** noon-midnight Mon-Thur, Sun; noon-1am Fri, Sat. **Average** £20 incl £1.50 cover. **Set meal** £12.50 per person (minimum two) incl service. **Service** 15%. **House wine** £10 bottle, £2.50 glass. **Mineral water** £1.75 bottle, £1 glass. **Credit** A, AmEx, DC, JCB, £$TC, V.
A gracious Lebanese restaurant next to Holland Park. Pristine white linen, sparkling glassware and velvet seating generate an atmosphere of restrained opulence. Food – a mixture of meze (hors d'oeuvres) dishes and traditional meat main courses – is superbly fresh.

Tageen
12 Upper St Martin's Lane, WC2 (071 836 7272). Leicester Square underground. **Lunch served** noon-2.30pm Mon-Sat. **Dinner served** 6-11pm Mon-Thur; 6-11.30pm Fri, Sat. **Average** £16 incl 90p cover. **Set meals** (noon-2.30pm, 6-7pm) £5.80 one course, £8.60 two courses, £11.50 three

courses. **House wine** £9 bottle, £2 glass. **Mineral water** £3.20 bottle. **Credit** A, AmEx, DC, V.
Courtly cooking and an eastern ambience are this Moroccan restaurant's hallmarks. Many of the dishes are special occasion recipes; less esoteric are the tagines (Moroccan casseroles), and the couscous. Staff are happy to talk novices through the menu.

Scandinavian

Anna's Place
90 Mildmay Park, N1 (071 249 9379). Canonbury BR/38, 73, 141, 171A, 236, 277 bus. **Lunch served** 12.15-2.15pm, **dinner served** 7.15-10.45pm, Tue-Sat. **Average** £22. **Service** 10%. **House wine** £7 bottle, £1.85 glass. **Mineral water** £1.75 bottle, 75p glass. **No credit cards**.
Swedish food with a modern bent served in cottage parlour surroundings. Fish, excellently prepared, looms large on the menu. Anna, the proprietress, is usually in evidence to keep an eye on things.

Spanish

Albero & Grana
Chelsea Cloisters, 89 Sloane Avenue, SW3 (071 225 1048/1049). Sloane Square or South Kensington underground.
Restaurant **Lunch served** noon-4pm, **dinner served** 7.30-11.15pm, daily. **Average** £25.
Bar **Open** noon-4pm, 6pm-midnight, daily. **Average** £11. **Set regional menu** £20.
Both **Service** 10% for parties of seven or more. **House wine** £8.50 bottle, £1.85 glass, 90p ½ glass. **Mineral water** £3 bottle, £1 glass. **Credit** A, AmEx, DC, £PtaTC, V.
A design-led bar and restaurant, serving contemporary variations on traditional dishes. Roast suckling pig is sometimes available, puddings are wonderful, and a set menu showcases a different Spanish regional cuisine every two months. Tapas are available from the bar.

Thai

Bahn Thai
21A Frith Street, W1 (071 437 8504). Leicester Square or Tottenham Court Road underground/29, 38, 55 bus.
Brasserie **Meals served** noon-midnight daily. **Average** £10. **Minimum** £4.50. *Restaurant* **Lunch served** noon-2.45pm Mon-Sat; 12.30-2.30pm Sun. **Dinner served** 6-11.15pm Mon-Sat; 6.30-10.30pm Sun. **Average** £20 incl 75p cover. *Both* **House wine** £7.95 bottle, £1.65 glass. **Mineral water** £2.25 bottle, 75p glass. **Credit** A, AmEx, DC, £TC, V.
The ground floor holds a small brasserie where bar snacks and one-dish meals are served; the first floor restaurant has a wide-ranging menu that includes some esoteric dishes, such as catfish salad. The cooking is brilliant and authentic.

Chiang Mai
48 Frith Street, W1 (071 437 7444). Piccadilly Circus or Tottenham Court Road underground. **Lunch served** noon-3pm, **dinner served** 6-11pm, daily. **Average** £22. **Set lunches** £5.50, £6.50, £7.75, three courses incl coffee. **Set dinners** £18.40-£21.40, all per person (minimum two), incl coffee. **Service** 12½%. **House**

Bahn Thai. *See* **review** page 144.

wine £7.80 bottle, £1.80 glass. **Mineral water** £2.95 bottle, £1 glass. **Credit** A, AmEx, £TC, V.
Distinguished cooking is on display at this pleasant restaurant – meat eaters should try kratong thong (curried meat enclosed in batter cases). There's a separate vegetarian menu, and a wider range of soups than in most Thai restaurants.

Khun Akorn
136 Brompton Road, SW3 (071 225 2688). Knightsbridge underground. **Lunch served** noon-3pm daily. **Dinner served** 6.30-11pm Mon-Thur; 6.30-11.30pm Fri-Sun. **Average** £22. **Set lunch** £12.50 three courses incl coffee. **Set dinner** £17.50 three courses incl coffee. **House wine** £9.80 bottle, £2.60 glass. **Mineral water** £3 bottle, £1.50 half bottle. **Credit** A, AmEx, DC, TC, V.
Outstandingly good food and superb presentation make Khun Akorn a must. Even a humble pad Thai is packed with goodies and decorated with an egg 'lace basket'. The interior is (still) undergoing cosmetic changes.

Sri Siam
14 Old Compton Street, W1 (071 434 3544). Leicester Square underground. **Lunch served** noon-3pm Mon-Sat. **Dinner served** 6-11.15pm Mon-Sat; 6-10.30pm Sun. **Average** £18. **Set lunch** £9. **Set dinners** £14.95 per person (minimum two) three courses. **Service** 12½%. **House wine** £8.50 bottle, £2.20 glass. **Mineral water** £2.70 bottle, £1.35 glass. **Credit** A, AmEx, DC, £TC, V.
A bustling and fun Thai restaurant. The inventive menu lists many excellent dishes, some of them vegetarian. Toong thong (sort-of spring rolls with plum sauce), neua pad prik (pan-fried beef) and any of the curries are recommended.
Branch: Sri Siam City 85 London Wall, EC2 (071 628 5772).

Turkish

Lezzet Lokanta
330 Essex Road, N1 (071 354 1162). Essex Road BR/38, 73, 277 bus. **Meals served** noon-12.30am Mon-Thur; noon-1am Fri-Sun. **Average** £12 incl 50p cover. **Set meal** £12 incl coffee, service. **House wine** £6.75 bottle, £1.50 glass. **Mineral water** 75p glass. **Credit** A, LV, £TC, V.
A comfortable restaurant with a takeaway area at the front. The mixed meze, served with warm home-made

pide bread, is worth ordering, as are the kebabs. Service is chatty.

Sofra
18 Shepherd Street, W1 (071 493 3320). Green Park or Hyde Park Corner underground. **Meals served** noon-midnight daily. **Average** £20 incl £1.50 cover. **Set lunch** £8.45. **Set dinner** £9.95. **House wine** £9.95 bottle, £2.25 glass. **Mineral water** £2 bottle. **Credit** A, AmEx, DC, £TC, V.
A spotlessly clean, stylish establishment. The standard of cooking – from meze dishes (hors d'oeuvres), to grills and kebabs – is well above average.

Vietnamese

Vietnamese
34 Wardour Street, W1 (071 494 2592). Leicester Square underground. **Meals served** 11.30am-11.30pm daily. **Average** £10. **Service** 10%. **House wine** £7.20 bottle, £1.80 glass. **Mineral water** £1.20 glass. **Credit** A, AmEx, DC, MC, V.
The place to sample pho (noodle soup) – £3 for a small bowl, £3.70 large. Otherwise, from a massive menu avoid anything too Chinese-sounding and go for the Vietnamese specialities listed at the end. Pho, the sister café around the corner, is cheaper, but far more basic.
Branch: Pho 2 Lisle Street, W1 (071 437 8265).

Vegetarian

Mildred's
58 Greek Street, W1 (071 494 1634). Tottenham Court Road underground. **Open** noon-11pm Mon-Sat. **Average** £8.50. **House wine** £6.75 bottle, £1.85 glass. **Mineral water** £2.25 bottle, 60p glass. **Credit** LV, £TC.
A small, Spartan café with a congenial atmosphere. The food is a cut above the vegetarian norm – it's certainly never worthy. There's always a stir-fry served with a good satay sauce, and a few of the dishes contain fish. No smoking.

Neal's Yard Dining Room
First floor, 14 Neal's Yard, WC2 (071 379 0298). Covent Garden underground. **Meals served** noon-8pm Mon; noon-8pm Tue-Fri; noon-6pm Sat. **Average** £10. **Unlicensed. Corkage** no charge. **Mineral water** 85p glass. **Credit** £TC.
The menu at this plain but attractive room above Neal's Yard features dishes from around the globe. Quality ingredients go into the likes of Turkish meze, Indian thali (both are set meals) and Egyptian falafel (chickpea fritters). All are excellent, and the puddings, such as Polish cheesecake, deserve special mention. No smoking.

The Place Below
St Mary-le-Bow, Cheapside, EC2 (071 329 0789). St Paul's underground. **Meals served** 7.30am-3.30pm Mon-Wed; 7.30am-3.30pm, 6.30-9.30pm, Thur, Fri. **Average** £10 lunch. **Set dinners** £14.50 two courses, £16.50 three courses, incl coffee and service. **Unlicensed. Corkage** no charge (dinner only). **Mineral water** £2.25 bottle, 75p glass. **Credit** LV, £TC.
A splendid venture housed in a cleverly-lit crypt. It's self-service at lunch-time; waiter service in the evening. The lunch menu is soup, salad and quiche-based; the set evening menus are more sophisticated, but all dishes are inventive and light. No smoking.
Branch: St Marylebone Café St Marylebone Crypt, 17 Marylebone Road, NW1 (071 935 6374).

Cafés, Pubs & Bars

London is blessed with many superb old pubs, but the city is also acquiring a Continental-style café culture.

There are between five and six thousand examples in London of Britain's greatest gift to the world: the pub. From time immemorial, Londoners have met, espoused ludicrous 'pub-philosophy' and drunk in these fine institutions. Nowadays, fruit machines and piped music make an all-too-common intrusion into the conversation, but pubs are still the best places to observe Londoners at play.

What is commonly known in Europe and America as beer, the British call lager. British lagers tend to be a pale imitation of German lagers. If you want something with an extra bite, ask for export lager or pilsner. However, Britain's national drink is bitter or ale. This is served at room temperature and varies in strength from 2 per cent to about 6 per cent alcohol. Low-alcohol lagers and bitters are now widely available, and cider is becoming increasingly fashionable (though you'll rarely find genuine farmhouse cider – 'scrumpy' – in London pubs; for that you must travel to southwest England).

Large, national breweries have almost gained a monopoly of pubs in central London, but there are still places where you can find the nectar produced by London's two remaining independent breweries, Young's (based in Wandsworth, SW18; 081 870 0141) and Fuller's (based in Chiswick, W4; 081 994 3691; *see chapter* **London by Area: West**).

Since the licensing laws were liberalised in 1988, all-day drinking has finally become possible (except on Sunday, when between 3pm and 7pm drinks may only be served with food). This has led to the growth of trendy, Continental-style bars and brasseries, particularly in central London. Beers tend to be bottled (rather than draught) and more expensive at these establishments, and the division between eating and drinking places is gradually becoming less marked. But the easing of the law doesn't mean that every pub, bar and brasserie in the capital has flung open its doors for day-long drinking bouts, so check the opening times carefully if you're craving alcohol in

the afternoon. Unfortunately, the law still dictates that pubs must close at 11pm (10.30pm on Sundays) unless they have a special licence. To find a late-night drinking hole *see chapter* **Early Hours**. (When somewhere is unlicensed, we say so in the listings.)

Central

The American Bar
Savoy Hotel, Strand, WC2 (071 836 4343). Aldwych underground/Charing Cross underground/BR. **Open** 11am-3pm, 5.30-11pm, Mon-Sat; noon-3pm, 7-10.30pm, Sun. **Credit** A, AmEx, DC, £$TC, V.
Smart dress (a jacket and tie for men) is required at this subdued, art deco-ish bar. Prices are high (this *is* the Savoy) but the bartenders are first class. Concoctions include Black Russian (vodka and Kahlúa), Prevention (a non-alcoholic fruit juice mix) and a cracking choice of champagne cocktails. Pianist 7-10pm Mon-Sat.

Aroma
36A St Martin's Lane, WC2 (071 836 5110). Leicester Square underground/Charing Cross underground/BR. **Open** 8am-11pm Mon-Fri; 9am-11.30pm Sat; noon-9pm Sun. **Unlicensed. Credit** A, LV, £TC, V.
A gaudily-painted venue for serious caffeine addicts. Customers are treated to loud South American music, slightly uncomfortable chairs, brightly painted pottery and excellent coffee. Sandwiches, cakes and a few hot dishes make up the menu.
Branches: 1B Dean Street, W1 (071 287 1633); 273 Regent Street, W1 (071 495 4911).

Bar Crêperie
21 South Row, The Market, WC2 (071 836 2137). Covent Garden underground. **Open** 9am-midnight daily. **Credit** A, AmEx, LV, £TC, V.
The outdoor seating – under a canopy, and with a good view of the Covent Garden Piazza – pulls in the punters here. Crêpes aren't cheap, but there's lots of choice, and on a warm day it's a winner.

Brixtonian Backayard
4 Neal's Yard, WC2 (071 240 2769). Covent Garden underground. **Open** noon-midnight daily (women only 7pm-midnight Sat). **Credit** A, AmEx, DC, £TC, V.
A sizeable room, arrestingly decorated with vibrantly coloured chairs and a good-looking bar lined with bottles (mainly rum). Cocktails cost about £5; beers (Sapporo and Zambezi) just over £2. Caribbean bar snacks are available; there's a small restaurant upstairs. Jazz 7.30-10.30pm nightly.

Caffe Piazza
16-17 Russell Street, WC2 (071 379 7543). Covent Garden underground. **Open** noon-11.45pm Mon-Sat; noon-11pm Sun. **Credit** A, AmEx, £TC, V.
A pleasant Italian brasserie with a large biscuit-coloured interior, that's good for people-watching. Should you decide to eat, antipasti cost around £3; more substantial new-wave Italian dishes about £6. Wines are Italian.

Coffee Gallery
23 Museum Street, WC1 (071 436 0455). Holborn or Russell Square underground. **Open** 8am-5.30pm Mon-Fri; 10am-5.30pm Sat; 12.30-6.30pm Sun. **Unlicensed. Credit** £TC.
This bright and sunny, Italian-run café-cum-gallery is very handy for the British Museum. Brilliant southern Italian dishes and mouth-watering patisseries and desserts are served on rustic-looking plates. The coffee is good.

Endell's
69 Endell Street, WC2 (071 240 2108). Covent Garden underground. **Open** 9.30am-8pm Mon-Fri; 10am-8pm Sat; 11am-7pm Sun. **No credit cards**.
A small café, idiosyncratically-decorated (tapestries, and chairs attached to plaster pilasters). Amiable chaos prevails at busy times, but sandwiches, salads and quiches are top-notch. Drinks include ultra-strong cappuccino and a small choice of beers.

Freuds
198 Shaftesbury Avenue, WC2 (071 240 9933). Covent Garden or Tottenham Court Road underground. **Open** 11am-11pm Mon-Sat; noon-10.30pm Sun. **Credit** £TC.
A groovy but welcoming basement bar, sporting bare plaster walls, slate tables, black fans and uncomfortable seats. It's dozy during the day, but the pace and noise levels are cranked up at night. Fashionable beers, classic cocktails and so-so snacks are served throughout.

Kudos
10 Adelaide Street, WC2 (071 379 4573). Charing Cross underground/BR. **Open** noon-11pm Mon-Sat; noon-10.30pm Sun. **Credit** A, £TC, V.
Primarily a gay bar/café, Kudos doesn't discourage straights. Food is nothing special, but the drinks list is varied (flavoured vodkas, celebrity beers and so on) and the atmosphere is welcoming. Mighty crowded at night.

Lamb and Flag
33 Rose Street, WC2 (071 497 9504). Covent Garden underground. **Open** 11am-10.45pm Mon-Sat; noon-3pm Sun. **Credit** LV, £TC.
A small, rickety pub, tucked up a narrow alleyway. In the seventeenth century, Dryden was beaten up here for writing offensive verse – now it's a popular meeting place. The upstairs bar (where not-bad bar food is served) is normally the quietest spot.

Old Crown
33 New Oxford Street, WC1 (071 836 9121). Holborn or Tottenham Court Road underground. **Open** noon-midnight Mon-Sat. **Credit** A, AmEx, DC, V.
A pub that has been transformed into a Continental bar: the light, clean interior makes it a relaxing spot during the day; at night it's pretty lively. The food ranges from croissants to full (international) meals during the day; in the evening it's Mexican.
Branch: **Old Parr's Head** 46 Upper Street, N1 (071 226 2180).

Pelican
45 St Martin's Lane, WC2 (071 379 0309). Charing Cross underground/BR. **Open** 11am-1am Mon-Sat; 11am-3pm, 7-10.30pm, Sun. **Credit** A, AmEx, DC, £TC, V.

A large, urbane, recently refurbished brasserie which caters for most requirements. The menu is all-encompassing (from breakfast to late suppers); the wine list is heavily biased towards France. Pianist nightly.

Pret à Manger
77/78 St Martin's Lane, WC2 (071 379 5335). Leicester Square underground/Charing Cross underground/BR. **Open** 8am-10pm Mon-Fri; 8am-11pm Sat; 10am-8pm Sun. **Unlicensed. Credit** LV.
A rapidly-expanding chain of designer sandwich bars. Surroundings are functional fast-food joint; sandwiches, salads, cakes and savouries are in a different league – as the four types of sushi demonstrate. Listed below are the branches with seating.
Branches: 12 Kingsgate Parade, Victoria Street, SW1 (071 828 1559); 17 Eldon Street, EC2 (071 628 9011); 23-28 Fleet Street, EC4 (071 353 2332); 298 Regent Street, W1 (071 637 3836).

West End

For more pubs in Soho, *see chapter* **London by Area: West End**.

Argyll Arms
18 Argyll Street, W1 (071 734 6117). Oxford Circus underground. **Open** 11am-11pm Mon-Sat. **No credit cards.**
There are precious few pubs this close to Oxford Street, but the Argyll is one of the best. It's housed in a fine Victorian building with engraved glass partitions and giant mirrors. Liberties, the Palladium, and Oxford Circus tube are all within two minutes' walk.

Caffe Nero
43 Frith Street, W1 (071 434 3887). Leicester Square or Tottenham Court Road underground. **Open** 8am-1am Mon-Fri; 9am-1am Sat; 9am-11pm Sun. **Unlicensed. Credit** £TC.
Sited opposite Bar Italia (*see chapter* **London by Area: West End**) the Nero has more outside seating and better Italian cakes, but less atmosphere, despite the designer interior (all beaten metal and chrome). The coffee is definitely worth drinking.
Branch: 66 Old Brompton Road, SW7 (071 589 1760).

dell 'Ugo
56 Frith Street, W1 (071 734 8300/fax 071 734 8717). Leicester Square underground. Café **Open** 11am-11pm Mon-Sat. **Credit** A, AmEx, £TC, V.
The café is on the ground floor (the next two floors hold the restaurant). It's loud and lively and offers a Mediterranean-style menu. The quality of the dishes is inconsistent, but this is a fun place for a drink and a snack.

The Dog House
187 Wardour Street, W1 (071 434 2116). Tottenham Court Road underground. **Open** 12.30-11pm Mon-Fri; 6-11pm Sat. **Credit** A, AmEx, £TC, V.
Full of hip young things, but welcoming nonetheless, this cramped basement bar is a medley of dark, clashing colours. Bar staff are friendly and competent; drinks are cocktails and cult beers. Above-average bar snacks are served all day.

The Edge
11 Soho Square, W1 (071 439 1223). Tottenham Court Road underground. **Open** 8am-midnight Mon-Fri; 10am-midnight Sat; noon-10.30pm Sun. **Credit** A, AmEx, £TC, V.
This welcoming cafe/bar attracts a mix of gay and straight customers. The décor is modern, the menu is

long and accommodating, and includes baguettes, cakes, pasta dishes, burgers and full meals.

The Fountain
Fortnum & Mason, 181 Piccadilly, W1 (071 734 8040, ext 492). Green Park or Piccadilly Circus underground. **Open** 7.30am-11pm Mon-Sat. **Credit** A, AmEx, DC, £STC, V.

The Fountain restaurant is decked out in Fortnum's green, with chandeliers, *trompe-l'oeil* panels, starched white napery and uniformed waitresses. Meals are served all day, but tea – cakes, scones, sandwiches, ice-creams and seven different types of tea, plus 13 different sundaes – is the one to go for.

George
55 Great Portland Street, W1 (071 636 0863). Oxford Circus underground. **Open** 11am-11pm Mon-Fri; 11am-6pm Sat; 7-10.30pm Sun. **Credit** A, AmEx, V.

This comfortable old pub is much used by workers from nearby BBC Broadcasting House. Standard pub food (fish and chips, burgers) is served at lunchtimes.

Häagen-Dazs on the Square
14 Leicester Square, WC2 (071 287 9577). Leicester Square underground. **Open** 10am-midnight Mon-Thur, Sun; 10am-1am Fri, Sat. **Unlicensed. Credit** £TC.

The international smart-but-bland surroundings can't detract from the excellence of the ice-cream served here. Further options include frozen yoghurt or pastries and a choice of soft drinks, coffees and tea. Takeaway service. **Branches:** 75 Hampstead High Street, NW3 (071 794 0646); Unit 6, The Piazza, WC2 (071 240 0436); 138A King's Road, SW3 (071 823 9326).

Hardy's
53 Dorset Street, W1 (071 935 5929). Baker Street underground. **Open** 12.30-3pm, 5.30-10.30pm, Mon-Fri. **Credit** A, £TC, V.

The décor (yellow rag-rolled walls hung with gilded mirrors, plus bare boards and unadorned tables) and the calibre of the food mark this wine bar out. The wine list is short, and like the food, on the pricey side.

Maison Bertaux
28 Greek Street, W1 (071 437 6007). Leicester Square underground. **Open** 9am-8pm daily. **Unlicensed. No credit cards.**

An unadorned, rather pokey but much-loved café that's been here for decades. Baked on the premises, cakes, patisserie and savoury quiches are luscious; coffee is café au lait.

Patisserie Valerie
44 Old Compton Street, W1 (071 437 3466). Piccadilly Circus or Tottenham Court Road underground. **Open** 8am-8pm Mon-Fri; 8am-7pm Sat; 10am-5.30pm Sun. **Unlicensed. Credit** LV, £TC.

Larger than Maison Bertaux, but just as crowded, this Soho old-timer continues to dispense succulent patisserie and sustaining cappuccino to an assortment of Soho bohos. **Branches:** 215 Brompton Road, SW3 (071 823 9971); **Patisserie Valerie at Maison Sagne** 105 Marylebone High Street, W1 (071 935 6240).

Ranoush Juice Bar
43 Edgware Road, W2 (071 723 5929). Marble Arch underground. **Open** 8am-2am daily. **Unlicensed. No credit cards.**

A hubbub of activity with a juice bar along one wall, a snack counter opposite, and seating at the back around a fountain. Juices include melon and tamarind, as well as orange, grapefruit and carrot; snacks are Middle Eastern.

Soho Soho
11-13 Frith Street, W1 (071 494 3491). Leicester Square or Tottenham Court Road underground. Café/bar/rôtisserie **Open** 8am-12.30am Mon-Fri; noon-12.30am Sat. **Credit** A, AmEx, DC, £TC, V.

The open-plan ground floor bar and brasserie is a prime Soho meeting and greeting spot – the noise can be relentless, but it's fun. In contrast the décor is cool and bleached. The cuisine is South of France-inspired.

Spice of Life
6 Moor Street, W1 (071 437 7013). Leicester Square underground. **Open** 11am-11pm Mon-Sat; noon-3pm, 7-10.30pm, Sun. **No credit cards.**

A noisy pub just off Cambridge Circus on the edge of Soho. It's a popular haunt for art students and just about anyone else who wants to meet up for a night on the town.

Star Café
22B Great Chapel Street, W1 (071 437 8778). Tottenham Court Road underground. **Open** 7am-5.30pm Mon-Fri. **Credit** LV, £TC.

Caff meals with a touch of class. Sandwiches, omelettes, salads and hot meals of heart-stopping proportions come at very nice prices for the area. Vintage metal advertising signs decorate the ground floor and basement.

Three Greyhounds
25 Greek Street, W1 (071 734 8799). Piccadilly Circus or Tottenham Court Road underground. **Open** noon-11pm Mon-Sat; 7-10.30pm Sun. **Credit** A, V.

A charmingly spruced up pub that hasn't lost any character. A simple snack menu of sandwiches and really good home-cooked food (served all day) highlights the contrast with the average boozer.

Le Tire Bouchon
6 Upper James Street, W1 (071 437 5348). Piccadilly Circus underground. **Open** 8am-9.30pm Mon-Fri. **Credit** A, AmEx, LV, £TC, V.

A small brasserie, serving a short menu of French standards, in surroundings that are authentic but most definitely not themed. Coffee is good. Service is thoroughly Gallic.

The Yard
57 Rupert Street, W1 (071 437 2652). Piccadilly Circus underground. **Open** noon-3pm, 6-10pm, Mon-Sat. **Credit** A, AmEx, V.

This attractive café-bar is primarily, though not exclusively, a gay venue. Light, modern dishes cost about £5, and a good selection of drinks includes Continental lagers and New World wines. **Branch: Village Soho** 81 Wardour Street, W1 (434 2124).

West

Beach Blanket Babylon
45 Ledbury Road, W11 (071 229 2907). Notting Hill Gate underground. **Open** 11am-11pm Mon-Sat; 11am-10.30pm Sun. **Credit** A, V.

A dauntingly fashionable bar adorned with a Gaudi-esque design and swarms of beautiful people. Arrive before 8pm or you might not get in. There's a restaurant too.

Brasserie du Marché aux Puces
349 Portobello Road, W10 (081 968 5828). Ladbroke Grove underground/15, 52, 295 bus. **Open** 10am-11pm Mon-Sat; 11am-4pm Sun. **Credit** £TC.

An unassuming brasserie at the fag end of Portobello Road. It's possible to just have a drink, but a shame to miss the food. Dishes are eclectic and can sound unlike-

Hip but hospitable: the **Dog House**. *See* **review** *page 147.*

ly, but are always stunningly successful – for example, spinach pancake with fennel and Dolcelatte.

Café Laville
453 Edgware Road, W9 (071 706 2620). Edgware Road or Warwick Avenue underground/6 bus. **Open** 10am-7pm daily. **No credit cards**.
The Laville backs onto the canal, and you can sit outside and watch the boats go by. The menu is a pleasing mishmash of cakes, sandwiches, full meals, omelettes and soups. The coffee is worth having.

Café Minema
43 Knightsbridge, SW1 (071 823 1269). Hyde Park Corner or Knightsbridge underground. **Open** 9am-11.15pm Mon-Sat; 11am-7pm Sun. **Credit** A, AmEx, DC, TC, V.
A two-storey, glass-fronted café with views out over Hyde Park, above the cinema of the same name. Smart-but-pricey café dishes are served in modish surroundings. Equally chic drinks include espresso and champagne.

Daquise
20 Thurloe Street, SW7 (071 589 6117). South Kensington underground. **Open** 10am-11.30pm daily. **Credit** LV, £TC.
Avoid the over-hearty main meals at this Polish café and

you won't go far wrong. The cakes, coffee and flavoured vodkas are all first rate and the crowded, cluttered upstairs room is a splendid restorative after a heavy morning at the local museums.

Dove
19 Upper Mall, W6 (081 748 5405). Ravenscourt Park underground. **Open** 11am-11pm Mon-Sat; noon-3pm, 7-10.30pm, Sun. **No credit cards**.
Occupying a small seventeenth-century building within a whisker of the Thames, this pub has good food and fine ales (brewed by Fuller's). Graham Greene and Ernest Hemingway drank here; and the writer of *Rule Britannia* lived upstairs.

Ebury Wine Bar
139 Ebury Street, SW1 (071 730 5447/fax 071 823 6053). Sloane Square underground/Victoria underground/BR. **Open** 11am-11pm Mon-Fri. **Credit** A, AmEx, DC, £TC, V.
A pleasant wine bar that fills up quickly after office hours, plus a quieter dining room where the menu lists reasonably-priced, mainly British dishes. There are lots of wines by the glass. **Branches: Carriages** 43 Buckingham Palace Road, SW1 (071 834 0119); **Draycotts** 114 Draycott Avenue, SW3 (071 584 5359).

Fifth Floor Café
*Harvey Nichols, Knightsbridge, SW1 (071 235 5000).
Knightsbridge underground.* **Open** 10am-10.30pm Mon-
Sat; 11am-4.30pm Sun. **Credit** A, AmEx, DC, TC, V.
The café/bar lies between the food hall and the
restaurant on this Julyan Wickham-designed fifth floor.
Prices for the designer salads and the blow-out teas
aren't bad, given the surroundings. At peak times
turnover is fast and furious.

Julie's Bar
*137 Portland Road, W11 (071 727 7985). Holland
Park underground.* **Open** 11.30am-midnight daily.
Credit A, AmEx, £TC, V.
A warren of rooms with churchy-Gothic fittings, and a
mellow atmosphere. Food (unexciting but reliable) and
drink (some interesting bottles) are priced high.

Lisboa Patisserie
*57 Golborne Road, W10 (081 968 5242). Ladbroke
Grove underground.* **Open** 8am-8pm daily. **No credit
cards.**
One of the oldest and certainly the most popular
Portuguese pastelaria. Inside has a beautiful tile painting and a hissing Gaggia. Pasteis de camarão (shrimp
pasty) is one of the few savoury snacks; cakes are baked
on the premises and are moreish.

Maison Pechon
*127 Queensway, W2 (071 229 0746). Bayswater
underground.* **Open** 8am-7pm Mon-Wed; 8am-8pm
Thur-Sat; 8.30am-7pm Sun. **Credit** LV.
Pierre Pechon's patisserie française is a long, thin and mirrored room with a patisserie counter running the length
of one side. Patisseries (from 60p) are of course the main
event, but there is also a short list of hot dishes.

Mesón Doña Ana
*37 Kensington Park Road, W11 (071 243 0666).
Ladbroke Grove underground.* **Open** noon-11.30pm
daily. **Credit** A, TC, V.
The three tapas bars in this small chain have the same
menu, similar attractive décor, and share a lively-but-
comfortable atmosphere. The quality of the food here is
slightly better, but all three are great places for a drink
and a snack.
Branches: Mesón Don Felipe 53 The Cut, SE1 (071
928 3237); **Mesón Don Julián** 125-127 Dawes Road,
SW6 (071 386 5901).

Le Metro
*28 Basil Street, SW3 (071 589 6286). Knightsbridge
underground.* **Open** 10.30am-11pm Mon-Sat. **Credit** A,
AmEx, DC, £TC, V.
A small, soberly decorated basement brasserie serving excellent food and wine. From a lengthy, worldwide choice, ten bottles at any one time are available
by the glass.

Star Tavern
*6 Belgrave Mews West, SW1 (071 235 3019). Hyde
Park Corner or Knightsbridge underground.* **Open**
11.30am-3pm, 5-11pm Mon-Sat; noon-3pm, 7-10.30pm,
Sun.
A highly popular pub that occupies two storeys of a
Georgian building in a cobbled mews off Belgrave
Square. Food is served noon-2pm and 6.30-8.45pm Mon-
Fri. Fuller's beer is on draught.

Windsor Castle
*114 Campden Hill Road, W8 (071 727 8491). Notting
Hill Gate underground.* **Open** 11am-11pm Mon-Sat;
noon-3pm, 7-11pm, Sun. **Credit** A, AmEx, £TC, V.
The dark, old-wood interior, pretty, walled garden and

good, British pub food are the attractions here. The steak
and kidney pudding is one of the best in London and
costs around a fiver.

South

Alma
*499 Old York Road, SW18 (081 870 2537).
Wandsworth Town BR.* **Open** 10am-11pm Mon-Sat;
11am-3pm, 7-10.30pm, Sun. **Credit** A, AmEx, TC, V.
While it remains a pub, rather than a restaurant, the
attractions of Youngs beer, a pinball machine and the
authentic, dark wood interior pale beside the marvellous
food on offer. Dishes have a French flavour, and prices
are at pub level.
Branch: Coopers Arms, 87 Flood Street, SW3 (071
376 3120); **Ship** *see below.*

Anchor Bankside
*34 Park Street, SE1 (071 407 1577). Monument
underground/Cannon Street or London Bridge
underground/BR.* **Open** 11.30am-11pm Mon-Sat; noon-
3pm, 7-10.30pm, Sun. **Credit** A, AmEx, DC, LV, £TC, V.
A Forte-run pub serving adequate food and a reasonable
choice of beers. The attraction is the fine views over the
Thames – patrons can enjoy a drink at one of the tables
on the large, paved area at the front. There's also a
restaurant upstairs.

Annabel's Patisserie
*33 High Street, SW19 (081 947 4326). Wimbledon
underground/BR.* **Open** 9am-7pm Mon, Sun; 9am-
11pm Tue-Sat. **Credit** A, £TC, V.
This charming old-fashioned patisserie expanded from tea
room into fully-fledged brasserie in January 1993.
However, the cakes and patisserie remain as good as ever.

Café Portugal
*5A & 6A Victoria House, South Lambeth Road, SW8
(071 587 1962). Vauxhall underground/BR.* **Open**
10am-10.30pm daily. **No credit cards.**
Portugal has been recreated here with remarkable success. There's an ice-cream parlour next door, a basement
restaurant, and a ground floor bar which serves cakes,
coffee, beers and Portuguese liqueurs.

Forget-me-not Teas
*45 High Street, SW19 (081 947 3634). Wimbledon
underground/BR/93 bus.* **Open** 10.30am-5.30pm Tue-
Fri; 10.30am-5.45pm Sat, Sun. **Unlicensed. Credit** £TC.
A traditional tea room, with starched and embroidered
tablecloths and a collection of Victorian china. Choose
from five different set teas or a long list of hot savouries,
salads, sandwiches and cakes.

The Depot
*Tideway Yard, Mortlake High Street, SW14 (081 878
9462). Barnes Bridge or Mortlake BR.* **Open** noon-
3pm, 6-11pm, Mon-Sat; 12.30-3.30pm, 6-10.30pm, Sun.
Credit A, AmEx, LV, £TC, V.
A tremendously popular venue with magnificent riverside views. The laid-back atmosphere and brasserie-style
menu make it a relaxing place. A favourite with families.

The Fire Station
*150 Waterloo Road, SE1 (071 401 3267). Waterloo
underground/BR.* **Open** 11am-11pm Mon-Sat. **Credit**
LV, TC.
A converted fire station, simply decorated, which operates as a bar/brasserie. Dishes are affordable Modern
British; drinks are wines (all available by the glass), plus
Young's bitter and scrumpy on draught. A fine addition
to the area.

Flumbs

67-69 Abbeville Road, SW4 (081 675 2201). Clapham South underground. **Open** 10am-11pm Mon-Sat; 10am-10.30pm Sun. **Credit** A, AmEx, V.
A cosy spot with the ambience and décor of a typical wine bar. The menu runs from breakfast to supper, brasserie style. The global wine list has half a dozen wines available by the glass, and there's a sizable choice of international beers.

The Hothouse Café Bar

9 Station Approach, Richmond, Surrey (081 332 1923). Kew Gardens underground/BR. **Open** 10am-7pm daily. **Credit** £TC.
A congenial, haphazardly decorated joint where the coffee comes in nearly 30 different guises. The menu is varied and flexible; breakfast is served all day, and there's beer as well as cakes and teas.

Off the Rails

Greenwich Station, 187 Greenwich High Road, SE10 (081 293 4512). Greenwich BR. **Open** 7am-7pm Mon-Fri; 9.30am-7pm Sat, Sun. **Unlicensed**. **Credit** LV, £TC.
A small pink-painted café in a room off Greenwich Station. The range of food is small, but it's all good, home-made stuff, and includes cakes, sandwiches, pizzas and quiches.

Pierre

11 Petersham Road, Richmond, Surrey (081 332 2778). Richmond BR. **Open** 9am-10.30pm daily. **Credit** £TC.
French and Lebanese ownership has resulted in a patisserie that also serves Middle Eastern snacks and simple grills. The pastel-pink premises are tiled and bright, although the chandelier lights are dimmed at night.

La Rueda

66-68 Clapham High Street, SW4 (071 627 2173/071 498 0547). Clapham North underground. **Open** noon-3pm, 6.30-11.30pm, Mon-Fri; 12.30-11.30pm Sat; 1-10.30pm Sun. **Credit** A, AmEx, DC, V.
Not unlike a traditional Spanish *mesón*, with a long wooden bar and wine bottles laid out on racks above the diners' heads. The tapas, almost 40 in number, are full of rich and earthy flavours.
Branch: 642 King's Road, SW6 (071 384 2684).

The Ship

41 Jews Row, SW18 (081 870 9667). Wandsworth Town BR/28, 95, 291 bus. **Open** 11am-11pm Mon-Sat; noon-3pm, 7-10.30pm, Sun. **Credit** (food only) A, AmEx, £TC, V.
Good food is served every lunchtime (noon-2.45pm) and evening (6.30-10pm) at this popular riverside pub, but the barbecues in the summer are overpriced and overcrowded.

Tea-time

21 The Pavement, SW4 (071 622 4944). Clapham Common underground/35, 37, 45, 88, 137, 155 bus. **Open** 10am-6pm Mon-Wed; 10am-10pm Thur-Sat; 10am-6.30pm Sun. **Unlicensed**. **No credit cards.**
Pleasantly nostalgic décor (Lloyd Loom chairs and mismatched crockery) and sweet and savoury tea-time dishes are the attractions here. Thursday to Saturday nights it operates as a bistro (bring your own booze).

White Cross Hotel

Water Lane Riverside, Richmond (081 940 6844). Richmond underground/BR. **Open** 11am-11pm Mon-Sat; noon-3pm, 7-10.30pm, Sun. **Credit** A, LV, V.
A popular riverside haunt, with excellent views and Victorian front parlour decoration. Above-average pub fare is served alongside fine ales and a decent choice of wines.

City

For more City supping houses, *see chapter* **London by Area: The City**.

Bleeding Heart

Bleeding Heart Yard, off Greville Street, EC1 (071 242 8238/fax 071 831 1402). Chancery Lane underground/Farringdon underground/BR. **Open** noon-10.30pm Mon-Fri. **Credit** A, AmEx, DC, £TC, V.
This rambling, historic wine bar has smart French staff and a menu with a Gallic emphasis. The wine list is overlong (27 pages), but at least there are plenty of bottles for under £15.

Diana's Dining Room

30 St Cross Street, EC1 (071 831 7261). Farringdon underground/BR. **Open** 8am-4pm Mon, Tue; 8am-8pm Wed-Fri. **Credit** A, LV, V.
Just out of earshot of Leather Lane market, this family-run snackbar has a reputation for serving freshly prepared food with a Middle Eastern bent. Salt beef sandwiches and pasta dishes are further options.

Eagle

159 Farringdon Road, EC1 (071 837 1353). Farringdon underground/BR/19, 38, 171A bus. **Open** noon-11pm Mon-Fri. **Credit** £TC.
One of the best up-dates of the traditional British boozer. It's a large, bright interior that still looks like a pub, but the food is a delight, and there are half a dozen wines by the glass, plus a range of beers. Very crowded.

Lamb Tavern

10-12 Leadenhall Market, EC3 (071 626 2454). Liverpool Street underground/BR. **Open** 11am-9pm Mon-Fri. **Credit** A, V.
A fine setting in Leadenhall Market and the quality of the lunch-time roast beef sandwiches make this pub worth a visit. The downstairs bar is packed with besuited workers; food is served on the first floor, in a less frenetic atmosphere.

Leith's at the Institute

Chartered Accountants' Hall, Moorgate Place, Moorgate, EC2 (071 920 8626). Moorgate underground/BR. **Open** noon-2.30pm Mon-Fri. **Credit** A, AmEx, V.
Prue Leith's latest project is housed in a cavernous basement. The attractively decorated, split-level room is home to sustaining, capable food and a concise, well-balanced wine list. Her original (expensive) restaurant remains at 92 Kensington Park Road, W11 (071 229 4481).

Ye Olde Mitre

1 Ely Court, Ely Place, EC1 (071 405 4751). Chancery Lane underground/Farringdon underground/BR. **Open** 11am-11pm Mon-Fri. **Credit** LV.
A dark, ancient pub hidden in an alleyway off Ely Place, peopled by lawyers and business types. The two, alcoved bars are wondrously snug, but the food is very basic.

East End & Docklands

Barley Mow

44 Narrow Street, E14 (071 265 8931). Limehouse DLR. **Open** 11am-11pm Mon-Sat; noon-3pm, 7-10.30pm, Sun. **Credit** A, AmEx, LV, V.
What was the dockmaster's house has been turned into a pub. It's a great setting – there's a superb view of the Thames and seating outdoors on a balcony. The food is standard pub grub.

Mayflower

117 Rotherhithe Street, SE16 (071 237 4088).
Rotherhithe underground. **Open** noon-3pm, 6-11pm,
Mon-Fri; 11am-11pm Sat; noon-3pm, 7-10.30pm, Sun.
Credit A, V.
A fine, old pub, dark and snug inside, with views over the
Thames from its jetty. The food alone isn't worth the trip,
but it is slightly more adventurous than average.

Prospect of Whitby

57 Wapping Wall, E1 (071 481 1095). Wapping
underground. **Open** 11.30am-3pm, 5.30-11pm, Mon-
Sat; noon-3pm, 7-10.30pm, Sun. **Credit** (food only) A,
AmEx, £TC, V.
One of the oldest surviving drinking houses in London.
The terrace and restaurant have superb views over the
river, but the beer (Courage) is pricey, and the pub is
often crowded. Food is served noon-2pm Mon-Fri, Sun;
7-9.30pm Mon-Sat.

Town of Ramsgate

62 Wapping High Street, E1 (071 488 2685). Wapping
underground. **Open** 11.30am-11pm Mon-Sat; noon-
3pm, 7-10.30pm, Sun. **No credit cards**.
This unpretentious pub was where Judge Jeffreys, who
was fond of hanging all and sundry, was saved from a
lynch mob in 1688. There's a (slightly dingy) riverside
garden, and at low tide you can see the post to which
smugglers and pirates (including Captain Kidd in 1701)
were condemned to hang in chains until three tides
washed over them. Standard pub food is served at
lunchtimes and early evenings.

Whitechapel Café

Whitechapel Gallery, 80 Whitechapel High Street, E1
(071 377 6182). Aldgate East underground. **Open**
11am-3.30pm Mon; 11am-4.30pm Tue, Thur-Sun; 11am-
6.30pm Wed. **No credit cards**.
An independent adjunct to the gallery, this sparsely decorated café has a certain style. Fresh ingredients are
employed in the making of cakes and a small choice of
meat and vegetarian hot dishes.

North

Alfredo's

4-6 Essex Road, N1 (071 226 3496). Angel
underground/38, 56, 73 bus. **Open** 7am-2.30pm Mon-
Fri; 7am-noon Sat. **Unlicensed. Credit** LV, £TC.
A cherished caff which has been serving cheap British
food – pies, fry-ups and puddings drowned in custard –
since its art deco fittings were new in the 1920s.

Bar Gansa

2 Inverness Street, NW1 (071 267 8909). Camden
Town underground. **Open** 10.30am-11.30pm Mon-Sat;
10.30am-10.30pm Sun. **Credit** A, TC, V.
A durable, unthemed tapas bar in the thick of one of
Camden's markets. The good quality tapas aren't particularly authentic, with the happy result that there's lots of
choice for vegetarians. The bar is packed to bursting
point at weekends.

Café Mozart

17 Swains Lane, N6 (081 348 1384). Gospel Oak
BR/214, C2 bus. **Open** 9am-5.30pm Mon; 9am-10pm
Tue-Sun. **Credit** A, £TC, V.
A cheery, haphazardly-decorated café that manages to
be most things to most people. Rich patisserie, all-day
breakfasts, pancakes and hot dishes with a central
European slant are dispensed in a relaxed atmosphere.

The Coffee Cup

74 Hampstead High Street, NW3 (071 435 7565).
Hampstead underground. **Open** 8am-midnight Mon-
Sat; 9am-midnight Sun. **Unlicensed. Credit** LV, £TC.
A cosy, wood-panelled café (with tables outdoors) where
the varied menu is very flexible. Have as little as a cof-
fee or an ice-cream, or as much as no-holds-barred
English breakfast.

Cosmo

4-6 Northways Parade, Finchley Road, NW3 (071 722
1398). Finchley Road or Swiss Cottage underground.
Open 8.30am-11pm daily. **Credit** A, AmEx, DC, £TC, V.
Old world charm distinguishes this central European coffee bar. Décor is functional, but the atmosphere more
than compensates. Try the creamy scrambled eggs.

Cottons Rhum Shop, Bar & Restaurant

55 Chalk Farm Road, NW1 (071 482 1096). Chalk
Farm underground/31, 168 bus. **Open** 5-11.45pm Mon;
noon-11.45pm Tue-Sun. **Credit** A, £TC, V.
Drink potent cocktails in an atmospheric setting of
flaky, rough coloured plaster and distressed shuttering.
The food is Caribbean, and is the least reliable part of
the equation.

Crown & Goose

100 Arlington Road, NW1 (071 485 2342). Camden
Town underground. **Open** 11am-11pm Mon-Sat;
10.30am-3pm, 7-10.30pm, Sun. **Credit** LV.
A successful pub conversion, all scrubbed wood and
green paint, that attracts a youngish crowd. Food is no-
nonsense, high-quality stuff, such as a burger in ciabatta
bread.

The Flask

77 Highgate West Hill, N6 (081 340 7260). Highgate
underground/43, 271 bus. **Open** 11am-11pm Mon-Sat,
Bank Holidays; noon-3pm, 7-10.30pm, Sun. **Credit**
(food only) A, TC, V.
The pub's name refers to the containers in which the
salubrious Highgate spa water was sold. The building
was first erected in 1663, with additions in 1767. William
Hogarth, used to sketch scenes of drunken revelry here.
Good, traditional pub food is served noon-2pm, 6-9pm,
Mon-Fri; noon-2.30pm Sat, Sun (though there's usually
something to eat in the afternoons and later evenings).
There's a beer garden for the summer.

Gill Wing Café

302-304 St Paul's Road, N1 (071 226 2885). Highbury
& Islington underground/BR. **Open** 10am-10.30pm
Mon-Fri; 9.30am-10.30pm Sat, Sun. **Credit** £TC.
Restful, undemanding surroundings and an enticing
brasserie menu make this place a winner. Dishes run from
tea and toast to game pie with trimmings. Newspapers are
provided.

Golders Hill Park Refreshment House

North End Way, NW3 (081 455 8010). Golders Green
or Hampstead underground. **Open** *April-Sept* 10.30am-
sunset daily. **No credit cards**.
A superior park canteen, decorated with hanging baskets and tubs of flowers. Gelati are dispensed from a
hatch at one side; inside, a sort-of self-service canteen
doles out delicious home-made Italian food.

Holly Bush

22 Holly Mount, NW3 (071 435 2892). Hampstead
underground. **Open** 11am-3pm, 5.30-11pm, Mon-Fri;
11am-4pm, 6-11pm, Sat; noon-3pm, 7-10.30pm, Sun.
Credit LV.
An idyllic pub, tucked away up a narrow lane. There are
several dark, low-ceilinged rooms arranged around an

ancient wooden bar. The splendid collection of beers far outshines the tired pub fare.

Lansdowne

90 Gloucester Avenue, NW1 (071 483 0409). Chalk Farm underground/31, 168 bus. **Open** 6-11pm Mon; 11am-11pm Tue-Sat; noon-3pm, 7-10.30pm, Sun. **Credit** £TC.
Bare boards, fresh flowers and world music make this reworked pub an engaging place. What brings in the crowds is the splendid cooking – dishes are eclectic, but with a Middle Eastern bias. Wine is also a strong point.

Magpie & Stump

132 Stoke Newington Church Street, N16 (071 275 9407). Bus 73. **Open** 11am-11pm Mon-Sat; noon-3pm, 7-10.30pm, Sun. **No credit cards.**
A pleasant bare-boards boozer with an easy-going atmosphere. Food is only served at lunch-time, but it's a cut above the competition. There's a small garden at the back, and a tiny restaurant on the first floor.

Marine Ices

8 Haverstock Hill, NW3 (071 485 3132). Chalk Farm underground/31, 168 bus. **Open** 10am-10.45pm Mon-Sat; 11am-9pm Sun. **Credit** LV, TC.
Just up the road from Camden market, this gelateria has been run by three successive generations of the Mansi family since it opened in 1931. There's an inexpensive Italian restaurant too, but it's the ices that are renowned, especially the sublime sorbets.

Patisserie Bliss

428 St John Street, EC1 (071 837 3720). Angel underground/19, 38, 43, 56, 73, 171A, 279 bus. **Open**

8am-7pm Mon-Fri; 9am-6pm Sat, Sun. **Unlicensed. No credit cards.**
A minute Islington patisserie where splendid bread and pastries are baked on the premises. Strong cappuccinos come from the Gaggia, or there's a range of teas. Service is chaotic.

Primrose Patisserie

136 Regent's Park Road, NW1 (071 722 7848). Chalk Farm underground. **Open** 8am-10.30pm Mon-Sat; 9am-10.30pm Sun. **Unlicensed. Credit** £TC.
It's Polish-run – specialities are poppy seed cake and thick-based cheesecake, plus hot dishes like goulash or spinach and dill soup.

Spaniard's Inn

Spaniard's Road, NW3 (081 455 3276). Hampstead underground/210, 268 bus. **Open** 11am-11pm Mon-Sat; noon-3pm, 7-10.30pm, Sun. **Credit** (food only) A, £TC, V.
Part of the Spaniards pub dates from 1585, and through the years, highwayman Dick Turpin, Byron, Keats, Shelley and that inveterate tippler Charles Dickens have supped here. They had good taste. In the winter, you can huddle around an open fire; in the summer there's a classic English garden. The restaurant has a hot and cold buffet and traditional pub food.

Wisteria

14 Middle Lane, N8 (081 348 2669). Bus 14A, W2, W3, W7. **Open** 11.30am-6pm Tue-Fri; 10am-6pm Sat; 11am-6pm Sun. **Unlicensed. No credit cards.**
A charming, if ramshackle tea room serving homemade cakes, sandwiches and inventive tea-time savouries. No smoking.

Heaven in Hampstead: the **Holly Bush.** *See* **review** *page 152.*

Shops
& Services

London for sale: from arty antiques to the best boutiques; plus London at your service, from the hippest health-salons, to the fastest photo-processors – here we list the pick of the bunch.

Contents

Shopping Area Index

Central

FASHION/DESIGNER: Christopher New (p159); Duffer of St George (p159); John Richmond (p159); Jones (p160); Michiko Koshino (p160); Paul Smith (p160); Space NK (p160).

FASHION/MEDIUM-RANGE: Boxfresh (p161); French Connection (p161).

FASHION/DESIGNER DISCOUNT: 70 (p162).

FASHION/LEATHER: Natural Leather (p162).

FASHION/SECOND-HAND: Flip (p163).

FASHION/LARGE SIZES: Base (p163).

FASHION/HATS: The Hat Shop (p163).

FASHION/JEWELLERY: Contemporary Applied Arts (p164).

FASHION/SHOES: Plum Line (p165); Red or Dead (p165).

ANTIQUES & COLLECTABLES: Grosvenor Prints (p165); London Silver Vaults (p165).

BOOKS/DEPARTMENTAL BOOKSHOPS: Books Etc (p166); Dillons The Bookstore (p166); Foyles (p166); Waterstones (p166).

BOOKS/ONE-OFFS: Dillons Arts Bookshop (p166); Edward Stanford (p166); Murder One (p166); Sportspages (p166).

BOOKS/SECOND-HAND/ ANTIQUARIAN: Bertram Rota (p167); Henry Pordes (p167); Skoob (p167).

FOOD & DRINK/CHEESE: Neal's Yard Dairy (p169).

FOOD & DRINK/CHOCOLATES: Bendicks (p169).

FOOD & DRINK/DELICATESSENS: Carluccio's (p171).

FOOD & DRINK/HEALTH FOODS: Neal's Yard Wholefood Warehouse (p171).

FOOD & DRINK/WINE, BEER & SPIRITS: The Bloomsbury Wine and Spirit Company (p171).

FURNISHINGS & ACCESSORIES: Habitat (p171); Heal's (p172).

GIFTS: James Smith & Sons (p172); Naturally British (p172).

HEALTH & BEAUTY: Culpeper Herbalists (p172); Neal's Yard Remedies (p172); Penhaligon's (p172).

RECORDS, TAPES & CDS: Black Market (p175); Ray's Jazz Shop (p175).

STAMPS: Stanley Gibbons (p175).

West End

FASHION/DEPARTMENT STORES: Fortnum & Mason (p157); John Lewis (p158); Liberty (p158); Marks & Spencer (p158); Selfridges (p158); Simpson (p158).

Central (column 2)

FASHION/DESIGNER: Browns (p159); Margaret Howell (p160); Mulberry (p160); RM Williams (p160); Whistles (p161); Vivienne Westwood (p161).

FASHION/MEDIUM-RANGE: American Retro (p161); Sonico (p161).

FASHION/CHEAP: Miss Selfridge (p161); River Island (p161); Top Shop (p162).

FASHION/DESIGNER DISCOUNT: Paul Smith (p162); Vivienne Westwood (p162).

FASHION/LARGE SIZES: Evans (p163).

FASHION/SMALL SIZES: Debenhams (p163); Miss Selfridge (p163); Next Petite (p163); Principles (p163); Wallis Petite (p163).

FASHION/JEWELLERY: Aalto (p164); Jess James (p164).

FASHION/SHOES: Shelley's (p165).

AUDIO & HI-FI: Hi-Fi Care (p166).

BOOKS/SECOND-HAND/ ANTIQUARIAN: Maggs Brothers (p167).

FOOD & DRINK/FOOD HALLS: Fortnum & Mason (p167).

FOOD & DRINK/CHEESE: Paxton & Whitfield (p169).

FOOD & DRINK/CHOCOLATES: Charbonnel & Walker (p169).

FOOD & DRINK/DELICATESSENS: Fratelli Camisa (p171); Lina Stores (p171).

FOOD & DRINK/TEA & COFFEE: Algerian Coffee Stores (p171); H R Higgins (p171).

FOOD & DRINK/WINE, BEER & SPIRITS: Berry Bros & Rudd (p171).

GIFTS: Waterford-Wedgwood (p172).

HEALTH & BEAUTY: Floris (p172); A Nelson & Co (p172).

MARKETS/CRAFTS MARKETS: Piccadilly Crafts Market (p173); St Martin-in-the-Fields Market (p173).

MARKETS/GENERAL: Berwick Street Market (p173).

RECORDS, TAPES & CDS: HMV (p174); Tower Records (p174); Virgin Megastore (p175); Reckless Records (p175); Stern's African Record Centre (p175); Vinyl Experience (p175).

TOYS: Hamleys (p175).

West

FASHION/DEPARTMENT STORES: Harrods (p157); Harvey Nichols (p157); Peter Jones (p158).

FASHION/DESIGNER: A La Mode (p159); Issey Miyake (p159); Joseph (p160); Katharine Hamnett (p160).

FASHION/MEDIUM RANGE: American Retro (p161); Jigsaw (p161); Soldier Blue (p161).

West (column 3 continued)

FASHION/DESIGNER DISCOUNT: Designers Sale Studio (p162).

FASHION/INDOOR CLOTHES MARKETS: Hyper-Hyper (p162); Kensington Market (p162).

FASHION/SECOND-HAND: Merchant of Europe (p163).

FASHION/OPTICAL: Arthur Morris (p164); Cutler & Gross (p164).

FASHION/SHOES: Patrick Cox (p165).

FOOD & DRINK/FOOD HALLS: Harrods (p169); Harvey Nichols (p169).

FURNISHINGS & ACCESSORIES: Conran Shop (p171); General Trading Company (p171).

GIFTS: The Crafts Council (p172).

HEALTH & BEAUTY: Crabtree & Evelyn (p172).

MARKETS/WEEKEND: Portobello Market (p174).

RECORDS, TAPES & CDS: Honest Jon's (p175).

South

MARKETS/ANTIQUES MARKETS: Bermondsey (New Caledonian) Market (p173).

MARKETS/CRAFTS MARKETS: Gabriel's Wharf Market (p173).

MARKETS/GENERAL: East Street Market (p173).

RECORDS, TAPES & CDS: Dub Vendor (p175).

North

FASHION/LARGE SIZES: 1647 (p163).

FASHION/SECOND-HAND: Glorious Clothing Company (p163).

FASHION/BELTS: Gohil's (p163).

FASHION/SHOES: Emma Hope (p164).

ANTIQUES & COLLECTABLES: Gallery of Antique Costume & Textiles (p165).

AUDI & HI-FI: Grahams Hi-Fi (p165).

BOOKS/ONE-OFFS: Compendium (p166).

FOOD & DRINK/WINE, BEER & SPIRITS: The Beer Shop (p171).

GIFTS: Richard Kihl (p172).

MARKETS/GENERAL: Ridley Road Market (p174).

MARKETS/WEEKEND: Camden Markets (p174).

MUSICAL INSTRUMENTS: Blanks (p174).

East End & Docklands

FASHION/SECOND-HAND: The Cavern (p162).

FASHION/HATS: Fred Bare (p163).

FOOD & DRINK/BAGELS: Brick Lane Beigel Bake (p169).

MARKETS/WEEKEND: Brick Lane Market (p174); Columbia Road Market (p174); Petticoat Lane Market (p174).

Shopping

With its marvellous markets, bountiful bookstores and fabulous fashion boutiques, London always comes up with the goods.

Whether you're soaking up the atmosphere while picking up a few bargains in a street market, or strolling down the trendy streets of the West End, you'll find London is one of the world's great shopping cities. On the whole, Londoners are friendly, but if you're unfamiliar with the currency or prices, avoid being conned and stick to reputable shops. For a start, forget the souvenir shops: instead try scouring some of the many antique and junk stores for inexpensive, good quality, real British bargains.

Because of the city's immense size, shopping in London may seem daunting. But certain types of store are often grouped together in specific areas. Most of the large bookstores, for example, are gathered on and around Charing Cross Road, WC2. Hi-fi outlets populate Tottenham Court Road, W1, while musical instrument shops have congregated on Denmark Street, WC2. Antiques shops also proliferate in specific districts (*see below* **Antiques & Collectables**). Clothes shops, too, cluster together depending on type of fashion and price range (*below* **Fashion**). But because of escalating rents in central London, and a pernicious, persistent recession, many shops were forced out of business in the early nineties. Even in Oxford Street, shops stand empty, though not usually for long, as store-squatters often move in.

SALES

London's stores have twice-yearly sales, the biggest just after Christmas into February, then another in June/July. Prices are cut in a bid to shift old stock, and bargains can be found in the large department stores. Harrods has the most famous sale, and the queue for the start of the sale is almost a tourist attraction in itself.

FAULTY GOODS

As the law stands, you're entitled to a full refund or replacement if a purchase turns out to be faulty in some way. Notices such as 'No refunds given' are misleading, so don't be put off, even if a repair is offered. If, however, you have a change of heart after buying something in perfect condition, then legally you won't have a leg to stand on if you demand an exchange or money back. Always keep the receipt after every purchase, just in case there's cause to return the goods.

Department Stores

Fortnum & Mason

181 Piccadilly, W1 (071 734 8040). Green Park or Piccadilly Circus underground. **Open** 9.30am-6pm Mon-Sat. **Credit** A, AmEx, DC, JCB, £$TC, V, most foreign currencies.
It's so old-fashioned it's like a theme park. Upstairs in hushed and thickly carpeted rooms, Fortnum's stocks dependable British clothing at exotic prices, some phenomenally expensive foreign designers' clothing, and lots of evening wear. While you're observing how the other half live, keep an eye out for Fortnum's own-brand toiletries: they are beautifully packaged, reasonably priced, and make great gifts. *See also below* **Food Halls**. *Antique valuations. Catalogue. Café and restaurants. Delivery. Export bureau. Mail and telephone credit order.*

Harrods

Knightsbridge, SW1 (071 730 1234). Knightsbridge underground. **Open** 10am-6pm Mon, Tue; 10am-7pm Wed-Fri; 9am-6pm Sat. **Credit** A, A/c, AmEx, DC, SC, £$TC, V, most foreign currencies.
There are more than 60 fashion departments with clothes for all occasions here, but somehow that's not enough to make Harrods an exciting place to shop for clothes. It's better for silverware, home accessories, glassware, kitchenware and cutlery; it has a fabulous magazine department with every fashion title you can imagine; London's best selection of greeting cards in the basement; the sort of toy floor that makes kids (and grown-up kids) think they've died and gone to heaven; and a zoo (really). In fact, Harrods is wonderful as long as you don't mind being told how to carry your bag (even Chanel ruck sacks have to be held in the hand), how to dress (occasional mindless restrictions about wearing shorts can be imposed), and meeting all the tourists who aren't at Buckingham Palace or The Tower. *See also below* **Food Halls**.
Baby-changing facilities. Bureau de change. Cafés and restaurant. Car park. Delivery. Export bureau. Hair salon. Interior design consultancy. Mail and telephone credit order. Store map from Customer Services, 4th floor. Ticket shop.

Harvey Nichols

109-125 Knightsbridge, SW1 (071 235 5000). Knightsbridge underground. **Open** 10am-7pm Mon, Tue, Thur, Fri; 10am-8pm Wed; 10am-6pm Sat. **Credit** A, AmEx, DC, SC, £$TC, V.
Harvey Nichols is serene but never boring and its fashion and accessory buyers really know their stuff. Come and browse through rack upon rack of Dolce & Gabbana, Calvin Klein, Dries van Noten and just about any other designer of merit. All the top Brits are here – don't miss John Rocha's wonderful tailoring or young Londoner Nicholas Knightley's cool, calm women's-wear. The store's own Harvey Nichols Collection is worth a look for basic jackets, shirts and trousers which share the styling – but not the pricing – of designer equivalents. You'll find the best of designer men's-wear in the basement, an excellent selection of contemporary British jewellery on

the ground floor and the sort of luggage and leather goods that last a lifetime (at lifetime-repayment prices). A store with real class. *See also below* **Food Halls**. *Baby-changing facilities. Bureau de change. Cafés and restaurant. Car park. Delivery. Export bureau. Mail and telephone credit order.*

John Lewis

Oxford Street, W1 (071 629 7711). Oxford Circus underground. **Open** 9am-5.30pm Mon-Wed, Fri, Sat; 9.30am-8pm Thur. **Credit** SC.

We all love John Lewis because we know we won't be able to buy identical goods cheaper anywhere else (that's the whole point of the store). It's renowned for its vast selection of fabrics, and staff who can answer all your sewing queries – though the fashion is very humdrum. It's brilliant for unsexy and mundane household goods: electrical stuff, an astonishingly good kitchenware section, luggage, and basic fashion accessories like gloves and socks.
Alterations to own goods. Baby-changing facilities. Delivery. Export bureau. Mail order. Restaurants. Wheelchair access and toilets for the disabled.

Liberty

Regent Street, W1 (071 734 1234). Oxford Circus underground. **Open** 9.30am-6pm Mon-Wed, Fri, Sat; 9.30am-7.30pm Thur. **Credit** A, AmEx, DC, JCB, SC, £$TC, V.

Liberty's Arts and Crafts heritage still suffuses every inch of the store. It has a wonderfully warm carved wood interior that's lovingly cared for and full of everything you can imagine in the famous Liberty prints – from handkerchief holders and notebooks to sofas. Women's fashion on the first floor is usually a pretty good mix of the very expensive (Koji Tatsuno, Workers For Freedom) with the more reasonable (Liberty's own range, Tehen). The second-floor fabric department will take any seamstress's breath away. The basement has a fantastic selection of china, glass and kitchenware, all sold by helpful, knowledgeable staff, and the modern furniture is worth a look.
Café. Delivery. Export bureau. Mail order. Restaurant. Toilets and lifts for the disabled.

Marks & Spencer

458 Oxford Street, W1 (071 935 7954). Marble Arch underground/25, 30, 74 bus. **Open** 9am-7pm Mon-Wed, Sat; 9am-8pm Thur, Fri. **Credit** SC, £$TC.

It doesn't matter who you are, if you're British this is where you buy your underwear. M&S clothes may not be the height of fashion but they're inexpensive and well made, especially the basic knitwear ranges. The men's-wear often seems streets ahead of the women's – it's worth both sexes looking in that department. Some larger stores now have fitting rooms, but money is always refundable on (unworn) mistakes, so you can wait until you get home to try things on properly. The home furnishings might be good quality, but they are desperately middle-of-the-road in design; it's a smarter idea to linger in the lingerie department.
Bureau de change. Delivery. Export bureau. Mail and telephone credit order. Wheelchair access.

Peter Jones

Sloane Square, London SW1 (071 730 3434). Sloane Square underground. **Open** 9am-5.30pm Mon, Tue, Thur-Sat; 9.30am-7pm Wed. **Credit** SC, £$TC.

Peter Jones is a sister store to **John Lewis** (*see above*). It's run on the same 'never knowingly undersold' policy, but thanks to its glamorous location and the fact that it occupies a superb 1934 landmark building, it has the smooth, sophisticated air of a real old department store.
Baby-changing facilities. Café and restaurant. Delivery. Export bureau. Mail and telephone credit order.

Selfridges

Oxford Street, W1 (071 629 1234). Bond Street underground. **Open** 9.30am-7pm Mon-Wed, Fri, Sat; 9.30am-8pm Thur. **Credit** A, AmEx, DC, EC, JCB, Sears, Switch, £$TC, V.

A massive building worth entering simply for the quantity and variety of household and fashion goods. The food hall on the ground floor is impressive, with different counters for different countries. Selfridges will refund the difference if you find the same item cheaper elsewhere.
Baby-changing facilities. Café. Delivery. Disabled facilities. Export scheme. Free catalogue. Mail and telephone credit order. Restaurant. Services arcade (in basement). Wheelchair access.

Simpson

203 Piccadilly, W1 (071 734 2002). Piccadilly Circus underground. **Open** 9am-6pm Mon-Wed, Fri, Sat; 9am-7pm Thur. **Credit** A, AmEx, DC, JCB, SC, £$TC, V.

Seven floors of mainly classic British fashion goods for men and women, including the DAKS label (Simpson's own). Accessories are also worth a scan. On the whole, high quality is matched by high prices. If you feel the need for relief from the relentless Britishness of it all, there's a sushi bar in the basement.

Sending goods abroad

Visitors who live outside the European Community (EC), and who stay no longer than three months, can claim back the Value Added Tax (VAT, currently 17½ per cent) charged on most goods in Britain: the catch is that you'll probably have to spend over £50 or £75 first, depending on the shop. The procedure is simple: take along your passport, then fill in a form at the shop which the assistant will stamp (there may be a small service charge), and hand the completed document to the customs office at the airport or port (officials may want to see the goods, so keep them somewhere handy). There's normally a six-week wait before you get the money back, and payment will be by cheque or by accreditation to your credit card. Not all shops offer this scheme, so it's best to check first before spending any money. If you are having your goods shipped directly by the shop, you can usually persuade them to deduct the VAT prior to payment. But not all shop assistants are as well-informed about this system as they should be.

Delivery. Export scheme. Free catalogue. Gift wrapping services. Mail and telephone credit order. Restaurant/sushi bar. Wine bar/café.

Fashion

London's fashion shops tend to be grouped in the West End and the west of the city. South Molton Street, Sloane Street, Knightsbridge, West Soho and St Christopher's Place are known for costly designer gear, whereas Oxford Street is the home of the chainstore, offering a wide selection of middle-of-the-road fashion. Kensington High Street has both chainstores and trendy street fashion.

But it is the area around Covent Garden that has seen most growth in its number of fashion stores in the past couple of years. The Central Market, Covent Garden, holds scores of shops selling smart mid-range clothing, and lots of knick-knacks for visitors; it's unashamedly commercial, oriented towards tourists, and gets impossibly crowded in the peak visitor season. If you're looking for more interesting shops, cross Long Acre to Neal Street. Although rents on Neal Street itself have been rocketing, it still contains outlets for some of the top London designers, including **Christopher New** and **John Richmond**. But the latest developments have taken place in the area off Neal Street; take a good look around in Endell Street, Shorts Gardens, Monmouth Street, Seven Dials and the recently-opened shopping mall (the Thomas Neal's Centre) between Monmouth Street and Shorts Gardens for innovative and unusual small fashion stores. *See also chapter* **London by Area: Central London.**

Designer

You'll find just about every top designer in London, from the overblown glamour of Gianni Versace to the ascetic refinement of Comme des Garçons. We list some of the best below, but it's worth consulting the phone book, or calling the big stores, to find out what else is around.

A La Mode

36 Hans Crescent, SW1 (071 584 2133). Knightsbridge underground. **Open** 10am-6pm Mon, Tue, Thur-Sat; 10am-7pm Wed. **Credit** A, AmEx, DC, £$TC, V.
With names like Prada, Isaac Mizrahi, Hervé Leger and Amanda Wakeley, we're talking serious money here. A La Mode picks out the best of every season's collections, but it's not exactly a fun place. Feel the chilly breeze as the assistants swish past.
Export scheme. Free alterations to own goods. Mail order. Postal delivery. Wheelchair access.

Browns

23-27 South Molton Street, W1 (071 491 7833). Bond Street underground. **Open** 9.30am-6pm Mon-Sat. **Credit** A, AmEx, DC, £$TC, V.
If you want men's and women's high fashion, go straight

to Browns. Top names such as Jil Sander, Donna Karan and Chloé preside, with top price-tags to match. This is the flagship store of an ever-expanding empire which includes the G Gigli shop across the street at No.38, where you'll find the Romeo Gigli diffusion range with many pieces costing under £100. The Browns Own Label store at No.50 stocks the company's new range of more realistically priced women's wear from its own design team, Bill Amberg's superbly simple leather bags (up to £250) and Simon Day's beaten silver jewellery. By the time you read this, these should have been joined by yet another outlet devoted to Romeo Gigli. The arrogance of Brown's staff is something of a London legend, so prepare to be disappointed; these days the assistants are incredibly nice and helpful.
Alterations to own goods. Export scheme for goods over £100. Postal delivery (£2 postage).
Branches: 6 Sloane Street, SW1; **G Gigli** 38 South Molton Street, W1; **Romeo Gigli** 50 South Molton Street, W1; **Browns Own Label** 45 South Molton Street, W1.

Christopher New

56 Neal Street, WC2 (071 379 1024). Covent Garden underground. **Open** 10.30am-7pm Mon-Fri; 10.30am-6.30pm Sat. **Credit** A, AmEx, DC, JCB, £$TC, V.
Christopher New creates clothes for men who aren't frightened off by a dash of colour or the joys of decorative embroidery and buttons. This is a good place to look for casual jackets, T-shirts and accessories; shirts are priced around the £50-£70 mark.
Delivery. Export scheme.

Duffer of St George

29 Shorts Gardens, WC2 (071 379 4660). Covent Garden underground. **Open** 10.30am-7pm Mon-Fri; 10.30am-6pm Sat; noon-4.30pm Sun. **Credit** A, AmEx, DC, £TC, V.
Where the city's seriously hip males go for image maintenance. Duffer provides up-to-the-minute street clothes, at fairly un-street prices. Jeans are around the £50 mark, but knitwear can hit £200. Still, it all comes with an absolute guarantee that you won't get arrested by the fashion police.
Delivery.
Branch: 27 D'Arblay Street, W1 (071 439 0996).

Issey Miyake

270 Brompton Road, SW1 (071 581 3760). South Kensington underground. **Open** 10am-6pm Mon-Sat. **Credit** A, AmEx, DC, £$TC, V.
Issey Miyake's inimitable designs are created in unique fabrics such as twisted silks that take years to perfect. This store stocks mostly women's fashion – and the American visitors reel in shock when they see the prices.
Delivery. Export scheme.

John Richmond

62 Neal Street, WC2 (071 379 6020). Covent Garden underground. **Open** 10.30am-7pm Mon-Sat; 1-6pm Sun. **Credit** A, AmEx, £TC, V.
If his clothes are anything to go by, John Richmond is obsessed with sex, rock 'n' roll and motorbikes (and indeed if his family life is anything to go by: his son is called Harley Davidson). He isn't the most innovative of designers, but he does have his finger firmly on the pulse of London fashion, and is now strengthening his collections to meet with the demands of showing in Paris, which he started doing in 1993. Look for the trademark mixed-fabric tailored jackets in the men's and women's shops and the really clubby – and cheaper – stuff in Boutique Destroy over the road. These are the clothes that pop stars wear: you can have the same jacket as Lisa Stansfield.
Delivery. Export scheme.
Branches: 2 Newburgh Street, W1 (071 734 5782); **Boutique Destroy** Neal Street (071 379 1896).

Paul Smith: classic men's-wear. *See* **review**.

Jones
13 Floral Street, WC2 (071 240 8312). Covent Garden underground. **Open** 10am-6.30pm Mon-Sat; 1-6pm Sun. **Credit** A, AmEx, DC, JCB, £$TC, V.
Quite the trendiest of the London shops, Jones marks the way ahead with names such as deconstructivists Martin Margiela and Ann Demeulemeester on its racks and old favourites like Jean Paul Gaultier and John Galliano. Don't take it personally if the assistants disappear at your approach. They're just too damn tired after the previous night's rave even to think about serving you. A glance at the price tags might make you feel a bit weary, too.
Alterations to own goods. Export scheme. Delivery.

Joseph
77 Fulham Road, SW10 (071 823 9500). South Kensington underground. **Open** 10am-6.30pm Mon, Tue, Thur; 10am-6pm Sat; 10am-7pm Wed; noon-5pm Sun. **Credit** A, AmEx, DC, £$TC, V.
Joseph's largest outlet, at Brompton Cross, is a calm and cavernous Eva Jiricna-designed space on two floors. Upstairs there's a good mix of Joseph's own label – suits, jackets (about £300), jeans (about £60), leggings and, of course, the famous Joseph Tricot knitwear (£100-£400) – and fabulous designer apparel by the likes of Prada, Yohji and Alaia. Downstairs it's the same, but for the boys. A well-cut Joseph suit will set you back £300, but if you don't find this too shocking, you'll be delighted to know that Joseph also stocks Helmut Lang, Dolce & Gabbana and other bank-breakers.
Alterations. Café. Export scheme for goods over £100.

Katharine Hamnett
20 Sloane Street, SW1 (071 823 1002). Knightsbridge underground. **Open** 10am -6.30pm Mon, Tue, Thur; 10.30am-6pm Sat; 10am-7pm Wed. **Credit** A, AmEx, DC, £TC, V.
After a few faltering steps at the end of the eighties, Katharine Hamnett is rapidly regaining lost ground. The women's denim range is good fun, dead clubby and starts as low as £50, while smart suits go way off the other end at around £600. But it's the men's wear that's her real success, from beautifully cut suits and dazzlingly decorative waistcoats to the most relaxing casual wear you'll find anywhere.
Alterations to own goods. Delivery. Mailing list.

Margaret Howell
24 Brook Street, W1 (071 495 4888). Bond Street underground. **Open** 10am-6pm Mon-Sat. **Credit** A, AmEx, DC, JCB, £$TC, V.
Quintessentially English, Howell creates men's and women's clothes for tall Rangey types with deep pockets. Her crisp, white shirts are the best in town and hover both sides of the £100 mark.
Alterations to own goods. Export scheme. Gift-wrapping. Tea and coffee.

Michiko Koshino
70 Neal Street, WC2 (071 497 0165). Covent Garden underground. **Open** 11am-7pm Mon-Sat. **Credit** A, AmEx, DC, V.
The clothes here could never be criticised for being unadventurous and neither could anything else about the store. If you are undaunted by the shop assistants, the store's design and the thumping music, you'll love the fierce, fast fashion. A good place to pick up club fliers and eye-up fashion victims.
Export scheme. Mail order.

Mulberry
11-12 Gees Court, W1 (071 493 2546). Bond Street underground. **Open** 10am-6pm Mon-Wed; 10am-7pm Thur; 10am-6pm Fri, Sat. **Credit** A, AmEx, DC, £TC, V.
Mulberry's instantly identifiable leather goods – from wash bags to Filofaxes – are much loved. Bags start at £30 for the neatest little shoulder strap number to £500 for the mother of all suitcases. Clothing crosses the board from cruise wear to tailored separates – England's Ralph Lauren.
Alterations to own goods. Export scheme. Luggage repair service. Postal delivery.

Paul Smith
41-44 Floral Street, WC2 (071 379 7133). Covent Garden underground. **Open** 10.30am-6.30pm Mon-Wed, Fri; 10.30am-7pm Thur; 10am-6.30pm Sat. **Credit** A, AmEx, DC, JCB, £TC, V.
Classic men's-wear, enlivened by witty details, ranges from sportswear to formal clothing. Clothes and accessories at No.43 are divided into the flamboyant, such as jazzy silk ties, and the timeless: wool cardigans and linen shirts. At Nos.41-42 there are cashmere blazers and beautifully-cut suits; and sports and casualwear is to be found at No.44. A women's collection is being launched in 1994: our guess is that, like the men's-wear, it will be classic, in great fabrics and fabulous colours, and just a little on the expensive side.
Accessory repairs. Alteration to own goods. Brochure. Export scheme. Postal delivery.

RM Williams
179-181 Regent Street, W1 (071 434 0061). Oxford Circus underground. **Open** 9.30am-6.30pm Mon-Wed, Fri; Sat; 10am-6.30pm Thur. **Credit** A, AmEx, DC.
This is the original Aussie bushmen's outfitters, for that classically masculine Crocodile Dundee look. The clothes and accessories aren't cheap, but the quality is second to none. The trouser belts, boots, rain-jackets, and moleskin trousers are some of the more wearable items; staff also sell bush hats and pack saddles.
Export scheme. Mail order.
Branch:15 Kensington Church, W8 (071 937 4333).

Space NK
41 Earlham Street, WC2 (071 379 7030). Covent Garden underground. **Open** 11am-7pm Mon-Sat; 1-6pm Sun. **Credit** A, AmEx, DC, £$TC, V.
When Space NK opened in 1993 it made all sorts of embarrassing announcements about shaping the new shopping environment of the nineties. Well it does incor-

porate a sort of hippy café, but more importantly it's rounded up some of Britain's young design talents, such as Abe Hamilton, Pascale Smets and Sonnentag Mullen to showcase their very wearable collections. Good karma, at a price.
Alterations. Export scheme. Make-up advice. Postal delivery.

Whistles
12-14 St Christopher's Place, W1 (071 487 4484). Bond Street underground. **Open** 10am-6pm Mon-Wed, Fri, Sat; 10am-7pm Thur. **Credit** A, AmEx, £$TC, V.
Whistles has garnered together a combination of mid-priced and designer women's-wear. The store's own label is what lots of fashion-conscious London women wear to face the daily grind. The labels are fairly safe with names like Ghost, Idem and Marcel Marongiu.
Branches: 1 Thayer Street, W1 (071 935 7013); 14 Beauchamp Place, SW3 (071 581 4830); 20 The Market, WC2 (071 379 7401); 27 Sloane Square, SW1 (071 730 9819); 303 Brompton Road, SW3 (071 823 9134).
Export scheme. Postal delivery.

Vivienne Westwood
6 Davies Street, W1 (071 629 3757). Bond Street underground. **Open** 10.30am-6pm Mon-Wed, Fri, Sat; 10.30am-7pm Thur. **Credit** A, AmEx, DC, JCB, £$TC, V.
Come here to pay homage to the undisputed queen of British fashion, and to be surprised. Vivienne's reputation might be for crazy old English eccentricity, but many of her beautifully tailored clothes are extremely wearable. Others are just works of art. *See also below* **Sale Shops**.
Branches: World's End 430 King's Road, SW3 (071 352 6551).

Medium-Range

American Retro
35 Old Compton Street, W1 (071 734 3477). Piccadilly Circus underground. **Open** 10.15am-7pm Mon-Sat. **Credit** A, AmEx, £TC, V.
Don't be fooled by the name, there's nothing remotely retro here. The Ben Kelly-designed interior dates from autumn 1993, and stock includes Dolce & Gabbana underwear and swimwear, Smedley knitwear and American Retro's own range of bags – pared down designs that are a real bargain at £20-£50. This is where style and quality come together without making unreasonable demands on your wallet.
Export scheme. Postal delivery.
Branch: 14 Pembridge Road, W11 (071 243 2393).

Boxfresh
2 Short's Gardens, WC2 (071 240 4742). Covent Garden underground. **Open** 11am-6.30pm Mon-Wed, Fri, Sat; 11am-7pm Thur. **Credit** A, AmEx, JCB, £TC, V.
Hip and helpfully priced jeans, jackets and T-shirts from the Boxfresh label and other current favourites like Carhartt. An essential stop-off for funky boys and girls.
Mail order catalogue. Postal delivery.

French Connection
Men's Shop, 56 Long Acre, WC2 (071 379 6560). Covent Garden underground. **Open** 10.30am-6.30pm Mon-Wed, Fri, Sat; 10.30am-8pm Thur; noon-6pm Sun. **Credit** A, AmEx, £TC, V.
French Connection is a fast mover, whipping looks both off the designer catwalks and the street and into its shops in record time. It's a big chain, but that doesn't stop it combining quality and inspired ideas and managing to get many of the goods on to the racks for £50, or less, a piece. The men's-wear, especially, can look deceptively expensive.
Alterations. Export scheme. Postal delivery.

Branch: French Connection Women's Shop 11 James Street, WC2 (071 836 0522).

Jigsaw
31 Brompton Road, SW3 (071 584 6226). Knightsbridge underground. **Open** 10am-7pm Mon, Tue, Thur-Sat; 10am-8pm Wed. **Credit** A, AmEx, £TC, V.
Practical clothes for sensible women. Jigsaw is where you go for basic linen trousers, a plain T-shirt or a cost-effective work jacket, not for a fashion *frisson*. The Knightsbridge store's exuberant interior, designed by Nigel Coates, with its curving vertebral staircase and flamboyant décor, rather steals the thunder. Some branches, including the one at Covent Garden, now stock equally sensible men's-wear.
Alterations. Export scheme. Postal delivery.
Branches: St Christopher's Place, W1 (071 495 9169); Kensington High Street, W8 (071 937 3573); Covent Garden, WC2 (071 340 3855).

Soldier Blue
184A King's Road, SW3 (071 352 7556). Sloane Square underground/11, 19, 22 bus. **Open** 9am-6pm Mon-Sat; 10am-4pm Bank Holidays. **Credit** A, AmEx, £TC, V.
If the label says Levi's, Soldier Blue stocks it. Jeans start at £38 and are guaranteed good quality. You'll find all the right tags and an easy atmosphere. Wranglers, Lee and Pepe jeans are also available.
Export scheme.

Sonico
47 Oxford Street, W1 (071 734 7958). Tottenham Court Road underground. **Open** 10am-6.30pm Mon-Wed, Fri, Sat; 10am-8pm Thur. **Credit** A, AmEx, DC, £TC, V.
Several stores in this part of Oxford Street sell expensive Levi's seconds – and don't even have the grace to tell you they're imperfect. The busy but well-informed staff at Sonico, in sharp contrast, sell the best Levi's at very competitive prices – certainly a lot cheaper than an 'official' Levi's store. Sonico has outlets throughout London, selling Levi's, Lee, Wrangler and other name-brand jeans at pretty good prices.
Branches: 47 Oxford Street, W1 (071 734 7958); 65 Kings Road, SW3 (071 730 6575); 106 Camden High Street, NW1 (071 267 5268); 404 Mare Street, E8 (081 985 7388).

Cheap

Miss Selfridge
Duke Street, W1 (071 629 1234). Bond Street underground. **Open** 9.30am-7pm Mon-Wed, Fri, Sat; 9.30am-8pm Thur. **Credit** A, AmEx, £TC, V.
A teenage paradise with no age limit. Miss Selfridge adapts all the very latest fashions as quickly and cheaply as possible – faster than anyone else, in fact – slings them into the shops, and then reduces them in a matter of months to clear the decks for the next trend. Crap quality, but absolutely brilliant fun.
Brochure. Export scheme. Postal delivery.
Branches: 75 Brompton Road, SW3 (071 584 7814); 221 Oxford Street, W1 (071 434 0405); 42 Kensington High Street, SW1 (071 938 4182).

River Island
283 Oxford Street, W1 (071 493 7359). Oxford Circus underground. **Open** 10am-6.30pm Mon-Wed, Fri, Sat; 10am-8pm Thur. **Credit** A, AmEx, DC, £$TC, V.
A pretty predictable selection, but at incredibly low prices and in some quite good colours. Skip the polyester lines, hunt out basics like T-shirts, and save yourself some pennies.
Export scheme.

Top Shop/Top Man

214 Oxford Circus (071 636 7700). Oxford Circus underground. **Open** 10am-6.30pm Mon-Wed, Fri-Sat; 10am-8pm Sun. **Credit** A, AmEx, DC, JCB, V.

More like a fairground than a clothing store, this vast flagship branch of Top Shop pulsates with chart music and heaves with young fashion. Smashing sunglasses for a fiver! Crop tops for £4! 'Ethnic' trousers for under £20! The quality's not brilliant, but it smells like teen spirit to us; a nirvana for the fashion-conscious on a low budget.

Designer Discount

70

70 Lamb's Conduit Street, WC1 (071 430 1533). Holborn or Russell Square underground. **Open** 10am-6pm Mon-Fri; 10am-5pm Sat. **Credit** A, AmEx, £TC, V.

It's hard to tell what you'll turn up here, and since these are the most publicity-shy retailers in London, they're not about to tell us. But in the past we've found incredible reductions on Smedley knitwear and Junior Gaultier. It's mostly men's-wear, but women are beginning to get more of a look in. Ask no questions....

Designers Sale Studio

241 King's Road, SW3 (071 351 4171). Sloane Square underground/11, 19, 22 bus. **Open** 10am-7pm Mon-Fri; 10am-6pm Sat; noon-6pm Sun. **Credit** A, AmEx, DC, £STC, V.

End-of-lines and cancelled orders bearing some glittering Italian names are up for grabs at the Designers Sale Studio. If you're lucky, you might bag something by Genny, Complice, Armani and Versace at up to 60% off, and it could even be this season's.
Delivery. Export scheme.

Paul Smith

23 Avery Row, W1 (071 493 1287). Bond Street underground. **Open** 10am-6pm Mon-Fri; 10am-5pm Sat. **Credit** A, AmEx, DC, £STC, V.

The end of the line for all those classic men's clothes, with the possibility of monster reductions.
Export scheme.

Vivienne Westwood

40-41 Conduit Street, W1 (071 439 1109). Oxford Circus underground. **Open** 10.30am-6pm Mon-Wed, Fri, Sat; 10.30am-7pm Thur. **Credit** A, AmEx, DC, JCB, £STC, V.

Fab gear at **The Cavern.** *See* **review.**

Queen Viv at knockdown prices. Items from the current collection that have been used in shoots or paraded down the catwalk will be down 30% (and let's face it, where else are you going to get this close to Naomi or Linda?) You can snap up last season's look for as much as 75% off. *See also* **Designer Fashion** *above.*
Export scheme.

Indoor Clothes Markets

Hyper-Hyper

26-40 Kensington High Street, W8 (071 938 4343). High Street Kensington underground. **Open** 10am-6pm Mon-Wed, Fri, Sat; 10am-7pm Thur. **Credit** stalls vary.

Over 70 young British designers are given first exposure in Hyper-Hyper. Indoor stalls sell original clothes, shoes, hats, jewellery, belts and other accessories. For the fastest injection of club fashion in town, head for Sign of the Times – there's no knowing what it'll be stocking by the time you read this, but it'll be groovy as hell. Rina da Prato, at unit A6, sells knitwear to die for: unfortunately perfection doesn't come cheap.
Café.

Kensington Market

49-53 Kensington High Street, W8 (071 938 4343). High Street Kensington underground. **Open** 10am-5.30pm Mon-Wed, Fri, Sat; 10am-6pm Thur. **Credit** stalls vary.

Cheap denim, second-hand clothes and leather are things to look out for in Kensington Market's many stalls. Americano stocks second-hand seventies clothing, Rock-a-cha has fifties-style and The Salvage Company has second-hand stuff. The mood of the Wild West features at Western Styling, and Johnsons sells cowboy boots and stetsons.
Café.

Leather

There are hundreds of stores selling inexpensive leather jackets in London, but the best place for a bargain are the shops of Brick Lane, where many of them are made. You can pick up a decent-quality leather biker jacket for as little as £60. *See chapter* **London by Area: East End & Docklands.**

Natural Leather

33 Monmouth Street, WC2 (071 240 7748). Covent Garden underground. **Open** 11am-7pm Mon-Sat. **Credit** A, £STC, V.

This well-established shop stocks all styles of leather jackets, jeans and bags in good-quality hide. Jackets range from £100 to £300. Even better, the woman who makes them is there to help you, so alterations or having goods made to order is no problem.
Alterations, cleaning and repair service. Clothes made to order. Export scheme. Mail order.

Second-Hand

See also below **Markets.**

The Cavern

154 Commercial Street, E2 (071 247 1889). Liverpool Street or Aldgate East underground. **Open** 10am-6pm Tue-Thur; 10am-7pm Fri; noon-6pm Sat; noon-3pm Sun. **No credit cards.**

Welcome to the fab gear centre of the world. Deidre Crowley and Bill del Monte have been stockpiling unworn originals – the hits and a few of the misses from

the last few decades – and drag them out for your delight when their time comes round again. This was the one and only place to come for last year's seventies revival, but with a warehouse packed full of perfect goods they'll always have something that's just right for the moment. A lot of it won't even cause a cash-flow problem.
Alterations. Catalogue. Mail order.

Flip
125 Long Acre, WC2 (071 836 4688). Covent Garden underground. **Open** 10am-7pm Mon-Wed, Fri, Sat; 10am-8pm Thur; noon-6pm Sun. **Credit** A, AmEx, DC, £TC, V.
Definitely not the most glamorous of shopping environments, but you can sometimes find a bargain. Flip's always heaving with worn checked shirts and a huge variety of used Levi's from £5-£38. If you've got time, patience and an overdraft, it should be on your list.
Export scheme.

Glorious Clothing Company
60 Upper Street, N1 (071 704 6312). Angel underground. **Open** 11am-6.30pm Mon-Sat. **Credit** A, £TC, V.
A firm favourite with fashion stylists and victims alike, Glorious offers up the best of the not-so-old. We're talking sixties and seventies here; knee-length boots seem to be a speciality.

Merchant of Europe
Portobello Road, W11 (071 221 4203). Notting Hill Gate underground. **Open** 10.30am-6pm Mon-Fri; 10.30am-6.30pm Sat. **Credit** £TC.
Second-hand clothing is hunted down throughout Europe, re-conditioned and then sold on at this knowingly trendy outlet in Portobello. They turn up some brilliant pieces and some real oddities. You pay the price.

Women's Fashion: Large Sizes

Don't despair. Once upon a time large and small sizes meant a trip to a dowdy specialist shop, or mail-order catalogue selling horrible gear. Now, the big chains are wooing the little and large of discerning women. As the stock changes quickly, we only give rudimentary listings here – phone for more details. Men's large and small sizes in fashionable styles are generally much easier to find.

1647
69 Gloucester Avenue, NW1 (071 722 1647). Camden Town or Chalk Farm underground/Primrose Hill BR. **Open** 10am-6pm Mon-Sat. **Credit** A, AmEx, £TC, V.

Base
55 Monmouth Street, WC2 (071 240 8914). Covent Garden underground. **Open** 10am-6pm Mon-Sat. **Credit** A, AmEx, DC, £TC, V.

Evans
538-540 Oxford Street, W1 (071 499 5372). Marble Arch underground. **Open** 9.30am-7pm Mon-Wed, Fri; 10am-8pm Thur; 9am-6pm Sat. **Credit** A, AmEx, DC, £TC, V.

Women's Fashion: Small Sizes

Debenhams
334-338 Oxford Street, W1 (071 580 3000). Bond Street underground. **Open** 9.30am-7pm Mon, Tue; 10am-8pm Wed; 9.30am-8pm Thur, Fri; 9.30am-7pm Sat. **Credit** A, AmEx, DC, SC, £$TC, V.

Miss Selfridge
40 Duke Street, W1 (071 629 1234). Bond Street underground. **Open** 9.30am-7pm Mon-Wed, Fri, Sat; 9.30am-8pm Thur. **Credit** A, AmEx, DC, JCB, £$TC, V.

Next Petite
160 Regent Street, W1 (071 434 2515). Oxford Circus or Piccadilly Circus underground. **Open** 10am-6.30pm Mon-Wed; 10am-8pm Thur; 10am-7pm Fri, Sat. **Credit** A, AmEx, DC, £$TC, V.

Principles
419 Oxford Street, W1 (071 629 9152). **Open** 10am-7pm Mon-Wed, Fri, Sat; 10am-8pm Thur. **Credit** A, AmEx, DC, £TC, V.
Branches are too numerous to list here. For details of your nearest stockist, phone (071 927 1443).

Wallis Petite
272-274 Oxford Street, W1 (071 499 1900). Oxford Circus underground. **Open** 10am-6.30pm Mon, Tue; 10am-7pm Wed, Fri; 10am-8pm Thur. **Credit** A, AmEx, £TC, V.

Fashion Accessories

Belts

Gohil's
246 Camden High Street, NW1 (071 485 9195). Camden Town underground. **Open** 11am-6pm Tue-Sun. **Credit** A, AmEx, DC, £TC, V.
You won't find anything out of the ordinary here, just plain black and brown leather belts – the sort that you're always looking for but can never find. Since they're all made on the premises they're cheap and can be created on the spot to your specification. Basic brass buckles start at £1.60, decorative ones at £6.50, and a chunky Harley Davidson motif will set you back about £10; belts cost about £10-£15. The staff must be the nicest in London.
Repairs.

Hats

Fred Bare
118 Columbia Road, E2 (071 729 6962). Old Street underground/BR/6, 35, 55 bus. **Open** 9am-2pm Sun. **Credit** A, AmEx, £TC, V
London hatters Fred Bare produce delightful casual headwear in velvet, straw, suede, embroidered felt and knits at a £20-£100 tariff. It's open on Sundays, so you can combine your visit with a wander round the gorgeous flower market (*see below* **Markets**).
Delivery.

The Hat Shop
58 Neal Street, WC2 (071 836 6718). Covent Garden underground. **Open** 10am-6pm Mon, Tue; 10am-7pm Wed-Fri; 10.30am-6pm Sat. **Credit** A, AmEx, £TC, V.
Probably the only shop in London that you have to queue to get in to. Once inside the poky room you'll find a vast selection of both casual and formal millinery, and an army of assistants who like to whip things away before you've finished trying them on.
Export scheme.

Jewellery

If you're carat counting, head for Hatton Garden, EC1, the traditional area for diamond trading. Otherwise, try these stores, which con-

*Designer chic gets in the frame at **Arthur Morris**. See **review**.*

tain some of the most imaginative designs for contemporary jewellery in the city.

Aalto
8 Ganton Street, W1 (071 439 8320). Oxford Circus underground. **Open** 10am-6pm Mon-Fri; 10am-2pm Sat. **Credit** A, AmEx, £TC, V.
Contemporary and post-war Scandinavian pieces happily sit side by side in this small Soho retailer's. Current work is provided by European designers including Mark Newell and Kirsten Nolte. It's interesting how many of the older Swedish and Danish designs look more modern, and can still generate more excitement.
Export scheme.

Contemporary Applied Arts
43 Earlham Street, WC2 (071 836 6993). Covent Garden underground. **Open** 10am-6pm Mon-Wed, Fri, Sat; 10am-7pm Thur. **Credit** A, AmEx, £TC, V.
Among the ceramics and other decorative pieces you'll find top contemporary jewellers including Gerda Flöckinger, Wendy Ramshaw's famous ring sets and the perfect restraint of Elisabeth Holder.
Export scheme. Overseas delivery.

Jess James
3 Newburgh Street, W1 (071 437 0199). Oxford Circus underground. **Open** 11am-6.30pm Mon-Wed, Fri; 11am-7pm Thur; 11am-6pm Sat. **Credit** A, AmEx, DC, £$TC, JCB, V.
Lots of contemporary British jewellers' work shown to advantage in careful displays under good lighting. Names like Sian Evans, Jacqueline Rabun, Dinny Hall and Wright & Teague cover a pretty wide price range.
Mailing list.

Optical

Here we concentrate on fashionable eyewear. For a top-notch optician dealing with eye care problems, *see chapter* **Services: Contact Lens Specialist.**

Arthur Morris
13 Beauchamp Place, SW3 (071 584 4661). Knightsbridge underground. **Open** 9.30am-6pm Mon-Sat. **Credit** A, AmEx, DC, JCB, £TC, V.
A little gem of a shop, beautifully designed and offering a wide range of designer frames, from classics by Armani and Oliver Peoples to the avant-garde creations of Proksch's. There's also a counter-full of old frames – including fabulous fifties up-sweeps and real tortoiseshell – which can cost anything from £20 to £300. Arthur Morris, a fully qualified optician, will be on hand to help you make the difficult decision.
Catalogue. Contact lenses fitting service. Export scheme. Prescription sunglasses. Repair. Tinted lenses.

Cutler & Gross
16 Knightsbridge Green, SW1 (071 581 2250). Knightsbridge underground. **Open** 9.30am-6pm Mon-Sat. **Credit** A, AmEx, DC, £$TC, V.
This is where you'll find the sunglasses that grace the pages of every British fashion magazine. Cutler & Gross is quick to pick up on what's happening, producing a large collection of new frames every year. Prices range from £60 to £100; styles from wacky plastics to wearable classics.
Catalogue. Customised frames. Export scheme. Fully qualified dispensing optician available. Mail order. Prescription sunglasses. Repairs.

Shoes

Emma Hope
33 Amwell Street, EC1 (071 833 2367). Angel underground or King's Cross underground/BR. **Open** 10am-6pm Mon-Wed, Fri, Sat; 10am-7pm Thur. **Credit** A, £TC, V.
If you're getting married in white or going to a ball, or you just hanker for the world's most feminine footwear, Emma Hope's for you. Choose from luxurious materials, embroidery, luscious colours, and 15 styles of bridal shoes. Prices start at £130.
Catalogue. Export scheme. Specialist wedding service.

Patrick Cox

8 Symons Street, SW3 (071 730 6504). Sloane Square underground. **Open** 10am-6pm Mon-Sat. **Credit** A, AmEx, DC, JCB, £TC, V.

Patrick Cox produces exquisitely crafted high fashion footwear for men and women and sells it from small premises which nestle behind Peter Jones in Sloane Square. The interior is full of old-fashioned charm (the shop manager sits behind an antique desk); the shoes are the last word in style. Expensive, but simply the best. *Export scheme. Mail order. Repairs.*

Plum Line

55 Neal Street, WC2 (071 379 7856). Covent Garden underground. **Open** 10am-6pm Mon, Tue; 10am-7pm Wed-Fri; 10am-6.30pm Sat; noon-5.30pm Sun. **Credit** A, AmEx, £STC, V.

The flagship shop for Freelance shoes in Britain also carries Luc Berjen and Armando Pollini. This is a place for people who feel pretty brave about what they wear on their feet and don't mind dipping deeply into their pockets. It's a shame that the assistants are so much less exuberant than the merchandise. Don't miss the wonderful leather floor at the back of the shop. *Export scheme. Mail order.*

Red or Dead

33 Neal Street, WC2 (071 379 7571). Covent Garden underground. **Open** 10.30am-7.30pm Mon-Fri; 10am-7pm Sat; 12.30-7pm Sun. **Credit** A, AmEx, DC, £TC, V.

London's greatest success story, Red or Dead started as a stall on Camden Market and now puts on a catwalk show in London Fashion Week. Despite the fashion fame, the basic shoes are still the thing – clumpy styles, many for about £60. *Export scheme. Mail order.*

Branches: 36 High Street Kensington, W8 (071 937 3137); 186 Camden High Street, NW1 (071 482 4423).

Shelley's

159 Oxford Street, W1 (071 437 5842). Oxford Circus underground. **Open** 9.30am-6.30pm Mon-Fri; 9.30am-8pm Sat. **Credit** A, AmEx, DC, £TC, V.

Selling everything from baseball boots and Doc Marten's to the extremes of platforms and stilettoes, Shelley's also collaborates with top-name designers to create new styles. Okay, so style comes before quality here, but you'll be paying rock-bottom prices and you probably won't want the whimsical choices to last more than a season anyway. *Catalogue.*

Branches: 266 Regent Street, W1 (071 287 0939); 19 Foubert Place, W1 (071 287 0593); 44 Carnaby Street, W1 (071 437 6757).

Antiques & Collectables

Good areas of London to browse for antiques are **Camden Passage**, N1, **Church Street**, NW8 (especially at Alfie's Antiques Market, Nos.13-25; 071 723 6066), **King's Road**, SW6 (west from the junction with Sydney Street), **Kensington Church Street**, W8, **Portobello Road**, W11, and the area around **Bond Street**, W1 (especially Gray's Antiques Market, 58 Davies Street, W1; 071 629 7034). Here we've highlighted a handful of interesting shops. *See also below* **Markets**.

Gallery of Antique Costume & Textiles

2 Church Street, NW8 (071 723 9981). Edgware Road

underground or Marylebone underground/BR. **Open** 10am-5.30pm Mon-Sat. **Credit** A, AmEx, £TC, V.

The Gallery specialises in antique clothing and textiles. The reasonably-priced stock is spread over two floors and comes from all over the world.

Grosvenor Prints

28-32 Shelton Street, WC2 (071 836 1979). Covent Garden underground. **Open** 10am-6pm Mon-Fri; 11am-4pm Sat. **Credit** A, AmEx, V.

Grosvenor contains a huge selection of antique prints and engravings – London's largest, claims the staff. Prices start at £10 and keep rising.

London Silver Vaults

Chancery House, 53-64 Chancery Lane, WC2 (071 242 3844). Chancery Lane underground. **Open** 9am-5.30pm Mon-Fri; 9am-1pm Sat. **Credit** vaults vary; check with individual dealers.

These top-security vaults were built in 1883 and are 42ft (12.6m) underground. The casual visitor might receive a less-than-friendly reception from the dealers, but if you know what you want, it's worth persevering. As well as antique and modern silver, traders sell gold and silver jewellery, and even ceramics.

Audio & Hi-Fi

Tottenham Court Road is the customary hunting ground for cheap bits of hi-fi, but don't expect great service or even a demonstration before you're cajoled into buying. If you want to be treated as if you've got ears as well as a wallet, try **Grahams**.

Grahams Hi-Fi

Canonbury Yard, 190A New North Road, N1 (071 226 5500). Old Street underground/BR or Essex Road BR/271 bus. **Open** 10am-6pm Tue-Thur; 9am-6pm Fri, Sat. **Credit** A, AmEx, £TC, V.

Quite simply the best place to buy quality hi-fi equipment in London (ie £500 plus for a system). The prices are the same as anywhere else, but the quality of service is superior, and great attention is paid to seeing you get something tailored to your needs, not those of a theoretical audiophile. Our only criticisms concern the bias

Fancy footwear at **Patrick Cox**. *See* **review**.

towards vinyl-based (as opposed to CD-based) systems, and towards expensive British-made 'name' equipment (Linn, Rega, Naim etc). Grahams also stocks a range of general interest records and CDs.
Delivery and installation (free for systems). Demonstration facilities. Export scheme. Record-cleaning service. Repair and testing service. Wheelchair access.

Hi-Fi Care
245 Tottenham Court Road, W1 (071 637 8911). Goodge Street or Tottenham Court Road underground. **Open** 9am-6pm Mon-Sat. **Credit** A, AmEx, DC, £TC, V.
Hi-Fi Care sells a lot of video accessories these days, but also has an impressive range of hi-fi bits and bobs. Cartridges from Audio Technica, Ortofon, Shure and many others can be picked up, as can CD cleaning kits, speaker and equipment stands (including the entire Target range), microphones, jacks, and an army of cables. The staff know their stuff, and can find products easily despite the seeming disarray.
Export scheme. Mail order.

Books

Departmental Bookshops

Books Etc
120 Charing Cross Road, WC2 (071 379 6838). Tottenham Court Road underground. **Open** 9.30am-8pm Mon-Sat; noon-6pm Sun. **Credit** A, AmEx, BT, DC, £TC, V.
With a permanent bargain basement and modern, clear layout, Books Etc claims to attract the foot-weary refugee from Foyles, as well as a somewhat younger crowd. The selection is strong on fiction, cookery, gardening and sport. A friendly atmosphere prevails.
Mail order. Postal delivery (free in London area).
Branches are too numerous to list here. Check the telephone directory for your nearest.

Dillons The Bookstore
82 Gower Street, WC1 (071 636 1577). Goodge Street underground. **Open** 9am-7pm Mon, Wed-Fri; 9.30am-7pm Tue; 9.30am-6pm Sat. **Credit** A, AmEx, BT, £TC, V.
Dillons is considered by many to be the best bookshop in town. It has approximately 250,000 books in stock, so it's safe to assume that if the book's in print and well-thought-of, it will be here. Displays are clearly labelled and each department has an enquiry desk. Dillons rarely feels crowded, and the staff are helpful, well-informed and efficient. There's a bias towards academic books.
Catalogues of new titles for medical, nursing, business, education and ELT subjects. Mail order. Wheelchair access; lifts and toilets for the disabled.
Branches are too numerous to list here. Check the telephone directory for your nearest.

Foyles
119 Charing Cross Road, WC2 (071 437 5660). Leicester Square or Tottenham Court Road underground. **Open** 9am-6pm Mon-Wed, Fri, Sat; 9am-7pm Thur. **Credit** A, AmEx, £$TC, V.
Everyone has heard of Foyles, either because of its vast selection of titles or the illogical and frustrating layout. It takes two long waits to buy a book; you need to queue for the purchase slip and then join another line to pay for it. There are compensations however. The range of books is extensive and you're sure to stumble across innumerable weird and wonderful publications that better-run shops will have returned to the publishers months ago. If you like a rummage, it's worth a visit.
Export scheme for records and tapes. Magazine (monthly). Mail order. Postal delivery.

Waterstones
121-131 Charing Cross Road, WC2 (071 434 4291). Tottenham Court Road underground. **Open** 9.30am-8pm Mon-Sat; noon-7pm Sun. **Credit** A, AmEx, BT, £TC, V.
This shop is a good example of a dozen branches throughout London that usually stock a well-chosen selection of books. It has recently expanded to include an enormous fiction section.
Book-finding service. Mail order from Milsom Street, Bath, BA1 1DA. Seasonal catalogue of new titles.
Branches: are too numerous to list here. Check the telephone directory for your nearest.

One-offs

Compendium
234 Camden High Street, NW1 (071 485 8944/071 267 1525/fax 071 267 0193). Camden Town or Chalk Farm underground. **Open** 10am-6pm Mon-Sat; noon-6pm Sun. **Credit** A, BT, £TC, V.
The depth and range of left-leaning and New Age books – particularly of imported titles – at Compendium puts many, much larger, bookshops to shame. The ground floor holds fiction, poetry, journals, comics, and books on film, pop music, semiotics, women's issues, psychology, alternative healing and the like. In the basement are the libertarian and alternative departments, with Third World development, environmentalism and green politics particularly well represented. The assistants know and care about the stock, and there are regular talks and signings. Many people's favourite London bookshop.
Book lists. Booksearch. Mail order including overseas. Wheelchair access to ground floor only.

Dillon's Arts Bookshop
8 Long Acre, WC2 (071 836 1359). Covent Garden or Leicester Square underground. **Open** 9.30am-10pm Mon-Sat; noon-7pm Sun. **Credit** A, AmEx, £TC, V.
This arts bookshop is well laid out, with plenty of space for browsers. Downstairs boasts good poetry and performing arts sections, while upstairs tends to be devoted to visual arts. There's also a fine selection of postcards plus beautiful wrapping paper.
Mail order. Overseas delivery. Wheelchair access to ground floor.

Edward Stanford
12-14 Long Acre, WC2 (071 836 1321). Covent Garden or Leicester Square underground. **Open** 10am-6pm Mon, Sat; 9am-7pm Tue-Fri. **Credit** A, £TC, V.
Street maps of Cairo, wine maps of France, topographical maps of rural India, ocean bottoms, the moon, and just about anywhere else you might or might not want to go are kept at this travel bookshop; if Stanford's doesn't stock it, chances are no-one does. The books section is also impressive.
Delivery overseas. Mail order. Wheelchair access to ground floor.

Murder One
71-73 Charing Cross Road, WC2 (071 734 3485). Leicester Square or Tottenham Court Road underground. **Open** 10am-7pm Mon-Wed; 10am-8pm Thur-Sat. **Credit** A, AmEx, £TC, V.
All manner of detective stories, true crime volumes, American imports and second-hand crime books can be found in this brightly-lit shop. Note that book tokens are not accepted.
Mail order.

Sportspages
Caxton Walk, 94-96 Charing Cross Road, WC2 (071 240 9604/fax 071 836 0104). Leicester Square or

There's a world to discover at **Edward Stanford**'s. See **review** page 166.

Tottenham Court Road underground. **Open** 9.30am-7pm Mon-Sat. **Credit** A, AmEx, DC, £TC, V.
Easily the best shop for sports books and publications, Sportspages has the largest selection of football fanzines in Britain, including *The Absolute Game*, from north of the border, and the best-selling *When Saturday Comes*. The most popular sports have the depth of coverage you might expect, but the great strength of the shop is the books and periodicals on minority sports such as ice-hockey or underwater soot-juggling. Some sports can be found on video.
Delivery overseas. Mail order (specialist sports' lists available). Wheelchair access.

Second-Hand/Antiquarian

In addition to the shops listed below, Cecil Court (*see chapter* **London by Area: Central London**) is renowned for its high concentration of quality second-hand bookshops. The roads around Great Russell Street, WC1, near the British Museum, are also worth exploring.

Bertram Rota
9-11 Langley Court, WC2 (071 836 0723). Covent Garden underground. **Open** 9.30am-5.30pm Mon-Fri. **Credit** A, V.
Modern first editions are the business of this shop hidden down an alleyway off Long Acre. Prices are on the high side and the atmosphere doesn't encourage lingering. *Mail order.*

Henry Pordes Books
58-60 Charing Cross Road, WC2 (071 836 9031). Leicester Square underground. **Open** 10am-7pm Mon-Sat. **Credit** A, V.
A major second-hand bookshop in the heart of London's book quarter, Pordes is distinguished by its musty smell

and its basement crammed with old fiction. Prices start at 50p. There's 10% discount for students.

Maggs Brothers
50 Berkeley Square, W1 (071 493 7160). Green Park underground. **Open** 9.30am-5pm Mon-Fri. **Credit** A, £TC, V.
Now run by the fourth and fifth generations of the Magg's family, this is London's best antiquarian book-shop. Staff are experts in their field; it is best to first make an appointment with one of them. You will then be shown into one of several studies lined with rare and beautiful first editions. Prices might soar to thousands of pounds for a unique, seventeenth-century volume.

Skoob
15 Sicilian Avenue, Southampton Row, WC1 (071 404 3063). Holborn underground. **Open** 10.30am-6.30pm Mon-Sat. **Credit** A, AmEx, V.
One of the best second-hand bookshops in London. Although books are a little more expensive than else-where, they are invariably in good condition. There's a student discount of 10%.

Food & Drink
Food Halls

Fortnum & Mason
181 Piccadilly, W1 (071 734 8040). Green Park or Piccadilly Circus underground. **Open** 9.30am-6pm Mon-Sat. **Credit** A, AmEx, CB, DC, JCB, £STC, V.
This theme park capitalises on its olde worlde image – the food hall staff even wear fancy dress (well, tail coats). Fortnum & Mason is renowned for its stock of exotic and dubious culinary wonders. In 1886 it ordered Mr Heinz's entire stock of new-fangled canned food. Today, Fortnum's no longer sells chocolate-covered ants, but any true (and

rich) connoisseur will advise you to buy your provisions from Harrods, and your indulgences from Fortnum's. *Christmas catalogue. Delivery. Export scheme. Restaurants.*

Harrods
Knightsbridge, SW1 (071 730 1234). Knightsbridge underground. **Open** 10am-6pm Mon, Tue; 10am-7pm Wed-Fri; 9am-6pm Sat. **Credit** A, A/c, AmEx, DC, SC, £$TC, V, most foreign currencies.
Easily the best in London, and one of the best in the world. The spectacular food halls at Harrods offer a comprehensive range of delicacies. The halls are divided into Grocery, Fruit, Flowers, Meat, Poultry, Bakery, Confectionery and Wines & Spirits. If you can't find that special ingredient somewhere among all this, the staff might be able to order it for you (at a price). It's worth visiting just to admire the fresh fish sculpture.

Harvey Nichols
109-125 Knightsbridge, SW1 (071 235 5000). Knightsbridge underground. **Open** 10am-7pm Mon-Fri; 10am-6pm Sat. **Credit** A, AmEx, DC, SC, £$TC, V.
This recently refurbished food hall sells some desirable victuals (black pasta, truffle oil, balsamic vinegar and the like) in very classy packaging. There are more dried goods than fresh, and some incongruous everyday brand-name groceries (such as Kellogg's corn flakes) among the fancier stuff. It's good, and much improved, but still lags way behind Harrods or even Fortnum's. *Cafés. Car park. Delivery. Export scheme. Mail order. Restaurant.*

Bagels

Brick Lane Beigel Bake
159 Brick Lane, E1 (071 729 0616). Aldgate East or Shoreditch underground. **Open** 24 hours daily. **No credit cards.**
Immensely popular, day and night, this is the most notable of the bagel shops in the area. Always fresh and

very cheap, the range of filled bagels includes the classic: smoked salmon and cream cheese. Combine it with a visit to **Brick Lane Market** (*see* **Box: Markets**).

Cheese

Neal's Yard Dairy
17 Shorts Gardens, WC2 (071 379 7646). Covent Garden underground. **Open** 9am-7pm Mon-Sat; 11am-5pm Sun. **Credit** A, £TC, V.
Randolph Hodgson buys immature cheeses from farms in Britain and Ireland, then brings them to peak condition in his shop's store rooms. He lists over 70 cheeses, 40 to 50 of which are in stock at any time. *Mail order. Price list.*

Paxton & Whitfield
93 Jermyn Street, SW1 (071 930 0259). Green Park or Piccadilly underground. **Open** 9am-6pm Mon-Fri; 9am-4pm Sat. **Credit** A, AmEx, DC, £TC, V.
Paxton & Whitfield is one of the best cheese merchants in London with over 250 types of British and Continental cheese. The sense of genteel tradition is a peculiarly British joy, and the staff provide unfailingly proper service. *Mail order. Price list.*

Chocolates

Bendicks
7 Aldwych, WC2 (071 836 1846). Covent Garden underground. **Open** 9.30am-7.30pm Mon-Sat. **Credit** A, V.
Bendicks's fancy dark handmade chocolates make great gifts; the after-dinner mints are certainly one-up on After Eights.
Branches: 20 Royal Exchange, EC2 (071 283 5843); 31 Fleet Street, EC4 (071 583 4702); 9 Curzon Street, W1 (071 629 4389).

Charbonnel et Walker
1 Royal Arcade, 28 Old Bond Street, W1 (071 491 0939). Green Park or Piccadilly Circus underground.

Sexy supplies of fashion food at **Carluccio's***. See* **review** *page 170.*

Open 9am-5.30pm Mon-Wed, Fri; 9am-6pm Thur; 10am-4pm Sat. **Credit** A, AmEx, DC, £TC, V.
Despite the Franglais name, this English chocolate maker has been fattening the London nobility since 1875. Presentation is the strongest point; boxes of chocs are satinned and silked, ruched and ruffled to such an extent that even Barbara Cartland might have a saccharine overload.
Catalogue. Delivery service. Gift-wrapping. Mail order. Personalised packaging.

Delicatessens

Fratelli Camisa (1A Berwick Street, W1; 071 437 7120) and nearby, **Lina Stores** (18 Brewer Street, W1; 071 437 6482) are two of the best, old-style Italian delicatessens in London. *See also chapter* **London by Area: West End.**

Carluccio's
28 Neal Street, WC2 (071 240 1487). Covent Garden underground. **Open** 11am-7pm Mon-Thur; 10am-7pm Fri; 10am-6pm Sat. **Credit** A, AmEx, £TC, V.
A far cry from the traditional Italian deli, this shop stocks only the most desirable, sexy, and expensive of Italian foodstuffs, smartly packaged. It's the stuff that gifts are made of; truffle oil, brilliant focaccia, black pasta, balsamic vinegars, crisp crostini; if it's fashionable, Carluccio's will have it. Mmmm.
Bespoke catering. Delivery service. Gift packaging and customisation.

Health Foods

Neal's Yard Wholefood Warehouse
off Short's Gardens, WC2 (071 836 5151). Covent Garden underground. **Open** 9am-7pm Mon-Wed, Fri; 9am-7.30pm Thur; 9am-6.30pm Sat; 10am-5.30pm Sun. **Credit** A, £TC, V.
A wide selection of wholefoods are on sale in this clean and well laid out shop. It isn't cheap, but the quality and selection of goods is of a high standard.

Tea & Coffee

Algerian Coffee Stores
52 Old Compton Street, W1 (071 437 2480). Leicester Square or Piccadilly Circus underground. **Open** 9am-7pm Mon-Sat. **Credit** A, A/c, AmEx, DC, JCB, £TC, V.
Despite its name, the teas at this Soho store now outnumber the coffees. With mouth-watering names like Japanese Cherry and Mocha Parfait, these beverages will make a change from your usual cuppa.
Delivery (free within W1). Mail order. Price list.

H R Higgins
79 Duke Street, W1 (071 629 3913/071 491 8819). Bond Street underground. **Open** 8.45am-5.30pm Mon-Wed; 8.45am-6pm Thur, Fri; 10am-5pm Sat. **Credit** A, £TC, V.
Higgins has more than 30 original and blended coffees, a fine selection of teas and knowledgeable service: it's easy to see why the Queen gets her supplies here. Wood panelling and the aroma of roast coffee (the Chagga is particularly good) combine to give the shop the ambience of a gentleman's club.
Coffee and tea lists. Mail order from 10 Lea Road Industrial Park, Waltham Abbey, EN9 (0992 768254). Newsletter.

Wine, Beer & Spirits

See also **Fuller Smith & Turner Brewery** *listed in chapter* **London by Area: West.**

The Beer Shop
8 Pitfield Street, N1 (071 739 3701). Old Street underground/BR. **Open** 11am-7pm Mon-Fri; 10am-4pm Sat. **Credit** A, £TC, V.
Hundreds of bottled beers, from around the world and around Britain, are squeezed into this ace ale shop. Cider makes an appearance, as does home-brew equipment. You can also buy beer by the barrel.

Berry Bros & Rudd
3 St James's Street, SW1 (071 839 9033). Green Park underground. **Open** 9am-5.30pm Mon-Fri. **Credit** A, A/c, AmEx, DC, V.
This famous shop first opened as a general grocer's in 1699. It now houses an excellent and efficient wine merchant's, tops on information and service. Ancient Madeiras, crusty ports and venerable clarets, plus an array of New World wines, are kept in the cellars.

The Bloomsbury Wine and Spirit Company
3 Bloomsbury Street, WC1 (071 436 4763/4). Tottenham Court Road underground. **Open** 9.30am-6pm Mon-Fri; 10.30am-3.30pm Sat. **Credit** A, A/c, AmEx, DC, JCB, £TC, V.
This shop doesn't look like anything special, but it stocks one of the best selections of Scottish malt whiskies in town. Pure malt whiskies are made only from malted barley, and come from one distillery; they give great variation in taste. There should be something here to satisfy the most demanding connoisseur: over 175 malts are stocked.
Delivery service (free in central London). Mail order. Price list.

See also above **Department Stores,** especially **Liberty.**

Conran Shop
Michelin House, 81 Fulham Road, SW3 (071 589 7401). South Kensington underground/14, 49 bus. **Open** 9.30am-6pm Mon, Sat; 10am-6pm Tue; noon-5pm Sun. **Credit** A, AmEx, £TC, V.
Everything from hand-crafted notebooks and bottles of balsamic vinegar to huge dining tables and chi-chi gardening equipment is sold at this design Mecca. Housed in the lovingly restored Michelin Building, it's all in the best possible taste. *See chapter* **Restaurants.**

General Trading Company
144 Sloane Street, SW1 (071 730 0411). Sloane Square underground. **Open** 9am-5.30pm Mon, Tue, Thur-Sat; 9am-7pm Wed. **Credit** A, £TC, V.
A youngish, upwardly mobile, slightly (but not overly) adventurous clientele is being courted here. Stock ranges from furniture to knick-knacks; quality is assured.

Habitat
196 Tottenham Court Road, W1 (071 631 3880). Goodge Street underground/24, 29, 73, 134 bus. **Open** 10am-6pm Mon-Wed; 10am-8pm Thur; 10am-6.30pm Fri; 9am-6pm Sat; noon-5.30pm Sun. **Credit** A, AmEx, £TC, V.
Having recently pulled itself out of the design doldrums, this store seems more in tune with the times than it has for years. Goods (designed in-house) include furniture,

kitchen equipment and china, along with bedding and soft furnishings. Prices are reasonable.
Branches: 206-222 King's Road, SW3 (071 351 1211); King's Mall, King Street, W6 (081 741 7111); 191-217 Finchley Road, NW3 (071 328 3444).

Heal's

196 Tottenham Court Road, W1 (071 636 1666). Goode Street underground/24, 29, 73, 134 bus. **Open** 10am-6pm Mon-Wed; 10am-8pm Thur; 10am-6.30pm Fri; 9am-6pm Sat. **Credit** A, AmEx, £TC, V.
Next door to Habitat (*above*), Heal's represents the next level of aspiration and contains several floors of household durables. Whole houses can be kitted out here, plus there's an entire floor of gifts and accessories.

Gifts

The Crafts Council Shop

Victoria & Albert Museum, Cromwell Road, SW7 (071 589 5070). South Kensington underground. **Open** noon-5.30pm Mon; 10am-5.30pm Tue-Sun. **Credit** A, AmEx, £TC, V.
An excellent source of classy presents by contemporary craftspeople. The stock changes regularly, but includes ceramics, domestic pottery, glass, wood, textiles, jewellery and metalwork. Prices start at a few pounds and rise sharply.

James Smith & Sons

53 New Oxford Street, WC1 (071 836 4731). Tottenham Court Road underground. **Open** 9.30am-5.25pm Mon-Fri; 10am-5.25pm Sat. **Credit** A, £TC, V.
Not far from the British Museum, this umbrella shop is distinguished by its Victorian frontage. Inside there's a huge number of (mostly traditional) umbrellas, sticks and canes.

Naturally British

13 New Row, WC2 (071 240 0551). Covent Garden or Leicester Square underground. **Open** 11am-7pm Mon-Sat; noon-5pm Sun. **Credit** A, AmEx, DC, £TC, V.
Everything sold here is made in Britain. The diverse stock includes cards, knitwear, jewellery and knick-knacks – it's all good quality, but don't expect anything avant-garde.

Richard Kihl

164 Regent's Park Road, NW1 (071 586 3838). Chalk Farm underground. **Open** 9.30am-5pm Mon-Fri; noon-5pm Sat. **Credit** A, AmEx, V.
Wine accessories galore are the speciality of this unique shop. Decanters and corkscrews come in both new and antique versions.

Waterford-Wedgwood

173 Piccadilly, W1 (071 629 2614). Green Park or Piccadilly Circus underground. **Open** 9am-6pm Mon-Fri; 9am-4pm Sat. **Credit** A, AmEx, DC, JCB, £STC, V.
As the name suggests, Wedgwood china and Waterford crystal are the stock in trade, although other bone china goods are also sold. If traditional, well-made British domestic-ware is what you're after, look no further.

Health & Beauty

For late-night pharmacies, *see chapter* **Early Hours**.

Crabtree & Evelyn

6 Kensington Church Street, W8 (071 937 9335). High Street Kensington underground. **Open** 9.30am-6pm

Mon-Wed, Fri, Sat; 9.30am-7pm Thur. **Credit** A, AmEx, £TC, V.
The strongly perfumed scents, body lotions, and bath gels make this an intoxicating shop to visit. None of the products is tested on animals.
Branches: 30 James Street, WC2 (071 379 0964); 134 King's Road, SW3 (071 589 6263).

Culpeper Herbalists

8 The Market, Covent Garden Piazza, WC2 (071 379 6698). Covent Garden underground. **Open** 10am-8pm Mon-Thur; 9am-8pm Fri, Sat; 10am-6pm Sun. **Credit** A, AmEx, £TC, V.
A small shop filled with the massed scents of the herbs, spices, pot-pourris, oils, creams, bath salts and soaps on sale. Products are made from herbs grown by Culpeper in Suffolk.
Branch: 21 Bruton Street, W1 (071 629 4559).

Floris

89 Jermyn Street, SW1 (071 930 2885). Piccadilly Circus underground. **Open** 9.30am-5.30pm Mon-Fri; 9.30am-5pm Sat. **Credit** A, AmEx, DC, £STC, V.
Traditional toiletries are dispensed in a dignified atmosphere here. Colognes, perfumes, soaps and candles employ old-fashioned scents such as Rose or Lily of the Valley.

Neal's Yard Remedies

15 Neal's Yard, WC2 (071 379 7222). Covent Garden underground. **Open** 10am-6pm Mon, Tue, Thur, Fri; 10am-5.30pm Wed, Sat; 11am-4pm Sun. **Credit** A, V.
Homoeopathic remedies and herbal medicines are sold alongside beauty products at this fragrant shop. Less essential items include soaps, shampoos, massage oils and essential oils.

A Nelson & Co

73 Duke Street, W1 (071 629 3118). Bond Street underground. **Open** 9am-5.30pm Mon-Fri; 9am-4pm Sat. **Credit** A, V.
A homoeopathic pharmacy. Over 4,000 remedies derived from herbs, minerals and other natural substances are offered. Staff are happy to advise.

Penhaligon's

41 Wellington Street, WC2 (071 836 2150). Covent Garden underground. **Open** 10am-6pm Mon-Sat. **Credit** A, AmEx, £TC, V.
Classic fragrances are the speciality of this upmarket perfumery. The setting is deliberately old-fashioned, and there are products for men, women and the home.

Markets

London's markets are a joy. Packed with life and bustle, they're worth visiting as much for the spectacle as for the spectacularly low prices to be found. Markets are remarkably resilient; many have been on the same site for over a century, surviving the Blitz, the planners, and the development of the chainstore. During the recent recession, they have been thriving, as shoppers deserted stylish stores and headed for the streets to find bargains. Watch out for pickpockets, take a good dose of scepticism (those 'Levi's' for a tenner might not be all they seem) and enjoy the vitality.

Camden Markets: *expanding, but still exciting. See* **review** *page 174.*

Antiques Markets

Camden and **Portobello** markets both contain scores of antiques stalls. For Islington's Camden Passage Market, *see chapter* **London by Area: North.**

Bermondsey (New Caledonian) Market
Bermondsey Square, SE1. Borough underground or London Bridge underground/BR. **Open** 5am-2pm Fri, starts closing at noon.
Smart antiques collectors arrive at Bermondsey Square before dawn on Fridays. They come to root through the astonishing array of goods: from paintings and old jewellery to rabbits' feet and urine-testing kits (we're not taking the piss). There are few giveaway bargains: traders here are old-hands and know the value of their stock. But, as much of their haul has come direct from house clearances, or consists of curios snapped up for a snip at car-boot sales, prices are generally lower than you'd find in the shops.

Crafts Markets

For Greenwich Market *see chapter* **London by Area: South.**

Gabriel's Wharf Market
Gabriel's Wharf: north side of Upper Ground, east of LWT building, SE1 (071 620 0544). Waterloo underground/BR. **Open** Mar-Dec 11am-3pm Fri.
The new and rather contrived crafts market at Gabriel's Wharf is still trying to find its feet. Shops displaying ceramics, paintings and jewellery surround a bandstand where jazz groups sometimes play in the summer. A few stalls are set up around the courtyard selling ethnic clothing (including Turkish khilims and Andean knitwear), handmade jewellery and pottery.

Piccadilly Crafts Market
Courtyard of St James's Church, Piccadilly W1. Green Park underground. **Open** 10am-5pm Thur-Sat.

The churchyard of Wren's beautiful St James's church provides the setting for this newish crafts market. Aimed mostly at tourists, merchandise ranges from silly souvenirs to genuine nineteenth-century prints. Knitwear, handmade greetings cards and a few antiques stalls can also be found. Come to escape the traffic madness of Piccadilly, and to take a bite to eat at the Wren wholefood café.

St Martin-in-the-Fields Market
Courtyard of St-Martin-in-the-Fields Church, off Trafalgar Square, WC2. Charing Cross underground/BR. **Open** 11am-5pm Mon-Sat; noon-5pm Sun.
Thread your way through the tacky souvenirs (T-shirts, football scarves and the like) to reach the more interesting collection of clothing, jewellery and artefacts from around the world: Russian dolls and Peruvian knitwear are highlights.

General

For Brixton Market *see chapter* **London by Area: South**, and for Chapel Market *see chapter* **London by Area: North.**

Berwick Street Market
Berwick Street, Rupert Street W1. Piccadilly Circus underground. **Open** 9am-6pm Mon-Sat.
If you haven't the time to leave the West End, and want to see a traditional London street market, free from tourist traps and trappings, beetle over to Soho's Berwick Street. Its boisterous costermongers sell the cheapest, most eclectic range of fruit and vegetables in central London. Look out for Dennis's mushroom and veg stall: it's a work of art. Fabrics are the market's other forte. Prices are higher on Rupert Street and the traders are more subdued.

East Street Market
East Street, SE17. Elephant & Castle underground/BR, then 12, 35, 40, 45, 68, 171, 176 bus. **Open** 8am-3pm Tue-Thur, Sun; 8am-5pm Fri, Sat.
East Street celebrated its centenary in 1980, and con-

tinues to flourish by catering for south London workers. Every Sunday over 250 stalls fill the narrow street, and a plant and flower market takes place on Blackwood Street. A horde of clothes (mainly new, some second-hand), electrical, and household goods go on sale. Fruit and veg traders are relatively rare. The rumour that you can have your watch lifted at one end of the street and sold back to you at the other is not entirely unfounded.

Ridley Road Market
Ridley Road, E8. Dalston Kingsland BR/22, 30, 38, 149 bus. **Open** *9am-3pm Mon-Wed; 9am-noon Thur; 9am-5pm Fri, Sat.*
Jews, Asians, Turks and West Indians all live in this cosmopolitan area, and Ridley Road reflects the mix well. Green bananas and reggae records (the latter being played at bone-resonating volume) are sold from dilapidated shacks, pulses and olive oil from the Turkish lock-ups, and bagels from a 24-hour bakery. Add to this the colourful drapery stalls and the very cheap fruit and vegetables, and you have one of London's best and most exuberant local markets.

Weekend

Brick Lane Market
Brick Lane, E1. Aldgate East or Shoreditch underground. **Open** *5am-2pm Sun.*
Half the East End, it seems, takes to the streets for a weekly knees-up at Brick Lane. For a dose of Cockney culture, it has no equal. Venture into the Cheshire Street lock-ups, packed to the rafters with shoddy furniture and old books; or pick through the farrago of junk sold along the Bethnal Green Road. Dodgy spivs proffer gold on Bacon Street, while Sclater Street is good for pet provisions. Off Cygnet Street is a stretch of wasteland, taken up by yet more stalls: new bicycles, and butchers with a superb line in banter are the highlights. Brick Lane itself is dull in comparison, with cheap fashion and leather goods for sale. The rest of the week, Brick Lane is a centre for the Bangladeshi community, and has some of the best curry houses in town (*see chapter* **London by Area: East End & Docklands**).

Camden Markets
Camden High Street to Chalk Farm Road, NW1. Camden Town underground/24, 28, 31, 68 bus. **Open** *8am-6pm Sat, Sun.*
Since opening in 1974, Camden's Markets have expanded rapidly, and now have outposts in every bit of space on and off the Chalk Farm Road from Camden Town tube to beyond Hawley Road (the Stables market is the latest addition). Handmade crafts, new and second-hand street fashions, wholefoods, books, records and antiques form the bulk of the goods sold, but thousands of young people come here just for the atmosphere. This is enhanced by buskers and street performers who draw crowds to the cobbled area near the canal. Be warned – it can get mighty crowded on a fine weekend.

Columbia Road Market
Columbia Road (east of Ravenscroft Street), E2. Shoreditch underground or Old Street underground/BR. **Open** *8am-12.30pm Sun.*
Walking distance from **Brick Lane** (*see above*) is London's best retail flower market. Columbia Road is where to go for cut flowers, plants, shrubs, seedlings and pots. You'll know you're getting near when you spot a procession of hardy perennials being carried along the street.

Petticoat Lane Market
Middlesex Street, E1. Aldgate or Aldgate East

underground or Liverpool Street underground/BR. **Open** *9am-2pm Sun.*
Swarms of visitors and Londoners swoop on Middlesex Street for London's most famous Sunday market. There's plenty of cheap fashion, household goods and knick-knacks from the bizarre to the banal. Prices can be higher here than at other markets, don't forget to haggle. Look out for the impressive array of leather goods.

Portobello Market
Portobello Road, W11. Ladbroke Grove, Notting Hill Gate or Westbourne Park underground/12, 28, 31, 52, 88 bus. **Open** *fruit and vegetables 8am-5pm Mon-Wed, Fri, Sat; 8am-1pm Thur; general 8am-3pm Fri; 8am-5pm Sat; antiques 8am-5pm Sat.*
Though there's a small market most days on Portobello Road, Saturday is the time to visit. From early morning, the Notting Hill Gate end becomes crammed with antiques, sold from scores of shops and hundreds of stalls on and off Portobello Road and Westbourne Grove. Jewellery, paintings, musical instruments: almost anything old and collectable is for sale. The area is very touristy: dodgy foreign-exchange booths pepper the street; buskers entertain the crowds. The market's character changes beyond Elgin Crescent. Fruit and veg stalls cater for locals, then under the Westway, there's second-hand everything (including plenty of clothes). Stick around here to avoid tack and high prices.

Musical Instruments

The place to head for is the north end of Charing Cross Road, and around Denmark Street, WC2. There's a dozen shops selling all kinds of instruments, sheet music, amplification equipment, and everything connected with the creation of music. If you can't find what you want there, try **Blanks**.

Blanks
271-273 Kilburn High Road, NW6 (071 624 1260/071 624 7777). Kilburn underground/Brondesbury BR. **Open** *10am-5.30pm Mon-Sat.* **Credit** *A, £$TC, V.*
Blanks is the biggest music shop in London and contains virtually every instrument invented. African talking drums share space with authentic Scottish bagpipes. *Export scheme. Installment payment scheme. Part-exchange. Repairs. Tuning.*

Records, Tapes & CDs
Megastores

HMV
150 Oxford Street, W1 (071 631 3423). Oxford Circus or Tottenham Court Road underground. **Open** *9.30am-7pm Mon-Wed, Fri, Sat; 9.30am-8pm Thur.* **Credit** *A, AmEx, DC, £$TC, V.*
Bright, loud, and clearly laid out, HMV's main floor stocks mainstream pop, rock and soul. Downstairs there's an impressive specialist selection, with plenty of jazz (often at reduced prices), classical, and world music from every conceivable part of the globe. Despite the move away from vinyl, there's still a fair number of titles on LP as well as a good choice of 12" singles. *Mail order.*

Tower Records
1 Piccadilly Circus, W1 (071 439 2500). Piccadilly Circus underground. **Open** *9am-midnight Mon-Sat;*

11.30am-7.30pm Sun incl Bank Holidays. **Credit** A, AmEx, Connect, £TC, V.

It can be tiring just walking from one section to another in this vast emporium. All types of music are stocked and thoughtfully displayed, but if it's vinyl you're after you'll be disappointed – virtually everything is kept on CD or tape only. Tower's specialist departments are the best of all the megastores, with particularly fine collections of soundtracks and stage shows, blues, country and jazz.

Export scheme. Mail order. Wheelchair access.

Virgin Megastore

14-30 Oxford Street, W1 (071 631 1234). Tottenham Court Road underground. **Open** 9.30am-8pm Mon, Wed-Sat; 10am-8pm Tue; noon-7pm Sun; 9.30am-6pm Bank Holidays. **Credit** A, AmEx, £TC, V.

The massive ground floor contains a vast selection of music, mainly on CD. However, the confusing lay-out of the store often makes it hard to find what you're looking for. It's strongest on new releases, especially 12" singles, and good for back-catalogue rock, pop and soul. There's plenty to keep you happy besides the music, including T-shirts, videos and computer games.

Café. Export scheme. Listening facilities. Mail order. Wheelchair access.

Specialist Record Shops

Black Market

25 D'Arblay Street, W1 (071 437 0478). Tottenham Court Road underground. **Open** 10am-7pm Mon-Sat. **Credit** A, AmEx, £TC, V.

If it's happening on the dancefloor, you're likely to find it here, in advance of anywhere else. Most of the business is in import 12" singles; upstairs is devoted to House/Euro and some rap and swing, while downstairs is techno. At the back of the shop are stocks of T-shirts, baseball caps and the like. It's also a good place to find out where to buy tickets to this week's most fashionable club.

Dub Vendor

274 Lavender Hill, SW11 (071 223 3757). Clapham Junction underground/BR. **Open** 9am-6.30pm Mon-Wed; 9am-7pm Thur-Sat. **No credit cards.**

Dub is a reggae specialist stocking the latest pre-release singles hot off the plane from Jamaica, as well as 12" singles and LPs. There's a fine back-catalogue selection from the greats (Bob Marley, Gregory Isaacs and Freddie McGregor). Staff also offer an efficient mail-order service with well-produced lists packed with information and reviews.

Listening facilities. Mail order.
Branch: 150 Ladbroke Grove, W10 (081 969 3375).

Honest Jon's

278 Portobello Road, W10 (081 969 9822). Notting Hill Gate underground. **Open** 10am-6pm Mon-Sat; 11am-5pm Sun. **Credit** A, £TC, V.

A wonderful selection of carefully-chosen records guaranteed to excite any Black Music fan. Upstairs there's soul, jazz-funk, and reggae LPs and 12" singles. In the backroom, 'Reggae Revive' has an unsurpassed choice of rare 7" singles. In the basement there's collectable jazz including a large number of coveted records on the Blue Note label.
Catalogue. Listening facilities. Mail order.

Ray's Jazz Shop

180 Shaftesbury Avenue, WC2 (071 240 3969). Tottenham Court Road underground. **Open** 10am-6.30pm Mon-Sat. **Credit** A, £TC, V.

New and second-hand jazz mainly on LP (although there are some CDs), from early New Orleans to modern

avant-garde. Prices are reasonable, particularly for second-hand items, although rare records are priced accordingly. It's all beautifully organised, with records classified by artist and musical style. The staff are friendly, knowledgeable and happy to offer advice.
Books. Listening facilities. Wheelchair access.

Reckless Records

30 Berwick Street, W1 (071 437 4271). Piccadilly Circus underground. **Open** 10am-7pm Mon-Sat. **Credit** A, £TC, V.

Everything's second-hand. Rock, soul and jazz are the main lines, but selections of country, classical and reggae can also be found. There are also large stocks of 12" dance singles including imports. Prices for records in good condition start high, but these are reduced regularly according to how long they've been in the shop. The Islington branch has a basement catering for the committed collector, with many rare titles.
Branch: 79 Upper Street, N1 (071 359 0501).
Listening facilities. Mail order.

Stern's African Record Centre

116 Whitfield Street, W1 (071 387 5550). Goodge Street underground. **Open** 10.30am-6.30pm Mon-Sat. **Credit** A, £TC, V.

A great place for the world-music enthusiast, boasting fair prices, a vast selection of African music on all formats, and extremely knowledgeable staff. They're happy to let you listen to records before you buy. Other parts of the planet are not neglected, so if it's samba, salsa or zouk you're after, pay Stern's a visit.
Export scheme. Listening facilities. Mail order.

Vinyl Experience

18 Hanway Street, W1 (071 636 1281/071 637 1771). Tottenham Court Road underground. **Open** 10am-6.30pm Mon-Sat. **Credit** A, AmEx, £TC, V.

Catering for the serious collector, Vinyl Experience specialises in rare vinyl and memorabilia. Downstairs the record section covers mainstream acts including a strong selection of hard-to-find Beatles items as well as progressive rock, indie, and some soul and jazz. Upstairs there's an incredible selection of posters, photos, autographs and 35 years of assorted ephemera that'll please any dedicated fan.
Branch: 3 Buck Street, NW1 (071 267 5228).
Listening facilities. Mail order. Wheelchair access.

Stamps

Stanley Gibbons

399 Strand, WC2 (071 836 8444). Charing Cross underground/BR. **Open** 8.30am-6pm Mon-Fri; 10am-4pm Sat. **Credit** A, AmEx, £TC, V.

A long established (1856) stamp shop, selling and collecting stamps from all over the world. The range and depth of stock (both stamps and accessories) is impressive.
Catalogues. Mail order.

Toys

Hamleys

188 Regent Street, W1 (071 734 3161). Oxford Circus underground. **Open** 10am-6.30pm Mon-Wed, Fri; 10am-8pm Thur; 9.30am-6.30pm Sat; noon-6pm Sun. **Credit** A, AmEx, £TC, V.

London's biggest toy shop. If you can't find what you want on the six floors of toys and games, you probably won't find it anywhere. *See also chapter* **Children**.

Services

Your suitcase has broken, your shoes leak, and you've a backache. Fear not: London is there to serve you.

Virtually anything you want can be made, mended or delivered in London; the trick is to find the reputable places, because for every painstaking hairdresser, meticulous repair shop or sensitive beauty clinic there will be a score who are far less professional. Inevitably, the highest standards cost more, but this is one city where you can find the best.

Consumer services are also listed in other chapters of this Guide. For police, fire, ambulance and other emergency services (plumbing, glazing, for instance) *see chapter* **Survival**. Details of transport services are listed in *chapter* **Getting Around**; services for business people are in *chapter* **Business**; and large department stores also offer many services, so check in *chapter* **Shopping**. A reputable childminding agency is listed in *chapter* **Children**.

Antiques Valuations

The London and Provincial Antique Dealers Association (LAPADA) is worth contacting, if you want to find your way around the British antiques world. Phone the Association (071 823 3511) and ask for its booklet *Buying Antiques in Britain*, which gives details of all members as well as good advice on buying antiques, customer's protection, antique markets and export services. For packing and shipping of antiques *see below* **Packing and Removals**.

Christies South Kensington
85 Old Brompton Road, SW7 (071 581 7611). South Kensington underground. **Open** 9am-7.30pm Mon (valuations until 7pm); 9am-5pm Tue-Fri; 10am-1pm Sat (viewing and valuations only).
The expert valuers at Christie, Manson & Woods will give free estimates on anything from toys to textiles. Vintage wine, furniture, silver and an array of collectables are among the myriad goods sold at this South Kensington branch in the course of more than 350 auctions every year. Go to the head office at King Street to bid for Van Goghs and the like.
Branch: 8 King Street, SW1 (071 839 9060).

Phillips
101 New Bond Street/7 Blenheim Street, W1 (071 629 6602). Bond Street underground. **Open** 8.30am-5pm Mon-Wed, Fri; 8.30am-8pm Thur; 2-5pm Sun (viewing only).
Verbal valuations are mostly free. Each branch has its own speciality: Glendining's at the Bond Street branch are the coin experts; valuers at Salem Road have the gen

on collectables, textiles, pianos and furniture. Sales at both branches are open to the public.
Branch: 10 Salem Road, W2 (071 229 9090).

Sotheby's
34-35 New Bond Street, W1 (071 493 8080). Green Park underground. **Open** 9am-4.30pm Mon-Fri.
Sotheby's is the biggest and oldest fine-art auctioneer's in the world and covers all aspects of art. Bring your antiques in for a valuation or for larger pieces call out one of the experts to your home. Either way the service is free. There are up to three sales a day with everything from Islamic art to vintage wine going under the hammer. All sale goods are put on view three days prior to the auction (the premises are often open at weekends for viewings) and there's an Auction Line (071 409 2686) to find out roughly when each item will be sold.

Book Search

Dillons Rare Book Department
Dillons Direct, PO Box 1992, Epping, Essex (0992 524 554). **Open** 9am-5pm Mon-Fri. **Credit** A, V.
Don't despair if the book you've set your heart on is out of print. Dillons book-finding service has an excellent success rate and isn't madly expensive. There's also a book-binding service, the cost of which depends on the book: a minor repair could cost under £50; major work can run into hundreds of pounds.

Clothing & Shoes

For minor clothing repairs, ask your nearest dry-cleaner's if it offers a mending service.

Dress Hire

Contemporary Wardrobe
The Horse Hospital, Colonnade, Bloomsbury, WC1 (071 713 7370). Russell Square underground. **Open** 10am-6pm Mon-Wed, Fri; 10am-7pm Thur by appointment. **Credit** A, AmEx, £$TC, V.
Each design here is unique. Full-length gowns and cocktail dresses are made from luxurious fabrics such as silk, taffeta, chiffon and georgette. It costs from £69 to £89 to hire a dress and matching bag for three days, with a returnable £200 deposit. Rentable jewellery and evening gloves start at £5.75. Robe Noire's evening dresses can be made to order.

Costume Studio
6 Penton Grove, N1 (071 388 4481). Angel underground. **Open** 9.30am-6pm Mon-Fri; 10am-5pm Sat. **Credit** A, AmEx, £$TC, V.
For fancy dress, there's no better place to come. This warehouse is chock-a-block with everything from the usual pirates, vampires, nuns, and French maids, to some truly wonderful period clothing. Most costumes cost from £35 to £45 to hire for a couple of days. The

Full steam ahead at **Tothills**. *See* **review**.

staff are patient and friendly; dressing up has never been so much fun.

Moss Bros

27 King Street, WC2 (071 497 9354). Covent Garden or Leicester Square underground. **Open** 9am-6pm Mon-Wed, Fri, Sat; 9am-7pm Thur. **Credit** A, AmEx, £TC, DC, V.

The hire departments here and at Regent Street hold thousands of suits between them. Prices are reasonable: most outfits cost between £35 and £45 to hire, although a classic morning suit complete with top hat, wing-collar shirt, cravat, pin and handkerchief costs just under £63 (plus a £50 deposit). Full Highland Dress costs £47.85 plus a £100 deposit. Women's-wear for hire is limited to bridal gowns (phone for details).
Branch: 88 Regent Street, W1 (071 494 0666).

Dry Cleaning

Sketchley

49 Maddox Street, W1 (071 629 1292). Bond Street or Oxford Circus underground. **Open** 8.30am-6pm Mon-Fri. **Credit** A, AmEx, V.

You're never far from a Sketchley: there are 40 branches in central London. The firm is better than many of its high street equivalents. It offers fast turnaround, a Golden Service for garments that require individual attention, and a comprehensive repair service. Sketchley is gradually replacing its stock of dry-cleaning machines with ozone-friendly perchloroethylene machines.
Branches are too many to list here. Check the phone book for your nearest.

Tothills

8 Lower Belgrave Street, SW1 (071 824 8389/collection service 071 252 0100). Victoria underground/BR.

Open 8.30am-5.30pm Mon-Fri; 8.30am-1.30pm Sat. **Credit** A, £TC, V.

Tothills takes over when Jeeves runs out of steam; there's no better dry-cleaner in the country. The latest equipment, best chemicals and conscientious staff make sure that your designer suit or wedding dress will come back in tip-top condition. There's a collection and delivery service from anywhere in central London; the standard turnaround time is one week, but 24-hour and 48-hour express services are possible for a supplementary charge. The prices are high; a standard man's two-piece suit costs around £15, an elaborate evening gown £85 or more. Tothills has just installed the latest planet-friendly machine from Germany.

Laundry

Self-service launderettes can be found in many residential districts of London (try Tulthorpe's at 1 Brunswick Shopping Centre, WC1; 071 837 0182); make sure you have plenty of 20p, 50p and £1 coins to use. Often the supervisor at these establishments is willing (for a few pounds) to do a 'service wash': if you leave your unwashed garments in the morning, they will be washed and dried for you to pick up that evening. But if you want to splash out, contact **DEL**.

Danish Express Laundry (DEL)

16 Hinde Street, W1 (071 935 6306). Baker Street or Bond Street underground. **Open** 8.30am-5.30pm Mon-Fri; 9.30am-noon Sat. **Credit** A, A/c, AmEx, V.

DEL can collect and return your laundry for as little as £2 during its opening hours; staff are generalists who

can launder a shirt for £2.29, a pair of jeans for £2.69, or even dry-clean a kaftan for a rather overpriced £14.30. An express same-day service is available for a 50% surcharge; a next-day service costs an extra 33%; standard dry-cleaning takes a week. General repairs and alterations can also be taken care of; collars can be turned (from £20). Regular customers are encouraged to open accounts.
Collection and delivery service (express).
Branch: Janet's Laundry 281A Finchley Road, NW3 (071 435 6131).

Repair & Alteration

British Invisible Mending Service
32 Thayer Street, W1 (071 935 2487). Baker Street or Bond Street underground. **Open** 8.30am-5.45pm Mon-Fri; 10am-1pm Sat. **No credit cards.**
Woven fabrics are carefully repaired by removing threads from unseen hems and re-weaving them into the damaged area. This takes about three days a garment, and prices vary according to the texture of the material. The menders cannot repair velvet, fine cottons or silks. Savile Row suits or sequined and beaded costumes constitute much of the repair work here. Staff also do alterations.

Natural Leather
33 Monmouth Street, WC2 (071 240 7748). Covent Garden underground. **Open** 11am-7pm Mon-Sat. **Credit** A, £TC, V.
Proprietor Bella Mani is keen on helping customers with alterations, repairs and cleaning of leather goods. She cleans goods by hand and can recolour by hand, replace linings, and restitch. Having garments made to order is no problem. Prices are reasonable.
Export scheme. Mail order.

General Leather Company
56 Chiltern Street, W1 (071 935 1041). Baker Street underground. **Open** 10am-6pm Mon-Fri; 10am-5pm Sat. **Credit** A, AmEx, DC, £STC, V.
Staff at this leatherwear shop specialise in bespoke work but can also alter and repair suede, leather and sheepskin. They cannot, however, clean, oil or recolour garments. Relining a jacket costs from around £90, while tear repairs start from £15. New panels can be fitted where damage is severe. The work is good, but the prices high.

Stitchcraft
7 South Molton Street, W1 (071 629 7919). Bond Street underground. **Open** 9am-5pm Mon-Fri; 9.30am-3pm Sat. **No credit cards.**
Pop in to Stitchcraft if your fashionable South Molton Street garment needs a little reworking. Remodelling and alteration of both men's- and women's-wear is undertaken. Quotes for the work are given on the spot, but prices start at about £8.

Shoe Repairs

The Crispins Cobbler
5 Chiltern Street, W1 (071 935 7984). Baker Street underground. **Open** *cobblers* 8.30am-4.30pm Mon-Fri; *shoe shop* 10am-6pm Mon-Wed, Fri; 10am-7pm Thur; 9.30am-4.30pm Sat. **Credit** A, AmEx, DC, £STC, V.
Crispins repairs, valets and renovates any kind of leatherwear. We have been using the firm regularly for years and can vouch for the quality of work. The catch? The cost reflects the work.
Postal service.

Jane Packer Floral Design
56 James Street, W1 (071 935 2673). Bond Street underground. **Open** 9am-6pm Mon-Sat. **Credit** A, AmEx, DC, JCB, £TC, V.
Jane Packer specialises in the 'no-rules' school of floristry so expect artistic licence if you come here. Crushed velvet, tartan ribbon, ornamental gourds, fruits and nuts are just some of the things you might find in one of her arrangements. Bouquets and arrangements start from around £30.

Back Care

Barry Pluke
Bodyshift, 1 Hillside, Highgate Road, NW5 (answerphone 081 677 3694). **Appointments** by arrangement. **No credit cards.**
Done your back in carrying luggage, or by prolonged sitting on a coach? Barry Pluke practises 'Bodyshift', a very rapid back and joint treatment that can get you up and mobile again. You can visit his clinics in Highgate, Kentish Town (071 284 4614), or Chiswick (081 747 3448), or he will visit you. We've used him a few times, always with positive results. The catch is the price. Home (or hotel) visits cost as much as £50, but you can pay as little as £15 for a brief (but effective) session at a clinic.

British School of Osteopathy
1-4 Suffolk Street, SW1 (071 930 9254). Piccadilly Circus underground. **Open** 9am-6pm Mon-Fri; 10am-1pm Sat (emergencies and sports clinic only). **Credit** A, AmEx, £TC, V.
The BSO is a training school for osteopaths, therefore assessments and treatments of back- and joint-pain are closely supervised and reasonably priced. You need to book an appointment days in advance, though the Saturday clinic is open for 'emergencies'. Treatments cost about £5 to £15 and take around 40 minutes.

Contact Lens Specialist

Nigel Burnett Hodd
7 Devonshire Street, W1 (071 636 2444/5209/fax 071 637 3847). Great Portland Street underground. **Open** 8.30am-5.30pm Mon, Wed-Fri; 8.30am-6.30pm Tue, by appointment only. **Credit** A, £TC, V.
Nigel Hodd is recognised as one of the country's leading contact lens practitioners. If you have had to give up lenses because of discomfort, Mr Hodd is probably the one who can restore your sight. Next-day emergency appointments are possible, and emergency replacement lenses can be swiftly provided for visitors to London. The service is second-to-none, but prices are commensurate. An emergency consultation can cost £60 or more. Weekly-disposable lenses, the kindest on your eyes, are £400 including the cost of plenty of regular checks, but excluding solutions.

Hairdressers

Eggison Daniel
Lansdowne House, 23 Berkeley Street, W1 (071 495 7777). Green Park underground. **Open** 8.30am-6.15pm Mon-Fri; 8.30am-5.30pm Sat. **Credit** A, V.
Two former employees of Vidal Sassoon have put their business faith in the old barber-shop tradition. This is a unisex salon, but 75% of the customers are male, and the

environment is relentlessly masculine, with an interior that mixes marble with grey slate and copies of the *Financial Times*. For a charge of £24 to £35, clients are treated to a haircut, hot towels, aftershave gel and a post-cut rinse to get rid of stray hairs. Comb-on colour is popular.
Treatments *hairdressing, manicure, shaving*.

Geo F Trumper
9 Curzon Street, W1 (071 499 1850). Green Park underground. **Open** 9am-5.30pm Mon-Fri; 9am-1pm Sat. **Credit** A, AmEx, DC, £TC, V.
A staunchly conservative, traditional barber's where army majors and cabinet ministers have their locks trimmed: groovy John Major was a regular prior to greatness. The prices are no snip at £17.50 for a haircut and shampoo, and from £11 for a shave and hairbrush, but the place is great for old world atmosphere. The shaving accessories and men's toiletries look good and are used by the Royal Family, but they're expensive.
Wheelchair access.
Branches: 20 Jermyn Street, SW1 (071 734 1370/6553); at **Simpson**, Piccadilly, SW1 (071 734 2002; ext 342).

Harrods' Long Hair Clinic
Fifth floor, Hair & Beauty Salon, Harrods, Knightsbridge, SW1 (071 584 8881/071 581 2021). Knightsbridge underground. **Open** 10am-6pm Mon, Tue; 10am-7pm Wed-Fri; 9am-6pm Sat. **Credit** A, A/c, AmEx, DC, JCB, SC, £$TC, V.
Harrods' hair clinic specialises in styling, cutting and general care for long hair and hair of one length. On the first visit your hair is analysed (free of charge), and then an individual hair-care programme is devised. Innovative cleansing methods, massages, protein-enriched heat

treatments, setting and blunt cuts are the usual offerings. A dry cut costs £18, a cut and blow-dry costs £36.
Wheelchair access.

Molton Brown
58 South Molton Street, W1 (women's 071 629 1872/men's 071 493 5236). Bond Street underground. **Open** 10am-5.30pm Mon-Wed, Fri; 10am-6.30pm Thur; 9am-4.30pm Sat. **Credit** A, £$TC, V.
We can recommend the herbal speciality treatments, and natural-look perming and tinting techniques for which this salon is famed. According to previous satisfied customers, it's worth forking out up to £65 for the Molton Brown finish. But if you only need an unfussy shampoo and cut, you'll be wasting your money here. It costs £35 for a cut by an 'ordinary' stylist, and up to £65 for the attention of the 'top' MB employees. Men's cuts cost from £26 to £30.
Beauty treatments. Bridal service. Catalogue. Mail order. Price list. Wheelchair access.
Branches: 54 Rosslyn Hill (071 794 2022); 19 High Street, Wimbledon, SW19 (081 946 9684).

Splinters
27A Maddox Street, W1 (071 493 5169). Oxford Circus underground. **Open** 10am-6pm Mon; 9am-6pm Tue, Wed, Fri; 9am-8pm Thur; 9am-4pm Sat. **Credit** A, AmEx, DC, £TC, V.
One of the longest-established black hairdresser's in the West End, Splinters was founded over 20 years ago. The salon is very busy but experienced staff and an eager bunch of younger helping hands, plus the latest in soul/reggae sounds, makes everything run smoothly. Because of its central London location, you'll probably pay slightly more than at a local salon.
Extensions. Price list.

Contact **Nigel Burnett Hodd** *with contact-lens problems. See* **review** *page 178.*

Toni & Guy

34 Southampton Street, WC2 (071 240 7342). Covent Garden or Charing Cross underground. **Open** 10am-6.30pm Mon-Wed; 10am-7.30pm Thur, Fri; 9am-5.30pm Sat. **Credit** A, AmEx, DC, V.

These ferociously trendy salons are modern and monochrome. But staff soon put you at ease, and listen carefully to your needs before cutting your hair: at £23-£27 for men and between £31 and £35 for women they ought to. Students at the Toni & Guy Educational Centre in St Christopher's Place, where you can be a model for a snip of the price (£2.50 for a cut). The service is less expert and can be incredibly slow, but supervision is good. Book in advance for the school.

Branches: 10-12 Davies Street, W1 (071 629 8348); 49 Sloane Square, SW1 (071 730 8113/4313); Kensington Barracks, Kensington Church Street, SW1 (071 937 0030); **Toni & Guy Educational Centre** 33 St Christopher's Place, W1 (071 486 0047).

Trevor Sorbie

10 Russell Street, WC2 (071 379 6901). Covent Garden underground. **Open** 9am-6pm Mon, Tue; 9am-7pm Wed; 9am-7.40pm Thur, Fri; 9am-5.30pm Sat. **Credit** A, AmEx, £TC, V.

This is a high fashion salon with a friendly atmosphere, a rare combination. Staff go out of their way to make you comfortable. And they do magnificent cuts. A cut and blow-dry for both men and women costs from £34 to £43; colouring costs from £16 to £89.

Vidal Sassoon

60 South Molton Street, W1 (071 491 8848). Bond Street underground. **Open** 9am-6pm Mon, Tue, Fri, Sat; 9am-6.45pm Wed, Thur. **Credit** A, £TC, V.

Because of the large number of staff employed by this internationally famous salon, the quality of the hairdressing does vary considerably, especially at the schools. A haircut and blow-dry at the main branches costs from £33 to £48 for women and £31 to £38.50 for men, depending on the level of the stylist you choose: regular stylist, top stylist, senior stylist, manager, or creative team. A perm costs between £38 and £70 and colouring is from £31.50 to £37.50. The staff also give free hair consultations – but so do many competitors. *Manicure and pedicure.*

Branches: 130 Sloane Street, SW1 (071 730 7288); **The Sanctuary** 11 Floral Street, WC2 (071 240 6635); 54 Knightsbridge, SW1 (071 235 7791); **Whiteleys of**

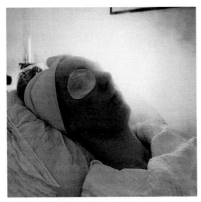

The **Helena Harnik Clinic***. See* **review***.*

Bayswater 151 Queensway, W2 (071 792 2741).
Schools: *men* 56-58 Davies Mews, W1 (071 629 1752); *women* 17 Queen Street, W1 (071 499 5808).

Hair Problems

Institute of Trichologists

228 Stockwell Road, SW9 (071 733 2056). Stockwell underground. **Open** 9am-5pm Tue, Fri; 9am-7pm Wed, Thur; 9am-1pm Sat. **Credit** V.

The Scalp and Hair Hospital, within the Institute building, is busy, slightly down-at-heel, but friendly. Consultations take place in the privacy of an upstairs room, last up to an hour, and cost £22. There's no quackery; treatment involves steam, pine-tar shampoo, and heat lamps (£12). We can vouch for its success.

Men's Beauty Salon

Daniel Rouah

7A Station Approach, Baker Street, NW1 (071 935 4362/helpline 071 487 3198). Baker Street underground. **Open** 9am-6pm Mon-Wed, Fri, Sat; 9am-7pm Thur. **Credit** £TC.

Frenchman Daniel, who runs this barber's shop under Baker Street station, specialises in shaving problems. Call in for a shave and he'll happily dispense friendly advice on dealing with shaving rash, and offer tips to avoid nicking yourself. You don't need to buy the products he touts (substitutes will do), but the advice is sound. There's a range of other treatments available, and advice on hair care, acne and skin problems is well within his scope. Frequent visitors are placed on the mailing list and receive lots of special offers.

Treatments *ear-piercing, electrolysis, eye-care, facials, haircare, manicure, pedicure, scalp massage, shaving, waxing.*

Unisex Beauty Salons

Helena Harnik Clinic

19 Upper Berkeley Street, W1 (071 724 1518). Marble Arch underground. **Open** 9.30am-6pm Tue-Thur; 9.30am-5pm Fri, Sat. **Credit** A, £TC, V.

Helena Harnik is a specialist in dealing with problem skins, and can treat acne, broken veins, rough skin, and warts. We've used this clinic for deep-cleansing facials, and for electrolysis; both were effective, and the service utterly professional. Facilities are discreetly private, and very smart. Almost half of the clients are men. It takes 15 minutes of electrolysis to remove a moustache from a woman, or to partition a man's single eyebrow; the cost is £13.50. Six or so treatments may be needed for strong hair growth. A bikini wax costs £7.50, and facials are around £50.

Treatments *bleaching, chiropody, cleansing, electrolysis, facials, eye-lashes, wart removal.*

Tao Clinic

5 Sloane Street, SW1 (071 235 9333). Knightsbridge underground. **Open** 10am-6pm Mon, Fri; 10am-7pm Tue-Thur; 9am-4pm Sat. **Credit** A, £TC, V.

One of the original pioneers in the field of electrolysis, the Tao Clinic has expanded to include many other body treatments, and now has 15 branches across the country. A ten-minute electrolysis session costs between £10.95 and £12.75. A half-leg wax (both calves, not just the one leg) costs £12.50, and make-up (eg for weddings) is possible by arrangement.

Treatments *aromatherapy, ear-piercing, electrolysis, eye-lashes, facials, make-up, manicure, massage, neck treatment, pedicure, Slendertone and waxing.*

Women's Beauty Salon

Steiner
25A Lowndes Street, SW1 (071 235 3154).
Knightsbridge or Sloane Square underground. **Open**
9.30am-8pm Mon-Fri. **Credit** A, AmEx, DC, £TC, V.
Each of the Steiner's four rooms are completely private
and luxurious, albeit lacking natural light. The service is
impeccable. Therapists are both polite and attentive, and
top practitioner Arsho Grimwood is completely dedicated to her art. Records are kept of your skin type for reference on subsequent visits.
Treatments *Bio-peel, electrolysis, eye-care, facials, make-up,*
manicure, pedicure and waxing.

Luggage Repairs

Barnards
10 Old Brompton Road, SW7 (071 584 4084). South
Kensington underground. **Open** 8.30am-6.30pm Mon-
Sat. **Credit** A, AmEx, DC, JCB, £TC, V.
Mr Justin and his staff undertake repairs on backpacks,
holdalls, trunks and handbags as well as suitcases.
Delivery. Embossing.

Leather Guild
111 Kingsway, WC2 (071 831 8718). Holborn
underground. **Open** 9am-5.30pm Mon-Fri. **Credit** A,
AmEx, DC, £STC, V.
Be prepared to wait up to one month for the work to be
completed, as this is one of the only firms that specialises in the repair of leather goods. The staff will replace
zips and locks as well as relining or restitching goods in
disrepair. They also undertake quality shoe repairs,
which take under a week.

Mayfair Trunks
3 Shepherd Street, W1 (071 499 2620). Green Park
underground. **Open** 9.30am-5.30pm Mon-Fri. **Credit**
A, AmEx, DC, £TC, V.
Mayfair Trunks supplies luggage to members of the Royal
Family (and there's been plenty of bag-packing in that
household recently). It also repairs damaged bags and
cases. Prices are steep, but may be worth it if you want a
good-quality suitcase or bag mended. Phone for a quote.

Packing & Removals

The Packing Shop
Unit L, London Stone Business Estate, Broughton Street,
SW8 (071 498 3255). Battersea Park BR/137 bus. **Open**
9am-6pm Mon-Fri. **Credit** A, AmEx, DC, £STC, V.
The Packing Shop offers a unique service. It specialises
in the custom-packing and delivery of small and fragile
goods, though staff are more than capable of organising
the delivery of larger objects too. Same-day delivery is
possible in Britain; deliveries to Europe and North
America could take as little as 48 hours.
Brochure. Export scheme.

L J Roberton
Marlborough House, Cook's Road, E15 (081 519 2020).
Stratford underground/BR. **Open** 9am-5pm Mon-Fri.
No credit cards.
Specialising in overseas removals and the packing and
transporting of antiques, Roberton also undertakes
removals in this country. Free estimates and storage
facilities are available.

SBS Freight Agencies
Unit 2, Staples Corner Business Park, 1000 North
Circular Road, NW2 (081 208 1677/081 554 8333).
Brent Cross underground. **Open** 8.30am-8pm Mon-Fri;
8.30am-noon Sat; 10am-2pm Sun. **Credit** A, AmEx, DC,
£TC, V (also currency of destination country).
The minimum shipment that SBS will pack and ship to
anywhere in the world is a suitcase. There's substantial
storage facilities in NW2, and effects will be collected from
London postal districts (free of charge), and also from any-
where in the UK (on a sliding scale of charges). Cars can
be shipped with insurance arranged. Free estimates.
AIR member.

Photographic & Video Services

For a 24-hour photo-processing service, *see*
chapter **Early Hours**.

Camera & Video Repair & Hire

Keith Johnson & Pelling
93 Drummond Street, NW1 (071 380 1144). Euston
underground/BR. **Open** 9am-5.30pm Mon-Fri. **Credit**
A, AmEx, DC, £TC, V.
You can hire anything from a Polaroid to an SLR system
here. If you decide to buy a new camera within 28 days
of having hired a similar model, the company will give a
50% refund on the hire charge. Technicians undertake
repair jobs on the premises.

Leeds Film and Hire
20-22 Brunswick Centre, WC1 (071 833 1661). Russell
Square underground. **Open** 9am-5pm Mon-Fri. **Credit**
A, DC, £TC, V.
Hire charges at Leeds are slightly cheaper than elsewhere, although the stock available is less extensive. The
knowledgeable and friendly staff attempt to undertake
all camera repairs in-house. All repairs carry a three-
month guarantee.

Passport Photos

You'll find fast passport photo booths in many
train stations, airports, department stores, and
some of the larger branches of Boots The
Chemist.

Passport Photo Service
449 Oxford Street, W1 (071 629 8540). Bond Street
underground. **Open** 9am-6pm Mon-Fri; 9am-2pm Sat.
No credit cards.
This family business has been established in Oxford
Street for over 40 years. There's a ten-minute wait and a
£5.50 charge for three passport-sized photographs, £7.50
for six, or if you're really doing the rounds, £18.50 for 50.
It's not at all like an instant photo-booth; there's a proper photographer, negatives and high-quality printing. Old
photographs can also be copied or you can have them
enlarged. Appointments aren't necessary.

Rapid Photo Processing

Boots The Chemist
44 Piccadilly Circus, W1 (071 734 6126). Piccadilly
Circus underground. **Open** 8.30am-8pm Mon-Fri; 9am-
8pm Sat; noon-6pm Sun. **Credit** A, AmEx, £TC, V.
Most major branches of Boots (and they're all over
London) offer a one-hour turnaround on photos. A roll
of 36, printed 6" by 4" (15.2cm by 10.2cm) will cost £7.49.
A next-day service is £5.99. Next day 7" by 5" (17.8cm by
12.7cm) costs £7.49.

Galleries
& Museums

Few cities can compete with London's haul of world-class museums and renowned art galleries, but the city also holds scores of small, fascinating collections that together embrace the avant-garde and the ancient, the Old Masters and the modern.

Contents

Art Galleries

London's world-renowned galleries let you examine the expressionists, peek at Picassos (and square up to a cubist), or even ogle Old Masters. Others have a forte in photos.

The fact that all the publicly funded art galleries and museums are free (with the notable exception of special exhibitions) and that they run extensive free lecture and film programmes means that even the most impoverished visitors to London can get their fill of art and education.

The entire history of western art, with very few major exceptions, can be followed at the **National Gallery** (*listed under* **Collections**). While the **Tate Gallery** (*under* **Collections**) contains a curious and unmissable hybrid of historic British art (from Hogarth to Hockney and beyond), together with the nation's modern and contemporary collection (from the post-impressionists to the weirder end of current post-conceptual practice). And if this bemuses you, then go to the Tate's daily lunchtime lecture at 1pm in the galleries on Millbank.

The **Royal Academy of Arts** on Piccadilly has a major programme of international exhibitions throughout the year (but you do have to pay, and queue); while the **Whitechapel Gallery** in east London shows mainly twentieth-century art and has a particular bent for contemporary British painters like Michael Andrews and Lucian Freud. The **Serpentine Gallery** in Hyde Park is probably the most beautiful space in London in which to view mainly contemporary international art (*all under* **Public Galleries**).

The commercial galleries are of course free, although it can be pretty intimidating to push open those heavy glass doors and enter the sleek white interiors. The area around Cork Street is still the most densely populated gallery district in London, with the three sites owned by the **Waddington Gallery** at the core, showing work by painters like Patrick Heron and Sean Scully, as well as having a substantial holding of early twentieth-century masters, from Picasso and Matisse to Giacometti and Dubuffet – and all for sale if you dare to ask for the price list.

Hard-core seekers after the avant-garde should venture up to Dering Street and then Lisson Grove where the **Anthony d'Offay** and **Lisson Galleries** are to be found. Here, the best of the celebrated British sculpture can be seen. Richard Long, Tony Cragg, Richard Deacon, Anish Kapoor are represented by these two galleries, as are Joseph Beuys, Gilbert and George, Sol LeWitt, Anselm Kieffer, George Baselitz and even Jeff Koons.

It's well worth going out east, too. **Flowers East**, near London Fields, shows war artists Peter Howson and John Keane, among others, and when the recession all but obliterated the Cork Street scene, Angela Flowers expanded her operation, buying a large space on the other side of Richmond Road. The **Paton Gallery** has capitalised on the cheaper space available here, too, and moved into bigger premises for its showings of experimental art. And out to the west, around Portobello Road, galleries such as the **Todd** are good hunting grounds for smaller names that are set to get bigger.

Late June and early July is the time to catch the fine art degree shows at the London colleges: you'll find details in the press. Chelsea and the Slade are going strong, but the Royal College of Art's painting department seems to be suffering a lack of direction. Goldsmith's, in south-east London, is still the place to seek out tomorrow's art heroes today.

ART PUBLICATIONS

There is a plethora of writing to help you work out what's happening on the London art scene. All the daily and Sunday papers have their art critics, but some of them have been around a little too long. The most authoritative of the younger generation, Andrew Graham-Dixon, champions the avant-garde in the *Independent*, while you'll find the die-hard modernist Tim Hilton in its sister paper, the *Independent on Sunday*.

At the other end of the scale, Brian Sewell expounds his vehemently anti-avant-garde views in the daily *Evening Standard*, even going so far as to exhort sponsors to withdraw funding from the shows of which he disapproves (usually the more fascinating exhibitions). For a solid, respected and decidedly didactic stance, check out Richard Cork in *The Times*. He was conceptualism's greatest supporter in the 1970s, and now puts his energies into patiently explaining the avant-garde to his readers.

Read one of the very few women to be given a voice in the art world, Sarah Kent, in the *Time Out* weekly magazine, which also carries reviews of current exhibitions and up-to-date listings of what's on.

Other magazines include *Frieze* (£3.50, monthly) – hip and utterly wonderful to hold and behold. Its expansive brief means it happily embraces areas such as fashion, photography and film, alongside painting and sculpture. But it can be wilfully dense and self-conscious. *Tate* (£3), which was launched by the gallery in September 1993, and appears three times yearly, aims to be equally trendy, but with more nods to the mainstream and with a greater emphasis on accessibility.

If you fancy something more middle-brow look for *Modern Painters* (£4.50, quarterly), the glossy magazine made infamous by the contentiously reactionary views of its founder Peter Fuller, who died a couple of years ago. And for the best of the earnest brigade, buy *Art Monthly* (£2.25, monthly), for a safe and scholarly look at the art world.

Magazines are for sale in most gallery shops. But even better is Dillon's Art Bookshop at 8 Long Acre, WC2 (071 836 1359). It sells more art, photography, fashion and culture journals than you'll ever have the time to read.

Waddington's. See **review** page 188.

Collections

Courtauld Institute Gallery

Somerset House, Strand, WC2 (071 873 2526). Covent Garden underground. **Open** 10am-6pm Mon-Sat; 2-6pm Sun. **Admission** £2.50; £1 under-15s, OAPs. **Credit** A, £TC, V.

The Courtauld Collection is now housed in the Strand block of George III's Somerset House, allowing 80 per cent of its hoard to be hung. This is the largest collection of post-impressionist works in London. To get round the 32 Rubens paintings, Bellinis, Veroneses and impressionists, it's worth buying a guide, or booking a guided tour.

Dulwich Picture Gallery

College Road, SE21 (081 693 5254). North or West Dulwich BR; P4, 12, 37, 78, 176 bus. **Open** 10am-1pm, 2-5pm, Tue-Fri; 11am-5pm Sat; 2-5pm Sun. **Admission** £2; £1 under-15s, OAPs. **No credit cards**.

Having negotiated the South Circular and endless grey suburbs, you will find Dulwich a rare treat. The first national gallery to be built, by Sir John Soane in 1817, it is as famous for its architecture as for the important seventeenth- and eighteenth-century works it houses. The paintings are still densely hung, just as Victorian visitors would have seen them, with some impressive Gainsboroughs, Van Dycks and Rubens, and Rembrandt's *Girl leaning on a Window* among them.

Iveagh Bequest, Kenwood

Hampstead Lane, NW3 (081 348 1286). Hampstead underground/Golders Green underground then 210 bus. **Open** 1 April-30 Sept 10am-6pm daily; 1 Oct-31 Mar 10am-4pm daily. **Admission** free, donations gratefully received.

Approaching the First Earl of Mansfield's neoclassical home, with its proud Robert Adam façade, you feel like you're in deep countryside, not half an hour from central London. It's in the part of Hampstead Heath known as Kenwood, which is much loved by Londoners as a week-end retreat. During the week you'll just meet joggers and dog-walkers. The First Earl of Iveagh left the house and his collection of eighteenth-century paintings to the nation in 1927. Look out for Rembrandt's self portrait, a rare Vermeer in the dining room, and Gainsborough's *Mary Countess Howe*. There's also Wright of Derby's painting of children under candlelight. The English Heritage staff are knowledgeable and friendly, so do ask questions. *Audio cassettes £1. Wheelchair access to the ground floor and car parking. Facilities for the hard of hearing, educationally challenged. Foreign language guides. Group tours. Open-air summer concerts, indoor recitals (071 413 1443). School visits. Coach House restaurant, open noon-2.30pm daily. Old Kitchen restaurant open noon-2.30pm daily April-Sept; Sunday lunchtimes throughout the year.*

Leighton House Museum

12 Holland Park, W14 (071 602 3316). High Street Kensington underground/9, 93 bus. **Open** 11am-5.30pm Mon-Sat. **Admission** free but donations appreciated.

The painter Lord Leighton – a true nineteenth-century Renaissance man – realised his dream to build his own 'house beautiful' when he sold his classical painting, *Dante in Exile*, in 1864. Now it houses his strong collection of pre-Raphaelite and High Victorian work as well as paying homage to the East, which fascinated Leighton. The Arab Hall is startling. It's an Islamic tiled, wooden-latticed room, based on a Moorish palace in Palermo, that even had its own underfloor heating. The souvenir guide is beautifully illustrated and an enjoyable read. The audio cassettes are entertaining, but don't always work.

National Gallery

Trafalgar Square, WC2 (071 839 3321). Leicester Square or Piccadilly Circus underground/Charing Cross underground/BR. **Open** 10am-6pm Mon-Sat; 2-6pm Sun. **Admission** free. **Credit** A, AmEx, £STC, V.

Founded in 1824 with just 38 pictures, the National Collection now contains over 2,000 western European paintings from the thirteenth to the twentieth century, including works by all the major schools of art. The leather Chesterfield-style sofas, marble, and creaking wooden floors add to the old-world atmosphere. There is a guided tour for the daunted, which concentrates on the major paintings on the ground floor. Robert Venturi and Denise Scott Brown's Sainsbury Wing, opened in 1991, provides breathtaking exhibition space for the fine

collection of early Renaissance works. And don't miss the Micro Gallery, where at the touch of the screen you can see any painting in the collection.
Bookshop. Brasserie: lunch 11.45am-2.45pm Mon-Sat; tea 2-5pm daily. Café. Wheelchair access Orange Street/Sainsbury Wing. Films. Lectures. Guided tours. Micro Gallery open 10am-5.30pm Mon-Sat; 2-5.30pm Sun. Parent/baby room.

National Portrait Gallery
2 St Martin's Place, WC2 (071 306 0055). Leicester Square underground or Charing Cross underground/BR. **Open** *10am-5pm Mon-Fri; 10am-6pm Sat; 2-6pm Sun.* **Admission** *free.* **Credit** *A, AmEx, DC, £TC, V.*
The National Portrait Gallery is an entertaining social and cultural history lesson. Founded in 1856 to collect pictures of royal and political figures, it houses the only known portrait of William Shakespeare and a coronation picture of Elizabeth I, with uncharacteristically loose hair. Start on level 4 – the Medieval landing – and work chronologically down. The present generation of the royal family is on Level 2, with the well-known early eighties portrait of the Princess of Wales by Brian Organ. Early on a Saturday is the quietest time to visit. A new gallery of twentieth-century portraiture will open in November 1993, with a photography gallery and a new exhibition space.
Bookshop. Group visits by prior appointment. Lunchtime lectures. Talks. Videos.

Queen's Gallery
Buckingham Palace, Buckingham Palace Road, SW1 (071 930 4832/recorded information 071 799 2331). St James's Park underground. **Open** *10am-5pm Tue-Sat; 2-5pm Sun.* **Admission** *£2.50; £1.80 OAPs; £1.20 under-17s.*
The Queen heads a committee that decides which paintings to show from her vast collection. From March to December 1994, it's the turn of the Gainsboroughs. We don't yet know how the opening of Buckingham Palace will affect this gallery.

Saatchi Collection
98A Boundary Road, NW8 (071 624 8299). St John's Wood underground/159 bus. **Open** *noon-6pm Fri, Sat.* **Admission** *free.*
Adman Charles Saatchi is a powerful self-publicist, London's most influential mover of modern art, and nothing if not controversial. The debate about his role in shaping the contemporary art scene just keeps on going. His stunning 27,000-foot (8,230m) purpose-built gallery has been the location for some brilliant and emotion-arousing shows. Of the two a year, one tends to concentrate on fresh talent straight out of the art colleges – especially Goldsmith's. The names for 1993 were Sarah Lucas, Mark Wallinger, Rose Finn-Kelcey and Marc Quinn. See them rise. A visit to the gallery is a must.

Tate Gallery
Millbank, SW1 (071 821 1313). Pimlico underground/C10, 77A, 88 bus. **Open** *10am-5.50pm Mon-Sat; 2-5.50pm Sun.* **Admission** *free; special exhibitions £3; £1.50 OAPs, under-15s.*
The Tate Gallery is the museum of British art, as well as the holder of the national collection of international contemporary painting. It is a beautiful and restful gallery with large airy spaces and some wonderful work, including an especially good cubist collection. Unfortunately, limited space means that there are more paintings not on display here than in any other gallery. New Displays hopes to combat this, by placing paintings by artists such as Picasso, Matisse and Stubbs on temporary display alongside loans from other galleries. The Duveen sculpture galleries are excellent and now

contain Rodin's *The Kiss*. The Turner collection is housed in James Stirling's postmodern Clore Gallery, while The Turner Prize, awarded annually to a modern British artist, attracts some excellent entries (previous winners include Anish Kapoor and Richard Long) which are exhibited in November.

Wallace Collection
Hertford House, Manchester Square, W1 (071 935 0687). Bond Street underground. **Open** *10am-5pm Mon-Sat; 2-5pm Sun.* **Admission** *free.* **Credit** *A, £TC, V.*
Housed in the impressively restored Hertford House – with its rare Louis XV iron and bronze balustrade – the collection contains some superb eighteenth-century French paintings, with a few Boucher, and Fragonard's *Girl on a Swing* among them. The Old Masters are represented by Rembrandt, Titian and Poussin. A fascinating haven, just minutes walk from Oxford Street.
Library. Public lectures. Tours and study days (contact education officer).

Public Galleries

Barbican Art Gallery
Level 8, Barbican Centre, Silk Street, EC2 (071 638 4141 ext 306/recorded information 071 588 9023). Barbican underground or Moorgate underground/BR. **Open** *10am-6.45pm daily.* **Admission** *£4.50; £2.50 OAPs, under-15s.* **Credit** *A, AmEx, £TC, V.*
The Barbican art gallery can defeat the most determined of visitors even before they get to the art. It's impossible to find (follow the yellow painted arrows), and housed in a grim, concrete space with partitioned walls and corridor-shaped areas. The main gallery is on Level 8 and has two or three contemporary, historical or thematic shows a year staged by outside curators. The Concourse Gallery on Level 5 has temporary exhibitions organised by the Barbican itself.

Camden Arts Centre
Arkwright Road, corner of Finchley Road, NW3 (071 435 2643). Finchley Road underground. **Open** *noon-8pm Tue-Thur; noon-6pm Fri-Sun.* **Admission** *free.* **Credit** *A, V.*
The community arts centre for the borough of Camden has three great gallery spaces, which have hosted contemporary exhibitions by artists such as Julian Opie and Mark Rothko. School groups come in the morning and there are educational tours. Talks are given on Sundays at 3pm by artists, usually responding to the current exhibition.

Chisenhale Gallery
64-84 Chisenhale Road, E3 (081 981 4518). Bethnal Green or Mile End underground/D6, 8, 277 bus. **Open** *1-6pm Wed-Sun.* **Admission** *free.*
This is an enormous exhibition space from which great things emerge. Rachel Whiteread and Rose Finn-Kelcey were both commissioned first by the Chisenhale. Richard Deacon and Grenville Davey have been shown here. Whether it's British or international, painting, sculpture or installation, the emphasis is on contemporary, innovative work.

Crafts Council
44A Pentonville Road, N1 (071 278 7700). Angel underground. **Open** *11am-6pm Tue-Sat; 2-6pm Sun.* **Admission** *free.* **Credit** *(shop) A, AmEx, V.*
Now housed in an elegantly converted Georgian house in Islington, the Council's gallery showcases the nation's crafts output. The exhibitions have often been unconvincingly curated, but if you're lucky you'll catch something as good as 1992's Lucy Rie show.

Hayward Gallery

Belvedere Road, South Bank Centre, SE1 (071 928 3144/recorded information 071 261 0127). Waterloo underground/BR. **Open** 10am-6pm Mon, Thur-Sun; 10am-8pm Tue, Wed. **Admission** £5; £3.50 OAPs, under-18s. **Credit** A, V.

Part of the South Bank Centre, the Hayward is London's most important venue for temporary exhibitions of both contemporary and historical art. Its strength is the choice of excellent shows, which have recently included Magritte, the art of ancient Mexico, and the controversial sculpture show 'Gravity and Grace'. It gets very crowded at the beginning of a show's run; early on Sunday morning is a good time to visit. Shows to watch out for include Dali's early works (March-May 1994), and the German Romantic Movement (September 1994-January 1995).

ICA Gallery

The Mall, SW1 (071 930 3647/membership enquiries 071 930 0493/recorded information 071 930 6393). Piccadilly Circus underground or Charing Cross underground/BR. **Open** noon-8pm daily. **Admission** free with membership. **Membership** £18 per year; £9 per year OAPs; £1.50 per day. **Credit** A, AmEx, DC, £TC, V.

At its opening in 1948, Herbert Read hailed the Institute of Contemporary Arts as, 'Not another museum, another bleak exhibition gallery', and it has managed to maintain the reputation of being a challenging and avant-garde centre for all forms of artistic expression. The Upper Gallery is a superb airy space, in which installation, expressionist and abstract works are shown. The Concourse Gallery attracts more attention because of its position by the café. Many leading artists had their first London exhibitions at the ICA, including Moore, Picasso, Ernst, Helen Chadwick and Steven Brisley.
Bar. Bookshop. Café. Cinema. Group discount. Lectures. Workshops.

RIBA

66 Portland Place, W1 (071 580 5533). Oxford Circus underground. **Open** 9.30am-5.30pm Mon-Fri; 10am-1.30pm Sat. **Credit** A, V.

The Royal Institute of British Architects is housed in a monumental edifice built by Grey Wornham in 1934. The gallery exhibits the great and the good: Nicholas Grimshaw, Tadao Ando and Santiago Calatrava, to name a few.

Riverside Studios

Crisp Road, W6 (081 741 2251). Hammersmith underground. **Open** 1-8pm Tue-Sun. **Admission** free.
This Hammersmith arts centre concentrates on film and theatre, but also has 10 art shows a year in the gallery and foyer space. Sculpture, paintings, drawings and installations by young British unknowns and high-profile international artists are shown.

Royal Academy of Arts

Burlington House, Piccadilly W1 (071 439 7438). Green Park or Piccadilly underground. **Open** 10am-6pm daily. **Admission** £3-£5. **Credit** A, AmEx, £TC, V.

Britain's first art school (it opened in 1768), the Royal Academy of Arts also held the country's first annual open exhibitions of living artists. This persists as the Summer Exhibition (*see chapter* **London by Season**) where thousands of paintings, sculptures and architectural works are on view, and visitors number around 150,000 each year. Whatever the exhibition, the RA's reputation and history ensures huge crowds of weekend gallery wanderers, and long queues to get in. Early on Sunday morning is the quietest time at the weekend. Exhibitions for 1994 include Modigliani drawings, Goya, Belgian Post-Impressionists and, of course, the 226th Summer Exhibition. The RA's postgraduate school stages its Premium Show every January.

Serpentine Gallery

Kensington Gardens, Hyde Park, W2 (071 402 6075). Lancaster Gate or South Kensington underground. **Open** 10am-6pm daily. **Admission** free.
Sister gallery to the Hayward until 1987, the Serpentine has the same fresh innovative approach to the exhibitions it organises, and the same adoring London following. The gallery was formerly a tea pavilion and has a wonderfully relaxing Hyde Park location. There are some excellent art, photography, installation and video shows. Informal talks given by artists on Sunday afternoons are very lively.

Whitechapel Gallery

Whitechapel High Street, E1 (071 377 0107). Aldgate East underground. **Open** 11am-5pm Tue, Thur-Sun; 11am-8pm Wed. **Admission** free.
The Whitechapel is an innovative contemporary gallery in every sense – it is independent and puts on a good mix of exciting temporary shows. The gallery has a number of artists-in-residence who give lectures and run workshops for the local community. The annual Whitechapel Open is the only major show of East London artists.

Commercial Galleries

Central: Cork Street

Cork Street is worth more than ten minutes sandwiched between the Royal Academy and a cream tea. The galleries remain wedded to established modern art, steering clear of the trend towards multi-media extravaganzas. A renewed artistic spirituality has been apparent in recent shows, along with a little less of the self-consciousness that marked the early nineties. Most of the galleries are closed in August.

Bernard Jacobson Gallery

14A Clifford Street, W1 (071 495 8575). Green Park or Piccadilly Circus underground. **Open** 10am-6pm Mon-Fri; 11am-5pm Sat. **No credit cards.**
Bernard Jacobson, a Cork Street veteran, celebrated his 25 years of residency in the area by declaring 1993 Landscape Year – his way of encouraging modern abstract artists to look away from more sterile subjects and towards the landscape for inspiration. The gallery was formerly an old gaming club, and the ornate stucco ceiling contrasts with the abstract sculptures of Ivor Abrahams and Glen Williams, and the paintings of Sutherland and Spencer.

Marlborough Fine Art

6 Albermarle Street, W1 (071 629 5161). Green Park underground. **Open** 10am-5.30pm Mon-Fri; 10am-12.30pm Sat. **No credit cards.**
This gallery concentrates on contemporary British figurative works, but has also had some strong abstract shows. The annual summer show is generally considered to be worth a look; in the past it has featured Lucian Freud, David Hockney and Francis Bacon. About six shows a year are held in this long, cool space, while the print room shows the Marlborough's own artists including Frank Auerbach, Christopher Bramham and Lynn Chadwick.

Raab Gallery

9 Cork Street, W1 (071 734 6444). Green Park underground. **Open** 10am-6pm Mon-Fri; 10am-4pm Sat. **Credit** A, AmEx, V.
Lively and colourful international figurative works on

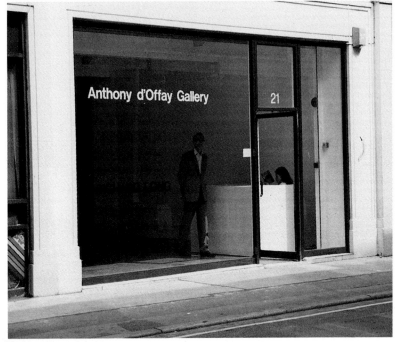

Anthony d'Offay *has a stable of star artists. See* **review**.

large canvasses are the Raab's speciality. Its impressive European stable includes Luciano Castelli and Pierre et Gilles. The principal Cork Street gallery concentrates on well-established artists such as Rainer Fetting, while its newer space near the Tate shows younger British talent.
Branch: 6 Vauxhall Bridge Road, SW1 (071 828 2588).

Salama-Caro
5-6 Cork Street, W1 (071 734 9179). Green Park or Piccadilly Circus underground. **Open** 10am-6pm Mon-Fri; 10am-1pm Sat. **Credit** (books and catalogues only) A, AmEx, V.
Salama-Caro has a healthy representation of American and British conceptual artists and stages some excellent single and mixed shows. In spring 1993, the 'Irony and Ecstasy' mixed American show breathed new life into the contemporary art scene, and a similar British contemporary mixed show is planned. It's a great space, too; don't forget to look downstairs.

Victoria Miro
5-6 Cork Street, W1 (071 734 5082). **Open** 10am-5.30pm Mon-Fri; 11am-1pm Sat. **No credit cards**.
Victoria Miro's versatile space does justice to the excellent international minimalist abstraction she shows. Artists such as Peter Doig, Thomas Bernstein, Alan Charlton and Yoko Terauchi have been exhibited.

Waddington's
5, 11, 12 & 34 Cork Street, W1 (071 437 8611). Green Park or Piccadilly Circus underground. **Open** 10am-

5.30pm Mon-Fri; 10am-1pm Sat (34 Cork Street closed in August). **No credit cards**.
The Waddington Galleries are a powerful force in modern art. The flagship space at number 12 shows the major stars – Picasso, Magritte, Miro, Hockney – and larger sculptural pieces. Number 34 puts on six or seven international shows a year, from the multi-media works of Michael Craig-Martin to Ian Davenport's abstract paintings. And number 11 holds solo shows, often of British artists.

Central: Dering Street

Annely Juda Fine Art
23 Dering Street, W1 (071 629 7578). Bond Street underground. **Open** 10am-6pm Mon-Fri; 10am-1pm Sat. **No credit cards**.
This gallery has great natural light from its glass roof. It has about ten shows a year – mainly non-representational work, with a number of contemporary sculpture shows. Anthony Caro, Michael Kenny, Alan Reynolds and Eduardo Chillida are all represented here.

Anthony d'Offay
9, 21 & 23 Dering Street, W1 (071 499 4100). Bond Street underground. **Open** 10am-5.30pm Mon-Fri; 10am-1pm Sat. **Credit** (books.and catalogues only) A, AmEx, V.
Since opening in 1980 with Joseph Beuys and Gilbert & George, d'Offay has forged ahead with strong shows of international star-status artists. If Jeff Koons, Andy Warhol, Mark Rothko or Jackson Pollock are on show in London, then it'll be here. Because of London's dimin-

ishing importance, however, d'Offay is now showing more and more of his stable abroad. The most bewitching space of the three is 23 Dering Street, where international contemporary work is shown. Plans for expansion mean that a new space should open in 1994.

Anthony Reynolds Gallery
5 Dering Street, W1 (071 499 4100). Bond Street underground. **Open** 10am-5.30pm Mon-Fri; 10am-1pm Sat. **Credit** A, AmEx, V.
Anthony Reynolds has been showing since 1967 but this space opened in 1985. It shows a variety of British and international works from the figurative to the abstract, and from 26- to 70-year-old artists.

Fine Art Society
148 New Bond Street, W1 (071 629 5116). Bond Street underground. **Open** 9am-5.30pm Mon-Fri; 11am-4pm Sat. **Credit** A, V.
The Fine Art Society feels like yet another anachronism on a street that's littered with them. The furniture around the art is a mixture of twenties, thirties and forties pieces. The art itself, concentrating on British nineteenth- and twentieth-century, is pretty hit and miss, but every now and again something really noteworthy such as its John Downton exhibition, comes along.

Gimpel Fils
30 Davies Street, W1 (071 493 2488). Bond Street underground. **Open** 9.30am-5.30pm Mon-Fri; 10am-1pm Sat. **No credit cards.**
Gimpel Fils are out there on their own, enjoying the flamboyant and sticking to their origins by representing Europeans based in London. They have shown the watercolour works of Louis le Brocquy, Antoni Malinowski's luminous brushstrokes, and abstracts by Alan Davie and Albert Irvin. Three female American artists are also supported by them: Pamela Golden, Susan Hiller and Andrea Fisher. The gallery space can show off large canvases to full effect, and generally does.

Central: Other Galleries

Austin/Desmond Fine Art
Pied Bull Yard, 15A Bloomsbury Square, WC1 (071 242 4443). Holborn underground. **Open** 10am-5.30pm Mon-Fri. **No credit cards.**
John Desmond and John Austin specialise in modern British painting, and carry a wide selection of contemporary prints which are mostly abstract, although some are traditional.

Le Chat Noir
63 Neal Street, WC2 (071 379 0876). Covent Garden underground. **Open** 4.30-8pm Mon-Fri; 11am-6pm Sat; or by appointment. **No credit cards.**
This is a tiny Covent Garden basement space that only opened in 1991, but has already attracted a great deal of attention. It shows predominantly British work, such as Felicity Shillingford's quirky constructions on birth and motherhood. Owners Matthew Breslin and Nicole Tinero are intent on a serious approach to art; it looks like their gallery is here to stay.
No wheelchair access.

Frith Street
60 Frith Street, W1 (071 494 1550). Tottenham Court underground. **Open** 10am-6pm Tue-Fri; 11am-4pm Sat. **No credit cards.**
Six shows a year are held in this beautiful wooden-panelled interior, and the gallery has built up a stable of very bankable artists including Callum Innes, Craigie Horsfield, Tim Head and newcomer Katrine Herian.

Karsten Schubert
41, 42 Foley Street, W1 (071 631 0031). Goodge Street underground. **Open** 10am-5.30pm Tue-Fri; 11am-5pm Sat. **No credit cards.**
A visit here is essential if you want to keep up with the latest developments. Artists shown include Michael Landy, Bridget Riley, and Rachel Whiteread.

Burger-off: one of the flamboyant collection of sculptures at **Gimpel Fils**. *See* **review**.

Laure Genillard Gallery

38A Foley Street, W1 (071 436 2300). Goodge Street underground. **Open** 11am-6pm Tue-Fri; 11am-3pm Sat. **No credit cards.**
The small space is unsatisfactory, but there are some good British and American abstracts shown here, with an emphasis on installations.

New Arts Centre

41 Sloane Street, SW1 (071 235 5844). Knightsbridge underground. **Open** 9.30am-6pm Mon-Fri; 11am-3pm Sat. **No credit cards.**
This gallery specialises in twentieth-century British contemporary art and sculpture. Famous names such as Henry Moore, Barbara Hepworth, Kenneth Armitage and William Turnbull are shown alongside younger artists – Tim Harrisson, Tim Hadfield and Paul Roberts-Holmes. New sculptors are often first shown in the sculpture garden in Wiltshire.

Rebecca Hossack

35 Windmill Street, W1 (071 409 3599). Tottenham Court Road underground. **Open** 10am-6pm Mon-Sat. **No credit cards.**
Rebecca Hossack has a roster of interesting young artists, including Tim Allen, Rebecca Salter and Chris Drury. She shows work as varied as jeweller Simon Costin's exquisite featherworks and the African Bushmen. Expect to see more African art here in 1994, as well as British work, and visit the city's first central sculpture garden next to St James's Piccadilly.

West

Anderson O'Day

255 Portobello Road, W11 (071 221 7592). Ladbroke Grove underground/7, 15, 23, 52 or 52A bus. **Open** 10am-5.30pm Thur-Sat; then by appointment. **No credit cards.**
Started seven years ago by Anderson O'Day print publishers, this is a good place to see contemporary art and sculpture. Don't be put off if the gallery looks closed, for reasons of security the door is often locked.

England & Co

14 Needham Road, W11 (071 221 0417). Bayswater or Notting Hill Gate underground. **Open** 11am-6pm Tue-Sat. **Credit** A, AmEx, V.
Jane England, an art historian by profession, has a small, friendly gallery with no schmaltz, and a following dedicated to her historic re-appraisals of artists like Ralph Rumney and Paule Vézelay. She was involved in the Barbican's controversial show 'The Sixties Art Scene in London', setting a parallel show in her gallery. Her annual international 'Art in Boxes' show is very popular. Nip over the road to the larger space in Pentagram's reception.

London Print Workshop

421 Harrow Road, opposite Bravington Road, W10 (081 969 3247). Westbourne Park underground/18, 31, 36 bus. **Open** 2-6pm Mon; 10.30am-9pm Tue; 10.30am-6pm Wed-Fri; 1-5pm Sat. **No credit cards.**
The workshop has six exhibitions a year, and offers open access to artists. The shows are wide and varied, and often affiliated to other galleries such as Flowers East. Recently Ken Kiss and Harvey Daniels have been among the artists shown here.

Todd Gallery

1-5 Needham Road, W11 (071 792 1404). Bayswater or Notting Hill Gate underground. **Open** 11am-6pm Tue-Fri; 11am-4pm Sat. **No credit cards.**
Jenny Todd defected from Portobello Road in 1991 to take over this fabulous 1,000-foot (305m) purpose-built space, which can take even the enlarged sculptural forms of Gerard Williams. She shows work by young British abstract painters such as David Leapman, Rosa Lee and Maria Lalic.

Minimalism reaches new heights at **Frith Street.** *See* **review** *page 189.*

South West

Anna-Mei Chadwick
*64 New King's Road, SW6 (071 736 1928). Parsons
Green underground.* **Open** 10am-6pm Mon-Fri; 10am-
5.30pm Sat. **Credit** A, V.
Anna-Mei Chadwick opened her gallery in 1986, to offer
'affordable' art (£1,000-£3,000) to those who want an original painting by a living artist. She packs in 17 exhibitions
a year, mostly of figurative works, with lesser known
artists often having their first solo show with her.

North

Lisson Gallery
*67 Lisson Street, NW1 (071 724 2739). Edgware Road
underground.* **Open** 10am-6pm Mon-Fri; 10am-5pm
Sat. **Credit** A, AmEx, V.
It's in an off-beat location, but this C-shaped gallery plus
its recent, seriously minimalist extension, is well-worth a
visit. The Lisson offers space to the young and established, and represents a number of sculptors of international repute including Tony Cragg and Anish Kapoor. At
weekends it tends to be packed with chattering tourists.

East

Flowers East
*199-205 Richmond Road, E8 (081 985 3333). Bethnal
Green underground/6, 35, 55, 106, 253 bus.* **Open**
10am-6pm Tue-Sun. **Credit** A, V.
With three spaces – Flowers East, London Fields and
Silver Place – Flowers has plenty of room to show its 30-
strong stable. The art is mostly British and ranges from
the abstract to the figurative. Those represented here
include Peter Howson, John Keane and Patrick Hughes.
Branches: London Fields 282 Richmond Road, E8
(081 533 5554); **Silver Place** 5 Silver Place, W1 (071
287 8328).

Paton Gallery
*London Fields, 282 Richmond Road, E8 (081 986
3409). Bethnal Green underground/106, 253 bus.*
Open 11am-6pm Tue-Sat; noon-6pm Sun.
No credit cards.
The dynamic Graham Paton moved his gallery to larger
premises in London Fields in 1993. With double the
space, he hopes to expand beyond his core artists and
show some more experimental works.

Photography Galleries

The Association Gallery
*The Association of Photographers, 9-10 Domingo Street,
EC1 (071 608 1441). Barbican or Old Street
underground.* **Open** 9.30am-6pm Mon-Fri; noon-
4.30pm Sat. **Admission** free. **Credit** A, AmEx, V.
The two-floored gallery opened in 1986 to showcase work
commissioned for advertising and editorial purposes and
puts on an annual show of Association of Photographers'
award winners each February. In 1993, it included gold-
award recipient John Claridge's documentary of the last
US cowboys, and Nick Georghiou's manipulated images.

Camerawork
*121 Roman Road, E2 (081 980 6256). Bethnal Green
underground.* **Open** 1-6pm Tue-Sat.
Camerawork's brief is a worthy one: to show adventurous, challenging, issue-based work. The 1994 programme includes a group show of artists' responses to
regeneration in the urban environment (Jan-Mar), an

England & Co. *See* **review** page 190.

examination of the Eurocentric images of beauty propa-
gated by the media (July), and an installation investigat-
ing the identity of Asian Americans by Alann de Souza
and Yong Soon Min.

Hamilton's
*13 Carlos Place, W1 (071 499 9493). Bond Street or
Green Park underground.* **Open** 10am-6pm Mon-Fri;
11am-5pm Sat. **Admission** free. **Credit** A, AmEx,
£STC, V.
Rubbing shoulders with Mayfair's fine-art galleries,
Hamilton's has always had an exclusive international
clientele and exhibited high-profile photographers. It
shows photography as fine art; prints start at about £250
and go on upwards. Choose from over 3,000 prints by
names like Bailey, Irving Penn, Richard Avedon and
Helmut Newton. It's a great space and has excellent exhibitions, concentrating on more fashionable contemporary names, from Linda McCartney's sixties pop stars to
the controversial Joel-Peter Witkin.
Large print room. Wheelchair access.

Photofusion
*17A Electric Lane, SW9 (071 738 5774). Brixton
underground/BR.* **Open** 1.30-5.30pm Tue-Fri; noon-
4pm Sat. **Admission** free. **No credit cards.**
This is a revamped version of the former Photo Co-op,
which is now in larger Brixton premises. Aided by council and commercial grants, it has kept to its community
roots and concentrates on social documentary photography, showing some probing, often hitherto unseen
images of London's communities. At the same time, it
has widened its scope to show work by international photographers at the cutting edge of documentary photography, such as Wen Danqing's portrayal of workers in
rural China and Miro Svolik's playful abstract studies of
the body, based on old Czechoslovak fables and theatre.

While exclusive Mayfair has **Hamilton's** *(see* **review** *page 191), trendy Notting Hill is home to the* **Special Photographers' Company**. *See* **review**.

The gallery is a showcase, but Photofusion's real work is the debates, talks and educational events it runs, which have created a south London photography forum. *Courses, events, talks. Children's workshops. Darkroom and studio facilities by prior appointment. Monthly membership available. Picture library open 9.30am-5.30pm Mon-Fri. Wheelchair access, chair-lift entrance & toilets.*

Photographers' Gallery

5 Great Newport Street, WC2 (071 831 1772). Leicester Square or Covent Garden underground. **Open** *11am-7pm Tue-Sat.* **Admission** *free.* **Credit** *A, AmEx, DC, V.*
In 1971 the Photographers' Gallery, entirely devoted to photography, was the first of its kind to open in England. It has been promoting contemporary photography ever since, especially social documentary and reportage, and has been instrumental in encouraging national galleries to hold photographic shows. It has 24 shows a year, which have included Gordon Parks' photographic portrait of Black America, Danny Lyon the Civil Rights photographer, and British photographers such as Paul Reas and Martin Parr.
Café. Facilities for the deaf and elderly. Membership available. Print room. Reference library. Shop. Wheelchair access. Workshops, illustrated talks, discussions, teachers' evenings.

Special Photographers' Company

21 Kensington Park Road, W11 (071 221 3489). Notting Hill Gate or Ladbroke Grove underground. **Open** *10am-6pm Mon-Fri; 11am-5pm Sat.* **Admission** *free.* **Credit** *A, V.*
Opened in the eighties in the heart of trendy Notting

Hill, this gallery aimed to represent the work of serious photographers, while taking advantage of the growing market of wealthy thirtysomethings looking for entertaining and beautiful images to hang on the wall. It seems to have achieved this, by exhibiting a wide range of work from Joyce Tenneson to Clare Park and Herman Leonard's classic jazz images. Not limited by a specifically fine-art or documentary tradition, the gallery holds a large collection of prints from landscape to abstract, which start at £60, and a number of Spanish images, including startling work by the fashion photographer Javier Vallhonrat. Remember to look in the spacious downstairs gallery, too.
No wheelchair access downstairs. Print room, no appointment necessary.

Zelda Cheatle Gallery

8 Cecil Court, WC2 (071 836 0506). Leicester Square or Charing Cross underground/BR. **Open** *10am-6pm Tue-Sat; by arrangement Mon.* **Admission** *free.* **Credit** *A, AmEx, V.*
When Zelda Cheatle broke away from the Photographers' Gallery in 1989, she took with her a background in documentary work and a following of serious, especially US, collectors. Her small gallery shows some excellent British, American and European photography. Predominantly exhibiting portrait, documentary, landscape and abstract work, the gallery has featured Helen Levitt's images of New York in the forties, the familiar faces captured by *Observer* photographer Jane Bown and contemporary computer-based work by young practitioners. The print collection includes Calum Colvin, Annie Liebowitz, Robert Doisneau, vintage Czechoslovak and modern Mexican works.
No wheelchair access downstairs.

Museums

Gleaming gadgets and orating actors have replaced fusty cabinets and creaky curators at London's interactive museums.

Musty old corridors of dusty, glass-cased exhibits are thankfully a thing of the past in many of London's museums. Visitors are more often met with high-tech, interactive displays, like the fabulous Dinosaur and Ecology galleries in the **National History Museum**. These more accessible and informative galleries have been born out of a need to become more commercial. Until recently, sponsors were more interested in funding art galleries (Sainsbury's fabulous, high-profile extension of the National Gallery, for example), as these would get greater publicity and have a wider appeal. But museums are now actively marketing themselves, instead of waiting in vain for Arts Council grants. Some have successfully encouraged commercial giants such as Hanson and Hotung to plough mega-bucks into refurbishment projects.

This wave of commercialism also means that museums are desperately trying to appeal not just to educational parties and specialists, but to the general public. Being all things to all people has worked for the **British Museum** and the **Imperial War Museum** because they both cover large chunks of fascinating social and political history. The smaller galleries, like the **National Army Museum**, have yet to realise that technical specialist jargon and cases full of cluttered regalia do little to woo the public. The **Victoria & Albert Museum**, despite its new Chinese, Japanese and Korean galleries, still seems very inaccessible to the inexperienced gallery-goer.

But there are many critics of the new slick image that museums have had to adopt. Huge information desks, piled high with guides to cutting corners and 'doing' the museum in the minimum time, have taken over beautiful old foyers, and a museum trip has become as undemanding as an airport check-in – you just need to know where to go. It has been argued that this does not encourage creative educational exploration. Should it be that increasing the number of visitors is the only goal? The **Horniman Museum** and the **Geffrye Museum** – small, community-based museums – are very informative and still accessible and lively, as well as being excellent places for small children.

It is really up to individual visitors to see as much as they want. London offers an abundance of exhibits from all over the world: relics, booty and imperial treasures from ancient times through to the twentieth century; so, despite growing commercialism, there's still a wealth of history and knowledge to be enjoyed.

Major Museums

The British Museum

Great Russell Street, WC1 (071 636 1555/recorded information 071 580 1788). Holborn, Russell Square or Tottenham Court Road underground. **Open** 10am-5pm Mon-Sat; 2.30-6pm Sun; 6-9pm first Tue every month except Jan. **Admission** free but donations welcome. **Exhibitions** £3; £2 children, OAPs, students, UB40s. **Credit** (shop only) A, AmEx, DC, £$TC, US currency, V.

This is the largest museum in Britain, containing thousands of examples of every aspect of international cultural history from the pre-historic Egyptian Rosetta Stone through to modern British coins and contemporary Oriental vases. Two and a half miles (4km) of 94 galleries are set in a neo-classical building, designed in the style of an Ionic temple in Asia Minor. The King's Library, built in 1826 to house George III's 56,000 books, now contains a copy of virtually every Western book from the original Magna Carta manuscripts to Beatles scores. When the museum is packed, it can be like pushing through King's Cross station in the rush hour, so it's worth going on the 90-minute Highlights Tour (£6). An expert guide will take you on a colourful journey around the most famous treasures: the Ancient Assyrian human-headed bulls; the pop art Parthian sculptures; and the Lindow Man, preserved since medieval days. The newly refurbished Hotung Gallery of Oriental Antiquities (best approached from the Montague Place entrance) is not covered on the tour yet has some exquisite carvings and figures from China, Asia and India that are beautifully displayed. New galleries opening are pre-historic Egypt (December 1993); Renaissance (February 1994); Hellenic (1995) and Mesopotamia (1995/1996).

Bookshop. Buffet/restaurant (open 10.15am-4.30pm; lunch served 11.45am-2.45pm). Café (open 10.15am-4.30pm Mon-Sat; 2.30-5.30pm Sun). Parent and baby room. Reading room access only with educational pass. Schools and groups book in advance (071 323 8511/8854). Shop. Sketching: contact information desk (071 636 1555). Touch tours for the partially sighted. Tours, lectures, gallery talks, including free tours. Wheelchair access (information 071 637 7384).

Museum of London

150 London Wall, EC2 (071 600 3699). Barbican, St. Paul's underground or Moorgate underground/BR. **Open** 10am-6pm Tue-Sat, Bank Holidays; noon-6pm Sun. **Admission** £3; £1.50 OAPs, under-15s.

London from 400,000BC to 1993 is a pretty long slice of history to cover in an interesting and accessible way. But the Museum of London manages it, taking in archi-

Museums

Time Out London Guide **193**

tecture (including the building of Westminster Abbey, the Tower of London and St Paul's), politics and the development of various areas (such as Spitalfields from its silk-weaving roots onwards). Exhibits are clearly explained, and full of fascinating detail: in 1875 it took 10,000 women to make the required quantity of lace Valentine's Day cards; the 1870s equivalent of a package holiday was a hop-picking trip. It takes a good two hours to go round, but tickets last three months, which makes it very popular with Londoners. Children from five years upwards can visit; Saturday morning is a good time to avoid them.

Braille guide and taped commentary for the visually impaired. Films. Lectures (induction loop for the hard of hearing). Restaurant (10am-5pm Tue-Sat; noon-5pm Sun). Shop. Wheelchair access; toilets for people with disabilities. Workshops.

National Maritime Museum

Romney Road, SE10 (081 858 4422). Greenwich or Maze Hill BR/Island Gardens DLR then Greenwich foot tunnel/1, 177, 188 bus/boat to Greenwich Pier. **Open** *Mar-Oct* noon-6pm Mon-Sat; 2-6pm Sun. *Nov-Feb* 10am-5pm Mon-Sat; 2-5pm Sun. **Admission** passport to all sections £6.95; £4.95 disabled, OAPs, students, UB40s, under-16s; £13.95 family ticket; free under-7s. *Any one of National Maritime Museum, Queen's House, East Wing Exhibition or Old Royal Observatory* £3.50; £2.50

disabled, OAPs, students, UB40s, under-16s. **Credit** A, AmEx, £TC, V.

The museum is a famous landmark for both tourists and Londoners, partly because many people make a pilgrimage down-river to see the famous Meridian Line – Greenwich Mean Time – in the Old Royal Observatory up on the hill *see chapter* **Tudors & Stuarts**. However, the museum itself has a lot more to offer: the largest collection in the world of marine art, a plethora of ship models, the whole history of Britain and the sea, trade, navigation and war. The Twentieth Century Sea Power gallery's Gulf War and Falklands displays give the museum a more modern appeal, but it can still get quite tedious spending the recommended two hours looking at boat relics. However, 600,000 people find it worth a visit every year. Greenwich is an idyllic spot, and looks especially impressive when approached by river.

Educational department. Group discount. Library. Restaurant. Shop. Wheelchair access to ground floor only.

Natural History Museum

Cromwell Road, SW7 (071 938 9123/recorded information 042 692 7654). South Kensington underground. **Open** 10am-5.50pm Mon-Sat; 11am-5.50pm Sun. **Admission** £4; £2.30 OAPs, UB40s; £2 under-17s; £10.50 family (two adults and four children); season tickets available. Free after 4.30pm

The Victoria & Albert Museum

The airy elegance and lavish Edwardian splendour of the V&A – designed by Aston Webb in 1890 and opened in 1909 – create the perfect setting for the world's greatest collection of decorative art and design pieces. Together, the four million or more exhibits cover every conceivable aspect of the subject, and include early Korean bronze, a 200-metre (220-yard) plaster cast of Trajan's Column, Rodin sculptures, delicate eighteenth-century Chinese lacquer-ware, ancient and modern jewellery, and a new collection of architectural drawings. Staggeringly, nearly all these works are on view to the public, even the 500,000 prints in the largely unexplored Print Gallery.

The V&A's sheer size can be intimidating to the uninitiated, especially as the visitors' information is fairly unhelpful. There are free introductory tours to point out the main landmarks, but they tend to concentrate on works in the British sculpture, Medieval Treasury, and Plaster Casts galleries. Groups can be too large and guides get stuck on their own pet interests. Be your own guide, starting with the major galleries on the ground floor.

Not to be missed are the TT Tsui Gallery of Chinese Art, a fascinating display illuminating all facets of Chinese daily life and worship; and the adjacent Toshiba Gallery of Japanese Art which contains lethal but beautiful seven-

teenth-century swords, plus a few contemporary sculptured ceramics. The famed Dress Gallery starts with a seventeenth-century doublet and trunk hose, and ends (at the time of writing) with the Naomi Campbell-defying platform shoes from Vivienne Westwood's autumn/winter 1993 collection.

The new and much-publicised Frank Lloyd Wright Gallery houses the actual office that the American architect designed for Edgar J Kaufmann in the 1930s. The Raphael Cartoons gallery re-opened in December 1993, and the Ironworks gallery will do so in autumn 1994. One of the latest additions to the V&A is the Glass Gallery which opened in January 1994. The museum is at its busiest in the early afternoon and at weekends. The café is spacious and serves good, but expensive, food.

The Victoria & Albert Museum, *Cromwell Road, SW7 (071 938 8500/recorded information 071 938 8441). South Kensington underground.* **Open** noon-5.50pm Mon; 10am-5.50pm Tue-Sun. *Print Room* 10am-4.30pm Tue-Fri; 10am-1pm, 2-4.30pm, Sat. **Admission** free, donation requested: £2; 50p OAPs, students, UB40s, under-16s. **Credit** (shop only) A, AmEx, £TC, V.

Children's tours. Craft workshops. Education department. Language tours can be booked in advance. Library facilities. Short courses. Specialised gallery talks 2.30pm Mon-Sat. Study days. Restaurant (open noon-5pm Mon; 10am-5pm Tue-Sun). Sunday jazz brunch. Wheelchair access by prior arrangement.

ECOLOGY

THE
SIMPSON

ur hands...

he future of natural dive
e essential connections
flourish here on Earth.

weekdays; 5pm weekends, Bank Holidays. **Credit** (shop only) A, AmEx, £TC, V.

Waterstone's finest neo-gothic building stands in all its Victorian glory, the terracotta exterior still gleaming from its 1970s clean up. Early on weekday mornings is a good time to avoid the crowds. Every year 1.6 million visitors are lured in primarily by the new Dinosaur Gallery, the Blue Whale, and the Creepy-Crawlies Gallery. The curators have introduced new multi-media and visually stunning displays. In the Ecology Gallery you get to clamber through an epidermis and 'feel' the heat of an illuminated sun. The upstairs rooms are more traditional and the preserve of enthusiasts; Discovering Mammals, showing some of the biggest and rarest mammals in the world, is a good display. Back downstairs, scientists can be seen restoring an Ichthyosaurus in a 'goldfish bowl' laboratory.

Bookshop. Café and restaurant (open 10am-5pm Mon-Sat; 11am-5pm Sun). Discovery centre. Gallery shops. Group visits by prior appointment. Library facilities. Multilingual souvenir guides. School party. Wheelchair access.

Victoria & Albert Museum

See **Box** p195.

Armed Services

These museums appeal principally to army buffs and cater only for them, with jargon-filled, technical explanations of exhibits which can be quite unintelligible to the casual visitor. The **Imperial War Museum** is a notable exception, attracting fewer lone gentlemen than the others and a lot of families.

Imperial War Museum

Lambeth Road, SE1 (071 416 5000). Lambeth North underground, Elephant & Castle or Waterloo underground/BR. **Open** 10am-6pm daily. **Admission** £3.70; £2.75 OAPs, students, UB40s; £1.85 under-16s; free under-5s; £9.50 family (two adults, two children). **Credit** (shop only) A, V.

The Royal Bethlehem Hospital had, by Shakespeare's time, become known as Bedlam, a lunatic asylum and byword for confusion and uproar. These premises were built to house its inmates in 1815. It is perhaps appropriate that in 1920, following the most destructive (and some say the most insane) war in Britain's history, it was decided to house the national museum of twentieth-century war here. The collection includes colourful, well-illustrated displays that dwell as much on the human face of war as the mechanics. A lively and emotive approach to the subject has been taken. Visitors can experience the feeling of being in a country at war with the Blitz Experience (climb inside a dark shelter and listen to a dramatic air-raid happen around you), and 'ride' in an RAF plane with Operation Jericho. The Trench Experience is pretty frightening, and not for those with heart conditions. Voted Museum of the Year in 1990, it attracts enormous numbers of visitors. Late afternoon seems the quietest time to visit.

Films. Group discounts. Lectures. Library. Nursing mother facilities. Research facilities. Restaurant. Shop. Wheelchair access; toilets for people with disabilities.

Opposite: *the fine neo-gothic structure of the* **Natural History Museum** *houses an array of stunning displays, among them the Ecology Gallery. See* **review** *page 195.*

Guards' Museum

Wellington Barracks, Birdcage Walk, SW1 (071 414 3271). St James's Park underground. **Open** 10am-4pm daily. **Admission** £2; £1 ex-guardsmen, OAPs, students; under-16s; £4 family (two adults, three children). **No credit cards.**

The museum, which opened in 1988, celebrates the 300-year history of the five Guards regiments, including the Scots, Coldstream and Grenadier Guards. Pomp and circumstance come together daily at 11.30am with the Changing of the Guard, when the new guard marches from the Wellington Barracks to Buckingham Palace. The museum itself has an olde-worlde feel and is geared towards the ceremonial buff, with stirring pipe music, and cases of uniforms and pikes. Enthusiasts should go on curator Captain Horn's guided tour.

Group discount. Tour by prior arrangement. Toy soldier shop. Wheelchair access; toilets for people with disabilities.

Museum of Artillery

The Rotunda, Repository Road, SE18 (081 316 5402). Woolwich Dockyard BR. **Open** *Nov-Mar* noon-4pm Mon-Fri; 1-4pm Sat, Sun. *Apr-Oct* noon-5pm Mon-Fri; 1-5pm Sat, Sun. **Admission** free. **No credit cards.**

Thousands of arms, mostly field pieces, are here, from a Napoleonic war cannon to a 25-pound (11.4kg) SAS cannon used in the Yemen. The John Nash building, one of the first purpose-built museums ever, deserves as much attention as the contents. The museum was started in an old forge in the Arsenal in 1780 by Sir William Congreave (an old Captain), before moving to the present site in 1822. There are models all over the grounds of cannons and ammunition. Swords, photographs and regimental regalia are kept on the other side of Woolwich Common in the old military academy.

Shop. Wheelchair access.

National Army Museum

Royal Hospital Road, SW3, next to Royal Hospital (071 730 0717). Sloane Square underground/11, 19 or 239 bus. **Open** 10am-5.30pm daily. **Admission** free. **No credit cards.**

The Gulf War media coverage brought war live to our screens, radically changing public perception of the armed forces in action and encouraging more interest in modern military technology and strategies. Perhaps the most fascinating, if chilling, sight of this museum is the huge Russian D-30 Howitzer anti-aircraft gun that was captured from the Iraqis during the war and now stands outside. But the US desert-coloured arms carrier, also used in the war, is equally intriguing. These stark pieces of warfare 'memorabilia' were collected on a scavenging mission by museum staff only days after the Gulf War ended. Enthusiasts and specialists may find the explanations on the history of weapons, the army, and the uniforms of officers clear enough, but the general public may not.

Reading room (open Tue-Sat by appointment two weeks in advance). Reception and conference facilities. School talks arranged. Shop. Wheelchair access.

Royal Air Force Museum

Grahame Park Way, NW9 (081 205 2266/recorded information 081 205 9191). Colindale underground/Mill Hill Broadway BR (Thamesline)/32, 226, 292 bus. **Open** 10am-6pm daily. **Admission** £4.90; £2.45 OAPs, students, UB40s, under-15s; registered disabled free; £12 family (two adults, two children; £1.10 per additional child). **Credit** (shop only) A, £TC, V.

This is where flight first began, or at least where Claude Grahame White – the first man in flight – had his factory. The RAF was formed in 1917, and the museum covers the history of flight from White onwards. Aircraft

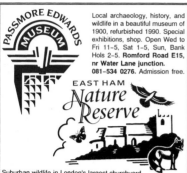

from World War I bombers to modern Harrier jets fill the original hangar. A guided tour of the (grounded) planes includes a look at Battle of Britain fighters. *See chapter* **The World Wars**.
Car park (free). Classroom. Educational films. Restaurant (10am-5pm daily). Shop. Tour by prior arrangement. Wheelchair access.

Art & Design

Design Museum
Butlers Wharf, Shad Thames, SE1 (071 407 6933/recorded information 071 407 6261). Tower Hill underground or London Bridge underground/BR/15, 78 bus. **Open** 10.30am-5.30pm daily. **Admission** £3.50; £2.50 children, OAPs, students, UB40s. **Credit** (shop only) A, V.
The white and glass modernist building on Butlers Wharf is the ideal venue for a collection of innovative design. Sir Terence Conran, who brought design into the British High Street, was the driving force behind the museum. Inside are spacious, airy galleries. The Review Gallery on the first floor showcases new international design – from a Jasper Morrison sofa to Rodney Kinsman's seating designed for the British Pavilion in Seville at Expo '92. The rather small section at the back is for temporary exhibitions. Upstairs, the Collection Gallery takes a historical look at cultural and technological influences on design and the development of mass-produced consumer objects. It won't take you long to get round, but it's worth coming here for the great river views and a quick overview of 1980s architecture in the surrounding streets. The Blueprint Café which shares the building, with its balcony overlooking the Thames, is a rare find (*see chapter* **Restaurants**).
Bar/café. Education programme for schools. Guided tours by prior arrangement. Research library (open 10.30am-1.30pm, 2.30-5.30pm, daily). Shop and mail order (to check availability telephone 071 403 4933). Wheelchair access.

Fan Museum
12 Crooms Hill, SE10 (081 305 1441/081 858 7879). Greenwich BR/boat to Greenwich Pier/1, 177, 180, 185, 188, 286 bus. **Open** *workshop* by appointment; *museum* 11am-4.30pm Tue-Sat; noon-4.30pm Sun. **Admission** £2.50; £1.50 OAPs, students, under-16s; free OAPs 2-4pm Tue. **Credit** A, V.
Mr and Mrs Alexander opened the Fan Museum two years ago in this Georgian town house that was donated to them. The only museum in the world dedicated to fans, it has a vast collection from the seventeenth century to the present day. Not all of them can be on display at once, however, and some are too fragile to be left out for long. The permanent exhibition on the ground floor has explanations of how fans are made and what the different types are, and there are three temporary exhibitions a year. Fan-making lessons are given by an expert conservator in the workshop on the first Saturday of every month.
Shop. Tour by prior arrangement. Wheelchair access; toilets for people with disabilities.

Geffrye Museum
Kingsland Road, E2 (071 739 9893/recorded information 071 739 8453). Old Street underground exit 2, then 243 bus/Liverpool Street underground, Bishopsgate exit, then 22B, 48, 67 or 149 bus. **Open** 10am-5pm Tue-Sat; 2-5pm Sun, Bank Holidays. **Admission** free, under-8s must be accompanied by an adult.
A dedicated band of staff have made this unique exhibition of English lived-in interiors – from Elizabethan oak panelling, to 1950s pre-fab – accessible to all.

The **Geffrye Museum**. *See* **review**.

People's Cars

view

Children are eager to follow the work-sheet trail; adults are fascinated by the detail given with each room. There is a lot to learn here, even for art historians, designers and architects, in keeping with the museum's original aim to educate the surrounding Spitalfields carpenters and craftsmen. Don't miss John Evelyn's splendid 1652 'curiosities chest' intricately carved in ebony, and the painful-looking Regency correction chair. The curators' Period Room talks are excellent – some keen visitors even listen twice. Ask, and you'll discover all sorts of things.

Coffee bar. Facilities for people with disabilities. Herb garden. School and group tours by prior appointment. Shop. Talks 2pm, 3.30pm Sat.

Percival David Foundation of Chinese Art

53 Gordon Square, WC1 (071 387 3909). Euston, Euston Square, Goodge Street or Russell Square underground. **Open** 10.30am-5pm Mon-Fri; closed Bank Holidays. **Admission** free, but donations welcome.
Children under 14 must be accompanied by an adult.

Sir Percival David's vast 17,000-piece Chinese ceramic collection is on display right in the middle of the academic buildings of the University of London, just as he wished when he donated it to the University in the late 1950s. The museum has a rather academic feel, with its glass cases which leave the impressive objects from the Song, Yuan, Ming and Qing dynasties to speak for themselves. Many of the ceramics provide an important historical record of the dynasties, as the inscriptions on them date the emperor and dynasty quite precisely. The most famous pieces are near the entrance: the 1351 blue and white David vases of Jingdezhen. The striking Ming bowls – in yellow and red copper glaze – have a familiar look to the modern eye, clearly demonstrating the strong Chinese influence on modern Western tableware. Only those studying Chinese porcelain will want to stay more than half an hour, but a quick visit is recommended.

Catalogues, slides, postcards all sold at the entrance. Group visits by prior arrangement. Library facilities available (£25 per week/£35 per year), with permission from the curator.

Botanical

Chelsea Physic Garden

66 Royal Hospital Road, SW3 (071 352 5646). Sloane Square underground/11, 19, 22, 239 bus. **Open** Apr-Oct 2-5pm Wed, Sun. **Admission** £2.50; £1.30 students, UB40s, under-16s. **No credit cards.**
Designed by the Society of Apothecaries in 1673, and developed by the famous physician Sir Hans Sloane with the aid of his undaunted gardener Philip Miller, these herb, plant, water and rock gardens were grown to study the therapeutic properties of plants for medicinal purposes. Today, it's still a vital centre for botanical research and education. The gardens are sheltered by high brick walls and the surrounding square of houses, making it warm enough for a Crimson Bengal to flower continually, a nineteenth-century Olive tree (Olea eurpaea) to fruit, peonies to bloom in spring, and eastern herbs to grow in the oldest rock garden in Europe.

Guided tours by appointment (£10 inclusive price, up to 25 people). Shop. Tea (3.15-4.45pm). Wheelchair access.

Opposite: *the* **Design Museum,** *a compendium of modern innovation. See* **review** *page 199.*

Museum of Garden History

St Mary-at-Lambeth, Lambeth Palace Road, SE1 (071 261 1891). Waterloo underground/BR/507, C10 bus. **Open** mid Mar-mid Dec 11am-3pm Mon-Fri; 10.30am-5pm Sun. **Admission** free; donations requested.
Credit A, £STC, V.
Sited inside St Mary-at-Lambeth church, this museum was founded in 1977 in commemoration of the Tradescant family – gardeners to Charles 1 – who are partly responsible for the great variety of trees and flowers found in Britain today. It gives the chance of a sedate look at the history of gardening and cultivation, and has space for special exhibitions. A replica of a seventeenth-century garden has been created in the tiny church courtyard, which is an attractive, secluded spot in which to sit and chat.

Café. Lectures. Shop. Tour by prior arrangement. Wheelchair access.

Childhood

Bethnal Green Museum of Childhood

Cambridge Heath Road, E2 (081 980 3204/recorded information 081 980 2415). Bethnal Green underground/BR/8, 8A, 106, 253 bus. **Open** 10am-5.50pm Mon-Thur, Sat; 2.30-5.50pm Sun. **Admission** free. **No credit cards.**
Itself a child of the V&A, this museum is housed in a nineteenth-century building in the East End and contains a mammoth number of dolls, doll's houses, trains, cars, children's clothes, books and puppets. According to the staff everything is worth seeing, but the sheer scale of looking at endless glass cases means that it's easier to stick to the doll's houses on the ground floor and the international doll collection on the first floor. The doll's houses in cabinets, originating in seventeenth-century Holland, and the new Japanese ceremonial dolls, must be seen.

Lectures by prior arrangement. Shop (open 10am-5.20pm Mon-Thur; 10.15am-1pm, 2-5.20pm, Sat; 2.30-5.20pm Sun). Wheelchair access by prior arrangement. Workshops (11am, 2pm Sat, phone for details).

London Toy and Model Museum

21 Craven Hill, W2 (recorded information 071 262 7905/940). Queensway underground or Paddington underground/BR/12, 15, 94 bus. **Open** 10am-4.30pm daily. **Admission** £3.50; £2.50 OAPs, students, UB40s; £2 under-16s; £6 family (two adults, two children); free under-fives. **Credit** £TC.
After a hefty admission charge, it's annoying having to pay extra to work nearly all the exhibits, from the 1960s penny machines to the model village, especially since they're not very interesting when at rest. The penny slot machines. Among the most popular attractions are the Bernard Hall doll's house, the 1920s Tootsie toys and Dinky cars, and the old teddy collection (including the famous Aloysius bear from the television adaptation of *Brideshead Revisited*. Outside, the puffing old toy steam train and children's carousel add to the fun on a sunny day. Enter the toilets at your own risk.

Activity room. Café. Garden. Group discount. Shop. Tour by prior arrangement. Videos. Worksheets. Workshop.

Pollock's Toy Museum

1 Scala Street, W1 (071 636 3452). Goodge Street underground/14, 24, 29, 73 bus. **Open** 10am-4.30pm Mon-Sat. **Admission** £2 adults; 75p under-18s; under-3s free. **Credit** (shop only) A, AmEx, V.
'If you love art, folly, or the bright eyes of children, speed to Pollock's,' said Robert Louis Stevenson. How right he was. Tucked away behind Goodge Street, the museum looks like the Gingerbread House, and you half expect a

THE·HORNIMAN·FREE·MVSEVM

FOLLOW
ME TO
SANTIAGO

MASKS

wizened white-haired toymaker to descend the steep stairs. Instead, there's Mrs Fawdy who collects Pollock's old toy theatres and puts on live model theatre shows. The oldest teddy bear, born in 1906, lives here, along with some colourful Mexican and Indian dolls. The excited voices of seven- to 12-year-olds show what a fine place this is.
Shop. Toy theatre (during school holidays).

Ethnography

Commonwealth Institute
Kensington High Street, W8 (071 603 4535). High Street Kensington, Holland Park or Earl's Court underground/9, 10, 27, 28, 31, 49 bus. **Open** 10am-5pm Mon-Sat; 11am-5pm Sun. **Admission** £4 adults; £2 under-14s. **No credit cards.**
It's housed in an uninspiring 1960s edifice, but never mind: the Institute is a mine of information. Each country of the Commonwealth organises and funds its own exhibition, presenting a fascinating subjective view of its own history, culture and traditions. The Indian exhibition is particularly diverse, charting the country's history from 2500BC to 1950, with a mud-walled hut you can peep into, a great map of India showing distances with European equivalents, and a marriage pavilion from Gujarat. There is also an extensive educational programme with workshops and lectures. National Commonwealth festivals are celebrated throughout the year, and there are some excellent temporary exhibitions. Hoards of school children visit in the morning. The shop sells everything from Oriental apricot chutney to hand-blown Maltese glass ducks.
Art gallery. Educational resource centre. Group visits/coach bookings by prior arrangement. Restaurant. Schools reception and dining room. Shop. Wheelchair access.

Horniman Museum
London Road, SE23 (081 699 1872; education dept ext 124/recorded information 081 699 2339). Forest Hill BR/176 bus. **Open** 10.30am-5.30pm Mon-Sat; 2-5.30pm Sun. **Admission** free. **Credit** A, V.
Frederick Horniman, an ardent nineteenth-century collector of ethnic artefacts and zoological specimens, amassed a diverse assortment of international treasures through his Quaker missionary and tea merchant contacts. He presented this art-nouveau style museum to the City of London for the 'instruction and enjoyment' of its people, and today it's still an active, thriving educational centre for the surrounding community and well worth a trip out of central London. Exhibits are still in traditional glass cases, but well-displayed with some fascinating information, including: how African masks are made; the history of Tibetan Buddhas; an explanation of Jainism. The Living Waters Aquarium, actively conserving London's remaining aquatic life, delights young children. In the new high-tech music room, you can touch, play and hear the sounds of Bolivian guitars, Sudanese bowl-lyres and more modern keyboards and guitars.
Café. Reference library (except Mondays). Shop. Wheelchair access; toilets for people with disabilities.

Museum of Mankind
6 Burlington Gardens, W1 (071 437 2224/recorded information 071 580 1788). Green Park, Oxford Circus or Piccadilly Circus underground. **Open** 10am-5pm

Mon-Sat; 2.30-6pm Sun. **Admission** free. **Credit** (shop only) A, AmEx, DC, £$TC, US currency, V.
Ethnography – the scientific description of races and cultures of mankind – is as vital a part of Western education as it was in 1970, when the Ethnography department at the British Museum became the Museum of Mankind. Sadly, due to a lack of space and funding, most of the 300,000 exhibits, including 600 pre-Columbian pieces, are deep in storage, and plans to return to the British Museum site have been delayed. Still, an enjoyable hour can be spent browsing through these rooms. Highlights include fine Tibetan trumpets, Native American carvings, and Torday's booty from the heart of the African Congo, first exhibited in 1910 and judged remarkably unprimitive. Look out for the dramatic magical 'Wishi' mask worn in Tetelu-Sungu, and the Kwilu skirts woven by the men. The restaurant is a surprisingly smart, expensive brasserie. The shop is well-stocked with ancient-Mexican and African anthropological guides.
Activity room. Bookshop. Café (open 10am-4.30pm Mon-Sat; 2.30-5pm Sun). No tours/guides. Sketching permits might be required. Wheelchair access.

Film

Museum of the Moving Image (MOMI)
South Bank, SE1 (box office 071 928 3232/recorded information 071 401 2636/administration 071 928 3535). Embankment underground or Waterloo underground/BR. **Open** 10am-6pm daily; last entry 5pm. **Admission** £5.50; £4.70 students; £4 children, OAPs, UB40s; £16 family ticket (two adults, four children). **Credit** A, V.
Watching moving images was popular entertainment long before the arrival of Hollywood. So MOMI looks back 3,000 years to when Oriental shadow plays were performed with intricate shadow puppets and the history of the moving image began. The museum takes you through early optical toys such as the revolving Praxinoscope, the first Wet Plate camera, a display of the Cinématographe that started in a Parisian café, and lots of other pre-history before moving on to the glitzy world of early Hollywood glamour. Actor guides are trained to provide colourful illustrations of the various exhibits, although it can be difficult to ask them questions with queues of children wanting their autographs. Quieter times to visit are either 10am or 4pm. No guide book is needed, just read the information boards. The recommended visiting time is two hours, but you could easily spend all day here (there's no re-entry), watching old news reel footage, the early developments of television drama and classic Eisenstein. Children love creating their own animation, appearing on television opposite Barry Norman or reading the news.
Audio cassettes for the visually impaired. Bookshop. Films shown in evenings. Foreign language guides. Regular exhibitions and events. Shop. Sign interpreted tours (contact Education dept). Wheelchair access and help points.

Historical Figures

Other residences that are open to the public include **Hogarth's House** and **Dr Johnson's House** (for both *see chapter* **Georgian London**), and **Dickens's House** (*see chapter* **Victorian Times**).

Baden-Powell Museum
Queen's Gate SW7 (071 584 7030). South Kensington or Gloucester Road underground/C1, 74, bus. **Open**

Opposite: *the **Horniman Museum** houses a fascinating collection of exhibits, from startling masks to stuffed mammals. See* **review**.

8am-8.30pm daily; closed for two weeks over Christmas. **Admission** free. **Credit** A, V.

Lord Baden-Powell started scouting in 1907 by taking 20 boys to Brownsea Island near Poole. Fifty years later, nine million boys and five million girls in 100 countries had sworn to be 'good citizens'. Quotes from Baden-Powell, pictures of jamborees worldwide, original Akela badges and 200 cigarette cases commemorating scouting provide a clear, colourful background to the movement's history. The joys of camping are widely promoted and altogether it's a very jolly place, with hundreds of green-shorted, yellow-badged, knobbly-kneed boys running around the exhibition.

Accommodation bookable in the hostel for any scout or guide worldwide (single £23.40; double £18.10). Restaurant. Shop. Wheelchair access.

Carlyle's House

24 Cheyne Row, SW3 (071 352 7087). Sloane Square underground. **Open** 11am-5pm Wed-Sun. **Admission** £2.30; £1.10 under-16s. **No credit cards.**

Unlike many of its National Trust counterparts, this Queen Anne house where essayist Thomas Carlyle came to live in 1834, is easily accessible to the public. Sit in his Victorian chairs, touch the piano where Chopin played, or take the sun in the walled garden. The warm and friendly informality of the volunteers and the live-in curator's colourful anecdotes make this a perfect way to while away a wet Sunday. The house has barely been altered since opening to the public in 1895. Mrs Carlyle's lily-of-the-valley curtains still hang in the back room.

Limited wheelchair access. Souvenirs.

Florence Nightingale Museum

St Thomas's Hospital, 2 Lambeth Palace Road, SE1 (071 620 0374). Westminster underground or Waterloo underground/BR/12, 53, 77, 109, 170, 171, 171A, 184, 196, 507, C1 bus. **Open** 10am-4pm Tue-Sun. **Admission** £2.50; £1.50 OAPs, students, UB40s, under-16s; £5 family (two adults, two under-16s). **Credit** A, AmEx, V.

The 'Lady of the Lamp' is famous for her heroism in the Crimean War, but this exhibition also shows her work at King's College Hospital. Look for the quaint black and white photograph of the nurses at lunch. A worthy attempt has been made to animate the museum, with a mock-up of an amputation scene. Present-day Nightingale nurses occasionally come to give talks.

Film. Group discount. Shop. Study and resource centre on application to curator.

Freud's House

20 Maresfield Gardens, NW3 (071 435 2002/5167). Finchley Road underground/Finchley Road and Frognal BR/2B, 13, 31, 46, 82, 113, C11 bus. **Open** noon-5pm Wed-Sun. **Admission** £2.50; £1.50 OAPs, students, UB40s; under-12s free. **Credit** A, AmEx, V.

Having escaped from the Nazis in 1938, Freud came to live in this ordinary suburban street in north London, where he recreated his lost Viennese home. The library piled with books, the collections of Greek, Egyptian and Japanese archaeological pieces and, of course, the famous couch are still here. Stop and listen to the crackling voice of Anna Freud, his daughter, recounting his last few years. The house has been maintained by the dedication of his loyal supporters.

Guided tours by prior arrangement. Lectures. Shop. Videos.

Keats's House

Wentworth Place, Keats Grove, NW3 (071 435 2062/recorded information 071 794 6829). Hampstead underground. **Open** Apr-Oct 10am-1pm, 2-6pm Mon-Fri; 10am-1pm, 2-5pm Sat; 2-5pm Sun. *Nov-Mar 1-5pm*

Mon-Fri; 10am-1pm, 2-5pm Sat; 2-5pm Sun. **Admission** *voluntary donations* £1.50; 75p children.

Keats, a leader of the Romantic Movement, wrote one of his most famous poems, *Ode to a Nightingale*, under a tree in the front garden of this house. It's not difficult to imagine; the building is situated in Hampstead just off the Heath. Charles Armitage Brown invited Keats to live with him after his brother Tom died, and Keats lived here until his premature death in Rome in 1821. The house has been restored and contains little of the original furniture, but many of Keats's letters, old copies of works by Chaucer and Shakespeare, and many mementos of Keats's love for his fiancée, Fanny Brawne, who lived next-door. There are some interesting 'ambrotypes', early 1850s photographs, of Fanny and her children. The museum tells you little about Keats or his work, and the few staff are rather aloof.

Audio cassettes. Poetry recitals, book in advance (071 794 6829). Wheelchair access severely limited.

William Morris Gallery

Lloyd Park, Forest Road, E17 (081 527 3782/081 527 5544 ext 4390). Blackhorse Road underground or Walthamstow Central underground/BR then 34, 97, 215, 257, 275 buses from Terminal C. **Open** 10am-1pm, 2-5pm, Tue-Sat; 10am-noon, 2-5pm, first Sun every month. **Admission** free.

This memorial gallery opened in 1950 in Water House, Morris's eighteenth-century childhood home. Morris was a leading nineteenth-century designer and craftsman, socialist and poet. His wallpapers and fabric prints have survived changing fashions and are still popular today. You might leave this museum feeling a bit dissatisfied by how little of his actual work is on display, although an extension to the ground floor is planned to allow more of his furniture, prints and wallpaper to be exhibited. Designs are also on display by his associates, Burne-Jones, Rossetti and Philip Webb, and followers such as Mackmurdo of Century Guild, who designed furniture based on his ideas.

Guided tours by arrangement. Lectures. Mail-order service. Reference library, by prior arrangement. Shop. Wheelchair access to ground floor only.

Livery Companies

Livery companies are descended from the guilds of artisans and merchants that were formed in medieval times in the City of London. Their role is now mainly social, with many administering charities. *See also* **By Area: The City.**

Clockmakers' Company Museum

The Clockroom, Guildhall Library, Aldermanbury, EC2 (071 606 3030 ext 1865). Bank, Mansion House, Moorgate or St Paul's underground. **Open** *museum* 9.30am-4.45pm Mon-Fri; *library* 9.30am-5pm Mon-Sat. **Admission** free. **No credit cards.**

The Clockmakers' Museum has some of the finest hand-designed watches from the seventeenth century onwards. The constant tick-tock of the long-case grandfather clocks provides a great background to the history of the craft. The company is still active today. The museum is unsupervised and the only information is contained within a slim pamphlet, so enthusiasts should book for curator Mr White's tour.

Library. Toilets for the disabled. Wheelchair access.

Freemasons' Hall

Great Queen Street, WC2 (071 831 9811). Covent Garden or Holborn underground. **Open** 10am-5pm

Mon-Fri; 10.30am-1pm Sat. **Admission** free. **No credit cards.**
The sixteenth-century traditions of the Stone Masons are still an important part of modern-day Masonic ritual. The Masons' headquarters, called the Grand Lodge, are in this dark grey art-deco building, which also acts as the central meeting place and advisory centre on Masonic procedure for the 8,500 Masonic 'lodges' (local centres) throughout the UK. The Library and Museum are the only parts on view, but the guided tour will take you to the Grand Temple, with its 12-foot (3.7m), 11.25-tonne doors, which swing open to reveal 123 feet (37.5m) of white marble and rare jade. Look for the case of eighteenth-century, hand-embroidered aprons (still part of the regalia worn today). Souvenirs are available at Letchworth's next door.
Guided tours. Wheelchair access.

Merchant Taylors Hall
30 Threadneedle Street, EC2 (071 588 7606). Bank or Monument underground. **Open** tours arranged by appointment only (contact three weeks in advance). **Admission** free.
The Merchant Taylors can trace its roots to 1327 when it began life as a religious and social guild for the Taylors and Linen Armourers (linen was worn under armour), controlling the measurement of cloth in the City of London. Now the guild concentrates on maintaining alms houses for the elderly and educational grants and scholarships. It has been in 'Thread needle' Street since 1347, and most of the library, court room and great kitchen has survived the Blitz and the Great Fire. The central point is the Cloisters Hall, rebuilt in the late 1940s, and used for livery dinners and conferences. Part of the organ housed here dates back to 1722. But all rooms have been beautifully restored; another highlight is the kitchen – three floors high and in use since 1425, with the original stone wall still visible.
Wheelchair access.

Religions & Societies

The Jewish Museum
Woburn House, Tavistock Square, WC1 (071 388 4525). Euston Square or Russell Square underground/Euston underground/BR. **Open** 10am-4pm Tue-Thur; 10am-12.45pm Fri, Sun; closed on Jewish festivals. **Admission** £1; 50p OAPs, students, UB40s; children free.
From spring 1994 moving to: *129 Albert Street, NW1. Camden Town underground.* **Open** 10am-5pm Mon-Thur, Sun. **Admission** £2; £1 OAPs, students, UB40s; children free.
Housed at present in this grim, granite building, the museum is moving to more spacious, airy premises which will do greater justice to its large collection of ceremonial art, Anglo-Jewish artefacts and eighteenth-century prints. Gems of the collection include silver-work by Oliveira, an eighteenth-century silversmith; and the lush red flannel Ark curtain, delicately embroidered. The eighteenth-century circumcision set, with its two knives, is eye-wateringly fascinating. For non-Jewish visitors the festivals are explained clearly.
Bookshop in old premises. Extended shop in Camden. Group visits by appointment. School workshops with audio-visuals.

Museum of Methodism and John Wesley's House
Wesley Chapel, 49 City Road, EC1 (071 253 2262). Old Street underground. **Open** 10am-4pm Mon-Sat; after 11am service Sun. **Admission** *museum and house* £3; £1.50 OAPs, students, UB40s; £8 family ticket; 10% reduc-

tion for groups over 20. Second visit free with ticket (same month).
John Wesley, a passionate apostle, founded the first Methodist church (the Wesley Chapel) in 1778, after he was thrown out of the Anglican Church for being 'over enthusiastic'. Methodist was the nickname given by the other students to his fervent Bible groups at Oxford University, and it stuck. Today Methodism has a following of 32 million in the USA, and three million in Asia. The museum layout is lively, clearly explaining Methodist history with audio-visual displays and the famous Wedgewood jugs and teapots. Go over to the house to see Wesley's travelling preacher gear, his warm-looking night cap, and even the last tree trunk he preached under. For a drink or snack it's best to go one stop on the Northern line to Angel and explore Islington.
Films. Groups must book in advance. Shop. Tours. Wheelchair access to museum only.

Museum of the Order of St John
St John's Gate, St John's Lane, EC1 (071 253 6644). Barbican or Farringdon underground. **Open** 10am-5pm Mon-Fri; 10am-4pm Sat. Grand Priory Church and other Gate House rooms open only on guided tours (11am, 2.30pm Tue, Fri, Sat). **Admission** free, donations appreciated.
The sixteenth-century gates of St John's (complete with flags flying) will come as a pleasing surprise after the surrounding, grimy EC1 streets. From 1140 until the Dissolution in 1540, the old mission of the medieval Knights of the Order of St John lived on this site. They cared for the poor and for visiting pilgrims, but periodically also galloped off in defence of Christendom against the Muslims. The highlights of the museum are undoubtedly the Flemish diptych, and the intricate model of Jerusalem's Holy Sepulchre, dating back to the seventeenth century and carved in Syrian wood, ivory, ebony and mother of pearl. The modern Order of St John founded the St John's Ambulance in 1877, and there are interesting displays connected with the service. The twelfth-century crypt of the building is also worth visiting.
Groups must book in advance. Reference library open by appointment. Shop. Wheelchair access.

Science

Science Museum
Exhibition Road, SW7 (071 938 8008/8080/recorded information 071 938 8123). South Kensington underground. **Open** 10am-6pm Mon-Sat; 11am-8pm Sun. **Admission** £4; £2.10 OAPs; £17 family (two adults, four children); season tickets available; free entry after 4.30pm. **Credit** (shop only) A, £TC, V, AmEx.
Children of the 1980s and 1990s, brought up on a diet of Super Nintendo and Game Boy, prefer some active participation when it comes to the educational process: something that the Science Museum understands. Flight Lab allows children to test the principles of flight for themselves – climbing into a cockpit to take the controls. A hot-air balloon rises up when heated with a blow torch. The Launch Pad, which looks like an over-run playground, shows how technology works: you can push bubbles through silicone oil or whizz round on a turntable. Staff are called 'Explainers'. Talks on flight, space and power are enthusiastic and lively. Buy the recently updated guide and avoid the less interesting galleries. Miss the school parties by visiting early morning.
Bookshop. Café (open 10am-5pm, lunch served noon-2.30pm, daily). Facilities for the visually impaired. Foreign language guides. Group discounts. Library. Tours, free for schools. Wheelchair access by prior arrangement.

Kew Bridge Steam Museum

Green Dragon Lane, Brentford, Middlesex (081 568 4757). Gunnersbury underground/Kew Bridge BR/27, 65, 237, 267 bus. **Open** 11am-5pm daily. **Admission** Mon-Fri £1.70; 90p OAPs, students, under-16s; £4.75 family (two adults, three children); *Sat, Sun, Bank Holidays* £2.50; £1.40 OAPs, students, under-16s; £7.25 family. **No credit cards.**

Volunteers work the steam engines, making the nineteenth-century pumping-station building hiss, and smell of oil and grease. To see all the engines in action would take 90 minutes, but you'll get to see one or two in operation during a shorter visit. The 1846 100-inch (2.54m) Cornish Beam engine – the Grand Junction Engine – is the most impressive. Climb up to its top for a bird's eye view.
Group discount. Guided tour by prior arrangement. Shop. Tour tapes included in admission fee. Wheelchair access is limited.

Vintage Wireless Museum

23 Rosendale Road, SE21 (081 670 3667). West Dulwich BR/2, 3 bus. **Open** by appointment only 11am-7.30pm Mon-Sat. **Admission** free (donation requested). **No credit cards.**

Gerry Wells is the keen organiser of the museum – a radio enthusiasts' paradise – which has the original crystal 1920s radios, the first ever television set, old telephones and original news footage. His love for the subject shines through on the two-and-a-half-hour tour, which takes in some of the thousands of pieces on display. Wells also runs a repair service to help pay for the museum. Give him a hand by making a donation.
Lectures. Restoration and repair service. Tea and biscuits on the hour. Wheelchair access.

Sport

MCC Museum

Marylebone Cricket Club, Lord's Ground, NW8 (071 289 1611). St John's Wood underground. **Open** tours (phone 071 266 3825 for availability) noon, 2pm daily; match days 10am, noon, 2pm. **Admission** guided tours £4.50; £3 OAPs, students, UB40s, under-16s. **Credit** (shop only) A, V.

Connoisseurs of cricket cannot possibly miss this museum. The noble game's origins are traced with the help of countless paintings, photos, old relics and battered bats. In 1936 a ball bowled here hit a sparrow, killing it instantly. The bird was stuffed, the ball kept, and the whole scene has been gorily recreated. The Ashes are also kept here. Any self-respecting Aussie or Pom will appreciate the importance of the little urn, the symbolic prize for which England and Australia have battled for over a century. (The ashes are, in fact, those of a bail from the second series of Tests held in 1882 between the two sides). The guided tour lasts 90 minutes and takes in other aspects of the grounds as well; there's a Real tennis court, where a cross between lawn tennis and squash is played. Then there's the Long Room, the holiest of cricketing shrines and strictly boys-only territory. Non-members (and no women can be members) are still banned from here on match-days. But if you're a cricket buff, the sense of occasion is enormous, treading the floor that Bradman, Richards, Botham and other hallowed icons crossed on their way to bat.

Opposite: *the* **Wimbledon Lawn Tennis Museum** *serves up the history of the sport and its ace stars. See* **review**.

Guided tour. Shop (open 10am-5pm Mon-Fri, match day weekends). Wheelchair access to ground floor only.

Rugby Football Union Museum

Gate 7, Rugby Football Union Stadium, Rugby Road, Twickenham (081 892 8161 ext 246/tours 081 892 5161). Twickenham BR or Hounslow East underground, then 281 bus. **Open** 9.30am-1pm, 2.15-5pm, Mon-Fri. **Admission** free; tours £1; 50p students, children, OAPs, UB40s. **Credit** (shop only) A, V.

Rugby is an activity, some say an assault, that's not easily represented by a static display. The museum makes a sorry attempt to capture the excitement and social history of the game. There is an abysmal clutter of nineteenth-century velvet caps, lethal 1830s boots, team colours and touch flags. The highlights are sets of black and white team photographs: all crossed arms and bland expressions. The tour, from the dressing rooms to the hallowed ground itself, is excellent. Combined tours with **Wimbledon Lawn Tennis Museum** (*see below*) are also run; book two- to three weeks in advance.
Tours (normally 10.30am-2.15pm Mon-Fri; book in advance). Shop (open 9am-5pm Mon-Fri).

Wimbledon Lawn Tennis Museum

Church Road, SW19 (081 946 6131). Southfields underground/39, 93, 200 bus. **Open** 10.30am-5pm Tue-Sat; 2-5pm Sun. *During Championships (spectators only)* 10.30am-7pm daily. **Admission** £2; £1 OAPs, under-16s. **Credit** (shop only) A, V.

Over 150 years of social and sporting history, dating from the invention of the lawn mower in the 1830s, is encapsulated in this newly re-designed, well-lit museum. More interesting than the rows of cases filled with rackets and balls, is a mock-up of an Edwardian tennis party, touch-button commentaries on past and present Wimbledon stars, and videos of past championships. It's packed with unusual information: yellow balls were first used in 1986; they are kept at 20°C and can reach a speed of 140mph (220kmh). For tennis groupies, the collection includes more personal memorabilia such as Pat Cash's headbands and Boris Becker's autograph.
Café (10am-5pm Tue-Sat). Library open by prior arrangement. Shop. Wheelchair access.

Theatre

The theatre museums have limited funds and are constantly threatened with further grants cuts. This means that adventurous schemes can simply evaporate. At the time of writing it's still unclear whether the ambitious Globe Theatre Centre project will be completed as planned by April 1994.

Shakespeare Museum

Beer Gardens, Bankside, London SE1 (071 928 6342). Mansion House underground or London Bridge underground/BR. **Open** 10am-5pm Mon-Sat; 2-5.30pm Sun. **Admission** £3; £2 OAPs, students, UB40s, under-16s. **No credit cards.**

Bankside – the Soho of the sixteenth century with its bear-baiting, brothels and bands of merry players – has once again become a hive of activity. Both the archaeological excavation of the 1587 Rose Theatre and the much-thwarted project to rebuild Shakespeare's Globe Theatre, have caused new interest in the area. It is hoped that the new International Shakespeare Globe Centre will open in April 1994. Regular daytime plays are due to take place in the open-air Globe Theatre. The Centre will also house the indoor Indigo Jones Theatre; a permanent exhibition of Elizabethan theatre; a restaurant; and the

Globe Education Centre. Until then, the small Globe Museum hardly does justice to the colourful history of Elizabethan drama with a remarkably bland and text-based exhibition and just a few theatrical costumes. The Theatre Gallery upstairs has a display on the archaeological remains of the Rose Theatre. The Museum Theatre below holds regular lunchtime and evening concerts and schools workshops.

Education programme: conferences, workshops, courses, lectures. Group visits, phone Globe education (071 602 0202). Shop. Wheelchair access.

Theatre Museum

1E Tavistock Street, WC2, entrance off Russell Street, (071 836 7891/071 836 2330/First Call credit card bookings 071 497 9977). Covent Garden underground. **Open** 11am-7pm Tue-Sun. **Admission** £3; £1.50 OAPs, students, UB40s. **Credit** A, £TC, V.

Sadly, in a capital boasting more than 200 theatres, most tourists think of English theatre as ranging from *Cats* to *Miss Saigon*. This National Museum of Performing Arts tries to correct the impression, with a vast historical display that covers all the arts: ballet, opera, theatre, circus, even rock and pop. It's a seemingly never-ending round of colourful well-lit cases. See a blow-by-blow audio-visual display of the National Theatre's *Wind in the Willows* production, as it progresses from page to stage. Staff at the Art of Stage Make-Up exhibition give free make-ups – obviously a great favourite with children. On the ground floor, in keeping with the museum's active rather than purely curatorial role, a Royal Opera House display aims to get some support for its million-pound modernisation scheme. *Celebrity interviews, phone box office for details. Play readings in the Painters' Gallery. Regular productions in the Studio theatre. Shop. Study days. Study room by appointment only. Wheelchair access. Workshops.*

Transport

London Transport Museum

39 Wellington Street, WC2 (071 379 6344). Covent Garden underground. **Open** 10am-6pm daily. **Admission** £3.95; £2.50 children, OAPs, students, UB40s; free for under-5s and registered disabled; £10 family (two adults and two children). **Credit** (shop only) A, V.

Most Londoners – subjected to London Transport's antiquated system on a daily basis – will be unexcited by the news that the LT Museum has received a £3.5 million facelift. Like its namesake, the museum (housed in what was a Victorian flower market) badly needed updating. The new layout is clearer, with more interactive videos. Actors add animation to the previously empty trains and buses. But the museum's fascination lies in its depiction of London's rapid nineteenth-century expansion, which led to the pioneering development of underground transport. Look out for temporary black and white photography exhibitions on the top floor. During weekends and holidays, the museum can get rather crowded.

Café. Foreign language guides. Guided tours weekends and school holidays. Information centre. School room. Shop. Wheelchair access; lifts and toilets for people with disabilities.

North Woolwich Old Station Museum

Pier Road, E16 (071 474 7244). North Woolwich BR/pedestrian tunnel/ferry from Woolwich BR. **Open** 10am-5pm Mon-Wed, Sat; 2-5pm Sun, Bank Holidays. **Admission** free. **No credit cards.**

This museum is dedicated to the Great Eastern Railway, which ran from the East End of London to Suffolk and Norfolk and back into Liverpool Street station. On the

first Sunday of every month there are steam engines working outside. Inside, trains, tickets, station signs and a 1920s ticket office are on display.

Lectures by prior arrangement. Shop. Wheelchair access.

Other Specialist Museums

Crystal Palace Museum

Anerley Hill, SE19 (081 676 0700). Crystal Palace BR/2B, 3, 63, 108B, 122, 137, 157, 227, 249 bus. **Open** 11am-5pm Sun, Bank Holidays. **Admission** free (donation requested). **Credit** A, AmEx, V.

Crystal Palace aimed to educate the public about architecture, history and science. The original 1851 Great Exhibition building moved from Hyde Park to this site in Sydenham, later to be named Crystal Palace. The museum is housed in one of the few original buildings left on site, the old engineering school, where Baird invented the television. It tells the history of the original Crystal Palace (burnt down in 1936) with a display of archive photographs. Its devoted staff don't manage to liven up the dull exhibits, but the 1850s models of prehistoric animals dotted around the gardens do, and are a reminder of just how quirky Crystal Palace was.

Tour by prior arrangement (£1; 50p children, OAPs, students, UB40s). Shop.

Musical Museum

368 High Street, Brentford, Middlesex (081 560 8108). Gunnersbury underground/Kew Bridge or Brentford Central BR/65, 237, 267 bus. **Open** *Apr-June, Sept-Oct* 2-5pm Sat, Sun; *July, Aug* 2-5pm Wed-Sun. **Admission** £2; £1.50 OAPs, under-16s. **No credit cards.**

Occupying a converted church, the museum concerns itself with musical devices of all types, shapes and sounds. On the 90-minute tour by dedicated guides, you can hear some of the most celebrated instruments, such as the Steinway Duo-Art grand piano or the Wurlitzer cinema organ. There's also a series of popular summer concerts.

Education service. Group discount. Guided tour/demonstration (2pm, 3.30pm; free). Sat evening concerts, phone for details. Shop. Wheelchair access.

National Postal Museum

King Edward Building, King Edward Street, EC1 (071 239 5420). Barbican or St Paul's underground. **Open** 9.30am-4.30pm Mon-Fri. **Admission** free. **No credit cards.**

The history of Britain's postal system appeals mostly to school parties, and the museum is well-equipped for them, with a film and a tour. The three floors of this Edward VII building cover everything from the history of uniforms and telegraph services, to stamps, seals, and delivery. It's worth pulling out the case on addresses, as some of the seventeenth-century seals and lettering are fascinating.

Shop. Tour by prior arrangement. Wheelchair access by prior arrangement.

Public Records Office Museum

Chancery Lane, WC2 (081 876 3444). Chancery Lane underground. **Open** 9.30am-5pm Mon-Fri. **Admission** free. **No credit cards.**

These national archives in the heart of the law courts contain a large collection of legal, governmental and Palatine (local authority and feudal) records, from the Norman Conquest to the present day. A tiny selection are on display, notably the Domesday Book (literally the Day of Judgement book), a record of the lands of England made in 1086, which has been painstakingly written by one scribe. But there's little else to keep you here long.

Shop.

Arts &
Entertainment

Nowhere else will you find the diversity, dynamism, and delectation that London's entertainment scene offers. We explore the spectrum, from sports to opera, covering venues both cramped and cavernous.

Contents

Media

From the gutter to the Sky, Britain's media will be beamed at you 24-hours a day. We separate the class from the crass.

When visiting this country, you'll probably hear the British assert that their television and radio are the best in the world. They have been told this by myriad visiting Europeans, Americans and Australasians and have begun to believe it. And it is probably true. Although game-shows, chat shows, sit-coms and soaps are in danger of swamping early-evening schedules, there are still plenty of excellent documentaries, imaginative arts programmes, provocative dramas, and in-depth news coverage to provide enough stimulation to counteract the stupefaction.

The British Broadcasting Corporation (BBC) is responsible for transmitting some of the best programmes (though there are worries about it plunging down-market). Funded by a TV licence fee, it is editorially independent and carries no advertising. The result is an expensive output of plays, documentaries and worldwide news on both radio and TV.

If you want to know what's happening back home, then consult *chapter* **Survival** for stockists of overseas newspapers and magazines.

Newspapers

If the British can be proud of their television output, they should surely be ashamed of their press. Over a third of the readers of national dailies buy papers controlled by one man, Rupert Murdoch. Expect to find these news-sheets giving extensive and unwarranted coverage to the latest News International takeover and Sky Sports scoops.

At the quality end of the market, the press keeps a loyal readership with the occasional good story, job advertisements and cartoons. Towards the gutter, there are the romps and frolics of clerics, mountainous mammary glands and more cartoons. The odd British sense of humour invades the papers on 1 April, 'April Fool's Day'; most print bizarre, semi-believable, but false stories. The sober *Guardian* is usually inspired, but tabloid journalism is so debased that you often can't guess which is the April Fool story.

Downmarket

Rupert Murdoch's **Sun** is the best-selling paper with over three and a half million readers. A tabloid of slavering right-wing politics, its SHOCK HORROR headlines are mostly about soap opera characters. It is rabidly anti-

Labour, anti-Europe and, surprisingly, anti-Royalty. More left-of-centre is the **Daily Mirror**, with just under three million readers. First Robert Maxwell, then David Montgomery, have seen off most writers with any integrity, but the *Mirror* is still the tabloid most likely to uncover the dirty-doings of miscreant ministers. The **Daily Star**, selling less than a million, was an attempt by the *Daily Express* Group to break into the sewers. Originally touted as an independent tabloid, it swiftly went the way of the rest. The **Daily Sport** is an offshoot of the **Sunday Sport**: a repository of breasts, balderdash and banner headlines.

Tabloids with Aspirations

Perhaps the nastiest of Britain's newspapers is the **Daily Mail**. In the 1930s, its proprietor helped to finance the British Union of Fascists. To the *Mail*, the poor are scroungers, shop-lifters should be hanged, and the rest of the world's ills can be blamed on unmarried mothers. It's all the worse for taking itself so seriously. The **Daily Express** also crusades against anything that doesn't fit its (Conservative) world view. **Today** was Britain's first colour daily. It has taken a very surprising lurch away from the right since being bought by Rupert Murdoch, of all people. The London **Evening Standard** is owned by Associated Newspapers (publishers of the *Mail*), but as it has the monopoly of London's evening newspaper market, it does manage to attract features by notable writers. Its news pages aren't above hiding behind bigoted, screaming headlines, though.

Quality Broadsheets

If you're from outside Britain and you've only heard of one of its newspapers, chances are it will be **The Times**. Which is a pity, as these days, it is by far the poorest of the 'quality' broadsheets. Since being taken over by Murdoch, the 'Thunderer' has become a whimperer, sometimes seeming to be little more than an advertising sheet for News International's other interests. During the summer of 1993 it embarked on a price-cutting war, aimed at reviving its flagging circulation. The **Guardian** remains the Bible of the Hampstead literary set, maintaining the softest of soft-left positions and taking itself rather seriously. Steve Bell's cartoons are a notable exception. The **Independent** proclaims that its name tells its politics, but often merely sits on the fence. It is known for its excellent (lack of) royal coverage. The leader pages can be pithy, but the best writing is found in its Saturday editions. The **Daily Telegraph** openly supports the Conservative Party. It was getting old with its million readers; as the crusty colonels died off, so the paper's circulation declined. This trend was reversed by its gung-ho Editor, Max 'Falklands Factor' Hastings. The paper has good coverage of British sports. The pink **Financial Times** (not owned by Murdoch) dominates the world of money. It also has remarkably good arts coverage.

Sunday Tabloids

The **News of the World** (just under five million readers), **People** and **Sunday Mirror** are even more outraged and outrageous than their weekday counterparts, obsessed with footballers and bimbos, or vicars and choirboys. The **Sunday Sport**, appropriately owned by a porn publisher, is for you if you really believe that Marilyn Monroe is alive and living with Elvis on the moon with a bust the size of Mars. But just try not smiling at its headlines.

Middle-brow Sunday Tabloids

The **Mail on Sunday** and the **Sunday Express** are more populist on the day of rest than during the week. The gossip columns are one of the main reasons they sell about two million each.

Quality Sunday Broadsheets

The quality Sundays aspire to serious investigative journalism and fairly good arts coverage. The **Sunday Times** has the thunderous impact of a falling tree and weighs almost as much. It runs some solid investigative journalism, but only on selective (Murdoch-friendly) topics. The **Observer** is leftish and has recently been taken over by the *Guardian*. It has some witty writers but continues to struggle. The **Sunday Telegraph** is not as physically weighty as the opposition, but the writing is ponderous. The financial pages are good for those with money; the arts pages are improving. The **Independent on Sunday**, launched in January 1990, has attracted some of the best writers from other papers. It's now probably the best of the Sunday broadsheets, if you can ignore the occasional outbreaks of pomposity and banality.

Magazines

The eighties saw a proliferation of magazines; the early nineties witnessed even more closures. One such departure means that **Time Out** magazine is now the only independent listings guide to what's on in London, detailing events on stage, screen and street.

Satirical magazines

The doings of the above papers, and of all public figures, are scathingly dissected in **Private Eye**. A bi-weekly satirical magazine, it attracts many libel suits, often exhorting its readers to contribute to legal funds. It celebrated 30 years of establishment-bashing in 1991. **Punch**, once its chief rival, finally went belly-up in March 1992. The monthly adult comic, *Viz*, has accelerated to a readership of one million by being as offensive as possible. With characters Sid the Sexist, the Fat Slags and the Pathetic Sharks, it parodies tabloid papers in the style of the *Beano* (a venerable comic for kids). More City businessmen read *Viz* than the *Financial Times*.

Lifestyle magazines

GQ, **Arena** and **The Face** are all designed (a word not used lightly in these publications) for the dedicated follower of fashion. All watched nervously as one of their main rivals, *Blitz*, went under in the early nineties. Americans *may* be pleased to hear that **Vanity Fair** launched a British edition in 1991; but they won't find it any different from its stateside parent. **Esquire**, huffing into life at the same time, is a slightly better read. **i-D** (owned by Time Out) has referred to itself as the most pretentious magazine in the universe. It takes its street fashion seriously but is self-deprecating in its editorial and design.

Women's magazines

Best, **Bella**, **More**, **Woman's Own**, **Prima**, and **Woman** specialise in triumph-over-tragedy stories, advice columns, recipes and invented horoscopes. They tend to appeal to middle-aged and married women. **Elle**, **Marie Claire**, **Cosmopolitan** and **Company** aim themselves at the 18-30 market. Ostensibly appealing to the 'liberated

woman', they are obsessed with sex, supermodels and psychotherapy. Politics, interviews and reviews take a supporting role.

Serious magazines

The **Economist** has good coverage of financial, political and foreign news. The **Spectator** promotes a crusty, old-fashioned conservatism, with entertaining columns by Taki and Jeffrey Bernard. The **New Statesman & Society** has a centre-left editorial policy, but it's righteous and a little dull. **The Big Issue** is a success story of the 1990s. Sold by, and partly written by, homeless people, it highlights London's housing problems as well as carrying more general articles.

Radio

British radio is undergoing its biggest-ever expansion. New stations are popping up all over the wavebands, and closing down just as fast. Many overseas visitors to London are astonished to discover that until the end of the eighties, Europe's biggest city was served by only nine stations, six of them provided by the BBC. Throughout the UK, new stations are being created for ethnic and specialist audiences. Licences are being handed out and London has benefited from the new output of stations such as **Kiss**, **Spectrum Radio** and **Jazz FM**. However, the listening public is learning that it doesn't take long for new stations, whatever their original intentions, to make a beeline for middle-of-the-road, safe programming.

London also has many pirate radio stations, but as they are illegal, we're unable to list them – a trawl up the FM waveband is the best way to keep up with their activities. For details of the new legal stations and for advance news of selected programmes, consult *Time Out* magazine; extensive listings are given in *Radio Times*.

Station Information

BBC Greater London Radio (GLR)

206m/1458kHz (MW); 94.9mHz (FM).
The BBC's local station for London, GLR serves 25 to 45 year olds with album-oriented rock. Some of the presenters are pretty inexperienced, but the two drive-time shows are a pleasing mix of news bites and ad-free music. The station is set to become more speech-orientated.

BBC Radio 1

275m/1089kHz and 285m/1053kHz (MW); 98.8mHz (FM).
Producers say that the most vital factor in making a hit is 'Radio 1 airplay'. Bland teen music rules in the daytime, but programming is more grown-up and varied after dark, when John Peel and others promote new and independent bands.

BBC Radio 2

89.2mHz (FM).
Radio 2 aims middle-of-the-road music at the over-45s. But many younger listeners value it as a relief from the follies of day-time Radio 1. Its evening output is a strange and endearing farrago of quizzes, comedies and affectionate shows of pre-Beatles music.

BBC Radio 3
247m/1215kHz (MW); 91.3mHz (FM).
This classical music station has a tiny audience, a huge budget, and a chorus of critics of its non-populist approach. Yet, even listeners uninterested in classical music will find much to enjoy in its high-quality discussion and drama shows.

BBC Radio 4
1500m/198kHz (LW); 417m/720kHz (MW); 93.5mHz (FM).
The BBC's main speech station is probably the quickest way for overseas visitors to discover the pre-occupations of Britain's chattering classes. Plays, phone-ins, discussions, humour and news programmes follow each other seamlessly. Millions of Britons habitually wake up to the station's morning news show, *Today* (6.30am-9am Mon-Sat). The nation's major obsession is covered by *Gardener's Question Time*. From April 1994, Radio 4 will carry educational programmes (refugees from the defunct Radio 5) and during the summer, the long-wave frequency is to be the new home of the incomparable Test Match Special (ball-by-ball cricket commentary interspersed with rain-stopped-play ruminations): an English institution.

BBC Radio 5
433m/693kHz and 330m/909kHz (MW).
The BBC has decided that news and sport never take place at the same time. So in April 1994, Radio 5 is to be replaced by a 24-hour news and sports station. If the Queen abdicates during the FA Cup Final, Gawd help them.

BBC World Service
463m/648kHz (MW).
Britain's equivalent of Radio Moscow or the Voice of America, is funded by the Foreign Office and is transmitted worldwide. Fortunately, it's little affected by its propaganda role and plays a weird mix of pop music, drama, comedy, features and inordinate quantities of news. From 12.45am to 5.45am it can be heard on the Radio 4 long-wave frequency (*see above*).

Capital FM
95.8mHz (FM).
A London-only commercial station which – with some specialist music shows and concerts – concentrates on perky presenters and current hits.

Capital Gold
194m/1548kHz.
Exclusively hit records of the last 35 years, played by DJs so old they spun the discs when they were new.

Choice FM
96.9mHz (FM).
All-day soul and dance music over south and central London.

Classic FM
100.9mHz (FM).
A new station with a menu of popular classics, and humable arias. The diet can become irritating (especially when Mozart is followed by an ad for cat food), but it has tempted many away from Radio 3.

Jazz FM
102.2mHz (FM).
Jazz across London 24-hours a day. A bit bland during the day, but perks up considerably after 10pm.

Kiss
100mHz (FM).
Dance, dance and more dance in all its multifarious forms, all day, every day.

London Country Radio
A country-music station that is set to start broadcasting from January 1994. Check *Time Out* for frequency information.

LBC Newstalk
97.3mHz (FM).
As LBC has lost its licence to broadcast, this station will close in October 1994. Its successor London News Radio plans a similar menu of phone-ins interspersed with news bulletins.

London Talkback
261m/1152kHz (MW).
A 24-hour phone-in station that is also run by LBC. In October 1994 it will be replaced by another station providing more of the same.

Melody FM
104.9mHz (FM).
Easy listening music of the kind your mum likes, for 24 hours a day.

Spectrum Radio
538m/558kHz (MW).
Programmes produced by and for London's ethnic minorities.

Sunrise
212m/1413kHz (MW).
An English-language breakfast show is followed by Asian-orientated day-time schedule.

Virgin Radio
247m/1215kHz (MW).
Offering national competition to Radio 1, but with a slightly more grown-up feel, Virgin started broadcasting in 1993.

Bush House, home of the **BBC World Service***. See* **review***.*

Television

British television is experiencing its greatest series of changes since John Logie Baird invented the medium. The arrival of satellite TV more than doubled the number of channels available at the beginning of the nineties, causing the competition for advertising revenue to hot-up. And the BBC has not been protected from the wind of change. The Corporation is having to re-apply for its licence to broadcast (which expires in 1996), a fact that is causing considerable trepidation, and has already led to cuts in staffing.

New laws have ushered in new channels and are making fundamental changes to the way the industry is financed. The British have long enjoyed the reputation of making the best TV programmes in the world – there's enormous anxiety that this will not be the case for long. Visitors don't come to London to watch television, but it's worth having a look at the all-powerful medium. And remember, if the pessimists are right, this will be regarded as the golden age of British television.

For detailed station information, news and features, pick up a copy of *Time Out*, *TV Times* or *Radio Times*.

BBC1
The oldest channel in this country, BBC1 has long had a reputation for quintessential Britishness. The BBC channels are funded by a licence fee and therefore do not need to take commercials to pay their way. BBC1 provides a mass-market mix of comedies, drama, soaps, game-shows and current affairs. The main news broadcasts are at 1pm, 6pm and 9pm.

BBC2
The BBC's cultural channel has a greater emphasis on arts, music and minority audiences. Music recitals and dance are regularly transmitted at prime time on Saturdays. This is also the channel which carries the classic drama serials for which the BBC is best known. Since it began commissioning films for TV transmission, it has produced some gems. An impressive regular is *Newsnight* – a nightly (10.30pm Mon-Fri) news and current affairs compendium.

ITV
This is the main commercial channel and is regarded by many as unremittingly populist. The tag is not entirely deserved (there are some fine documentaries), although it does have more than its fair share of nudge-nudge comedies and banal game-shows. Carlton TV took over the weekday franchise at the beginning of 1993; London Weekend Television continues to broadcast at the weekends. The main news bulletin of the day currently goes out at 10pm, weekdays, though programme planners are hoping to shift it to early evening.

Channel 4
Starting its broadcasts in 1982, Channel 4 quickly gained respect for providing programmes for those viewers whose needs were not being met. This has produced a varied diet which caters to supposed minority interests – from coarse fishing to black politics. It has become more mainstream after having to become completely self-financ-

ing. The longest and most analytical news programme available on terrestrial TV is *Channel 4 News* (7pm on weekdays). The Big Breakfast (weekdays 7-9am) currently provides the hippest way of waking up. Channel 4 also runs interesting, off-beat movies as well as commissioning its own films, which have included Peter Greenaway movies, *Mona Lisa* and *A Room With A View*.

Satellite TV

Britain began receiving satellite signals which could be picked up by small roof-top aerials in early 1989, when Rupert Murdoch, the US-Australian media magnate, launched a bundle of channels aimed at Britain. Although it has been running for five years, Satellite TV has only recently begun to make a profit. For details of the stations listed below, together with those of other satellite channels (the number continues to expand), check the national press or *Radio Times*.

CNN
News and features, 24-hours a day.

Comedy Channel
Canned laughter in 57 varieties.

Eurosport
Sporting events culled from European broadcasters – including the BBC – are transmitted with coverage of fixtures which often get squeezed on terrestrial TV.

MTV
The original 24-hour music channel with wall to wall videos. Very much modelled on its American sister, although the European version is a little more adventurous.

Sky Movies
Various first-run and re-run movies 24-hours a day, with the emphasis on mainstream blockbusters. There's also a Sky Movies Gold channel.

Sky News
Britain's first 24-hour news channel which delivers bulletins every hour on the hour. The rest of the time is filled with documentaries and discussion programmes. Bear in mind that Sky proprietor Murdoch is also the owner of the right-wing *Sun* and *Times* newspapers.

Sky One
A general entertainment channel, which kicks off with kids' programmes in the mornings and goes on to game shows and soaps – largely bought from America and Australia – plus TV movies.

Sky Sports
Major sports events, mostly soccer. Has caused much anger among the British populace by gaining sole rights to screening certain big boxing fights and soccer matches, thus preventing the dish-free majority from watching them.

UK Gold
Soaps, game-shows and sit-coms; mostly vintage productions that were shown on the terrestrial channels ages ago.

UK Living
A day-time channel for people at home which devotes itself to cookery and magazine programmes, interspersed with soaps and game shows.

Comedy

No but seriously, folks, there are over 50 cabaret venues in London and any number of new comics prepared to brave the capital's heartless audiences.

Before 1979, if you wanted an evening of 'cabaret', all that would be on offer would be high-kicking, semi-clad chorus lines or a succession of awful jokes about a (male) comic's mother-in-law. And then the **Comedy Store** opened, a radically new venue with a different agenda. Since then, what became known as 'alternative cabaret', or more recently 'new comedy', has grown to the point where there are well over 50 different venues in London.

Stand-up comedians are the backbone of new comedy; but they are just one of the styles on offer. You'll also be confronted by singers, magicians, musicians, jugglers, and the frankly indefinable. Comedians come in many different forms, ranging from political radicals to surrealists, from the reflective to the fiercely aggressive, as well as the downright silly. Names to look out for are: Jo Brand, Arthur Smith, Eddie Izzard, Alan Parker, John Shuttleworth, Jack Dee and John Hegley. But there's a huge pool of talent in London, so you shouldn't worry about the quality of the bill.

By its very nature, the cabaret circuit is not entirely predictable. Venues come and go and even long-established clubs suddenly bite the dust when premises are redeveloped or a pub is taken over by an unfriendly landlord. And over half the regular venues close down dur-ing late July and the whole of August, when many comedians head off to the **Edinburgh Festival** (*see chapter* **London by Season**). You'd be well advised to check the weekly listings in *Time Out* before you risk a trek to NW6 or SW11.

Unless it's specifically stated, you can assume that none of the clubs accept credit cards, although most do offer concessions.

Central

Chuckle Club
Shakespeare's Head, Carnaby St, W1 (071 476 1672).
Oxford Circus underground. **Open** 7.45pm Fri.
Performances 8.30pm. **Admission** £5; £4 students, UB40s.
Resident host Eugene Cheese brightens a fairly unprepossessing room through his silliness and sheer amiability. His high standing on the comedy circuit means that quality acts get booked.

Comedy Campus
The Roadhouse, 35 The Piazza, Covent Garden, WC2 (071 240 6001). Covent Garden underground. **Open** 5.30pm Sat. **Performances** 8pm. **Admission** £5; £4 students, UB40s.
American-style bar, all Harley-Davidson motorbikes and tequila slammers, but with some top Saturday night line-ups.

Comedy in Tatters
Tattershall Castle paddle steamer, Victoria Embankment, WC2 (071 733 6322). Embankment

Book two weeks ahead to be ring-side at **Jongleurs at the Cornet**. *See* **review** page 215.

underground. **Open** 8pm Sun. **Performances** 8.45pm. **Admission** £4; £3 students, UB40s.
London's only comedy club on a boat. It's an unexpectedly comfortable venue, but be prepared for plenty of jokes to make you feel queasy.

Comedy Store
28A Leicester Square, WC2 (0426 914 433). Leicester Square underground. **Open** 7pm Tue-Thur; 8pm, 11pm, Fri, Sat; 7.30pm Sun. **Performances** 8pm Tue-Thur; 8pm, midnight, Fri, Sat; 8.30pm Sun. **Admission** £7-£8.
The place where alternative comedy began is still the most famous comedy club in the country. The crowds queue for stand-up performances on Fridays and Saturdays, but there's more chance of getting in at the last minute on Thursdays. The infinitely talented Comedy Store Players stage improvised comedy on Wednesdays and Sundays.

Hurricane Club
The Black Horse, 6 Rathbone Place, W1 (071 580 0666). Tottenham Court Road underground. **Open** 8.30pm Sat. **Performances** 9pm. **Membership** 50p. **Admission** £5; £4 students, UB40s.
The only central London club to provide a mixture of stand-up comedy and improvisation from a regular team on Saturday nights.

Oranje Boom Boom
De Hems Dutch Coffee Bar, Macclesfield Street, W1 (081 694 1710). Leicester Square or Piccadilly Circus underground. **Open** 8pm Wed. **Performances** 8.45pm. **Admission** £5; £4 students, UB40s.
One of the first coffee bars to be penetrated by cabaret (but don't panic, alcohol is also sold). You're likely to see a fair number of newish acts, along with those who've already established their reputation.

Soho Ho
The Crown & Two Chairmen, 31 Dean Street, W1 (information 081 579 5414). Leicester Square underground. **Open** 8pm Sat. **Performances** 8.30pm. **Admission** £5; £4 students, UB40s.
This is a typical pub venue in the heart of Soho with shows featuring a combination of new and established acts.

West

Acton Banana
The King's Head, Acton High Street, W3 (081 673 8904). Acton Town underground. **Open** 8.30pm Fri. **Performances** 9pm. **Admission** £5; £3 students, UB40s.
West London offshoot of the enterprising Banana Cabaret (*see* **South West**). It's a comfortable and spacious pub room with a relaxed atmosphere.

Canal Café Theatre
The Bridge House, Delamere Terrace, W2 (071 289 6054). Warwick Avenue underground. **Performances** times vary. **Membership** £1 per year. **Admission** £4-£5.
Improvised comedy and scripted pieces are more usual than cabaret bills at this fringe theatre beside the canal in Little Venice. It's also the home of Newsrevue, a group which mounts revues based on topical events.

South West

BAC
Battersea Arts Centre, Old Town Hall, Lavender Hill, SW11 (071 223 2223). Battersea Park or Clapham Junction BR. **Performances** times vary. **Admission** £4-£6.
A mixed bag of different kinds of comedy and cabaret shows are a regular feature of the programming at this venue. *See* chapter **London by Area: South.**

Banana Cabaret
The Bedford, 77 Bedford Hill, SW12 (081 673 8904). Balham underground/BR. **Open** 8.30pm Fri; 8pm Sat. **Performances** 9pm. **Admission** £5; £3 students, UB40s.
One of the most enterprising and enjoyable clubs in London. Downstairs, the large, circular domed room looks like a stage set. Upstairs, a smaller space with wooden panels provides a cosier atmosphere. Promoter Andy Waring books excellent cabaret entertainment in both. Although your entertainment depends on the quality of the acts, this is one comedy club that it is a pleasure to visit.

Cartoon at Clapham
The Plough Inn, 196-198 Clapham High Street, SW4 (071 738 8763). Clapham Common underground. **Open** 8.15pm Fri, Sat. **Performances** 9pm. **Admission** £5; £4 students, UB40s.
A large pub venue with plenty of tables. It's relatively comfortable and generally good value. The bar is open until midnight.

Sir Laughalot
Barflies, 280 Streatham High Road, SW16 (081 940 0652). Streatham BR. **Open** 7pm Wed. **Performance** 8.30pm. **Admission** £2.50.
A late bar, a happy hour, and some of the most inventive turns on the circuit.

Jongleurs at The Cornet
49 Lavender Gardens, SW11 (071 924 2766). Clapham Common underground then 45 bus/Clapham Junction BR. **Open** 8pm Fri, Sat. **Performances** 9.15pm. **Admission** £8; £6 students, UB40s.
One of the most popular clubs on the circuit – you're advised to book well in advance. Top acts appear every week, the food is reasonable, the bar is open until 1.30am, and the audience is often very lively indeed.

Screaming Blue Murder
Leather Bottle, 277 Kingston Road, SW19 (081 339 0506). Wimbledon underground/BR. Also at: White Lion, 14 Putney High Street, SW15 (081 339 0506); Putney Bridge underground/Putney BR. **Open** 8pm Thur-Sun. **Performances** 8.30pm. **Admission** £4; £3.
Long running and widely respected clubs that bring comedy to the wild western extremities of the capital.

South East

Aztec Comedy Club
The Borderland, 47-49 Westow Street, SE19 (081 771 0885). Crystal Palace BR. **Open** 8.30pm Fri, Sun. **Performances** 9.30pm Fri; 9pm Sun. **Admission** £4; £3 students, UB40s.
The comedy shows take place in the pleasant upstairs room above a Mexican restaurant. You can eat while you watch (there's table service) or in the main restaurant beforehand.

East Dulwich Cabaret
The East Dulwich Tavern, 1 Lordship Lane, SE22 (081 299 4138). East Dulwich BR. **Open** 8.30pm Thur-Sat. **Performances** 9.30pm. **Admission** £4.50; £3.50 students, UB40s.
A pub venue that has line-ups of reliable quality in an area of London which isn't blessed with many comedy clubs. The bar is open until midnight.

Up the Creek
302 Creek Road, SE10 (081 858 4581). Greenwich BR. **Open** 8pm Fri; 7.30pm Sat, Sun. **Performances** 9pm Fri-Sun. **Admission** £7; £5 students, UB40s.
A purpose-built comedy and music club in a popular

tourist area. The talented line-up comes with an extra attraction in the shape of earthy comic Malcolm Hardee who runs the venue.

East

Comedy Café
66 Rivington Street, EC2 (071 739 5706). Old Street underground/BR. **Open** for meals, throughout the day. **Performances** 8.30pm Tue-Sat. **Admission** £4.50 Tue; free Wed, Thur; £5 Fri, Sat, £4 students, UB40s.
A pleasant restaurant/café on the edge of the East End. You can dine and watch top quality comedy at very reasonable prices.

Hackney Empire
291 Mare Street, E8 (081 985 2424). Hackney Central or Hackney Downs BR/22, 35, 38, 55, 106, 253 bus. **Open** Oct-Easter 7pm Sat. **Performances** 8.30pm. **Admission** £5-£10. **Credit** A, V.
One of London's famous old variety theatres is now a home for new comedy of every kind. The spectacular mock-Turkish interior is almost as beguiling as the shows, which range from star-studded cabaret bills to special solo performances by big names. *See chapter* **Early Twentieth Century**.

North

Bound & Gagged
The Fox, 413 Green Lanes, N13 (081 208 1983). Palmers Green underground. **Open** 8.30pm Fri. **Performances** 9.30pm. **Admission** £5; £3 students, UB40s.
Out in the wilds of inner suburbia, but worth the trek. The bills are invariably strong and there's a late bar until 1am. No admission after 10.30pm.

Comedy at the Garage
20 Highbury Corner, N5 (071 607 1818). Highbury & Islington underground/BR. **Open** 7.30pm Fri. **Performances** 8.30pm. **Admission** £6; £4 students, UB40s.
Popular rock music club with a twist of comedy every Friday. Entrance to the disco until 2am is included and there is food and a late bar.

Downstairs at the King's Head
2 Crouch End Hill, N8 (081 340 1028). Finsbury Park underground/BR then W7 bus. **Open** 8pm Sat; 7.45pm Sun. **Performances** 8.30pm. **Membership** 50p per year. **Admission** £4; £3 students, UB40s.
The longest-established comedy venue in London. Run by Peter Grahame, one of the most respected promoters in the capital, the club is well equipped and the audiences are genial. Recommended.

Jackson's Lane
269A Archway Road, N6 (081 341 4421). Highgate underground. **Performances** times vary; phone for details. **Admission** £3-£6.
A community arts centre, based in a former church. Comedy is well represented in the programme of events, but the Lane is just as well known for its comedy classes where some of today's finest acts have sharpened their material and stagecraft. If you fancy your chances, this is the place to start learning.

Opposite (clockwise from top left): Arthur Smith, Jo Brand, Eddie Izzard *and* John Hegley – *four of the top club comedians in suitably merry mood.*

Jongleurs Camden Lock
Dingwalls Building, Middle Yard, Camden Lock, NW1 (0426 933711). Camden Town underground. **Open** 7.30pm Fri; 7pm Sat. **Performances** 8.45pm Fri; 8.15pm Sat. **Admission** £8; £6 students, UB40s.
A purpose-built club with late bar and food and the spirit that makes **Jongleurs Battersea** (*see above* **South West**) so popular and successful. Entrance to the dance club afterwards is included.

Meccano Club
The Market Tavern, 2 Essex Road, N1 (081 800 2236). Angel underground. **Open** 8.30pm Fri, Sat. **Performances** 9pm. **Admission** £5; £4 students, UB40s.
There's a very low ceiling here and the intimacy often brings out the best from comedians. Also worth looking for here are the occasional nights when established comedians try out their new jokes: watch as they squirm while routines they have honed for months die a silent death.

Red Rose Cabaret
129 Seven Sisters Road, N7 (071 281 3051). Finsbury Park or Holloway Road underground. **Open** 8pm Fri, Sat. **Performances** 9pm. **Membership** 50p per year. **Admission** £4.75; £3.50 students, UB40s.
The Red Rose Cabaret is a club that rivals top venues for the quality of the entertainment on offer at half the admission price of the Comedy Store – and the drink is cheaper too. Sit at the long, raised table at one end of the room and you can imagine you're part of a tableau representing The Last Supper.

North West

Punchline Comedy Club
The Railway, West End Lane, NW6 (071 482 6534). West Hampstead underground/BR. **Open** 8pm Sat. **Performances** 8.30pm. **Admission** £5; £4 students, UB40s.
A justifiably popular venue that was an R&B club in the sixties and a punk dive in the seventies, but has now settled down to comedy. The performances are mainly stand-up and the bar is licensed until midnight.

Outside London

Cabaret at the Square
Fourth Avenue, Harlow, Essex (0279 417029), Harlow Town BR (from Liverpool Street). **Open** 7.30pm Thur. **Performances** 9.15pm. **Membership** £1. **Admission** £3.
John Mann continues to attract some of London's best comedians to Harlow on a week night. Considering how Essex has suffered at the hands of lesser comics recently, it's no mean feat.

Jesters Comedy Club
92 High Street, Rickmansworth, Herts (0923 896 363). Rickmansworth underground/BR. **Performances** 9pm Wed. **Admission** £3; £2 students, UB40s.
At the northern extremities of the Metropolitan Line is a lively and popular club that usually has a big-name headliner, a couple of promising comedians and a newcomer on a try-out spot.

Splatt!
Royal Bell, 175 High Street, Bromley, Kent (081 778 9412). Bromley North/Bromley South BR. **Open** 8.30pm Thur. **Performances** 9pm. **Admission** £4; £3 students, UB40s.
A suburban venue that can attract big names out of the city for a night. The late bar is just an added extra to the usual bill of two stars from the London circuit.

Children

Take a handful of young nippers, a batch of banknotes and a stack of stamina, and get ready to start the adventure of exploring London. Izzy whizzy let's get busy.

Making a sojourn in London fun for the children in your care without reducing yourself to the point of exhaustion and near bankruptcy requires careful planning. Some suggestions for child-friendly excursions are listed below, with prices, where applicable. The places chosen are a representative sample of the scores of sights, activities and special events laid on for young visitors to London all year round. More attractions are listed every week in the 'Children' section of *Time Out* magazine.

It is often the case that what children pronounce 'wicked', their adult companions reckon to be 'bloody criminal'. Take the **London Dungeon**. Paying £6 to see a batch of gruesome instruments of torture and to hear taped, blood-curdling screams may not be your cup of tea, but the average nine-year-old talks about it for days afterwards. There has to be give and take in any relationship: take comfort in the fact that once a child has had a bellyful of London's seamier side, there's always acres of parkland and the wholesome domains of London's city farms to be explored. The major museums and tourist attractions have a great deal to offer children, and though their admission prices may seem a bit steep at first glance, places like the **Science Museum**, with all their interactive displays and commitment to the 'hands on' approach, take at least half a day to get round and so give good value.

Children for whom a journey usually means being strapped into the family saloon, get a kick out of London's public transport system. A journey on a big red double-decker bus, the capital's mascot, can be an adventure in itself, especially if the vehicle trundles past some of the city's major sights. The number 15, for example, takes in the West End before going on to St Paul's via Piccadilly Circus and Trafalgar Square, providing a happy half-hour's sightseeing for the price of a bus ticket. Buy the children a one-day travelcard and you can ride the tube, which is also a source of fascination for young children.

Finally, a word about crowds. The rush hour (8.30-9.30am and 4.30-6.30pm) is not a sensible time to be on public transport unless your journey is essential. Bear in mind that crowds are especially bewildering if you're only three feet high. Keep a careful eye on small children at all times when you're out and about.

Meet the Animals

Cheeky grey squirrels and scruffy sparrows can be persuaded to eat out of your hand in the inner city parks; pigeons mob you in Trafalgar Square, but few visitors are aware of the variety of wildlife that can be seen in the capital. Richmond Park has herds of deer, there are herons in Regent's Park and a waterbird sanctuary in St James's Park. Then there are the city farms — 17 altogether — the biggest of which is **Mudchute City Farm** (*see chapter* **By Area: East End & Docklands**). For a full list send a stamped, addressed envelope to the National Federation of City Farms, AMF House, 93 Whitby Road, Brislington, Bristol BS4 3QF.

Battersea Dogs' Home
4 Battersea Road, SW8 (071 622 3626). Vauxhall underground/BR/Battersea Park BR/44, 170 bus. **Open** 10.30am-4.15pm Mon-Fri; 10.30am-3.15pm Sat, Sun. **Admission** 50p adults; 20p under-16s; free under-5s.
Britain's most famous — and heartrending — canine collection welcomes visitors, so much so that a cafeteria is provided for light refreshment after browsing. Adults have to brace themselves for the inevitable pleas from children to provide a sanctuary for the inmates they see here. Those that weaken and decide to rescue a pet are required to fill in a questionnaire and receive a visit from Dogs' Home staff, just to check that the animal is going to a suitable home.

Kentish Town City Farm
1 Cressfield Close, Grafton Road, NW5 (071 916 5421). Chalk Farm underground/Kentish Town underground/BR/Gospel Oak BR/24, 46, 134, 214, C11 bus. **Open** 9am-5.30pm Tue-Sun. **Admission** free.
London's original city farm is set on five acres (two hectares) of land, and boasts a riding club for young Camden residents. There are six horses, two cows, sheep, goats and numerous free-range chickens. The staff are extremely good with young children.

Living Waters
at the **Horniman Museum** (*see listings below* **Museums & Collections**).
This very wonderful free museum has much to recommend it, not least its enchanting aquatic conservation centre for endangered species. Children can look at favourites of the British pond, such as leeches, frogs, minnows and water fleas, all of which are succumbing to the

*A **one o' clock club**. See **review** page 224.*

adverse effects of intensive agriculture and pollution. There are also aquariums for sea life, including seahorses, starfish, coral reef varieties and shellfish. Other glass homes contain spiders, land snails, snakes and tree frogs. Outside in the gardens is a mini zoo, housing goats, a turkey, ducks, rabbits, guinea pigs and wallabies.

London Butterfly House

Syon Park, Brentford, Middlesex (081 560 0378). Gunnersbury underground then 237, 267 bus. **Open** *Oct-Apr* 10am-3.30pm daily; *May-Sept* 10am-5pm daily. **Admission** £2.40 adults; £1.50 under-16s, OAPs; £6.80 family (two adults, four children). **Credit** A, V, £TC.
The extensive grounds of Syon Park, seat of the Duke of Northumberland, have become home to a hot-house full of foliage and thousands of gorgeous butterflies. Children fritillary away their pocket money on butterfly-inspired souvenirs at the shop. There's also an aquarium with a huge fish tank. *Café. Restaurant. Shop.*

London Zoo

Regent's Park, NW1 (071 722 3333). Camden Town underground. **Open** *Apr-Sept* 10am-5.30pm daily; *Oct-Mar* 10am-4pm daily. **Admission** £6.50 adults; £4 under-15s; under-4s free. **Credit** A, AmEx, £$TC, V.
A £1 million gift from the Emir of Kuwait, drastic cuts in staff numbers and vastly improved attendance figures have breathed new life into Britain's largest zoological gardens. With the emphasis now on conservation and education, the zoo is a brighter, livelier place. Children are drawn to the insect and reptile houses, the wonderful zoo shop and the aquarium, with its mean-looking piranhas. *Education centre. Films. Group discount for 20 or more. Lectures. Restaurant. Shop. Wheelchair access to most areas.*

Surrey Docks Farm

Rotherhithe Street, SE16 (071 231 1010). Surrey Quays underground/P11, 225 bus. **Open** *term time* 10am-5pm Tue-Fri; 10am-1pm, 2-5pm, Sat, Sun. *School holidays* 10am-1pm, 2-5pm, Tue-Thur; 10am-1pm, 2-5pm, Sat, Sun. **Admission** free.
A small, neat city farm amid the new developments of Surrey Quays. The friendly young farmers tend to their goats, sheep, free-range chickens, sows and ducks, and answer any questions you may have. They also keep bees, which live in a fantastic observation beehive. The bees' honey is for sale, as are free-range eggs, subject to availability. A fragrant corner of the small-holding is given over to herbs, and plants for natural dyes.

Horrors & Spooks

Below is a selection of horrible sights and spooky tours for those children with a well-developed sense of the macabre. Young children and those prone to nightmares should avoid them at all costs.

Chislehurst Caves

Old Hill, Chislehurst, Kent (081 467 3264). Chislehurst BR. **Open** *Easter-Sept* 11am-5pm daily. *Oct-Easter* 11am-4.30pm daily (closed Christmas Day). **Admission** *short tour* £2.50 adults; £1.20 under-15s; under-5s free. *Long tour* (Sun, Bank Holidays only) £4 adults; £2 under-15s; no under-5s.
Take a spooky lamplight tour (lasting 45-50 minutes) through this maze of chalk tunnels and caves, dug out and used by man since the Stone Age. Previous occupants include the druids, the Romans and war-time Londoners sheltering from the air-raids. More recently it was used as a pirate radio station and sixties disco. The whole place is largely untouched and unspoilt and there are chilling stories of druid sacrifices and ghosts. Snacks are served in the small hut near the entrance. Active adults and older children can try the no-holds-barred tour, on Sundays and Bank Holidays only at 2.30pm. It lasts 1½ hours, and – as you would expect – is more adventurous than the standard tour, covering extra exhibits and taking you through low tunnels.

London Dungeon

28-34 Tooley Street, SE1 (071 403 0606). London Bridge underground/BR. **Open** 10am-5.30pm daily (last admission one hour before closing). **Admission** £6 adults; £4 under-14s, OAPs; £5 students; free entry for under-5s and people in wheelchairs. **Credit** A, AmEx, £TC, V.
Grisly waxwork displays of torture, execution, murder, plague and other incidents of foul play make this one of the worst places to take a young child with a nervous disposition. Older children lap it up, even the all-new Jack the Ripper Experience. *Café. Group discount. Wheelchair access.*

Madame Tussaud's

Marylebone Road, off Baker Street, NW1 (071 935 6861). Baker Street underground. **Open** *May-Sept* 9am-5.30pm daily. *Oct-Jun* 10am-5.30pm Mon-Fri; Sat, Sun 9.30am-5.30pm. **Admission** £7.40 adults; £4.75 under-16s; £5.50 OAPs. *Combined ticket with Planetarium* £9.40 adults; £6 under-16s; £6.40 OAPs; no under-5s. **Credit** A, AmEx, £TC, V.
The hefty admission price proves that this is one of the most popular of all the tourist attractions, and the one that goes down best with children. It consists of life-size statues of the famous and infamous cast in wax with questionable accuracy. There are pop stars, royalty, sports personalities (and Steve Davis), actors and – the main event for most children – the Chamber of Horrors, where waxworks of murderers and villains frozen in their barbarous acts grimace at the visitors and scare the pants off young children. The excellent, if short, new Dark Ride takes you on a whistle-stop tour of London's history in a so-called time taxi. *Café. Group discount. Wheelchair access by prior arrangement.*

Museums & Collections

These museums run special activities for young visitors. Others are listed in *chapters* **Sightseeing** and **Museums**.

Bethnal Green Museum of Childhood
Cambridge Heath Road, E2 (081 980 2415/3204/4315). Bethnal Green underground. **Open** 10am-5.50pm Mon-Thur, Sat; 2.30-5.50pm Sun. **Admission** free.
A collection of toys, dolls and dolls' houses, games and puppets belonging to the Victoria & Albert Museum. Saturday is a good day to visit if you have young children, because the staff run art workshops (11am-1pm, 2-4pm). *See also chapter* **Museums**.

Cabaret Mechanical Theatre
33 The Market, Covent Garden Piazza, WC2 (071 379 7961). Covent Garden underground. **Open** *Easter-Sept* 10am-7pm daily. *Oct-Easter* noon-6.30pm Mon; 10am-6.30pm Tue-Sun.* **Admission** £1.75 adults; £1 under-16s, OAPs, students, UB40s; under-5s free; family ticket £4.25 (two adults, three children). **Credit** A, AmEx, DC, £TC, V.
More than 40 push-button machines and automata make up this bizarre collection. As well as the permanent show, there is usually some kind of exhibition from leading contemporary inventors. Many of the machines are for sale. *Group discount. Shop.*

Horniman Museum
100 London Road, SE23 (081 699 2339/1872). Forest Hill BR. **Open** *museum* 10.30am-5.30pm Mon-Sat; 2-5.30pm Sun. *Gardens* 8am till dusk daily. **Children's club open** *term time* 10.30am-12.30pm Sat; *school holidays* 10.30am-12.30pm Mon-Sat. **Admission** free. **No credit cards.**
This eccentric museum is a magical place to take children, whatever their age. Inside the building, with its strangely rounded clocktower, there's a collection of masks and costumes from all over the world, as well as musical instruments and cases of stuffed birds, mammals and insects. Pride of place goes to a gigantic stuffed walrus. The shop is excellent for gifts. *See also above* **Living Waters**. *Café. Shop. Toilet for people with disabilities.*

Livesey Museum
682 Old Kent Road, SE15 (071 639 5604). **Open** 10am-5pm Mon-Sat. **Admission** free.
A small local museum with a rather dog-eared look about it, but with a good line in hands-on exhibitions for the under 12s. Themes change regularly, ranging from food to space exploration, involving feely-boxes, button-oper-

ated machines and other interactive educational aids. There's also a soft play area for the very young.

Science Museum
Exhibition Road, SW7 (071 938 8000/8080/8008). South Kensington underground. **Open** 10am-6pm Mon-Sat; 11am-6pm Sun. **Admission** £4 adults; £2.10 under-16s, students, UB40s, OAPs; free under-5s, registered disabled; £17 family (two adults, four children). **Credit** A, AmEx, £TC, V.
Even toddlers get a buzz out of this museum, which boasts five floors of scientific inventions and interactive exhibitions. There's Launchpad, full of do-it-yourself experiments; Flight is the new aeronautics gallery and Food for Thought explains the impact of science and technology on food.
Café (10.30am-5pm Mon-Sat; 11.30am-5pm Sun). Group discount. Lectures by prior arrangement. Library. Dillons bookstore. Wheelchair access.

Activities & Sports

See also chapter **Sport & Fitness**.

The Arches Leisure Centre
Trafalgar Road, SE10 (081 858 0159). Maize Hill BR/177, 180, 286 bus. **Open** *leisure pool term-time* 2-7.45pm Mon; 2-7pm Tue; 2-8pm Wed; 2-8.45pm Thur; 2-6pm, 7-9pm Fri; 9.30am-5.30pm Sat; 9am-5.30pm Sun. *Holidays* from 10.30am. *Family splash (£1 admission)* 7-9pm Fri. **Admission** £2 adults; £1.10 under-16s. **No credit cards.**
This is a family leisure centre with two pools. The one children seem to prefer is full of outlandish aqua delights, including a water cannon, an erupting volcano, a foaming spring and a cascade. The beach area makes it ideal for the very young.

Brass Rubbing Centre
Crypt of St Martin-in-the-Fields Church, Trafalgar Square, WC2 (071 437 6023). Charing Cross underground/BR. **Open** 10am-6pm Mon-Sat; noon-6pm Sun. **Admission** free. **Brass rubbings** according to size £2.35-£11.50. **Credit** (shop) A, AmEx, £TC, V.
The Brass Rubbing Centre is housed in one of London's most famous churches, off Trafalgar Square. Children can rub replicas of medieval church brasses and so follow a tradition that has been popular in Britain for generations. Try to steer them towards the smaller exhibits; you pay according to size.
Gift shop. Wheelchair access.

Britannia Leisure Centre
40 Hyde Road, N1 (071 729 4485). Old Street underground/141, 271 bus. **Open** 9am-8.45pm Mon-Fri; 9am-5.45pm Sat, Sun. **Admission** £2.50 adults; £1.20 under-16s; free under-5s. **No credit cards.**
This swimming pool is a large, aquatic playground. Serious swimmers avoid it because it's all water chutes, fountains, flumes and a wave machine. Children love it. Adults huddle in the café, which overlooks the pool so they can make sure their water babies are behaving themselves.
Poolside Café. Bar.

Playscape
Clapham Kart Raceway, Triangle Place, SW4 (081 986 7116). Clapham Common underground. **Open** 10am-10pm daily. **Fee** £17.63 per half hour; £30 full hour. **Credit** A, AmEx, V.
For a really special treat, take the children to the go-kart race track. If they're over eight years old, they can get behind the wheel of a powerful 150cc mean machine and receive expert tuition in how to drive it. The company

The **Horniman Museum**. *See* **review**.

Karting at **Playscape**. *See* **review** *page 220.*

also runs courses for children, and accepts group bookings for a party of child racers.
Branch: Hester Road, SW11 (081 986 7116).

Shops & Markets

Young children and shops don't mix, but the over-fives enjoy blowing their pocket money on unsuitable items. Many get a good deal of mileage out of Woolworth's and bankrupt stock tat shops, nevertheless, they should find something to interest them from the choice below. Direct teenagers to **Camden Market, Portobello Road Market** (for both *see chapter* **Shopping: Markets**), and Carnaby Street, W1, where they can lose themselves in a welter of bashed leather jackets and other statement-making gear.
See also chapter **Shopping: Children.**

Beatties
202 High Holborn, WC1 (071 405 6285/8592). Holborn underground. **Open** 10am-6pm Mon; 9am-6pm Tue-Fri; 9am-5.30pm Sat. **Credit** A, AmEx, £TC, V.
As well as being the biggest name in train sets and associated merchandise, Beatties has a huge selection of remote-controlled and model cars, boats and planes, an impressive Lego selection and a wide range of other toys, both pocket-money priced and otherwise.

Davenport's Magic Shop
Charing Cross Underground Shopping Arcade, Strand, WC2 (071 836 0408). Embankment underground or Charing Cross underground/BR. **Open** 10.15am-5.30pm Mon-Fri; 10.15am-4pm Sat. **No credit cards.**
London's oldest magic shop, stocking all the tricks for professional magicians and enthusiasts, plus masks and hundreds of practical jokes. It is best reached from the William IV Street entrance to Charing Cross underground station.

Eric Snook's Toyshop
32 The Market, Covent Garden Piazza, WC2 (071 379 7681). Covent Garden underground. **Open** 10am-6.30pm Mon-Fri; 10am-7pm Sat; 11am-6pm Sun. **Credit** A, AmEx, £TC, V.
You won't find any loud or vulgar toys in this smart and

selective Covent Garden shop. Instead there are Beatrix Potter characters such as Jemima Puddleduck, and hand-made wooden soldiers sitting proudly in a carriage.

Frog Hollow
15 Victoria Grove, W8 (071 581 5493). High Street Kensington underground. **Open** 9am-5.30m Mon-Sat; 11am-5.30pm Sun. **Credit** A, AmEx, £TC, V.
This extremely attractive toy and gift shop has a wealth of pocket-money-priced toys to buy as a reminder of a trip to London. Soft-toy addicts may find it hard to resist the teddies and other cuddlables.

Hamleys
188 Regent Street, W1 (071 734 3161). Oxford Circus underground. **Open** 10am-6.30pm Mon-Wed, Fri; 10am-8pm Thur; 9.30am-6.30pm Sat. **Credit** A, AmEx, DC, JCB, £$TC, V.
'The most famous toy shop in the world' is a paradise for children, with five floors filled with toys and games of every imaginable description – radio-controlled cars and planes, computer games, magic tricks, model kits, puzzles and puppets, miniature railways, sports equipment, dolls and (of course) plenty of teddy bears. There are dozens of working models and demonstrations, so the whole place is like a gigantic playground.
Baby-changing facilities. Restaurant.

Museum of the Moving Image Gift Shop
South Bank Arts Centre, South Bank, SE1 (071 928 3535 ext 569). Waterloo underground/BR. **Open** 12.30-9pm daily. **Credit** A, AmEx, DC, £TC, V.
This is where you'll find the merchandising of the film of the moment. At the time of writing it is groaning with dinosaur-related toys and gift. There are also posters, mugs, cards and badges printed with the film star of your dreams.

Puffin Bookshop
1 The Market, Covent Garden, WC2 (071 379 6465). Covent Garden underground. **Open** 10am-6.30pm Mon, Wed-Sat; 10.30am-6pm Tue; noon-6pm Sun. **Credit** A, AmEx, £TC, V.
All Puffin titles are stocked in this well laid-out book store. You will also find a great breadth of classics, fiction, non-fiction, poetry and picture books.

Skate Attack
95 Highgate Road, NW5 (071 485 0007). Tufnell Park underground/Gospel Oak BR. **Open** 10am-6pm Mon-Fri; 9am-6pm Sat. **Credit** A, AmEx, £TC, V.
This shop has the biggest selection of roller skates and related equipment in Europe. If you fancy a skate round the park of your choice, the staff will hire you a pair of skates for £10 per day (or a whole weekend) plus £100 deposit (they accept credit cards for this). Body protection (pads, helmet) is included in the hire price. The roller-crazy staff are a mine of information about the best places to skate.

Entertainment

Details and previews of shows and films for children taking place each week are printed in *Time Out* magazine. The following venues usually have something on.

Barbican Children's Cinema Club
Barbican Centre (cinema 1), EC2 (071 638 8891). Barbican or Moorgate underground. **Admission** £3 adults; £2.50 under-15s. **Membership** £3 per year. **Credit** A, AmEx, £TC, V.

Davenport's. *See* **review** page 221.

The cinema club runs on Saturday afternoons. Films generally start at 2.30pm.

Little Angel Marionette Theatre
14 Dagmar Passage, off Cross Street, N1 (071 226 1787). Angel underground/Highbury & Islington underground/BR. **Performance** times vary, phone for details. **Admission** £4.50 adults; £4 under-16s. **No credit cards.**
The only permanent puppet theatre in London. It's a delightful place, with seating for 110, and is hidden away in Islington. There are regular weekend and holiday performances, and a visiting company is usually booked for August.

Lyric Theatre Hammersmith
King Street, W6 (081 741 2311). Hammersmith underground. **Performance** 11am Sat. **Admission** £2.50. **Credit** A, AmEx, DC, £TC, V.
Children's entertainment, from plays and puppets to clowns and workshops, is put on every Saturday. *Wheelchair access by prior arrangement.*

National Film Theatre
South Bank, SE1 (071 928 3232). Waterloo tube/BR. **Admission** £3.95 adults; £2.75 under-16s. **Credit** A, AmEx, £TC, V.
Matinées for children are held here on Saturday and Sunday at 4pm. *See also chapter* **Film**.

Nomad Puppet Studio
37 Upper Tooting Road, SW17 (081 767 4005). Tooting Bec underground. **Performances** 11.30am, 2.30pm, Sat; closed for six weeks mid Jul-Aug (phone to check). Private parties by arrangement. **Admission** £2.25 adults; £2 children.
A small, friendly theatre which provides excellent entertainment in the form of short puppet stories (acted out by the puppets Jo Jo, Scruffy and their friends) particularly suited to the under fives. Squash and biscuits are provided.

Polka Theatre for Children
240 The Broadway, SW19 (081 543 0363/4888). Wimbledon South underground/Wimbledon BR. **Open** *box office* 9.30am-4.30pm Tue-Fri; 11am-5.30pm Sat. **Admission** £2.50-£4.50. **No credit cards.**
A purpose-built complex for the under-12s, which has a charming playground with slides, a beautiful rocking horse and play house, a café and a little shop for pocket-money priced toys. Specially commissioned children's shows take place in the attractive main theatre, with shows for the under-fives usually taking place in the smaller Adventure Room.
Café. Induction loop for the hard of hearing. Wheelchair access.

Rio Cinema
107 Kingsland High Street, E8 (071 249 2722/071 254 6677). Dalston Kingsland BR. **Admission** £2.50 adults; £1.50 under-15s. **No credit cards.**
The Rio cinema Club takes place on Saturdays at 11am — you can drop your children off and collect them after the film.

Tricycle Theatre
269 Kilburn High Road, NW6 (box office 071 328 1000/information 071 372 6611). Kilburn underground. **Performances** *winter* 11.30am, 2pm Sat; extra matinées during Christmas and summer holidays. **Admission** £2.25 in advance; £2.75 on the day. **Credit** A, AmEx, DC, £TC, V.
The Tricycle continues staging superb children's shows and after-school and holiday workshops. On Saturdays, the café's children's menu is good value.
Bar. Café. Wheelchair access.

Unicorn Theatre for Children
6 Great Newport Street, WC2 (071 836 3334). Leicester Square underground. **Open** *box office* 10am-8pm Mon-Sat. **Performances** *(term-time)* 1.30pm Tue-Fri; 2.30pm Sat school holidays (phone to confirm). **Admission** £3-£6 plus 20p temporary membership. **No credit cards.**
Founded in 1948, this is London's oldest professional children's theatre. It puts on an adventurous programme of specially commissioned plays and other entertainment (puppets, magic, music) for 4-12 year olds. The Children's Club organises weekend and holiday workshops through the year.
Café.

Annual Events

Teddy Bear's Picnic
Battersea Park, SW11 (081 871 6349). Battersea Park BR/49 bus. **Date** Friday afternoon early in August. **Admission** free.
An annual picnic is held for thousands of children plus their cuddly friends. Accompanying activities range from face-painting to donkey rides.

Summer in the City
Barbican Centre, Silk Street, EC2 (071 638 4141). Barbican underground. **Date** first three weeks in August. **Admission** £4 adults; £1 under-16s.
One of London's major arts centres holds this annual jamboree of events for 2-10 year olds. It takes place both indoors and out with performances of music, comedy and theatre specifically for the under-11s. Phone for details.

Eating Out

Most restaurant managers are unwilling to refuse children admission, but few restaurants do much to make them feel welcome. Young diners who can't sit still very long are particularly frowned upon. Fast food outlets, Happy Eaters, and department store restaurants welcome children with plates of burgers and chips. The restaurants listed below go out of their way to make lunch with children fun for everyone.

Benihana
100 Avenue Road, NW3 (071 586 7118/9508). Swiss Cottage underground. **Lunch served** 12.30-3pm Tue-

Sun. **Dinner served** 6.30pm-midnight Mon-Sat; 6.30-11.30pm Sun. **Average** £30. **Credit** A, AmEx, DC, V. The charming staff at this Japanese restaurant are happy to cater for children on a Sunday lunch-time. No-one has to eat raw fish and noodles if they object to deeply Japanese fodder; a suitable spread for a child could include corn-on-the-cob, chicken breast with a side dish of sauce, and rice, with ice-cream to follow. Puppet shows take place on a Sunday and there's a garden to run about in.

The Chicago Pizza Pie Factory
17 Hanover Square, W1 (071 629 2552). Oxford Circus underground. **Open** 11.45am-11.30pm Mon-Sat; noon-10.30pm Sun. **Credit** A, AmEx, £TC, V.
Every Sunday (noon-5pm) this big, brash burger and pizza joint holds Sunday Funday, with children's disco, storytelling, face-painting and entertainments from the Arts Theatre Workshop.

Glaister's Garden Bistro
4 Hollywood Road, SW10 (071 352 0352). Fulham Broadway underground. **Open** noon-3pm, 7.30-11.30pm, daily **Sunday lunch** £6.95. **Credit** A, AmEx, DC, £TC, V.
On Sundays (12.30-4.30pm), parents can leave their small children in the crèche next door (dubiously named Nipper Snippers), then slope off for lunch in this bistro. Children in the crèche get a sandwich lunch, and entertainments such as videos, Nintendo games, painting and loads of toys.

Holland Park Café
Ilchester Place, Holland Park, W14 (071 602 2216). Holland Park or Kensington High Street underground. **Open** 10am-30 mins before sunset daily. **Average** £4.50 adults; £1.50 children. **No credit cards.**
This delightfully situated café has plenty of outside seating. Wholesome, homemade Italian food – soup, pizza, ice-cream – is on the menu. A child's portion of spaghetti costs just £1.10.

Marine Ices
8 Haverstock Hill, NW3 (071 485 3132). Chalk Farm underground. **Open** *ice-cream parlour* 10.30am-10.45pm Mon-Sat; 11am-8pm Sun. **No credit cards.**
The Mansi family run this gelateria, and have done so since 1931. A scoop of the homemade ice costs 85p from the hatch; if eating-in, the price goes up to £1 a scoop. Ice-cream-based puddings can be as large and elaborate as you can imagine, but bear in mind that nearly all children's eyes are bigger than their stomachs.

PJ's Grill
30 Wellington Street, WC2 (071 240 7529). Covent Garden underground. **Open** noon-1am Mon-Sat; noon-5pm Sun. **Average** £12. **Credit** A, AmEx, DC, £TC, V.
Uncle PJ's fun club provides a special menu, toys, entertainers, high-chairs and other delights for children who lunch here with their parents on Saturdays and Sundays.

Smollensky's Balloon
1 Dover Street, W1 (071 491 1199). Green Park underground. **Open** noon-midnight Mon-Sat; noon-10.30pm Sun. *Family lunches* noon-3pm Sat, Sun. **Average** £17 adults; £6 children. **Credit** A, AmEx, DC, V.
Family Affair at Smollensky's takes place on Saturdays, Sundays and Bank Holiday Mondays. The children's menu costs £3.95 and there's a magic show as well as video games, balloons, a raffle and toys to keep the mites amused once they've trodden their fish fingers into the carpet.

Uncle Ian's Deli Diner
8-10 Monkville Parade, Finchley Road, NW11 (081 458 3493). Golders Green underground. **Open** 9am-11.30pm Mon-Thur, Sat, Sun; 9am-4pm Fri. **Average** £7.50. **Credit** A, £$TC, V.
Provisions for children at this bustling restaurant include

Dressed up to the nines for the weekend party at **PJ's Grill**. *See* **review**.

high chairs and free lollipops. There are reduced-price children's portions and servings are generous. It's so popular, especially for family lunches, that you may have to queue.

Staying Up Late

Parents may need some persuading but evenings are a great time for window shopping. **Covent Garden** (*see chapter* **By Area: Central**) stays lively in the evening, and wandering around **Chinatown** (*see chapter* **By Area: West End**) is especially exciting. The brightly-lit restaurants and supermarkets, full of strange and exotic delicacies, don't close till late.

Some sports centres and swimming pools also stay open during the evening (*see chapter* **Sport & Fitness**). But if you're looking for entertainment, remember the **Guinness World of Records** and **Rock Circus** (*see chapter* **Sightseeing**) are open every night until 10pm. Many museums have occasional early-evening sessions (*see chapter* **Museums**).

During the weeks running up to Christmas, dark evenings are magic in central London. **Selfridges** and **Hamleys** are famous for their window displays; there are Christmas lights and decorations through Oxford Street, Regent Street, Carnaby Street, Covent Garden Market, Piccadilly and Burlington Arcade; and a giant tree (London's annual Christmas present from Norway) in Trafalgar Square.

Under-Fives

One o' clock clubs are play clubs within parks where pre-school children can play in safety. Most have sandpits, Wendy houses, paints, toys to ride on, slides and climbing frames. As Councils find it increasingly hard to make ends meet, provision for the under fives has been subject to cost-cutting, but most Greater London Boroughs run a one o' clock club in their larger parks. Children playing in these enclosed, dog-free places must be accompanied by an adult. A selection is listed below.

Barnard Park
Barnsbury Road, N1 (071 278 9494). Angel underground/Caledonian Road & Barnsbury BR. **Open** *one o'clock club* noon-3.30pm Mon-Fri.

Battersea Park
Albert Bridge Road, SW11 (081 871 6349). Battersea Park/Queenstown Road BR/19, 39, 44, 45, 49, 130, 137, 170 bus. **Open** 1-4pm Mon-Fri; *adventure playground* 11am-6pm Mon-Fri (closed Mon during term-time.
Children's Zoo *(081 871 7540).* **Open** 11am-5.30pm daily. **Admission** adults 80p; under-15s 30p.

Crystal Palace Park
Crystal Palace Park Road, SE26 (081 778 4487).

Open *Park Farm* 11am-5pm Mon-Fri; 11am-5.30pm Sat, Sun. **Admission** £1 adults; 50p under-15s.

Holland Park
Abbotsbury Road Entrance, W8 (071 603 2838). Holland Park underground. **Open** *one o'clock club* 12.30-4pm Mon-Fri.

Paddington Recreation Ground
Randolph Avenue, W9 (071 625 7024). Maida Vale underground. **Open** phone for details of under-5s club.

Peckham Rye Common
Peckham Rye, SE15 (no phone). Peckham Rye BR/12, 37, 63, 78, P2, P3, P12 bus. **Open** *one o'clock club* 1-4pm Mon-Fri.

Taking a Break

A babysitter or childminder can be found in a hurry from one of these reliable organisations. They are not cheap, but they're worth it for the peace of mind that comes from knowing your child is in capable hands.

Childminders
9 Paddington Street, W1 (071 935 2049/9763). Baker Street underground. **Open** 8.50am-1pm, 2-5.20pm, Mon-Fri; 9am-1pm, 2-4.30pm, Sat. **Membership** £35 plus VAT per year, or £5 visitors' booking fee. **Fees** £3.85 per hour day-time; £2.65-£3.45 per hour evenings (minimum 4 hours), plus travel expenses.
A large agency with over 1,000 babysitters (all with references; mainly nurses and infant teachers) who live all over London and the suburbs.

Pippa Pop-ins
430 Fulham Road, SW6 (071 385 2458). Parsons Green underground. **Open** by appointment. **Fees** £20 for a morning or afternoon; £30 all day. **Credit** A, AmEx, £TC, V.
In a large, bright and airy, specially adapted house and garden, Pippa and her team of NNEB- and Montessori-trained nursery teachers and nannies run a crèche, nursery school, children's hotel and babysitting service. They welcome children two years old and over. *See also chapter* **Accommodation**.

Information

Circusline
(0891 343341). **Open** 24 hours daily.
Recorded information on circuses around the country. Calls are charged at 36p a minute cheap rate, 48p a minute standard rate.

Kidsline
(071 222 8070). **Open** *term-time* 2-6pm Mon-Fri.
Information on films, shows, attractions and activities all over London.

London Tourist Board 'What's On' Line
(0839 123 404).
A recorded service giving details of events and exhibitions for children. Calls are charged at 36p per minute cheap-rate (after 6pm weekdays and all day Sat and Sun); 48p per minute all other times. The 'Places to Visit' line (0839 123424; same price) gives details of where to see animals, plus tourist attractions and museums.

Clubs

'Raise your arms in the air, and shake them like you just don't care.'
The capital's club scene panders to all party animals on the prowl.

Although London may not yet be able to claim 'round-the-clock city' status (and as more clubs become licensed for dancing 'til dawn that accolade cannot be far away), it has arguably the most cosmopolitan club scene to be found anywhere in the world. A brief glimpse may give the impression that everyone and everywhere is obsessed with House and Techno music, but, if those aren't your bag, rest assured that there are venues to suit every taste in music, fashion and atmosphere.

All-night clubbing was legalised in 1990. Now clubbers are so used to venues staying open as late as 10am at weekends, that many don't bother going out until well after midnight. Unfortunately, the new timetable only applies to the dance floor. At the bar we're stuck with antiquated licensing laws, so after 3am alcohol gives way to fruit juices and 'psycho-active' drinks – stimulating, eco-friendly beverages to keep you going.

As a result of later music and dance licences, weekend clubbing is more expensive than ever. Admission is often about £10 on Fridays and Saturdays, at least until 3am, when the price drops to encourage club crawling.

New **one-nighter clubs** are continually opening up, each with its own sharply defined profile. They used to be exclusive parties hosted by flamboyant personalities for their trendy clique. Now they are mainly inspired by the latest dance music, and the DJ is the main attraction. Most nights of the week you can hustle at seventies party nights; do the bruck wine to a ragga beat in Brixton; learn to dance like a Brazilian; sweat on down to rap; or practise lindyhopping to big band swing.

While the vanguard of the dance music scene is mainly of interest to the younger crowd, there are plenty of intimate (and sober) venues where it's possible to communicate without shouting. The mature clubber may feel comfortable at some of the smarter, more expensive clubs in the West End, Mayfair, Kensington or Chelsea.

In London you can dance to anything from African to zydeco – if you know where to go. Every week you'll find listings of about 150 different clubs and one-nighters in the 'Clubs' section of *Time Out* magazine. In the mean-

time, bear in mind a number of suggestions to ensure that your night on the town lives up to expectations.

MEMBERSHIP
Venues are prohibited from selling alcohol after 11pm unless they have either a music-and-dance licence or a club licence. Most opt for the latter, since it gives them the freedom to select members. However, most clubs' membership regulations are quite flexible. Many venues include a membership fee as part of the admission price, while most one-nighters only claim to be 'Members Only' if they don't think you would 'fit in'.

DRESS CODE
Most nightspots have a vague 'smart but casual' dress code. Jeans, T-shirts and trainers (sneakers) are frowned upon at the smarter venues, but are the 'uniform' elsewhere. Although fashion isn't as important as it used to be, bear in mind that if a club has a reputation for a particular kind of music there's usually a style to go with it. Turn up in a suit to a club full of goths, and you might be glad if the bouncers refuse you entry.

TRANSPORT
Unless you can dance until breakfast time, you'll usually leave a club well after the underground network has stopped running. Taxis can be hard to find early in the morning, so if at all possible it's worth arranging homeward transport in advance. You could take a 'minicab' – although it may be unwise for a single woman to do so; reputable cab companies are listed in *chapter* **Getting Around**. Night buses are the cheapest means of transport (*see chapter* **Early Hours** and *chapter* **Getting Around**), and they offer an entertaining ride home. We've listed the night buses for clubs in districts outside central London, but if you're in the West End, head for Trafalgar Square, from where nearly all night buses depart.

The Clubs

Astoria
157 Charing Cross Road, WC2 (071 434 0403).
Tottenham Court Road underground. **Open** 7pm-11pm Mon-Thur; 11pm-3am Fri; 10pm-6am Sat. **Admission** £8-£10. **Credit** A, AmEx, DC, V.

HALF PRICE TICKETS
LEICESTER SQUARE

The Half-Price Ticket Booth
A great way to save money and enjoy one of the true highlights London has to offer, the West End theatre!

The Leicester Square Half-Price Ticket booth sells tickets for a wide selection of West End shows on the day of the performance only, at half price.

Centrally located in the clock tower building on the south side of Leicester Square, the Booth is open Monday to Saturday from 12 noon for matinees and from 2.30 pm - 6.30 pm for evening performances. Tickets are limited to 4 per person, for cash only plus a service charge of up to £1.50 per ticket.

Kinky Gerlinky at **Equinox**. *See* **review**.

Although it has never been properly adapted for nightlife use, this former theatre does have a huge balcony and an enormous dance floor. It's always packed with a young, indie/goth convention at weekends. Various live concerts and one-nighters take place on other nights. *See* chapter **Music: Rock, Folk & Jazz.**

Bass Clef
35 Coronet Street, N1 (071 729 2476). Old Street underground/BR/N96 bus. **Open** 8pm-2am daily. **Admission** £4-£7. **Credit** A, AmEx, DC, V.
This small, atmospheric club is one of London's best live jazz venues, and one of the hardest to find (down a dingy side-street). It specialises in live jazz sessions (Wed, Thur), Latin jazz (Fri), and African (Sat), with excellent complementary turntable sounds. Very popular, especially at weekends. *See chapter* **Music: Rock, Folk & Jazz**.

The Borderline
Orange Yard, Manette Street, WC2 (071 734 2095). Leicester Square or Tottenham Court Road underground. **Open** 11.30pm-3am Mon-Sat. **Admission** £6-£10. **No credit cards.**
A stylish subterranean venue underneath a Tex-Mex restaurant. Lively, unpretentious dance nights and live performance clubs are run. Bands play at weekends. *See* chapter **Music: Rock, Folk & Jazz.**

Busby's
157 Charing Cross Road, WC2 (071 734 6963). Tottenham Court Road underground. **Open** 10.30pm-3am Mon-Sat. **Admission** £4-£7. **No credit cards.**
Mainstream disco is on the menu at Busby's, which is popular for its central location rather than its chrome and mirror furnishings. A variety of one-nighters take place.

Café de Paris
3 Coventry Street, WC1 (071 287 3602). Leicester Square or Piccadilly Circus underground. **Open** 10pm-6am Fri, Sat. **Admission** £10-£12. **No credit cards.**
A stylish ballroom in the West End that specialises in weekend all-nighters and excellent occasional mid-week parties.

Camden Palace
1A Camden Road, NW1 (071 387 0428). Camden Town underground/N2, N29, N90, N93 bus. **Open** 9pm-2.30am Tue-Thur, Sat; 9pm-6am Fri. **Admission** £2-£10. **No credit cards.**
This former music hall is one of the most popular tourist venues in town – and none the worse for that. The spacious dance floor is always crowded, and there are lavish lights and great sound. Hidden amid the myriad levels and passages, you might find a cocktail bar and a restaurant. Indie, '60s, rock, rave, and mainstream disco all take their turns here.
Wheelchair access.

Electric Ballroom
184 Camden High Street, NW1 (071 485 9006). Camden Town underground/Camden Road BR/N2, N29, N90, N93 bus. **Open** 10pm-3am Fri, Sat. **Admission** £5. **No credit cards.**
A large, basic, two-tiered venue (with a huge dance floor) that should have been refurbished long ago but that still draws crowds for weekend dance sessions. DJs will mix anything from rock and glamour punk to trash disco and House. Each level usually has a different brand of music. *Restricted wheelchair access.*

Equinox
Leicester Square, WC2 (071 437 1446). Leicester Square underground. **Open** 9pm-3.30am Mon, Wed, Thur; 9pm-2.25am Tue; 9pm-4am Fri, Sat. **Admission** £5-£7 Mon-Thur; £8-£10 Fri, Sat. **Credit** A, AmEx, V.
Revamped to the tune of almost £2 million in 1992, Equinox now looks like a 1970s disco with 1990s touches. The outrageous drag-fest Kinky Gerlinky takes place here every month, but the best weekly events are on Saturdays, and Tuesday's student night.

Fish
37-39 Oxford Street, W1 (071 437 7945). Tottenham Court Road underground. **Open** 11pm-6am Mon, Fri, Sat; 11pm-3.30am Tue; 11pm-4am Thur. **Admission** £7. **No credit cards.**
Fortunately for everyone, the Fish funk is fresh, especially at the weekend all-nighters, and the piscine sound system is pumping.

The Fridge
Town Hall Parade, Brixton Hill, SW2 (071 326 5100). Brixton underground/BR/N2, N78 bus. **Open** 11pm-3am Tue, Wed; 10pm-3am Thur-Sat. **Admission** £8. **No credit cards.**
Always adventurous and interesting, The Fridge is also the best large dance venue in town. It pioneered multimedia nightlife entertainment with films and visuals, allied to live performance and go-go dancers. The club has a small, cheap-and-cheery café where you can escape the sound of music and the baloney that gives an extra dimension to the club. It attracts a young, trendy assembly, reflecting Brixton's multi-racial culture. A rigorous security check at the door may come as a surprise at first, but on reflection is reassuring.
Restaurant. Wheelchair access by arrangement.

The Garage
22 Highbury Corner, N5 (071 607 1818). Highbury and Islington underground/N19, N73, N96. **Open** 7.30pm-2am daily. **Music** 9pm. **Admission** £6. **Credit** A, V.

Straightforward, popular local club that presents bands in the evening and carries on with a club into the night. Indie rocking a speciality.

The Gardening Club
4 The Piazza, WC2 (071 497 3154). Covent Garden underground. **Open** 10pm-3.30am Mon-Sat. **Admission** £4-£8. **No credit cards.**
A hot and sweaty club with a good range of one-nighters. Regular House nights can keep the place open until 6am.

Gossips
69 Dean Street, W1 (071 434 4480). Leicester Square or Tottenham Court Road underground. **Open** 10pm-3.30am Mon-Sat. **Admission** £4-£6. **No credit cards.**
The archetypal mid-eighties one-nighter venue: a dark cellar, home to all sorts of dance music, from psychedelia or heavy metal, to ska, dance music and ragga.

Heaven
Underneath the Arches, Villiers Street, WC2 (071 839 3863). Embankment underground or Charing Cross underground/BR. **Open** 10pm-3am Mon; 10.30pm-3am Tue-Sat. **Admission** £6-£7.50. **Credit** A, £TC, V.
A giant aerodrome of a venue under Charing Cross Station, Heaven is London's major gay club (*see chapter* **Gay**). It's also one of the best dance venues in town, featuring a maze of bars, corridors and large dance floors with excellent lasers, sound systems and lightshows. Gay nights are held at the weekends and there are some massive one-nighters during the week.

The Hippodrome
Cranbourn Street, WC2 (071 437 4311). Leicester Square underground. **Open** 9pm-3am Mon-Sat. **Admission** £8 Mon-Thur; £6-£10 Fri, Sat. **No credit cards.**
This centrally-sited club has superb lighting and sound systems, but it has the bizarre appearance of a chrome-clad disco dinosaur. The club usually offers a 'commercial' mix of dance music for a smartly-dressed crowd (of out-of-towners and tourists), although there may be a heavy-rock night or avant-garde poseurs' parade, depending on your luck.

Iceni
11 White Horse Street, off Curzon Street, W1 (071 495 5333). Green Park underground. **Open** 10pm-3am Wed-Sat. **Admission** £5-£8. **Credit** A, AmEx, V.
Disco, cabaret, rock, funk and board games might all be on offer on the same night at Iceni's three-storey premises. If you're the good-looking, hard-dancing type, it's the place to be.

Jazz Café
5 Parkway, NW1 (071 916 6000). Camden Town underground/N2, N29, N90, N93 bus. **Open** 7pm-midnight Mon-Thur, Sun; 7pm-2am Fri, Sat. **Admission** £5-£6. **Credit** A, V.
Some of the best music in the capital (from Afro-Latin to rap) can be heard at this cool club, which is scantily clad in 1980s minimalism. There are a couple of fun funk nights at the weekend to expand the experience. *See also chapter* **Rock, Folk & Jazz**.

Legends
29 Old Burlington Street, W1 (071 437 9933). Green Park or Piccadilly Circus underground. **Open** 10pm-3.30am Wed-Sat. **Admission** £3-£15. **Credit** A, AmEx, DC, £TC, V.
A sleek nightclub venue, host to various very good one-nighters (especially at weekends) that attract a mixture of Mayfair trendies, smart Sloanes, wild dancers and snappy dressers.

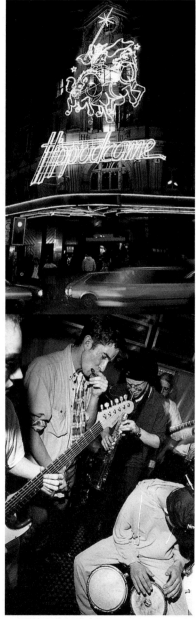

Top: *glitz at the* **Hippodrome**. **Above**: *jamming at the Iceni. See* **reviews**.

Clockwise: the **Ministry of Sound**, **Raw**, *and* **Maximus** – *providing soul for all seasons*. *See* **reviews**.

Limelight

136 Shaftesbury Avenue, WC2 (071 434 0572).
Leicester Square underground. **Open** 10.30pm-3am
Mon-Thur; 10.30pm-3am Fri, Sat. **Admission** £5-£8
Mon-Thur; £10 Fri, Sat. **Credit** A, V.
Once a church, now a temple of funk (and garage and
House). There are two dance floors in the bass-ment
(sic) and the dome. The Limelight can be dull early in
the week, but its sound system is excellent. Worth a visit
towards the weekend, especially if you like designer
beers and vodka cocktails.

Maximus

14 Leicester Square, WC2 (071 734 4111). Leicester
Square underground. **Open** 10.30pm-3.30am Wed;
10pm-3am Thur; 10.30pm-6am Fri; 11pm-6am Sat;
9.30pm-3am Sun. **Admission** £5-£10. **No credit cards**.
A classic example of mirror-tiled seventies disco kitsch.
Maximus is populated by passing tourists, and those who
still think cocktails are glamorous. The dance floor is small,
but there's acres of alcoved seating. Music is mainstream
disco, but occasional one-nighters redeem matters.

Ministry of Sound

103 Gaunt Street, SE1 (071 378 6528). Elephant &
Castle underground/BR/N12, N53, N62, N65, N72,
N77, N78, N82, N85, N86. **Open** midnight-8am Fri;
midnight-9am Sat. **Admission** £12 Fri; £15 Sat.
No credit cards.
Garage, House and club classics all throb out of the
Ministry's superb sound system. It's only open weekends,
it's prohibitively expensive, it's huge, but it's always
packed. An all-night cinema, and famous name DJs are
among the attractions; the lack of a drinks licence is a
detraction (for some), though an application is in progress.

Moonlighting

17 Greek Street, W1 (071 734 6308). Leicester Square
or Tottenham Court Road underground. **Open** 9pm-
3.30am Mon, Wed-Sat. **Admission** £5 Mon, Wed,
Thur; £6 Fri; £8 Sat. **Credit** A, AmEx, V.
What was formerly Le Beat Route is now a comfortable
disco-venue. It attracts a smarter, older crowd who
slide on the (very slippery) dance floor to a commercial dance mix.

Le Palais

242 Shepherd's Bush Road, W6 (081 748 2812).
Hammersmith underground/N11, N97 bus. **Open**
9.30pm-2.30am Wed; 9.30pm-3am Thur; 9pm-3am Fri,
Sat. **Admission** £3-£7. **Credit** A, AmEx, DC, V.
Redecorated in tacky, art deco revival style, west
London's major disco comes complete with the requisite
lightshow, lasers, video walls and a restaurant. But it's
still like a dance hall in an aircraft hangar.
Wheelchair access.

Paradise Club

1-5 Parkfield Street, N1 (071 354 9993). Angel under-
ground/N19, N73, N92, N96. **Open** 11pm-4am Fri;
10pm-10am Sat. **Admission** £5-£13. **No credit cards**.
If you can absorb 12 hours of brain-bursting bass lines,
Paradise can be paradise right up to breakfast time at
weekends. There's a 24-hour party licence.

RAW

112A Great Russell Street, WC1. Tottenham Court Road
underground. **Open** 10pm-4am Thur; 10.30pm-5am Fri,
Sat; 10.30pm-6am Sun. **Admission** £5-£8.
No credit cards.
Somewhere below the earth's crust and the YMCA, is an
aquatically furnished, Atlantis of a venue. Fashionable clubbers throng onto the spacious dance floor at weekends.

Clubs

Samantha's
3 New Burlington Street, W1 (071 734 6249). Oxford Circus or Piccadilly Circus underground. **Open** 9pm-3.30am Mon-Sat. **Admission** £3 Mon; £5-£7 Tues-Sat. **No credit cards.**
A comfortable mainstream disco with plenty of alcoved seating, two floors, two dance floors, a fish pond and swing seats hanging on chains at the bar. Smart dress is expected; over-40s won't feel inhibited.

Stringfellow's
16 Upper St Martin's Lane, WC2 (071 240 5534). Covent Garden or Leicester Square underground. **Open** 9pm-3.30am Mon-Sat. **Admission** £8-£10 Mon-Thur; £10-£15 Fri, Sat. **Credit** A, AmEx, DC, £$TC, V.
This is where the stars go, in theory. Well, you may be lucky, but you're more likely to meet a computer programmer from Basildon, trying to look glamorous amid the glitz. The restaurant is a mite pricey.
Wheelchair access.

Subterrania
12 Acklam Road, W10 (081 960 4590). Ladbroke Grove underground/N18, N50 bus. **Open** 8pm-2am Mon-Thur; 10pm-3am Fri, Sat. **Admission** £7. **Credit** A, V.
Although it's hard to find and in an unlikely location, Subterrania is worth rooting out. It's one of the very few clubs in London to have benefited from late-1980s décor. There's a European atmosphere, a great sound system and cold beer. Designer clothes are much in evidence.
Wheelchair access.

SW1
197 Victoria Street, SW1 (071 828 7455). Victoria underground/BR/night buses from Victoria. **Open** 9pm-

6am Wed; 10pm-3am Thur; 10pm-6am Fri; 10.30pm-5am Sat. **Admission** £10. **No credit cards.**
There's a bizarre contrast between the setting and the sounds at SW1. The venue: an Edwardian dance hall with traditional oak panelling. The music: Tough House. The attractions: serious dancers, chunky sound.

Tokyo Joe
85 Piccadilly, W1 (071 409 1832). Green Park underground. **Open** 8.30pm-3.30am Mon-Sat. **Admission** £10 Mon-Sat. **Credit** A, AmEx, DC, V.
A plush nightclub with an accompanying restaurant. Unsurprisingly, it tends to attract well-heeled patrons.

United Kingdom
Buckhold Road (at the side of the Arndale Complex), SW18 (081 877 0110). Wandsworth Town BR/N88. **Open** 10pm-6am Fri, Sat. **Admission** £10. **No credit cards.**
Established in July 1993, the outrageously popular UK shook up all conventional wisdom about clubs by opening in untrendy Wandsworth. It's worth the trip just to see the dance floor, the kitsch décor, and the beds in the chill-out bar. The sound system and the DJs are equally attractive.

The Wag Club
35 Wardour Street, W1 (071 437 5534). Leicester Square or Piccadilly Circus underground. **Open** 10.30pm-3.30am Mon-Thur; 10.30pm-6am Fri, Sat. **Admission** £4-£6 Mon-Thur; £8 Fri; £10 Sat. **Credit** £TC.
For five years after it opened in the early eighties, the Wag was the place to be. Now the 'Wag crowd' has moved on, and today the club responds to trends rather than creating them. Nonetheless, the dance crowd are young, trendy and friendly – unlike the bouncers, who can be unnecessarily choosy at the popular weekend nights.

United Kingdom: *land of hope and glory (and a chill-out bar). See* **review**.

Dance

Pirouetting around London's premier dance venues needn't send your wallet reeling.

There's every kind of dance performed in London in every type of venue. Tickets can cost £200, or just £2. Famous ballet companies from the US and the CIS regularly visit London, but there's also plenty of physical activity from a plethora of troupes based in the capital. The diverse menu ranges from the greatest of classics, such as *Swan Lake* and *The Sleeping Beauty*, to contemporary masterpieces, world premières and radical experimentations that spotlight the latest ideas.

Dance in London is surprisingly affordable and sometimes even ludicrously cheap. Although the best seats in the major theatres can cost from about £15 to £30, stand-by tickets, concession prices, and restricted view seats can bring even the most lavish spectacles within the realms of the impoverished. At the fringe venues throughout London, the ticket prices are kept as low as possible. Even so, a ticket for visiting companies such as the Bolshoi Ballet can cost in excess of £50.

Here's a rundown of the major London venues, from the plush and grand expanses of the **Coliseum** to the intimate bonhomie of **The Place**.

Major Venues

ICA
The Mall, SW1 (071 930 3647/membership enquiries 071 930 0493). Piccadilly Circus underground or Charing Cross underground/BR. Open *box office* noon-9.30pm daily; noon-6pm for advance bookings. **Tickets** prices vary – phone for details. **Credit** A, AmEx, DC, £TC, V.
Much of the dance presented at the ICA belongs to the genre known as performance art. Tending to be radical, eclectic and non-conformist, performance art breaks down conventional notions through an uninhibited mix of movement, music, text, mime and design. The result is a hybrid that often can't be confined within standard definitions of either dance or theatre. The Institute is a beehive of activity, with galleries, a cinema, an extensive video library, a bookshop, a bar and a restaurant. The ICA theatre has seating for approximately 200 people. *See also chapters* **Art Galleries**, **Film** *and* **Theatre**. *Bar. Bookshop. Café. Group discount. Lectures. Workshops.*

The London Coliseum
St Martin's Lane, WC2 (071 836 3161/credit card bookings 071 240 5258/recorded information 071 836 7666). Leicester Square underground or Charing Cross

underground/BR. Open *box office* 10am-8pm Mon-Sat. **Tickets** £8-£43. **Credit** A, AmEx, DC, £STC, V.
This 2,530-seat theatre, London's biggest, is home to the English National Opera. During the summer months, while the opera is off, dance moves in. **English National Ballet** is here for two summer weeks. It's one of London's most spacious and attractive theatres and is the first choice of visiting foreign companies. The Bolshoi and Kirov Ballets are frequently seen here. The Dance Theatre of Harlem and the National Ballet of Spain have also played the 'Collie'. Champagne and coffee bars are dotted around the theatre, but sandwiches and dessert goodies are on sale in the Edwardian ambience of the Dutch Bar, hidden away in the cellar. Stand-by tickets are sold at reduced prices on the day of performance. *See also chapter* **Music: Classical & Opera**. *Group & family discount (071 836 0111 ext 318). Shop (10am-7.30pm Mon-Sat). Toilets for the disabled. Wheelchair access.*

The Place
17 Duke's Road, WC1 (071 380 1268). Euston underground/BR. Open *box office* noon-6pm Mon-Fri; Sat, when there is a performance. **Tickets** £4-£12.50; concessionary rates for Camden residents, OAPs, students, UB40s. **Credit** A, £TC, V.
Cheap ticket prices and an intimate performance space (it only seats 300) have helped keep The Place one of the most exciting dance spots in the country. The building is home to the London Contemporary Dance School, which explains the full-length mirrors in the foyer – it's a classroom by day. The programming over recent years has included regular seasons such as: *Spring Loaded* (new British dance); *The Turning World* (the best from Europe); *Vivarta* (showcasing the new face of South Asian dance and performance); and **Dance Umbrella** *(see below* **Special Attractions**). The Video Place is a major resource centre for students and professionals. *Wheelchair access.*

Riverside Studios
Crisp Road, W6 (081 748 3354/081 741 3602/credit card bookings 081 563 0331). Hammersmith underground. Open *box office* noon-8pm daily. **Tickets** £7-£9 and concessions. **Credit** A, V.
Originally from the BBC studios where such cosy, olde worlde series as *Dixon of Dock Green* were filmed, the Riverside has become an exciting, if troubled, arts complex. Two performance spaces, including one of the largest stage areas in the country, host regular programmes of exciting contemporary dance. There are also a gallery, cinema, restaurant and bar to keep your attention. *See also chapters* **Art Galleries** *and* **Theatre**. *Bar. Bookshop. Café. Restaurant. Wheelchair access.*

Royal Opera House
Covent Garden, WC2 (071 240 1066). Covent Garden underground. Open *box office* 10am-8pm Mon-Sat. **Tickets** £2-£57. **Credit** A, AmEx, DC, V.
This handsome 2,000-seat house, home to the **Royal Ballet**, produces some of the most memorable classical performances the world of dance can offer. Prestige and

*The non-conformist **ICA** is a beehive of bohemian activity. See **review** page 232.*

quality mean that tickets are in demand, but even if you arrive in town and want to see a show that night, there are always 65 rear amphitheatre seats held back for sale on the day. Even if an event is a sell-out, 50 standing room places are available, although it is worth considering that some performances are three hours long. Getting a stand-by space often means queuing outside the box office in Floral Street at daybreak, and tickets are restricted to one per person. Once you get in, though, you can munch expensive sandwiches and rub elbows with lots of well-heeled champagne-guzzlers. To complete the experience, there is the Royal Opera shop on James Street which sells books, videos and recordings. *See also* chapters **Sightseeing** and **Music: Classical & Opera**. *Opera and ballet education officers. Shop. Wheelchair access; toilets for people with disabilities.*

The Royalty Theatre
Portugal Street, WC2 (071 494 5090). Holborn underground. **Open** *box office* 10am-8pm Mon-Sat (till 6.30pm when there's no performance). **Tickets** prices vary; phone for details. **Credit** A, AmEx, V.
This modern, 1,000-seat West End theatre sometimes is a venue for visiting dance and ballet companies. It has been playing an increasingly prominent role in bringing dance events to central London since 1991. The stage is large and the sightlines are excellent. *Wheelchair access to some seats.*

Sadler's Wells Theatre
Rosebery Avenue, EC1 (071 278 8916). Angel underground. **Open** *box office* 10.30am-7.30pm Mon-Sat (till 6.30pm when there's no performance). **Tickets** *main theatre* £7.50-£35; *Lilian Baylis theatre* £4-£10. **Credit** A, AmEx, DC, £TC, V.
The Sadler's Wells remains one of London's most eclectic dance theatres, even though the Sadler's Wells Royal Ballet moved to Birmingham in 1990 and became the Birmingham Royal Ballet. This historic 1,500-seat theatre doesn't have the world's largest stage, but sightlines are exceptional, particularly in the dress circle. Major dance companies from home and abroad pay regular visits to the Wells: from flamenco and Lindsey Kemp, to London Contemporary Dance Theatre and the National Ballet of Cambodia. There are three bars, all of which get crammed on busy nights. The de Valois wine bar serves snacks both before and after performances. The theatre has a policy of reserving 50 stalls tickets for sale on the day of performance only. They're sold from 10.30am at the advance box office, on the corner across the road. The Lilian Baylis Theatre (*see chapter* **Theatre**), is situated in Arlington Way, behind the main theatre. Opened in October 1988 and named after the woman

who saved the theatre from extinction in 1931, it holds just over 200 people. Tickets for Baylis performances are rock bottom in price for often experimental, small-scale dance, theatre and music performances. *Restaurant. Toilets for the disabled. Wheelchair access to main theatre.*

South Bank Centre
South Bank, Belvedere Road, SE1 (box office 071 928 8800/general information 071 928 3002).Waterloo underground/BR/Riverbus. **Open** *box office* 10am-9pm daily. **Tickets** £2.50-£30, some free events and children events. **Credit** A, AmEx, DC, V.
This central riverside complex includes three separate theatres which are used for dance and music. Built to commemorate the Festival of Britain in 1951 (*see chapter* **Post War**), the **Royal Festival Hall** holds 3,000 people and offers excellent viewing no matter where you sit. Each year, English National Ballet presents a month-long season of *The Nutcracker,* which opens on Boxing Day. It also puts on a summer season that lasts between three and six weeks. The **Queen Elizabeth Hall** holds 1,000 people and is designed like a lecture hall. However, the sightlines are good, even if the atmosphere is as clinical as an operating-theatre. The intimate **Purcell Room** – which shares the same foyer as the Queen Elizabeth Hall – holds only 375 people. Every August the complex is home to the Ballroom Blitz, a dance extravaganza that takes in performances and classes in everything from flamenco to belly-dancing. *See also chapter* **Music: Classical & Opera**.
Car Park. Free exhibitions. Front seats for the partially sighted by prior arrangement. Guided tours. Infra-red audio for the hard of hearing. Poetry library. Restaurants & cafés. Shops for books, music, records and gifts. Toilets for the disabled. Wheelchair access.

Special Attractions

Broadgate Arena
Corner of Liverpool Street and Eldon Street, EC2 (071 588 6565). Liverpool Street underground/BR. **Performances** May-Sept 12.30-2pm Mon-Fri. **Tickets** free.
This outdoor site in the middle of the massive Broadgate complex becomes an amphitheatre during the summer. Used mainly as a music venue, it also presents some dance companies. The format includes free lunch-time performances that run for an hour. From November to April the Broadgate Arena becomes Britain's only open-air ice rink (*see chapters* **Sport & Fitness** and **London by Area: The City**).
Toilets for the disabled. Wheelchair access.

Dance Books

9 Cecil Court, WC2 (071 836 2314). Leicester Square underground. **Open** 11am-7pm Mon-Sat. **Credit** A, £TC, V.
A stock of books and periodicals, plus videos, records, photos, out-of-print volumes and memorabilia, make this shop a popular venue for dance fans. Dance Books also publishes its own, invariably handsome, books.

Dance Umbrella

20 Chancellor's Street, W6 (081 741 4040). Hammersmith underground. **Tickets** £9-£25. **Credit** A, V.
Now in its second decade, Umbrella is recognised as one of the most exciting showcases for new dance anywhere in the world. The autumn season runs for about six weeks from mid-October and takes place in a variety of venues all over London, including **The Place**, the **Riverside Studios**, the **ICA**, the **South Bank Centre** and **Sadler's Wells Theatre** *(see above for all)*. The programme is filled with premières of the best and most creative work from young British choreographers, together with productions by innovative companies from around the globe. Dance Umbrella, in association with *Time Out*, also sponsors the annual **London Dance and Performance Awards**, which honour the exceptional creative talents working in new dance and performance art.

Holland Park Theatre

Holland Park, Kensington High Street, W8 (box office 071 602 7856/information 071 603 1123). High Street Kensington underground. **Performances** 7.30pm or 8pm, June-Aug. **Tickets** £5-£9. **Credit** A, £TC, V.
A 600-seat open-air theatre in the middle of lush gardens, close to woods, peacocks, and picnickers. Throughout the summer there are outdoor opera, dance and theatre performances; for those rare occasions when it rains, a canopy stretches across the audience and the stage, so you won't be drenched.
Toilets for the disabled. Wheelchair access.

One way to hail a taxi: students go through their paces at **The Place**. *See* **review** *page 232.*

Film

Cineastes can savour anything from art-house to Animal House in one of a myriad movie houses around the metropolis.

The prime jamboree for the capital's film buffs is the **London Film Festival,** which grows in importance each year. It is mainly based at the **National Film Theatre** (*see below* **Repertory**), and takes place in November.

But throughout the year, there is plenty to view in the city's cinemas – over 250 new films are premièred every 12 months in London. Of these, the vast majority are of course American, with around 30 per cent split between Britain and the rest of the world.

After the doldrums of the sixties and seventies, when many picture houses were converted into bingo halls, cinema-going boomed in the late eighties. The greatest innovation has been the building of new multiplex 10- and 12-screen cinemas around Britain. By paying more attention to audience comfort, these houses have found they can tempt people away from the TV and video. Contoured chairs, plus wine, coffee and ice-cream bars, are replacing frayed furniture and steamy hot-dog stands of the old 'flea-pits'. Nearly all cinemas are now entirely no-smoking.

There are five certificates: **'U'** (universal) – suitable for all; **'PG'** – parental guidance advised; **'12'** (no-one under 12 allowed) – a degree of violence and a hint of sex might be present; **'15'** (no-one under 15 allowed) – these can be a little more explicit and might include swear words; **'18'** (no-one under 18 allowed) – most horror movies are given this classification, the language can be enlightening, and (God and the censors preserve us) there might be nudity.

First-Run

West End cinemas are the best places to see mainstream movies, but are also the most expensive. Latest releases are often screened in 70mm and Dolby Stereo, in a spacious auditorium. To avoid queuing at some of the larger cinemas, you can book in advance by credit card over the phone. But you often won't be able to pay by plastic on the door. *Time Out* magazine's 'Film' listings give details of current programmes.

Barbican
Silk Street, EC2 (071 638 8891). Barbican underground or Moorgate underground/BR. **Tickets** £6; £3 Mon, students, OAPs, UB40s. **Credit** A, AmEx, V.
A modern two-screen cinema that has the misfortune to

occupy part of the Barbican concrete jungle. Recently it has moved away from featuring foreign movies, and veered towards the mainstream. Films are often linked to Barbican exhibitions.
Advance booking. Car park. Cafés. Restaurant. Shops. Toilets for the disabled. Wheelchair access.

Camden Plaza
211 Camden High Street, NW1 (071 485 2443). Camden Town underground. **Tickets** £5; £3.80 first show daily; £2.30 OAPs, students, UB40s, first show daily. **Credit** (only accepted for last show) A, AmEx, V.
Primarily a local cinema, the Plaza has sombre décor, but a spacious auditorium and plenty of leg-room. Foreign-language films and unusual British productions are screened, as well as some Hollywood blockbusters.
Advance booking.

Chelsea Cinema
206 King's Road, SW3 (071 351 3742). Sloane Square underground. **Tickets** £6, £5.50; £4 first show daily; £2.50 OAPs, students, UB40s first show daily. **Credit** A, £TC, V.
High-class movies are shown in these high-class surroundings. The atmosphere can be forbidding, but there's a wine bar, attractive seating and an impressive foyer. Prestigious art-house movies are often screened.
Advance booking.

Curzon Mayfair
Curzon Street, W1 (071 465 8865). Green Park underground. **Tickets** £7, £6. **Credit** A, AmEx, V.
Programming and prices at this plush, large-screened cinema reflect the Mayfair area in which it's located. Highly regarded foreign-language films provide much of the entertainment.
Advance booking.

Curzon Phoenix
110 Charing Cross Road, WC2 (071 240 9661). Leicester Square or Tottenham Court Road underground. **Tickets** £5. **Credit** A, AmEx, DC, V.
Admirable British and European pictures, plus the odd offbeat American film are shown at this luxury single-screen cinema hidden just off the Charing Cross Road.
Advance booking.

Empire
Leicester Square, WC2 (071 437 1234/credit card booking 071 497 9999). Leicester Square underground. **Tickets** £8, £6.50; £4 first show daily; £4 under-14s. **Credit** A, AmEx, DC, V.
A luxury three-screen cinema with luxury prices. Major money-earners are shown on a vast screen with amazing THX Lucasfilm sound. Tacky laser shows are put on before each show. The Empire is often used to stage glitzy premières.
Advance booking. Coffee bar. Video bar. Weekend late shows.

Gate Cinema
87 Notting Hill Gate, W11 (071 727 4043). Notting Hill Gate underground. **Tickets** £5.50; £3 OAPs,

students, UB40s first show Mon-Fri (not Bank
Holidays). *Sunday matinées £4; £3 OAPs, students,
UB40s.* **Credit** A, V.
A wonderful cinema, where baskets of papier mâché fruit
adorn the foyer. Unusual movies, mainstream blockbusters and independent films are screened throughout
the week, but it's also worth a visit for the Sunday matinée double-bills.
Advance booking. Weekend late shows. Wheelchair access.

ICA Cinema
*Nash House, The Mall, SW1 (071 930 3647).
Piccadilly Circus underground or Charing Cross
underground/BR.* **Membership** £20 per year.
Tickets (incl day membership) £6; £5 OAPs,
students, UB40s Mon, first show Tue-Fri. **Credit** A,
AmEx, DC, £TC, V.
Modern and archive work from Asia, Europe, the Soviet
Union and America can be seen during the week, while
cinematic treats for young children are shown at the
weekend. Day membership allows you to visit the exhi-
bitions and café.
*Advance booking. Bar. Bookshop. Café. Group discount.
Lectures. Workshops.*

Lumière
*42 St Martin's Lane, WC2 (071 836 0691). Leicester
Square underground.* **Tickets** £7, £6; £5 first show
daily; £3 OAPs, students, UB40s first show daily.
Credit A, AmEx, £TC, V.
Film critics have been known to rave about this luxurious but relaxing cinema, one of the finest in the capital.
Major new foreign-language films are an important part
of the programme.
*Advance booking. Weekend late shows. Wheelchair
access.*

Metro
*11 Rupert Street, W1 (071 437 0757). Piccadilly
Circus or Leicester Square underground.* **Tickets** or £6;
£4 Mon, nurses, OAPs, students, UB40s, under-16s.
No credit cards.
A two-screen cinema showing independent English-lan-
guage films alongside Indian, Chinese and European
successes. It's also the home of the London Latin
American Film Festival.
Advance booking.

MGM Haymarket
*Haymarket, W1 (071 839 1527/credit card bookings
081 970 6016 – subject to booking fee). Piccadilly Circus
underground.* **Tickets** £6.50; £3.25 Mon; £3.50 before
6pm Tue-Fri. **Credit** A, V.
A three-screen cinema with standard blockbuster-type
programmes, small seats and a bold sixties-style interior.
Weekend late shows.

MGM Panton Street
*Panton Street, SW1 (071 930 0631/credit card bookings
081 970 6021 – subject to booking fee). Piccadilly Circus
underground.* **Tickets** £5; £2.50 Mon; £3.50 before 6pm
Tues-Fri. **Credit** A, V.
A four-screen complex which occasionally shows more off-
beat films than the other MGM branches. Unfortunately,
the screens are tiny and the atmosphere claustrophobic.

MGM Piccadilly
*Piccadilly, W1 (071 437 3561). Piccadilly Circus
underground.* **Tickets** £6; £3 Mon; £3.50 before 6pm
Tues-Fri. **No credit cards.**
Two screens with 150 seats each. The gay programmes
attract a loyal following. No advance booking.
Weekend late shows.

MGM Shaftesbury Avenue
*135 Shaftesbury Avenue, WC2 (071 836 6279/credit
card booking 081 970 6021 – subject to booking fee).
Leicester Square or Tottenham Court Road
underground.* **Tickets** £6.50; £3.25 Mon; £3.50 before
6pm Tues-Fri. **Credit** A, V.
A comfortable two-screen cinema that's frequented by
theatre trendies who come to see what are often critically-acclaimed English-language films.
Advance booking.

MGM Tottenham Court Road
*30 Tottenham Court Road, W1 (071 636 6148/credit
card booking 081 970 6032 – subject to booking fee).
Tottenham Court Road underground.* **Tickets** £6; £3
Mon; £3.50 before 6pm Tues-Fri. **Credit** A, V.
This small, three-screen theatre looks like a flea-pit out-
side, but has a surprisingly clean and modern interior.
Hidden around the corner from the mainstream MGM
Oxford Street, it doesn't attract long queues. European
and independent US and British films form the main
programme.
Weekend late shows.

Minema
*45 Knightsbridge, SW1 (071 235 4225). Hyde Park
Corner or Knightsbridge underground.* **Tickets** £6.50;
£3.50 first two shows Mon-Fri (not Bank Holidays);
£3.50 OAPs, students, UB40s. **Credit** A, AmEx, V.
A small independent cinema specialising in quality films
that have won the critics' praise.
Advance booking.

Notting Hill Coronet
*Notting Hill Gate, W11 (071 727 6705). Notting Hill
underground.* **Tickets** £5.50, £2.75 OAPs; £2.75 under-
14s before 6pm. **Credit** A, V.
The last smoking cinema in London, the Coronet's shabbiness is part of its charm. The programming was adventurous once, but mainstream American blockbusters are
the only films ensuring survival nowadays. One screen,
600 (reclining) seats.

Odeon Haymarket
*Haymarket, W1 (0426 915353/credit card bookings
071 839 7697). Piccadilly Circus underground.*
Tickets £6-£8; OAPs, students £3 off before 5pm
Mon-Fri. **Credit** A, V.
A pleasant, single-screen cinema with a small bar. Some
distributors insist on their films being shown here first,
because of the cinema's reputation for screening criti-
cally-acclaimed mainstream works.
Advance booking.

Odeon Kensington
*High Street Kensington, W8 (0426 915353/credit card
bookings 071 371 3166). High Street Kensington
underground.* **Tickets** £6.30, £5.80; £3.50 OAPs,
students before 6pm, under-15s. **Credit** A, V.
There's not much in the way of refreshments at this four-
screener. Hollywood hits are the order of the day, but
films tend to stay for a longer run than in the West End.
This means flops outstay their welcome.
*Advance booking. Weekend late shows. Wheelchair
access to Screens 2, 3 and 4.*

Odeon Leicester Square
*Leicester Square, WC2 (0426 915683/credit card
bookings 071 930 3232). Leicester Square or Piccadilly
Circus underground.* **Tickets** £7-£9; £4-£6 OAPs early
afternoon. **Credit** A, V.
Famed for its black art deco façade and tower, this is the
largest cinema in London. The Royal Family comes here

The **Electric Cinema**: *London's oldest. See* **review** *page 238.*

to see films premièred. Major Hollywood films are the order of the day (and night).
Advance booking. Toilets for the disabled. Weekend late shows. Wheelchair access.

Odeon Marble Arch
10 Edgware Road, W2 (0426 914501/credit card bookings 071 723 2011). Marble Arch underground. **Tickets** £6-£8. **Credit** A, V.
Battle through massive weekend queues to watch Hollywood blockbusters shown on London's biggest screen. The best views are from the balcony; the sound is superb everywhere.
Advance booking. Weekend late shows.

Plaza
17-25 Lower Regent Street, SW1 (071 437 1234/credit card bookings 071 497 9999). Piccadilly Circus underground. **Tickets** £6.50; £4 under-14s, first performance Mon-Fri. **Credit** A, AmEx, DC, V.
American and British money-makers are shown at this US-style, four-screen movie house. It is one of the few cinemas with a sufficient number of ticket booths.
Advance booking. Weekend late shows.

Prince Charles
Leicester Place, WC2 (071 437 8181). Piccadilly Circus or Leicester Square underground. **Tickets** £1.20-£1.99. *Lates* £6. **No credit cards**.
With the cheapest seats in London, the Prince Charles screens a programme of recent American movies, classic revivals and European imports.
Weekend late shows.

Renoir
Brunswick Centre, Brunswick Square, WC1 (071 837 8402). Russell Square underground. **Tickets** £5.50; £4 first show daily; £2.50 OAPs, students, UB40s first show daily. **Credit** A, AmEx, V.
Even though this cinema was built under a housing estate, its off-beat British pictures and critically-acclaimed foreign-language films draw cinema-goers away from Leicester Square.
Advance booking.

Screen on Baker Street
96 Baker Street, NW1 (071 935 2772). Baker Street underground. **Tickets** £5; £3.50 Mon (not Bank Holidays), first two shows Tue-Thur. **Credit** A, V.
Quality independents and British movies are shown at this small, two-screen theatre.
Advance booking. Sat late show.

Screen on the Green
83 Upper Street, N1 (071 226 3520). Angel underground. **Tickets** £5; £3.50 Mon (not Bank Holidays), first show Tue-Fri. *Lates* £4.50. **Credit** A, V.
A distinctive cinema, reminiscent of a picture palace of old. Its name is strikingly displayed in pink and green neon, the exterior is bold and white, pillars frame the entrance. The programme is selected to bring in the money, but redeems itself with a few impressive films. Good snacks and coffee are sold.
Advance booking. Weekend late shows.

Screen on the Hill
203 Haverstock Hill, NW3 (071 435 3366). Belsize Park underground. **Tickets** £5; £3.50 Mon (not Bank Holidays), first show Tue-Fri. *Lates* £5. **Credit** A, V.
Mainly American and British releases of artistic note are screened in this small but comfortable local cinema which has high-quality cakes and coffee.
Advance booking. Weekend late shows. Wheelchair access.

UCI Whiteleys 8 Cinema
Whiteleys of Bayswater, Queensway, W2 (box office 071 792 3303/recorded information 071 792 3332/credit card bookings 071 792 3324). Bayswater or Queensway underground. **Tickets** £5.75; £3.50 before 3pm daily; £3 OAPs before 5pm Mon-Fri, under-14s. **Credit** A, £TC, V.
London's first multiplex cinema provides a stream of blockbusters on each of the eight screens. It has two foyers with enough ticket booths to prevent long queues. All cafés in the adjoining shopping centre remain open until the last show. The largest auditorium seats 330 and has ear-shattering THX (Lucasfilm) sound.

Advance booking. Toilets for the disabled. Wheelchair access.

Warner West End
Leicester Square, WC2 (071 437 3484/recorded information 071 437 4347/credit card bookings 071 437 4343). Leicester Square underground. **Tickets** £7; £4 before 5pm, OAPs, students, UB40s, under-12s. **Credit** A, £TC, V.
Originally opened in 1938, the West End had a complete £15 million overhaul before re-opening in September 1993 as a multiplex. Its nine screens are as big as any in the West End and are spread over eight levels.
Advance booking. Wheelchair access.

Repertory

Repertory cinemas screen an array of new and vintage English and foreign-language films, cult oddities, art-films and classics, often with programmes changing daily. At least, that is the theory. Commercial pressures have meant that several now rely on showing films that have only just completed their West End runs. Recently, a number of reps that refused to follow this policy have gone out of business. Some repertory cinemas will only admit members, but the fee is often about 50p per year, payable with your ticket. Consult *Time Out* magazine for current programmes.

Electric Cinema
191 Portobello Road, W11 (071 792 2020/recorded information 071 792 0328). Ladbroke Grove or Notting Hill Gate underground/7, 15, 52 bus. **Tickets** £4.50; £3.50 OAPs, students, UB40s. *Children's matinées* £2. **Credit** A, V.
The oldest surviving purpose-built cinema in London, beautifully restored and technically the equal of the major chains. Everything from mainstream American to obscure foreign-language imports is shown at this 437-seat picture palace. Concessionary rates are available Mon-Fri, and before 4.30pm Sat.

Everyman
Hollybush Vale, NW3 (071 435 1525). Hampstead underground. **Membership** 60p per year. **Tickets** £4.50; £3.50 nurses, OAPs, students, UB40s; £2.50 under-15s. *Season tickets* £32 for ten tickets.
No credit cards.
London's oldest repertory cinema, with plush seating, good food and friendly staff. European and English-language favourites intermingle with cult films and directorial seasons. First-run and major revivals are also shown, in double- and triple-bills. Concessionary rates are available Mon-Fri and before 4.30pm Sat, Sun.
Café. Toilets for the disabled. Wheelchair access.

French Institute
17 Queensberry Place, SW7 (071 589 6211). South Kensington underground. **Tickets** £3.50; £2.50 OAPs, students, UB40s. **No credit cards.**
New and classic French films are shown on a large screen two or three times a week. Booking in person is essential. There's also a café-bar and exhibition area.

Goethe Institute
50 Princes Gate, Exhibition Road, SW7 (071 581 3344). South Kensington underground. **Tickets** £1.50.
No credit cards.

German celluloid triumphs from as early as 1913 are screened twice weekly, often without subtitles. The occasional US classic has been known to sneak in.
Personal & postal bookings only.

ICA Cinemathèque
Nash House, The Mall, SW1 (071 930 3647). Piccadilly Circus underground or Charing Cross underground/BR. **Membership** £20 per year, £1.50 per day. **Tickets** £4 (incl day membership). **Credit** A, AmEx, DC, V.
A small, but ambitious cinema that screens seasons of directors' work, together with horror, animated, and political films and videos. Day membership allows you to visit the ICA's exhibitions and café.
Advance booking. Bar. Bookshop. Café. Group discount. Lectures. Workshops.

National Film Theatre
South Bank, SE1 (071 928 3232). Waterloo underground/BR. **Membership** £13.50 per year (student membership £8; daily membership 40p). **Tickets** £3.95; £2.75 disabled, OAPs, students, UB40s. **Credit** A, AmEx, £TC, V.
Widely varied programmes are shown at the two screens inside the confusing NFT structure, plus the new one at **MOMI** (*see chapter* **Museums**). Seasons dedicated to directors or to countries, genres or themes are featured alongside classics. The British Film Institute Awards are held here in October; the London Film Festival in November.
Advance booking. Bar, café and restaurant. Toilets for the disabled. Wheelchair access.

Phoenix
52 High Road, N2 (081 444 6789/recorded information 081 883 2233). East Finchley underground. **Tickets** £4; £3 Mon; £3 students, UB40s; £2 OAPs, under-15s. *Children's cinema club* £2. **No credit cards.**
European, American and Asian cinematic successes are shown in this comfortable old auditorium, often in double bills. The programme changes several times a week and there's a children's cinema club on Saturday mornings. No concessionary rates after 6pm Sat.
Advance booking. Wheelchair access by prior arrangement.

Rio
107 Kingsland High Street, E8 (071 249 2722/recorded information 071 254 6677). Dalston Kingsland BR/67, 76, 149, 243 bus. **Tickets** £4.50; £3.50 OAPs, students, UB40s; £2.50 under-15s. *Lates* £4.50 (no concs).
Children's cinema club £1.50 (£2.50 adults). *Classic matinées* £3; £2.50 under-15s; £1.25 OAPs & carers.
No credit cards.
A decaying old theatre that's dilapidated enough to be charming. Everything from acclaimed European films to cult American pictures is shown as double-bills here, with a children's film club on Saturday mornings. Price reductions for screenings on Mon, and before 5.30pm Tue-Fri.
Toilets for the disabled. Weekend late shows. Wheelchair access.

Riverside Studios
Crisp Road, W6 (081 748 3354). Hammersmith underground. **Tickets** £3.75; £2.60 nurses, OAPs, students, UB40s, under-16s. **Credit** A, V.
A converted film studio hidden in an arts centre, the Riverside screens a surprising choice of films. Recent British work is shown alongside classics, art-house, cult and the best of the rest. It's the home of the BP Expo Student Film and Video Festival. *See also chapters* **Art Galleries**, **Dance** and **Theatre**.
Advance booking. Bar. Bookshop. Café. Restaurant. Wheelchair access.

Music: Classical & Opera

How long can London's orchestras continue to triumph, under a government that doesn't know its arts from its elbow?

*The first night of the Proms at the **Royal Albert Hall**. See **review** page 241.*

For quality, quantity and variety London has the highest standard of classical music of any western capital. Only New York approaches it. Some have complained that the city's plethora of full-scale symphony orchestras leads to cut-throat competition, over-safe programming and audiences spread too thinly. Conventional wisdom has it that the cream of London's orchestras could combine for a super-band on the level of Berlin or Vienna; London would have a world-beater instead of five merely good orchestras (that's counting the BBC Symphony Orchestra).

No musician, native or foreign, agrees with this. Visiting conductors point out that each of London's symphony orchestras has evolved its own character and its specialities. The Phil-

harmonia has even carved out a base in the most culturally chauvinistic society in the world: though officially snubbed in London, it plays regularly in Paris to the annoyance of French artistic bureaucracy and the pleasure of mere music-lovers. On a good night, given enough rehearsal (blame official philistinism for cheeseparing economies in time and resources), they have all been known to reach the highest international standards. Besides, as every musician points out, great orchestras aren't created by political diktat. France has discovered this over the past 30 years. Unlimited money, prestige and politicising have managed to make the artificially-created Orchestre de Paris into a respectable band, but not the rival to Chicago or Leningrad as originally envisaged.

At the time of writing, London's orchestral life is in a tangle, thanks to official meanness, indifference and crass ignorance. The government funding body, the Arts Council, enjoys provoking a financial judgement of Solomon while chickening out of the sort of artistic decisions that should be its business. Operatic life is also in a state of wait-and-see, though things are more optimistic here. The administration of the **Royal Opera House** (ROH) in Covent Garden has had a welcome shot of new and expert blood; while at the **Coliseum** the English National Opera (ENO) settles down in the first season of new management. Over the past few years the Royal Opera has come in for brickbats: the institution we love to hate for its élitism, high prices, lack of artistic policy and the ill-judged property development proposals that have led it into a financial morass not to mention the fury of the environmental lobby. Supporters point out that the ROH is merely doing what it must to survive in Britain's ludicrously underfunded arts scene, according to the fishwife political tenets of Thatcherite market-forces. But the audiences of braying non-musical socialites and snoozing businessmen sponsors, allied with the General Director Jeremy Isaacs' frequently abrasive PR manner, make it hard to sympathise.

Meanwhile ENO, in the vanguard of 'people's opera' and opera-as-theatre, holds its breath to see how the former administration's slightly jaded trio of ageing whizzkids (theatrical, musical, managerial) will be succeeded by a new managing director, the bravely chosen Sìan Edwards (both young *and* female), and Dennis Marks – ominously, perhaps, another high-powered executive from television, like Isaacs at the ROH.

The one undoubted success of the past year has been the refurbished **Wigmore Hall**. The beloved old venue, cherished for its friendliness and intimacy by performers and audiences alike, has had the architectural equivalent of hormone-replacement therapy, to emerge with new restaurant and bar space and backstage facilities. The much-publicised theft of Victoria de los Angeles' jewels showed up shortcomings in security; certain safeguards are necessary when dealing with that eccentric breed, famous sopranos who carry a fortune round the world with them in a handbag. Otherwise the Wigmore's Sunday morning coffee-concerts are still the most bearable way to start a London sabbath.

For detailed information of performances, times and places see *Time Out*'s 'Classical Music' listings.

Major Venues

Barbican Centre
Silk Street, EC2 (071 638 8891). Barbican underground (closed Sun) or Moorgate

Lunchtime music amid the City's mayhem at **St Bride's**. *See* **review** page 244.

underground/BR. **Open** *box office* 9am-8pm daily.
Admission £5-£20. **Credit** A, AmEx, V.
This grim cultural stalag was the City's gift to London's
arts world. And London never stops grumbling about it.
The Barbican concert hall is home to the London
Symphony Orchestra and the English Chamber
Orchestra – though both bodies hop across the river to
the **South Bank** (*see below*), for large-scale choral and
orchestral works that the Barbican's designers neglected to plan for. Among its many festivals, theme-cycles
and series, the Barbican has at least one biggie every
year. The LSO is planning a series for Jessye Norman,
the great American soprano, in March 1994, a Mahler
season for autumn 1994 and celebrations for the birthday of Russian composer Alfred Schnittke in November.
Old and new are excitingly balanced with Nikolaus
Harnoncourt conducting the Chamber Orchestra of
Europe in Beethoven, Schumann and Brahms (11
March, 1994) and young pianist Joanna Macgregor
devising a festival of new music (28 April-4 May).
'Platform 4: 1994' includes jazz and improvisation besides
contemporary classical music. Visiting great bands
(book early) include the legendary Leipzig Gewandhaus
under Kurt Masur (21, 22 April) and the Royal
Concertgebouw from Amsterdam conducted by
Riccardo Chailly (24 April). Not to be missed in 1994:
young piano phenomenon Yevgeny Kissin (15 May),
Anne Sophie Mutter (7 October), Itzhak Perlman (27
October) and Andras Schiff (11 December).
*Car Park. Restaurant & cafés. Shops. Toilets for the
disabled. Wheelchair access.*

The London Coliseum

*St Martin's Lane, WC2 (box office 071 836 3161/credit
card bookings 071 240 5258/recorded information 071
836 7666). Leicester Square underground or Charing
Cross underground/BR.* **Open** *box office* 10am-8pm
Mon-Sat. **Tickets** £8-£42.50. **Credit** A, AmEx, DC,
£TC, V.
The Coliseum's lovely Edwardian auditorium first rang
to the sound of the Sadler's Wells Opera in 1968. The
company stayed, and is now the English National Opera
(ENO). Performances are in English, but there is nothing parochial about them. The company has toured
abroad and its home-grown stars include Valerie
Masterson (a success in French opera) and John
Tomlinson (who has played Wotan at the Bayreuth
Festival). Among the established stars is international
Wagnerian Norman Bailey. ENO productions range
through the repertoire, from Monteverdi to the moderns,
but above all, they exist as theatre – sometimes controversial, sometimes outrageous, sometimes a brilliantly
successful gamble. The new General Director should
keep up the adventurous policy; Dennis Marks has made
a name for innovative opera coverage at the BBC. The
1994 repertory emphasises the company's strong theatre
tradition: Jonathan Miller returns for a new *Der
Rosenkavalier* (Feb and March), rubbing shoulders with
Nicholas Hytner's witty success with Handel's *Xerxes* and
David Pountney's production of Verdi's *Falstaff* which
changes from *Dynasty*-style costumes to authentic
Elizabethan before our eyes. April sees the world première of *Blond Eckbert* by acclaimed Scots composer
Judith Weir. New productions include *Così fan tutte*
(May), a *Bohème* from director Stephen Plimlott, and
Jenufa by Janácek, a composer close to ENO's heart
(June). And watch out for Britten's *Peter Grimes* (May),
a stylised production by another theatre-cum-opera
director, Tim Albery. The opera boom in London owes
more to the Coli than to the glossy, expense-account
appeal of the ROH. Parents take children to their first
opera here. Sandwiches and coffee in the Dutch Bar take
the place of Covent Garden's champagne and smoked
salmon. The nearby Coliseum shop has an excellent

selection of records, videos, libretti, books and magazines. *See also chapter* **Dance**.
*Group & family discount (071 836 0111 ext 318). Shop
(10am-7.30pm Mon-Sat). Toilets for the disabled.
Wheelchair access.*

Royal Albert Hall

*Kensington Gore, SW7 (information 071 589 3203/box
office 071 589 8212). High Street Kensington or
Knightsbridge underground/9, 73 bus.* **Open** *box office*
9am-9pm daily. **Tickets** £3.50-£30. **Credit** A, AmEx, V.
The Royal Albert Hall is the major host of the best music
festival in the world, the BBC Henry Wood Promenade
Concerts. The Proms run from mid-July to mid-
September and include a variety of orchestras, ensem-
bles and performers from all over the world; tickets are
at subsidised prices. The hall is rich in atmosphere and
has been a well-loved venue for over a century. It has had
acoustical problems but there have been improvements
in recent times. The old place comes into its own with
massed choirs and big orchestral forces.
*Guided tours (May-Oct). Induction loops for the hard of
hearing. Toilets for the disabled. Wheelchair access by
prior arrangement.*

Royal Opera House

*Covent Garden, WC2 (071 240 1066). Covent Garden
underground.* **Open** *box office* 10am-8pm Mon-Sat.
Tickets £1.75-£113. **Credit** A, AmEx, DC, £TC, V.
The Royal Opera House is London's answer to La Scala,
the Met, the Bastille, and the Vienna Staatsoper. This is
where you might see Domingo and Pavarotti, if they
bother to turn up. Government cuts have meant that seat
prices have risen to levels previously unheard of in
London. The audience now has a high proportion of
block business subscribers. Foreign-language performances are translated in subtitles over the proscenium.
Bar staff are still among the best in the world – fast, efficient and courteous. The Royal Opera has painted itself
into a Thatcherite corner by its emphasis on private funding, sponsorship, and business support. There are signs
that the ROH has taken criticisms to heart and is struggling to be more accessible, but prices are still out of
reach for the average music-lover, and a repertory which
tends to comprise star-vehicles and obscure insipidity
adds to the incentive to save your pennies. Whether the
new production of Massenet's *Chérubin* will amount to
any more than a *précieux* museum-piece, a lacy valentine
(première 14 Feb, 1994), remains to be seen. And no self-
respecting opera house should bother with that prepos-
terous old piece of hokum, Giordano's *Fedora* (9 May),
even as a vehicle for a star tenor (Careras). Rossini's
Mosè in Egitto (23 May) continues the Royal Opera's fix-
ation with the more inept works of the Swan of Pesaro.
Both Italian works are co-productions with foreign theatres – forced economic marriages that frequently result
in disaster, as one country's art is another race's kitsch.
Try Trevor Nunn's production of *Katya Kabanova*
(March 1994): more Janácek from a master-opera (and
Shakespeare- and musical-) director. Two undisputed
successes, Harrison Birtwistle's *Gawain* and Puccini's
Fanciulla del west should be caught in spring and early
summer; and the new *Aida* reminds us of the ROH's new
Verdi initiative – to stage all the composer's works leading up to the centenary of his death in 2001.
*Opera and ballet education officers. Shop. Toilets for the
disabled. Wheelchair access.*

St James's Church, Piccadilly

*Piccadilly, W1 (071 734 4511). Piccadilly Circus
underground.* **Admission** *lunchtime* donation of £2
appreciated; *festivals* £8-£15; tickets available at the
door one hour before performance starts. **Credit** A, V.
Designed by Christopher Wren, St James's provides a

Simon Rattle, conductor of the CBSO.

peaceful oasis in the middle of London. Young musicians give lunchtime recitals Wed-Fri each week, and concerts are slotted in among such activities as talks, discussions and healing sessions. The Lufthansa Festival (a regular summer event) yields a feast of baroque music which attracts some of the best international performers of early music. Contact Tony Goodchild (081 940 7835) for information (box office 071 434 4003). The RTZ Festival of Young Musicians takes place here during October 1994.

St John's Smith Square

Smith Square, SW1 (071 222 1061). Westminster underground. **Open** *box office* 10am-5pm Mon-Fri; till start of concert on concert nights. **Tickets** £5-£15. **Credit** A, £TC, V.

Situated within belching distance of Conservative Party headquarters, St John's church is a happy example of conversion to other uses. The musical fare is similar to the **Wigmore**'s (*see below*), though slightly more space means that chamber orchestras figure more prominently here. BBC lunchtime concerts provide a frequent bargain (Mondays at 1pm). *Restaurant.*

South Bank Centre

South Bank, Belvedere Road, SE1 (box office 071 928 8800/recorded information 071 633 0932). Waterloo underground/BR/Riverbus. **Open** *box office* 10am-9pm daily. **Tickets** £2-£50 **Credit** A, AmEx, DC, V.

The windy wastes of concrete detract from this fun-palace complex. The **Royal Festival Hall** is the largest concert hall on the South Bank, ideal for orchestral concerts and large-scale choral works. The **Queen Elizabeth Hall** is smaller – a good space for chamber orchestras – and is convertible into a temporary theatre for visiting opera productions. The smallest hall, the **Purcell Room**, hosts the debut recitals of many young artists. The South Bank Arts Centre has come to emphasise the 'theme' series as a way of beating the jaded palates of the musically over-fed. The complex, which includes book and record shops and a

variety of eating places far preferable to the Barbican's, is also the home of Opera Factory whose abrasive productions under director David Freeman frequently shock, jolt and even – as with their *dolce vita* beach-bum version of *Così fan tutte* – prove a revelation. In 1994 there are two new productions, including Stravinsky's *The Rake's Progress* (May). Meanwhile the London Philharmonic, the South Bank's precarious resident orchestra, contributes to the Luciano Berio Festival (late April-May) and an extensive festival devoted to German Romanticism that includes a vast exhibition at the Hayward Gallery (Sept-Nov). The superb Alban Berg Quartet gives recitals throughout the year; international piano recitalists include the veteran Tatyana Nikolaeva, Alfred Brendel, Krystian Zimerman, Maurizio Pollini and Stephen Hough. Simon Rattle and his world-class Birmingham band, the CBSO, celebrate the 1930s in the latest instalment of their progress *Towards the Millenium* (March). And after last year's success, the summer junket of avante-garde, *Meltdown* (June-July), ranging through different forms and artistic experiences, will be worth catching. *See also chapter* **Dance**.

Car Park. Free exhibitions. Front seats for the partially sighted by prior arrangement. Guided tours. Infra-red audio for the hard of hearing. Poetry library. Restaurants & cafés. Shops for books, music and records. Toilets for the disabled. Wheelchair access.

Wigmore Hall

36 Wigmore Street, W1 (071 935 2141). Bond Street underground. **Open** *box office* 10am-8.30pm (10am-5pm when no concert) Mon-Sat; *Dec-Mar* 10.30am-1pm, 3.15-5.30pm, Sun; *Apr-Oct* 10.30am-1pm, 6.15-8.30pm, Sun. **Performances** 7.30pm Mon-Sat; *Dec-Mar* 11.30am, 3pm Sun; *Apr-Oct* 11.30am, 7pm, Sun. **Tickets** £3-£18. **Credit** A, AmEx, DC, V.

Artists love the Wigmore for its consoling acoustics and immediate contact with the audience. The hall is a favourite location for recitals and chamber music and offers the most civilised pastime for Sunday morning (sex and newspapers notwithstanding) in its mid-morning concerts which include coffee or sherry. Evening concerts are held seven nights a week, apart from the summer closure, and include intimate music (chamber, instrumental, vocal) from every period in every style. Prices tend to be cheap, but popular concerts sell out fast.

Restaurant (open noon-3pm, 5.30-8pm, Mon-Fri; 5.30-8pm Sat; noon-4pm Sun). Café/bar (open 11.30am-one hour after performance, 5.30pm-one hour after performance, Mon-Fri. Wheelchair access.

Lunchtime Concerts

One of the great pleasures of London's musical life is the tradition of performances in churches, not just as part of the service but in concert and recital, especially at lunchtime. Tired shoppers, workers enjoying their break, curious tourists and casual passers-by are all welcome. Concerts are usually free though donations are customary and sometimes collections are taken. Artists include young professionals, students and established musicians. Standards are usually high.

All Souls

Langham Place, W1 (071 580 3522). Oxford Circus underground.

All Souls is patronised by the BBC (aren't we all?). It specialises in organ music recitals and there's often an admission charge.

St Anne and St Agnes

Gresham Street, EC2 (071 373 5566). St Paul's underground.

St Anne and St Agnes not only puts on lunchtime concerts (starting at 1.10pm Mon and Fri) but has performances of liturgical music in the church services. As a Lutheran church it excels in the music of Bach, performed as part of the Sunday service as originally intended. *Wheelchair access with assistance.*

St Bride

Fleet Street, EC4 (071 353 1301). Blackfriars underground/BR.

Lunchtime concerts are frequently held here. They feature either professional musicians or senior students. Performances start at 1.15pm and last for 35 minutes. They stop during Lent and Advent. *Wheelchair access to ground floor only.*

St Lawrence Jewry

Guildhall, EC2 (071 600 9478). Bank or St Paul's underground.

A handsome Wren church (1678) which has a rather unusual Mander organ made out of parts saved from the Blitz. Lunchtime piano recitals are held on Mondays, and organ recitals on Tuesdays, both at 1pm. During August, there's a lunchtime festival, with a concert every weekday. *Wheelchair access with assistance.*

St Margaret

Lothbury, EC2 (071 606 8330). Bank underground.

Adjacent to the Bank of England, the church contains a recently restored English pipe organ of 1801, one of the finest in London. Frequent lunchtime recitals (1.10pm Thur) feature guest organists as well as other vocal and instrumental combinations.

St Martin-in-the-Fields

Trafalgar Square, WC2 (071 930 0089). Charing Cross underground/BR.

St Martin-in-the-Fields has given its name to an excellent chamber orchestra. Young artists give two or three lunchtime recitals a week and there are occasional evening concerts. The café in the crypt is especially recommended. *Bookshop. Café. Toilets for the disabled. Wheelchair access.*

St Martin-within-Ludgate

Ludgate Hill, EC4 (071 248 6054). St Paul's underground or Blackfriars underground/BR.

A striking church with a magnificent spire that was completed by Wren in 1684. Recitals are given on Wednesday lunchtimes at 1.15pm, and cover a wide spectrum, from classical to Palm Court.

St Mary-le-Bow Church

Cheapside, EC2 (071 248 5139). St Paul's underground.

This beautiful church provides a sympathetic environment for early, medieval and Renaissance music. Recitals are on Thursdays, starting at 1.05pm. On Tuesday at 1.05pm the Bow Dialogue takes place: a discussion between the vicar and a prominent personality.

St Michael's

Cornhill, EC3 (071 626 8841). Bank underground.

St Michael's excellent series of Monday lunchtime organ recitals is now an integral part of the City's musical life. *Guided tours by arrangement.*

St Olave's

Hart Street, EC3 (071 488 4318). Tower Hill underground/Fenchurch Street BR.

St Olave's lunchtime chamber music recitals, every Wednesday and Thursday at 1.05pm, feature a selection of solo, duo and trio instrumentalists.

St Sepulchre-without-Newgate

Holborn Viaduct, EC1 (071 248 1660). Chancery Lane or St Paul's underground/Holborn Viaduct BR.

St Sepulchre's is known as 'The Musicians' Church' –

St John's Smith Square: *a champion of chamber music. See* **review** *page 243.*

we're prepared to bet that it is the only church in the world where Mimi from *La Bohème* is depicted in a stained-glass window. Sir Henry Wood, founder of the Proms, is also commemorated here.

Around & About

Almeida
Almeida Street, N1 (071 359 4404). Angel underground or Highbury & Islington underground/BR or Essex Road BR. **Open** *box office* 10am-6pm Mon-Sat. **Performances** 8pm Mon-Sat; *matinées* 4pm Sat. **Tickets** £7.50; £5 students, OAPs. **Membership** £10 per year. **Credit** A, AmEx, DC, V.
This is perhaps the London venue most deserving of the adjectives 'avant garde' and 'international'. It has been condemned by its local authority for not being international enough. Such idiocies are the stuff of local arts commissars. Through the year, drama alternates with occasional weekend concerts. The high-powered international music festival has a worthy descendant in Almeida Opera, a festival of new stage works interspersed with concerts, now run in conjunction with English National Opera in July.
Restaurant. Toilets for the disabled. Wheelchair access.

Blackheath Concert Halls
23 Lee Road, Blackheath, SE3 (box office 081 318 9758/information 081 463 0100). Blackheath BR/54, 75, 89, 108 bus. **Open** *box office* 8am-7pm Mon-Sat. **Tickets** £3-£15. **Credit** A, V.
A venue for high-powered series and cycles. International artists often perform here. See *Time Out* magazine's listings for details.
Educational projects. Shop (open for concert events only). Wheelchair access to ground floor only.

British Music Information Centre
10 Stratford Place, W1 (071 499 8567). Bond Street underground. **Open** 10am-5pm Mon-Fri. **Recitals** 7.30pm Tue, Thur. **Tickets** £2-£3.
A unique collection of scores, taped music, records, compact discs and videos about composers are kept here. There's usually a recital (predominantly new British music) on Tuesday and Thursday evenings – although not in August.

Burgh House
New End Square, NW3 (071 431 0144). Hampstead underground.
Regular concerts by local musicians are given in this museum venue. There's no set evening for music, so check *Time Out* magazine's listings for details. Tickets average £3. *See also chapter* **By Area: North**.

Dulwich Picture Gallery
College Road, SE21 (081 693 5254). West Dulwich BR/P4, 12, 37, 78, 176 bus. **Open** 11am-1pm, 2-5pm, Tue-Fri; 11am-5pm Sat; 2-5pm Sun. **Admission** *gallery* £2; £1 OAPs, students, UB40s; free under-15s. *Concerts* £5-£10. **No credit cards.**
The oldest art gallery in England is also a venue for promenade concerts on one Saturday a month at 11.30am. Recitals are held in the evenings (at 8pm), also about once a month; phone for details. *See also chapter* **Art Galleries**.
Guided tours. Lectures. Wheelchair access.

Fenton House
Hampstead Grove, NW3 (071 435 3471). Hampstead underground. **Open** 1-6.30pm Mon-Wed; 11am-5.30pm Sat, Sun. **Admission** £6; £12 for celebrity concerts.
Fenton House contains the treasured Benton Fletcher

Jessye Norman, appearing at the **Barbican Centre**. *See* **review** *page 240.*

collection of early keyboard instruments. First-class musicians give recitals of baroque music on occasional Wednesday evenings between May and September.
Wheelchair access to ground floor only.

Kenwood Lakeside Concerts
Kenwood House, Hampstead Lane, NW3 (081 348 1286). Archway, Highgate or Hampstead underground. **Tickets** £3-£7.50; concessions for children, OAPs, students, UB40s. Book through Ticketmaster (*071 379 4444*) or on the night two hours before the concert begins. **Dates** Sat June-Aug. **Credit** A, AmEx, DC, V.
The Lakeside Concerts take place in a magical setting among the trees at the side of Kenwood lake. Take a picnic hamper, pray it doesn't rain, settle in a deckchair and let the classical melodies soothe away the city blues. The concerts tend towards safe, popular classics, but they're by top orchestras. Audibility is not first-rate, but never mind the music. The evening ends with a firework display.
Wheelchair access.

Lauderdale House
Waterlow Park, Highgate Hill, N6 (081 348 8716/081 391 2032). Archway underground. **Open** 11am-4pm Tue-Fri. **Tickets** £3.50-£6. **No credit cards.**
You can treat children to a fair or a puppet show on Saturday morning, and enjoy a recital in the evening at this family venue. Performances might be by a local professional trying out a programme before appearing at the Wigmore Hall. Saturdays and Sundays tend to be the music days, but phone for details.

National Sound Archive
29 Exhibition Road, SW7 (071 589 6603). South Kensington underground. **Open** 9am-5pm Mon-Wed, Fri; 9am-9pm Thur.
The proverbial Aladdin's cave, housing millions of items of recorded sound from the 1890s to the present, plus over 80,000 musical scores to use with recordings. If you want to hear Beatrice Harrison playing her cello to the nightingale in her garden, you must book in advance.

Music: Rock, Folk & Jazz

Seven nights a week, in pubs, clubs, halls and ballrooms, London raps, raggas and rocks on relentlessly.

It may go against the prevailing belief that live music is dying on its feet, but London's concert circuit has never been more active. There are certainly more gigs in an average week than ever before – whether in pubs where the carpet sticks to your shoes, or in the plush stalls of a legitimate theatre that's gone pop for the night. Few major performers (Elvis apart) can sustain a career without treading the boards at one of London's auditoriums. On any day you might be able to catch, say, Michael Jackson at Wembley, The Levellers at the Academy, Betty Carter at Ronnie Scott's or the Ramones at the Forum. Things are a little quieter in January (post-Christmas, no spare cash) and August (all the bands are on the outdoor festival circuit), but only relatively so – the beat goes on all year round. And even if your fave megastars aren't in town, you can swoon over their effigies at the **Rock Circus** (*see chapter* **Sightseeing**).

There is one warning that should be highlighted: the practice of 'booking fees'. Superficially, a handling charge to cover administration costs, they have become a way of squeezing more money from music fans paying up to £25 for a night out. Whenever possible, buy tickets from the concert venue, which should charge face value. It is also not unknown for an extra £2 to be added to the cost of each ticket if you pay by credit card, so use cash or cheques. If there is any extra charge, query it: if you are not satisfied with the explanation ask to speak to the manager – such action could lead to the charge being waived.

Where venues are open late into the night, we have given details of night buses. Apart, that is, for those in the West End, in which case you should head for Trafalgar Square, where virtually all Night buses stop.

Jools Holland *and his crazy, honky-tonk piano.*

Major Venues

Academy Brixton
211 Stockwell Road, SW9 (071 326 1022). Brixton underground/BR. **Open** 7-11pm daily. **Admission** £8.50-£15. **Credit** A, V.
A majestic venue with extraordinary décor, just a few minutes' walk from Brixton underground. The large crowds (capacity roughly 4,000) can usually convince themselves that it is an intimate club despite the setting, so the atmosphere is worth experiencing. Great views, plenty of bars, seats upstairs, and, mostly, bands with a sense of adventure. There are few venues as big with this much soul.

Astoria
157 Charing Cross Road, WC2 (071 434 0403). Tottenham Court Road underground. **Open** 7-11pm Mon-Thur; 11pm-3.30am Fri; 10pm-6am Sat. **Admission** £8-£10. **Credit** A, AmEx, DC, V.
This capacious theatre, with a large dance floor and upstairs seating, doesn't take full advantage of its central location. It does have an open-minded programming policy – from R&B to indie and reggae – and is popular with clubbers on Friday and Saturday nights. *See chapter* **Clubs.**

Forum
9-17 Highgate Road, NW5 (071 284 2200). Kentish Town underground/BR/N2 bus. **Open** 7-11pm. **Admission** £7-£12. **Credit** A, V.
Formerly the wonderful Town & Country Club, this 'new' venue is still one of the most popular spots in town. Normally everything clicks into place here, you can get a great view no matter where you stand and the PA is top notch.

The Grand
Clapham Junction, St Johns Hill, SW11 (071 738 9000). Clapham Junction BR. **Open** 7-11pm various nights. **Admission** £8-£12. **Credit** A, V.
Another venue in the ever-expanding Mean Fiddler chain, which continues the tradition of attention to detail, staging good bands in pleasant surroundings. Programming is varied in a rock vein. The highlight for many people seems to be the view of the stage that you get from the bar.

Hammersmith Apollo
Queen Caroline Street, W6 (081 741 4868). Hammersmith underground. **Open** 7.30-10.30pm various nights. **Admission** £10-£16. **No credit cards.**
The Apollo (which gained fame as the Odeon) is one of London's live music landmarks, and the biggest mainstream names play here. It's a bit old-style – crowded bars and dodgy hotdogs – but, if you don't mind sitting, the sound and views are worth the inconveniences.

Marquee
105 Charing Cross Road, WC2 (071 437 6601). Leicester Square or Tottenham Court Road underground. **Open** 7-11.30pm Mon-Thur; 7.30-10.30pm, 11pm-3am, Fri. **Music** 8pm. **Admission** £5-£7 discounts before 8pm. **Credit** V.
While its current activities no longer justify its fame, the Marquee is still pulling in the punters for its rock and indie nights. Dalliances with gospel, soul and jazz, plus the rare secret dates by the likes of Keith Richard, will probably keep this amiable dinosaur's reputation as sound as it was in the 1960s (when Keef's band first played on its Soho site).

Royal Albert Hall
Kensington Gore, SW7 (071 589 8212). Gloucester Road, Knightsbridge or South Kensington underground/9, 10, 52 bus. **Open** box office 9am-9pm daily. **Credit** A, AmEx, DC, V.

A famous Victorian venue that's architecturally way ahead of any other London hall. More famous for classical promenade concerts (*see chapter* **Music: Classical & Opera**), but New Order, Van Morrison and Bob Dylan have done their things here too.

Wembley Arena
Empire Way, Wembley, Middlesex (081 900 1234). Wembley Park underground or Wembley Central underground/BR. **Open** 6.30-11pm various nights. **Music** 7.30pm. **Admission** £9-£25. **Credit** A, AmEx, DC, V.
The largest indoor venue in London – and only for dedicated fans. Chances are that if you like the band, you'll overlook the venue's faults, such as the lack of atmosphere, the transport difficulties, the sound problems and the extortionately-priced merchandise and refreshments.

Wembley Stadium
Empire Way, Wembley, Middlesex (081 900 1234/081 902 8833). Wembley Park underground or Wembley Central underground/BR. **Open** 7.30-11pm various nights. **Admission** £14-£25. **Credit** A, AmEx, DC, V.
Also the English national football stadium, and you'll leave believing the gig was a dull 0-0 draw. Admittedly, it is the best venue if you suffer from claustrophobia, but the wide open spaces are a symptom of a far greater problem. Atmosphere? Forget it. Anyway, you'll need binoculars to see what's happening and the sound is dreadful. The weather probably will be too. Madonna, Michael Jackson, U2 and the Stones have played here in recent summers.

Pubs & Wine Bars

Bull & Gate
389 Kentish Town Road, NW5 (071 485 5358). Kentish Town underground/BR. **Open** 11am-3pm, 5.30-11pm, Mon-Fri; 11am-11pm Sat; noon-3pm, 7-10.30pm, Sun. **Music** 8-11pm Mon-Sat. **Admission** £3.50. **No credit cards.**
A traditional pub that picks up trade from concert-goers at the nearby Forum. It was once London's most notorious indie spawning ground and still puts on around 15 bands a week, most of them revelling in ineptitude.

Dover Street Wine Bar
8-9 Dover Street, W1 (071 629 9813). Green Park underground. **Open** noon-3pm, 5.30pm-3am, Mon-Fri; 7pm-3am Sat. **Music** 10.15pm, midnight Mon-Sat. **Admission** free early evening, £3-£8 later. **Credit** A, AmEx, DC, £TC, V.
A friendly, candle-lit basement brasserie, with seating for 200, featuring jazz, R&B, soul, blues and a small dance floor for those with an urge to do more than tap their toes.

Dublin Castle
94 Parkway, NW1 (071 485 1773). Camden Town underground. **Open** 11am-midnight daily. **Music** 8.30pm. **Admission** £3-£5. **No credit cards.**
Classic old man's pub with a music policy that books anyone who can promise a wild night out, especially if it's rock 'n' roll, blues, ska or soul.

Falcon
234 Royal College Street, NW1 (071 485 3834). Camden Town underground. **Open** 5.30-11pm Mon-Sat; 7-10.30pm Sun. **Music** 9pm. **Admission** £3.50. **No credit cards.**
One of London's dingier haunts for the rock and indie-music fraternity. The last obstacle on the independent road to fame for some lucky could-become-giants.

Half Moon
93 Lower Richmond Road, SW15 (081 780 9383). Putney Bridge underground. **Open** 11am-11pm Mon-*

*Blues in the basement at the **Dover Street Wine Bar**. See **review** page 248.*

Sat. **Music** 8.30pm Mon-Sat. **Admission** £2.50-£6. **No credit cards.**
Very popular for minor guitar heroes and ex-members of lesser-known R&B bands. Good-time boogying guaranteed most nights of the week. There's also plenty of jazz and soul.

King's Head

115 Upper Street, N1 (071 226 1916). Angel underground or Highbury & Islington underground/BR/N92 bus. **Open** 11am-midnight Mon-Sat; noon-3pm, 7-10.30pm, Sun. **Music** 9.30pm daily. **Admission** free. **No credit cards.**
An easy-going but crowded pub in the heart of Islington, this is a popular haunt for solo and acoustic duos. Gigs start when the theatre (in a room behind the bar) empties out.

Plough Stockwell

90 Stockwell Road, SW9 (071 274 3879). Clapham North or Stockwell underground/N87 bus. **Open** 11am-3pm, 6.30pm-midnight, Mon-Sat; noon-3pm, 7pm-midnight, Sun. **Music** 9.30pm Wed-Sun; 12.30pm Sun. **Admission** £3. **No credit cards.**
A very popular south London venue with rock residencies, standard R&B and sixties revivalists.

Station Tavern

41 Bramley Road, W10 (071 727 4053). Latimer Road tube/295 bus. **Open** 11am-11pm Mon-Sat; noon-3pm, 7-10.30pm, Sun. **Music** 9pm. **Admission** free. **No credit cards.**
More blues than a paint catalogue. Whether you like it acoustic, folk or R&B style, this is west London's home for anyone who wanted to be born around Memphis, Tennessee.

Swan

1 Fulham Broadway, SW6 (071 385 1840). Fulham Broadway underground/N11, N14 bus. **Open** noon-3pm, 5pm-midnight, Mon-Sat; noon-3pm, 7-10.30pm,

Sun. **Music** 9pm Mon-Sat; 1pm, 9pm, Sun. **Admission** £5. **No credit cards.**
A traditional pub with traditional pub rock 'n' roll from favoured regulars.

Club Venues

In many venues, the division between live music and pure dance clubs is no longer distinct. A word of warning: some trendier spots will be fussy about attire and may give problems on the door. Drinks tend to be more expensive than in pub venues and even in the freezing winter months bouncers like to develop a long queue, just because it looks good.

Borderline

Orange Yard, Manette Street, WC2 (071 734 2095). Leicester Square or Tottenham Court Road underground. **Open** 8-11pm Mon-Sat. **Music** 9.30pm. **Admission** £5. **No credit cards.**
A central venue popular with record companies putting on gigs to break-in new acts. All sorts of pre-mega stardom bands play here, from Texas to Was Not (Was), and the crowds usually contain a high proportion of music biz insiders.

Camden Palace

1A Camden Road, NW1 (071 387 0428). Camden Town underground/N2, N93 bus. **Open** 9pm-3am Tue-Thur; 8pm-3am Fri, Sat. **Music** midnight. **Admission** £5. **Credit** A, AmEx, £TC, V.
Dancing, rather than concerts, is the architecturally exquisite Palace's forte, although Tuesday night's Feet First is probably the best indie night of the week and usually features a couple of happening bands. *Wheelchair access.*

Another quiet night at the **Robey**. *See* **review**.

Garage
20-24 Highbury Corner, N5 (071 607 1818). Highbury & Islington tube/N92 bus. **Open** *7.30pm-2am daily.* **Music** *9pm.* **Admission** £6. **Credit** A, V.
Catch-all venue with good sound, views and recommended club nights. There are bands most nights, rock, pop and indie being favoured, although comedy fills Friday evening.

Mean Fiddler
24-28A High Street, Harlesden, NW10 (081 961 5490). Willesden Junction tube/BR/N18 bus. **Open** *8pm-2am Mon-Sat; noon-3pm, 8pm-1am, Sun.* **Music** *9.30pm.* **Admission** £5-£8. **Credit** A,V.
Good sound, good beer and good music are reasonable foundations for success and, coincidentally, what the Fiddler strives for. Two venues in one: the Acoustic Room lives up to its name and the main hall has just a whiff of country about it.

Orange
3 North End Crescent, North End Road, W14 (071 603 4317). West Kensington underground/N11, N31, N97. **Open** *8.30pm-midnight daily.* **Music** *9.30pm.* **Admission** £5. **No credit cards.**
Small west London club, popular with Australians. Live music daily, with club nights featuring songwriters on Monday, indies on Wednesday and funk on Fridays. Views are not great so get there early.

Powerhaus
1 Liverpool Road, N1 (071 837 3218). Angel underground/N92, N96 bus. **Open** *8pm-2am Mon-Thur; 8pm-3am Fri, Sat; 7-11pm Sun.* **Music** *9pm.* **Admission** £4-£6.
Indie club with up to three bands on every night of the week, plus drinking and dancing afterwards. It's excellent for finding out which band to name-drop.

Robey
240 Seven Sisters Road, N4 (071 263 4581). Finsbury Park underground/BR/N21, N29, N90 bus. **Open** *5pm-*
2am Mon-Sat; 7-10.30pm Sun. **Music** *9.30pm.* **Admission** £5. **No credit cards**.
A large, dark pub that hosts all-day festivals in honour of the greats of goth, grebo, ska and punk. Little to recommend any of the bands in the way of musical proficiency, but that's beside the point. Late opening and up to six sweaty bands a night.

Rock Garden
The Piazza, Covent Garden, WC2 (071 836 4052). Covent Garden underground. **Open** *7.30pm-3am Mon-Sat; 7.30pm-midnight Sun.* **Music** *8.30pm.* **Admission** £4. **Credit** A, AmEx, DC, V.
Right in the heart of Covent Garden, bands on the one-way trip to nowhere get a chance to showcase their abilities. The young U2 played here.

Subterrania
12 Acklam Road, Ladbroke Grove, W10 (081 960 4590). Ladbroke Grove underground/N18, N50 bus. **Open** *8pm-2am Mon-Thur; 10pm-3.30am Fri, Sat.* **Music** *9pm.* **Admission** £5-£8. **Credit** A, V.
Funk, jazz, soul and rap have dominated the programme recently in this functional but lively small club with good sound. One of the best clubs in town if you're a groover.

Underworld
174 Camden High Street, NW1 (071 482 1932). Camden Town underground/N2, N93 bus. **Open** *8pm-1am daily.* **Music** *9.30pm.* **Admission** £5-£8.
Intimate, though underused, gig space that extends under London for what may seem like miles. Drinks are pricey, but on the other important matters (views, sounds and bands) it scores highly. Advance tickets can be bought from the World's End pub upstairs.

The Venue
2A Clifton Rise, New Cross, SE14 (081 692 4077). New Cross underground/BR/N77 bus. **Open** *7.30pm-2am Fri, Sat.* **Music** *9.30pm.* **Admission** £5. **Credit** A,V.
A grubby indie den. And one of the best, although you probably won't get a great view of the band. You can dance until late afterwards.

Folk & Roots Venues

Africa Centre
38 King Street, WC2 (071 836 1973). Covent Garden tube. **Open** 9.30pm-3am Fri. **Music** 10.30pm. **Admission** £7. **No credit cards.**
The relaxed and often anarchic atmosphere makes this the favourite venue for visiting African bands. Once a week there is a part of Covent Garden that will forever be uptown Lagos, Kinshasa or Dakar. Great DJs too.

Cecil Sharpe House
2 Regent's Park Road, NW1 (071 485 2206). Camden Town underground/N2, N29, N93. **Open** 9am-6pm Mon-Sat; 7.30-11pm Fri, Sat. **Music** 7.30pm. **Admission** £4. **No credit cards.**
A hub of folk activity, staging traditional dancing, fayres, regular singers' nights and special guest evenings. It's cheap, friendly and set in a canal-side building. For earnest English folk aficionados, there's also a shop open during the week.

Halfway House
142 The Broadway, West Ealing, W13 (081 567 0236). Ealing Broadway underground/N50, N89. **Open** 11am-11pm Mon-Thur; 11am-midnight Fri, Sat; noon-3pm, 7-10.30pm, Sun. **Music** 9.30pm Fri-Sun. **Admission** free. **No credit cards.**
Specialising in Irish and country music, Halfway House has a resident roster that includes hot country through to Cajun and blues.

Hare & Hounds
181 Upper Street, N1 (071 226 2992). Highbury & Islington underground/BR/N92 bus. **Open** 11am-midnight Mon-Sat; noon-3pm, 7-10.30pm, Sun. **Music** 9.15pm. **Admission** £1-£3. **No credit cards.**
A good place to see honky-tonk and country-rock foot-tapping bands.

Swan
215 Clapham Road, SW9 (071 274 1526). Stockwell underground/N87 bus. **Open** 11am-11pm Mon-Wed; 11am-2am Thur-Sat; noon-3pm, 7-10.30pm, Sun. **Music** 9pm. **Admission** free-£2. **No credit cards.**
Popular traditional Irish bands have made this Stockwell pub their base. A good time, a good drink and a good sing-along. At weekends, there is a disco or live music long into the night.

Weavers
98 Newington Green Road, N1 (071 226 6911). Highbury & Islington tube. **Open** 8.30pm-midnight Mon-Sat; 7.30-10.30pm Sun. **Music** 9pm. **Admission** £2-£6. **No credit cards.**
Great venue for traditional and contemporary acoustic roots music. Within these parameters, the choice is diverse and internationally flavoured – Cajun, Celtic, folk and country are regular features.

Jazz Venues

Most of the places listed here are well-established haunts for jazzers but there are many other restaurants and pubs that have trad jazz while you eat. Watch out for the distinction between trad jazz venues and places that stage more improvisational artists.

100 Club
100 Oxford Street, W1 (071 636 0933). Tottenham Court Road underground. **Open** 7.30pm-midnight Mon-Wed; 8pm-1am Thur; 8.30pm-3am Fri; 7.30pm-1am Sat; 7.30-11.30pm Sun. **Admission** £5-£7. **No credit cards.**
The Sex Pistols staged one of their first London gigs in this basement in Oxford Street. Although it's hard to get a view of the stage, it's a fun place. These days you're more likely to hear trad and modern jazz, rockabilly, blues and swing.

606 Club
90 Lots Road, SW10, (071 352 5953). Fulham Broadway underground/11, 22, N11 bus. **Open** 8pm-2am Mon-Sat; 8.30pm-midnight Sun. **Music** 9.30pm. **Admission** £4. **Credit** A, V.
Tiny basement with an open-minded policy that encourages young musicians to jam along with established names in any style from Latin to bebop. Non-members welcome.

Bass Clef
35 Coronet Street, N1 (071 729 2476/071 729 2440). Old Street underground/N96 bus. **Open** 8pm-2am daily. **Music** 9pm. **Admission** £4-£7. **Credit** A, AmEx, DC, V.
The Bass Clef brings a Left Bank atmosphere to Hoxton, and plays host to well-known jazz, Asian, African and Latin artists from Britain and abroad. The capacity is limited: arrive early or book. *See also* **Tenor Clef** (*below*). *Restaurant.*

Bull's Head Barnes
Barnes Bridge, SW13 (081 876 5241). Hammersmith underground then bus 9/Barnes Bridge BR/N14, N65 bus. **Open** 11am-11pm Mon-Sat; noon-3pm, 7-10.30pm, Sun. **Music** 8.30pm daily. **Admission** £4-£8. **No credit cards.**
If you're prepared to travel outside central London, catch the Bull's Head for some of the best jazz in Britain in convivial, riverside surroundings.

Duke of Wellington
119 Balls Pond Road, N1 (071 249 3729). Highbury & Islington underground/BR/Dalston Junction BR/N19 bus. **Open** 6pm-midnight Mon-Fri; 1pm-midnight Sat; 7-11pm Sun. **Music** times vary. **Admission** free. **No credit cards.**
A pub venue with a respected reputation for staging adventurous contemporary jazz and free-improvisation combos. It's small and there's no booking, so arrive early.

Jazz Café
5 Parkway, NW1 (071 916 6000). Camden Town underground/N93 bus. **Open** 7pm-midnight Mon-Thur, Sun; 7pm-2am Fri, Sat. **Music** phone for details. **Admission** £5-£12. **Credit** A, V.
The programme is jazz, but at its widest interpretation, including soul, Latin, African and rap. There are bands every night.

Palookaville
13A James Street, WC2 (071 240 5857). Covent Garden underground. **Open** 5.30pm-1am Mon-Wed; 5.30pm-2am Thur-Sat; 7pm-midnight Sun. **Music** 8pm. **Admission** free to diners, £3 after 9.30pm Thur-Sat. **Credit** A, AmEx, DC, V.
Admission is free to this cosy restaurant/wine bar which has mellow live jazz during the week and R&B and Latin at weekends. There's a small dance floor if you feel like shaking a leg.

Pizza Express
10 Dean Street, W1 (071 437 9595). Tottenham Court Road underground. **Open** 8pm-midnight daily. **Music** 9.15pm. **Admission** £6-£13.50. **Credit** A, AmEx, DC, V.
Well-known venue in the cellar of a pizza restaurant which has its own resident band. Popular mainstream

MC Kinky: *a blooming star.*

combos, from Georgie Fame to Clark Tracey, also make appearances. You have to eat, but these are some of the best pizzas in town.

Pizza on the Park
11 Knightsbridge, Hyde Park Corner, SW1 (071 235 5550). Hyde Park Corner underground. **Open** 8am-2am daily. **Music** 9.15pm. **Admission** £8-£17.50. **Credit** A, AmEx, DC, V.
An elegantly-designed restaurant with sets from popular names in mainstream jazz.

Ronnie Scott's
47 Frith Street, W1 (071 439 0747). Leicester Square, Piccadilly Circus or Tottenham Court Road underground. **Open** 8.30pm-3am Mon-Sat. **Music** 9.30pm. **Admission** £12. **Credit** A, AmEx, DC, £STC, V.
This legendary jazz venue in the heart of Soho still attracts all the major visiting jazz heroes. The sound and atmosphere are excellent; unfortunately, the charges for food and drink are extortionate. The club gets crowded most nights, so book in advance to get a table with a good view. Sunday nights are for rock/soul/world music bands.

Tenor Clef
1 Hoxton Square, N1 (071 729 2440/2476). Old Street underground/BR/N96 bus. **Open** 8pm-2am daily. **Admission** £3-£7.50. **Credit** A, AmEx, DC, V.
Directly above the **Bass Clef** (*see above*), this jazz club-cum-art gallery offers live Latin, African and rare groove seven nights a week. It's smaller, cooler and more upmarket than its sister.

Vortex
Stoke Newington Church Street, N16 (071 254 6516). Stoke Newington BR/67, 73, 76, 106, 243 bus. **Open** 11am-midnight Mon-Sat; noon-10.30pm Sun. **Music** 8.30pm daily. **Admission** £1.50-£6. **Credit** A, V.
A civilised, friendly club with a great attitude towards putting on local jazz musicians. Often closed on Mondays, so phone in advance.

Other Venues

Check *Time Out* magazine for details of forthcoming gigs. During term-time, universities and colleges often have name bands playing at low prices in their student unions. *See chapter* **Students**.

Dominion
Tottenham Court Road, W1 (071 580 8845). Tottenham Court Road underground. **Open** 7-11pm daily. **Admission** £10-£25. **Credit** A, AmEx, V.
The conveniently placed Dominion is enjoying a healthy revival as an occasional music venue. Although it's seating-only, and is more commonly given to musicals (*42nd Street, Grease*), this theatre attracts some of the more sedate rock acts and cocktail crooners. Nonetheless, a comfortable venue with few hassles.

Electric Ballroom
184 Camden High Street, NW1 (071 485 9006). Camden Town underground/N2, N29, N90, N93 bus. **Open** 10.30pm-2am Fri, Sat. **Admission** £5. **No credit cards**.
This under-used and run-down venue in Camden is the site for record fairs, clubs and an indoor market at weekends. Its medium-sized capacity is equally suited to jazz or new-wave bands.

Fairfield Halls
Park Lane, Croydon, Surrey (081 688 9291). East Croydon BR. **Open** 10am-8pm Mon-Sat. **Admission** £4-£20. **Credit** A, AmEx, DC, V.
Mainstream popular acts, many of them has-beens, stop-off at this plush theatre is relive their glory days. Reasonably priced and relaxing.

London Palladium
8 Argyll Street, W1 (071 494 5020). Oxford Circus underground. **Open** 6.45-10.30pm. **Music** 7.30pm. **Admission** £8.50-£29. **Credit** A, AmEx, V.
This sedate theatre, more often associated with tacky cabaret and pantomimes, has been home to *Joseph and the Amazing Technicolor Dreamcoat* since the dawn of time. However, acts like Elvis Costello and Lou Reed have occasionally made use of the intimate atmosphere. *See chapter* **Theatre**.

National Ballroom Kilburn
234 Kilburn High Road, NW6 (071 328 3141). Kilburn underground/N8, N94 bus. **Open** 9.30pm-1am Mon; 9.30pm-1.30am Fri; 9.30pm-1.45am Sat. **Music** 11pm Mon, Fri, Sat. **Admission** £4-£6. **No credit cards**.
An under-exposed and under-used venue. A pity, because the splendid ballroom interior has played host to some terrific rock gigs in the past. In the main, it's the local Irish community which makes most use of it.

South Bank Centre
South Bank, Belvedere Road, SE1 (box office 071 928 8800/general information 071 928 3002/recorded information 071 928 3191). Waterloo underground/BR/Riverbus. **Open** *box office* 10am-10pm daily. **Tickets** £5-£25 **Credit** A, AmEx, DC, V.
One of the major London venues, with three large, all-seating music theatres, it's the location for major jazz festivals (*see also chapters* **Dance** *and* **Music: Classical & Opera**).
Car Park. Free exhibitions. Front seats for the partially sighted by prior arrangement. Guided tours. Infra red audio for the hard of hearing. Poetry library. Restaurants & cafés. Shops for books, music and records. Toilets for the disabled. Wheelchair access.

Sport & Fitness

Fancy a whizz through the waves on waterskis, an invigorating hack on horseback, or an amiable amble round a golf course? This city can supply it.

Far from being a metropolis of concrete and cars, London is in fact crammed with sporting opportunities for men and women of all aspirations and levels of fitness – whether it's getting in shape at an aerobics class or playing a gentle game of tennis.

London is also the place to be if you want to watch top-level sporting action. There are numerous professional football clubs in the city, while Lord's and the Oval host county and Test match cricket. Leading teams in rugby union, basketball, hockey and athletics are based in London, while there's a host of competitions in sports both major and minor going on every day.

The week's events are listed and previewed in *Time Out* magazine's 'Sport' section, where you'll also find contacts enabling you to take part in virtually an entire alphabet of activity – from archery to yoga. Alternatively, phone **Sportsline** (071 222 8000), a free information service.

Participation Sports

Archery

Mike Parry's 'The' London School of Archery
34A Ponsonby Place, SW1 (071 383 5022).
Membership £40 per year.
If you've always imagined yourself as a budding Robin Hood, try one of Mike Parry's regular three-hour evening taster courses at the Fatima Centre, Commonwealth Avenue, W12 at a cost of £15. Coaching with a qualified instructor is then available to improve your bowpersonship.

Athletics

Many of the capital's sports centres serve as bases for running groups, who take to London's streets and parks and welcome new members of all standards. Women runners might be interested in joining the **Sisters Network**, which encourages more females to take up the sport by matching newcomers ('Little Sisters') with experienced partners ('Big Sisters'). The scheme, organised through the pages of *Running* magazine (£1.75), has spawned a number of informal groups – and female runners of all abilities are welcome to join the regulars on the first Saturday of every month, 9.45am, at the Cassac Club, Lloyd Park, Coombe Road, Croydon. South Croydon BR from Victoria.

You can train for track and field athletics at the following venues, all of which have resident clubs and host regular meetings in the National and Southern Leagues. The tracks are open from dawn to dusk during the summer months.
Barnet Copthall Stadium, *Great North Way, NW4 (081 203 4211). Mill Hill East underground.*
Croydon Sports Arena, *Albert Road, SE25 (081 654 3462). Norwood Junctioin BR.*
Crystal Palace National Sports Centre, *Ledrington Road, SE19 (081 778 0131). Crystal Palace BR.*
Mayesbrook Park, *Lodge Avenue, Dagenham (081593 3539). Upney underground.*
New River Stadium, *White Hart Lane, N22 (081 881 2310). Wood Green underground.*
Paddington Recreation Ground, *Randolph Avenue, W9 (071 798 3642). Maida Vale underground.*
Parliament Hill, *Highgate Road, NW5 (071 435 8998). Gospel Oak BR.*
Queen Elizabeth Stadium, *Donkey Lane, Enfield (081 363 7398). Enfield Town BR.*
Terence McMillan Stadium, *Maybury Road, E13 (no phone). Plaistow underground.*
Tooting Bec Track, *Tooting Bec Road, SW17 (no phone). Tooting Bec underground.*
West London Stadium, *Du Cane Road, W12 (081 743 4030). White City underground.*

Baseball

British Baseball Federation
66 Belvedere Road, Hessle, North Humberside HU13 9JJ (0482 643551).
The BBF runs the National League, which has a Premier Division and three regional 'Conferences'. There are lower divisions in the Southern League, catering for players of all standards, with games played every Sunday afternoon during the summer. Phone or write (with a stamped, addressed envelope) for details of your nearest club.

Croquet

Hurlingham Club
Ranelagh Gardens, SW6 (information 071 736 3148). Putney Bridge underground.
The manicured lawns of Hurlingham are croquet's spiritual home, and the venue for the British Open Championships held every July. Phone or write (with a stamped, addressed envelope) for details of other fixtures, or contacts at local clubs, should you wish to play.

Cycling

Cycle Tracks
Eastway Cycle Circuit, *Temple Mills Lane, E15 (081 534 6085). Leyton underground.* **Open** 9am-dusk daily.
Admission £1.60 for 2 hours with own bike.

Herne Hill Stadium *Burbage Road, SE24 (071 737 4647). Herne Hill BR.* **Open** 10am-noon Sat; noon-4pm Sun. **Admission** *Sat* £2.50; £1 under-16s. *Sun* £1; 50p under-16s; £2 family.
Eastway is a collection of purpose-built cycle tracks catering for BMX, road racing and cyclo-cross, with events in one discipline or another taking place most weekends. Herne Hill is the only velodrome in London, an 800m (880yd) banked track that's well-used by local clubs for training and competitions. Phone both venues for details of forthcoming events, and for access if you want to have a ride yourself. Bikes can be hired for £2.50 per session.

Dance

Dance Attic
212-214 Putney Bridge Road, SW15 (081 785 2055). Putney Bridge underground. **Open** 9am-10pm Mon-Fri; 9am-5pm Sat, Sun. **Membership** £20 for six months; £1.50 per day. **Classes** £2.50-£3.
This popular Putney centre has a gym and a dance studio, and offers tuition in ballet, jazz, contemporary, tap, flamenco, historic dance, lambada and rock and roll, together with Pilates, fitness and aerobics classes. Phone

for the full timetable, which has classes scheduled at 10am, 1pm and from 6pm in the evenings.

Danceworks
16 Balderton Street, W1 (071 629 6183). Bond Street underground. **Open** 8am-10.30pm Mon-Fri; 9.30am-5.30pm Sat, Sun. **Membership** £75 per year (£35 students, nurses, UB40s); £22 per three months. **Classes** £4.
Almost every form of dance is available here, including capoeira – a thrilling Brazilian blend of movement and martial arts – with teaching of a uniformly high standard. Also available at the same venue is Physioworks, a private physiotherapy practice specialising in the aches, pains and ailments brought about by dance and sport.

Pineapple Dance Centre
7 Langley Street, WC2 (071 836 4004). Covent Garden underground. **Open** 9.30am-9pm Mon-Fri; 9.30am-6pm Sat; 10.30am-3.30pm Sun. **Membership** £65 per year; £35 per year Equity, students, UB40s; £4 per day. **Classes** £4.
Pineapple was synonymous with the 1980s boom in fitness and dance, and is still popular with those who take their activity seriously. There are classes in most dance forms, with teachers considered among the best in town.

The Sporting Year

January **Basketball** WICB Tournament, Crystal Palace. **Rugby Union** Five Nations International Championship starts, Twickenham (081 892 8161).

February **Snooker** Benson & Hedges Masters, Wembley Arena (081 900 1234).

March **Badminton** All-England Championships, Wembley Arena (081 900 1234). **Football** Coca-Cola League Cup Final, Wembley Stadium (081 900 1234). **Rowing** University Boat Race, River Thames (071 379 3234).

April **Athletics** London Marathon. **Ice Hockey** British Championships, Wembley Arena (081 900 1234). **Rugby Union** County Championship Final, Twickenham (081 892 8161). **Squash** British Open, Wembley Conference Centre (081 900 1234).

May **Cricket** One-Day International, Lord's (071 289 8979). **Equestrianism** Royal Windsor Horse Show, Windsor Great Park (0753 860633). **Football** FA Cup Final, Wembley Stadium (081 900 1234). **Golf** Volvo PGA Championship, Wentworth (0344 842201). **Rugby League** Challenge Cup Final, Wembley Stadium (081 900 1234). **Rugby Union** Pilkington Cup Final and Middlesex Sevens, Twickenham (081 892 8161).

June **Cricket** Lord's Test match (071 289 8979). **Greyhound Racing** Greyhound Derby Final, Wimbledon (081 946 5361). **Horse Racing** Derby meeting, Epsom (0372 726311); Royal Ascot (0344 22211). **Rowing** Henley Regatta (0491 572 153). **Tennis** Stella Artois Championship, Queen's Club (071 225 3733); All-England Championship, Wimbledon (081 946 2244).

July **Cricket** Benson & Hedges Cup Final, Lord's (071 289 8979). **Croquet** British Open, Hurlingham (071 736 8411). **Motor Sport** British Formula One Grand Prix, Silverstone (0327 857273). **Polo** Cartier International, Guards Club (0784 434 212).

August **American Football** American Bowl, Wembley Stadium (081 900 1234). **Football** Charity Shield, Wembley Stadium (081 900 1234); League season starts.

September **Cricket** NatWest Trophy Final, Lord's (071 289 8979).

October **Equestrianism** Horse of the Year Show, Wembley Arena (081 900 1234).

December **Equestrianism** Olympia International Show Jumping Championship, Olympia (071 373 8141). **Rugby Union** Varsity Match, Twickenham (081 892 8161).

Golf

Courses

Airlinks, *Southall Lane, Hounslow (081 561 1418).*
Hayes & Harlington BR. **Course** 18 holes. **Fee** £10 per
round Mon-Fri; £13 Sat, Sun.
Beckenham Place, *Beckenham Hill Road, SE6 (081
650 2292). Beckenham Hill BR.* **Course** 18 holes. **Fee**
£8.70 per round Mon-Fri; £14 per round Sat, Sun.
Brent Valley, *Church Road, Cuckoo Lane, W5 (081
567 1287). Hanwell BR.* **Course** 18 holes. **Fee** £7.95
per round Mon-Fri; £12 Sat, Sun.
Chingford, *Bury Road, E4 (081 529 5708). Chingford
BR.* **Course** 18 holes. **Fee** £8.30 per round Mon-Fri,
£11.50 Sat, Sun.
Picketts Lock, *Picketts Lock Lane, N9 (081 803
3611). Ponders End BR.* **Course** 18 holes. **Fee** £8.50
per round Mon-Fri; £10.50 Sat, Sun.
Richmond Park, *Roehampton Gate, Richmond Park,
SW15 (081 876 3205). Barnes BR.* **Course** two 18-
hole courses. **Fee** £9 per round Mon-Fri; £12.50 per
round Sat, Sun.
Stockley Park, *Stockley Park Golf Course, Heathrow
(081 813 5700). Heathrow Terminal 1, 2, 3
underground, then U5 bus.* **Course** 18 holes. **Fee** £17.50
per round Hillingdon residents, £25 non-residents, daily.

English Golf Union

*1-3 Upper King Street, Leicester LE1 6XF (0533
553042).* **Open** 9am-5pm Mon-Fri.
The EGU publishes a booklet (price £1 inc p&p) which
explains the handicapping system, one of the keys to
gaining membership of a private club.

Regent's Park Golf School

*Outer Circle, Regent's Park, NW1 (071 724 0643).
Baker Street underground.* **Open** 8am-9pm daily.
Use of the school's popular driving range costs £60 per
year plus £2 for 15 minutes, while access to non-members
is via a £5 day card. A 30-minute lesson with the club pro
costs £16 (£14 members), or you can book a course of six
for £70. You can have your swing computer-analysed for
£35, and the fee is waived if you buy a set of clubs.

Ice Skating

Broadgate Ice Rink

*Eldon Street, EC2 (071 588 6565). Liverpool Street
underground.* **Open** *Nov-end Mar.* **Sessions**
noon-3pm Mon-Fri; 4-7.30pm Tue-Thur; 4-8pm Fri;
11am-1pm, 2-4pm, 5-7pm, Sat, Sun. **Admission** £5;
£3.50 under-16s. **Skate hire** £2; £1 OAPs.
A tiny outdoor circle of ice open only in the winter and
surrounded by the high-tech architecture of Broadgate,
this is the newest and most pleasant rink in London. It
also plays host to broomball, a game similar to ice hockey in which teams from the surrounding offices attempt
to 'sweep' a football into goals using brooms.

Queens Ice Skating Club

*17 Queensway, W2 (071 229 0172). Queensway or
Bayswater underground.* **Sessions** 11am-4.30pm, 7.30-
10pm, Mon-Fri; 10am-12.30pm, 2.30-5pm, 7.30-
10.30pm, Sat; 10am-12.30pm, 2.30-5pm, 7-10pm, Sun.
Admission £3.50-£5; free OAPs; £2.30-£5 under-15s.
Skate hire £1.50.
The most famous rink in London is popular with serious
skaters and the disco crowd alike, the former for the
good standard of tuition and the latter for the bar overlooking the ice.

Streatham Ice Rink

*386 Streatham High Road, SW16 (081 769 7771).
Streatham BR.* **Sessions** 10am-4pm, 7.30-10.30pm,
Mon-Fri (4.30-10pm family night on Tue); 11am-
4.45pm, 8-11pm, Sat; 11am-4.45pm, 7.30-10.30pm, Sun.
Admission £4.80 Mon-Fri, £5.30 Sat, Sun; £3.80
children (both incl skate hire).
For years the most down-at-heel of London's rinks,
Streatham is currently being refurbished. Also taking
advantage of the large rink are the Streatham Redskins,
who play English League ice hockey every Sun at 6pm.

Karting

Karting has become popular for company
nights out, and the indoor tracks listed below
are all equipped to cater for parties as well as
individuals seeking a spin.
National Karting Association, *John Fielding, 66
Oaklands Avenue, Brighton, East Sussex (0273
300989).* Contact the Association for information
about the sport and details of your nearest circuit.
Daytona & Indianapolis Raceways, *54 Wood Lane,
W12 (081 749 2277). White City underground.* **Fee**
£25-£32 per person plus VAT. **Sessions** 9am, 1pm,
6pm daily.
Fast Lane Leisure, *Knight Road, Strood, Rochester,
Kent (0634 713383). Strood BR.* **Fee** £25 per person.
Sessions 9am, 2pm, 7pm daily.
Playscape, *Clapham Kent Raceway, Triangle Place,
SW4 (071 498 0916). Clapham Common underground.*
Fee £30-£33 per person plus VAT. **Sessions** 9.30am,
2pm, 6pm daily.
Spitfire Karting *Browells Lane, Feltham, Middlesex
(081 893 2104). Feltham BR.* **Fee** £25-£35 per person.
Sessions 10am, 1pm, 6.30pm daily.
Trak 1 Racing *Unit 2A, Wyvern Way, Barnsfield
Place, Uxbridge, Middlesex (0895 258410). Uxbridge
underground.* **Fee** £34.50 per person. **Sessions** 10am,
1.30pm, 6.30pm daily.

Martial Arts

British Council of Chinese Martial Arts

*14 Stevenson Way, Larkfield, Aylesford, Kent ME20
6UN (0732 848065).*
Can answer queries about martial arts organisations and
clubs.

British Karate Federation

*Smalldrink, Parsonage Lane, Begelly, Kilgetty, Dyfed
SA68 0YL .*

Venues

Central School of Tai Chi Chuan, *52-53 Dean
Street, W1 (071 287 2001). Tottenham Court Road
underground.* The School uses sports centres in
various parts of London for its regular weekly
beginners classes, which offer a well-planned
introduction to the most gentle of the martial arts.
Finsbury Leisure Centre, *Norman Street, EC1
(071 253 4490). Old Street underground.* The
British Ki-Aikido Association runs regular courses
for martial artists of all standards at Finsbury. A
five-week beginners course costs £25. Contact 071
281 0877.
London School of Capoeira *22 Highbury Grove,
N5 (071 354 2084). Highbury & Islington
underground/BR.* Capoeira is an exciting blend of
dance and martial arts that's still not widely known
in the UK. The School runs free demonstrations
every Sat, 3.30pm, while a four-week beginners
course costs £90. *See also above* **Danceworks** *listed
under* **Dance**.

Riding

Belmont Riding Centre
The Ridgeway, NW7 (081 906 1255). Mill Hill East underground. **Open** 9am-9pm Tue-Fri; 9am-5pm Sat, Sun. **Lessons** £13.50 per hour (group); £19 per hour (private).
Located in the centre of Mill Hill, Belmont has access to 150 acres (60 hectares) of parkland and a cross-country course. It has a good reputation in schooling riders for competitions and hunting.

Hyde Park Stables
63 Bathurst Mews, W2 (071 723 2813). Lancaster Gate underground. **Open** 7.30am-4.30pm Mon, Wed, Fri; 7.30am-6pm Tue, Thur; 9am-4.30pm Sat, Sun. **Lessons** £25 per hour (group); £35 per hour (private).
Situated behind Lancaster Gate tube, Hyde Park Stables caters for a well-heeled clientele who find compensation for the high prices through the pleasure of riding in the park.

Wimbledon Village Stables
24 High Street, SW19 (081 946 8579). **Open** 8am-5pm daily. **Lessons** £19 per hour (group); £26 per hour (private).
The chance to hack across Wimbledon Common and Richmond Park is the attraction of this small, informal stables which is reputed to have the best horses in London for nervous riders.

Rollerskating & Skateboarding

Skate Attack City Track
Spitalfields Old Market, Brushfield Street, E1 (071 377 6169). Liverpool Street underground. **Open** 10am-6pm Mon-Fri; 10am-3pm Sun.
Situated within the old Spitalfields fruit and vegetable market is a 1,000ft (303m) track with a tarmac surface specially designed for In-Line rollerskates, and ramps and half-pipes for skateboarders. There's free instruction available, a well-equipped shop, and regular competitions for the hordes of cool kiddies who populate the place.

Softball

National Softball Federation – Greater London Region
Contact Bob Fromer, Birchwood Hall, Storridge, Malvern, Worcs WR13 5EZ (0886 884203).
Softball is still a popular summer pastime for London's office workers, many playing in teams and leagues connected with their professions. Write (with stamped, addressed envelope) or phone Bob Fromer for details of any competitions that may be suitable for you. Most of the capital's major softball tournaments are now played at the University of Westminster Sports Ground, Grove Park, Cavendish Road, W4.

Swimming

London is awash with public swimming pools, far too many to mention here. To find your nearest, look in *Yellow Pages* or phone **Sportsline** (*see* **Introduction**).

Gurnell Baths
Ruislip Road East, W13 (081 998 3241). Ealing Broadway underground. **Open** 8am-7pm Mon, Fri; 8am-9pm Tue-Thur; 8am-4.45pm Sat, Sun. **Admission** £2; £1 children.

The **Oasis**. *See* **review** page 258.

At 50m (55yd) this is one of the longest pools in London, which makes it a regular venue for league water polo matches. There are good changing facilities for people with disabilities and families with small children, while aqua-aerobics, parent-and-baby classes and highly-rated lessons for learners and improvers are also on offer.

Highbury Pool
Highbury Crescent, N5 (071 226 4186). Highbury & Islington underground. **Open** 7.30am-8.30pm Mon-Fri; 7.30am-5pm Sat, Sun. **Admission** £1.90; 85p children.
This modern pool is excellent for adult swimmers who want to improve, as there is lane-only swimming every morning from 7.30-9am and a full programme of lessons. Women-only sessions run on Tuesday from 6.30pm, and include aqua-aerobics.

Ironmonger Row Baths
Ironmonger Row, EC1 (071 253 4011). Old Street underground. **Open** 7.30am-7.30pm Mon-Fri; 9am-4.30pm Sat; 9am-noon, 2-5pm, Mon-Fri; 9am-noon Sat); 85p children.
This is one of London's older pools, a 30m (33yd) 1930s-look tank with lane swimming, parent and toddler classes and tuition available – phone for details and times.

Latchmere Leisure Centre
Latchmere Road, SW11 (081 871 7470). Clapham Junction BR. **Open** 7.30am-9pm Mon-Thur, Sat, Sun; 7.30am-5.30pm Fri. **Admission** £1.90 (£1.65 off-peak: 9am-5pm Mon-Fri); £1.20 children.
The pride and joy of Wandsworth, this impressive leisure centre includes a free-form pool with a 25m (27.5yd) straight area. There's all the paraphernalia for water-

Set course for east London, to Windsurf.

based fun such as slides and inflatables, but kids are only admitted after 9am on weekdays so adults can fit in a few unfettered lengths before catching the train into town.

Marshall Street Leisure Centre
14-16 Marshall Street, W1 (071 287 1022). Oxford Circus underground. **Open** 7.30am-7pm Mon; 7.30am-9pm Tue-Fri; 8.30am-7pm Sat; closed Sun. **Admission** £2.20; 85p children.
Tucked away in a quiet corner of west Soho, this is a delightful old pool with a glass roof, housed in a listed building.

The Oasis
32 Endell Street, WC2 (071 831 1804). Covent Garden underground. **Open** 7.30am-8pm Mon-Fri (7.30am-6.45pm indoor pool); 9.30am-5pm Sat, Sun. **Admission** £2.30; 75p children.
The outdoor pool is a popular summer posing place for Covent Garden trendies, although both this and the indoor pool can get hopelessly cramped with local office workers when the weather is hot. Late afternoon is the best time to visit if you want to swim in relative peace.

Tennis

There are public courts in many London parks, most operating a booking system for busy

times (usually the month around Wimbledon). It costs about £3 per hour to play, and some run registration schemes which allow members to reserve courts up to a week in advance. The Lawn Tennis Association Trust has produced a guide, *Where to Play Tennis in London*, which lists the facilities in each London borough and outlines the coaching opportunities available. Write for a copy (with stamped, addressed envelope) to: The LTA Trust, Queen's Club, W14 9EG (071 385 4233). **Sportsline** (*see above* **Introduction**) also holds extensive details of local clubs, court charges and coaching courses.

Islington Tennis Centre
Market Road, N7 (071 700 1370). Caledonian Road underground. **Open** 8am-10pm Mon-Fri; 9am-10pm Sat, Sun. **Courts** *outdoor* £5.30-£12 per hour; *indoor* £6-£10.20 per hour.
Created as part of the Lawn Tennis Association's Indoor Tennis Initiative, the Islington centre offers three indoor, three outdoor and three mini-courts in an effort to get more people from a non-traditional tennis area playing the game. Six-week coaching courses for players of all standards, juniors and women-only, are regularly available, and cost around £35.

Kensington & Chelsea Sports Development Team
LTA-qualified instructors offer six-hour, one-weekend intensive group coaching courses at venues throughout the borough. It costs £40. Individual tuition is also available at £18 per hour. Phone 071 221 3749 for details.

Tennis Network
195 Battersea Church Road, SW11 3ND.
This organisation aims to match players of similar ability in their local area. Write to them, enclosing a stamped, addressed envelope, for details.

Water Sports

There are plenty of places for Londoners to mess about on, in and under the briny. The gradual opening up of Docklands in particular has created a huge resource for water sports addicts. *See also above* **Swimming**.

Discover Scuba
7 Capricorn Centre, Cranes Farm Road, Basildon, Essex SS14 3JJ (0268 272272). **Open** 9am-5.30pm Mon-Fri.
This company runs introductory diving evenings and beginners' courses at various pools in north London. A trial lesson costs £15.

Docklands Watersports Club
Gate 15, King George V Dock, Woolwich Manor Way, E16 (071 511 7000). North Woolwich BR. **Open** 10am-dusk Mon, Tue, Thur-Sun.
This is the place to go if you want to hire a jet ski or wet bike and indulge in two of the most fashionable water sports. It costs £20 for 30 minutes, which includes tuition, a wetsuit and use of the club's facilities.

Lea Valley Watersports Centre
Greaves Pumping Station, North Circular Road, E4 (081 531 1129). Angel Road BR. **Open** 10am-dusk daily.
The Lea Valley centre is 21 years old this year, and offers

windsurfing, dinghy sailing, water skiing and canoeing on the 90-acre (36-hectare) Banbury Reservoir. There are RYA-approved coaching courses in all activities, and comprehensive programmes for kids.

Royal Docks Waterski Club
Gate No.16, King George V Dock, Woolwich Manor Way, E16 (071 511 2000). North Woolwich BR. **Open** 10am-dusk daily.
Situated opposite the runway at London City Airport, the Royal Docks club is proud of the fact that its water is tested regularly and conforms to EC standards. There are two courses set out, instruction is included in the 20-minute trial lesson (£15; course of four costs £52), and the club runs open days and competitions.

Royal Yachting Association
RYA House, Romsey Road, Eastleigh, Hampshire SO5 4YA (0703 629962). **Open** 9am-5pm Mon-Fri.
The RYA is the governing body for all water-based activities, and can put you in touch with your nearest facilities or answer any questions.

Women's Rowing Centre
The Promenade, Duke's Meadows, W4 (081 840 4962).
The centre runs courses on the Thames for complete beginners. Leave a message on the answerphone if there's no-one in the office.

Fitness Clubs

Albany Fitness
St Bede's Church, Albany Street, NW1 (071 383 7131). Great Portland Street underground. **Membership** £500 per year plus £199 joining fee.
A beautifully designed club in the shell of a deconsecrated church, the Albany has a well-appointed gym, separate free weights and cardio-vascular fitness rooms, a lovely top-floor dance studio, and a calm, relaxing atmosphere.

Gym at the Sanctuary
11 Floral Street, WC2 (071 240 0695). Covent Garden underground. **Fees** £95 per year; £5 per visit, plus £1-£2.50 classes.
A splendid pool is the main attraction of this small women-only club in the heart of London, along with a gym, steam-room, sauna and range of exercise classes.

Health Haven
40 Vauxhall Bridge Road, SW1 (071 834 2289). Victoria underground/BR. **Membership** £495 per year.
A friendly if rather cramped women-only club that combines mainstream fitness (step classes, gym) with luxurious pampering (Rene Guinot facials, aromatherapy and Swedish massage).

Sequinpark
134 Stoke Newington Church Street, N16 (071 241 1449). Canonbury BR. **Membership** £380 per year.
There are now three women-only Sequinpark clubs in North London, each providing a friendly and unpretentious atmosphere together with a gym, workout studio and health suite. A plus point is the lack of joining- or class-fees. The other clubs are at 240 Upper Street, N1 (071 704 9844); and 17 Crouch Hill, N4 (071 272 6857).

Sports Centres

There are public sports centres in all London boroughs – look in the telephone directory or contact **Sportsline** (071 222 8000; *see above* **Introduction**) for details of your nearest.

Jubilee Hall Leisure Centre
30 The Piazza, WC2 (071 836 4835). Covent Garden underground. **Open** 7.30am-10pm Mon-Fri; 10am-5pm Sat, Sun.
Popular with famous faces – Boy George and Betty Boo work out here – this streetwise centre has just been refurbished. The gym is large and well-equipped, though busy during the week. There's a good selection of exercise and dance classes (£3.50), and you can play five-a-side football, badminton, or try one of the many martial arts practised here.

London Central YMCA
112 Great Russell Street, WC1 (071 637 8131). Tottenham Court Road underground. **Open** 7am-10.30pm Mon-Fri; 9am-9pm Sat, Sun.
For £32.50 per week you can have access to the most comprehensive range of sports facilities in town, along with a magnificent swimming pool and exercise classes from the instructors whose job it is to teach the latest moves to their colleagues. The London Central YMCA Bobcats basketball team is based at the 'Y', and plays National League matches here on Sat, 6pm. The centre has a cosmopolitan, buzzy atmosphere and is popular with the gay community.

Queen Mother Sports Centre
223 Vauxhall Bridge Road, SW1 (071 798 2125). Victoria underground/BR. **Open** 7.30am-7.30pm Mon-Thur; 7.30am-8.30pm Fri; 9am-5.30pm Sat; 9am-5.15pm Sun.
A 25m pool (£1.70 per swim), badminton (£5.70 per court) and squash (£4 for 30 mins) are the main attractions at this small, easy-going centre that's popular with people who work in the area.

Seymour Leisure Centre
Seymour Place, W1 (071 723 8019). Edgware Road or Marble Arch underground. **Open** 7.30am-9pm Mon, Tue, Thur, Fri; 7.30am-9pm Wed; 7.30am-7pm Sat; 9am-6pm Sun.
This well-run central leisure centre has a large games hall and swimming pool, the highly-rated 'Move It' programme of exercise classes (£3.50), and a new cardio-vascular fitness room (£2.50).

Spectator Sports

Basketball

The slam-dunk game is growing in popularity in Britain, and you can see many of this country's best players in action in the capital. National League games are played every Saturday and Sunday – phone each club for details of its forthcoming matches. London Towers is one of the top men's teams, while London Central YMCA Bobcats and London Jets play in the women's Division One.
London Towers, *Michael Sobell Sports Centre, Hornsey Road, N7 (071 609 2166). Holloway Road underground.*
Brixton Topcats, *Brixton Recreation Centre, Station Road, SW9 (071 274 7774). Brixton underground/BR.*
Crystal Palace, *Crystal Palace National Sports Centre, Ledrington Road, SE19 (081 778 0131). Crystal Palace BR.*
London Central YMCA Bobcats, *London Central YMCA, 112 Great Russell Street, WC1 (071 637 8131). Tottenham Court Road underground.*

London Jets, *Summit Sportcomplex, Sedgwick Centre, Colchester Street, E1 (071 481 5123). Aldgate East underground.*

Boxing

York Hall
Roman Road, E2 (081 980 2243). Bethnal Green underground.
Many of the pubs along the Old Kent Road, SE1 – such as the Thomas A' Becket and the Henry Cooper – have boxing gyms upstairs where the stars work out. Details of big fights are usually fly-posted around the capital; seats cost from around £15 up to £150 for a world title contest. Regular locations include the Royal Albert Hall, SW7; Battersea Town Hall, SW11; Olympia, W14; and Lewisham Theatre, SE6. The most atmospheric of London's venues is the cramped York Hall, in the boxing heartland of the East End.

Cricket

Lord's
St John's Wood Road, NW8 (Middlesex 071 289 8979/Marylebone Cricket Club – national administrative body – 071 289 1611). St John's Wood underground.
Lord's is the home of cricket, but is also HQ for Middlesex, and the county plays Championship and Sunday League matches here on a regular basis during the summer. Admission to these games costs £6-£7, and there's no need to book in advance. The ground also hosts one Test match and often a one-day international per year (in 1994 both New Zealand and South Africa will play here) together with all the limited-overs cup finals. Booking tickets for these games is essential, at a cost of £15-£40.

Foster's Oval
SE11 (071 582 6660). Oval underground.
The Oval, as its downmarket sponsorship might suggest, is a far less pretentious venue than Lord's. Nevertheless it has one of the best batting tracks in the country, and the annual Test match staged at the ground attracts genuine cricket fans. Booking tickets in advance is again vital, although you can watch Surrey play its Championship and Sunday League cricket there for £7.

Football

The season runs from mid-August to May. If you've never been to a game before, we advise you to pay for a seat; the view is generally better than from the terraces.

FA Carling Premiership
Arsenal, *Arsenal Stadium, Avenell Road, N5 (071 226 0304). Arsenal underground.* **Tickets** *seats £10-£23.*
Chelsea, *Stamford Bridge, Fulham Road, SW6 (071 385 5545). Fulham Broadway underground.* **Tickets** *standing £9-£10; seats £10-£30.*
Queens Park Rangers, *Rangers Stadium, South Africa Road, W12 (081 743 0262). White City underground.* **Tickets** *standing £8-£10; seats £11-£25.*
Tottenham Hotspur, *White Hart Lane, High Road, N17 (081 808 3030). White Hart Lane BR.* **Tickets** *standing £10; seats £13-£22.*
West Ham United, *Boleyn Ground, Green Street, E13 (081 472 2740). Upton Park underground.* **Tickets** *standing £9; seats £11-£17.*

Wimbledon, *Selhurst Park, Park Road, SE25 (081 771 2233). Selhurst BR.* **Tickets** *standing £7-£8; seats £13-£20.*

Endsleigh Insurance League Div 1
Charlton Athletic, *The Valley, Floyd Road, SE7 (081 293 4567). Charlton BR.* **Tickets** *seats £12-£14.*
Crystal Palace, *Selhurst Park (see Wimbledon above; 081 653 1000).* **Tickets** *standing £9; seats £13-£25.*
Millwall, *The New London Stadium, Senegal Fields, Zampa Road, SE16 (071 231 9999). South Bermondsey BR.* **Tickets** *seats £10-£20.*

Golf

Both the famous courses listed below are on the circuit for major international events, with the Volvo PGA Championship something of a regular at Wentworth every May. Admission charges vary.
Sunningdale *Ridgemount Road, Sunningdale, Ascot (0344 21681). Sunningdale BR.*
Wentworth Golf Club *Wentworth Drive, Virginia Water, Surrey (0344 842201). Virginia Water BR.*

Greyhound Racing

Thousands of punters 'go to the dogs' every week. All of the tracks have a bar and restaurant. Admission costs from £2.50.
Catford Stadium *Ademore Road, SE26 (081 690 2261). Catford Bridge BR.* **Races** *7.30pm Mon, Thur, Sat.*
Hackney Stadium *Waterden Road, E15 (081 986 3511). W15 bus.* **Races** *11am Sat; 1pm Tue.*

*Still waiting for a cross: **Tottenham**'s Teddy Sheringham. See **review**.*

Walthamstow Stadium *Chingford Road, E4 (081 531 4255). Walthamstow underground.* **Races** 7.30pm Tue, Thur, Sat.
Wembley Stadium *Stadium Way, Wembley (081 902 8833). Wembley Park underground.* **Races** 7.30pm Mon, Wed, Fri.
Wimbledon Stadium *Plough Lane, SW19 (081 946 5361). Wimbledon Park underground.* **Races** 7.30pm Tue, Thur-Sat.

Hockey

Hockey has been a boom sport in Britain recently, with the success of the men's and women's teams in the Olympic Games encouraging many new players to pick up their sticks. Games in the respective national leagues are played on Saturday or Sunday afternoons; below we list the home venues for London's senior clubs:
Hounslow *Riverside Drive, Duke's Meadows, Great Chertsey Road, W4 (081 994 9470). Chiswick BR.*
Indian Gymkhana Feltham School, *Browells Lane, Feltham (081 890 8882). Feltham BR.*
Old Loughtonians *Luxborough Lane, Chigwell (081 504 7222). Chigwell underground.*
Southgate Broomfield School, *Sunningdale, off Wilmer Way, N14 (081 361 2932). Arnos Grove underground.*
Teddington School, *Broom Road, Teddington (081 977 0598). Teddington BR.*

Horse Racing

A day at the races can be a thrilling experience – if you manage to pick all the winners, that is. You can bet on the state-run Tote, which gives no odds until all bets have been placed and

Hell for leather at **Epsom.** *See* **review.**

divides the pool between those who have forecast correctly; or with one of the bookies who stand along the track rail. The bookies make their own odds, demand a larger minimum stake (often £5), and usually accept only 'win only' bets; whereas you can back a horse to finish in a 'place' with the Tote.

Ascot
High Street, Ascot (0344 22211). Ascot BR. **Admission** *Silver Ring £3; Grandstand £9; Club £15.*
The Royal Meeting in June is Ascot's annual high spot (*see chapter* **London by Season**), but the historic course has more than 20 flat and jumps race days throughout the year. There's good, if expensive, food available in all areas of the course.

Epsom
Racecourse Paddock, Epsom (0372 726311). Epsom BR. **Admission** *Enclosure £4; Grandstand £13.*
Meetings have been held on Epsom Downs since the 1640s, and although the course now hosts fewer than ten race days a year, it still stages two Classics: the Derby and the Oaks (at the beginning of June), when the crowds are at their height. There are drinks and snack bars throughout, and you can view from the winning post in the Lonsdale Enclosure.

Kempton Park
Staines Road East, Sunbury-on-Thames (0932 782292). Kempton Park BR. **Admission** *Silver Ring £4; Tattersalls £9; Club £13 .*
The closest course to London had a facelift a few years ago, and is now a pleasant though unexceptional venue for both flat and jumps meetings. There's a series of popular summer evening meetings.

Sandown Park
The Racecourse, Esher Station Road, Esher (0372 463072). Esher BR. **Admission** *Silver Ring £3; Grandstand £9; Club £13.*
Voted 'Racecourse of the Year' no fewer than seven times in the last 14 years, Sandown Park is always well-organised and accessible – it's just off the A307, and Esher BR station adjoins the course. At least 25 flat and jumps race days are staged each year, and there's good viewing of the oval track from all points together with ample snack bars and restaurants.

Windsor
Maidenhead Road, Windsor (0753 865234). Windsor & Eton Riverside BR. **Admission** *Silver Ring £4; Tattersalls £8; Club £12 .*
Windsor takes full advantage of its Thames-side setting, with a shuttle boat service operating from Barry Avenue Promenade in the town before and after racing. The well-frequented summer evening meetings are probably the best to attend. The course, which stages both flat and jumps meetings, has an amiable, slightly tatty-at-the-edges feel about it – but there are good restaurants and bars in the Club Enclosure.

Motor Sport

Silverstone Circuit
Silverstone, near Towcester, Northants (0327 857271). Northampton BR.
Silverstone has taken over the mantle as this country's premier motor racing circuit now that it stages the British Formula One Grand Prix each July (admission around £60, grandstand seats £115). There's also a full

programme of club and championship car, bike and truck racing most weekends of the year.

Wimbledon Stadium
Plough Lane, SW17 (081 946 5361). Wimbledon Park underground. **Admission** £6 adults; £3 children.
Banger racing is Wimbledon's stock-in-trade: a noisy, smoky spectacle held every Sunday, 6pm, from July to May. There are glass-fronted grandstands, and plenty of bars and restaurants to help you enjoy the mayhem.

Polo

The Guards Polo Club
Smiths Lawn, Windsor Great Park, Englefield Green, Egham (0784 437797). Windsor & Eton Central BR.
Polo is an undeniably glamorous sport with more than a dash of elitism, but it still provides a pleasant day out in the shadow of Windsor Castle. There are matches every Saturday and Sunday at 3pm, with the Cartier International in July a highlight. Admission is from £15 per car, which includes all occupants.

Rugby League

London Crusaders
Barnet Copthall Stadium, Great North Way, NW4 (081 203 4211). Mill Hill East underground.
In 1993, the London Crusaders moved from their former home at Crystal Palace to the north London suburbs in an effort to build a regular audience for the 13-man form of rugby. Their survival as the only southern club in a professional sport strongest in the north-west of England has always been precarious, but the Crusaders are one of the stronger teams in Division Two of the national Stones Bitter Championship.

Rugby Union

Club Rugby
Blackheath *Rectory Field, Charlton Road, SE3 (081 858 1578). Blackheath BR.* Div 3.
Harlequins *Stoop Memorial Ground, Craneford Way, Twickenham (081 892 0822). Twickenham BR.* Div 1.
London Irish *The Avenue, Sunbury-on-Thames (0932 783034). Sunbury BR.* Div 1.
London Scottish *Athletic Ground, Kew Foot Road, Richmond (081 332 2473). Richmond underground/BR.* Div 2.
Richmond *Athletic Ground, Kew Foot Road, Richmond (081 940 0397). Richmond underground/BR.* Div 2.
Rosslyn Park *Upper Richmond Road, Priory Lane, SW15 (081 876 1879). Barnes BR.* Div 3.
Saracens *Bramley Ground, Chase Side, N14 (081 449 3770). Cockfosters underground.* Div 2.
Wasps *Repton Avenue, Sudbury (081 902 4220). Sudbury Town underground.* Div 1.
The club rugby season runs from September to May, and games are played every Saturday afternoon. Admission is around £3-£6 and you will be able to see many top international players in action, especially for Harlequins, Wasps and London Irish. Even though the game is tough on the pitch, the atmosphere off it is good-natured and convivial with spectators welcomed into the clubhouse afterwards for a beer and a burger. Above, we list the clubs playing in the top three divisions of the national Courage League.

Twickenham
Whitton Road, Twickenham (081 892 8161). Twickenham BR.
This is the spacious, well-appointed ground where

England plays its international fixtures, and where other representative games and cup finals are staged. Tickets for matches in the Five Nations Championship, which runs from January to March, are distributed through clubs and are almost impossible for casual spectators to obtain. However, the finals of the Pilkington Cup for clubs, and the County Championship are also played here; the box office will have details of these and all Twickenham's other games for which gaining admission is less difficult.

Tennis

All England Lawn Tennis Club
Church Road, SW19 (081 944 1066/ticket information 081 946 2244). Wimbledon Park or Southfields underground.
If you're lucky enough to have a pair of centre court tickets with lunch and tea in a hospitality tent, then a day out at Wimbledon is a dream. If not, then you may find yourself utterly frustrated by the queues, the restrictions, and the price of strawberries and cream. Tickets for the show courts are allocated by ballot, and you should write (with stamped, addressed envelope) to the club between 1 September and 31 December for an application form. A limited number of tickets is also available at the gate each day, but there are usually people prepared to camp out all night to get them. A better bet is to turn up after 5pm when ground admission is reduced, some centre court seats may have been vacated by the sozzled recipients of free champagne, and you could enjoy three hours of top-class tennis for a fiver.

Queen's Club
Palliser Road, W14 (071 385 2366/ticket information 071 497 0521). Barons Court underground.
Queen's is the venue for the Stella Artois Championship, which is held in early June and is the most important of the men's pre-Wimbledon grass-court tournaments. Despite its increasing popularity with spectators, the competition has retained a civilised, low-key atmosphere with none of the stuffy snobbishness that so bedevils the All-England event.

Major Stadiums

Crystal Palace National Sports Centre
Ledrington Road, SE19 (081 778 0131). Crystal Palace BR. **Open** box office 9.30am-5pm Mon-Fri.
The Palace is Britain's longest-established athletics venue, and hosts a Grand Prix meeting every summer. The sports centre itself stages major championships in activities ranging from basketball to weightlifting, diving to judo. Phone for details of forthcoming events.

Wembley Complex
Empire Way, Wembley, Middlesex (081 900 1234). Wembley Park underground. **Open** box office 9.30am-9pm Mon-Sat; 10am-6pm Sun.
Despite constant criticisms of inadequate toilet facilities and poor views, the 80,000-capacity Wembley Stadium is still one of the world's most famous sports arenas. The Coca-Cola and FA Cup finals are staged here in March and May respectively. The Rugby League Challenge Cup final and American football's London Bowl are also played here in May and August, while there's dog racing for the local punters on three nights a week (*see above* **Greyhound Racing**). Wembley Arena is the venue for top-level gymnastics, ice hockey, boxing and basketball events. Tickets for the entire Wembley complex are available from the box office number listed above, or from booking agencies throughout London.

Theatre

From a feast of thespians, to a ham in a pub, London provides a banquet of theatrical talent. We throw some light on the dramatic scenery.

For years, Londoners were used to the idea of posh, professional West End theatres offset by the cheap, youthful, experimental Fringe. But in 1993, *Time Out* magazine single-handedly reorganised the London theatre scene by proclaiming a new middle category of Off-West End.

The new category is a measure of the Fringe's success. Gone are the days when all Fringe theatres occupied the seedy backrooms of seedier pubs. The difference between Off-West End and Fringe theatres is the difference between venues with a management that produces plays, and those venues that are simply hired out to visiting companies to do with as they will.

The West End is the centre of excellence it has always been. No other major city in the world can boast such a diverse, dramatic heritage, from the repertory productions at the **National Theatre**, to the long-running blockbuster musicals around Shaftesbury Avenue. Still, audiences have dwindled in the past few recession-hit years, and backers have been reluctant to invest money in anything but near-certain hits.

We list below the principal companies, long-running shows, and important West End, Off-West End and Fringe theatres. **LIFT**, the London International Festival of Theatre, is a major biennial event, featuring the best of innovative, contemporary theatre from around the world, as well as new British work. The eighth festival takes place in July 1995 at venues all over London. Information from 23 Neal Street, WC2 (071 836 7186/7433).

Information & Tickets

Tickets for West End musicals are the most expensive (£9-£30) and can be the most difficult to obtain. In association with many theatre box offices, Ticketmaster (071 344 4444) provides tickets in advance for all West End shows. Expect to pay a booking fee for some productions.

Ten tips for cheap theatre-going

1 Go to the **SWET** half-price ticket booth in Leicester Square (*see below* **Information & Tickets**).

2 Go to a matinée performance if there is one. The tickets are cheaper but the performances may be lack-lustre compared with the evening, and understudies may replace the stars.

3 Pay for a restricted-view seat in the stalls (not all theatres have them), then move to a more expensive seat further forward as soon as the lights go down.

4 Sit in the 'gods' at the top of the theatre (higher even than the balcony) and take a pair of binoculars.

5 Buy tickets direct from the box office to save credit-card charges and agency commissions.

6 Go to a preview (West End and some Off-West End only). Tickets are cheaper as critics haven't had a chance to pan the show.

7 Go to the **National Theatre** early in the morning on the day of the show you want to see. A number of tickets are sold on the day from 10am at the box office: 40 for the Olivier; 40 for the Lyttelton; 20 for the Cottesloe. People queue from 8am for the popular shows.

8 At the **Royal Court** in Sloane Square, all tickets are £4 on Monday nights.

9 Pay concessionary prices (for OAPs, students and children) or enquire about the availability of standby tickets (usually also concessionary) at the West End.

10 Look out for special offers in the back of *Time Out* magazine.

Theatre

Artsline

5 Crowndale Road, NW1 (071 388 2227). Mornington Crescent or Camden Town underground/Camden Road BR. **Open** 10am-4pm Mon-Fri.
A free advice and information service for disabled people on access to arts and entertainment in London. Ask staff to send you the free monthly arts listings magazine, *Disability Arts in London.*

Society of West End Theatre (SWET)

Ticket Booth Leicester Square, WC2 (no phone). Leicester Square or Piccadilly Circus underground. **Open** 2.30-6.30pm Mon-Sat; noon-6.30pm on matinée days. **Tickets** for some shows half price plus £1.50 service charge. **No credit cards.**
The SWET ticket booth in Leicester Square has a limited number of tickets for some West End shows on the day of performance at half price (cash only). Tickets are restricted to four per person and you cannot return tickets to the booth, though the theatre might accept returns. The new booth is identifiable by its long queue. A list of theatres that operate SWET's standby scheme is available from SWET, Bedford Chambers, The Piazza, Covent Garden, WC2 (071 836 0971); open 10am-5.30pm Mon-Fri.

Major Theatre Companies

The National Theatre

South Bank, SE1 (box office 071 928 2252/information 071 633 0880). Waterloo underground/BR **Open** box office 10am-8pm Mon-Sat. **Performances** 7pm or 7.30pm Mon-Sat, plus 2.30pm or 3pm matinées, usually Tue-Thur. **Tickets** *Olivier and Lyttelton* £7-£21; *Cottesloe* £13.50.
Britain's first state-subsidised theatre has established itself as the nation's leading theatrical hot-house, given first voice to writers such as Peter Shaffer and David Hare, and achieved national notoriety when Mary Whitehouse tried unsuccessfully to sue it for the depiction of homosexual rape in Howard Brenton's *Romans in Britain.* The current director Richard Eyre assumed the position in 1988. The building itself comprises three theatres: the Olivier (large, open-platform stage), the Lyttelton (proscenium arch) and the Cottesloe (small, flexible studio space).
Restaurants and cafes. Bookshop. Gallery. Wheelchair access. Toilets for the disabled.

Old Vic

Waterloo Road, SE1 (071 638 8891/recorded information 071 928 7618). Waterloo underground/BR. **Open** box office 10am-9pm Mon-Sat. **Performances** 7.45pm Mon-Sat; matinées 3pm Wed, Sat. **Tickets** £10-£29.50 (cheapest seats may have restricted view). **Credit** A, AmEx, DC, TC, V.
Though the building has been a theatre since 1818, it was not until the eccentric South African Lilian Baylis took over in 1914 that the Royal Victoria Theatre really came into its own. Baylis ran the theatre until her death in 1937, and with actors such as John Gielgud, Laurence Olivier and Sybil Thorndike, Baylis founded the Old Vic Theatre Company, the nucleus of which, in 1963, became the **National Theatre Company** under Olivier (*see above*). Today it is owned by Canadian businessman 'Honest' Ed Mirvish who has restored its eighteenth-century splendour. Large-scale revivals of classics are its staple.

Royal Court (English Stage Company)

Sloane Square, SW1 (071 730 1745). Sloane Square underground. **Open** box office 10am-8pm Mon-Sat. **Performances** ring for times. **Tickets** £5-£15. **Credit** A, AmEx, DC, £TC, V.
The Royal Court theatre situated in arty, once Bohemian Chelsea, has always been the bad boy of West End the-

atre. In the early years of the century, writers like Shaw, Pinero and Granville-Barker established it as a centre of new drama, a reputation it has never lost. More recently, writers such as Caryl Churchill, Edward Bond, and Timberlake Wertenbaker have made their names here. Above the main house, the Theatre Upstairs is one of the principal Off-West End venues.
Educational workshop by prior arrangement (082 960 4041). Group discount (071 730 5174). Tour by prior arrangement (071 328 7558). Induction loop. Disabled assistance (071 730 5174). Wheelchair access.

The Royal Shakespeare Company

Barbican Centre, Silk Street, EC2 (071 638 8891/information 071 628 2295). Barbican underground/Moorgate underground/BR. The RSC in Stratford, Warwickshire (0789 295623). Stratford-upon-Avon BR (from Paddington BR).
The RSC has two homes, one in London at the Barbican Centre (incorporating the Barbican Theatre and The Pit) and the other in Shakespeare's birthplace of Stratford-upon-Avon (*see chapter* **Trips Out of Town**). Stratford's Royal Shakespeare Theatre is the only venue that puts on nothing but Shakespeare. The others all have an equal commitment to other classics and to new writing. What is seen in Stratford one season, comes to London the next. The Barbican Centre in London has the reputation of being very hard to find, but the confusing modernist interior lay-out is due to be revised this year.
Car park. Restaurants & cafes. Shops. Wheelchair access; toilets for people with disabilities.

Theatreless Theatre Companies

Age Exchange

The Reminiscence Centre, 11 Blackheath Village, SE3 (081 318 9105).
The actors in this ten-year-old theatre company make it their business to record the anecdotes, tales and memories of those of advancing years, to turn them into drama and to act them out.

Black Mime Theatre

61 Collier Street, N1 (071 833 3785).
A three-man theatre group which won the Charlie Award at the London International Festival of Street Entertainers in 1991. Hit shows include *Superheroes*, a parody of comic book clichés and *Rainbow*, an exploration of what it's like to be young, black and diagnosed schizophrenic.

Cheek By Jowl

Alford House, Aveline Street, SE11 (071 793 0153).
Adventurous, award-winning theatre company founded in 1981 by Declan Donnelan (director) and Nick Ormerod (designer) and acclaimed for its innovative productions of world classics. The company is renowned for its single-sex productions, including an all-male *As You Like It*, with a memorable Rosalind played by six-foot black actor, Adrian Lester, who won a *Time Out* best actor award.

Paines Plough

121 Tottenham Court Road, W1 (071 380 1188).
Paines Plough has also long been known as 'the writers' company'. It was founded in 1974 to produce new works only, and to support the development of writers at all stages. All productions are directed by Pip Broughton. These include Kay Adshead's *Such as women*, and William Gaminara's *Germinal*.

The People Show

St James the Great Institute, Pollards Row, E2 (071 729 1841).
An anarchic 20-year-old company, so egalitarian that not

even individual words are permitted to have prominence. Each show is numbered, not titled, and is more spectacle than drama, but always memorable.

Ra Ra Zoo
Diorama Arts Centre, 34 Osnaburgh Street, NW1 (071 916 5268).
With attendances waning at traditional big-top circus entertainments, avant-garde, animal-free circuses like Ra Ra Zoo have come into their own. Performers include trapeze artistes, stilt-walkers, dancers, tumblers, and chain-saw handlers.

Really Useful Group
22 Tower Street, WC2 (071 240 0880).
The Andrew Lloyd Webber production company responsible for the long-running productions of *Cats, Starlight Express, Phantom of the Opera, Joseph and the Amazing Technicolour Dreamcoat* and now *Sunset Boulevard* as well as other non-Lloyd Webber shows such as *Daisy Pulls it Off* and *Lend Me a Tenor*. Prince Edward once worked for the company.

Renaissance Theatre Co
83 Berwick Street, W1 (071 287 6672).
Kenneth Branagh's successful, unsubsidised, touring theatre company. Productions of Shakespeare and other classic texts.

Snarling Beasties
27 Grovesnor Road, Harbourne, Birmingham (021 427 5171).
This three-person company (two actors and an administrator) was founded by writer/performer Debbie Isitt. She has made a virtue of imbuing serious subjects – wife beating in *Punch and Judy*, transvestism in *Femme Fatale* – with the spirit of comedy. The group won the 1989 Independent Theatre Award.

Strathcona TC
c/o Strathcona Social Education Centre, Strathcona Road, Wembley, Middx (081 451 7419).
This extraordinary company was founded in 1982 and produces professional drama using handicapped actors (some severely so). A comic group, it is not too self-reverential to make jokes at its own expense.

Tara Arts
356 Garratt Lane, SW18 (081 871 1458).
Tara Arts is the country's leading Asian theatre company, albeit with an ethnically mixed cast. Formed in 1976 and led by the charismatic director Jatinder Verma, it is characterised by a mix of English and Punjabi languages, on-stage percussion instruments, and exaggerated thespian gestures. Re-interpretations of classic texts are the mainstay.

Theatre de Complicité
20 Eden Grove, N7 (071 700 0233).
Complicité's approach is inspired by a determination to enjoy and exploit the business of standing on stage in front of an audience. Its work, all of which is conceived through improvisation, is characterised by great invention, expansive minimalism, duplicitous inanity, a Breughel-like attention to detail, frothy cerebral antics and grossly overweight press packs. A latter-day *commedia dell'arte* without the pedantry.

Trestle Theatre Co
47-49 Wood Street, Barnet, N14 (081 441 0349).
This is the country's principal masked theatre company. The group's style of theatre is as remarkable as it is expressive.

Women's Playhouse Trust
5 Leonard Street, EC2 (071 251 0202).
A 21-year-old group of female performers that commissions and performs work by female writers. Tours nationally.

London's Long Runners

Blood Brothers
Tickets £9.50-£25.
Musical by Willy Russell and Bob Tomson which is now at the **Phoenix Theatre**. It's a grand, ambitious melodrama, lined with sentiment and memorable songs, and is now ten years old. A pair of twins are separated at birth, one remaining with his family in working-class-dom, the other farmed out to a middle-class couple unable to have kids of their own.

Buddy
Tickets £8-£24.
A musical by Alan Janes that occupies the **Victoria Palace**. Buddy is a staged biography of the bespectacled rock and roll star who was killed in a plane crash. A must for the nostalgic.

Cats
Tickets £10.50-£30.
The most successful Andrew Lloyd Webber musical of all, having occupied the **New London Theatre** since 1981. It's a dancing moggie show with a text taken from T S Eliot's *Old Possum's Book of Cats*. It has long since cruised past the record for London's longest-running musical.

Five Guys Named Moe
Tickets £5-£27.50.
This jazz musical by Clarke Peters is now in its third year at the **Lyric Theatre, Shaftesbury Avenue**. It's a high-spirited tribute to the late Louis Jordan's versatile repertoire and pragmatic, home-grown philosophies about life and women. The joint never stops jumping.

It Runs in the Family
Tickets £5-£18.50.
Traditional British farce by Ray Cooney, which has been playing at the West End's only dinner-drama restaurant (the **Playhouse**) since 1991. The world conspires against a top surgeon when the illegitimate 18-year-old son he never knew he had, turns up to claim his birthright. A well-executed romp.

Joseph and the Amazing Technicolour Dreamcoat
Tickets £8.50-£29.
A revived and much lengthened production of the first musical success by Andrew Lloyd Webber and Tim Rice which has taken over the famous **London Palladium**. This is a seductive staging, propped up by an orchestra which swings knowingly from Pharaoh's blue-suede rockabilly to gospel.

Les Miserables
Tickets £7-£30.
An RSC production of Alain Boublil's and Claude-Michel Schonberg's epic adaptation of Victor Hugo's novel, that has resided at the **Palace Theatre** for more than five years. Easy melodies, comprehensible lyrics, virtuous paupers, obvious villains and seamless scenes are the ingredients.

Miss Saigon
Tickets £8.50-£30.
For the past four years this musical by Alain Schonberg and Claude-Michel Schonberg has occupied the **Theatre Royal Drury Lane**. It's a sumptuous updating of the *Madame Butterfly* tragedy in which an American GI falls in love with and impregnates a Vietnamese prostitute.

The **Adelphi**, *home to Lloyd Webber's latest:* Sunset Boulevard.

The Mousetrap

Tickets £8-£20.

The long-runner of long runners, Agatha Christie's thriller, directed by David Turner, has now been in the West End for 42 years, and at its present home in the **St Martin's Theatre** for 22 years. It's a charming institution of a play that continues to stroll along at a sedate 1930s pace.

The Phantom of the Opera

Tickets £9-£30.

Andrew Lloyd Webber's *Phantom* has just about made **Her Majesty's Theatre** its own. It's an enormously successful, lavish musical based on the tale of the monster who falls in love with an opera singer.

Starlight Express

Tickets £9-£28.

An Andrew Lloyd Webber production that is now in its eleventh year at the **Apollo Victoria**. It's the world's only roller-skating musical, performed at high speed on tracks before, round and above the nightly packed audience. The show has its faults, but steams along at a fair old lick.

The Woman in Black

Tickets £8.50-£18.50.

This ghost story by Susan Hill has been the staple at the **Fortune Theatre** for the past five years, gaining a cult following that has helped make it the theatre's longest running show ever.

Venues

West End

Adelphi Theatre, *Strand, WC2 (Ticketmaster 071 344 0055). Charing Cross underground/BR.* **Open** *box office* 24-hours daily.

Albery Theatre, *St Martin's Lane, WC2 (071 867 1115/credit-card bookings 071 867 1111). Leicester Square underground.* **Open** *box office* 9.30am-8pm Mon-Sat.

Apollo Shaftesbury, *Shaftesbury Avenue, W1 (071 494 5070). Piccadilly Circus underground.* **Open** *box office* 10am-8pm Mon-Sat.

Apollo Victoria, *Wilton Road, SW1 (071 828 8665). Victoria underground/BR.* **Open** *box office* 10am-8pm Mon-Sat.

Barbican Centre, *Silk Street, EC2 (071 638 8891/24-hour information 071 628 2295). Barbican underground or Moorgate underground/BR.* **Open** *box office* 9am-8pm daily.

Comedy Theatre, *Panton Street, SW1 (071 867 1045/credit-card bookings 071 867 1111). Piccadilly Circus underground.* **Open** *box office* 10am-7.30pm Mon-Sat.

Criterion Theatre, *Piccadilly Circus, WC2 (071 839 4488). Piccadilly Circus underground.* **Open** *box office* 10am-7.30pm Mon-Sat.

Dominion Theatre, *Tottenham Court Road, W1 (071 580 8845/credit-card bookings 071 580 9562). Tottenham Court Road underground.* **Open** *box office* 10am-6pm Mon-Sat.

Drury Lane Theatre Royal, *Catherine Street, WC2 (071 494 5062). Covent Garden underground.* **Open** *box office* 10am-8pm Mon-Sat.

Duchess Theatre, *Catherine Street, WC2 (071 494 5075). Covent Garden underground.* **Open** *box office* 10am-8pm Mon-Sat.

Duke of York's, *St Martin's Lane, WC2 (071 836 5122). Leicester Square underground.* **Open** *box office* 10am-8pm Mon-Sat.

Fortune Theatre, *Russell Street, WC2 (071 836 2238). Covent Garden underground.* **Open** *box office* 10am-8pm Mon-Sat.

Garrick, *Charing Cross Road, WC2 (071 494 5085). Leicester Square underground.* **Open** *box office* 10am-8pm Mon-Sat.

Globe Theatre, *Shaftesbury Avenue, W1 (071 494 5065/6/7). Piccadilly Circus underground.* **Open** *box office* 10am-8pm Mon-Sat.

Haymarket Theatre Royal, *The Haymarket, SW1 (071 930 8800). Piccadilly Circus underground.* **Open** *box office* 10am-8pm Mon-Sat.

Her Majesty's, *Haymarket, SW1 (071 494 5050). Piccadilly Circus underground.* **Open** *box office* 10am-8pm Mon-Sat.

London Palladium, *Argyll Street, W1 (071 494 5020). Oxford Circus underground.* **Open** *box office* 10am-8.30pm Mon-Sat.
Lyric Shaftesbury Avenue, *Shaftesbury Avenue, W1 (071 494 5045). Piccadilly Circus underground.* **Open** *box office* 10am-8pm Mon-Sat.
National Theatre, *South Bank, SE1 (071 928 2252). Waterloo underground/BR.* **Open** *box office* 10am-8pm Mon-Sat.
New London, *Drury Lane, WC2 (071 405 0072). Covent Garden or Holborn underground.* **Open** *box office* 10am-8pm Mon-Sat.
Old Vic, *Waterloo Road, SE1 (071 928 7616/recorded information 071 928 7618). Waterloo underground/BR.* **Open** *box office* 10am-9pm Mon-Sat.
Palace, *Shaftesbury Avenue, W1 (071 434 0909). Leicester Square underground.* **Open** *box office* 10am-8pm Mon-Sat.
Phoenix, *Charing Cross Road, WC2 (071 867 1044). Leicester Square underground.* **Open** *box office* 10am-8pm Mon-Sat.
Playhouse Theatre, *Northumberland Avenue, WC2 (071 839 4401). Embankment underground or Charing Cross underground/BR.* **Open** *box office* 10am-8pm Mon-Sat.
Prince Edward Theatre, *Old Compton Street, W1 (071 734 8951). Leicester Square underground.* **Open** *box office* 10am-8pm Mon-Sat.
Prince of Wales, *Coventry Street, W1 (071 839 5972). Piccadilly Circus underground.* **Open** *box office* 10am-7pm Mon-Sat.
Queen's Theatre, *Shaftesbury Avenue, W1 (071 494 5040). Leicester Square underground.* **Open** *box office* 10am-6pm Mon-Sat.
Royal Court, *Sloane Square, SW1 (071 730 1745). Sloane Square underground.* **Open** *box office* 10am-8pm Mon-Sat.
RSC Barbican, *Barbican Centre, Silk Street, EC2 (071 638 8891). Barbican underground (closed Sun) or Moorgate underground/BR.* **Open** *box office* 9am-8pm daily.
St Martin's, *West Street, Cambridge Circus, WC2 (071 836 1443). Leicester Square underground.* **Open** *box office* 10am-8pm Mon-Sat.
Shaftesbury Theatre, *Shaftesbury Avenue, WC2 (071 379 5399). Holborn or Tottenham Court Road underground.* **Open** *box office* 10am-8pm Mon-Sat.
Strand Theatre, *Aldwych, WC2 (071 930 8800). Aldwych underground.* **Open** *box office* 10am-7pm Mon-Sat.
Vaudeville, *The Strand, WC2 (071 836 9987). Charing Cross underground/BR.* **Open** *box office* 10am-8pm Mon-Sat.
Victoria Palace, *Victoria Street, SW1 (071 834 1317). Victoria underground/BR.* **Open** *box office* 10am-8pm Mon-Sat.
Whitehall, *Whitehall, SW1 (071 867 1119). Charing Cross underground/BR.* **Open** *box office* 10am-8pm Mon-Sat.
Wyndhams, *Charing Cross Road, WC2 (071 867 1116). Leicester Square underground or Charing Cross underground/BR.* **Open** *box office* 10am-8pm Mon-Sat.

Off-West End

Almeida, *Almeida Street, N1 (071 359 4404). Angel underground or Highbury & Islington underground/BR.* **Open** *box office* 10am-6pm Mon-Sat.
BAC, *176 Lavender Hill, SW11 (071 223 2223). Clapham Junction BR.* **Open** *box office* 10am-6pm Mon; 10am-10pm Tue-Sun.
The Bush, *Shepherd's Bush Green, W12 (081 743 3388). Goldhawk Road or Shepherd's Bush*

underground. **Open** *box office* 10am-7pm Mon-Sat.
The Cockpit, *Gateforth Street, NW8 (071 402 5081). Edgware Road underground or Marylebone underground/BR.* **Open** *box office* 10am-6pm Mon-Sat.
Donmar Warehouse, *Thomas Neal's, Earlham Street, WC2 (071 867 1150). Covent Garden underground.* **Open** *box office* 10am-8pm Mon-Sat.
Drill Hall, *16 Chenies Street, WC1 (071 637 8270). Goodge Street underground.* **Open** *box office* 10am-8pm Mon-Fri; 12.30-8pm Sat.
The Gate, *The Prince Albert, 11 Pembridge Road, W11 (071 229 0706). Notting Hill Gate underground.* **Open** *box office* 10am-6pm Mon-Fri.
Hampstead Theatre, *Avenue Road, NW3 (071 722 9301). Swiss Cottage underground.* **Open** *box office* 10am-7pm Mon-Sat.
ICA Theatre, *The Mall, SW1 (071 930 3647). Piccadilly Circus underground or Charing Cross underground/BR.* **Open** *box office* noon-6pm daily.
King's Head, *115 Upper Street, N1 (071 226 1916/8561). Angel underground or Highbury & Islington underground/BR.* **Open** *box office* 10am-8pm Mon-Sat; 10am-6pm Sun.
Orange Tree, *1 Clarence Street, Richmond, Surrey (081 940 3633). Richmond underground/BR.* **Open** *box office* 10am-7pm Mon-Sat.
Riverside Studios, *Crisp Road, W6 (081 748 3354). Hammersmith underground.* **Open** *box office* 10am-8pm daily.
Theatre Royal Stratford East, *Gerry Raffles Square, E15 (081 534 0310). Stratford underground/BR.* **Open** *box office* 10am-6pm Mon-Fri; 10am-3pm Sat.
Tricycle, *269 Kilburn High Road, NW6 (071 328 1000). Kilburn underground.* **Open** *box office* 10am-8pm Mon-Sat.

Fringe Venues

Arts Threshold, *170 Gloucester Terrace, W2 (071 262 1629). Lancaster Gate or Royal Oak underground/Paddington underground/BR/27 bus.* **Open** *box office* 10am-5pm Mon-Sat.
La Bonne Crêpe, *539 Battersea Park Road, SW11 (071 228 5070). Clapham Junction BR.* **Open** *box office* 10am-midnight daily.
Bridge Lane, *Bridge Lane, off Battersea Bridge Road, SW11 (071 228 8828). Clapham Junction BR.* **Open** *box office* 10am-6pm Mon-Sat.
Etcetera Theatre, *Oxford Arms, 265 Camden High Street, NW1 (071 482 4857). Camden Town underground.* **Open** *box office* 10am-8pm Mon-Sat.
The Finborough, *Finborough Arms, Finborough Road, SW10 (071 373 3842). Earl's Court underground.* **Open** *box office* 11am-8pm Mon-Sat.
Hen & Chickens, *Highbury Corner, N1 (071 704 2001). Highbury & Islington underground.* **Open** *box office* noon-7pm Mon-Sat.
Man in the Moon, *392 King's Road, SW3 (071 351 2876/5701). Sloane Square underground, then 11, 19, 22 bus.* **Open** *box office* 10am-7pm Mon-Sat.
New End Theatre, *27 New End, NW3 (071 794 0022). Hampstead underground.* **Open** *box office* 10am-8pm Mon-Sat.
The New Grove, *Drummonds, 73-77 Euston Road, NW1 (071 383 0925). King's Cross underground/BR.* **Open** *box office* 24-hour answerphone.
Old Red Lion, *St John's Street, EC1 (071 837 7816). Angel underground.* **Open** *box office* 10am-11pm daily.
White Bear, *138 Kennington Park Road, SE11 (071 793 9193/071 735 8664). Kennington underground.* **Open** *box office* 24-hour answerphone.
Young Vic, *66 The Cut, SE1 (071 928 6363). Waterloo underground/BR.* **Open** *box office* 10am-6pm Mon-Sat.

Early Hours

Jazz at midnight, tenpin bowling at 2am, food at 4am: where London keeps working in the wee small hours.

Because of some draconian and prohibitive licensing laws, London has still to become a city with a 24-hour lifestyle. It may come as a shock to anyone with a European outlook, but what do you expect in a country where shops that open on Sundays can be taken to court? But matters are improving and, if you've got the stamina, there's no need to go to bed between Friday and early Wednesday. But unless you're in the centre of town in the early hours, you're unlikely to find much to do, although other centres of late-night action include Queensway, Earl's Court and the Old Kent Road.

Some of the places we've listed have been around for years, while others could well have shut down since we went to press. If you're ever short of inspiration for a late-night excursion, hail a black cab and ask the driver to take you to where it's happening.

For more information on what to do after hours, *see also chapters* **Shopping**, **Comedy**, **Film**, **Gay London**, **Music: Rock, Folk & Jazz** and **Clubs**. For 24-hour emergency services *see chapter* **Survival**.

Transport

Last trains from central London on the underground system are between midnight and 12.30am. London Regional Transport (LRT) operates a network of night buses until the tubes start again at about 6am (8-9am on Sunday). The focal point of this service is **Trafalgar Square**; most night buses run to and from there. British Rail runs an irregular service of trains to commuter stations on the outskirts of London through the night from Euston, King's Cross (main line and Thameslink stations), Victoria and Waterloo. For further information on times for the tubes, night buses and overland trains call the LRT enquiry service on 071 222 1234 which is open round the clock, or *see* **Night Bus Map**.

You can catch a taxi or minicab any time, day or night. Try waiting outside big hotels or at cab ranks; *see chapter* **Getting Around**.

Comedy

The **Comedy Store**, **Jongleurs at the Cornet**, **Jongleurs at Camden Lock**, and **Up the Creek** all provide mirth around midnight, and alcohol till the early-hours. *See chapter* **Comedy**.

Drinking

It's a widely held belief that English licensing laws only encourage alcohol abuse and a malevolent

Wow! That cappuccino gets you moving at **Bar Italia**. *See* **review** *page 271.*

atmosphere on the streets around 11pm, when everyone leaves the pub and looks for something else to do. Because of these laws, pubs where you can get a drink after 11pm, instead of being sociable, relaxed bastions of civilisation, are the last resorts of desperate drunks. If you happen to be around the City of London the situation is even worse: many pubs close at 8.30pm during the week and never open at weekends.

There are relatively few ways to drink after pub hours, although the situation is gradually getting better. The rule is: you can keep drinking if you have paid to do something else. So, if you go to dance, eat or watch comedy, keep drinking until thrown out. To get on the bandwagon, pubs throughout central London are employing DJs or musicians as entertainment and having their licences extended to two or three in the morning. Look for any pub or wine bar that charges £3-£5 entry fee. In effect they have transformed themselves into nightclubs

where you don't need to dance. Otherwise, see *chapters* **Comedy**, **Music: Rock, Folk & Jazz** and **Clubs** for late night bars disguised as entertainment hotspots.

To sample London nightlife at its purest and coarsest, take a trip to the Old Kent Road, SE1: the pubs are open until 2am and the scenes outside shortly afterwards will remind you of nothing so much as the Apocalypse.

Rocky's Bar

Thomas-à-Beckett, 320 Old Kent Road, SE1 (071 252 7605). Elephant & Castle underground/BR/53, 177, N77, N85 bus. **Open** 9pm-2am Fri, Sat. **Admission** £3 after 11pm.
The Thomas-à-Beckett complex celebrates London's boxing heritage; Rocky's bar looks more to the Hollywood version.

Eating

This is one part of London's nightlife which isn't lacking in quantity, or even in variety, but can

Breakfast

If you make it through the night and, in the cold, grey light of dawn, can't face any of the 24-hour shops, here are some places to help you cope with the new day.

Central

Fox and Anchor
115 Charterhouse Street, EC1 (071 253 4838). Farringdon underground/BR. **Open** 6am-3pm Mon-Fri. **No credit cards.**
Smithfield Market is well served by early opening pubs. Strictly speaking, alcohol can only be sold to market traders for whom 7am feels like late afternoon. After a night on the town, the full breakfasts hit the spot.

Goldrings of Holborn
2A Farringdon Road, EC1 (071 253 5488). Farringdon underground/N21, N83, N93 bus. **Open** 4am-3pm Mon-Fri. **No credit cards.**
Start your day healthily with fresh bread or sandwiches.

The Hope Tavern
94 Cowcross Street, EC1 (071 250 1442). Farringdon underground. **Open** 6-9am, 10.30am-3pm, 5.30-8pm, Mon-Fri. **No credit cards.**
Big breakfasts, lunches and snacks in this traditional Smithfield pub. Again, don't be surprised if they refuse to serve you alcohol.

West

Maison Pechon
127 Queensway, W2 (071 229 0746). Bayswater underground. **Open** 7am-7pm Mon-Wed; 7am-8pm Thur-Sun. **No credit cards.**

Traditional English breakfasts, plus an endless list of cakes and fresh drinks.

Perry's Bakery & Haminados Patisserie
151 Earl's Court Road, SW5 (071 370 4825). Earl's Court underground/N56, N97 bus. **Open** 6am-midnight daily. **No credit cards.**
An inviting patisserie with a few seats for eat-in snacks. Good, fresh bread and cakes.

South East

Off the Rails
Greenwich Station, 187 Greenwich High Road, SE10 (081 293 4512). **Open** 7am-7pm Mon-Fri; 9am-7pm Sat, Sun. **No credit cards.**
The commuter's friend: a station buffet with good cappuccino and sandwiches.

East

Gaffers
Eagle Studios, 49-50 Eagle Wharf Road, N1 (071 490 4099). Old Street underground/BR. **Open** 8am-9pm Mon-Fri. **No credit cards.**
Peaceful studio café that opens out onto a canal. Very relaxing.

North

Alfredo's
4-6 Essex Road, N1 (071 226 3496). Angel underground. **Open** 7am-2.30pm Mon-Fri; 7am-noon Sat.* **Credit** A, V.
Authentic, well-priced caff, still with its original art deco design.

often be short of quality. Most parts of London have at least one restaurant that stays open late and serves more imaginative fare than burgers. For a more detailed look at London's restaurant scene, buy the latest edition of the *Time Out Guide to Eating & Drinking in London.*

Central

Bar Italia
22 Frith Street, W1 (071 437 4520). Tottenham Court Road underground/Night buses from Trafalgar Square. **Open** 7am-very late (usually 4am) Mon-Fri; 24 hours Sat, Sun. **Unlicensed. No credit cards.**
An authentic blast of Italy in the middle of Soho. The décor (Formica and mirrors) never seems to change (recent renovations notwithstanding), nor does the excitable atmosphere. Enjoy simple snacks, pizzas and *Serie A* football on the TV.
Air-conditioning. Tables outdoors. Takeaway service. Vegetarian savouries.

Bar Madrid
4 Winsley Street, W1 (071 436 4649). Oxford Circus underground/N3, N6, N8 bus. **Open** 7pm-3am Mon-Sat. **Average** £16 restaurant; £12 tapas. **Licensed. Credit** A, AmEx, DC, V.
Once *the* tapas bar, now just a tapas bar, but open very late. It's more of a Latin club these days, but someone in there has great taste in music.

Ed's Easy Diner
12 Moor Street, W1 (071 439 1955). Leicester Square underground/Night buses from Trafalgar Square. **Open** 11.30am-midnight Mon-Thur; 11.30am-1am Fri; 9am-1am Sat; 9am-11pm Sun. **Licensed. Average** £7. **Credit** LV, £TC.
Looking down Old Compton Street is one of Soho's success stories. Ed's is decorated in a mock fifties American diner style, complete with mini-jukeboxes. The short menu of burgers and shakes should be enough to satisfy even the hugest appetite. Service is friendly without being obsequious and there's a healthy banter between the staff.

Häagen Dazs
14 Leicester Square, WC2 (071 287 9577). Leicester Square underground/Night buses from Trafalgar Square. **Open** 10am-midnight Mon-Thur, Sun; 10am-1am Fri, Sat. **No credit cards.**
A tobacco-, alcohol- and additive-free ice-cream parlour for folk in search of a late-night sensual experience.

Los Locos
24-26 Russell Street, WC2 (071 379 0220). Covent Garden underground/Night buses from Trafalgar Square. **Open** 5pm-3am Mon-Sat. **Average** £17. **Licensed. Credit** A, AmEx, DC, EC, £$TC, V.
This rowdy Mexican place has a long cocktail list and vegetarian dishes. There's a disco nightly at 11.30pm.

Men's Bar Hamine
84 Brewer Street, W1 (071 439 0785). Piccadilly Circus underground/Night buses from Trafalgar Square. **Open** noon-3am Mon-Fri; noon-2am Sat; noon-midnight Sun. **Average** £12. **Licensed. Credit** A, V.
Young, new-wave Japanese noodle bar: great food with karaoke thrown in.
Air-conditioning. Takeaway service. Vegetarian dishes.

Yung's
23 Wardour Street, W1 (071 437 4986). Leicester Square underground/Night buses from Trafalgar

Square. **Open** noon-4.30am daily. **Licensed. Credit** A, AmEx, DC, V.
Even at 4am the food is well above average in this popular Chinatown eaterie.
Air-conditioning. Booking advisable. Takeaway service. Vegetarian menu.

South West

Soraya
36 Gloucester Road, SW7 (071 589 5745). Gloucester Road underground/N67, N97 bus. **Meals served** 11am-1am daily. **Average** £15. **Licensed. Credit** A, £TC, V.
A well-loved Iranian restaurant. Here, you can listen to Persian songs, while eating kebabs or khoreshes – meat braised in thick sauces made with traditional blends of herbs, spices and fruit.
Air-conditioning. Book weekends. Dress: smart. Takeaway service. Vegetarian dishes.

East

Nazrul
130 Brick Lane E1 (071 247 2505). Aldgate East underground/N76, N95, N98. **Lunch served** noon-3pm Mon-Sat. **Dinner served** 5.30pm-midnight Mon-Thur; 5.30pm-1am Fri, Sat. **Meals served** noon-midnight Sun. **Average** £7. **Unlicensed. Corkage** no charge. **Credit** LV, £TC.
Nazrul is a typical Brick Lane curry house. Portions are huge, prices are low and the amiable hubbub is highly entertaining. Staff don't mind if you bring in drink from the off-licence next door.
Babies and children admitted. Takeaway service. Vegetarian dishes.

North

Seachef
87-89 Tollington Way, N7 (071 272 3397). Archway underground/17, 43, 271, N65 bus. **Open** 11.30am-3am Mon-Thur; 11.30am-4am Fri, Sat; 4pm-3am Sun. **No credit cards.**
A Cypriot-run, late-night fish and chip shop. Apart from its late hours, the place is also a useful shop for milk, eggs, fruit juice, cigarettes, etc.

WKD Cafe
18 Kentish Town Road, NW1 (071 284 3660). Camden Town underground/N1, N2 bus. **Open** noon-2am Tue-Sat; noon-11pm Sun. **Average** £14. **Service** 10%. **Licensed.**
It's a café, it's a restaurant, it's a music venue, it's a club. It's all-round entertainment.
Book lunch; dinner Fri. Vegetarian menu.

Film

Cinemas all over London provide late-night programmes, usually at weekends. For the best, see chapter **Film**.

Music

'Nightclubs' is a pretty self-explanatory description, so they have been excluded from this section (see *chapter* **Clubs** instead). This list includes the best clubs, restaurants and concert-halls for live music after-hours.

Central

100 Club
100 Oxford Street, W1 (071 636 0933). Tottenham Court Road underground/N1, N2, N5, N98 bus. **Open** 7.30pm-midnight Mon-Wed; 8pm-1am Thur; 8.30pm-3am Fri; 7.30pm-1am Sat; 7.30-11.30pm Sun. **Admission** £5-£7. **No credit cards.**
Punters wearing anything from zoot suits to bondage gear have disappeared into the basement of 100 Oxford Street over the years. An ever-changing programme of new and established acts has been drawing in the crowds for decades. At the moment it's trad jazz.

Brahms & Liszt
19 Russell Street, WC2 (071 240 3661). Covent Garden underground/Night buses from Trafalgar Square. **Open** noon-1am Mon-Sat; 7-10.30pm Sun. **Admission** free Mon, Tue, Sun; £3 Wed; £4 Thur; £5 Fri, Sat. **Credit** A, AmEx, DC, £TC, V.
Just off Covent Garden Piazza, this wine bar plays host to a lively selection of jazz, swing and R&B in the basement. The less rowdy can settle for a full meal in the ground floor restaurant.

Dover Street Wine Bar
8-9 Dover Street, W1 (071 491 7509). Green Park underground/N3, N8, N11, N97 bus. **Open** noon-3pm, 5.30pm-3am, Mon-Fri; 7pm-3am Sat. **Admission** free early evening, £3-£8 later. **Credit** A, AmEx, DC, EC, £TC, V.
Live music and a late licence ensure that this smartish, dimly-lit basement rendezvous is usually busy until the early hours. There's dancing from 10pm. No jeans.

Palookaville
13A James Street, WC2 (071 240 5857). Covent Garden underground/Night buses from Trafalgar Square. **Open** 5.30pm-1am Mon-Wed; 5.30pm-2am Thur-Sat; 7pm-midnight Sun. **Admission** free to diners; £3 after 9.30pm Thur-Sat. **Credit** A, AmEx, DC, EC, £TC, V.
This basement restaurant has an ordinary European menu. But there's jazz music every night.

Rock Garden
6-7 The Piazza, Covent Garden Market, WC2 (071 240 3961). Covent Garden underground/Night buses from Trafalgar Square. **Open** 7.30pm-3am Mon-Sat; 7.30pm-midnight Sun. **Admission** £4-£7. **Credit** A, AmEx, DC, £TC, V.
Tourists, students and devotees of raw, young rock groups mingle in the basement of this good quality, but very over-priced burger bar. The bands will either return to obscurity or one day make it very big (U2 and Talking Heads played here).

Ronnie Scott's
47 Frith Street, W1 (071 439 0747). Leicester Square, Piccadilly Circus or Tottenham Court Road underground/Night buses from Trafalgar Square. **Open** 8.30pm-3am Mon-Sat. **Admission** £12. **Credit** A, AmEx, DC, £STC, V.
London's premier jazz venue may not have terribly interesting food but it does book among the best and most innovative acts in the country. Mellow, smoky, unmissable. Tango, the upstairs club, has global dance music six nights a week.

North

Bass Clef
35 Coronet Street, N1 (071 729 2476/071 729 2440). Old Street underground/N83 bus. **Open** 8pm-2am daily. **Admission** £4-£7. **Credit** A, AmEx, £TC, V.

An off-beat and intimate basement jazz club with low ceilings and low-lighting. There's seating as well as room for dancing. Latin and African tunes ring out loud on certain evenings.

Garage
20-24 Highbury Corner, N5 (071 607 1818). Highbury & Islington tube/BR/N92 bus. **Open** 7.30pm-2am daily. **Music** 9pm. **Admission** £6. **Credit** A, V.
Catch-all venue for slightly older people who still relish left-field indie rock.

Mean Fiddler
24-28 Harlesden High Street, NW10 (081 961 5490). Willesden Junction underground/BR/N18 bus. **Open** 8pm-2am Mon-Sat; 8pm-1am Sun. **Admission** £5-£8. **Credit** A, V.
The location – and a fair amount of the bands – may seem obscure, but it's well worth the trek. Come here to see rock, country & western and folk bands. *Wheelchair access to ground floor.*

Powerhaus
1 Liverpool Road, N1 (071 837 3218). Angel underground/N92, N96 bus. **Open** 8pm-2am Mon-Sat; 7-11pm Sun. **Admission** £4-£6. **Credit** A, V.
Lively indie rock club where the stars hang out, finding out whether they are still stars. *Wheelchair access.*

Photo Processing

Joe's Basement
113 Wardour Street, W1 (071 434 9313). Piccadilly Circus underground/N2, N3, N67, N99 bus. **Open** 24 hours daily. **Credit** A, V.
Joe's Basement is a professional photographic laboratory, which can turn round a 35mm colour transparency film in two hours, and a black and white one in six hours; the cost is £4.50 plus VAT and £7 plus VAT respectively, for 36 exposures. All are done by hand, not machine. A 35mm colour print film can be processed in 24 hours and costs £4.50 plus VAT for 36 exposures. You can then decide which of your masterpieces you want printing.
Branch: 83-88 Clerkenwell Road, EC1 (071 253 6000).

Shopping
Pharmacists

Bliss
5 Marble Arch, W2 (071 723 6116/6219). Marble Arch underground/N3, N56, N99 bus. **Open** 9am-midnight daily. **Credit** A, AmEx, DC, £TC, V.
Branches: 33 Sloane Square, SW1 (071 730 4336); 149 Edgware Road (071 724 5750).

Boots
75 Queensway, W2 (071 229 9266). Bayswater underground/N12, N89. **Open** 9am-10pm Mon-Sat. **Credit** A, AmEx, V.
Branches: Earl's Court Road (071 370 2232), open 8.30am-9pm Mon-Sat; 10am-9pm Sun. Victoria Station (071 834 0676), open 7.30am-9pm Mon-Fri.

Warman Freed
45 Golders Green Road, NW11 (081 455 4351). Golders Green underground/N13 bus. **Open** 8.30am-midnight daily. **Credit** A, AmEx, DC, V.

Noodles in the night, from **Yung's**. *See* **review** *page 271.*

Groceries

The choice is simple, should you need to eat during the night. You can visit a petrol station, or one of the grocer's shops listed below.

7-Eleven

Selected branches:
Marylebone: *384 Edgware Road, W2 (071 723 2123). Edgware Road underground/N18, N56, N59, N79 bus.*
Archway: *35 Junction Road, N19 (071 272 1287). Archway underground/N65 bus.*
Hammersmith: *134 King Street, W6 (081 846 9154). Hammersmith underground/N11, N67, N92, N97 bus.*
South Kensington: *119 Gloucester Road, SW7 (071 373 1440). Gloucester Road underground/N14, N97 bus.*
Westbourne Grove: *112 Westbourne Grove, W2 (071 727 6342). Bayswater underground/N12, N89.bus.*

7-Eleven is an American chain of late-night supermarkets selling a range of 3am essentials – from frozen food to hot snacks. They are not cheap, but they are open 24 hours. They don't take credit cards.

Beigel Bake

159 Brick Lane, E1 (071 729 0616). Shoreditch or Whitechapel underground/N76, N95, N98 bus. **Open** 24 hours daily. **No credit cards.**
There's a constant queue of taxi-drivers and clubbers through the night for these unbeatable bagels.

Bestway

107 Edgware Road, W2 (071 723 6793). Marble Arch or Edgware Road underground/N18, N50, N56 bus. **Open** 24 hours daily. **No credit cards.**
There's hardly room to walk around in this supermarket, which has a variety of foods, drinks and household goods overflowing from the shelves.

Crispins

82 Holland Park Avenue, W11 (071 727 7332).
Holland Park underground/N89 bus. **Open** 8am-11pm
daily. **Credit** A, V.
A small grocer's and off-licence.

Europa Food & Wine

178 Wardour Street, W1 (071 734 4845). Oxford Circus
or Tottenham Court Road underground/Night buses
from Trafalgar Square. **Open** 8.30am-11pm Mon-Fri;
9am-11pm Sat, Sun. **No credit cards.**
A large grocery store, convenient for late-night shopping
in Soho.

Ladbroke Supermarket

171 Ladbroke Grove, W10 (081 968 6760). Ladbroke
Grove underground/N50 bus. **Open** 10am-
midnight daily. **No credit cards.**
Everything you'd expect to find in a supermarket, plus a
microwave to heat up the samosas.

Midnight Food Store

207 Sutherland Avenue, W9 (071 286 6084). Warwick
Avenue underground/N18 bus. **Open** 7am-midnight
daily. **No credit cards.**
Groceries, magazines, newspapers, cigarettes and
sweets.

Midnight Shop

223 Brompton Road, SW3 (071 589 7788).
Knightsbridge or South Kensington underground/N14,
N97 bus. **Open** 9am-midnight daily. **No credit cards.**
A friendly, small supermarket with a surprisingly large
selection of fresh vegetables, groceries and frozen food.

Portlands of Charing Cross

75-77 Charing Cross Road, WC2 (071 734 5715).
Leicester Square underground/Night buses from Trafalgar
Square. **Open** 24 hours daily. **Credit** A, £TC, V.
A good grocer's with a delicatessen, fresh vegetables,
frozen food, magazines and cigarettes.

Ridley Bagel Bakery

13-15 Ridley Road (071 241 1047). Dalston Kingsland
BR/N83 bus. **Open** 24 hours daily. **No credit cards.**
Diverse, multi-cultural and sleepless clientele. Terrific
filled bagels.

Riteway

57 Edgware Road, W2 (071 402 5491). Marble Arch
underground/N18, N56, N59, N79 bus. **Open** 24 hours
daily. **No credit cards.**
Groceries, magazines, newspapers, cigarettes and sweets.

Star Delicatessen

176 Earl's Court Road, SW5 (no phone/fax 071 244
7352). Earl's Court underground/N56, N97 bus. **Open**
9am-3am Mon-Thur, Sun; 9am-4am Fri, Sat.
No credit cards.
A general supermarket and delicatessen.

Presents

Last-minute shopping to solve your problems.
The streets around Leicester Square and
Covent Garden are your best bet in desperate
moments.

Cheapo Records

53 Rupert Street, W1 (071 437 8272). Piccadilly Circus
underground. **Open** 11am-10pm Mon-Sat. **No credit**
cards.
Three floors of jazz, rock, classical and blues records.

Covent Garden General Store

105-111 Long Acre, WC2 (071 240 0331). Covent
Garden underground. **Open** 10am-midnight Mon-Sat;
11am-9pm Sun. **Credit** A, AmEx, DC, EC, £TC, V.
An emporium of silly gifts such as novelty crockery,
crossword toilet rolls and executive toys. A lot of
goods that you hadn't realised you didn't want until
you saw them.

Pan Bookshop

158 Fulham Road, SW10 (071 373 4997). South
Kensington underground/14, 45 bus. **Open** 9.30am-
9.30pm Mon-Sat; 11am-9.30pm Sun. **Credit** A, AmEx,
£TC, V.
A paperback bookshop with a fair selection of fiction,
non-fiction and travel titles. Also a few good quality greetings cards.

Tower Records

1 Piccadilly Circus, W1 (071 439 2500). Piccadilly
Circus underground. **Open** 9am-midnight Mon-Sat;
11am-10pm Sun. **Credit** A, AmEx, £TC, V.
Megastore of music and video spread over four floors,
with particularly strong classical, world music and jazz
departments. Tower also sells T-shirts and computer
games, but is particularly noted for its collection of magazines.

Waterstone's

193 Kensington High Street, W8 (071 937 8432). High
Street Kensington underground. **Open** 9.30am-9pm
Mon-Fri; 9.30am-7pm Sat; 11am-6pm Sun. **Credit** A,
AmEx, £TC, V.
A late-opening branch of the excellent chain of arts-ori-
ented bookshops. Fortes in fiction and travel-related
titles.

Sport

Night Fishing

National Rivers Authority

King's Meadow House, King's Meadow Road, Reading
RG1 8HQ (0734 535 651).
A permit is needed for coarse night fishing. Contact the
NRA for details.

Snooker

Centre Point Snooker Club

Under Centre Point, New Oxford Street, WC1 (071 240
6886). Tottenham Court Road underground/N8, N21,
N98 bus. **Open** 11am-6am daily. **Membership** £20 per
year; £3.95 per hour.

New World Snooker Clubs

Telephone the head office (071 228 0934) after 6pm for
details of your local hall.

Tenpin Bowling

Lewisham Bowl

11-29 Belmont Hill, SE13 (081 318 9691). Lewisham
BR/N47, N53, N62, N72, N82, N85 bus. **Open** 10am-
midnight daily.

Rowans

10 Stroud Green Road, N4 (081 809 5511). Finsbury
Park underground/BR/N19, N21, N90 bus. **Open**
10am-4am Mon-Fri; 9am-6am Sat, Sun.

In Focus

Here we get down to particulars: specific listings for specific people. Whether you're searching for business advice, a gay bar, a student café, or a women's centre – you should find your destination here.

Contents

Business

London is the biz. Although it occupies only one per cent of the UK's area, this city creates over 20 per cent of the nation's GDP.

Well over half of London's ten million foreign visitors each year are involved in business of some sort and many are drawn not only by the international financial centre in the City but also by the relative probity of its supporting business services. Below we list a selection.

Banking

Arrange banking facilities with your own bank before leaving home: the chances are, it'll have a reciprocal arrangement with a British bank, and you may need to obtain references. The head offices of the 'big four' commercial banks are listed below. See *chapter* **Essential Information** for opening hours and further information.

Barclays Bank
54 Lombard Street, EC3 (071 626 1567). Bank underground.

Lloyds Bank
71 Lombard Street, EC3 (071 626 1500). Bank underground.

Midland Bank
Poultry, EC2 (071 260 8000). Bank underground.

National Westminster Bank
41 Lothbury, EC2 (071 726 1000). Bank underground.

Business Information

The *Financial Times* is the best newspaper to consult for an update on facts and figures in the City and all over the world.

American Chamber of Commerce
75 Brook Street, W1 (071 493 0381). Bond Street underground. **Open** 9am-5pm Mon-Fri; *library* 9.30am-1.30pm Mon-Thur.
The Chamber publishes a trade directory, but only member companies may use the library and research facilities. The commercial library of the American Embassy (071 499 9000) is also a good source of American business addresses.

Anglo-Japanese Economic Institute
Morley House, 314-322 Regent Street, W1 (071 637 7872). Piccadilly Circus underground. **Open** 9.30am-5.30pm Mon-Fri by appointment.
A good source of reference material on all Japanese economic matters. Each year it publishes the invaluable *Japanese Addresses in the UK* (£5).

Business Design Centre
52 Upper Street, N1 (071 359 3535/fax 071 226 0590).

Angel underground. **Open** 9am-5pm Mon-Sat.
A trade centre for commercial interior design, this impressive building contains show-rooms, an exhibition centre and a conference centre. The exhibitions display products used in commercial design, and usually change weekly.

Business Information Service
British Library, 25 Southampton Buildings, Chancery Lane, WC2 (071 323 7454). Chancery Lane underground. **Open** *library* 9.30am-9pm Mon-Fri; 10am-1pm Sat. *Telephone enquiries* 9.30am-noon, 1-5pm, Mon-Fri.
The most comprehensive collection of business information in the UK is held here, including company reports, house journals and CD-ROM services. There's a quick query service, on the number above, or a Priced Research Service, available (071 323 7457/fax 071 323 7453) which will undertake on-line searches of the library records, and provide market over-views, company profiles, distributor details, and mailing lists.

Chamber of Commerce and Industry
33 Queen Street, EC4 (071 248 4444/fax 071 489 0391). Mansion House underground. **Open** 9am-5.30pm Mon-Fri (export documents dept closed 12.30-1.30pm); *reference library* (members only) 9.15am-5.15pm Mon-Fri.
The largest Chamber of Commerce in the UK. It is open to members and overseas visitors only, who can avail themselves of the lounge and function rooms.

Design Centre
28 Haymarket, SW1 (071 839 8000/071 925 2130). Piccadilly Circus underground. **Open** 10am-6pm Mon-Sat; 1-6pm Sun.
Visit the Design Centre for full details of product, graphic and interior designers in Britain. Exhibitions and campaigns are held, and the wonderful bookshop has many books published by the Design Council, a government-sponsored organisation that runs the Centre.

EC Information Unit
8 Storeys Gate, SW1 (071 973 1992). St James's Park or Westminster underground. **Open** 10am-1pm Mon-Fri; also 2-5pm Mon-Fri by appointment.
The small London office of the EC will provide information on Brussels' initiatives. There's also a reference library open to all.

Extel Financial
Fitzroy House, 13-17 Epworth Street, EC2 (071 253 3400/fax 071 251 3525). Liverpool Street underground/BR or Moorgate underground/BR. **Open** *enquiries* 8am-6pm Mon-Fri; *help desk and computer desk* 24-hours daily.
Extel publishes financial data on easy-to-read sheets about more than 9,000 British and foreign businesses. It costs £29 to take one of these cards away. The firm also undertakes British and overseas company searches, and deals with all kinds of corporate financial queries and problems.

Taking the plunge: the Stock Market crash of 1987 as seen in the London Stock Exchange.

Financial Times Cityline
(recorded information 0891 123456/list of all lines 0898 123099/information 071 873 4378). **Open** 24 hours daily.
There are 28 FT Cityline recorded information services, updated constantly with news from financial markets.Calls cost 48p a minute peak time, 36p a minute cheap rate.

Jordan & Sons Company Information
Jordan House, 47 Brunswick Place, N1 (071 253 3030/fax 071 251 0825). Old Street underground/BR. **Open** 9am-5pm Mon-Fri.
A full company search costs £28.05, and takes 48 hours. Jordans also organises company formations (Britain and overseas); phone for a quote. A same-day search costs £4.

London Law Agency
84 Temple Chambers, EC4 (071 353 9471). Temple underground. **Open** 9am-5.30pm Mon-Fri.
If you want to form a company in the UK, this agency is one of many that can cut through the red tape, for a fee. It can also provide status reports on UK companies (£20 per company) so you can vet your potential trading partner.

London World Trade Centre
International House, 1 St Katherine's Way, E1 (071 488 2400). Tower Hill underground. **Open** 9am-5.30pm Mon-Fri.
In common with the other 240 or so Trade Centres around the world, complete office and business support services are offered here. The Centre will also provide

lists of prospective buyers or suppliers for your product in this country, trade leads, and business information.

Reference Libraries

For general reference libraries *see chapter* **Survival**.

Chamber of Commerce & Industry Reference Library
33 Queen Street, EC4 (071 248 4444/fax 071 489 0391). Mansion House underground. **Open** 9.15am-5.15pm Mon-Fri.
A comprehensive library open to members and overseas visitors. You'll find general commercial information and detailed information on export and international trade.

City Business Library
1 Brewers Hall Garden, EC2 (071 638 8215/recorded information 071 480 7638). Moorgate underground. **Open** 9.30am-5pm Mon-Fri.
The City Library has an excellent range of business reference works, including newspaper cuttings, Extel cards and world directories.

London Business School Library
Sussex Place, Regent's Park, NW1 (071 262 5050). Baker Street underground/BR. **Open** 9am-9pm Mon-Fri; also 9am-6pm Sat during term-time. **Admission** £20 a day.

The library has a collection of by-country and by-industry information files, plus a comprehensive stock of standard business reference works, including Extel and McCarthy press-cutting cards. The LBS Research Service (071 723 3404) will do the work for you at a rate of £60 per hour.

Communications

British Monomarks
Monomarks House, 27 Old Gloucester Street, WC1 (071 405 4442/071 404 5011/fax 071 831 9489). Holborn underground. **Open** 9.30am-5.30pm Mon-Fri; *telex bureau* 8am-8pm Mon-Fri. **Credit** A, AmEx, £$TC, V.
Here you can use a telex or fax machine, have mail forwarded, or arrange to use the 24-hour telephone answering service. Leave a deposit and telephone-in your telex messages, 24 hours a day.

Business Matters
203 High Street, SE13 1235/fax 081 318 1439). Lewisham BR. **Open** 8.30am-8.30pm Mon-Fri; 8.30am-noon Sat. **Credit** A, AmEx, DC, £TC, V.
Dictate a message over the phone and Business Matters will fax or telex it for you anywhere in the world. Its telephone answering service costs £30 a month plus VAT, paid in advance.

Hanway Print Centre
106 Essex Road, Islington, N1 (071 226 6868). Angel underground. **Open** 9am-5.30pm Mon-Fri. **Credit** A, £TC, V.
A comprehensive and reasonably priced copying and print service is offered here, including high speed xeroxing. You can also send a fax for £1 a page within the UK.

Company Legislation

Institute of Trading Standards Administration (ITSA)
4/5 Hadleigh Business Centre, 351 London Road, Hadleigh, Essex (0702 559922/fax 0702 559902). Hadleigh BR.
The Administration will provide details of your local Trading Standards Office, which is responsible for enforcing the legislation on fair and safe trading. It will also offer help and advice.

Patent Office
25 Southampton Buildings, WC2 (071 438 4700). Chancery Lane underground. **Open** 10am-4pm Mon-Fri.
It costs £25 to file a patent here, although the office recommends employing a qualified agent for its wording. The patent examiners also offer a Search and Advisory Service (SAS). For £200 or more, they will gather information from the world's largest single source of technical information. The library (open 9.30am-9pm Mon-Fri; 10am-1pm Sat) contains the national collection of patent documentation.

Conferences

London Tourist Board
26 Grosvenor Gardens, SW1 (no phone/fax 071 730 9367). Victoria underground/BR. **Open** 8am-7pm Mon-Sat; 8am-4pm Sun.
The LTB will assist with the organisation of conventions or exhibitions. Ask for the convention bureau or write or telephone for its free guide *Convention and Exhibition London*, which lists hotels and centres that host events, together with their facilities.

Queen Elizabeth II Conference Centre
Broad Sanctuary, SW1 (071 222 5000/enquiries 071 798 4060/fax 071 798 4200). St James's Park underground. **Open** 8am-6pm Mon-Fri; 24-hour conference facilities available.
This purpose-built centre has some of the best conference facilities in London. There's a choice of rooms with capacities from 12 to 1,000; communication equipment is available and there's a TV studio equipped to broadcast-specifications.

Couriers

Harley Street Runners
65 Great Portland Street, W1 (071 323 5595/fax 071 323 5867). Oxford Circus underground. **Open** 8am-7pm Mon-Fri; 8am-3pm Sat. **Credit** A, AmEx, DC, JCB, V.
A van, cycle, motorbike and foot messenger service. The couriers will go anywhere in mainland Britain for a fixed amount. The company can also organise direct-mailing, removals, Datapost and foreign deliveries.

Parcel Force Datapost
Dataport Service Centre, 4th floor, 20-23 Greville Street, EC1 (Freephone 0800 88 4422/fax 071 250 2938). Farringdon underground/BR. **Open** 8.30am-5.30pm Mon-Fri. **Credit** A, AmEx, DC, V.
Parcel Force Datapost is a Post Office parcel service. Use it to send packages anywhere in Britain; next-morning delivery is guaranteed. There's also an international service. Parcels are accepted at any main post office. Same-day delivery can often be arranged.

Equipment Hire

ABC Business Machines
59 Chiltern Street, W1 (071 486 5634). Baker Street underground. **Open** 9am-5.30pm Mon-Fri; 9.30am-12.30pm Sat. **Credit** A, £TC, V.
Answerphones, calculators and audio equipment are among the equipment you can hire from ABC. Electronic typewriters cost £25 a month, Betacom fax machines are £59 a month. Copiers and computers start at £90 a month.

Network Office Equipment
63 Lupus Street, SW1 (071 821 8186/fax 071 630 5160). Pimlico underground. **Open** 9am-5.30pm Mon-Fri. **Credit** A, AmEx, £$TC, V.
All types of office electrical equipment can be bought or hired from Network. Short-term rental charges (per month) start from £45 for electronic typewriters; £120 for basic Rank Xerox 7010 A4 fax machines; and £275 for IBM computers with laser printers.

Import & Export

Within EC countries, import licences are needed only for raw steel and restricted items (for example, firearms). Importers from outside the EC need licences for a wide variety of goods, including clothing and shoes, textiles, agricultural goods, foodstuffs, and ceramics. An application must be made for each product to be imported and takes from three to five days to clear. Licences are valid from three months to a year.

Commercial goods must always be declared on arrival, and an SAD (Single Administrative

Document) completed. But for merchandise carried as baggage (valued under £600), a customs declaration need not be needed. There's a standard rate of 17½ per cent Value Added Tax (VAT) on most imported goods, based on the value of the goods plus the duty payable.

The exporting of certain goods – such as arms, electronic equipment, and chemical equipment – requires licences issued by the **Department of Trade & Industry** (*see below*).

British Overseas Trade Board

123 Victoria Street, SW1 (office hours 071 215 5000 /5.30pm-9am 071 215 5000). **Open** 9am-5pm Mon-Fri. The OTB was set up in 1972 to advise the government on overseas trade. Over 200 experts are available to give practical advice to anyone wishing to export goods anywhere in the world.

Companies House

55-71 City Road, EC1 (general information 071 253 9393/company search 0222 380801). Old Street underground/BR. **Open** 9am-5pm Mon-Fri (last company search 3pm).
In order to export goods from Britain, you should register as a UK company (for taxation purposes) at Companies House. You can also gain access to information on companies, British and foreign (if registered here).

Customs & Excise

New King's Beam House, 22 Upper Ground, SE1 (071 620 1313, ext 3997/fax 071 865 5625). Waterloo underground/BR. **Open** 9am-5pm Mon-Fri.
The New King's Beam House deals with telephone enquiries only. You can call in person at Dorset House, Stanford Street, SE1, during office hours. Phone for the addresses of local London centres giving advice on VAT and excise.

Department of Trade & Industry (DTI)

Queensway House, West Precinct, Illingham, Cleveland, TS23 2NF (0642 364333/fax 0642 533557). **Open** 9am-5pm Mon-Fri.
Export Licensing Unit *Kingsgate House, 66-74 Victoria Street, SW1 (071 215 8070/fax 071 215 8564). Victoria underground/BR.* **Open** 9am-5pm Mon-Fri.
Contact the Illingham DTI office with enquiries about, or applications for, import licences. The Export Licensing Unit deals with enquiries on export controls and licences.

Export Market Information Centre

Department of Trade & Industry, Ashdown House, 123 Victoria Street, SW1 (071 215 5444/business statistics 0633 812973/fax 071 215 4231). Victoria underground/BR. **Open** 9.30am-5pm Mon-Fri.
Everything you could possibly want to know about exporting is kept here. The database – the British Overseas Trade Information System – provides information on products, markets, overseas agents and export opportunities.

Institute of Export

64 Clifton Street, EC2 (071 247 9812). Liverpool Street underground/BR. **Open** 9am-5.30pm Mon-Fri.
A professional body that aims to 'raise the standards of export management... through the exchange of information and ideas between exporters'. Membership enquiries are welcomed.

Institute of Freight Forwarders

Redfern House, Browells Lane, Feltham, Middx (081 844 2266/fax 081 890 5546). Hatton Cross

underground or Feltham BR. **Open** 9am-5pm Mon-Fri.
The IFF gives information about sending freight and baggage, and puts callers in touch with reputable companies who handle air and sea freight. Ask for the Air or Sea division.

Removals

Bishop's Move

102 Stewarts Road, SW8 (071 498 0300). Vauxhall underground/BR. **Open** 9am-5.30pm Mon-Fri. **Credit** by arrangement.
This reliable family-owned company has been shipping, removing and distributing goods for 140 years. It will undertake almost any scale of work, but specialises in handling valuable furniture.

Evan Cook

134 Queen's Road, SE15 (071 635 0224). Queen's Road Peckham BR. **Open** 9am-5pm Mon-Fri. **Credit** by arrangement.
A good London firm that has been specialising in office removals since 1893.

Secretarial

More typing services are advertised on bookshop noticeboards and in *Time Out* magazine's classified ads section.

Reed Employment, Staff Agency

181 Victoria Street, SW1 (071 828 2401/fax 071 821 5598). Victoria underground/BR. **Open** 8.45am-5.30pm Mon-Fri.
Reed supplies secretarial, computing, accountancy and technical services to registered companies.

Typing Overload

67 Chancery Lane, WC2 (071 404 5464/fax 071 831 0878). Chancery Lane underground. **Open** 9am-6pm Mon-Fri. **Credit** A, AmEx, DC, £STC, V.
Come here for a speedy and professional typing service for any job that can be done on a word-processor.
Branch: Knightsbridge Secretarial Services, 170 Sloane Street, SW1 (071 235 6855).

Translation

AA Technical & Export Translation

The London International Press Centre, 76 Shoe Lane, Fleet Street, EC4 (071 583 8690/fax 071 353 3133). Chancery Lane underground or Blackfriars underground/BR. **Open** 10am-6pm Mon-Fri. **No credit cards.**
AA provides native speakers of most languages; it has on its books 612 translators speaking 50 languages. Rates vary from £8 to £21 per 100 words depending on the language and complexity of the text. Interpreters cost between £220 and £500 per day. AA is a member of the Association of Translation Companies and holder of the International Export Association Seal of Approval.

Central Translations

2-3 Woodstock Street, W1 (071 493 5511). Bond Street underground. **Open** 9am-5pm Mon-Fri. **No credit cards.**
Conveniently situated in the West End, Central offers typesetting and proof-reading of pretty well every language under the sun, as well as translation and interpreters. Rates for translation into English range from about £8 to £25 per 100 words depending on how esoteric the copy is.

Where else

could you see premiéres by Bloolips,
Clyde Unity Theatre, Gloria,
Marga Gomez, Lea de Laria,
Music Theatre London,
Opera Factory, Pomo Afro Homos,
The Topp Twins,
The Ridiculous Theatrical Company?

☆ At The Drill Hall...

Holding a unique place in London's
cultural life, **The Drill Hall** *has a*
varied programme of theatre, opera and
music theatre from Britain and abroad,
championing in particular the work of gay,
lesbian and women artists.

☆ **The Drill Hall Arts Centre** ☆
☆ 200 seat theatre ☆ Exhibitions ☆
☆ Restaurant ☆ Bar ☆ Darkrooms ☆
☆ Free Creche ☆ Rehearsal Rooms ☆
☆ Courses and Classes ☆

---

16 CHENIES STREET (OFF TOTTENHAM COURT ROAD)
LONDON WC1
BOX OFFICE 071 637 8270
NEAREST TUBES: GOODGE STREET; TOTTENHAM COURT ROAD; WARREN STREET
REG CHARITY No. 290448

Gay London

**Gay life in London has never been brighter, with a burgeoning
network of shops, restaurants, clubs and bars. Relax and enjoy.**

London's busy gay scene rarely stands still. A
visitor to the city could easily feel overwhelmed
by the sheer volume of places to go, to say nothing of the variety on offer. While many venues
cater exclusively for gay men or (less often) lesbians, others are advertised as 'mixed'. A few
years ago, this would have stood for 'lesbian and
gay'. Nowadays, it's as likely to embrace 'sympathetic' straights. The club scene in particular
has geared itself away from Ghetto Heaven
towards the notion of a sexual melting pot. In
some cases this has worked extremely well, providing spaces where all people are tolerated,
provided they can dance to disco. In others, it
has marked a rapid descent into Hetero Hell.

Some of London's clubs and bars cater for a
specialist clientele (leather, rubber, drag, etc)
and operate strict dress codes. The majority
conduct a 'mix and match' policy, though as
with gay scenes everywhere, youth and beauty
still have the edge. Body culture is big, particularly on the club circuit. Sex and recreational
drugs are back in fashion, too. Increasing numbers of bars and clubs have unofficial darkrooms which, added to the popularity of outdoor
cruising spots like Hampstead Heath, ensure

that there's always somebody around to lend a
helping hand.

For women-only clubs, bars and information,
see chapter **Women's London**.

Clubs

Though the details here are correct at time of
writing, the commercial bar and club scene is
fast-moving and ever-changing. It's a wise pre-
caution to phone and check before setting out,
as well as scrutinising *Time Out* magazine's
'Gay' listings for the latest details.

The Anvil
*The Shipwright Arms, 88 Tooley Street, SE1 (071 407
0371). London Bridge underground/BR/N47, N70,
N89 bus.* **Open** 7.30pm-1am Mon-Wed; 7.30pm-2am
Thur-Sat; noon-3pm, 7pm-midnight, Sun.
No credit cards.
A late night bar-cum-club that caters for Real Men. The
bar is licensed until midnight (10.30pm Sun).

The Backstreet
*Wentworth Mews, Burdett Road, E3 (081 980 8557).
Mile End underground/N76, N98 bus.* **Open** 10pm-
2.30am Thur; 10pm-3am Fri, Sat; 9pm-1am Sun. **No
credit cards.**
London's most popular black leather/rubber, gay men's

Gay Soho

London's gay clubs, bars, restaurants and
cafés are spread out across the length and
breadth of the city. Earl's Court used to be the
nearest thing London had to a 'gay ghetto',
with a handful of gay bars and a gay shop or
two. But over the past year or so, attention has
shifted to Soho, which now boasts the highest concentration of gay businesses anywhere
in the capital. This square mile in the heart of
the West End contains half a dozen gay bars,
three gay life-style and fashion stores, several gay-run cafés, a gay travel company, a gay
financial adviser, a gay hairdresser's and a gay
beauty and sunbed centre.

Although **Comptons Of Soho** (on Old
Compton Street) has been attracting a loyal,
lively crowd for years, it was only when

Village Soho opened its doors on Wardour
Street in early 1992 that the 'queerification' of
the area really took off. **Clone Zone**, the gay
lifestyle chain store with branches in Earl's
Court and Manchester, was quick to follow
suit, rapidly followed by **Soho Men**, London's
first (and only) gay male grooming salon.

The most recent addition to Soho's 'gay village' is **The Yard**, a smart bar-complex on
Rupert Street, incorporating two bars and a
self-contained courtyard, and continuing the
trend towards more Continental-style watering holes. It is now possible to spend an
entire evening in Soho without staying in any
one place for longer than it takes to down a
pint of lager (or two bottled beers if you
decide to go European).

Soho's La Cage aux Folles: **Madame Jo Jo**. *See* **review**.

club has a very strict dress code, low lighting and designer-macho décor (chains, boots, and the like).

The Block

1-5 Parkfield Street, N1 (071 226 7453). Angel underground/N19, N65, N92 bus. **Open** 10pm-2.30am Mon; 10pm-4am Fri, Sat; 9.30pm-2am Sun. **No credit cards.**
Cruisey gay men's club with a strict dress code of black leather, rubber and uniform. Occasional theme nights are held.

Club Copa

180 Earl's Court Road, SW5 (071 373 3407). Earl's Court underground/N14, N31, N97 bus. **Open** 10pm-2am Mon-Thur; 9pm-2am Fri, Sat; 9pm-midnight Sun. **No credit cards.**
An Earl's Court institution. This was the first gay club in London with a no-smoking area. It remains a comfortable, busy, gay men's venue.

Heaven

Underneath the Arches, Villiers Street, WC2 (071 839 3852). Embankment underground or Charing Cross underground/BR/Night buses from Trafalgar Square. **Open** times and door charges vary Wed, Fri, Sat. **No credit cards.**
Britain's largest, busiest and most famous gay club features a huge cavernous dance floor, with impressive lights and lasers, a great sound-system and a small stage for frequent live shows. Upstairs, the Star Bar is a marginally quieter video lounge with a small dance

floor. The stylish Dakota Room is for the dressier cocktail crowd. The labyrinthine complex also includes a coat-check, snack bar and small shop selling cards, T-shirts, vests and condoms. Fruit Machine, the mixed lesbian and gay night (*see below* **Alternative & One-Nighters**) is held here on Wednesdays; Garage, a mixed gay/straight garage music night takes over every Friday; on Saturdays it's simply Heaven – a big, brash, lesbian and gay party night.

Madame Jo Jo

8-10 Brewer Street, W1 (071 734 2473). Piccadilly Circus underground/Night buses from Trafalgar Square. **Open** 10pm-3am Mon-Sat. **Credit** A, AmEx, £TC, V.
The heart of Soho is the setting for this plush, intimate, late-night cabaret bar-cum-club-cum-restaurant. It's camp, it's theatrical and it's very *La Cage Aux Folles* – though you may find yourself outnumbered by the Essex boys who come to gawp at the Barbettes.

Alternative & One-Nighters

Bang

at Busby's, 157 Charing Cross Road, WC2 (071 734 6963). Tottenham Court Road underground. **Open** 10.30pm-4am Mon, Sat. **Admission** £6; £5 with flyer. **No credit cards.**
DJs Dave Simmons and Jeremy Joseph play dance floor classics and bright, poppy numbers at this busy, friendly and unpretentious, gay club-night. Occasionally, there are theme nights and live entertainment.

Benjy's

562A Mile End Road, E3 (081 980 6427). Mile End underground/N76, N98 bus. **Open** 9pm-1am Sun. **Admission** £2. **No credit cards.**
A weekly gay men's disco session with DJs Tony Armstrong and Dave Simmons.

Ciao Baby!

at The Fridge, Town Hall Parade, Brixton Hill, SW2 (071 326 5100). Brixton underground/N2, N3, N78, N69 bus. **Open** 10pm-3am Tue. **Admission** £5; £3 before 11pm with flyer. **No credit cards.**
'Mama' Yvette hosts this ever-popular mixed lesbian and gay night in one of the city's best venues. Live entertainment includes DJs and go-go dancers, plus frequent theme parties and resident dancers, The Ciao Babies. Wild, hedonistic and always packed.

ff Club

at Turnmills, 63B Clerkenwell Road, EC2 (071 250 3409). Farringdon underground/N83 bus. **Open** 10pm-6am Sun. **Admission** £6; £4 students, UB40s before midnight. **No credit cards.**
A weekly lesbian and gay club run by the team behind *ff* magazine. It's always busy, and always wild and sexually orientated. Techno and hard beats are supplied by various DJs including the award-winning Mrs Wood.

Love Muscle

at The Fridge, Town Hall Parade, Brixton Hill, SW2 (071 326 5100). Brixton underground/N2, N3, N78, N69 bus. **Open** 10pm-6am Sat. **Admission** £8; £6 before midnight with flyer; £5 after 3am. **No credit cards.**
Hot and happening, this mixed gay party night is hosted by Yvette. Commercial house and dance classics are played by DJs Marc Andrews and Gareth. There's the added attraction of a 'smart' bar with psychoactive drinks to give a 'natural' buzz.

Trade

at Turnmills, 63B Clerkenwell Road, EC1 (071 250 3409). Farringdon underground/N83 bus. **Open** 3am-12.30pm Sat, Sun. **Admission** £10; £5 members. **Membership** £15. **No credit cards.**
If you still want to party when everywhere else is closed, get down to this weekly, wild, mixed gay/straight, late-late club hosted by Lawrence Malice. Dance music is purveyed by the self-proclaimed 'hottest mix-masters in town'. Breakfast is served from 6am.

Pubs & Bars

The Angel

65 Graham Street, N1 (no phone). Angel underground. **Open** noon-midnight Mon-Sat; noon-11.30pm Sun. **No credit cards.**
A popular lesbian and gay café-bar with food, coffee and a relaxed atmosphere. Free live music is staged every Sunday from 9pm.

The Bell

257-259 Pentonville Road, N1 (071 837 5617). King's Cross underground/N73, N96 bus. **Open** 9pm-1am Mon; 9pm-2am Tue, Wed; 9pm-2am Thur; 9pm-3am Fri, Sat; 5pm-midnight Sun. **Admission** £3 Fri-Sun. **No credit cards.**
Nightly discos are held at this busy, style-conscious, friendly bar. A young, mixed lesbian and gay crowd is attracted.

The Black Cap

171 Camden High Street, NW1 (071 485 1742). Camden underground/N1, N2, N5, N9, N29, N31,

N90, N93 bus. **Open** 1pm-2am Mon-Sat; noon-3pm, 7-midnight, Sun. **Admission** free Mon, Sun; £2 Tue-Thur; £3 Fri, Sat. **No credit cards.**
Drag institution with two bars and live acts nightly.

Bromptons

294 Old Brompton Road, Earl's Court, SW5 (071 370 1344). Earl's Court underground/N14, N31, N97 bus. **Open** 8pm-1am Mon-Wed; 8pm-2am Thur-Sat; 8pm-midnight Sun. **No credit cards.**
A popular gay men's bar with a record shop, videos and satellite TV, plus live DJs nightly.

Central Station

37 Wharfdale Road, N1 (071 278 3294). King's Cross underground/BR/N21, N56, N73, N90, N93, N96 bus. **Open** 5pm-midnight Mon-Wed; 5pm-3am Thur, 5pm-4am Fri; noon-4am Sat; noon-midnight, Sun. **Credit** A, £TC, V.
This cosy gay venue has two interconnecting bars, multi-video screens, cabaret, food, and a quiet bar. There's also a games room with pool tables.

The Coleherne

261 Old Brompton Road, SW5 (no phone). Earl's Court underground. **Open** noon-11pm Mon-Sat; noon-3pm, 7-10.30pm, Sun. **No credit cards.**
Love it or loathe it, London's most famous leather-scene bar is usually packed every lunchtime and evening.

Comptons Of Soho

53 Old Compton Street, W1 (no phone). Leicester Square or Piccadilly Circus underground. **Open** noon-11pm Mon-Sat; noon-3pm, 7-10.30pm, Sun. **No credit cards.**
This young gay men's bar has loud taped music, a central location and a frenetic atmosphere.

Crews

14 Upper St Martin's Lane, WC2 (071 379 4880). Leicester Square underground. **Open** noon-11pm Mon-Sat; noon-3pm, 7-10.30pm, Sun. **No credit cards.**
The biggest, busiest boys bar in the West End, with queues most nights. It's dark, clubby and hotter than a backroom full of sweating leather-queens. You can also ring 'Crewsline' on 071 240 1444 or 071 240 2121 and speak to a random member of the clientele who will answer your call in an old red telephone box.

Duke of Wellington

119 Balls Pond Road, N1 (071 249 3729). Angel underground then 38 bus/Highbury & Islington underground/BR then 277, 30 bus/Dalston Junction BR. **Open** 11am-midnight Mon-Sat; noon-3pm, 7-10.30pm, Sun. **No credit cards.**
A local lesbian and gay bar with frequent live entertainment. There's also a women-only bar.

The Edge

11 Soho Square, W1 (071 439 1223). Tottenham Court Road underground/Night buses from Trafalgar Square. **Open** 8am-1am Mon-Fri; 10am-1am Sat; noon-10.30pm Sun. **Credit** A, AmEx, DC, V.
You can get a great view of Soho Square from this smart, mixed (gay/straight) café-bar that's on two levels. A choice of breakfasts is available 8-11am Monday to Friday, there's a separate lunch menu, and snacks are served all day.

Hangar Bar

Soundshaft, Hungerford Lane (off Craven Street), WC2 (no phone). Embankment underground or Charing Cross underground/BR/Night buses from Trafalgar Square. **Open** 9pm-3am Mon-Wed. **No credit cards.**

It's bar prices with club style at this alternative cruise night, from the men who run Friday's Meat (also at this venue). DJs are in booths, go-go boys in cages and the cruising is multi-levelled.

King's Arms

23 Poland Street, W1 (071 734 5907). Oxford Circus underground. **Open** noon-11pm Mon-Sat; noon-3pm, 7-10.30pm, Sun. **No credit cards**.
A Soho gay men's pub with a lively atmosphere and friendly staff. Food is served at lunchtimes (until 3pm). Downstairs is always packed, upstairs is quieter and more relaxed.

Kudos

10 Adelaide Street, WC2 (071 379 4573). Charing Cross underground/BR. **Open** noon-11pm Mon-Sat; noon-10.30pm Sun. **Credit** A, AmEx, V.
Smart café-bar on two levels. The ground floor is spacious with ample seating and functions as a café during the day, attracting a mixed crowd of men and women. The basement is cruisier, and opens during the evenings for young, West End boyz.

London Apprentice

333 Old Street, EC1 (071 739 5949). Old Street underground (Exit 2)/N83 bus. **Open** 9pm-3am Mon-Thur; 9pm-5am Fri, Sat; 7pm-1am, Sun. **No credit cards**.
A popular, atmospheric macho bar on three levels, including a basement disco, and an air-conditioned coffee bar (first floor). There's an admission charge of £2.50 after 11pm Thur-Sat.

Market Tavern

'Market Towers', 1 Nine Elms Lane, SW8 (071 622 5655). Vauxhall underground/BR/N2, N68, N79, N87, N88 bus. **Open** 9pm-2am Mon-Thur; 9pm-3am Fri, Sat; 1-7pm, 9pm-midnight, Sun. **No credit cards**.
This very busy disco bar has a small dance floor, plus a back bar. It draws a loyal, cloney crowd.

Partner's Wine Bar

305 Kennington Road, SE11 (071 582 9900). Kennington underground. **Open** 5pm-midnight Mon-Fri; noon-midnight Sat; 2-11pm Sun. **No credit cards**.
A wine bar and restaurant for lesbians and gay men.

Sailing close to **The Edge**. *See* **review** *page 283.*

Hot and cold food is served and there's occasional live entertainment.

Royal Vauxhall Tavern
372 Kennington Lane, SE11 (071 582 0833). Vauxhall underground/BR/N2, N68, N79, N87, N88 bus. **Open** 8pm-1am Mon; 8pm-midnight Tue, Wed; 8pm-2am Thur-Sat; 7-10.30pm Sun. **No credit cards.**
There's live entertainment nightly at this busy south London drag-scene institution.

Substation
at Soho Theatre Club, Falconberg Court, W1 (071 287 9608). Leicester Square underground/Night buses from Trafalgar Square. **Open** 5pm-3am Mon-Thur; 5pm-4pm Fri;10.30pm-6am Sat; 7pm-1am Sun. **Admission** £1 for non-members. **Membership** £4. **No credit cards.**
Late night cruise bar, with low lighting, industrial décor and a pool table. On Saturdays Grit takes over (for men only).

Village Soho
81 Wardour Street, W1 (071 436 2468). Leicester Square underground. **Open** noon-11pm Mon-Sat; 4-10.30pm Sun. **No credit cards.**
Continental-style bar and café on two levels.

Village West One
38 Hanway Street, W1 (071 436 2468). Tottenham Court Road underground/Night buses from Trafalgar Square. **Open** 5pm-2am Mon-Sat; 7.30-10.30pm Sun. **Average** £8. **No credit cards.**
Hanway Street is a small side-street off Oxford Street. On it you'll find this two-storey gay bar and restaurant. The attractive, shorts-wearing staff are friendly, and there's a buzzy atmosphere. Recently refitted and fully air-conditioned.

The Yard
57 Rupert Street, W1 (071 437 2652). Piccadilly Circus underground. **Open** noon-11pm Mon-Sat. **Credit** A, AmEx, V.
This new, stylish bar complex from the Village crew, incorporates a downstairs courtyard/café bar plus an upstairs Loft Bar (open 6-11pm Mon-Sat). Food is served downstairs noon-3pm, 6-9pm. Two-pint jugs of lager (£4) or cocktails are available, and there's an early evening happy hour daily.

Out & About
Cafés & Restaurants

Many of London's gay bars also have restaurants attached, and still more serve substantial snacks. *See above* **Pubs & Bars**.

First Out Café/Bar
52 St Giles High Street, WC2 (071 240 8042). Tottenham Court Road underground. **Open** 11am-11pm Mon-Sat; noon-10.30pm Sun. **No credit cards.**
A well-liked lesbian and gay, Continental-style coffee house with licensed bar (downstairs).

Wilde About Oscar
30-31 Philbeach Gardens, SW5 (071 835 1858). Earl's Court underground. **Open** 7pm-1am Mon-Sat; 12.30-3.30pm Sun. **Average** £18. **Credit** A, AmEx, £STC, V.
Probably the best gay restaurant in town, with professional service and a small, classic French and Italian menu.

Saunas

Brownies
14 Gleneagle Road, SW16 (081 769 6998). Streatham BR/N69, N78, N87 bus. **Open** 2pm-midnight Mon-Thur, Sun; 2pm-2am Fri, Sat. **Membership** £10.50 per year. **Admission** £9.50 Mon-Thur; £10.50 Fri-Sun. **No credit cards.**
Gay men's sauna with steam room, masseurs, sunbeds, power-showers, lounge, satellite TV and snack bar.

Covent Garden Health Spa
29 Endell Street, WC2 (071 836 2236). Covent Garden underground. **Open** 11am-11pm daily. **Admission** £12.50; £6.25 students, UB40s. **Credit** A, £TC, V.
This stylish, comfortable and relaxed gay health spa is centrally located in the heart of Covent Garden. Facilities include a large new Jacuzzi, sauna, spa bath, solarium and snack bar. Mondays are for lesbian women only.

Shopping & Services

Clone Zone
64 Old Compton Street, W1 (071 287 3530). Leicester Square or Piccadilly Circus underground. **Open** 11am-10.45pm Mon-Sat; 1-7pm Sun. **Credit** A, AmEx, V.
A new multi-level store with a familiar range of leatherwear, sportswear, T-shirts, briefs and sweatshirts, together with cards and books.
Branch: 1 Hogarth Road, SW5 (071 373 0598). Open 10am-7pm Mon-Fri; 10am-8pm Sat; 1-7pm Sun.

Expectations
75 Great Eastern Street, EC2 (071 739 0292). Old Street underground (Exit 3). **Open** 11am-7pm Mon-Thur; 11am-8pm Fri; 11am-10.30pm Sat; noon-5pm Sun. **Credit** A, AmEx, £TC, V.
You'll find the city's widest choice of leather and rubberwear here, plus accoutrements displayed in atmospheric surroundings. Upstairs there's Lycra-, gym- and sports wear at *Sweat* (071 613 2383).
Branch: Sweat, 52 Dean Street, W1 (071 734 5363).

Gay's The Word Bookshop
66 Marchmont Street, WC1 (071 278 7654). Russell Square underground. **Open** 11am-7pm Mon-Fri; 10am-6pm Sat; 2-6pm Sun. **Credit** A, AmEx, DC, £TC, V.
London's best selection of new and second-hand, British and imported gay and lesbian books, plus magazines, videos, badges and cards.

Obsessions
30 Monmouth Street, WC2 (071 379 1740). Covent Garden underground. **Open** 11am-7pm Mon-Sat. **Credit** A, DC, £TC, V.
Goods based on traditional craftsmanship in leather and steel are sold at this upmarket store. Stock ranges from motorcycle jackets, Tom Ritts posters, mirrors, and luggage, to Calvin Klein, dressed teddy bears and designer gifts.
Branches: 1B Coleherne Road, SW10 (071 244 8220); 106 Heath Street, NW3 (071 794 7971).

Regulation
17A St Albans Place, N1 (071 226 0665). Angel underground. **Open** 10.30am-7.30pm Mon-Sat. **Credit** A, AmEx, £STC, V.
There's an array of PVC, rubber, leather and denim stocked at this fetish clothing shop. More unusual items include 1960s Pac-a-Macs and respirators. A bespoke service and wholesale is offered.

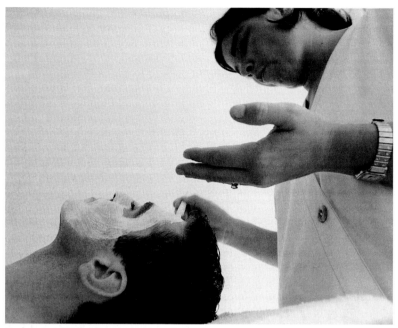

Fancy a facial? **Soho Men** *is the place. See* **review**.

Soho Men

Clone Zone, 64 Old Compton Street, W1 (071 287 3334). Leicester Square or Piccadilly Circus underground. **Open** 11am-8pm Mon-Sat. **No credit cards.**

A male health and beauty salon run by Adrienne Henshaw (cousin of Gary), which offers facials, waxing, eyebrow/eyelash tinting, manicures, pedicures, sunbeds and shiatsu massage. Prices range from £4 for an eyebrow tidy, to £35 for a 90-minute full facial. Gift vouchers also available.

Zipper Store

283 Camden High Street, NW1 (071 267 7665). Camden Town underground. **Open** 10.30am-6.30pm Mon-Thur; 10.30am-7pm Fri; 10am-6.30pm Sat; noon-5pm Sun. **Credit** A, AmEx, £TC, V.

London's only licensed gay sex store, recently refurbished and air-conditioned, manages to stock a surprisingly large variety of goods including sports, leisure and leatherwear, plus cards, accoutrements, novelties, books and mags.

Information

The first port of call for anyone wanting general advice or information on gay or lesbian matters should be the **Lesbian & Gay Switchboard** which operates a 24-hour service.

Bisexual Helpline

(081 569 7500). **Open** 7.30-9.30pm Tue, Wed.

Black Lesbian & Gay Helpline

(071 837 5364). **Open** 7-10pm Thur.
Advice, information and news.

Body Positive Helpline

(071 373 9124). **Open** 7-10pm daily.
Support for HIV-positive people.

GALOP (Gay London Policing Group)

(071 233 0854). **Open** 10am-6pm Mon-Fri.
Advice, counselling and support for gay men who have had problems with the police. There's a 24-hour answerphone service when the office is closed.

Lesbian & Gay Switchboard.

(071 837 7324).
A 24-hour advice and information service, with minicom facility for the deaf.

London Friend

(071 837 3337). **Open** 7.30-10pm daily.
Counselling for gay men and women. A women-only service is available on 071 837 2782 (open 7.30-10pm Tue-Thur).

National AIDS Helpline

(0800 567 123).
A 24-hour advice and information service. Phone calls are free.

Terrence Higgins Trust

(071 242 1010). **Open** noon-10pm daily.
Advice and information on AIDS, from a leading charity in the field, named after the first man to die of the disease in Britain.

Students

The British education system is in flux and students are having to ride the tide with scant resources. Thankfully, London offers a myriad diversions from study.

More people study in London than in any other city of the world. Over 500,000 students are registered at 140 different colleges throughout the capital. However, there is no discernible student district in the city. Student social life tends to be focused around individual colleges and various music and club venues. And students live anywhere they can find cheap accommodation.

That said, Bloomsbury, WC1, is the traditional heart of academia in London. Here you'll find several colleges of the University of London and its administrative offices, **Senate House**. Between Gordon Square, Russell Square and Gower St you'll find **Dillon's** (the University bookshop *see chapter* **Shopping**), the **University of London Union (ULU)** (*see* Box), the Vanbrugh Theatre (home to the Royal Academy of Dramatic Art), and the **British Museum** and Library (*see chapter* **Museums**).

The future of the University's federal structure has been in doubt since polytechnics were allowed to call themselves universities and award their own degrees. This move, the most radical shake-up in higher education since the sixties, has meant there are now many independent **New Universities** (*see below*) in the capital. Some colleges affiliated to the University of London are also considering independent status.

Yet the fundamental difference between the former polytechnics and the traditional universities, remains true: universities concentrate on academic research; polytechnics on vocational training.

The qualifications conferred by London's universities have also been changing rapidly. It's now possible to study for one degree at several different colleges, or over a period of several years at the same college. The key word has been 'modularity', whereby courses are taken in easily assessable and exchangeable parts. But given that student numbers are expected to increase by a third over the next ten years, the system is under considerable pressure.

The basic requirements for admission to courses remain much the same. Prospective students at the old universities usually need at least two A-levels or similar. Students claim a mandatory fixed grant (about £2,500 a year) towards

maintenance which can be supplemented with a loan. Generally grants still cover only the three-year duration of traditional degrees. Tuition fees for UK students are at present paid directly to the institution by the government. Overseas students can usually only receive funding if they have been resident in the UK for 3 years or more, and for purposes other than their education. Citizens of the EC, however, may be able to have tuition fees paid. Contact either the **British Council Information Centre** (*see below* Language Schools) or **UKCOSA** (*see below* Accommodation) for details on studying in the UK.

Universities

University of London

London University was founded in 1826 in response to the exclusion of non-denominational religious sects from Oxford and Cambridge universities (*see also chapter* **London by Area: Central**). **University College** was the first college to affiliate to the federal structure. It was rapidly followed by others, including **King's College**. Both are worth a visit for their impressive Victorian and Georgian buildings. The University now includes at least 40 colleges and institutions, and the 'external' system allows students from abroad or outside London to take a University of London degree.

Listed below are some of the larger colleges that make up the University. General enquiries should be addressed to University of London, Senate House, Malet Street, WC1 (071 636 8000). Open 9.30am-5.30pm Mon-Fri.
Goldsmith's College *Lewisham Way, SE14 (071 692 1406). New Cross underground/BR or New Cross Gate underground/BR.*
Imperial College *Prince Consort Road, SW7 (071 589 5111). South Kensington underground.*
King's College London *Strand, WC2 (071 836 5454). Aldwych or Temple underground.*
London School of Economics (LSE) *Page Building, Houghton Street, WC2 (071 405 7686). Holborn underground.*
Queen Mary and Westfield College *Mile End Road, E1 (071 980 4811). Whitechapel underground.*
University College London *Gower Street, WC1 (071 387 7050). Goodge Street or Russell Square underground.*

New Universities

Most of the other higher-education institutions in London were set up in the late sixties and early seventies to provide mainly vocational and technical training. All have active student unions which frequently stage events and live bands during term-time.

City University *Northampton Square, EC1 (071 247 1441). Barbican underground.*

South Bank University *Borough Road, SE1 (071 815 6041). Elephant & Castle underground/BR.*

University of East London *Stratford Campus, Romford Road, E15 (081 590 7722). Stratford underground/BR.*

University of Greenwich *Wellington Street, SE18 (081 855 0618). Woolwich Arsenal BR.*

University of Kingston *Penrhyn Road, Kingston, Surrey (081 549 1366). Kingston BR.*

University of Middlesex *Trent Park, Bramley Road, N14 (081 368 1299). Cockfosters or Oakwood underground.*

University of North London *166-220 Holloway Road, N7 (071 607 2789). Holloway Road underground.*

University of Westminster *104-108 Bolsover Street, W1 (071 911 5000). Great Portland Street or Oxford Circus underground.*

Accommodation

Cheap temporary accommodation in London is not as difficult to find as you might expect. Pimlico and the Cromwell Road are good areas to start looking for cheap hotels. For more inexpensive accommodation, contact **UKCOSA** (*listed below*) or *see chapter* **Accommodation**.

Centre Francais
61-69 Chepstow Place, W2 (071 221 8134). Notting Hill Gate underground. **Open** *24 hours daily.* **Rates** *single £23.20, dormitory £13.50, both incl breakfast.*

Indian YMCA
41 Fitzroy Square, W1 (071 387 0411). Warren Street underground. **Open** *24 hours daily.* **Rates** *£25.60, incl breakfast, dinner.*
You must be a YMCA member to sleep here, though you can join up on arrival. Book in advance as the hostel fills up quickly.

International House
Brunswick Square, WC1 (071 837 0746). Russell Square underground. **Rates** *about £17.*
Rooms can be rented during University of London vacation periods. Apply in writing in advance to the Bursar.

International Students House
229 Great Portland Street, W1 (071 631 3223). Great Portland Street or Regent's Park underground. **Open** *8.30am-11pm daily.* **Rates** *£11-£22.*
Single, double and triple rooms as well as dormitory accommodation is available at this friendly hostel. You can book-in anytime between 10am and 2pm.

London House
Mecklenburgh Square, WC1 (071 837 8888). Russell Square underground. **Open** *9am-5pm Mon-Sat (office booking hours).* **Rates** *single £17; double £34.*

Run by the London Goodenough Trust, London House has rooms for graduates from Europe and the Commonwealth countries (past or present). It's important to book in advance.

London Student House
Friendship House, 1 St Nicholas Glebe, Rectory Lane, SW17 (081 672 2262). Tooting underground/BR. **Rates** *about £10 per night.*
Re-opening in the spring of 1994 after major refurbishment, this south London hostel will be offering cheap temporary accommodation during vacations. Overseas students are particularly welcome.

UKCOSA
9-17 St Alban's Place, N1 (071 226 3762). Angel underground. **Open** *1-4pm Mon-Fri.*
The United Kingdom Council for Overseas Students' Affairs will provide a list of addresses providing student accommodation. Its staff are especially helpful if you are considering studying in Britain. Phone to make an appointment.

City Life

Many theatres, cinemas and galleries will give student discounts if you produce an **ISIC** (**International Student Identity Card**). To obtain a card, go to the **University of London Union** office (*see* **Box**) or **STA Travel** (*see chapter* **Survival: Travel & Driving**), with your student and personal identification, and ask for one. Others offer reduced rates to students on a stand-by basis. Ring the Student Theatreline on 071 379 8900 for information on availability. Details are updated daily after 2pm.

London's club scene changes fast and furiously, and often the prices are prohibitive to students. When cash is plentiful enough to venture beyond a student union bar, try the Camden Palace (1A Camden Road, NW1; 071 387 0428), where the Tuesday night 'Feet first' regularly packs in student punters. The Dome (178 Junction Road, NW5; 071 281 2195) is also popular with students. *See chapter* **Clubs** for more details on nightlife. And you can't leave the live-music capital of the world without seeing a band. There's an astonishing number of venues all over town. *See chapter* **Music: Rock, Folk & Jazz**.

London also has no shortage of second-hand shops selling cheap clothes, records and books. **Camden Lock** and **Portobello Road** are the best markets for clothes and records; specialist shops in both areas trade through the week. Camden Lock and the South Bank Book market (opposite the National Film Theatre under Waterloo Bridge) have trestle tables loaded with a hotchpotch of second-hand books, giving bibliophiles hours of happy browsing. **Brick Lane Market** in the East End also has new and second-hand book stalls hidden amid a welter of junk. For more details on London's shops and markets, *see chapter* **Shopping**.

During term-time the best places to go for inexpensive meals are the college canteens

Eat pie and chips in splendour at the **Great Dining Hall**. *See* **review**.

listed below. Otherwise, there are plenty of cheap cafés and restaurants listed in *chapter* **Eating & Drinking**.

The Great Dining Hall
London House, Mecklenburgh Square, WC1 (071 837 8888). Russell Square underground. **Breakfast served** 7-10am Mon-Fri; 8-10am Sat; 9-11am Sun. **Lunch served** 12.30-2pm, **dinner served** 6-8pm, daily. **No credit cards.**
Good square meals of the pie and chips variety are served up for less than £4 in the grand dining hall of the William Goodenough Trust for Overseas Graduates. It's open all year round.

Indian YMCA
41 Fitzroy Square, W1 (071 387 0411). Warren Street underground. **Breakfast served** 7.45-8.45am Mon-Fri; 8.30-9.30am Sat, Sun. **Lunch served** 12.30-1.45pm Mon-Fri; 12.30-1.30pm Sat, Sun. **Dinner served** 7-8pm daily. **Credit** £TC.
Visitors are welcome at this unusual canteen, which caters for Indians using the hostel. Food is dolloped out school-dinner style, but the spicing is good and the average price is only £6.

Malaysia Hall Dining Hall
46 Bryanston Square, W1 (071 723 9484). Marble Arch underground. **Open** noon-2.30pm, 5-9pm, daily. **No credit cards.**
Anyone can eat at this basement canteen for Malaysian students. The simple and extremely cheap set meal gives a choice of curries; you eat at refectory tables. Malaysian satay costs £2; the set meal is £1.70.

Mary Ward Centre
42 Queen Square, WC1 (071 831 7711). Russell Square or Holborn underground. **Open** 9.30am-9pm Mon-Thur; 9.30am-8.30pm Fri; 11am-4pm Sat. **No credit cards.**
Healthy wholefood meals at reasonable prices are served in the canteen of this central London Community Education Centre.

Palms Restaurant
University of London Union, Malet Street, WC1 (071 580 9551). Euston Square or Goodge Street underground. **Open** 9.30am-7pm Mon-Fri. **No credit cards.**
Good food at low prices and the chance to meet other students make this restaurant worth a visit. It closes for three weeks in August.

Work & Study

See chapter **Survival: Working in London**.

Language Schools

Language schools have mushroomed all over London, offering expensive and intensive courses in English as a foreign language. Be warned though; they are not all reputable educational establishments, so don't just walk into the first one you come across. Always check that the school you choose is recognised by the **British Council**, or is a member of **ARELS-FELCO** (*see below*). **FIRST** is a breakaway group of schools that has left ARELS-FELCO to form a professional body to promote excellence in English language schools.
The good schools have teachers with teaching certificates either from the Royal Society of Art (RSA) or International House (ITTI), run classes of no more than 15 students and usually use high-quality text books such as the *Cambridge* or *Meaning Into Words* series.

ARELS-FELCO
2 Pontypool Place, SE1 (071 242 3136). Waterloo underground/BR. **Open** 9.30am-5.30pm Mon-Thur; 9.30am-5pm Fri.
ARELS-FELCO, the Association for Recognised English

Language Teaching Establishments in Britain, is the professional body for language schools. It publishes *Learn English in Britain*, which lists its members and schools approved by the British Council.

British Council
10 Spring Gardens, SW1 (071 930 8466). Charing Cross underground/BR. **Open** *personal calls* 11am-4pm Mon-Fri; *phone* 9.30am-5pm Mon-Fri.
The British Council is the governing body covering language schools. The schools it approves are regularly inspected and are listed in *Learn English in Britain*, available from the Education Information Service Department (071 389 4383/071 389 4391).

Eurocentres
21 Meadowcourt Road, SE3 (081 318 5633). Lee or Blackheath BR. **Open** 9am-5pm Mon-Fri.
Recognised by the British Council, Eurocentres is a member of ARELS-FELCO and runs a range of classes all year round. It has three schools in London and affiliated establishments throughout the Continent. The summer intensive courses provide 25 hours' study a week, for three to four weeks, with morning and afternoon classes. They cost about £140 per week. All classes have a maximum of 16 pupils and staff can help find accommodation.
Branches: 56 Eccleston Square, SW1 (071 834 4155).

International House
106 Piccadilly, W1 (071 491 2598). Green Park underground. **Open** 8.30am-8.30pm Mon-Fri. **Credit** £TC.
Not merely an institute for English language teachers, International House has been running English language courses for 36 years. It's recognised by the British Council and has affiliated schools in 18 countries. An intensive summer course in August lasts four weeks, 25 hours per week, and costs £725. There's a maximum of 15 pupils a class but the average is ten. International

House also runs a two-week summer intensive course for mature students, with a maximum of six to a group, for 20 hours a week, costing £313.

Marble Arch Intensive English
21 Star Street, W2 (071 402 9273). Edgware Road or Paddington underground. **Open** 9am-5.30pm Mon-Fri. **Credit** £TC.
General English courses last a minimum of two weeks; classes hold no more than 14 students. On average a short course of half-days will cost £185 for two weeks (minimum two weeks), but the rate gets cheaper the longer the course. Full-day courses are also available. This ARELS-FELCO recognised centre also boasts a restaurant, language library, social programme and accommodation service, placing students in college halls or with families.

Libraries

University of London Library
Senate House, Malet Street, WC2 (071 636 4514). Goodge Street or Russell Square underground. **Open** *term-time* 8.30am-9pm Mon-Fri; 9am-5.30pm Sat; *holiday* 9.30am-5.30pm Mon-Sat.
This huge arts and humanities reference library holding about 1.5 million books can be used by visiting students on production of student ID. It costs £5 per day or £15 per week. There's also a cheap canteen. It's open 9.30-11.30am, noon-2pm, 3.30-4pm (until 5pm during term-time) Mon-Sat.

Westminster Central Reference Library
St Martin's Street, WC2 (071 798 2034). Leicester Square underground. **Open** 10am-7pm Mon-Fri; 10am-5pm Sat.
A general reference library open to the public, with extensive performing and fine-arts sections.

A blessed Union

The Student Union of London University represents about 60,000 students, making it the largest of its kind in Europe. The buildings in Bloomsbury have provided a meeting place for students from all the different colleges of the University since 1956. A plethora of facilities is provided here. Many of them can be used by visiting students, so long as they possess the relevant identification, or have made special arrangements beforehand.

During term-time there are dance-nights and regular live bands. You'll have to arrange entry as a guest of a member of the Union during the evenings as the place gets very crowded and does not have a public licence.

Apart from the array of ground-floor shops and services listed below, there's also a basement containing an Olympic-size swimming pool, a weights room and a gym. Use of these facilities is restricted, especially during term-time, but it's worth making enquiries.

Upstairs there's **Palms Restaurant** (*listed under* **City Life**).

ULU
Malet Street WC1 (071 580 9551). Goodge Street underground. **Open** 8.30am-11pm Mon-Fri; 9.30am-11pm Sat.
Unimart *(071 580 9551).* **Open** 10am-7pm Mon-Fri.
A general stationery store with writing equipment and computer software at reduced prices. Snacks and sandwiches are also sold.
Unisport *(071 580 9551).* **Open** 10am-7pm Mon-Fri.
Here you'll find reasonably priced racquets, footwear, rucksacks and general posing togs including University of London sweatshirts.
ULU Ticketshop *(071 343 5481).* **Open** 10am-7pm Mon-Fri; 11am-4pm Sat.
Using this ticket outlet for events at ULU, as well as for most other major venues in town, is a good way to avoid being ripped off by the innumerable ticket touts and agencies in the capital.
ULU Travel *(071 636 0271/636 1778).* **Open** 9.30am-6pm Mon-Fri; 10am-4pm Sat.
A travel agency that specialises in finding the best deals for students.

Women's London

Advice and sights, cafés and wild nights for all bluestockings, clubbers and businesswomen.

Personal security is less likely to be a concern in London than getting its citizens to tell you much more than the time of day. The notorious 'British reserve' is a fact. But whether you're in business meetings, sumptuous shops, rave clubs or visiting major historical sights, you should use a stranger's licence to brashness by starting a conversation. Often this will break down the barriers and you'll have a great time.

PRE-SUFFRAGE TO POST-FEMINISM

London was the centre of Britain's many-faceted suffragette movement by virtue of its role both as the social hub of the nation and the seat of Parliament. The success of this movement was due to key individuals and events stretching back more than a century – starting with Mary Wollstonecraft.

Described by Horace Walpole as 'a hyena in petticoats', Bloomsbury-based Wollstonecraft published *A Vindication of the Rights of Woman* in 1792; in it she said, 'It is time to effect a revolution in female manners, time to restore women to their lost dignity and to make them labour by reforming themselves to reform the world'.

By the middle of the next century, Barbara Bodichon had founded the Langham Place Group to fight for women's equal rights (to work, education, property and suffrage). She prompted John Stuart Mill to write *On the Subjection of Women* (in 1869) and petition on their behalf in Parliament. Mrs Emmeline Pankhurst (*see* **Box**), together with her daughters Christabel and Sylvia, declared that this soft approach got women nowhere. They formed the Women's Social and Political Union (WSPU), drew up 'Votes for women!' banners in white, purple and green, and embarked on guerrilla tactics that included window-smashing and arson around Westminster.

In 1918, women over 30 were given the right to vote, the Pankhursts had formally and acrimoniously split, and the suffragette movement, having won its primary aim (suffrage), fell apart. By the end of the 1960s, however, a powerful women's movement was emerging, championing women's rights to abortion (under NAC, the National Abortion Campaign) and campaigning for world peace

(the Greenham Common women later staked out a peace camp round the Greenham nuclear base to the west of London).

Meanwhile, Germaine Greer was developing her own brand of feminism, stating in the underground magazine, *Oz*, in 1970, 'The cunt must take the steel out of the cock and make it flesh again'. By the end of the decade Margaret Thatcher, who professed to 'hate those strident tones we hear from some Women's Libbers', had taken up residence in No.10 Downing Street as Britain's first woman Prime Minister.

As the eighties drew to a close, the backlash against feminism was entrenched. The supposed liberation of 'post-feminism' is now being questioned: in 1993, journalist Yvonne Roberts said, 'post-feminism is the bedpan of the male establishment in which women voluntarily piddle away their rights and aspirations. It's a con.'

Help & Information

See also chapter **Gay London**.

Drill Hall Arts Centre
16 Chenies Street, WC1 (071 637 8270). Goodge Street underground. **Open** *10am-11pm Mon-Sat.*
The Drill Hall has long been a first stop for lesbians and feminists seeking flyers on events, political and cultural, some of which take place at this venue. There's a women-only bar on Monday nights.

Fawcett Library
London Guildhall University, Old Castle Street, E1 (071 320 1000; ext 1189). Aldgate East underground. **Open** *term-time* 11am-8.30pm Mon; 10am-5pm Wed-Fri. *Holiday* 9am-5pm Mon-Fri. **Admission** £3; £1.50 students.
Named after the leader of the non-militant women's-suffrage movement, Millicent Fawcett, the national research library for women's studies is a fascinating repository of women's history. The emphasis is on Britain, but other countries are represented, including the Commonwealth and the Third World.

Federation of Business and Professional Women
23 Ansdell Street, W8 (071 938 1729/fax 071 938 2037). High Street Kensington underground. **Open** 9.30am-5pm Mon-Fri. **Membership** £40 per year.
This is a lobbying organisation and, if you join, gives you the chance to network with women from your profession and a cross-section of many others.

Gemma

BM Box 5700, London, WC1N 3XX.
Gemma is a 'friendship circle' for lesbian and bisexual women with or without a disability/illness (must be over 16 years old). Write with a stamped, addressed envelope for details.

Kidsline

(071 222 8070). **Open** *term-time* 9am-6pm, *holiday* 9am-4pm, daily.
A helpline mainly concerned with entertainment for children, but on a good day, phone operators will try and help with any queries.

Lesbian Artists Network

PO Box 2DL, London W1A 2DL (081 868 9103).
LAN aims to promote lesbian art in mainstream locations and fight discrimination by showing that the work bears

professional scrutiny. Contact the organisation for details of exhibitions.

Lesbian Line

(071 251 6911). **Open** 7-10pm Mon-Thur; 2-10pm Fri.
Counselling, information and advice is offered.

London Women's Centre (LWC)

Wesley House, 4 Wild Court (off Kingsway), WC2 (071 831 6946). Holborn underground. **Open** 8am-10pm Mon-Sat.
Amenities in this tucked-away resource centre include a computer centre, a video editing suite, a fitness centre, and nursery facilities. The LWC provides a phone referral service, but is also headquarters for various campaigning organisations: Feminist Forum, Justice for Women, Afro-Caribbean Older Sisters, Newham Asian Women's Project, Catholic Women's Group, Only

Women's trail

There's a great tradition of wild and magnificent London women – royals, writers, actresses, mistresses, and politicians. Here are just a few, with relevant sights to visit.

Boudicca (died AD 60). The queen, who led her Iceni tribe to war against the Romans reportedly shouting, 'Better masterless poverty than prosperous slavery!' is commemorated in a classic Victorian statue on the north side of Westminster Bridge.

Elizabeth I (1533-1603). The Virgin Queen's speech on the eve of the Spanish Armada in 1588 included the famous phrase, 'I know I have the body of a weak and feeble woman, but I have the heart and the stomach of a king'. One of her favourite portraits (by Hilliard) is at the **Tate Gallery** (*see chapter* **Art Galleries**).

Aphra Behn (1640-1689). The first woman in Britain to make her living by the pen was 'forced to write for bread' when she received neither payment nor recognition but instead a spell in prison for her labours as Charles II's spy. See her memorial stone in **Westminster Abbey** (*see chapter* **Sightseeing**).

Nell Gwyn (1651-1687). Orange-seller turned actress Nell Gwyn was housed by her lover Charles II at 79 Pall Mall, where her coachman explained when caught fighting a footman, 'He called you a whore, Mrs Nelly!' to which she reputedly replied, 'Well, I am a whore. Find something better to fight about.'

Elizabeth Barrett Browning (1806-1861). 'There is nothing to see in me, nor to hear in me,' she replied to Robert Browning after he had fallen in love with her having read her poems. She is commemorated with a plaque at 50 Wimpole Street, W1, where she was courted from her sick-bed by Browning.

Florence Nightingale (1820-1910). The mother of modern nursing was wilful. Lytton Strachey records that her mother wept 'We are ducks who have hatched a wild swan'; but, he counters, 'the poor lady was wrong: it was not a swan they had hatched: it was an eagle'. The Florence Nightingale Museum is in the St Thomas' Hospital precincts.

Florence Nightingale Museum, *Stangate House, Lambeth Palace Road, SE1 (071 620 0374). Westminster underground or Waterloo underground/BR.* **Open** 10am-4pm Tue-Sun. **Admission** £2.50 adults; £1.50 under-16s, OAPs.

Emmeline Pankhurst (1858-1928). 'Nothing has ever been got out of the British Government without something approaching a revolution,' claimed Ms Pankhurst. She was often imprisoned during her fight for women's rights, but is now commemorated with a statue in Victoria Tower Gardens, near the Houses of Parliament.

Nancy Astor (1879-1964). The first woman to sit in the House of Commons as an MP found the first years 'hell'. Known for her forthright approach, she once told Winston Churchill, 'If I were your wife, I'd put poison in your coffee.' 'If I were your husband,' he responded, 'I'd drink it.' The first woman to be elected to the Commons was Constance Markiewicz, an Irish Republican who did not take her seat in the chamber.

Mary Quant (born 1934). The woman whose innovations include the mini-skirt, geometric haircuts, white nail-polish and water-proof make-up, was awarded an OBE in 1966. A black and cream 1967 jersey Quant mini-dress is on display at the **Victoria & Albert Museum** (*see chapter* **Museums**).

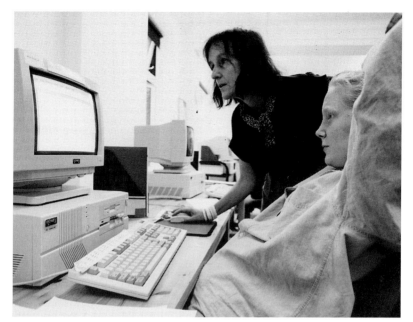

London Women's Centre: *a wealth of facilities for women. See* **review** *page 292.*

Women Press, Pensioners' Link and the Scarlet Theatre Company.

National Childbirth Trust (NCT)

(081 992 8637). **Open** 9am-5pm Mon-Fri.
Local branches of the NCT offer women who are pregnant, or who have young babies, advice and support.

Women Artists' Slide Library

Fulham Palace, Bishops Avenue, SW6 (071 731 7618/fax 071 384 1110).Putney Bridge underground. **Open** 10am-5pm Tue-Fri. **Admission** free.
The UK's largest reference source on women in the visual arts.

Accommodation

See also chapter **Accommodation**.

Blakes

33 Roland Gardens, SW7 (071 370 6701/fax 071 373 0442). Gloucester Road or South Kensington underground. **Rates** *single* £138.50 per night; *double* £185.50 per night; *junior suites* £230 per night; *deluxe double* £275 per night. **Credit** A, AmEx,.DC, £$TC, V.
Model/actress Anouska Hempel's hotel attracts media stars and expense-accounting businesswomen for its intimacy and individually designed, luxurious rooms.

No.7 Guest House

7 Josephine Avenue, SW2 (081 674 1880). Brixton underground. **Rates** *single* £28; *double* £42. **Credit** A, V.
No.7 is popular with gay men but is also lesbian-friendly. Although men may outnumber women, none of them will be heterosexual.

Women's Link

57 Great Russell Street, WC1 (071 430 1524). Tottenham Court Road underground. **Open** *personal calls* 11am-3pm Mon-Wed; 11am-7pm Thur; 1-3.30pm Fri; *telephone enquiries* 10am-4pm Mon-Wed; 10am-7pm Thur; 1-4pm Fri.
An information service that can provide a great deal of help in finding temporary, permanent or emergency accommodation for women. It produces a pamphlet, 'Hostels in London' (£2.50).

Clubs

Flyers handed out on Oxford Street saying things like 'girls go free' are generally invitations to cattle markets. If you want to spend a night in a club unhassled, head for venues with tables and slip the waiter a couple of pounds to see that you remain undisturbed. For news of the lesbian clubbing scene, pick up fliers at the cafés listed below *under* **Eating & Drinking**, or consult the gay press to find out about one-off and new clubs. For more clubs *see chapters* **Gay London** and **Clubs**. And always consult the listings in *Time Out* magazine.

Ace of Clubs

52 Piccadilly, W1 (071 408 4457). Green Park underground/Night buses from Trafalgar Square. **Open** 9.30am-4am Sat. **Admission** £3 before 10.30pm, £5 after.
If you want to explore all the ramifications of London's

lesbian scene, this friendly club is the place to start. Anything goes in terms of dress and age.

Clit Club

Central Station, 37 Wharfdale Road, N1 (071 582 8764). King's Cross underground/BR/N21, N73 bus. **Open** usually one Thur a month, phone for details.
This is no relation to the original New York Clit Club – it's leather/fetish and, many London lesbians say, terrifying. Well worth it if you're feeling courageous.

Ronnie Scott's

47 Frith Street, W1 (071 439 0747). Leicester Square or Piccadilly Circus underground/Night buses from Trafalgar Square. **Open** 8.30pm-3am Mon-Sat. **Admission** £12; £6 students Mon-Thur.
Perhaps the finest jazz club in London, with live music from major stars. Book a table in advance if you want to tuck yourself away in a quiet corner.

Venus Rising

at the Fridge, Town Hall Parade, Brixton, SW2 (071 326 5100). Brixton underground/BR/N2, N78 bus. **Open** 10pm-3am first Wed of the month. **Admission** £5.
London's entire lesbian community, plus a large number of politicised trendsters (in their twenties) save up for this monthly one-nighter. It's in a grandiose location and invariably involves a long night of dancing, cruising and drinking.

Wow Bar

The Brixtonian Backyard, Neal's Yard (off Short's Gardens), WC2 (071 240 2769). Covent Garden underground/Night buses from Trafalgar Square. **Open** 8pm-4am Sat. **Admission** £1.50.
There's Modern Caribbean food available at this stylish Jamaican Rhum shop, where Sue Wade hosts a weekly women-only club night.

Eating & Drinking

If you're dining on your own, it's best to avoid expensive and formal restaurants, where you're likely to be given a table tucked away by the toilet and then patronised by the waiters when it comes to the wine list. Cafés, grills, brasseries and bistros are a better bet: the staff are usually more laid-back and the layout less formal (you won't stick out like a sore thumb among the suits).

Angel Café

65 Graham Street, N1 (no phone). Angel underground. **Open** noon-midnight Mon-Sat; noon-11.30pm Sun. **No credit cards.**
Notoriously difficult to find (at night take a cab), this chi-chi north London bar and café has all the current event and club fliers plus free lesbian mags. It serves a good mix of healthy and trendy food. Sophisticated during the day, raging at night.

First Out

52 St Giles High Street, WC2 (071 240 8042). Tottenham Court Road underground. **Open** 11am-11pm Mon-Fri; noon-10.30pm Sun. **Average** £5. **No credit cards.**
Lesbians wanting to pick up club and event fliers and current free gay publications, use this central café regularly. The food's not spectacular, but the atmosphere's friendly. Ask the staff about women's bar nights.

Mildred's

58 Greek Street, W1 (071 494 1634). Leicester Square or Piccadilly Circus underground. **Open** noon-11pm Mon-Sat. **Average** £8.50. **House wine** £6.75 bottle, £1.85 glass. **Mineral Water** £2.25 bottle, 60p glass. **Credit** LV, £TC.
The vegetarian menu of this Soho café is a minefield of potential disasters as well as delights, but the place is ideal for women on their own, and it has an enthusiastic lesbian following.

Patisserie Valerie

44 Old Compton Street, W1 (071 437 3466). Leicester Square or Tottenham Court Road underground. **Open** 8am-8pm Mon-Fri; 8am-7pm Sat; 10am-5.30pm Sun. **Average** £4. **Unlicenced. No credit cards.**
Valerie is one of the best coffee-and-cake cafés that are so well-suited to women eating alone. Read the papers over a leisurely breakfast of croissants (some say they're the best in London), or take café au lait with a fresh cream and choux pasty concoction. If you can't face a formal restaurant in the early evening, come here for a light snack instead.
Branches: 215 Brompton Road, SW3 (071 823 9971); 105 Marylebone High Street, W1 (071 935 6240).

Rosanna's

17 Strutton Ground, off Victoria Street, SW1 (071 233 1701). St James's Park underground. **Open** noon-7pm Mon-Fri; *gay men* 7-11pm Mon, Tue; *single women* 7-11pm Wed; *gay women* 7-11pm Thur, Fri. **Average** £6. **House wine** £8 bottle, £1.85 glass. **Credit** A, AmEx, DC, £TC, V.
A very basic café that becomes a women-only bar on some evenings; cruised day and night by a designer dyke crowd.

Café Rouge

2 Lancer Square, off Kensington Church Street, W8 (071 938 4200). High Street Kensington underground. **Meals served** 10am-11pm Mon-Sat; 10am-10.30pm Sun. **Average** £15. **Set lunch** £6.95 two courses incl coffee. **Service** 12%. **House wine** £9.95 carafe, £2.65 glass. **Mineral water** £1 small bottle. **Credit** A, AmEx, V.
The Kensington branch of the Café Rouge chain is one of the nicest, as it's light and airy, and the Frenchness seems less contrived. You can eat anything from croque monsieur to entrecôte with fries at any time of the day, and there's a bargain *prix fixe* lunch. Waiting staff are attentive, and babies and children are welcome. *Wheelchair access.*

Tea Lounge

at Le Meridien, 21 Piccadilly, W1 (071 734 8000). Piccadilly Circus underground. **Open** 10am-11.30pm daily; *teas served* 3-6pm daily. **Average** £11. **House wine** £15 bottle. **Credit** A, AmEx, DC, £STC, V.
Hotel tea lounges make ideal places for informal business meetings (and save on conference-room fees), as well as being convivial and civilised places in which to take tea. Afternoon tea, dainties and crustless cucumber sandwiches may cost a pound or two more than in your local café, but the price is worth paying for the sense of occasion. Other tea lounges to investigate include those at **Browns** and **Claridges** (*see chapter* **Accommodation**).

TGI Friday's

6 Bedford Street, WC2 (071 379 0585). Charing Cross underground/BR. **Meals served** noon-11.30pm daily. **Average** £14. **House wine** £8.95 bottle, £3 glass. **Mineral water** £1.75 bottle, £1.25 glass. **Credit** A, AmEx, LV, TC, V.
This pseudo-American burger joint serves an unlikely

mix of functions: it's great for kids (there are place mats to colour and the staff are briefed to be child-friendly), and from around 9pm it can serve as a twentysomething preppy singles joint. Staff find out your name and occupation, chat, then if you want they'll introduce you to someone else at the bar.

Health

British Pregnancy Advisory Service

7 Belgrave Road, SW1 (071 222 0985). Victoria underground/BR. **Open** 9am-noon Mon, Sat; noon-7pm Tue; 9am-2pm Wed-Fri. **No credit cards**.
BPAS is a private clinic. Its services (contraception advice, contraceptives, pregnancy tests, abortions) don't come cheap, but many women prefer to come here for the speed, efficiency and friendly anonymity it affords.

Brook Advisory Centres

233 Tottenham Court Road, W1 (071 580 2991). Tottenham Court Road underground. **Open** noon-6.30pm Mon-Thur; 9.30am-2pm Fri.
Visit a Brooks Centre if you're under 21 and you want advice and contraceptive supplies in strict confidence. There are 13 centres – phone for information about your nearest.

Burnard Clinic

Charing Cross Hospital, Fulham Palace Road, entrance St Dunstan's Road, W6 (081 846 1577). Hammersmith or Baron's Court underground. **Open** 9.30am-12.30pm, 2-5pm, Mon-Fri.
A clinic that provides a friendly atmosphere for lesbian and bi-sexual women who need treatment for sexually transmitted diseases.

Family Planning Association

27-35 Mortimer Street, W1 (071 636 7866). Goodge Street underground. **Open** 10am-3pm Mon-Fri.
This is the information unit of the NHS Family Planning Association. Phone for the address of your local branch, where you can get family planning advice and contraceptives.

Marie Stopes Clinic

108 & 114 Whitfield Street, W1 (family planning 071 388 0662/sterilisation 071 388 5554). Warren Street underground. **Open** 9am-8pm Mon-Wed; 9am-5pm Thur, Fri; 9.30am-5pm Sat. **Credit** A, V.
An expensive private clinic that nevertheless has the advantage of speed and sensitivity. It was founded by the woman many consider the pioneer of family planning in Britain, Marie Stopes, who lectured in 1916 on a subject that was then unthinkable: 'women's spontaneous and natural sex drive'.

Pregnancy Advisory Service

11-13 Charlotte Street, W1 (071 637 8962). Goodge Street underground. **Open** *telephone enquiries* 8.30am-6pm Mon-Fri; *personal callers* 9am-5.30pm Mon-Fri; 9.30am-12.30pm Sat. **Credit** AmEx, £TC, V.
This is a non profit-making registered charity, and although you are charged for contraceptives and the abortion and counselling service, prices are lower than at private clinics.

Health Club

The Sanctuary

12 Floral Street, WC2 (071 240 9635). Covent Garden underground. **Open** 10am-6pm Mon, Tue, Sat, Sun; 10am-10pm Wed-Fri. **Admission** £39.50 per day, £27.50 after 5.30pm. **Credit** A, AmEx, £TC, V.

Pamper yourself at the women-only **Sanctuary**. *See* **review**.

The **Silver Moon Women's Bookshop**. *See* **review**.

Pay a day rate at the Sanctuary, and go from fluffy white bathrobe to plant-surrounded swimming pool, by way of a sauna or a Jacuzzi, in whatever order you feel like. Heavenly luxuries such as aromatherapy cost extra. The gym next door is also women-only; both places are clean and friendly.

Shopping

Hamleys

188 Regent Street, W1 (071 734 3161). Oxford Circus underground. **Open** 10am-6.30pm Mon-Wed, Fri; 10am-8pm Thur; 9.30am-6.30pm Sat. **Credit** A, AmEx, DC, JCB, £$TC, V.
Women with children should make a bee-line for this legendary children's store; there's plenty to amuse the mites, even if you buy them nothing. The store also has baby-changing facilities.

Harvey Nichols

109-125 Knightsbridge, SW1 (071 235 5000). Knightsbridge underground. **Open** 10am-7pm Mon, Tue, Thur, Fri; 10am-8pm Wed; 10am-6pm Sat. **Credit** A, AmEx, DC, SC, £$TC, V.
Once Harrods was the place to go, but now nearby Harvey Nich's has equal executive woman-appeal. Go to either store for personal shopper services, health and beauty treatments and products from deli food to cosmetics to stationery to lingerie.

Sh!

22 Coronet Street, N1 (071 613 5458). Old Street underground/BR (exit 2). **Open** 11.30am-6.30pm Mon, Wed-Sat. **No credit cards**.
A sex shop for women and their women friends that's often as much about friendly chatting and advice-swapping as selecting from the impressive range of sex accessories.

Silver Moon Women's Bookshop

64-68 Charing Cross Road, WC2 (071 836 7906). Leicester Square underground. **Open** 10am-6.30pm Mon-Sat. **Credit** A, AmEx, £TC, V.
Friendly staff, a central location and a wide range of stock including political feminist books and lesbian fiction are features of this pleasant, airy shop.

Transport

Women's Safe Transport

Women's Safe Transport for Hammersmith and Fulham (081 748 6036). Women's Safe Transport Lambeth (071 274 4641) for Lambeth; and **Lady Cabs** *(071 281 4803/071 272 3019) for most of north London.* **Open** 7.30am-12.30am Mon-Thur; 7.30am-1am Fri; 8.30am-2am Sat; 10am-midnight Sun. **No credit cards**.
The Metropolitan Police advises that women alone should take black cabs only, and not mini-cabs unless they come from one of these by-women-for-women mini-cab services.

Trips Out of Town

A great deal of England can be seen during a day-trip from London: stormy beaches, spectacular countryside, historic towns, good-looking villages. Read on to discover how to break out of the city.

Trips Out of Town

A cruise in the country, a trek round a town, a sojourn by the sea: decide on your destination and say so-long to the city.

Before escaping London, you should obviously work out what you want from your trip. Do you prefer to tread the tourist trail in Stratford or locate a literary bolt-hole in Cambridge? If London has failed to sate your royal-watching desires, then Windsor beckons. Bath has its Georgian architecture, while Brighton has its tacky coastal charms. And if the big city has really gnawed at your soul, you could flee to the lesser-known pastures of Salisbury, and then rejoin the tourist throng at Stonehenge. Or perhaps a spot of National Trust tranquillity and a quiet village pub seem more preferable? Who knows, you may even yearn for the sandy shores of Kent and find yourself a lone tourist on the beach at Margate.

Britain has a wealth of architecture. Such is the preponderance of medieval churches that the British are in danger of taking them for granted. Pointed-arched Gothic churches grace very many English villages; round-arched Norman buildings, over 800 years old, are by no means rare. An ancient town may even have foundations put down by the Romans, Britain's first major developers. Architecture buffs should head for the local library and consult the relevant volume of Nikolaus Pevsner's excellent *Buildings of England* series.

Many towns have grown around a medieval market square; some still have a weekly market, held on the same spot that it has occupied for half a millenium or more (contact the local Tourist Information Centre for details of market days). Towns such as **Bath** (*see below* **Town**) are famous for their eighteenth-century Georgian terraces; while Victorian civic buildings, monuments to the British Empire, can be spotted in nearly every town in the country.

GETTING STARTED

The best place to start your journey is at the **British Travel Centre** (*see below*). Here you can get guide books, free leaflets and advice on any destination, you can book rail, bus, air or car travel, reserve sightseeing tours, theatre tickets (without paying through the nose) and accommodation; there's even a bureau de change. The queues tend to be long in summer, though not at 9am.

The **Scottish**, **Wales** and **Northern Ireland Tourist Boards** provide a similar but more detailed service for their own countries. When you get to your destination, head for the local Tourist Information Centre, where you can find out what's on and pick up a useful map-cum-guide (often free). Always check opening times beforehand if you're going to see a specific sight: some venues are shut on Sundays; many close-down over Christmas and New Year Bank Holidays. Often, museums are closed all winter.

British Travel Centre

12 Lower Regent Street, SW1 (no phone). Piccadilly Circus underground. **Open** *May-Sept* 9am-6.30pm Mon-Fri; 9am-5pm Sat; 10am-4pm Sun; *Oct-Apr* 9am-6.30pm Mon-Fri; 10am-4pm Sat, Sun. **Credit** A, AmEx, V. Personal callers only.

Northern Ireland Tourist Board

12 Lower Regent Street, SW1 (071 839 8416/enquiries 071 493 0601). Piccadilly Circus underground. **Open** *May-Sept* 9am-6.30pm Mon-Fri; 9am-5pm Sat; 10am-4pm Sun; *Oct-Apr* 9am-6.30pm Mon-Fri; 10am-4pm Sat, Sun. **Credit** A, AmEx, V.

Scottish Tourist Board

19 Cockspur Street, SW1 (071 930 8661). Piccadilly Circus or Charing Cross underground/BR. **Open** *May-Sept* 9.30am-5.30pm Mon-Fri; 10am-4pm Sat, phone to confirm; *Oct-Apr* 9.30am-5.30pm Mon-Fri. **Credit** A, V.

Wales Information Bureau

12 Lower Regent Street, SW1 (071 409 0969). Piccadilly Circus underground. **Open** *May-Sept* 9am-6.30pm Mon-Fri; 9am-5pm Sat; 10am-4pm Sun; *Oct-Apr* 9am-6.30pm Mon-Fri; 10am-4pm Sat, Sun. **Credit** A, AmEx, V.

Rail Travel

Despite severe government cuts, the railway network is still an excellent way to explore the country, with some little-known local lines branching off from the main InterCity routes. A few of these pass through areas of spectacular beauty, often where no roads exist (especially in Scotland), and cross breathtaking Victorian viaducts. British Rail has produced a series of excellent free colour leaflets on the subject, available from the **British Travel Centre**, Regent Street (*see above* **Getting Started**), and major stations.

However rail tickets are expensive. If there are three or four of you, it may pay to hire a car (ask at the **British Travel Centre**, *see above*, or *see chapter* **Getting Around**). If travelling by rail, try to avoid rush hours when trains get very full.

Train Information

King's Cross
(071 278 2477). **Open** *phone lines* 7am-10.30pm daily.
For information about travel to West Yorkshire, the north-east and eastern Scotland.

Euston or St Pancras
(071 387 7070). **Open** *phone lines* 24-hours daily.
Information about travel to the Midlands, West Midlands, north Wales, the north-west and western Scotland.

Paddington
(071 262 6767). **Open** *phone lines* 24-hours daily.
Travel information about the west country and south Wales.

Charing Cross, Waterloo, Victoria and Liverpool Street
(071 928 510). **Open** *phone lines* 24-hours daily.
Information about travel to the south east, Essex and East Anglia.

Rail Travel Centres

Rail Travel Centres offer information on train services and local facilities; you can also book train tickets there. The main-line stations listed (*see above* **Train Information**) all have Travel Centres, and there are other offices dotted around London – personal callers only, no telephone enquiries. All accept Access, AmEx and Visa.

Heathrow Airport
Arrivals terminals. **Open** 7.45am-9pm daily.

Gatwick Airport
Main concourse. **Open** 7am-10pm daily.

SW1
14 Kingsgate Parade, Victoria Street. Victoria underground/BR. **Open** 7.15am-9.15pm daily.
Inside British Travel Centre, 12 Regent Street. Piccadilly Circus underground. **Open** 9am-5pm Mon-Fri.

EC4
87 King William Street. Bank or Monument underground. **Open** 9am-5pm Mon-Fri.

Fares & Tickets

Rail tickets can be bought right up until the moment of departure, but for InterCity routes at peak times it's wise to reserve a seat at least two hours in advance – otherwise you may end up standing all the way. Reservations can be made when buying the ticket, and cost £1 extra. Tickets can be bought from stations and Rail Travel Centres (*see above* **Rail Travel Centres**) or by phone with Access, AmEx and Visa from the relevant terminus. The fare structure breaks down thus: full-price **Standard Returns** can be used at any time of day; most people buy off-

peak **Super Saver Returns**, which have certain restrictions (no travel on Friday or Saturday) but are almost half the price. For Friday or Saturday travel, you'll need an ordinary **Saver**, which is up to £10 more expensive; both are valid for return within one month. For day-trips, **Cheap Day Returns** are best value. **First Class** is so expensive you might as well go by plane. Finally, avoid the Friday exodus at all costs and don't travel on a Sunday – because of engineering works, even InterCity services are appalling and can take hours longer.

Coach Travel

Coach travel is reasonably cheap and there's a comprehensive network, but you can find yourself stuck in motorway traffic watching your carefully planned day-trip go up in smoke. However, many long-distance routes offer 'luxury' services with videos and refreshments for a few pounds more. **National Express** (071 730 0202) has routes to all parts of the country, buses departing from Victoria Coach Station, Buckingham Palace Road, SW1, five minutes' walk from Victoria railway station. **Green Line Buses** (081 668 7261) has routes within Greater London: its major departure point is from Eccleston Bridge, off Buckingham Palace Road, SW1, behind Victoria railway station. In these days of cut-throat competition in bus travel there may well be competing services to your destination. National Express offers Rover Tickets which can make travel even cheaper.

Finding Accommodation

If you want to be sure to avoid spending a night in a railway station, it's advisable to book a room in advance, at least for the first day. The **British Travel Centre** (*see above* **Getting Started**) has a **Room Centre** which, for a small booking fee and a deposit, reserves appropriate accommodation anywhere in Britain. The Scottish, Welsh and Northern Ireland Tourist Boards do the same within their respective countries. If you do turn up somewhere without a room, make for the local **Tourist Information Centre**, which will reserve a bed in the area to suit your taste (and pocket). Most also provide a 'Book-a-Bed-Ahead' service, which means you can book the next night's hotel in another area. All these services are available to personal callers only.

Town

Whichever direction you take out of London, you're bound to find somewhere that stimulates: south to bustling Brighton, west to his-

*Georgian architecture, plus hot and cold running water at **Bath**. See **review**.*

toric Windsor or north to Shakespeare's Stratford. We list some of the more interesting places, and some of the ones you'll want to be able to say you've seen. These excursions are close enough to London to be covered in a day-trip, but in case you prefer to make the most of your journey by staying overnight, we've added a few suggestions for accommodation.

Bath

Bath is a mandatory visit on every whistle-stop tour of the country, but don't let that put you off. The reason everybody goes there is that it really is worth seeing. Why else would it be the only British city in its entirety to be designated a World Heritage Site? Avoid peak season weekends – if possible, go out of season or on a weekday.

Bath owes its existence to a hot spring. Legend has it that the leprous pigs of the banished King Bladud were the first visitors (circa 875 BC) to the healing waters of the future spa town. The Romans were the next to make regular use of the quarter of a million gallons of steaming water produced daily, and the **Roman Baths and Museum**, Stall Street, are unmissable – fasci-

nating underground remains with huge pools still filled with bubbling hot spring water (no bathing allowed). The Museum holds Britain's most detailed collection of Roman artefacts, complete with bronze ear-wax removers. The adjoining **Pump Room**, fashionable in Georgian times and immortalised in Jane Austen's *Northanger Abbey*, is still a civilised place for tea (to the accompaniment of string trios and jazz bands), but for cheaper refreshment sample the freshly pumped spa water. Facing it is the magnificent fifteenth-century **Bath Abbey**, known as the 'lantern of the west' on account of its many windows. Outside, Abbey Churchyard is the place to watch the world go by while listening to a wailing busker. Nearby in North Parade Passage is **Sally Lunn**'s, reputedly Bath's oldest house, and now a tiny cellar museum and over-subscribed tearoom where you can taste one of Ms Lunn's buns.

The **Guildhall Banqueting Room**, High Street, boasts a fine eighteenth-century interior, and the equally fine **Assembly Rooms**, Bennett Street, house the Costume Museum, a collection of fashion garb from the last four centuries. The excellent **Museum of English Naive Art** occupies the Countess of Huntingdon Chapel, The Vineyard/Paragon.

One of Bath's most famous architectural features is the **Royal Crescent**, the wonderful Georgian crescent of 30 houses and a total of 114 Ionic columns, where No.1 has been restored and is now one of Bath's 16 museums. Once occupied by the Grand Old Duke of York (who had ten thousand men), it was scandalously allowed to deteriorate into a near slum until the Bath Preservation Trust rescued it in the sixties. There is a splendid kitchen museum in the basement where you can see what really went on downstairs in a classy Georgian residence, and the dining room is laid out as if for a Georgian banquet.

Nearby, **The Circus** boasts the residences of Gainsborough and Pitt. Other interesting streets include Camden Crescent and Lansdown Crescent, steep climbs but a wonderful view; picturesque Pulteney Bridge with its tiny shops (guided river tours leave from here); and Riverside Walk, below the bridge – see the city from Roman level, and enjoy a beautiful vista of Pulteney Weir. There are daily walking and open-top bus tours and some excellent personal guides are available – details from the **Information Centre** (free walks from Abbey Churchyard).

History apart, Bath is a major shopping centre. Head for the area between Cheap Street and George Street, full of interesting little clothes and gift shops – some very exclusive and expensive – and try Northumberland Place and the little roads running off Old Bond Street. Food is sold at the Guildhall Market near High Street. Antique emporiums – a Bath speciality, naturally – congregate round Margaret's Buildings, Quiet Street, Queen Street and up Lansdown Road. There's an antique market in Guinea Lane every Wednesday morning (from 7am), and the Antique Centre, Bartlett Street, has many vendors under one roof. There's also a weekend flea market on Walcot Street.

Further Information

Getting there *by train* from Paddington, 80 minutes (longer on Sun)*; by bus* National Express from Victoria, 3 hours; *by car* M4 to exit 18; *local buses* Badger Line (0225 464446).

Eating and drinking *Pump Room* and *Sally Lunn's* apart, you can barely move for tearooms and restaurants. *The Moon And Sixpence*, Broad Street, is a popular bistro with a courtyard, conservatory and fountain; a more expensive alternative is *Woods*, Alfred Street. *Supannahong*, John Street, is an enjoyable Thai café. Vegetarians go to *Huckleberry's*, Broad Street. For an up-market Italian meal, book at the *Hole in the Wall*, George Street (0225 425242). **Pubs**; the *Volunteer Rifleman's Arms*, New Bond Street Place, and *Coeur de Lion*, Northumberland Place, vie to be 'Bath's smallest pub' (the latter is cosier); the *Grapes*, Westgate Street, is a bustling, ancient wine bar with a Jacobean beamed ceiling. In summer, drink on the riverside at the *Boater*, Argyle Street.

Events *Badminton Horse Trials* early May; *Bath Antiques Fair* May; *Bath International Festival* a major musical event, last week May, first week June; *Royal Bath & West Show* 4-day agricultural show, end of May-beginning of June. For music and nightlife, consult *Venue* magazine, sold in most newsagents.

If you want to stay *Haydon House* (0225 427351), *Paradise House* (0225 317723), or *Somerset House* (0225 466451) are good for bed and breakfast. If you want to indulge yourself in real luxury, *Lucknam Park* (0225 742777) is the place.

Tourist Information Centre

Ground Floor, Colonnades Shopping Centre, Bath Street, Bath, Avon (0225 462831). **Open** *June-Sept* 9.30am-6pm Mon-Sat; 10am-4pm Sun; *Oct-May* 9.30am-5pm Mon-Sat; (times on Sun and Bank Holidays subject to change, phone to confirm).

Brighton

Brighton used to be known as 'London by the sea', but whether that was because it was just as lively, just as dirty, or just packed with Londoners is hard to say. At first glance it's hard to see the attraction. The resort has acquired a faded look thanks to a steady decline in tourism and a rising population of young homeless. The beach is all pebbles and tar, and the sea's icy cold and none too clean – drinking the oceanic fluid was once highly recommended for those suffering from glandular disease. There's even a nudist cove for the truly foolhardy.

Forget swimming, though, and soak in the town's real asset – its atmosphere. With its homely summer seediness and raging nightlife, Brighton is the perfect remedy for those itching to escape the impersonality of the capital. The most famous area is The Lanes, quaint, twisty, traffic-free alleys between North Street and the seafront, packed with antiques, jewellery and clothes shops. However, these are often stuffy and over-priced, and the centre of fashion has shifted to the North Laine, a nineteenth-century conservation area between Trafalgar Street and North Street, where you'll find yet more, but cheaper, antique shops. Brighton is a junk-collector's paradise (especially the flea-markets at Upper Gardner Street on Saturday, and behind the station on Sunday).

One sight that must be seen is the many-domed **Royal Pavilion**, a fantastic, pseudo-oriental summer palace built by the celebrated Regency architect, John Nash, in 1823 for the Prince Regent (later George IV) and recently restored, at a cost of £10 million, to its original splendour. Once described as a 'minaret mushroom', it is a hybrid of Indian, Chinese, various Oriental and even Gothic styles. The overall result is a grand almost Disney-like extravaganza, capturing the spirit of Regency at play. Queen Victoria, however, was not amused with such frippery and sold the Pavilion to the town council in 1845. The rooms have been refurbished

Oh we do like to be beside the seaside at **Brighton***. See* **review***.*

with many splendid pieces of Regency design and the Chinese décor is well worth seeing.

Brighton Art Gallery and Museum, Church Street, is good for fashion and arts nouveaux and deco, and the former dolphinarium is now the dolphin-free but shark-infested **Sea-Life Centre** (0273 604234) in Madeira Drive. Alternatively, you could walk along the sweeping iron-fenced esplanade all the way from the Marina to Hove, Brighton's sister town. Or, for a shorter journey, catch an antique train on the country's first public electric railway, **Volk's Seafront Railway**, from the Marina to the wonderfully tawdry Palace Pier where you can lie back in a free deckchair, suck on some candyfloss and soak up the tackiness of Britain-on-Sea.

Further Information

Getting there *by train* from Victoria, 55 minutes; *by bus* from Victoria, two hours; *by car* A23, M23, A23; *local buses* Brighton and Hove Bus Co (0273 206666). **Eating and drinking** the Lanes is brilliant for pubs, restaurants (especially seafood places) and teashops, but one of the best places for your afternoon cuppa is the *Mock Turtle*, Pool Valley. *Food For Friends*, Prince Albert Street, sells above-average vegetarian fare. *Al Duomos*, Pavilion Gardens, is a cheap Italian place popular with locals. Preston Street is full of restaurants, but most are horrid tourist-traps. For a reliable meal, head out to the *French Cellar* on New

England Road (0273 603643). Late-night monster fry-ups can be had at the *Market Diner*, Circus Street. Good **pubs** include the *Frock and Jacket*, Prince Albert Street, a trendy cocktails-and-beer joint in The Lanes. *The Great Eastern*, Trafalgar Street, is small, sweet and book-lined. The *Sussex Yeoman*, Guildford Road, offers real ales and 32 types of sausage. **Events** *Brighton Festival* (0273 676926) 3 weeks of cultural events, second only to the Edinburgh Festival, first three weeks in May; *London to Brighton Bike Ride* June; *London to Brighton Veteran Car Run,* first Sunday in Nov. Also see *The Punter*, a listings magazine available in many shops and pubs. Marine Parade contains Brighton's trendiest **clubs**, the *Escape* and the *Zap*. **If you want to stay** Brighton has long had a reputation as a Mecca for dirty weekenders, and every other house seems to be a hotel or bed and breakfast. *The Adelaide* (0273 205286) is old, four-star and mid-priced; the *Hotel Brunswick* (0273 733326) enables you to enjoy a (pretty dilapidated) Regency building for the same price; the *Norfolk* (0273 738201) is in the expensive range; the no-less-comfortable *Marina House* (0273 605349) offers bed and breakfast from around £15; the *Oak Hotel* (0273 220033) is art deco and trendy (approx £30).

Tourist Information Centres

Room 20, Bartholomew Square, Brighton, East Sussex (0273 323755). **Open** *Easter-May* 9am-5pm Mon-Fri; 9am-6pm Sat; 10am-6pm Sun. *June, Sept* 9am-6pm Mon-Sat; 10am-6pm Sun. *July, Aug* 9am-6.30pm Mon-Fri; 9am-6pm Sat; 10am-6pm Sun. *Oct-Easter* 9am-5pm Mon-Sat; 10am-4pm Sun.

Town Hall, Church Road (0273 778087) and King Alfred Leisure Centre (0273 746100). Open Easter-Sept 9am-5pm daily; Oct-Easter 9am-5pm Mon-Fri.

Cambridge

The university town of Cambridge takes its name from the Romans who bridged the river Cam and built the first proper settlement, Camboritum, as an inland port. The town became a thriving market centre and in the thirteenth century, just as colleges were springing up all over Europe, learned men and students founded the first teaching institutions here. Cambridge is now famous for its **university**, and it's the colleges which make the town worth visiting. The grounds of these magnificent colleges are generally open to the public and they are empty of students in summer.

The oldest and most attractive colleges are all near the centre: **Trinity**, where Byron used to bathe naked in the courtyard fountain, is the largest and richest; second biggest is **St John's**, with its pseudo-Venetian enclosed Bridge of Sighs; **Emmanuel** has a Wren chapel. Others worth seeing are **Queens'** and **Jesus**; most awe-inspiring of all is **King's College Chapel**, one of the world's Gothic masterpieces, where Rubens' *Adoration of the Magi* (1639) adorns the altar. The best way to see the colleges is to do 'The Backs'; that is, meander along the serene lawns and riverside walks that run behind the colleges. Alternatively, hire a punt and mess around on the Cam for an hour or two – if you're worried about getting your pole stuck in the riverbed, chauffeured punts are available. But if you want to blend in with the locals, rent a bicycle from Mike's Bikes, 28 Mill Road.

The town centres on the ancient streets round Market Square. The thing to buy here is books of course – there are scores of new and second-hand bookshops, stocking everything from the latest bestseller to the most obscure of tomes. **Museums** include the **Fitzwilliam**, Trumpington Street, for classical antiquities and old masters including da Vinci and Michelangelo; the **Folk Museum**, Castle Street, for local history; **Kettle's Yard**, Castle Street, holds a wonderful collection of modern art in the former home of an art curator.

Further Information

Getting there *by train* from Liverpool Street or King's Cross, 75 minutes; *by bus* National Express from Victoria, 2 hours; *by car* on M11, exit 11, 1 hour; *local buses* Cambus (0223 423554).

Eating and drinking tea can be taken at *Fitzbillies*, 52 Trumpington Street. For posher food try *Midsummer House*, Midsummer Common (0223 69299) which has excellent (and expensive) British cuisine; or the *Blue Boar*, Trinity Street (0223 359590), for simpler, lower-priced lunches. More interesting is *Castle Tandoori* Castle Street (0223 312569), which serves good Indian

food. *The Old Spring* pub, Ferry Path off Chesterton Road, serves superb traditional homemade pies for lunch; local colour – drunken students – can be found at the *Baron of Beef*, Bridge Street during term time. *The Free Press*, Prospect Row, is run by an ex-rower, is registered as a boat club and is frequented by raucous boat crews; the *Fort St George*, Midsummer Common, is a part-Tudor pub on the riverside.

Events *May Week* two weeks of boat races, balls and open-air theatre, first two weeks in June; *Footlights Revue* future-famous entertainers make their debut, during May Week, though standards have plummeted since the Monty Python era; *Cambridge Folk Festival* last weekend in July; *Beer Festival* no fixed date.

If you want to stay try the moderately priced *Warkworth Guest House* (0223 63682); or *St Mark's Vicarage* (0223 63339). You'll need a bike or other transport if you decide on the *Old Rectory* at Swaffham Bulbeck (0223 811986), 6 miles (9km) from the city centre; for down-home bed and breakfast, try *Mrs Hatley,* Manor Farm, Landbeach (0223 860165); if you prefer a real hotel try the *University Arms*, Regent Street (0223 351241).

Tourist Information Centre

Wheeler Street, Cambridge, Cambridgeshire (0223 322640). Open Nov-Mar 9am-5.30pm Mon-Fri; 9am-5pm Sat. *Oct* 9am-6pm Mon, Tue, Thur, Fri; 9.30am-6pm Wed. *Easter-Sept* 9am-6pm Mon, Tue, Thur, Fri; 9.30am-6pm Wed; 10.30am-3.30pm Sun, Bank Holidays.

Canterbury

Long stretches of the **medieval walls** survive in Canterbury, one of Britain's oldest centres of habitation. It became the cradle of English Christianity: a new **Canterbury Cathedral** was built shortly after the Norman Conquest. Today it's the Mother Church of Anglicans worldwide, and has magnificent stained glass and a fascinating crypt.

The city centre is pretty, but very crowded and not notable for specialised shopping; it's much more interesting to go sightseeing. **Eastbridge (St Thomas's) Hospital**, High Street, dates from the twelfth century and contains a medieval mural, sundry treasures and a crypt; there's the remains of a Roman town house and mosaic floor at **Roman Pavement**, Butchery Lane; and the **Royal Museum, The Beaney**, High Street, covers the history of the area. **King's School** is where Elizabethan playwright Christopher Marlowe, author of *Dr Faustus*, was educated. **Canterbury Heritage**, at the medieval Poor Priest's Hospital, entails a walk through the city's past; **Canterbury Pilgrim's Way**, St Margaret's Street, is an animated interpretation of Chaucer's *Canterbury Tales*, recreating fourteenth-century sounds and smells; **St Augustine's Abbey** is an important ecclesiastical site, but there's little left to see. Horse-drawn carriage rides tour the city for the lazy or fat of wallet.

The only remaining gate, West Gate, now houses the **Museum of Arms and Armour**. Ancient houses overhang the lanes leading to Christ

The cathedral at **Canterbury**, *scene of a medieval murder. See* **review**.

Church Gate, the **cathedral**'s main entrance. A
plaque before the altar commemorates
Archbishop Thomas-à-Becket's murder at that
spot in 1170 by four over-zealous knights who'd
heard Henry II moaning, 'Will no-one rid me of
this turbulent priest?' Thomas's tomb has been a
site of pilgrimage ever since. **Trinity Chapel** contains the site of the original shrine, plus the tombs
of Henry IV and the Black Prince.

Further Information

Getting there *by train* from Victoria, 1 hour 20
minutes; *by bus* National Express from Victoria, 2
hours; *by car* on A2 direct, or on M2 to exit 7 then A2;
local buses East Kent Bus Co (0227 472082/information
0843 581333).
Eating and drinking *Tuo e Mio*, The Borough (0227
761471), is expensive, but its speciality pasta is worth
paying for. Try also *George's Brasserie* which is open all
day serving French-style food. *Café des Amis*, St
Dunstan Street, is a strangely named but good
Mexican restaurant. *Fungus Mungus*, St Peter Street, is
the only vegetarian restaurant in town. **Pubs** include
the fifteenth-century *Falstaff*, West Gate, very English
with good food; the traditional *Three Tuns*, Watling
Street; the *Seven Stars*, Orange Street, or the student-
packed *Simple Simon*, St Radigun Street.
Events *Chaucer Heritage Pilgrimage* one-week trek
from London, including costume cavalcades en route,
three-four weeks at Easter; *Chaucer Festival* April;
Canterbury Festival, three weeks of cultural events,
first three weeks of Oct. *Beer Festival* July. *The Penny
Theatre*, Northgate (0227 470512) is a lively new venue
for bands and occasionally theatre.
If you want to stay there's a good range of
moderately priced accommodation here: try *Pointers
Hotel* (0227 456846); the *Millers Arms Inn* (0227

456057) for a traditional beer and breakfast; or the
Thanington Hotel (0227 453227). A little cheaper are
the *London Guest House* (0227 765860) and in the
centre of town *The White House* (0227 761836). In the
expensive range is *The Pilgrim's Hotel* (0227 464531)
and the *County*, High Street (0227 766266).

Tourist Information Centre

*34 St Margaret's Street, Canterbury, Kent (0227
766567).* **Open** *summer* 9.30am-5.30pm daily; *winter*
9.30am-5pm daily.

Oxford

Oxford was established late in the Saxon period
as a fortified market town and flourished as a
centre of the wool trade (records of this period,
dating back to 1147, can be seen in the town
hall). At some indeterminate time in the twelfth
century it became a scholar's forum. By the end
of the century Oxford was firmly established as
the first university town in England. The city
grew up around the shrine of **St Frideswide**, a
royal nun. It centres on Carfax, where you can
ascend **Carfax Tower** for a commanding view
(Mar-Oct only); other rooftop vantage points are
St Mary the Virgin, High Street, and the roof
of Wren's neo-classical **Sheldonian Theatre**,
Broad Street. Browse around the immense
Blackwell's bookshop, Broad Street. **Alice's
Shop**, St Aldates, is where Alice bought barley-
sugar in *Through the Looking Glass*. Sadly, it now
sells Wonderland memorabilia. Park End Street,
near the train station, is home to two antiques

centres crammed with specialist dealers, **The Jam Factory** and the **Oxford Antique Trading Company**. The High Street contains most of the old-fashioned shops (Oxford Marmalade is a cheap souvenir) and the entrance to the **covered market** which contains classy butcher's shops, snack bars and plenty else.

Most visitors, however, head straight for the **colleges**; of the 30 or so, almost all are worth visiting (they are usually open to the public). **Christ Church** is the grandest, with its vast quad and chapel which doubles as Oxford's cathedral. **Magdalen** (pronounced Maudlin) is considered the most beautiful; **New College**, **Trinity**, and **Worcester** have lovely gardens. Other temples of knowledge are the **Ashmolean Museum**, Beaumont Street, Britain's oldest, featuring mainly art and archaeology; the **Bodleian Library**, stunning buildings containing one of the world's most important collections of books and ancient manuscripts, stacked along 81 miles (130km) of underground shelving; nearby, the domed **Radcliffe Camera**, an elegant circular reading room; the **Museum of Modern Art**, Pembroke Street; the fabulously Gothic **University Museum**, Parks Road, housing the University's natural history collections; and for the area's history, the **Museum of Oxford**, St Aldates. The University's history is recounted in **The Oxford Story**, Broad Street, a high-tech exhibition featuring a mini-train ride through 800 years of student life. Avoid the expensive bus tours and their superficial commentary blare – the town is much better visited on foot. During the summer, Oxford becomes overwhelmed by tourists; the undergraduate students return in October.

When you want to escape academia, stroll by the two rivers – the Cherwell (pronounced Charwell) and the Thames, known here as the Isis (from the Roman Thamesis). **Punts and rowing boats** can be hired from Folly Bridge, Magdalen Bridge and Cherwell Boathouse, off Bardwell Road. **Port Meadow** is a semi-wilderness mentioned in the *Domesday Book*, and the **university parks** are particularly peaceful.

Further Information

Getting there *by train* from Paddington, 1 hour; *by bus* Oxford Citylink (0865 711312) or Oxford Tube (0865 772250) from Grosvenor Gardens Victoria or Marble Arch, 1-2 hours; *by car* on M40, A40, A420 (or travel the pretty route via Windsor and Henley, A423). Use the park-and-ride off the A40 at the bottom of the Abingdon Road to avoid formidable parking problems; *local buses* Oxford Tube (0865 772250).

Eating and drinking *Browns*, Woodstock Road (0865 511995), serves reliable and generous meals at a reasonable price, and at the *Cherwell Boathouse*, Bardwell Road (0865 52746), you can sit near the riverbank and eat simple but delicious food. Raymond Blanc's internationally renowned *Le Manoir Aux Quat' Saisons* (0844 278881) is at nearby Great Milton – dinner

costs a fearsome £70 or so per person. The ancient *Turf Tavern*, Bath Place off Holywell Street, is Oxford's most distinctive **pub**; the *Bear*, Alfred Street, its oldest; the *Perch*, Binsey Lane, is a thatched riverside pub.

Events *Torpids* spring rowing races, Feb; *Eights Week* the great summer rowing races, end of May; *Encaenia* honorary degree awards, with procession, first Wed of Trinity term (May or June); *Oxford Regatta* Aug; *St Giles' Fair* old-fashioned two-day fun-fair, first Mon after 1 Sept.

If you want to stay the *Turf* has rooms which are best described as quaint. In the luxury class is the *Randolph*, Beaumont Street (0865 247481). *Oxford Moat House*, Godstow Road (0865 59933) is comfortable, while the *River*, Botley Road (0865 243475) is an efficient bed and breakfast. Outside the city, *Hill Farm* (08677 3944) offers bed and breakfast in more rural surroundings, and *Two Chimneys* (0865 739144) allows you to stay under a thatched roof.

Tourist Information Centre

St Aldates, Oxford, Oxfordshire (0865 726871). **Open** *May-Sept* 9.30am-5pm Mon-Sat; 10am-4pm Sun, Bank Holidays; *Oct-Apr* 9.30am-5pm Mon-Sat; 10am-4pm Sun, Bank Holidays. **Closed** Good Friday, Easter Sunday, Christmas and New Year.

Salisbury & Stonehenge

Legend has it that an arrow was fired randomly and **Salisbury Cathedral** was built where it fell. However, the thirteenth-century cathedral is carefully placed, soaring from a plain at the junction of five rivers. Its spire is the highest in Britain and its coffers contain the best preserved of the four surviving copies of the Magna Carta.

Most visitors come to Salisbury en route to Stonehenge, but the city is worth seeing in its own right. Because of its settled and prosperous history, Salisbury (officially called New Sarum) has a wealth of interesting architecture – medieval gabled houses and narrow alleys abound. Cathedral Close has the best buildings, including the **Bishop's Palace**, the Old Deanery and the Tudor **King's House**, where Richard III and James I both stayed. It now houses the local museum, which is strong on prehistoric remains. Also see superb **Mompesson House**, once a wealthy Georgian merchant's abode. There are more quaint streets round the market square (market days Tuesday and Saturday), dominated by **Poultry Cross**, a 600-year-old Gothic monstrosity.

Walk across the meadows to the River Avon and medieval Harnham Bridge; nearby is an old watermill. In the other direction, it's possible to follow the river to Old Sarum.

Stonehenge is 10 miles (16km) away, near Amesbury. It's the best British example of groups of ancient stone circles known as Druids' Circles. This is certainly one of the most remarkable works of prehistoric architecture in the world and it is estimated that it took a mind-blowing 30 million man-years to erect. The earliest stage of its construction dates back to 2800 BC, but whether it was used as a lunar calendar, a temple, an eclipse-predictor or an alien spacecraft hangar, is still a mystery and likely to remain so.

The site is now ringed by a perimeter fence, but you can still get a good view. Do not plan your visit to coincide with the summer solstice (21 June) unless you want to be branded a new-age traveller by the Wiltshire policemen who swarm around the area on the look-out for anyone attempting to stage a festival, or set foot on the site.

Buses to Stonehenge (route 3) run from Salisbury bus station, Endless Street, and are supposed to connect at the railway station with incoming London trains. Alternatively, go to Amesbury and get a 1, 5, 6 or 7 bus, or walk (check with the Information Centre for details). The site can be seen by car from the A303.

Further Information

Getting there *by train* from Waterloo, 1 hour 35 minutes; *by bus* National Express from Victoria, 2 hours 30 minutes; *by car* on M3, A303, A343, or A30; *local buses* Wilts & Dorset Bus Co (0722 336855). **Stonehenge** *(0980 623108).* **Open** *1 Apr-30 Sept* 10am-6pm daily; *winter* 10am-4pm daily. **Admission** £2.70; £1.30 under-16s; £2 OAPs, students, UB40s; group discounts.

Eating and drinking *Harpers*, Ox Row (0722 333118; no food Sun), is a restaurant which serves robust traditional fare and overlooks the vast market square. Also worth trying is *Crustaceans*, Ivy Street (0722 333948), which, as its name suggests, concentrates on seafood, or *Stoby's*, Fish Row, for grease-free fish 'n' chips. The *Haunch of Venison*, Minster Street, is the oldest of the city's 70 pubs, displaying a mummified hand clutching playing cards, that was found in 1905; the *King's Arms*, St John Street, is creakily Tudor; the *Red Lion*, Milford Street is a renovated coaching inn. Events *Salisbury Festival* arts, first two weeks Sept, includes a wine tasting festival; *Salisbury Charter Fair*, a fun-fair celebrating ancient servants' charter, mid-Oct; *From Darkness To Light* candle-lit Advent procession, late Nov.

If you want to stay *Stratford Lodge* is an inexpensive haven of peace (0722 325177). The *Rose & Crown*, Harnham Road (0722 327908) is more expensive, and sits in the shadow of the cathedral; in the same price range is the *White Hart*, St John Street (0722 327476). *Milford Hall,* Castle Street, (0722 417411) is good value. The *Red Lion*, Milford Street (0722 323334) is more basic.

Tourist Information Centre

Fish Row, Salisbury, Wiltshire (0722 334956). **Open** *Oct-Apr* 9.30am-5pm Mon-Sat; *May* 9.30am-5pm Mon-Sat; 11am-4pm Sun; *June, Sept* 9.30am-6pm Mon-Sat; 11am-4pm Sun; *July, Aug* 9.30am-7pm Mon-Sat; 11am-5pm Sun.

Stratford-upon-Avon

Make no mistake, you are now entering Shakespeare Country. It must be difficult being a resident of Stratford: Shakespeare's face beams down from every available surface, Saddam Hussein style, and the town is packed with Bard-lovers all year round. Yet despite the commer-cialisation, Stratford is still a very attractive place, and the sights are remarkably unspoilt.

There's been a settlement at Stratford-upon-Avon since the Bronze Age, and by William Shakespeare's time it was already an important market town. The main **Shakespeare** properties are: The **Birthplace Museum**, Henley Street; **Hall's Croft**, Old Town, where daughter Susanna lived; **New Place**, Chapel Street, the foundations of the Bard's last home (demolished in 1759 because the owner was fed up with visitors), set in an Elizabethan knot garden; **Mary Arden's House**, Wilmcote (three miles/5km away), the farmhouse where his mother grew up; and the picturesque **Anne Hathaway's Cottage** at Shottery, a mile (1.6km) away, his wife's lovely thatched home before she was married. The late medieval **Grammar School** where the Bard studied is still standing, as is riverside **Holy Trinity Church** where he and his family are buried.

Most sights can be 'done' by trooping along the **Town Heritage Trail**. Down on Waterside, 25 gaudy minutes can be spent experiencing **The World of Shakespeare** in a music-and-lights Elizabethan-England spectacular. To experience the real Shakespeare (ie a play), you'll need to book well in advance at any of Stratford's three theatres – the modern **Royal Shakespeare Theatre**, the smaller Jacobean-style **Swan Theatre** or **The Other Place** (booking information on 0789 295623; tickets £4.50-£39.50, no performances Feb, Mar). The Royal Shakespeare Company stages classics and modern works at the Swan and The Other Place; it produces nothing but Shakespeare at the Royal Shakespeare Theatre. If all seats are sold, try for returns or standing-room tickets, or console yourself with a backstage **theatre tour** and an inspection of the **RSC Collection** of props and costumes.

There's a walk along the **River Avon** from scenic Stratford Canal Basin, and **boat trips** are run in summer. Friday is Stratford's market day (held at the junction of Windsor and Wood Streets). **Guide Friday** (0789 294466) runs open-topped bus tours, and trips to nearby **Warwick Castle**, which is considered England's finest medieval castle (it can also be reached by buses 518 and X16).

Further Information

Getting there *by train* from Paddington, change at Leamington Spa, 2 hours; *by bus* National Express from Victoria, or late-night returns with *Guide Friday* from Euston, 2 hours 10 minutes, and *RSC Shuttle* (071 379 1564) from Russell Square, Park Lane, Victoria, Cromwell Road, approx 2 hours; *by car* M40 to junction 15, then A46; *local buses* Midland Red South Busline (0788 535555).

Eating and drinking The *River Terrace* sells light refreshments all day; *Shepherd's*, Sheep Street (0789

268233), is probably the best bet for good English food although it's pricey. *Sir Toby's*, Church Street, serves healthy café food, and *Giovanni's*, Ely Street (0789 297999), is a pretty good Italian place. The riverside **pub** the *Black Swan*, known locally as the Dirty Duck, is popular with actors; other theatrical hang-outs are the *Garrick*, High Street, and the *White Swan*, Rother Street, where William himself probably drank.

Events *Canals Celebration* March; *Shakespeare's Birthday Celebrations* closest Saturday to 23 April; *Stratford Regatta and Raft Race* June; *Stratford-upon-Avon Festival* July; *Mop Fair* mid-Oct, traditionally the venue for farm-hands looking for work for the coming year; *Runaway Fair* second Friday after Mop Fair, was for those labourers who, unhappy with their choice of master at the Mop Fair, had run away to choose another; *Shakespeare Run* vintage cars, Sept.

If you want to stay *Charlecote Pheasant Hotel* (0789 470333) is a converted eighteenth-century farmhouse, 4 miles (6.4km) from the town. For something more central, try the *White Swan Hotel*, Rother Street (0789 297022). Bed and breakfasts abound: you'll get a good breakfast at *Newlands*, 7 Broad Walk (0789 298449), and plenty of attention at the one-bedroom B&B at 211 Evesham Road (0789 299659). Alternatively, walk out of town along the B&B-lined Grove Road until you find a vacancy.

Tourist Information Centre

Bridgefoot, Stratford-upon-Avon, Warwickshire (0789 293127). **Open** Apr-Oct 9am-5.30pm Mon-Sat; 2-5pm Sun. Nov-Mar 10.30am-4.30pm Mon-Sat (opening hours under review).

Windsor

Windsor has been the home of royalty since medieval times. Edward the Confessor was a resident in the mid-eleventh century but it was William the Conqueror who first realised the military importance of this hill-side town overlooking the Thames. Four years after the Battle of Hastings, he had a fortress constructed here. **Windsor Castle** received substantial alterations during the reigns of subsequent monarchs, but it is still a royal home. The **State Apartments** have now reopened following the fire at the end of 1992 (Her Majesty's *annus horribilis*) and can be visited when the Windsors are out – the Queen's personal standard is flown if she is at home. Not to be missed is the finest dolls' house in the world, designed by the architect Edwin Lutyens for Queen Mary, wife of George V, and built over three years by 1,500 craftsmen. Take a very close look at the books and the paintings. Even the toilets flush.

The Perpendicular Gothic **St George's Chapel** is where Henry VIII is buried. There are other royal tombs – as well as the most beautiful roof you are likely to see. Evensong here is splendid, too. And if you missed the **Changing of the Guard** in London, you might want to catch it here at 10.25am every morning.

On sunny summer days Windsor gets packed with tourists, but you can always take a stroll by the river if the crowds get too much. **Eton College** lies near the Thames. Its buildings, some dating from the fifteenth century, are open in the afternoons. Schoolboys still wear tailcoats here.

Other attractions include walks in Windsor Great Park, or by the Thames to Runnymede or Cliveden House. And you can even see Queen Victoria arriving in Windsor for her Diamond Jubilee at the local branch of **Madame Tussaud's** in Windsor and Eton Central Railway Station (where the time is always 11.32am on 19 June 1897, the exact time of Victoria's arrival).

If you get fed up with all the royal lions, you can see the real thing at **Windsor Safari Park** (0753 869841), about two miles (3km) from the town centre; whales, exotic birds, monkeys and llamas also share the space.

Further Information

Getting there *by train* from Paddington to Windsor & Eton Central, change at Slough, 35 minutes, or from Waterloo to Windsor & Eton Riverside, 50 minutes; *by bus* Green Line 1 hour; *by car* M25, exit 13, then A308; *local buses* Beeline Buses (0344 424938).

Eating and drinking the *Dôme*, Thames Street, is a French bistro serving meals, snacks and drinks all day; the *Adam & Eve* **pub**, also on Thames Street, serves good pub lunches.

Events *Windsor Festival* late Sept/early Oct.

If you want to stay the *Harte & Garter*, facing the castle (0753 863426), is central, if expensive; a more moderately priced option is the *Clarence Hotel* (0753 864436) or for something cheaper and more homely try *Mrs Pliszka* at 64 Bolton Road (0753 860789) who runs one of the many bed and breakfasts in the town.

Tourist Information Centre

Windsor & Eton Central Station, Windsor (0753 852010). **Open** May-Sept 9.30am-6pm Mon-Sat; 10.30am-5pm Sun. Oct-Apr 9.30am-5.30pm Mon-Sat; 11am-4pm Sun.

York

York is unique among British cities in still having its entire **medieval walls** intact. The best way to see the city is to trudge along the high walls (hair-raising on a windy day as there are few railings). There are four interesting 'bars' (gates): **Monk**, **Bootham**, **Walmgate** and **Micklegate**, where traitors' heads were once impaled.

The Romans first formed a base here, then the Vikings moved in and developed Jorvik, as they called it, into a major trading centre. Most street names end in 'gate' – the Viking word for road. A re-creation of Viking life at a genuine underground archaeological site can be seen at the **Jorvic Viking Centre**, Coppergate. It's a marvellous sensory experience (latrine included), but the queues are long (up to four hours in peak season), it's expensive and it's over far too quickly.

If you're keen to keep away from the hurly-burly, you'd better take only a quick peek at **The Shambles**, a tiny street of overhanging half-timbered houses which made up the old butchers' quarter.

For peace, head for **York Minster**, seat of the Archbishop of York, and the largest Gothic cathedral in northern Europe. In 1984, it was struck by lightning, and the roof of the south transept caught fire. This happened shortly after the then Bishop of Durham, of the Archdiocese of York, had shocked many clerics by publicly casting doubts on the reality of biblical miracles. Divine wrath or just plain meteorological misfortune? The perfectly restored roof and gleaming stonework has probably not looked this good for centuries. The Minster's greatest glory is its stained glass, second only to that found in Chartres Cathedral, France. The Great East Window is the size of a tennis court and contains the world's largest piece of medieval stained glass in a single window. The old area round the Minster has a genuine serenity, especially at dusk.

Other interesting areas of York are medieval **Stonegate**, full of designer gift shops but still quaint; **Lady's Row**, Goodramgate, with some of York's oldest houses; narrow, crooked **High** and **Low Petergate**, full of interesting shops and restaurants; **Foss Street** with its antiques and book shops; and Micklegate, predominantly Georgian, with quirky collectors' shops. York's range of museums is impressive. The **National Railway Museum**, Leeman Road, houses the largest display of trains in the world and won a Museum of the Year award in 1991. Exhibits include models of Stephenson's Rocket and of the Transmanche Super Train soon to be gliding through the Channel Tunnel. The **ARC**, St Saviourgate, introduces ancient and high-tech archaeology in the setting of a beautifully restored Norman church. **York Castle Museum**, off Tower Street, is a real one-off. Housed in an eighteenth-century prison, it details everyday life over the past 400 years – there's a street full of nineteenth-century shops, and you can escape the tourism by watching the vintage comedy show *Hancock's Half Hour* on a 1950s television set.

Further Information

Getting there *by train* from King's Cross, 2 hours; *by car* M1 to Leeds then A64, or take the slower A1 or A1(M) past Leeds, then the A64. *Local buses* York City and District Bus Co (0904 624161).
Eating and drinking for snacks or lunch, try *Jane's Place*, York Arts Centre, Micklegate; *Bootham Bistro*, Bootham, big and friendly; *St Williams Restaurant*, College Street, right beneath the Minster. The *Bonding Restaurant*, Skeldergate Bridge, a warehouse by the river serves good English food. *Thomas Gent's*, off Stonegate, recreates an eighteenth-century coffee house with refreshments derived from original recipes. For dinner try *Lew's Place*, King's Staith (0904 628167),

a busy English bistro on the river-front; *Kites*, Grape Lane (0904 641750), unusual and traditional dishes. In the upper bracket are *The Judges Lodging*, Lendal (0904 638733), an historic building where expensive candle-lit dinners are served (you can get cheaper bar food in its eighteenth-century wine cellars); and the renowned *Middlethorpe Hall*, Bishopthorpe Road (0904 641241), serves modern cuisine in a grand 1699 mansion. The *Black Swan* **pub**, Peasholme Green, is a Tudor landmark; *Ye Olde Starre Inne*, Stonegate, is olde indeed, with good grub; the ancient *King's Arms*, King's Staithe, gets flooded sometimes and is the place to steady the nerves with a pint of Theakston's before stepping out on a ghost walk of old York, 8pm nightly; the *York Arms*, High Petergate, is liked by the gay fraternity.
Entertainment for forthcoming events see the *Yorkshire Post*, daily except Sun, and *York: What's On*, a free weekly guide.
Where to stay there are plenty of hotels in York, especially along the main roads leading away from the city gates, outside the walls – Bootham, Marygate, Fishergate and Tadcaster Road. The following are a selection: **budget** *Youth Hotel*, Bishophill Senior (0904 625904); **cheap** *Abcombe Road Guest House*, Abcombe Road, (0904 792321) and *River View Hotel*, Marlborough Grove (0904 626826); central; **medium** *Freshneys Hotel*, Lower Petergate (0904 622478) and *Bootham Bar Hotel*, High Petergate (0904 658516), both lovely houses; **expensive** *Mount Royale Hotel*, The Mount (0904 628856) and *The Judges Lodgings*, Lendal (0904 638733).
Events *Jorvik Viking Festival* battles and longship racing, Feb; *York Early Music Festival* last half July; *York Races* Ebor Handicap, Aug.

Tourist Information Centre

De Grey Rooms, Exhibition Square, York, North Yorkshire (0904 621756). **Open** *June-Sept* 9am-7pm Mon-Sat; hours vary Sun, phone to check. *Oct-May* 9am-5pm Mon-Sat.

Country

Taking in the great British countryside need not involve a week's expedition to the back of beyond. Pastoral scenes of timeless beauty lie in easy striking distance of the capital. However, picturesque villages within commuting distance of London are these days more likely to be filled with computer analysts and management consultants than cow-rearing yokels.

A useful companion on a bucolic foray is the *Good Beer Guide* (published by the Campaign for Real Ale and available at good bookshops, £8.99), which has details of local pubs and breweries around the country. Below we list those attractive rural spots that don't require a map and compass to be reached.

Cotswolds

Most places in Britain have at least one or two historic buildings dating back to Tudor times or even earlier, but in the Cotswolds you'll find whole towns and villages full of Tudor and Jacobean architecture. The buildings are constructed from honey-coloured Cotswold stone, which has been quarried in Gloucestershire and Oxfordshire for centuries. There are public gardens at Kiftsgate Court, near the beautiful wool town of **Chipping Campden**, and at nearby Hidcote Manor, where Major Lawrence Johnston created one of the finest gardens in Britain. For a walk on the wild side, amble about the woodlands of the Rococo Garden at Painswick, a recently restored six-acre (2.4 hectare) eighteenth-century affair. Also not to be missed is Barnsley House, a few miles north of **Cirencester**, with a garden restored by the writer Rosemary Verey.

The Cotswolds are extremely popular with tourists as they abound with beautiful villages, but the twin attractions of **Upper** and **Lower Slaughter** take some beating in the picture-postcard league. The two villages, divided by the river Eye, do not take their name from being a scene of medieval carnage – 'slohtre' is an old Anglo-Saxon word meaning 'muddy place'. Upper Slaughter is almost the village the twentieth century forgot – the last house to be built here was in 1904. But most of the stone dwellings pre-date this by at least 150 years.

Other places to be seen include the bustling **Broadway** with its twelfth-century church and sixteenth-century houses; **Stow-on-the-Wold**, surrounded by little Cotswold villages and with a fine market place and ancient grammar school; **Bourton**, which really is **on-the-Water** as the River Windrush winds through its main street. **Moreton in the Marsh** has yet more attractive buildings. The region is crammed with antiques shops, but don't expect any bargains.

Take the children to the Cotswold Wild Life Park at **Burford**, or the National Birds of Prey Centre at **Newent**, and visit **Blenheim Palace** (*see below* **Country Houses**); and Sudeley Castle, **Winchcombe**, where Henry VIII's last wife Catherine Parr is buried. On the edges of the Cotswolds are the cities of **Gloucester**, where you can visit the cathedral and Roman ruins, and **Cheltenham**, an immaculate Regency town with a famous race-course.

Further Information

Getting there *by train* from Paddington to Moreton in the Marsh, Cheltenham or Evesham; *local bus* Pulham's (0451 820369), based in Bourton-on-the-Water, but operating all over the Cotswolds and linking up with railway services at Moreton in the Marsh and town buses in Cheltenham. To tour this area properly you need a car, which can be hired in London or Oxford (*see chapter* **Getting Around**). Better still, hire a bike from Crabtrees, 50 Winchcombe Street, Cheltenham (0242 515291).
Eating and drinking *The White Hart*, High Street, Moreton in the Marsh (0608 650731), serves English cuisine at reasonable prices; in Broadway's High Street is *Hunters' Lodge* (0386 853247), a restaurant with a personal touch and quality cooking (closed Sunday evenings and all Monday). Nearly every village has a gem of a *pub*; in Bretforton near Evesham, try the *Fleece Inn*, which is owned by the National Trust.

Events *Cheltenham Gold Cup* three-day race meeting, mid-March; *Cheese rolling*, an ancient, occasionally violent ritual where locals hurtle down a hill after a wooden 'cheese', Stroud, early April; *Dover Games* strange sports including shin-kicking, late May/early June; *Cheltenham International Music Festival* classical music, first half of July.
If you want to stay and are feeling extremely flush, then the 400-year-old coaching inn *The Lygon Arms* (0386 852255) at Broadway may be a pleasant surprise; bed and breakfast at *The Orchard* (0386 852534) is a lot cheaper, and only just down the road; the Georgian *Old Rectory* (0386 853729), also at Broadway, is the sort of place where you forget you're in a hotel. *New Farm* (0608 50782), at Dorn near Moreton-in-the-Marsh, is a bed-and-breakfast worthy of mention.

Tourist Information Centres

Woolstaplers Hall High Street, Chipping Campden (0386 840289) **Open** *Easter-Oct* 11am-6pm daily.
Hollis House, The Square, Stow-on-the-Wold (0451 831082). **Open** *Apr-Oct* 10am-5.30pm Mon-Sat; *Nov-Mar* 9.30am-4.30pm Mon-Sat.
77 Promenade, Cheltenham (0242 522878). **Open** *May-Sept* 9.30am-6pm Mon-Fri; 9.30am-5pm Sat; 10am-4pm Sun. *Oct-April* 9.30am=5pm Mon-Sat.
The Almonry Museum, Vine Street, Merstow Green, Evesham (0386 446944). **Open** 10am-5pm Mon-Sat; 2-5pm Sun (*Aug* 10am-5pm Sun).

Seaside

While **Brighton** *(see above* **Town***)* is the most obvious seaside destination for Londoners, its pebbly beach is about as appealing to lie on as a bed of nails. For sandy shores within striking range of the capital, you need to head east to **Margate** on Kent's tacky Leisure Coast with its golden mile of occasionally sun-kissed beaches. Like so many east-coast towns, Margate has yet to shrug off its ambience of past glories, of days when the British flocked to what was considered the Blackpool of the south, prior to the take-off of the chartered jet and the package tour. Nowadays, many of the guest houses are boarded up or given over to the homeless, but there are plenty of attractions to keep you from having to swim in the chilled waters, notably the **Dreamland Theme Park** on the seafront.

Nearby **Broadstairs** takes you back still further in time to the nineteenth century when it was a favoured watering place of Charles Dickens. This quiet, attractive resort was where he wrote most of *David Copperfield*, atop the cliffs at **Bleak House**, which is now open to the public and filled with his letters, belongings and other memorabilia. The **Dickens House Museum** is also open to the public.

The neighbouring harbour town of **Ramsgate** has a decent beach and a bustling marina. But there's not much to do here, apart from taking a day-trip to the French port of Dunkirk.

Further Information

Getting there *by train* from Victoria, to Margate, 1 hour 40 minutes; *by car* M2, A299, two hours.

Day trips to the beach

Even if splashing about in the chilly waters off the south coast doesn't sound like your cup of tea, there are plenty of good beaches waiting within easy reach of London for those that do feel an urge to take the plunge. They're ideal for hardy bathers and some might even tempt inveterate landlubbers. Below we list some that are less polluted than many and that offer alternatives for when the weather proves unkind.

Bexhill-on-Sea

Getting there *by train* from Victoria, to Bexhill, 1 hour 30 minutes. *by car* A21 to Hastings, then A27 to Bexhill.

Two miles (3km) of pebbles (good for avoiding sand between the toes) and a ban on dogs from May to September make Bexhill a popular town resort for Londoners. Expect crowds in the summer. The amazing De La Warr Pavilion was built in 1935 overlooking the beach and has a restaurant, theatre and bar.

Botany Bay

Getting there *by train* from Victoria, to Margate, 1 hour 40 minutes, then bus to Cliftonville. *by car* M2 then A299 to Margate.

Chalk cliffs provide shelter from the wind on this secluded sandy beach near **Margate** (*see above*). A steep slope leads down to the sea from the cliff-tops. When the pleasures of bathing pall, take a walk along the cliffs to the Captain Digby pub overlooking Kingsgate Bay.

Camber Sands

Getting there *by train* from Victoria, to Rye, 1 hour 20 minutes; *by car* A21 to Hastings, then A259 to Rye. Miles of sandy beach, popular with holiday campers, make this a busy but typical British bathing spot. Buckets and spades, knotted handkerchief hats and rolled-up trousers are much in evidence. There's a café on the beach, and nearby Battle Abbey and Winchelsea are both worth exploring.

Cuckmere Haven

Getting there *by train* from Victoria, to Brighton, 1 hour, then bus to Eastbourne. *by car* M23 to Brighton, then coast road via Seaford to Eastbourne. One of the cleanest beaches on the South Coast, Cuckmere Haven is quite a walk away from the main road (though it's an enjoyable stroll alongside the River Cuckmere). The beach is shingle, and usually quiet. There's a Country Park Interpretative Centre, and food available at the Golden Galleon pub on the main road.

Dungeness

Getting there *by train* from Charing Cross, to Folkestone, 1 hour 40 minutes, then bus to Hythe, then local steam train (running Apr-Oct only, 0679 62353) to Dungeness; *by car* M20 to Folkestone, then A259 to New Romney and Dungeness.

Although it's not perfect for swimming, the largest shingle spit in Europe is worth the trek for its strange atmosphere. Is it the dilapidated fishing huts, the old lighthouse, the mile upon mile of shingle and scrub or the imposing nuclear power station that make up the peculiar charm of the place? The miniature-steam-train ride along the coast from Hythe never fails to delight children.

Eating and drinking Broadstairs has a couple of good, medium-priced restaurants in *Riviera* (0843 861223), a popular Italian on the High Street, and *Mad Chef's Bistro* (0843 869304) on the harbour. In Margate try *Chives* (0843 223223) in Marine Gardens and in Ramsgate *Melodys* (0843 595400) on King Street. Both serve a mix of continental dishes. Alternatively, pick up fish 'n' chips or jellied eels all over town. *The Happy Dolphin* pub (0843 296473) on Margate seafront (near the station) is a lively spot. In Broadstairs sample the quieter *Tartar Frigate* (0843 862013) on the harbour. **Events** Broadstairs Dickens Festival June; *Margate Carnival* second week Aug; *Broadstairs Folk Week* second week Aug; *Ramsgate Carnival* late Aug. Check the *Isle of Thanet Gazette* for further festivities.
If you want to stay *The Belview Guest House* (0843 293569) on Union Crescent, Margate is better than most. In Ramsgate, *Belvedere Guest House* (0843 588809), 26 Augusta Road, is near the centre. The *Bay Tree* (0843 862502) on Broadstairs' Eastern Esplanade is comfortable and will set you back £20 a head.

Tourist Information Centres

Margate *22 High Street, Margate (0843 220241).* **Open** *Jul, Aug* 9am-6pm Mon-Sat; 10am-4pm Sun. *Sept-Jun* 9am-5pm Mon-Sat.
Broadstairs *6 High Street, Broadstairs (0843 862242).* **Open** 10am-4pm Mon-Fri, Sun; 10am-5pm Sat.
Ramsgate *The Argyle Centre, Queen Street, Ramsgate (0843 591086).* **Open** *Sept-May* 9.30am-2pm, 2.50pm-5pm, Mon-Fri; 9.30am-5pm Sat. *Jun-Aug* 9.30am-2pm, 2.50pm-5pm, Mon-Fri; 9.30am-5pm Sat; 10am-4pm Sun.

Country Houses

England is replete with stately homes, where its ruling classes carried out their huntin', shootin', fishin' and frolicin' over the generations. Thanks to a few small doses of socialism over the past 60 years ('and the appalling cost of servants these days, my dear'), scores of these families now open their mansions to the public in order to raise cash to run the draughty places. Still more have given over their ancestral homes to the National Trust (36 Queen Anne's Gate, SW1, 071 222 9251; *London Information Centre* Blewcoat School, 23 Caxton Street, SW1). The Trust publishes a guide to the houses in its care, the *Historic Houses Handbook* (available from bookshops, priced £4.50). Below we list some of the best ancestral piles within easy striking distance of London.

Leeds Castle is the nearest England comes to a French chateau. Built by the Normans nearly 900 years ago, the castle straddles two small islands in the midst of a lake, surrounded by 500 acres (200 hectares) of trees and parkland. Take in the medieval furnishings, paintings, tapestries and, bizarrely, the world's finest (and presumably only) collection of antique dog collars, before crashing out in the grounds with a picnic and a loved one, to truly appreciate the romance of the setting.

South of London, standing on an escarpment of the North Downs near Westerham, is **Chartwell**, the home of Sir Winston Churchill until his death in 1965. Apart from the political memorabilia, there are spectacular views over the Weald of Kent, a terraced garden, and a wall built by Churchill. The fruits of his dabblings in oils can also be seen in the drawing room.

Blenheim Palace, the largest private home in England, also has Churchillian connections: the great leader was born here, in a closet in the middle of a party. The Palace was built between 1705 and 1722, a reward from Queen Anne to Winston's ancestor, John Churchill, Duke of Marlborough, for his great victory over Louis XIV at the Battle of Blenheim. Annual rent on the property was, and still is, one French flag payable to the Crown. The baroque Palace is set in 2,100 acres (850 hectares) of parkland, landscaped by 'Capability' Brown, and is noted for its Long Library and gilded state rooms. The village of Woodstock, a short walk from Blenheim, is ideal for a post-tourism drink. Try **The Bear**.

Ightam Mote is a medieval moated manor house belonging to the National Trust. The secluded setting makes it a peaceful place; check out the Fountain Garden or head off for a romantic walk in the woods. Nearby you'll find **Knole**, one of the finest Elizabethan country houses in the land. Its 52 staircases and 365 rooms are laden with rare seventeenth-century furniture and paintings. Outside you'll find an eighteenth-century walled garden, follies and a 1,000-acre (405-hectare) park where fallow and Japanese deer roam. **Hever Castle** is another Elizabethan house, famous for its connections with the ill-fated Anne Boleyn, wife of Henry VIII for 1,000 days before she lost her head in the Tower of London. Such grim associations have been considerably alleviated since the Astor family transformed the grounds with beautiful Italian gardens, a huge lake and an impressive rockery early this century. There's also an excellent maze in which to lose yourself, with at least a quarter of a mile (400 metres) of paths twisting between thick yew hedge.

CRUMBLING CASTLES

Further afield, an altogether different edifice worth a visit is **Bodiam Castle**. Children love exploring this ruined medieval castle with its turreted towers, thick walls, moat and drawbridge. In the same area you'll find **Bateman's**, which was the home of Rudyard Kipling from 1902 until his death in 1936. It was left to the nation by his widow and is hugely evocative of the great, imperial writer. The house dates from 1634 and has glorious gardens and Rudyard's Rolls, parked in the garage. Even so, there are very few gardens to compare to those at **Sissinghurst Castle and Gardens**, the home of those bastions of the Bloomsbury Set, Vita Sackville-West and Harold Nicholson. They bought the ruined sixteenth-century mansion in 1930 and transformed it into one of the loveliest places in Britain. The house is much as they left it; the gardens (Vita's pride and joy) are inspirational. The place is thick with visitors, so it's best to go early on a wet Monday morning.

North and west of London, there are several great houses which can easily be visited in a day. **Cliveden** is a flamboyant Italianate monument to early Victorian complacency in a spectacular setting high above the Thames at Taplow. Although now chiefly a hotel, three of the rooms and the extensive gardens are open to the public, and there's a sophisticated but expensive restaurant.

A genuine oddity of English architecture can be seen at **Waddesdon Manor** in Buckinghamshire where Baron de Rothschild gave extravagant expression to his love for eighteenth-century French art. This huge pastiche chateau overlooking the Vale of Evesham now houses much of his collection. Tucked away amid the landscaped gardens there's an extraordinary Victorian aviary.

Bateman's: *Rudyard Kipling's Empire building. See* **review**.

Bateman's
Burwash, Sussex (0435 882302). **Getting there** *by train* from Charing Cross, to Etchingham, 1 hour 30 minutes, then bus via Burwash; *by car* A21, then A265 to Burwash. **Open** *Apr-Oct* 11am-5pm Mon-Wed, Sat, Sun. **Admission** £3.50; £1.80 under-15s. **No credit cards.**

Blenheim Palace
Blenheim Palace, Woodstock, Oxfordshire (0993 811091). **Getting there** best combined with a visit to **Oxford** (*see above* **Town**) which is eight miles (13km) to the south by bus. **Open** *palace Mar-Oct* 10.30am-5.30pm daily; *park year round* 9am-5pm daily. **Admission** £6.50; £4.80 OAPs, students; £3 under-15s.

Bodiam
Bodiam, Robertsbridge, Sussex (0580 83436). **Getting there** *by train* from Charing Cross, to Robertsbridge, then bus to Hurst Green; *by car* A21 to Hurst Green. **Open** *Apr-Oct* 10am-5.30pm daily; *Nov-Mar* 10am-dusk Tue-Sun. **Admission** £2.50; £1.30 under-15s. **No credit cards.**

Chartwell
Westerham, Kent (0732 866368) **Getting there** *by train* from Charing Cross, to Sevenoaks, then bus 320 to Westerham; *by car* A233, or M25 junction 5, then A25. **Open** *Apr-Oct* noon-5pm Tue-Thur; 11am-5pm Sat, Sun. **Admission** *House and garden* £4.50; £2.30 under-15s; *garden only* £2; £1 under-15s. **No credit cards.**

Cliveden
Taplow, Maidenhead, Berkshire (0628 605069). **Getting there** *by train* from Paddington, to Burnham, 30 minutes; *by car* M4 to exit 7, then A4 to Maidenhead, Burnham. **Open** *gardens Mar-Sept* 11am-6pm daily; *Oct-Dec* 11am-4pm daily. *House Apr-Oct* 3-6pm Thur, Sun. **Admission** *gardens* £3.50; *house* £1. **No credit cards.**

Ightam Mote
Ivy Hatch, Sevenoaks, Kent (0732 810378). **Getting**

there *by train* from Charing Cross, to Sevenoaks, 30 minutes, then bus direction Reigate; *by bus* Greenline to Sevenoaks; *by car* A21 to Sevenoaks, then A25 to Ivy Hatch. **Open** *Apr-Oct* noon-5.30pm Mon, Wed-Fri; 11am-5.30pm Sun. **Admission** £4; £2 under-15s. **No credit cards.**

Leeds Castle
Leeds Castle, Maidstone, Kent (0622 765400). **Getting there** *by train* from Victoria to Bearsted (1 hour), then 10-minute coach transfer; *by bus* National Express, 1 hour 30 minutes, leaves Victoria 10am; *by car* A20, M20 junction 8. **Open** *Mar-Oct* 10am-5pm daily; *Nov-Feb* 10am-3pm daily. **Admission** £7; £6 OAPs, students; £4.80 under-15s; £4 disabled.

Knole
Sevenoaks, Kent (0732 450608). **Getting there** *by train* from Charing Cross, to Sevenoaks, 30 minutes; *by bus* Greenline to Sevenoaks; *by car* A21 to Sevenoaks. **Open** *Apr-Oct* 11am-5pm Wed, Fri, Sat, Sun; 2-5pm Thur. **Admission** £4; £2 under-15s; *garden only* 50p. **No credit cards.**

Sissinghurst Castle and Gardens
Sissinghurst, Cranbrook, Kent (0580 712850). **Getting there** *by train* from Charing Cross, to Staplehurst, 1 hour, then taxi or bus to Sissinghurst; *by car* A21 to Cranbrook. **Open** *Apr-Oct* 1-6pm Mon-Sat; 10am-4.30pm Sun. **Admission** £5; £2.50 under-15s. **No credit cards.**

Waddesdon Manor
Waddesdon, near Aylesbury, Buckinghamshire (0296 651211). **Getting there** *by train* from Marylebone, to Aylesbury, 1 hour, then bus to Waddesdon; *by car* M40 to junction 7, then join A41 at Long Crendon. **Open** *Apr-Jun, Sept, Oct* 1-6pm Wed-Sat; 11am-6pm Sun; *Jul, Aug* 1-6pm Thur-Sat; 11am-6pm Sun. **Admission** *house* £4; *gardens and aviary* £3 adults; £1.50 under-18s. **No credit cards.**

Survival

This massive metropolis can create a mass of needs. But fortunately London is well-served by agencies and services that will lend you a hand. If you've a toothache, you can smell a gas-leak, your car has broken down or you've lost your wallet – consult these pages.

Survival

**Got a problem? London is at your beck and call.
Here's how to survive in the city.**

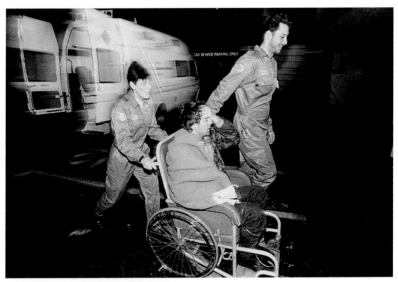

Need an ambulance? Phone 999.

Emergencies

The following emergency services are all open
24 hours daily. *See also below* **Health**.
Ambulance *(999)*.
Fire Service *(999)*.
Police *(999)*.
Samaritans *(24-hour helpline 071 734 2800)*. The
Samaritans will listen to anyone with emotional
problems, or who feels suicidal.
Women's Aid *(071 251 6537)*. **Open** 24 hours daily.
This organisation will help women in an emergency,
refer you to your nearest refuge, and provide advice
and counselling.

Emergency Repairs

See also below **Travel & Driving: Car Breakdown**.

Electrical

Phone your local area office if you have an electrical emergency. The day time number should
be dialled between 8.30am and 5pm Mon-Fri.

The number to ring depends on which postcode
your street is in. Find this out by consulting a
street atlas (*see chapter* **Essential Information:
Box**), asking anyone who lives locally, or (in
many older districts of London) looking at the
street sign.

Postcode
W1, W2, W6, W8, W10, W11, W12, W14, SW1, SW6,
SW7, SW10 **(071 730 9644)** day; **(071 274 1367)**
night.
SE1, SE5, SE11, SE15, SE16, SE17, SE21, SE22, SE24,
SE27, SW2, SW4, SW8, SW9, SW11-SW20 **(071 733
5611)** day and night.
SE2, SE3, SE4, SE6-SE10, SE12-SE14, SE18-SE20,
SE23, SE25, SE26, SE28 **(081 304 7144)** day and
night.
E1-E3, E6, E7, E10-E18 **(081 534 6677)** day; **(071
733 2161)** night.
WC1, WC2, EC1-EC4, N1, N4-N7, N16, N19, NW1-
NW6, NW8, NW10, E5, E8, E9, E11 **(071 251 5161)**
day; **(071 733 1930)** night.

Gas

Phone your local area office in an emergency.
The following numbers can be phoned at any

time. The number to ring depends on which postcode your street is in (*see above* **Electricity**).
Postcode
E1, E2, E5, E6, E8, E13, E14, N16 **(071 511 3296)**.
E4, E10, E17, E18 **(081 478 2244)**.
N9, N13, N14, N17, N18, N20, N21 **(081 447 1777)**.
N1-N8, N10, N12, NW4, NW7, NW11 **(081 346 9191)**.
NW2, NW3, NW6, NW8, NW9, NW10 **(081 423 4490)**.
W1, W2, W9, WC1, WC2, EC1-EC4, SE1, SE5, SE8, SE11, SE15, SE17 **(071 828 3299)**.
SW2, SW4, SW9, SW12, SW16, SE21, SE22, SE24 **(071 277 5500)**.
SW15, SW18, SW19, SW20 **(081 687 0747)**.
SE2, SE3, SE6, SE7, SE9, SE10, SE12, SE13, SE18, SE19, SE20, SE25, SE26, SE27 **(081 659 9599)**.
SW3, SW6, SW7, SW10, W6, W8, W14 **(071 828 3262)**.
W3, W4, W5, W7, W12, W13 **(081 878 7501)**.

Glaziers

Express Glaze
27 Old Gloucester Street, WC1 (071 242 4702). **Open** 24 hours daily. **Credit** A, AmEx, V.
Express claims to answer call-outs within the hour. Staff should be able to quote the cost over the phone.

Lloyd's
(081 764 5555/081 760 0760/0800 282103). **Open** 24 hours daily. **Credit** A, V.
A London-wide repair service. Calls are answered in one to two hours.

Locksmiths

If you've locked yourself out of your home or car, the following locksmiths charge a minimum of £16 to £30 and all run a 24-hour emergency service.

W2: Barry Bros
121-123 Praed Street, W2 (071 734 1001/071 262 9009). **Open** 24 hours daily. **Credit** A, AmEx, V.
Barry Bros will repair broken locks and doors and almost anything else to do with security, including car ignition keys. Minimum call-out fee is £45, which increases after 6pm to £60, and after midnight to £75.

SW1: Victoria Lock & Safe
4 Denbigh Street, SW1 (071 630 6500/24 hour emergency service 071 630 0917). **Open** 24 hours daily. **Credit** A, V.
The call-out charge depends on the area and the work to be done. The minimum charge is £30 plus VAT in central London; £35 plus VAT in the City; £29.50 incl VAT in SW1.

N4: North London Locksmiths
79 Grand Parade, Green Lanes, N4 (081 800 6041/ 3792/081 361 8614). **Open** 24 hours daily. **Credit** A, V.
This firm operates an emergency service. After 5.30pm the call-out fee for local (anywhere with a north London post-code) calls is £35; after midnight it goes up to £40, plus parts.

Plumbers

Thames Water
(071 837 3300).
Phone this number for Thames Water's emergency plumbing service and customer relations.

The Institute of Plumbing
64 Station Lane, Hornchurch, Essex RM12 6NB (0708 472791). **Open** 9am-5pm Mon-Fri.
Telephone or write for details of approved members in your area.

Embassies

Embassies, consulates and High Commissions are listed in the telephone directory under their respective countries and in *Yellow Pages* under 'Embassies'. Most close on British public holidays and those of their own countries.

American Embassy
24 Grosvenor Square, W1 (071 499 9000/visa information 0891 200 290). Bond Street or Marble Arch underground. **Open** 9am-6pm Mon-Fri; *Visa section* 8.30am-1pm, 2-4.30pm, Mon-Fri; *US citizens services* 8.30am-5.30pm, Mon-Fri. Seven-day, 24-hour phone line for emergency help.

Australian High Commission
Australia House, The Strand, WC2 (071 379 4334/visa information 0891 600333). Holborn or Temple underground. **Open** 10am-4pm Mon-Fri; *visa section* 10am-4pm Mon-Fri.

Canadian High Commission
Haut Commissariat du Canada, Macdonald House, 1 Grosvenor Square, W1 (071 258 6600 24-hour). Bond Street underground. **Open** 9am-3pm Mon-Fri; *visas* 8.45am-2pm Mon-Fri; *passports* 10am-3pm Mon-Fri.

Chinese Embassy
49-61 Portland Place, W1 (071 636 0380). Regent's Park or Oxford Circus underground. **Open** 9am-12.30pm, 2-3.6pm, Mon-Fri. *Visa section 31 Portland Place, W1 (071 631 1430/ recorded info 071 636 1835). Regent's Park or Oxford Circus underground.* **Open** 9am-noon Mon-Fri.

French Embassy
58 Knightsbridge, SW1 (071 201 1000). Knightsbridge underground. **Open** 24 hours daily. **Consulate General** *21 Cromwell Road, SW7 (071 838 2000). South Kensington underground.* **Open** 9am-noon Mon, Fri; 9am-noon, 1.30-3.30pm, Tue-Thur. *Visa section 6A Cromwell Place, SW7 (071 838 2050).* **Open** 8.45-11.30am Mon-Fri; visa collection 4-4.30pm Mon-Fri.

German Embassy
23 Belgrave Square, SW1 (071 235 5033). Hyde Park Corner or Knightsbridge underground. **Open** 8.30am-5pm Mon-Thur; 8.30am-3.30pm Fri; *Visa section* 9am-noon.

High Commission of India
India House, Aldwych, WC2 (071 836 8484). Holborn or Charing Cross underground/BR. **Open** 9.30am-5.30pm Mon-Fri; *visas* 9.30am-1pm Mon-Fri.

Jamaican High Commission
1-2 Prince Consort Road, SW7 (071 823 9911). South Kensington underground. **Open** 10am-5.30pm Mon-Fri; *visa section* 10am-3.30pm Mon-Fri.

Japanese Embassy
101-4 Piccadilly, W1 (071 465 6500). Green Park underground. **Open** 9.30am-1pm, 2.30-5pm, *visa section* 9.30am-12.30pm, 2.30-4.30pm, Mon-Fri.

New Zealand High Commission
New Zealand House, 80 Haymarket, SW1 (071 930 8422). Piccadilly Circus underground. **Open** 10am-noon, 2-4pm, *visa section (071 973 0366)* 12.30-4pm, Mon-Fri.

Pakistan High Commission
34-35 Lowndes Square, SW1 (071 235 2044). Knightsbridge underground. **Open** 9.30am-5.30pm Mon-Fri; *visa section* 10am-1pm, then 4.30-5.30pm for collection of visas, Mon-Fri.

Russian Embassy
13 Kensington Palace Gardens, W8 (071 229 3628). High Street Kensington or Notting Hill Gate underground. **Open** 9am-6pm Mon-Fri. **Consulate** *5 Kensington Palace Gardens, W8 (071 229 8027). High Street Kensington or Notting Hill Gate underground.* **Open** 10am-12.30pm Mon, Tue, Thur, Fri. Telephone enquiries 10am-6pm Mon-Fri.

Health

In an emergency, phone **999** and ask for an ambulance.

Free medical treatment under the National Health Service is available to:
* EEC Nationals – citizens of Belgium, Denmark, France, Germany, Greece, Italy, Irish Republic, Luxembourg, the Netherlands, Portugal and Spain.
* Nationals of the following countries, on production of a passport: Austria, Bulgaria, Finland, Gibraltar, Hungary, Malta, New Zealand, Norway, Sweden.
* Residents of the following countries: Anguilla, Australia, British Virgin Islands, Channel Islands, Czech Republic, Slovakia, CIS, Falkland Islands, Hong Kong, Iceland, Isle of Man, Montserrat, Poland, Romania, St Helena, Turks and Caicos Islands, NATO personnel.
* Anyone who at the time of receiving treatment has been in the UK for the previous 12 months.
* Students and trainees whose course requires them to spend more than 12 weeks in employment during their first year. Students and others living in the UK for a settled purpose for more than six months may be accepted as ordinarily resident and not liable to charges.
* People with HIV/AIDS at a special clinic for the treatment of sexually transmitted diseases. Treatment is limited to a diagnostic test and counselling associated with that test.

There are no NHS charges for district nursing, midwifery or health visiting; for ambulance transport; or for family-planning services.

Casualties: NHS

Casualty departments will treat injuries and sudden illness if you cannot wait to see a doctor. There are 24-hour walk-in casualty departments at:

WC1: University College Hospital *Gower Street (entrance Grafton Way), WC1 (071 387 9300). Euston Square or Warren Street underground.*
W6: Charing Cross Hospital *Fulham Palace Road (entrance St Dunstan's Road), W6 (081 846 1234). Baron's Court or Hammersmith underground.*
W12: Hammersmith Hospital *150 Du Cane Road, W12 (081 743 2030). East Acton underground.*
SW17: St George's Hospital *Blackshaw Road, SW17 (081 672 1255). Tooting Broadway underground.*
SE1: Guy's Hospital *St Thomas Street (entrance in Weston Street), SE1 (071 955 5000). London Bridge underground.*
SE1: St Thomas' Hospital *Lambeth Palace Road, SE1 (071 928 9292). Westminster underground.*
SE5: King's College Hospital *Denmark Hill (entrance in Bessemer Road), SE5 (071 274 6222). Denmark Hill BR.*
SE10: Greenwich District Hospital *Vanbrugh Hill, SE10 (081 858 8141). Maze Hill BR.*
SE13: Lewisham Hospital *Lewisham High Street, SE13 (081 690 4311). Ladywell or Lewisham BR.*
E1: London Hospital *Whitechapel Road, E1 (071 377 7000). Whitechapel underground.*
E9: Hackney and Homerton Hospital *Homerton Row, E9 (081 985 5555). Homerton BR/22B bus.*
EC1: St Bartholomew's Hospital *West Smithfield (entrance Giltspur Street), EC1 (071 601 8888). Barbican or St Paul's underground.*
N18: North Middlesex Hospital *Stirling Way, Edmonton, N18 (081 807 3071). Silver Street BR.*
N19: Whittington Hospital *St Mary's Wing, Highgate Hill, N19 (071 272 3070). Archway underground.*
NW3: Royal Free Hospital *Pond Street, NW3 (071 794 0500). Belsize Park underground/Hampstead Heath BR.*
NW10: Central Middlesex Hospital *Acton Lane, NW10 (081 965 5733). North Acton underground.*

Chemists: Late-Opening

If you have a prescription you need made up outside normal shopping hours, head for one of the following chemists:

W1: Bliss Chemist
5 Marble Arch, W1 (071 723 6116). Marble Arch underground. **Open** 9am-midnight daily. **Credit** A, AmEx, DC, £TC, V.

W2: Boots
75 Queensway, W2 (071 229 9266). Bayswater underground. **Open** 9am-10pm Mon-Fri; 9am-9pm Sat. **Credit** A, AmEx, V.
Branch: 114 Queensway, W4 (071 229 8625) Bayswater underground. **Open** 9am-10pm Mon-Sat; 10am-10pm Sun.

Contraception/Abortion

Family Planning advice, contraceptive supplies and abortions are free to British citizens on the National Health Service. This also applies to EC residents and foreign nationals living, working and studying in Britain. According to the 1967 Abortion Act, two doctors must agree to a woman having an abortion, whether on the NHS or not. If you decide to

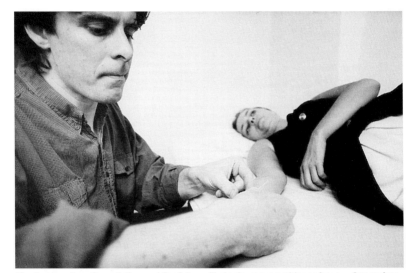

The **Acupuncture Association and Register** will pin down a practitioner for you. See **review** page 319.

go private, contact one of the organisations listed below.

British Pregnancy Advisory Service
7 Belgrave Road, SW1 (071 222 0985). Victoria underground/BR. **Open** 9am-5pm Mon, Wed, Thur, Fri; 9am-7pm Tue; 9am-2pm Sat.
Contraception advice, contraceptives and the morning-after pill are available here. The service carries out pregnancy tests and makes referrals to BPAS nursing homes for private abortions.
Branch: 160 Shepherds Bush Road, W4 (071 602 3804). Shepherds Bush underground. **Open** 9am-5pm Mon-Fri.

Brook Advisory Centres
233 Tottenham Court Road, W1 (071 323 1522). Tottenham Court Road underground. **Open** *office* 9am-7.30pm Mon-Thur; 9.30am-3pm Fri.
There are 13 Brook Advisory family planning clinics in London. Call the office to find your nearest one. Advice is given on contraception, sexual problems and abortion with referral to NHS or a private clinic.

Family Planning Association
27-35 Mortimer Street, W1 (071 636 7866). Oxford Circus underground. **Open** 9am-5pm Mon-Thur; 9am-4.30pm Fri.
There are more than 1,800 NHS-run Family Planning Clinics in Britain. Phone the FPA to find your nearest one, or drop in to pick up free leaflets.

Marie Stopes Clinics
Family Planning Clinic *108 Whitfield Street, W1 (071 388 0662/071 388 2585 for family planning/071 388 5554 for sterilisation). Warren Street underground.* **Open** 9am-8pm Mon-Wed; 9am-5pm Thur, Fri; 9.30am-1pm Sat.
The clinics provide contraceptives, treatment, and advice for gynaecological complaints, counselling for sexual problems and referral for abortion. Fees are: £30 for a family planning consultation; £40 for a pregnancy consultation; both plus costs of tests and medication.

Pregnancy Advisory Service
11-13 Charlotte Street, W1 (071 637 8962). Tottenham Court Road underground. **Open** 9.30am-6pm Mon-Wed, Fri; 9.30am-8pm Thur; 9.30am-12.30pm Sat. (Appointments necessary except in an emergency.)
A non-profit-making registered charity that provides the following services: pregnancy counselling; pregnancy tests (9.30am-5pm Mon-Fri); abortion advice and help; artificial insemination by donor; morning-after contraception; sterilisation; cervical smears; and post-abortion counselling. There's a branch at 17 Rosslyn Road, East Twickenham, Middlesex (081 891 6833).

Dental Services

Dental care is only free to British citizens who are receiving supplementary benefit. All other patients, whether National Health Service (NHS) or private, must pay. To find a dentist, get in touch with the local **Citizens Advice Bureau** (*see below* **Help & Information**) or **Family Practitioner Committee** (*see below* **Doctors**). Prices vary enormously, starting at about £14 for a filling on the NHS. Private dentists can charge whatever they like, there are no set charges. We list emergency services below.

Dental Emergency Care Service
(071 955 5000). **Open** 24 hours daily.
Callers are referred to a surgery open for treatment, whether it's private or National Health Service.

Eastman Dental Hospital
256 Gray's Inn Road, WC1 (071 837 3646). Chancery

Lane or King's Cross underground/BR. **Open** 8.30am-10pm Mon-Fri.
A free walk-in emergency dental hospital for anyone without a dentist in London. No appointment needed.

Guy's Hospital Dental School
St Thomas' Street, SE1 (071 955 5000). London Bridge underground/BR. **Open** 9am-4pm Mon-Fri.
A walk-in dental emergency service. Free treatment, except on Saturday and Sunday.

Doctors

If you're a British citizen visiting London or working in the city temporarily, you can go to any general practitioner (GP). You will most likely have to show your medical card or fill in a 'Lost Medical Card' form. Overseas students can register with an NHS doctor.

Great Chapel Street Medical Centre
13 Great Chapel Street, W1 (071 437 9360). Tottenham Court Road underground. **Open** 11am-12.30pm Mon, Tue, Thur; 2-4pm Mon-Fri.
A walk-in NHS surgery for anyone with no doctor.

Family Practitioner Committees
The various London boroughs provide lists of GPs, chemists, opticians and dentists. The telephone number of the borough committee and lists of local NHS doctors are available in libraries and post offices.

Medical Information

Healthline
(081 681 3311). **Open** 4-8pm Mon-Fri. 24-hour services are located at Hull *(0482 29933)* and Exeter *(0392 59191).*
A free telephone information service (except for the cost of the call). Phone and ask to listen to any of the 300-plus tapes on health topics. These give details of symptoms and contact names of groups involved with treatment or support for sufferers.

Medical Advisory Service
10 Barley Mow Passage, W4 (081 994 9874). **Open** 5-10pm Mon-Fri.
Advice over the phone.

Medication

Many drugs cannot be bought over the counter in Britain. A pharmacist will dispense medicines on receipt of a prescription from a doctor. An NHS prescription costs £4.75 at present. If you are not eligible to see an NHS doctor you will be charged cost price for all medicines prescribed by a private doctor.

Medicine: Complementary

The Acupuncture Association and Register
34 Alderney Street, SW1 (071 834 1012). Victoria underground/BR. **Open** 9am-5.30pm Mon-Sat.
Phone for your local registered specialist. The Association will provide lists of practitioners. A list and handbook are also available, price £2.30 plus p&p.

British Homoeopathic Association
27A Devonshire Street, W1 (071 935 2163). Baker Street or Great Portland Street underground. **Open** 9.30am-4.30pm Mon-Fri.
The BHA will give you the address of your nearest homoeopathic chemist and doctor (send a stamped addressed envelope for a list). The Association also provides a booklist of helpful information and has a library on the premises.

Mental/Emotional Health

Just Ask
46 Bishopsgate, EC2 (071 628 3380). Liverpool Street underground. **Open** 9.30am-9pm Mon-Thur, Sat; closed during August. 24-hour answerphone.
Make an appointment either by calling in or phoning. Counsellors help people with personal problems.

Mind
22 Harley Street, W1 (071 637 0741). Oxford Circus underground. **Open** 9.15am-5.15pm Mon-Fri; *general advice* 10am-12.30pm, 2-4.30pm, Mon-Fri; *legal advice* 2-4.30pm Mon, Wed, Fri.
This charity provides a useful starting point for anyone with general enquiries. Callers will be referred to one of 34 London groups. The legal service advises on maltreatment, wrongful detention and sectioning (involuntary hospitalisation). Phone for details.

National Association of Victims Support Schemes
Cranmer House, 39 Brixton Road, SW9 (071 735 9166 answerphone out of office hours). Oval underground. **Open** 9am-5.30pm Mon-Fri.
The Association helps victims of crime. Callers are put in touch with a volunteer who visits as soon as possible after the event to provide emotional and practical support.

Samaritans
(24-hour helpline 071 734 2800).
The Samaritans will listen to anyone with emotional problems. It's a popular service and you may have to phone several times before you get through.

Opticians

Eye Care Information Bureau
(071 928 9435). **Open** 9am-5pm Mon-Fri.
This service gives you information on the different kinds of eye-care specialists.

Physiotherapy

Chartered Society of Physiotherapy
14 Bedford Row, WC1 (071 242 1941). Chancery Lane or Holborn underground. **Open** 9am-5pm Mon-Fri.
This is the professional body of physiotherapists. The Society can check whether any practitioner is a qualified member.

Sexually Transmitted Diseases (VD)/AIDS/HIV Positive

The NHS Special Clinics listed below are affiliated to major hospitals. They specialise in genito-urinary conditions, treating sexually-transmitted diseases and non sex-related ones such as thrush and cystitis. They can also conduct a confidential blood test to determine HIV status. The Government pamphlets 'AIDS: The Facts'; 'Safer Sex and the Condom' and 'AIDS: The Test' are available from clinics and, with a stamped addressed envelope, by post from: Health Education Authority, Hamilton House, Mabledon Place, WC1.

AIDS Telephone Helpline
(0800 567 123). **Open** 24 hours daily.
A free and confidential help and information service for anybody worried or concerned about HIV/AIDS and safer sex. A Cantonese-speaking counsellor is available 6-10pm Tue (0800 282 446); a counsellor speaking Punjabi, Bengali, Hindi, Erdu and Gujarati is available 6-10pm Wed (0800 282 445); an Arabic-speaking counsellor is available 6-10pm Wed (0800 282 447); a Minicom service (for the hard of hearing) is available 10am-10pm daily (0800 521 361).

Body Positive
51B Philbeach Gardens, SW5 (071 835 1045/071 835 1046). Earl's Court underground. **Open** 11am-5pm Mon-Fri.
Run by and for people who are HIV positive, this is a drop-in centre. It also offers a helpline service (071 373 9124) between 7pm and 10pm daily.

Terence Higgins Trust
52-54 Gray's Inn Road, WC1 (helpline 071 242 1010/legal line 071 405 2381, 7-10pm Wed). **Open** noon-10pm daily for general advice.
The Trust advises and counsels those with HIV/AIDS, their relatives, lovers and friends. Free leaflets about AIDS are available. The Trust also gives advice about safer sex. Lines are constantly busy, so keep trying.

WC1: University College Hospital Special Clinic
Gower Street, WC1 (071 388 9625). Euston Square underground. **Open** 9-11.30am, 1-5pm, Mon-Fri. Appointment needed.

W2: St Mary's Hospital Special Clinic
Praed Street, W2 (071 725 1697). Paddington underground/BR. **Open** 9am-6pm Mon, Tue, Thur, Fri; 10am-6pm Wed (new patients should arrive before 5.30pm on all days).
No appointment necessary; free and confidential.

W6: Riverside Healthcare Special Clinic
Parsons Green, W6 (081 846 7834/6). Parsons Green underground. **Open** 9.30am-12.30pm, 2-5pm, Mon-Fri.
No appointment necessary.

Help & Information

Capital Helpline
(071 388 7575). **Open** 9.30am-5.30pm Mon, Tue, Wed, Fri; 9.30am-9pm Thur.
Run in conjunction with Capital Radio, this helpline tackles queries about anything. If the staff can't answer your query themselves, they'll put you in touch with someone who can. The line is always busy, so keep trying. They have an answerphone after the lines close and will call you back.

Citizens Advice Bureaux
Greater London Office, 136-144 City Road, EC1 (071 251 2000). **Open** 9.30am-5pm Mon-Fri.

Citizens Advice Bureaux are run by local councils and offer free advice on legal, financial and personal matters.

Consumer Problems

Statutory rights protect the consumer, and when you buy a large or expensive piece of equipment you should be provided with a guarantee by the vendor. **The Office of Fair Trading** *(see below)* publishes free leaflets on all aspects of consumer purchase covering goods and services. You can also obtain their leaflets at **Citizens Advice Bureaux** *(see above* **Help & Information**). Staff at the CAB should also be able to advise you of your rights under the law. The Consumer's Association publishes *Which?* magazine, *Which Car?* etc – well worth reading before a purchase is made.

Office of Fair Trading
Field House 15-25 Bream's Buildings, EC4 (071 242 2858). **Open** 8.30am-5.30pm Mon-Fri.

Financial Advice

Visitors from abroad who run into financial difficulties should contact their embassies for help *(see above* **Embassies**). But people on long-term stays who need counselling or advice can go to **Citizens Advice Bureaux** *(see above* **Help & Information**).

Gay & Lesbian

There's still a lot of prejudice against gays and lesbians, and violent attacks are on the increase. Be careful when leaving a gay or lesbian night-club on your own. More agencies that give advice and information to gay men and lesbians can be found in *chapter* **Gay London** and *chapter* **Women**, and for weekly events look in *Time Out* magazine.

Lesbian & Gay Switchboard
(071 837 7324).
A 24-hour advice and information service.

Legal & Immigration

You never know when you're going to need a lawyer or a solicitor. Contact your embassy, go to a **Citizens Advice Bureau** *(see above* **Help & Information**) or get in touch with one of the organisations listed below. Some people are eligible for Legal Aid. For a leaflet explaining how the system works write to **Legal Aid** *(see below)*.

Amnesty International
British Section, 99-119 Rosebery Avenue, EC1 (071 814 6200). Farringdon or Angel underground. **Open** 9am-6.30pm Mon-Fri.
Amnesty is a worldwide human rights movement working impartially for the release of prisoners of conscience. Staff can advise those seeking asylum.

Commission for Racial Equality
Elliot House, 10-12 Allington Street, SW1 (071 828 7022). Victoria underground/BR. **Open** 9am-5.45pm Mon-Fri.
The CRE was established by the 1966 Race Relations Act to work towards the elimination of discrimination and to promote equality of opportunity, irrespective of race. It offers free advice.

Law Centres Federation
(071 387 8570). **Open** 10am-6pm Mon-Fri.
There are about 25 Law Centres in London and this organisation will put you in touch. Centres can give free help with all aspects of the law to people who cannot afford to pay for legal advice.

Legal Aid
29-37 Red Lion Street, WC1 (071 831 4209). Russell Square underground. **Open** 9am-5pm Mon-Fri.
Apply to the head office of Legal Aid for the names and addresses of solicitors who act within the Legal Aid scheme. Staff at the office will listen to your problems and advise you on how to proceed.

Joint Council for the Welfare of Immigrants (JCWI)
115 Old Street, EC1 (071 251 8706). Old Street underground/BR. **Open** *personal callers* 10am-12.30pm, *telephone enquiries* 2-5.30pm, Mon, Tue, Thur.
The JCWI provides advice on immigration, takes up cases of people subject to deportation orders, and helps with legal representation. Phone for an appointment.

Release
388 Old Street, EC1 (071 729 9904). Old Street underground. **Open** 10am-6pm Mon-Fri.
Free legal advice is given by this organisation to anyone who has been arrested. Release is particularly helpful in cases involving illicit drugs, and gives confidential drugs counselling and referrals. It runs a 24-hour helpline on 071 603 8654, but during office hours contact the daytime number.

Reference Libraries

Guildhall Reference Library
Aldermanbury, EC2 (071 606 3030). Bank, Mansion House, St Paul's or Moorgate underground/6, 8, 9, 11, 25, 22B bus. **Open** 9.30am-5pm Mon-Sat. **Admission** free.
Most of the material kept here deals with the history of London. On the ground floor are printed books and on the first floor is a collection of maps, prints and manuscripts. *Wheelchair access limited.*

Westminster Central Reference Library
35 St Martin's Street, WC2 (071 798 2034). Leicester Square or Charing Cross underground/BR/24, 29 bus. **Open** 10am-7pm Mon-Fri; 10am-5pm Sat. **Admission** free.
A public reference library, with international telephone directories on the ground floor, a large collection of information on performing arts on the first floor and a register of companies trading in Britain and an arts library on the second floor.

Women

Sexual harassment is not as great a problem in Britain as it is in some other countries. In cafés and restaurants a woman alone won't really get bothered, but you may feel uncomfortable in pubs and nightclubs as men often assume that

The **Guildhall Reference Library**. *See* **review**.

any unaccompanied woman is looking for male companionship. *See also chapter* **Women's London** for more detailed information.

Feminist Library
5 Westminster Bridge Road, SE1 (071 928 7789). Lambeth North underground. **Open** 11am-8pm Tue; 2-5pm Sat, Sun.
London's main women's lending library, it stocks a wide range of feminist fiction and non-fiction, a research index and resource centre.

London Rape Crisis Centre
PO Box 69, WC1 (office 071 278 3956/24-hour phoneline 071 837 1600). **Open** 10am-12.30pm, 2.30-6pm, Mon, Wed, Fri; 10am-1pm, 2-6pm, Tue, Thur.
Run by women, Rape Crisis offers advice and support for women who have been raped or assaulted.

Women's Aid
(071 251 6537). **Open** 24 hours daily.
This organisation will help you in an emergency, refer you to your nearest refuge, and provide advice.

Left Luggage

Gatwick Airport *(081 763 2020).* **Office** open 24 hours daily. **Rates** up to 24 hours, £3 per item; £4 per day thereafter.
Heathrow Airport *(081 759 4321).* **Office** open *Terminal 1 (081 745 5301), 2 (071 745 6100),* 6am-10.30pm daily ; *Terminal 3 (071 745 4599)* 6am-10.30pm daily; *Terminal 4 (081 745 7460)* 6am-10pm daily. **Rates** £3 per item, per day.
London City Airport *(071 474 5555).* **Office** open 6.30am-9.30pm daily. **Rates** up to 6 hours, 50p per item; up to 24 hours, £1 per item; £1 for each subsequent day.
Euston Station *(071 928 5151).* **Office** open 24 hours daily. **Rates** £1.80 small, £2.50 large, per day.

Paddington Station *(071 262 6767/071 922 6773).* **Office** open *deposit* 7am-10pm daily; *collect* 7am-midnight daily. **Rates** £2 small, £3 large, per day.
Victoria Station *(071 928 5151).* **Office** open 7.30am-10.30pm daily. **Rates** £2.50 per day. There's also a locker service on platforms 7and 8; rates range from £2.50-£5 depending on size of locker.
Waterloo Station *(071 928 5151).* **Office** open 7am-10pm Mon-Sat. **Rates** £1.50 small, £2 large, per day.

Lost Property

Always inform the police if you lose anything (to validate any insurance claim). Go to the nearest police station. Only dial the emergency number (999) if violence has occurred. A lost passport should be reported to the police and to your embassy.

Airports

Gatwick Airport

(0293 503162). **Open** 8.30am-4.30pm daily.
The Lost Property Office is located below the Service Air check-in desk at the south terminal on the lower level. It's for property lost in the airport only. For property lost on the plane, contact the airline or handling agents dealing with your flight.

Heathrow Airport

(081 759 4321/lost property 081 745 7727). **Open** 9am-4pm daily.
The Lost Property Office is situated on the ground floor of Terminal 2 car park. It's for property lost in the airport only. For property lost on the plane, contact the airline by using the above number.

London City Airport

(071 474 5555). **Open** 6am-10pm daily.
The Lost Property Office is situated at the Information Desk for property lost in the airport only. For property lost on the plane, contact the airline on the same number.

Luton Airport

(0582 405100). **Open** 24 hours daily.
Report to the Airport Duty Manager's Office (directions from the Information Desk) for property lost in the airport only. For property lost on the plane, contact the airline on the same number.

British Rail

If it takes you as long to get through to the lost property offices as it did our researcher, claim on your insurance and buy new goods.
Charing Cross Station *(071 922 6061).* **Open** 7.50am-9.50pm daily. Lost property is deposited in the Information Office for seven days after which it goes to Waterloo Lost Property (*see below*).
Euston Station *(071 922 6477).* **Open** 7am-8pm daily.
King's Cross Station *(071 922 9081).* **Open** 9am-4.45pm daily.
Liverpool Street Station *(071 922 9189).* **Open** 7.30am-9pm daily.
London Bridge Station. Open 7am-7pm Mon-Fri.
Marylebone Station *(071 922 9543).* **Open** 6.20am-8pm Mon-Fri; 6.20am-1pm Sat.
Paddington Station *(071 922 6773).* **Open** 7am-10pm daily.
St Pancras Station *(071 922 6478).* **Open** 7am-10.30pm daily.

Victoria Station *(071 922 6216).* **Open** 9am-5pm Mon-Sat; 8am-4pm Sun.
Waterloo Station *(071 922 6135* answerphone*).* **Open** 24 hours daily. Leave your address, and staff will write to you if your property is found. Personal calls can be made to the office, situated below the station, 8.15am-6.45pm Mon-Fri.

Bus & Underground

London Regional Transport

Lost Property Office, 200 Baker Street, NW1 (071 486 2496 recorded information). Baker Street underground. **Open** 9.30am-2pm Mon-Fri.
Allow two days from the time of loss. If you lose something on a bus, and can remember which number or route it was, phone 071 222 1234 and ask for the phone numbers of the depots at either end of the route. You can pick up a lost property claim form from any underground station.

Taxis

Taxi Lost Property

15 Penton Street, N1 (071 833 0996). Angel *underground.* **Open** 9am-4pm Mon-Fri.
Things left in taxis work their way back to this central office, but it deals only with property found in registered black cabs. For property lost in a minicab you will have to call the office you hired the car from.

Lost/Stolen Credit Cards

Report lost or stolen credit cards to the police and the 24-hour services listed below. Inform your bank by phone and in writing.
Access *(Nat West 0532 778899/Lloyds 0800 585300).*
American Express *(Personal Card 0273 696933/Corporate Card 0273 689955/enquiries 071 222 9633).*
Barclaycard/Visa *(0604 230230).*
Co-operative Bank/Visa *(0695 26621)*
Diners Club/Diners Club International *(General Enquiries 0252 516261/Emergency 0252 513500).*
MasterCard/Eurocard *(0702 362988).*
Midland Gold MasterCard *(0702 352244).*
Bank of Scotland Visa *(0383 738866).*

Newspapers: Home & Abroad

Books Nippon

64-66 St Paul's Churchyard, EC4 (071 248 4956). St Paul's underground. **Open** 10am-7pm Mon-Fri; 10am-6pm Sat. **Credit** A, AmEx, DC, £TC, V.
A Japanese book and magazine importer and retailer offering popular Japanese dailies such as *Asahi*, weeklies such as *Shonen-Jump* and *Newsweek* in Japanese. CDs, videos, cassettes and gifts also sold.

Eman's

123 Queensway, W2 (071 727 6122). Bayswater *underground.* **Open** 24 hours daily. **No credit cards.**
A large collection of Middle Eastern newspapers and magazines are displayed in the shop.

Gray's Inn News

50 Theobald's Road, WC1 (071 405 5241). Chancery Lane or Holborn underground. **Open** 4am-5pm Mon-Fri. **No credit cards.**
The stock is varied, although it concentrates on

European titles. Good stock of local London newspapers and the specialities are finance, sport and leisure.

John Menzies
104-106 Long Acre, WC2 (071 240 7645). Covent Garden underground. **Open** 8am-8pm Mon-Fri; 8.30am-8pm Sat; 10am-6pm Sun. **Credit** A, £TC, V.
Newspapers from Europe and the USA, as well as a reasonable selection of American magazines such as *New Yorker* and *Vanity Fair*.

A Moroni & Son
68 Old Compton Street, W1 (071 437 2847). Piccadilly Circus or Leicester Square underground. **Open** 7.30am-7pm Mon-Sat. **No credit cards.**
A tiny shop that is over 100 years old. It stocks a superlative selection of foreign newspapers and magazines, but browsing is frowned upon.

DS Radford
61 Fleet Street, EC4. Blackfriars underground/BR. **Open** 7am-8pm daily. **No credit cards.**
If you're looking for European fashion magazines, this is the place. DS Radford sells US consumer magazines, as well as European newspapers.

Police & Security

In an emergency, if you are in danger or threatened in any way, dial **999** and ask for the police.

Practically the only public service that wasn't drained of resources during the Thatcher years was the police force. It's still fairly uncommon to encounter 'your friendly local bobby' patrolling his or her beat; more often they're roaring around in patrol cars, making high-speed arrests. Nevertheless, the police are a good source of information about the locality and are used to helping visitors find their way. If you've been robbed, assaulted or involved in an infringement of the law, look under 'Police' in the telephone directory for the nearest police station, or call directory enquiries on 142.

If you have a complaint to make about the police, then there are several things you can do. Always make sure that you take the offending police officer's identifying number, which should be prominently displayed on his or her shoulder lapel. You can then register a complaint with the **Police Complaints Authority**, 10 Great George Street, SW1 (071 273 6450). Alternatively, contact any police station or, if you'd rather not deal directly with the police, visit a solicitor or a law centre (phone directory enquiries on 142 for the nearest). Only dial 999 in an emergency.

You can feel relatively safe in London, but it's unwise to take any risks, especially as robbery and mugging (robbery with violence) have increased over the past decade. Thieves and pickpockets lurk in crowded places. Follow these basic rules:
• **Keep** your wallet and purse out of sight. Do not wear a wrist wallet (they are very easily snatched). Keep your handbag securely closed.

• **Don't** leave a handbag, briefcase, bag or coat unattended, especially in pubs, cinemas, department stores or fast-food shops, on public transport, at railway stations and airports, or in crowds.
• **Don't** leave your bag or coat beside, under or on the back of your chair. Hook the handle of your bag around the leg of the chair on which you're sitting.
• **Don't** put your bag on the floor near the door of a public toilet.
• **Don't** wear expensive jewellery or watches that can be easily snatched.
• **Late** at night, travel in groups of three or more. Avoid parks and commons after dark.
• **Don't** put your purse down on the table in a restaurant or on a shop counter while you scrutinise the bill.
• **Don't** carry a wallet in the back pocket of your trousers.
• **Don't** flash your money or credit cards around.

Post Offices

You can buy stamps and have letters weighed at all post offices, but stamps are also widely available at newsagents. **Stamp prices** are, at time of writing, 19p for second-class letters (inland only) and 25p for first-class letters to all EC countries. Charges for other letters and parcels vary according to the weight and destination. Courier services are listed under *chapter* **Business**; packaging and shipping under *chapter* **Shopping & Services**.

What's news? **A Moroni & Son**. *See* **review**.

Letters sent to you Poste Restante, London, can be collected from London Chief Post Office, King Edward Street, EC1. Bring your passport or ID card.

Post office opening hours are normally 9am-5.30pm Mon-Fri; 9am-noon Sat, although they do vary occasionally; we list the one office that opens late.

WC2: Trafalgar Square Post Office
24 William IV Street, WC2 (071 930 9580). Charing Cross underground/BR. **Open** 8am-8pm Mon-Sat.

Public Toilets & Baths

Many public swimming pools have bathrooms for hire, together with soap and a towel.

Kentish Town Pools
Prince of Wales Road, NW5 (071 267 9341). Kentish Town underground. **Open** 7.30am-9pm Mon-Fri; 9.30am-6pm Sat. **Admission** £1.95.

Oasis Sports Centre
32 Endell Street, WC2 (071 831 1804). Holborn underground. **Open** *indoor pool* 7.30am-6.45pm, *outdoor pool* 7.30am-8.30pm, Mon-Fri; *both pools* 9.30am-5pm Sat, Sun. **Admission** £2.30 adults, 75p under-15s.

Religion

Baptist

Bloomsbury Central Baptist Church
235 Shaftesbury Avenue, WC2 (071 836 6843/071 240 0544). Tottenham Court Road underground. **Open** *Office* 9am-6.30pm daily; *Friendship Centre* (closed Aug, Sept) 11.30am-2.30pm Tue; 6-8.30pm Wed; 10.30am-8.30pm Sun. **Services** 11am, 6.30pm Sun.

Buddhist

Buddhapadipa Temple
14 Calonne Road, SW19 (081 946 1357). Wimbledon Park underground. **Open** 1-6pm Sat; 8.30-10.30am, 12.30-6pm, Sun.

Catholic

Brompton Oratory
Brompton Road, SW7 (071 589 4811 enquiries). South Kensington underground. **Open** 6.30am-8pm daily. **Services** 7am, 7.30am, 8am (Latin mass), 10am, 12.30am, 6pm Mon-Fri; 7am, 7.30am, 8am, 10am, 6pm Sat; 7am, 8am, 9am, 10am (Tridentine), 11am (sung Latin), 12.30pm, 3.30pm (Vespers and Benediction), 4.30pm, 7pm Sun.

Westminster Cathedral
Victoria Street, SW1 (071 834 7452). Victoria underground. **Open** 7am-8pm daily. **Services** eight daily masses Mon-Fri; seven daily masses Sat; 7am, 8am, 9am, 10.30am, noon, 5.30pm, 7pm Sun.

Christian Scientist

Eleventh Church of Christ Scientist
1 Nutford Place, W1 (071 723 4572). Marble Arch underground. **Open** for services only. **Services** 11am,

7pm first Sun in month. **Testimony meetings** 7pm Wed. **Public Reading Room** *80 Baker Street, W1 (071 486 0759). Baker Street underground.* **Open** 9.30am-7.30pm Mon, Tue, Thur-Sat; 9.30am-6.30pm Wed; 2.30-6.30pm Sun.

Church of England

St Paul's Cathedral
EC4 (071 248 2705). St Paul's underground. **Open** 7.30am-6pm daily; *galleries* 9.45am-6pm daily; *services* 8am, 12.30pm (not Friday), 5pm (evensong) Mon-Fri; 8am, 10am (choral), 12.30pm, 5pm (choral) Sat; 8am, 10.30am (choral), 11.30am (choral), 3.15pm (evensong) Sun. Times vary because of special events, phone first to check.

Westminster Abbey
Dean's Yard, SW1 (071 222 5152). St James's Park or Westminster underground. **Open** *Royal Chapels* 9am-4pm Mon-Fri; 6-7.45pm Wed; 9am-2pm, 3-5pm, Sat. *Chapter House, Pyx Chamber, Abbey Museum* 10am-4pm daily. *Brass Rubbing Centre (071 222 2085)* 9am-5pm Mon-Sat. **Admission** *Royal Chapels* £3 adults; £1 under-16s; £1.50 students, OAPs. Guided tours £6 (including Royal Chapels, bookable on 071 222 7110). **Services** 7.30am, 8am (Holy Communion), 12.30am, 5pm (choral evensong, except Wed) Mon-Fri; 8am, 9.20am, 3pm (evensong) Sat; 8am, 10am (sung matins), 11.15am (abbey eucharist), 3pm (evensong), 4.45pm organ recital, 6.30pm (evening service), Sun.

Evangelical

All Souls Church
Langham Place, 2 All Souls Place, W1 (071 580 3522/071 580 6029). Oxford Circus underground. **Open** 9am-8pm Mon-Fri; 9am-9pm Sun. **Services** 9am Holy Communion, 11am, 6.30pm Sun.

Islamic

London Central Mosque
146 Park Road, NW8 (071 724 3363). Baker Street underground/74 bus. **Open** dawn-dusk daily. **Services** 3.18am, 1.06pm, 5.28pm, 9.22pm, 10.52pm (times vary, so phone to confirm).

East London Mosque
84-98 Whitechapel Road, E1 (071 247 1357). Aldgate East or Whitechapel underground. **Open** 8.30am-10.30pm daily. **Service** *Friday prayer* 1.25pm (1.10pm in winter).

Jewish

Liberal Jewish Synagogue
28 St John's Wood Road, NW8 (071 286 5181). St John's Wood underground. **Open** *enquiries* 9am-5pm Mon-Thur; 9am-3pm Fri. **Services** 6.45pm Fri; 11am Sat.

West Central Liberal Synagogue
109 Whitfield Street, SW1 (071 636 7627). Warren Street underground. **Open** 3pm Sat service.

Methodist

Central Church of World Methodism
Westminster Central Hall, Storeys Gate, SW1 (071 222 8010). St James's Park underground. **Open** *Chapel* 9am-5pm Mon-Fri. **Services** 11am, 6.30pm Sun.

Pentecostal

Assemblies of God, Pentecostal Church
141 Harrow Road, W2 (071 286 9261). Edgware Road underground. **Open** for services only. **Services** prayer meetings and Bible study 7.30pm Wed; Young People's Service 5.30pm Sat; 11am, 6.30pm Sun.

Presbyterian Church of Scotland

Crown Court Church of Scotland
Russell Street, WC2 (071 836 5643). Covent Garden underground. **Open** to visitors in Jun-Aug 11.30am-2.30pm Tue-Thur. **Services** 1.10-1.30pm Thur throughout the year; 11.15am, 6.30pm Sun.

Quakers

Religious Society of Friends (Quakers)
Friends House, 173-177 Euston Road, NW1 (071 387 3601). Euston underground/BR. **Open** 9am-5pm Mon-Fri. **Meeting** 11am Sun.

Unitarian Church

Rosslyn Hill Unitarian Chapel
Rosslyn Hill, NW3 (071 435 3506). Hampstead underground. **Open** for services only. **Service** 11am Sun.

United Reformed Church

United Reformed Church
Central office, 86 Tavistock Place, WC1 (071 916 2020). Russell Square underground or King's Cross underground/BR. **Open** 9am-5pm Mon-Fri.

Telephones

The red telephone call box is a famous symbol of Britain, but you may be surprised to hear that they are now very rare. Always easy to find, Giles Gilbert Scott's much-loved red boxes have almost all been replaced. The new smoke-grey cubicles are cleaner but invisible when you need to find one.

Public call boxes are usually cheaper to use than the telephones in hotel rooms, the charges for which are added to your bill. All call boxes display instructions for use. There are two types, one accepts money and the other only accepts a **Phonecard** (*see below*). Scattered throughout London you will see blue and grey **Mercury** telephone booths. In emergencies, dial **999** for police, fire or ambulance services.

Here's a phonetic guide to British telephone sounds. A steady *brrrrr* when you lift the receiver means go ahead and dial. A higher *brrr-brrr* pause *brrr-brrr* pause, etc means that the number's ringing. Quick, evenly-spaced *boop-boop-boop* means it's engaged (busy); a solid *woooo* means unobtainable.

Telecom Phonecards
Cards available from post offices and larger newsagents.

Cost 10p per unit; cards available in units of £1 to £20. **Credit** *phones in some stations accept credit cards:* A, AmEx, DC, V.
Call boxes with the green Phonecard symbol take pre-paid cards. A notice in the call box tells you where the nearest Phonecard stockist is. The phone's digital display shows how many units you have left.

Mercury Phonecards
(071 528 2000). Cards available from British Rail stations, post offices and larger newsagents. **Cost** 1p per unit; cards available in units of £2, £5 and £10. **Credit** *all phones accept cards* A, AmEx, DC, V.
British Telecom was privatised in November 1984, opening up the telecommunications market to competition. There were 1,550 Mercury phone booths in London by 1991, located at most train stations and throughout the capital. They don't take cash and work on the same principles as the Telecom Phonecards. Mercury calls (including international) are up to 20% cheaper than Telecom calls, partly because they're priced in 1p units: Telecom would charge 20p for an 11p call. Fewer people own Mercury cards, so the queues are usually shorter.

Operator Services

Directory Enquiries
Dial **142** to find London numbers, **192** for all other numbers in Britain. Each enquiry now costs 44p for two numbers, unless you're phoning from a public call box, in which case it's free.

International Directory Enquiries
Dial **153** if you've left your address book at home.

International Operator
Dial **155** if you need to reverse the charges (call collect) or if you can't dial direct. Dial direct if you can, as the service is very expensive.

Operator
Call **100** for the operator: when you have difficulty in dialling; for an early-morning alarm call; to make a credit card call; for information about the cost of a call; to reverse charges for a call (call collect); and for international person-to-person calls.

International Dialling Codes
Australia *(010 61);* **Canada** *(010 1);* **France** *(010 33);* **Eire** *(010 353);* **Germany** *(010 37);* **Italy** *(010 39);* **Netherlands** *(010 31);* **Spain** *(010 34);* **USA** *(010 1).*

International Telegrams/Telemessage
The traditional telegram, sadly, no longer exists in Britain; instead by calling **190** you can phone-in your message and the next day it is delivered by post. There is still a service for overseas telegrams. Call the same number if you urgently need to contact someone abroad or just like doing things in style.

Telephone Directories
There are three telephone directories for London, two for private numbers, divided into alphabetical sections A-K and L-Z, and one listing companies. These are available at post offices and some call boxes have copies. All hotels and guest houses have them and they are issued free to all residents with telephones, as is the *Yellow Pages* directory, which lists commercial establishments and services under category headings such as 'Boat Hire' and 'Minicabs'.

Travel & Driving

Public transport, car hire and so on are covered in *chapter* **Getting Around**. If you're thinking of travelling outside London look at *chapter* **Trips out of Town**.

London Regional Transport Travel Information Service

(071 222 1234). **Open** 24 hours daily.
Phone for information about travel by underground, bus and British Rail in Greater London.

Discounts

The Young Person's Railcard

This can be held by anyone aged 16 to 23 or those in full-time education. It costs £16 for one year, and entitles holders to a discount (usually a third off the off-peak standard fare, but more during special offer periods). Railcards are available from main British Rail stations. You'll need identification and a couple of passport-sized photographs. Students need a signature from their college.

The Student Coach Card

Costing £5, the Coach Card is for students only. It gives a 33% discount on fares and is valid for a year. The form is available from Victoria Coach Station, and needs to be stamped by your college.

The Inter-Rail Card

Suitable for all those aged under 26 who are planning a trip to Europe. For £249, the pass (available from British Rail stations) entitles holders to unlimited train travel in 24 countries for one month. You can buy more than one (they must run consecutively) and there's a small refund on return of your correctly filled-in card. There's now an Inter-Rail card for those aged over 26, but it doesn't include Spain, Portugal, Morocco, France, Belgium, Italy, or Switzerland. A 15-day card costs £209; a one-month card costs £269. Neither card is valid in the UK (if bought here).

STA Travel

74 & 86 Old Brompton Road, SW7 (Intercontinental 071 937 9962/European 071 937 9921). South Kensington underground. **Open** 9am-6pm Mon-Fri; 10am-4pm Sat.
A wide range of low-cost fares across five continents is offered here, with special rates for students, young people and academics. STA also has offices at 117 Euston Road, NW1 *(see chapter* **Students***)* and many other colleges throughout London.

Hitching

Hitching is easily the cheapest form of travel, although the journey may prove arduous and possibly dangerous. Single women should not hitch: the risk is not worth it. You're unlikely to get a lift within London except at the start of major roads and motorways.

Starting Points

M1 for the North ('change' at Watford Gap Services for the North West and Scotland, via the M6): Staples Corner (Brent Cross underground).
M2 for Dover: Rochester Way, A2 (Blackheath BR).
M3 for the South and South West: Chertsey Road at the junction with Whitton Road (Twickenham BR).
M4 for the West and South Wales: ('change' before Bristol for the M5 and the South West): Great West

Road, A4, at Hammersmith Flyover (Hammersmith underground); or at Chiswick (Gunnersbury underground/BR).
M11 for Cambridge and East Anglia: M11 junction with Eastern Avenue (Redbridge underground).
M20 for Folkestone: Sidcup Road junction with Court Road (Mottingham BR).
M23 for Brighton: Purley Way junction with Stafford Road (Waddon BR).
M40 for Oxford and the Midlands: Gipsy Corner, junction of Western Avenue and Horn Lane (North Acton underground).
A1 for A1(M) and the North: Watford Way at junction 2 with the M1 (Hendon Central underground).
A12 for Harwich and East Anglia: Gants Hill Cross (Gants Hill underground).

Parking

If you've heard that driving in central London is difficult, just wait till you try to find somewhere to park. If you park illegally (check the regulations in the *Highway Code*, available from newsagents), you'll probably get a £30 **parking ticket**. If you park illegally in central London your car will probably be immobilised by a yellow triangular wheel-clamp *(see below* **De-Clamping***)*. Vehicles may also be towed away and impounded. To retrieve your vehicle you have to go to a **Payment Centre** and pay a £105 tow-away fee and £12 storage for each day your car has been kept in the pound. Take the bus.

24-Hour Car Parks

W1: Arlington Street *(071 499 3312).* **Rates** £8.50 for 3 hours; £29 for 12 hours; £36 up to 24 hours.
W1: Brewer Street *(071 734 9497).* **Rates** £9.50 for 3 hours; £15.80 for 6 hours; £9.50 night rate.
W1: Denman Street *(071 734 5760).* **Rates** £5 for 2 hours; £15.80 for 6 hours; £9.50 night rate.
W1: Park Lane *(071 262 1814).* **Rates** £2.60 for 2 hours; £8.40 for 6 hours; £17 for 24 hours.
W8: Young Street *(071 937 7420).* **Rates** £3.20 for 2 hours; £9.60 for 6 hours; £1.40 night rate.
WC2: Cambridge Circus *(071 434 1896).* **Rates** £7.80 for 3 hours; £11.70 for 6 hours; £6.80 night rate.
SW1: Abingdon Street *(071 222 8621).* **Rates** £6.30 for 4 hours; £8.40 for 6 hours; £2.20 6pm-midnight; £3.30 midnight-9am.
SW1: Cadogan Place *(071 235 5106).* **Rates** £4 for 2 hours; £12 for 6 hours; £3.50 night rate.
SW3: Pavilion Road *(071 589 0401).* **Rates** £4.20 for 2 hours; £6.30 for 3 hours; £8.40 for four hours; £3.50 night rate.
SW5: Swallow International Hotel *Cromwell Road (071 370 4200).* **Rates** £4.80 for 4 hours; £15.50 for 24 hours.

De-Clamping

For years motorists ignored the thousands of tickets slapped on to their cars by traffic wardens and continued to park illegally, so the dreaded wheel clamp was introduced. However, it not only ruins the offender's day, but also guarantees the road will remain blocked until the clamped car is freed. If you've been clamped, there will be a label attached to the car telling you which of the **Payment Centres** (*listed below*) to visit. When you get there, you'll have to pay £38 on the spot for de-clamping and have 28 days in which to pay a £16 parking fine.

Now the fun starts. The staff at the payment centre promise to de-clamp your car within the next four hours but can't tell you exactly when. You are also warned that if you don't remove your car within one hour of its being de-clamped they will clamp it again. This means that you have to spend several hours, if not all day, waiting by your car.

Car Clamp Recovery Club

20 Newman Street, W1 (071 235 9901). **Open** 8am-10am Mon-Sat. **Membership** £30. **Credit** A, AmEx, DC, V.
If you're too busy to go through the de-clamp process yourself and want to have the car delivered to your door, pay the fine plus the membership fee for the first clamp; and an additional £18 for the second clamp.

Camden Police Car Pound and Payment Centre

Oval Road, NW1 (071 252 2222 ask for the Camden Car Pound). Camden Town underground. **Open** 8am-midnight Mon-Sat.

Hyde Park Police Car Pound and Payment Centre

Located in the NCP Car Park, Park Lane, W1 (071 252 2222 ask for the Hyde Park Car Pound). Marble Arch underground. **Open** 24 hours daily.

Warwick Road Police Car Pound and Payment Centre

245 Warwick Road, SW5 (071 252 2222 ask for the Kensington Car Pound). Earl's Court underground. **Open** 8am-midnight Mon-Sat.

24-Hour Petrol Stations

If you're driving late and are low on petrol don't panic, there are over 100 24-hour petrol stations throughout Greater London.
North: Elf Service Station, 109 York Way, N7 (071 267 5862).
South: Old Kent Road Filling Station, 420-432 Old Kent Road, SE1 (071 232 2957).
East: City Road Service Station, 309 City Road, EC1 (071 253 4059).
West: Star Service Station, 7 Pembridge Villas, W11 (071 229 6626).

Car Breakdown

The well-prepared visitor never travels without his/her membership card of a motoring organisation. But if you're not organised and disaster strikes, contact one of the following:

AA (Automobile Association)

Central London Office, Regis House, King William Street, EC4 (information 0345 500 600/freefone breakdown service 0800 887766/shop 071 623 4152/insurance 071 626 7787). **Open** office 8.30am-5.30pm Mon-Fri. **Breakdown service** 24 hours daily. **Credit** A, V.
You can call the AA out if your car breaks down. Become

a member on the spot: it will cost you £10 to join, £35 for the first year's membership, £25 for the relay service, £17.50 for homestart.

National Breakdown

(Head Office 0532 393434/Breakdown 0800 400 600/Membership 0532 3936661). **Open** 24 hours daily.
A non-member calling National Breakdown pays £32 call-out fee, mileage of 60p per mile plus parts and parts. To become a member, phone for details; degrees of cover vary from total protection (£72.50) to recovery (£24). National Breakdown will 'rescue' single women (non-members) and take them to the nearest recovery centre for safety.

Olympic Breakdown Service

(West London 071 286 8282). **Open** 24 hours daily. **Credit** A, AmEx, V.
This company is AA- and RAC-approved and operates a 24-hour London-wide recovery and roadside repair service. It will cost £35 plus VAT call-out charge, plus the price of any new parts. To be towed away costs £40 plus VAT within a three-mile (4.8km) radius and then £1.50 per mile. If you do need to be towed away you don't pay the call-out fee, only the tow charge.

RAC (Royal Automobile Club)

Motoring Services Ltd, PO Box 8, Marco-Polo House, 3-5 Lansdowne Road, Croydon (general enquiries 081 686 2314/membership 0345 331133). **Open** office 9am-5.30pm Mon-Fri; 9am-12.30pm Sat. **Breakdown service** 24 hours daily. **Credit** A, AmEx, DC, V.
Ring the general enquiries number and ask for the Rescue Service. Membership costs £58.50 (payable by credit card) or £67, which includes a £10 joining fee, only payable once. Describe your mechanical failure to the controller. An engineer will then be sent out to repair your car on the roadside or, if necessary, tow it away. A non-member calling breakdown services also pays a £25 surcharge and must then join.

Spare Parts

Barnet Brake & Clutch Services

120 Myddleton Road, N22 (081 881 0847). Bounds Green or Wood Green underground/N2, N21 Night bus. **Open** 24 hours daily. **Credit** A, V, £TC.
If you know what the problem is and just need parts, contact this 24-hour car spare parts shop.

Visitors with Disabilities

Things are improving (slowly) for disabled visitors to London. Many tourist venues now have wheelchair access; some councils are doing their best to improve the situation further. There are books and organisations which give useful information specifically for disabled people. The **London Tourist Board** publishes a leaflet, 'London For All', which covers transport, tours and hotels. It's available from **Tourist Information Centres** (*see chapter* **Essential Information**). For information about public transport, get a free copy of *Access to the Underground* from Tourist Information Centres, ticket offices or by post from the Unit for Disabled Passengers, 55 Broadway, SW1 (071 225 6000). *Access in London* is a booklet compiled by researchers with disabilities; it covers tourist spots, shopping, pubs, theatres and much more. It costs £3.50 from Books Etc, 120 Charing Cross Road, WC2.

Artsline
5 Crowndale Road, NW1 (071 388 2227).
Mornington Crescent underground/24, 29, 68, 253 bus. **Open** 9.30am-5.30pm Mon-Fri.
An organisation for disabled people which gives free information on arts and entertainment events in London and on adapted facilities at venues such as cinemas, art galleries and theatres. It produces a monthly publication.

British Sports Association for the Disabled
Solecast House, 13-27 Brunswick Place, N1 (071 490 4919). **Open** 9.30am-4pm Mon-Fri.
Disabled people interested in watching or participating in sports should contact the BSAD, a national organisation which puts people in touch with local sports groups and centres. The address is that of the Greater London regional office; there are regional branches throughout the country.

Greater London Association for Disabled People (GLAD)
336 Brixton Road, SW9 (071 274 0107). Brixton underground. **Open** 9am-5pm Mon-Fri.
The *London Disability Guide*, published by GLAD, is a comprehensive resource book covering subjects from education for disabled people to pregnancy and parenthood. It's available free by post, send an SAE.

Handicapped Helpline
Community Links, Canning Town Public Hall, 105 Barking Road, E16 (071 473 2270). **Open** 11am-3.30pm Tue-Fri for visits. Legal advice is given on the 1st and 3rd Tuesday of every month, 6.30-7.30pm.
Run by and for disabled people, the Helpline gives information and advice on a variety of subjects and counselling on careers. It can put you in touch with other organisations or specific associations and offers a drop-in service.

Royal Association For Disability and Rehabilitation (RADAR)
25 Mortimer Street, W1 (071 637 5400). **Open** 9am-5pm Mon-Thur; 9am-4.30pm Fri.
This is the central organisation for disabled voluntary groups. Through it you can get advice on virtually any aspect of life. The Association publishes *Contact*, a quarterly magazine which has features on disabled issues, and *Bulletin*, a monthly newsletter, which has articles on more news-orientated subjects such as housing, education and Acts of Parliament.

Shape
Shape London, 1 Thorpe Close, W10 5XL (081 960 9249).
Call Shape for very cheap tickets to accessible arts events in London. Shape also provides transport, drivers and escorts (where applicable).

Tripscope
The Courtyard, Evelyn Road, W4 (081 994 9294).
An advice service for the elderly and disabled. Jim Bennett's friendly service can help with all aspects of getting around London and the UK. It's chiefly an enquiry line, you can write in or visit by appointment if you have difficulty with the telephone.

Working in London

Finding a summer job in London, or temporary employment if you're on a working holiday, is a full-time job in itself. Despite frequent reports that the recession is over, there is precious little evidence of an increase in job vacancies.

But providing you can speak English well, are an EC citizen or have a valid work permit (*see* **Box**), you should be able to get work doing catering jobs, labouring, bar/pub work or shop work. Graduates with either English or a foreign language degree could try teaching. Other alternatives are: despatch riding (bike messengers need their own bike and a courageous disposition), distributing free magazines, or work in a betting shop. Also try summer work in tourist spots; local councils sometimes take on summer staff, such as playgroup leaders, assistants in homes for the elderly or swimming pool attendants. More ideas can be found in *Summer Jobs in Britain* published by Vacation Work, 9 Park End Street, Oxford, available from good bookshops. It costs £6.95 (£7.95 by post). The **Central Bureau for Educational Visits and Exchanges** (*see below* **Useful Addresses**) has other helpful publications.

To find work look in the *Evening Standard*, local and national newspapers, local newsagents' windows or Jobcentres. For temporary office work, sign on with temp agencies. If you have good shorthand, typing (40 words per minute upwards) or word-processing (WP) skills, and dress the part, agencies might find you well-paid office work.

If you're desperate, try a fast-food chain. You'll probably have to wear a hideous uniform and endure hyped-up competition to see who is the fastest burger-maker (and be made to don a badge if you are), but these establishments are always looking for staff (and no wonder).

Work for Foreign Visitors

With few exceptions, citizens of non-EC countries will need a work permit before they can legally get a job in the UK (*see* **Box**).

It's not easy meeting people in London. So one of the advantages of working here (apart from the money) is the opportunity to make friends with the natives. But for any work, it's essential that you can speak English of a communicable standard. Try catering – there's a **Jobcentre** at 3 Denmark Street, W1 (full-time work 071 497 2047/part-time work 33-35 Mortimer Street, W1 071 323 9190) dealing specifically in hotel and catering work. For office work you need a very high standard of English and office skills.

Au-pair work is another possibility. Try an au-pair agency in your own country or look in the *Yellow Pages* under 'Employment Agencies'.

Also look in *The Lady* magazine, which advertises au-pair and nanny jobs. The best thing about au-pairing is that you get free accommodation, but wages are often low.

Voluntary work in youth hostels will usually pay board and lodging and some pocket money, but there is a great demand for it. Voluntary work on social and community projects won't pay, but you might gain an insight into local life. Contact local councils (listed in phone directories). Work can also be found in shops, pubs and bars (*see above* **Working in London** for where to look).

Useful Addresses

Aliens Registration Office
10 Lamb's Conduit Street, WC1 (071 230 1208). Holborn underground. **Open** 9am-4.45pm Mon-Fri.
It costs £30 to be registered, if you already have a work permit.

Central Bureau for Educational Visits & Exchanges
Seymour Mews House, Seymour Mews, W1 (071 486 5101). Bond Street or Marble Arch underground. **Open** 9.30am-5.15pm Mon-Fri.
Funded by the Department of Education and Science, this office deals mainly with organising visits outside the UK. But contact it anyway for copies of the extremely useful books: *Working Holidays 1994* (£8.99), *Volunteer Work* (£7.99), *Home from Home* (£6.99) and *Study Holidays* (£7.95), available from bookshops and the Bureau itself (but only by post).

Department of Employment
Caxton House, Tothill Street, SW1 (071 273 3000). St James's Park underground. **Open** 9am-5pm Mon-Fri.
The government department dealing with all aspects of employment. The Overseas Labour Section can help with work permit enquiries (071 273 5336).

Home Office
Immigration and Nationality Department, Lunar House, Wellesley Road, Croydon, CR2 (081 686 0688). East Croydon BR. **Open** 8.30am-4pm Mon-Fri.
The immigration department of the Home Office deals with queries about immigration matters, visas and work permits for Commonwealth citizens.

Jobcentre
195 Wardour Street, W1 (071 439 4541). Oxford Circus underground. **Open** 9am-12.30pm, 1.30-5pm, Mon-Thur; 10am-12.30pm, 1.30-5pm, Fri.
Employers advertise job vacancies on noticeboards here and there's often temporary and unskilled work available. Most districts of London have a Jobcentre – they're painted bright orange so you can't miss them – and they're listed under 'Manpower Services Commission' in the telephone directory. The West End offices at 33 Mortimer Street, W1 (071 836 6622) and 3 Denmark Street, W1 (071 836 6622) both deal with catering vacancies only. All Jobcentres are run by the Department of Employment.

Work permits

EC citizens, residents of Gibraltar and certain categories of other overseas visitors don't need a work permit. All other visitors cannot work in the UK legally without one. Three government departments deal with work permits. Try any **Jobcentre**, where you can get an application form (form OW1), before going to the more bureaucratic **Department of Employment** or the **Home Office** (*see above* **Useful Addresses**). In most cases, you will need a UK employer to apply on your behalf and he/she must prove that no UK resident can do the work better. However, there is a 'training and work experience' scheme operated by the Department of Employment for 18- to 35-year-olds. This enables you to gain work experience or training in a certain field for a specific, limited period of time. A permit must be obtained by a UK employer on your behalf before you enter the country.

Citizens of Commonwealth countries aged between 17 and 27 years can get a passport stamp as a 'Working Holiday Maker' which allows you to do part-time work without a work permit for up to two years. Contact the British High Commission or Consulate in your country to obtain the stamp before entering this country. If applying for a visa extension while in Britain, you might convince the Home Office Immigration department (081 686 0688) or the Overseas Labour Section at the Department of Employment that you need part-time work and are not looking for full-time employment.

Visiting **students from the USA** can get a blue card enabling them to work for a maximum of six months. This is not difficult to obtain, but you must get it before entering the country. Contact the Work in Britain department of the Council on International Educational Exchange 205 East 42nd Street, New York, NY 10017 (0101 212 661 1414) for details. Alternatively, call BUNAC, 16 Bowling Green Lane, EC1 (071 251 3472), which is a non-profit making student club that organises work exchange programmes for students from America, Canada, Australia and Jamaica.

Index

London Guide

Features in this guide were written and researched by: **Introduction** Dominic Wells. **Essential Information** Charlie Godfrey-Faussett. **Getting Around** Charlie Godfrey-Faussett. **Accommodation** Shireen Jilla. **London by Season** Charlie Godfrey-Faussett, Ruman Chadhury, Philip Cornwel-Smith, Stephanie Hannerly, Albert Harwood. **Sightseeing** Charlie Godfrey-Faussett, Rick Jones, Philip Cornwel-Smith, Myra Hope Bobbit. **History** Dr Raymond Winch, Sarah McAlister, Rick Jones, Philip Cornwel-Smith, Phil Harriss. **London Today** Steve Grant. **London by Area** Phil Harriss. **Eating & Drinking** Sarah Guy. **Shopping & Services** Guy Dimond, Caroline Roux (fashion), Jeremy Brill (records). **Museums & Galleries** Shireen Jilla, Caroline Roux. **Media** Alkarim Jivani, Sid Smith, Hayden Williams, Phil Harriss. **Comedy** Malcolm Hay, David Hutcheon. **Children** Ronnie Haydon. **Clubs** Dave Swindells, David Hutcheon. **Dance** Allen Robertson, David Hutcheon. **Film** Joanna Berry, David Hutcheon. **Music: Classical & Opera** Martin Hoyle. **Music: Rock, Folk & Jazz** David Hutcheon. **Sport** Andrew Shields. **Theatre** Rick Jones. **Early Hours** David Hutcheon. **Business** Charlie Godfrey-Faussett. **Gay London** Paul Burston. **Students** Charlie Godfrey-Faussett. **Women's London** Josie Barnard. **Trips Out of Town** Mark Wareham, Grace Packham, Stephanie Hannerly. **Survival** Charlie Godfrey-Faussett, Steafan Hannigan, Conor McCutcheon, Phil Harriss.

The editors would like to thank:
The editors and staff of *Time Out* magazine, Rosamund Sales, Harry Boggis-Rolfe, Caroline Roux, Nick Royle.

The pictures in this Guide were taken by **Julian Anderson** with the exception of those on the following pages: **Barry J Holmes** piii, v, vi, 1, 11, 45, 127, 143, 155, 183, 209, 275, 297, 313, 215, 318; **Henry Wilson/Select** p27; **Trevor Ray Hart** p30; **Rex Features** p77; **Keith Bernstein/Select** p98; **Tricia de Courcy Ling** p131, 139, 145; **Dom Dibbs** p133; **F. Sanjar** p216; **Dave Swindells** p227, 229, 230, 231; **Aedan Kelly** p234; **BBC** p239; **Victoria Mihich** p243; **Virgin** p253; **Alex Livesey** p260; **Sporting Pictures** p261; **Link/Orde Eliason** p302; **Roger Perry** p310.

London Guide
Advertiser's Index
Please refer to the relevant sections for addresses/telephone numbers

Maps

Hungry?.....

Tired?........

Sick?........

Homesick?...

Lost?........

Broke?..

When you need money from home in a hurry, you have to know what to look for. Western Union. Because with Western Union Money Transfer, your friends and relatives can send you money in minutes, to any of 22,500 locations worldwide. Just call the numbers listed. We'll tell you exactly where to find us.

The fast way to send money worldwide.[SM]

AUSTRALIA
075 317 917

AUSTRIA
222 892 03 80

BELGIUM
02 722 3807

DENMARK
800 107 11

FRANCE
1 43 54 46 12

GERMANY
69 2648 201
681 9333328

GREECE
1 687 6575

IRELAND
1 800 395 395

ITALY
02 95 457 305

NETHERLANDS
0 6 0566

POLAND
2 2 31 70 08

SPAIN
34 1 522 9427

SWEDEN
20 741 742

UK
0800 833 833

US
1 800 325 6000

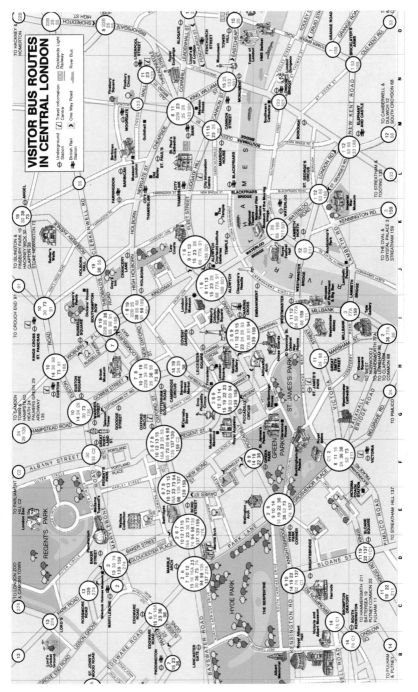

CENTRAL LONDON

London Underground line and station ....
British Rail line and station ....
Docklands Light Railway line and station .... DLR
Travel Information Centre .... *i*
Tourist Information Centre .... *i*
Place of Interest and/or Entertainment ....
Place of Entertainment (see index) ....
Principal Shopping Street ....
Covered Market ....
Street Market .... **M**
Hospital or College ....
Postal District and Boundary W1

0 ¼ ½ ¾ Mile
0 ¼ ½ ¾ 1 Kilometre

© Copyright Time Out Group

Time Out

takes you to the heart of the city

Amsterdam

Berlin

London

New York

Paris

Rome

Penguin Books

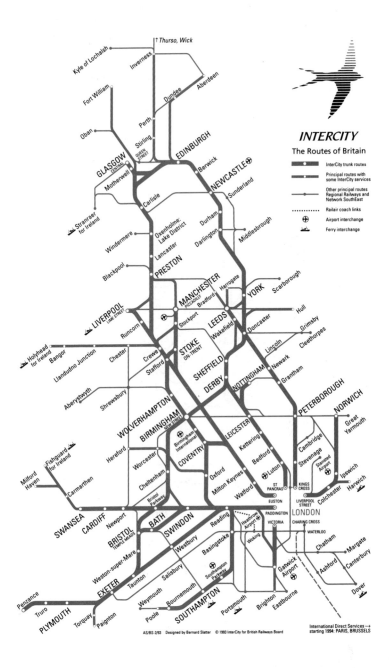

INTERCITY

The Routes of Britain

InterCity trunk routes

Principal routes with some InterCity services

Other principal routes Regional Railways and Network SouthEast

Railair coach links

Airport interchange

Ferry interchange

AS/BS-2/93 Designed by Bernard Slatter © 1993 InterCity for British Railways Board

International Direct Services →
starting 1994: PARIS, BRUSSELS

London: Underground

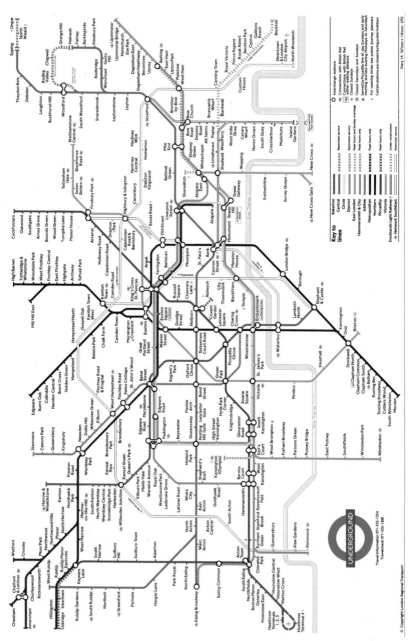

© Copyright London Regional Transport